The First

American Frontier

The First American Frontier

Advisory Editor: Dale Van Every

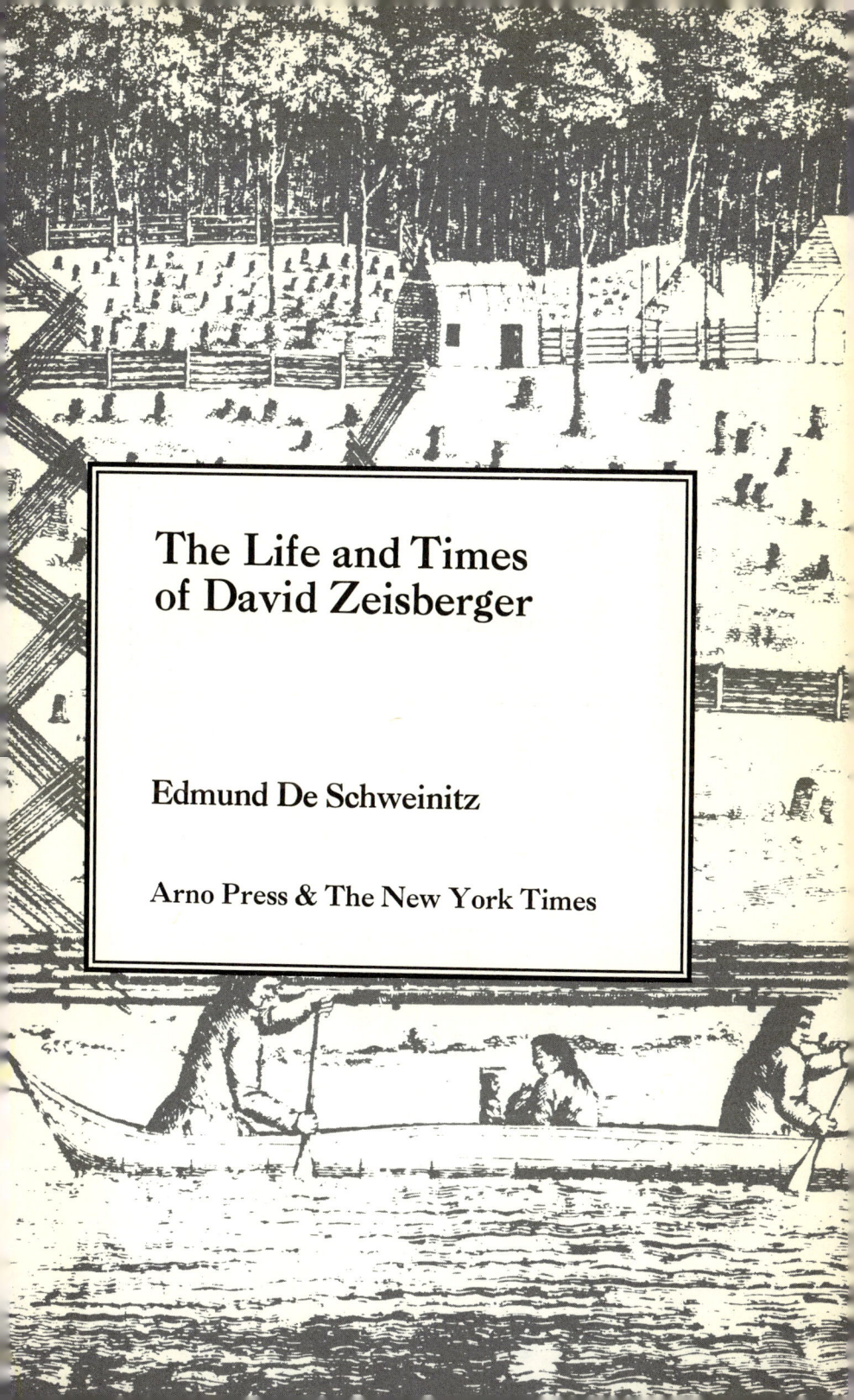

The Life and Times of David Zeisberger

Edmund De Schweinitz

Arno Press & The New York Times

Reprint Edition 1971 by Arno Press Inc.

Reprinted from a copy in
The State Historical Society of Wisconsin Library

LC # 70-146391
ISBN 0-405-02844-X

The First American Frontier
ISBN for complete set: 0-405-02820-2

See last pages of this volume for titles.

Manufactured in the United States of America

THE
LIFE AND TIMES
OF
DAVID ZEISBERGER

THE WESTERN PIONEER AND APOSTLE OF THE INDIANS.

BY

EDMUND DE SCHWEINITZ.

PHILADELPHIA:
J. B. LIPPINCOTT & CO.
1870.

Entered, according to Act of Congress, in the year 1870, by
J. B. LIPPINCOTT & CO.,
In the Office of the Librarian of Congress, at Washington.

PREFACE.

AMONG the philanthropists who dedicated themselves to the work of reclaiming the aborigines of our country and spreading civilization throughout the West, is a man who has remained comparatively unknown, although he deserves a prominent place in history. His name is DAVID ZEISBERGER. As a missionary and an Indian linguist he is the peer of John Eliot; while he far outranks him as a herald of the Gospel and a forerunner of the race that has since possessed the land in which he labored. As regards the frequency of his journeys among the Indians and the privations which he endured in his efforts to convert them, no one is his equal except the Jesuit Fathers of the seventeenth century.

I have attempted, in the following pages, to give a narrative of his life, devoting, for a number of years, such time to this work as was not occupied by official duties.

The only Life of Zeisberger which has been published is a small pamphlet of seventy-one pages, printed at Bielefeld, in 1849, in the German language, and written by J. J. Heim, a clergyman of Switzerland. It is an edifying production, but full of errors in all points relating to Indian history. In Loskiel's and Heckewelder's Histories of the Moravian Mission among the Indians, Zeisberger is a leading character, and much may be learned from these volumes concerning his labors.

The present work is based upon original manuscripts, preserved in the archives of the Moravian churches at Bethlehem and other places.

In addition to their regular correspondence with the Mission Board, Zeisberger and his fellow-missionaries wrote voluminous journals of their every-day life among the Indians, as also complete reports of any occurrences of special interest. These manuscripts, which are mostly in the German language and number many thousands of pages, have been preserved, and I have carefully studied them all. As a rule, references to them have been given in the foot-notes only in connection with events of unusual importance.

It has been my endeavor to weave into the narrative a full account of the manners, customs, character, and religion of the aborigines, without, however, entering into any critical investigations. In all cases I have reproduced what Zeisberger says upon

PREFACE. v

these subjects. His residence of sixty-two years among the Indians renders him an important authority. I have also set forth his life in close connection with the history of the Colonies and of the United States, from 1735 to 1808. Hence the Indian and other wars which broke out in our country during this long period all find a place in my work.

The narrative may seem, at times, to go too minutely into details. But this was unavoidable if I remained true to my purpose of writing not merely for the general reader, but also for the student of Moravian history among the Indians, and of furnishing a book of reference on this subject. I have endeavored to embody, as much as possible, biographical notices and local facts in the foot-notes. The details which I have given when treating of events of colonial or national interest, such as the Paxton Insurrection and the Western Border War during the Revolution, may be deemed important because they are mostly drawn from sources that have never before been used by the historian.

In the orthography of the Indian names, which varies so much that it cannot be subjected to rules, I have followed Zeisberger, who was guided by the German mode of pronunciation.

I have added a geographical glossary, setting forth the situation of those early settlements, Indian villages, forts, and the like which are mentioned in the work. This glossary, with the aid of an ordinary atlas of the United States, will answer all the purposes of a special map.

My sincere acknowledgments are due to the many friends who have, in various ways, assisted me in my researches, and I take pleasure in mentioning particularly John Jordan, Jr., Esq., of Philadelphia, and Jacob Blickensderfer, Jr., Esq., of Tuscarawas County, Ohio. Both these gentlemen have put me under the deepest obligations.

My object is not merely to bring out from obscurity an illustrious man, and to make prominent in the history of our country a name which should never be forgotten. I have a still higher aim in view. I humbly lay this work at the feet of that Divine Master whose glorious Gospel I am permitted to preach. If the following pages shall incite my readers to greater zeal and devotedness in the service of the Lord Jesus Christ, who is the only hope of America and of the world, and shall thus serve to promote His honor, I shall feel that my labors have not been in vain.

BETHLEHEM, PA., June 11, 1870.

ABBREVIATIONS IN THE FOOT-NOTES.

B. A. Archives of the Moravian Church at Bethlehem, Pennsylvania.
L. A. Archives of the Moravian Church at Litiz, Pa.
P. A. Archives of the First Moravian Church in Philadelphia.
G. A. Archives of the Moravian Church at Gnadenhütten, Ohio.

CONTENTS.

CHAPTER I.
The early Years of David Zeisberger.—1721–1743 . . . **PAGE** 13

CHAPTER II.
The Indians at the Time when Europeans began to settle on the North American Continent.—1497–1620 28

CHAPTER III.
New York and Pennsylvania about the year 1745.—Their Settlements and Indian Tribes 48

CHAPTER IV.
Government, Manners, Customs, Character, and Religion of the Delawares and Iroquois in the Times of Zeisberger . . . 75

CHAPTER V.
Missionary Operations among the Indians previous to Zeisberger's Times.—1549–1745 97

CHAPTER VI.
Zeisberger a Student at Bethlehem, a Prisoner at New York, and an Envoy to Onondaga.—1744, 1745 119

CHAPTER VII.
His Labors at Shamokin and in the Valley of Wyoming.—1745–1750 140

CHAPTER VIII.
Zeisberger and Cammerhoff on an Embassy to Onondaga.—1750 . 156

CHAPTER IX.
His Visit to Europe and first Labors after his Return.—1750–1752 . 176

CHAPTER X.
Zeisberger a Resident of Onondaga.—1752 187

CHAPTER XI.
Zeisberger a Resident of Onondaga.—1753–1755 . . . 204

CONTENTS.

CHAPTER XII.
The Months prior to the Indian War, and the Massacre at Gnadenhütten.—1755 220

CHAPTER XIII.
The French and Indian War.—1756–1761 241

CHAPTER XIV.
Zeisberger's first Labors after the French and Indian War.—1762, 1763 254

CHAPTER XV.
The Pontiac War and the Paxton Insurrection.—1763, 1764 . 274

CHAPTER XVI.
Zeisberger at Friedenshütten.—1765, 1766 307

CHAPTER XVII.
Zeisberger's Exploratory Tour to the Indians of the Alleghany River.—1767 321

CHAPTER XVIII.
Zeisberger a Missionary at Goschgoschünk.—1768, 1769 . . 336

CHAPTER XIX.
Zeisberger at Lawunakhannek.—1769, 1770 350

CHAPTER XX.
On the Beaver River, and first Visit to Ohio.—1770, 1771 . . 360

CHAPTER XXI.
The Susquehanna Converts settle in the West.—First Missionary Town in Ohio.—1771, 1772 368

CHAPTER XXII.
Zeisberger's Visits to the Shawanese.—Progress of the Mission in Ohio.—1772–1774 382

CHAPTER XXIII.
Dunmore's War.—1774 399

CHAPTER XXIV.
The Great Plans of Zeisberger and White Eyes.—1774 . . 410

CONTENTS.

CHAPTER XXV.
Religious Liberty in the Delaware Nation, and great Prosperity of the Mission.—1775 421

CHAPTER XXVI.
Lichtenau founded on the Muskingum.—1776 432

CHAPTER XXVII.
The Mission during the Western Border War of the Revolution.— 1776, 1777 441

CHAPTER XXVIII.
The Mission during the Western Border War of the Revolution (continued).—1778, 1779 460

CHAPTER XXIX.
Lichtenau abandoned and New Schönbrunn and Salem built.— 1779, 1780 472

CHAPTER XXX.
Zeisberger's Marriage and last Visit to the Settlements.—1781 . 480

CHAPTER XXXI.
Capture of the Missionaries, and Overthrow of the Mission on the Tuscarawas.—1781 486

CHAPTER XXXII.
The Missionaries and Christian Indians carried off to the Sandusky.—1781 513

CHAPTER XXXIII.
The Trial and Acquittal of the Missionaries.—1781 . . . 518

CHAPTER XXXIV.
The Missionaries at Captives' Town until their Remandment to Detroit.—1781, 1782 530

CHAPTER XXXV.
The Massacre at Gnadenhütten.—1782 537

CHAPTER XXXVI.
Zeisberger at Lower Sandusky and Detroit.—1782 . . . 558

CONTENTS.

CHAPTER XXXVII.
Second Campaign against the Christian Indians, and News of the Massacre in the States.—1782 564

CHAPTER XXXVIII.
Zeisberger at New Gnadenhütten, in Michigan.—1782–1786 . 578

CHAPTER XXXIX.
Zeisberger on the Cuyahoga, Ohio.—1786, 1787 590

CHAPTER XL.
Zeisberger founds New Salem on the Pettquotting.—1787–1789 . 600

CHAPTER XLI.
Zeisberger at New Salem amid the first Indications of War.—1789–1791 612

CHAPTER XLII.
Zeisberger at the Mouth of the Detroit River.—1791, 1792 . . 623

CHAPTER XLIII.
Zeisberger founds Fairfield, in Canada.—1792.–1795 . . . 631

CHAPTER XLIV.
Further Stay of Zeisberger at Fairfield.—1795–1798 . . . 644

CHAPTER XLV.
Zeisberger returns to Ohio and founds Goshen.—1798–1807 . . 652

CHAPTER XLVI.
The last Year of Zeisberger's Life.—1808 667

CHAPTER XLVII.
The literary Works of David Zeisberger 686

CHAPTER XLVIII.
The Indian Mission from the Death of Zeisberger to the present Time.—1809–1870 693

APPENDIX.
A Brief Sketch of the Moravian Church 698
Geographical Glossary 701
Index 717

LIFE AND TIMES
OF
DAVID ZEISBERGER.

CHAPTER I.

THE EARLY YEARS OF DAVID ZEISBERGER.—1721-43.

Zeisberger's birth.—Flees with his parents from Moravia to Saxony.—His parents emigrate to Georgia.—Zeisberger remains in Europe.—Becomes an errand-boy at Herrendyk, in Holland.—Being harshly treated, he runs away and joins his parents.—Zeisberger in Georgia and South Carolina.—Goes to Pennsylvania and helps to found Nazareth and Bethlehem.—Remarkable manner in which the plan of sending him back to Europe is frustrated.—Zeisberger's conversion.—He devotes himself to the mission among the North American Indians.

IN the eastern part of Moravia, where the Oder takes its rise, and the pastures are so luxuriant that the peasantry term the country *Kuhländl*, or Kine-land, there lies, in a beautiful valley inclosed by the spurs of the Middle Carpathians, a small village named Zauchtenthal. Formerly a sequestered spot, seldom visited by the stranger, it is now a station on the railroad from Cracow to Vienna. In this village David Zeisberger was born, on Good-Friday, the 11th of April, 1721.

His parents were David and Rosina Zeisberger, and their progenitors belonged to the ancient Church of the

Bohemian Brethren, founded, sixty years before the Reformation, by followers of John Huss. He came, therefore, of an ancestry that had been the first to kindle the torch of evangelical truth amid the darkness of the Middle Ages; and was born in a valley which had heard the stirring hymns of the Brethren, swelling in harmony from their modest sanctuaries, and making glad the day of the Lord.[1]

But when he saw the light of the world, the besom of persecution had, long since, swept the Church of his fathers from the land. The Reformers before the Reformation were forgotten, except by a few of their descendants, who groaned under the yoke of Romish oppression, and longed for the time when they would be free. That time was approaching. God had already sent His messenger to call the remnant from the land of bondage. One year after the birth of Zeisberger, ten Moravian emigrants, guided by Christian David, "the servant of the Lord,"[2] fled from their native country, under cover

---

[1] Biographical Sketch of David Zeisberger, written in German, by the Rev. John Heckewelder, MS. Library of Moravian Historical Society. The substance of this sketch is published in "Nachrichten aus der Brüdergemeine," and translated into English in "Periodical Accounts," vol. viii. London, 1821.

[2] Christian David (born December 31, 1690, at Senftleben, in Moravia; died February 3, 1751, at Herrnhut), a Roman Catholic, and by profession a carpenter, having been converted, became a zealous evangelist of Protestantism, and began a missionary work, in his native country, among the descendants of the Brethren, which resulted in a general awakening. Having received the promise from Count Zinzendorf of a home for Moravian refugees, he brought a number of them to Saxony, at various times. He afterward became an elder of the Church, and was one of her first missionaries to Greenland. In Moravian history he bears the title of "the servant of the Lord."

DAVID ZEISBERGER. 15

of the night, took their way to Saxony, and in Upper Lusatia, on an estate of Count Zinzendorf, founded Herrnhut, and formed the nucleus of a colony in the midst of which their venerable Church was renewed.[1]

When Zeisberger was five years old his parents escaped to this place of refuge, with their children (July, 1726). They had considerable possessions at Zauchtenthal, but sacrificed them all for the sake of religious liberty.

Herrnhut, however, was not to be their rest. In the year 1733, that noble-hearted philanthropist, James Oglethorpe, founded the colony of Georgia. It was an asylum for the oppressed. To that class the Moravians now belonged. They had fallen into disfavor with the Saxon Government, and it became a question whether they would be permitted to remain at Herrnhut. Hence Zinzendorf, himself an exile from his native country through the machinations of embittered enemies, secured other retreats. One of these was in Georgia, where Augustus Spangenberg[2] received

---

[1] For a brief account of Count Zinzendorf and the Moravian Church, see Appendix.

[2] Augustus Gottlieb Spangenberg (born July 15, 1704, at Klettenberg, in Prussia; died September 18, 1792, at Berthelsdorf, in Saxony) was a professor of the University of Halle, and an assistant director of the Orphan House. In 1733, he joined the Moravians, having been deprived of his offices at Halle, by a royal mandate, on account of his connection with their Church. He subsequently presided over the Church in America for nearly eighteen years. In 1762, he entered the General Executive Board of the Unitas Fratrum, and died in that office, in the eighty-ninth year of his age. He was known among Moravians as "Brother Joseph," and was one of her greatest men.

from the Trustees, for the Count, five hundred acres of land, and, for himself, fifty acres additional. The first of these tracts lay on the Ogeechee River; the other formed a part of the present site of Savannah.

Here a little company of Moravians settled (1735), planting the Church of their fathers in that Western World whose existence was unknown when, at the fiery stake of Constance, the blood of Huss became her seed. A second body of immigrants followed in 1736, led by Bishop Nitschmann.[1] They numbered twenty persons, and among them were David and Rosina Zeisberger. Soon after, the Moravians of Georgia organized a church (February 28, 1736), choosing Anthony Seyfert, a Bohemian by birth, as their pastor. Bishop Nitschmann ordained him, in the presence of John Wesley, who thought himself transported back to the times of the Apostles when he witnessed the impressive simplicity of the act, and the demonstration of power and of the spirit which accompanied it.[2] Thus, ten years after having fled from the fertile valley of their Moravian fatherland, where they had enjoyed temporal

---

[1] David Nitschmann (born December 27, 1696, at Zauchtenthal, Moravia; died October 8, 1772, at Bethlehem, Pa.) was the first bishop of the Renewed Moravian Church, consecrated at Berlin (March 13, 1735), by Bishop Daniel Ernst Jablonsky, Court-Preacher of the King of Prussia, and Bishop Christian Sitkovius, of Poland, the two survivors of the ancient Moravian Episcopate. John and Charles Wesley crossed the Atlantic with him and his party, which led to that fellowship whose results are identified with the early history of Methodism. After paying three visits to America, he settled here permanently in 1755.

[2] Wesley's Journal, i. 20.

prosperity but suffered spiritual bondage, Zeisberger's parents found themselves in a new world, amid primeval forests, pioneers of civilization and heralds of the Gospel of Christ.

David was not with them. He had been left at Herrnhut to finish his education. At school he distinguished himself by his talents and diligence. The ease with which he acquired Latin, in particular, gave early evidence of the extraordinary facility that he afterward displayed in learning the Indian languages. Courage and resoluteness were the prominent traits of his character.

When he was fifteen years of age, he attracted the notice of Count Zinzendorf, who took him to Holland, where, at the invitation of the Princess Dowager of Orange, the Moravians had established a settlement called Herrendyk, in the Barony of Ysselstein, near the City of Utrecht. In this settlement were shops belonging to the Church, and visited by the gentry of the surrounding country. David was employed as an errand-boy. Active, punctual, and mastering the Dutch with little trouble, he became a favorite among the customers.

But he was not happy. The educational principles of the Moravians were severe to a fault. Rigidly enforcing a system, they paid no regard to the disposition of the individual. Under this iron rule he suffered; and, on a certain occasion, was mercilessly beaten with the rod, although innocent of the fault imputed to him. Nor was this the greatest of his trials.

One day a gentleman of rank visited Herrendyk. Requesting a guide to Ysselstein, Zeisberger was sent with him, and so won his good-will that he offered him an unusually liberal fee. David had been forbidden to accept presents from visitors under any circumstances, and therefore declined the gift. "You must take it," said the gentleman, "I feel it to be my duty to give you this money. Keep it for yourself; it is yours!" And pressing the gold into the boy's unwilling hand, he turned away. Poor Zeisberger was in great perplexity. The stern prohibition in regard to fees was ringing in his ears. "If I conceal this occurrence," he reasoned, "it will be an act of disobedience; if I make it known, and deliver the fee, my story will not be credited." At last he concluded to keep one half of the money, and carry the other half to his employers. But the very suspicion which he wished, by these means, to avert, immediately fell upon him. "No stranger," said his frowning Brethren, "ever gives so large a reward as this to an errand-boy! You have not come honestly by this money. Hold! We will expose your wickedness." Two persons took him back to Ysselstein, in order to confront him with the gentleman. But he had left the place, and no one knew whither he had gone. Instead, therefore, of establishing his innocence, Zeisberger returned to Herrendyk, stigmatized as a liar and a thief.

This he determined not to brook. Finding a fellow-countryman, John Michael Schober, equally indignant with the tyranny they were enduring, he proposed to him to run away. Schober consented, and their attempt proved successful. The quiet settlement lay behind, the wide world before them. But they did not intend to misuse their freedom. Their fathers' God was still to be their God, and His people their people. Resolved no longer to submit to the yoke of Herrendyk, they were no less resolved to seek some other colony of the Brethren; but to which one they should bend their steps was a question that caused them no little disagreement. Zeisberger wanted to join his parents in Georgia; Schober was afraid of such an undertaking, and insisted upon going to Herrnhut. At last, however, he yielded. "That is right," said David; "you will see that God will prosper us." This was the hope with which the two friendless lads, not seventeen years of age, resolutely set their faces toward the Western World.

Having heard that General Oglethorpe, who was then in London, took an active interest in the Moravian colony of Georgia, they concluded to go to England and ask his assistance. They found a vessel which was on the point of sailing to that country, and secured a passage with the money which Zeisberger had retained of the amount given him by the stranger at Ysselstein. To this end that man had been prompted to reward him so liberally. His gold was to speed the future missionary to his field of labor.

Through the kind offices of the landlord of a German inn in London, they obtained an interview with General Oglethorpe, who no sooner heard the story of their wrongs than he warmly espoused their cause, gave them money, supplied them with clothing, and procured a free passage for them in a ship ready to weigh anchor for Savannah. Thus were Zeisberger's pious anticipations fulfilled.

Before embarking, he wrote a letter to David Heckewelder, one of the clergy at Herrendyk, and the father of the celebrated missionary, with whom he subsequently spent many years among the Indians, setting forth the cause of their flight, and informing him of their future plans.

The voyage across the Atlantic was expeditious. But Schober soon fell a victim to the climate and died. Zeisberger took up his abode with his parents; he had grown out of their recollection, and they were overwhelmed with astonishment when he announced himself to be their son.

Little did they anticipate that he was destined to become a chosen vessel unto the Lord, to bear His name before the gentiles. Yet such was the purpose of God. His overruling providence had brought the intrepid lad to America. While those traits of character were manifested, in this flight to the New World, which afterward distinguished the zealous missionary, whom no wilderness, however tangled, could keep from the Indians, and no peril, however imminent, could deter from duty, there are also revealed a divine plan and counsels more than human. In later years, Zeisberger himself acknowledged this. "From the day I left the Brethren in Holland," he writes, "to the day of my arrival in Georgia, the Lord graciously preserved me from all harm, in body and in soul. I was in great danger of being seduced to gross wickedness; but the Lord held His hand over me. At the time, I never realized this danger. Subsequently, however, it became plain to me, and I have often thanked my Saviour for His protection. Upon the whole, I see the finger of God in all that occurred; hence I can the more readily forgive the Brethren in Holland the injustice which I suffered at their hands. Indeed, I have forgiven them from my heart."

A few weeks after his arrival in Georgia he engaged in an adventure which again showed his fearlessness, but which nearly cost him his life. Hearing of the devastations committed by the deer in the rice-fields of the settlement, he went out one night, armed with a heavy rifle, to the place where they were accustomed to break through the inclosure, climbed up a tree, and fired at the approaching herd. The recoil of the weapon in his inexperienced hands was so great that he lost his balance, and fell senseless to the ground. In this state he remained for hours, with a deep and dangerous wound in his head. When consciousness at last returned, he dragged himself to the nearest cabin, where he was cared for.

Zeisberger's stay in Georgia was of great benefit to him; it taught him to endure privations. The settlers were poor, and although they did not actually suffer want, yet their mode of life was very different from that to which he had been accustomed in a luxurious country like Holland. He now received the training of an American pioneer and backwoodsman. At the same time his intercourse with Peter Boehler,[1] the pastor of the church, who took a particular interest in him, served to develop his mind. This was especially the case in the year 1739, the greater part of which Boehler spent at Purysburg, a small German settlement in South Carolina, twenty miles from Savannah, with the intention of preaching the Gospel to the negro slaves. After the death of his associate, Zeisberger was his sole companion for several months, and had the benefit of his daily instruction. In later years, Zeisberger often spoke of his abode in Georgia and South Carolina as a pleasant and profitable time.

It was, however, of short duration. War having broken out between England and Spain (1739), the Spaniards of Florida threatened to attack the Georgia colony, which flew to arms. The Moravians stood aloof, as the bearing of arms was contrary to their principles; and, eventually, in consequence of the disturbances which ensued, and the want of harmony among themselves, broke up their settlement. A remnant proceeded to Pennsylvania, arriving at Philadelphia in George

---

[1] Born, December 31, 1712, at Frankfort-on-the-Main, and celebrated as the agent, in God's hands, through whom John Wesley, the founder of Methodism, was converted. Having been educated at the Universities of Jena and Leipsic, he joined the Moravian Church in 1736, and in 1738 went to Georgia and South Carolina, where he labored until 1740, when he proceeded to Pennsylvania, and in the following year returned to Europe. In 1742 he came back to America, and remained until 1745. In 1748 he was consecrated a bishop, and labored in England, revisiting America in 1753, and continuing his work here until 1764, when he entered the General Executive Board of the Church in Saxony, and died in London, April 27, 1774, while on an official visit to England.

Whitefield's sloop (April 25, 1740), after a voyage of twelve days from Savannah.

Whitefield accompanied the party, and engaged them to build a school-house for negro children, on a tract of five thousand acres of land, which he had purchased in the "Forks of the Delaware," now Northampton County. Thither accordingly journeyed, on foot, with Peter Boehler at their head, seven men, two women, and two lads, one of whom was David Zeisberger, and, in the midst of a wilderness, began an edifice which is still standing, a venerable structure of unhewn stone, known as the *Whitefield House*.

Ere long, however, differences arose between him and the Moravians, fostered by the inhabitants of the Scotch-Irish settlements, and he ordered them to leave his land "forthwith."

In great distress, without money or friends, they asked God to help them. As if in answer to their prayers, Bishop Nitschmann arrived from Europe, bearing a commission to buy land in Pennsylvania and found a Moravian settlement. Ten miles to the south of Whitefield's improvements, a tract was selected on the Lehigh River. In spite of intensely cold weather and a deep snow, the now rejoicing immigrants began to clear the ground, and erected their first cabin. In September, 1741, Nitschmann laid the corner-stone for a chapel.[1] Three months later, Count Zinzendorf, who had mean-

---

[1] It was a large structure of logs, containing, besides the chapel, a number of dwelling-rooms. This house is still standing, on Church Street, at Bethlehem, but entirely remodeled.

while reached the country, celebrated Christmas with his Brethren, and gave to the new settlement the name of Bethlehem. This place soon became, and has always remained, the chief seat of the Moravian Church in America.[1]

In the following year a company of sixty-seven Moravians, from Saxony and England, arrived at Bethlehem. Those were stirring times for young Zeisberger. He loved the broad forests of Pennsylvania; he loved the hardy life he was leading; he loved to fish, to hunt, to fell trees, and build houses. It was, therefore, a bitter disappointment for him when the elders of the Church, with the consent of his parents, designated him as one of the escort which was to accompany Count Zinzendorf to Europe.[2]

On the 9th of January, 1743, the ship *James*, which had been chartered by the Church to bring immigrants to America, lay ready for her return-voyage. The Count was on board, surrounded by numerous friends, and

---

[1] Bethlehem, togetner with several other Moravian villages in its vicinity, constituted, at first, an altogether peculiar settlement. The inhabitants were united as one family, and established, not a community of goods, for each one retained his own private property, but of labor and housekeeping. All worked for the Church, at their respective professions; and the Church gave all a support, realizing, besides, sufficient means to pay for her land, and to sustain, in a great measure, the Mission among the Indians. This arrangement, which bore the name of "The Economy," was dissolved by common consent in 1762, after an existence of twenty years, and the individual inhabitants became owners of the real estate by purchase. Bethlehem is no longer an exclusively Moravian town, but a large and flourishing borough.

[2] Zeisberger lost both his parents a few years after this. His father died at Bethlehem, August 25, 1744, and his mother, at the same place, February 23, 1746.

engaged in animated conversation. Zeisberger stood, unnoticed and alone, in a retired part of the vessel, mournfully gazing upon the land of his choice, which he was about to leave perhaps forever. The signal for departure roused him from his reverie. With bursting heart he watched his associates, who had come to bid their friends farewell, as, one by one, they left the ship. "Cast off the cable!" commanded Captain Garrison.[1] In that moment Bishop Nitschmann, who had been the last to take leave of Zinzendorf, passed by, and, observing Zeisberger's dejected looks, stopped short.

"David," said he, "do you not return to Europe willingly?"

"No, indeed!" was Zeisberger's reply. "I would much rather remain in America."

"For what reason?"

"I long to be truly converted to God, and to serve Him in this country."

Surprised and rejoiced at this answer, the bishop said, "If this be so, and I were in your place, I would at once return to Bethlehem."

---

[1] Nicholas Garrison was born on Staten Island, in 1701, began life as a sailor in his twelfth year, and subsequently commanded various vessels and sailed to many parts of the world. In 1738, he made the acquaintance of Count Zinzendorf in St. Thomas, and after taking him to Europe in the *James*, traveled with him to Germany, where he joined the Moravian Church. In the course of time, he took the command of her missionary vessel, and served her faithfully in this capacity for a number of years, going as far as Greenland and Surinam. Having retired from the sea, he lived for some time in Germany. In 1763 he returned to America, and took up his abode at Bethlehem, where he died, at the age of eighty-one years, September 24, 1781.

Zeisberger did not wait to be told a second time, but hurrying with the bishop from the vessel in the last moment in which this was possible, went his way rejoicing to the quiet settlement amid the wilds of Pennsylvania.

The desire was sincere which he had expressed, of feeling in his own heart the regenerating power of the Gospel of Christ. He had experienced it for a long time, and it grew in intensity after his return to Bethlehem. In later years, when speaking of this period of his life, he said: "At that time my heart was not yet converted to God, but I longed to enjoy His grace, and that fully." A serious conversation, which his friend Büttner had with him, upon the subject of religion, deepened the impressions which he had received, and, at last, he passed from darkness into light.

One day, the young men of the community reverently united in singing, at their dinner-table, in the way of grace, a German hymn treating of the love of Christ.[1] Its words pierced his heart like a two-edged sword. He burst into tears, left the table, and spent the whole afternoon in weeping and praying, until he found the peace of God which passeth all understanding.

In the holy fire of his first love, he resolved to devote his life to the spread of the Gospel among the aborigines of his adopted country, and immediately made known this determination to the elders of the Church.

---

[1] An English translation of this hymn is found in the Hymn Book of the Moravian Church, No. 17.

Thus was the divine purpose, to which David Zeisberger had been foreordained, worked out by God himself, in His own time and way. As He had called John Eliot, in a former century, to be the apostle of the New England Indians, so he now set apart this young man to be the apostle of the Indians of the West.

CHAPTER II.

THE INDIANS AT THE TIME WHEN EUROPEANS BEGAN TO SETTLE ON THE NORTH AMERICAN CONTINENT.—1497-1620.

Obscurity of Indian history.—The generic stocks of the Indians east of the Mississippi.—Traditions of the Algonquins and Iroquois.—The Algonquin family.—The Iroquois Confederacy.—First European settlements.—Manner of life and character of the Indians in this period.—The Delawares made women by the Iroquois.—Traditions and history.—Population of the Indian tribes.

THE race, to the evangelization of which Zeisberger resolved to devote his life, stands forth among the savage nations of the earth a people of general interest and strange mystery. It is the theme of romance, the subject of the poet's song, the topic of the philosopher's speculations, and yet continues an unsolved problem in ethnography. Neither the origin of the Indians, nor their appearance upon the continent of America, has ever been satisfactorily explained.[1] Even that part of their history which immediately precedes the coming of the white man is shrouded in obscurity. The inquirer meets with nothing but traditions and fables. And when the European chronicler takes up the subject,

---

[1] Among the earliest Moravian missionaries the well-known theory prevailed, that the Indians are the descendants of the lost ten tribes of Israel. Zeisberger, however, seems not to have entertained this opinion. I have found no trace of it in any of his writings.

DAVID ZEISBERGER.   29

there ensue such widely different accounts, and such frequent changes among the natives, that the Indian, in many particulars, remains half hidden amid his forests.[1]

The present narrative will be confined to those aborigines who lived east of the Mississippi River. It will not enter into any critical investigations, but will serve merely as one part of the introduction which the history that we propose writing calls for; setting forth, in particular, as interesting relics, those traditions touching the early times of the Indians with which Zeisberger met.[2]

---

[1] By far the best records of the Indians in the seventeenth century are the so-called Jesuit *Relations*, consisting of the reports of the Jesuit missionaries transmitted, every year, to the Provincial of the order at Paris, and there published.

[2] Besides the various general sources—among which Schoolcraft's works are exceedingly unreliable, however necessary it is to consult them—and Bancroft's admirable chapter on the Indians, in his History of the U. S. (vol. iii. chap. xxii.), the above sketch is based, mainly, upon the investigations of Zeisberger himself, and of his fellow-missionaries. In the archives of the Church at Bethlehem, Pa., I was fortunate enough to find a voluminous German MS., buried out of sight. It was written by Zeisberger, in 1778, as is clear from its allusions to national events of that year, although it bears no date; and it contains a full account of the Indian nations with which he was acquainted. Internal evidences in Loskiel's work, as well as the acknowledgment which he makes (Preface, x.), prove conclusively that the entire first part of his history is based upon this MS. I have no doubt that Zeisberger wrote it specially for Loskiel's use. The latter lived in Europe, and had no personal knowledge of the Indians until after the publication of his work. This MS. has been invaluable to me. For the convenience of reference I shall call it "Zeisberger's History of the Indians." Published works are, "History of the Mission of the United Brethren among the Indians in North America, in three parts, by George H. Loskiel, translated from the German by Christian Ignatius Latrobe." London, 1794. "An Account of the History, Manners, and Customs of the Indian Nations who once inhabited Pennsylvania and the neighboring States, by Rev. John Heckewelder." Philadelphia, 1818.

These natives existed in a multitude of tribes and of smaller clans. Their generic stocks, however, were few in number, and may be reduced, upon the basis of radically distinct languages, to the following eight: the Mobilian, Natchez, Uchee, Cherokee, Catawba, Dahcota, Huron-Iroquois, and Algonquin.

The Cherokees had their seats in the upper valley of the Tennessee River, and among the mountains of Western Carolina, Georgia, and Alabama. It is a country that from its lofty hills proclaims the wonderful works of God. The Indian must have felt this in his day. Climbing over the moss-covered rocks of the peak now known as Mt. Mitchell, the highest summit in the United States east of the Rocky Mountains, and emerging from its deep forest of black balsams, the hunter beheld, as far as his eye could reach, one vast wilderness of mountains, crowned with chaplets of clouds, and standing, in silent majesty, the impregnable bulwarks of his country. The rich valleys abounded in game of every variety; and the winding streams, which he could see sparkling in the morning sun, teemed with fish. Within this secluded territory the Cherokee lived safe from every foe.

Not so favored were the Natchez. Their land stretched south of the Yazoo River, in the present State of Mississippi, and was a narrow country, with but four or five villages, where, few in number, the tribe worshiped the Great Sun, from which it claimed descent.

The Uchees, too, were a weak nation, dwelling southeast of the Cherokees, in the region above and below the town of Augusta. At an early period the Creeks subdued them, so that their right to a generic position rests upon traditionary sayings.

Far more numerous and powerful was the Mobilian or Floridian stock of Indians. To it belonged that wide territory which extends from the former seats of the Cherokees south, southeast, and west, to the Atlantic and the Gulf of Mexico, to the Mississippi, and where the waters of the Tennessee and of the Ohio mingle. In this region lived three confederacies,—the Chickasas, Choctas, and Creeks, embracing various subordinate tribes.

East of the Cherokees, in the midlands of Carolina, the Catawbas had their home. They did not count many warriors, but they were brave, and the inveterate enemies of the Iroquois, with whom they continually warred.

The Dahcotas dwelt, for the most part, west of the Mississippi, and belonged to a great and potent family; but bands of them pitched their camps in the prairies east of the river, and these must find a place in the present enumeration. They were the hereditary foes of the Chippewas, and are also and perhaps better known by the name of Sioux. A small branch of them, called the Winnebagoes, dwelt in the midst of Algonquin tribes on the western shore of Lake Michigan.

By far the most prominent nations, in the times of Zeisberger, were the Algonquins and the Huron-Iroquois. These, therefore, claim a more extended investigation.

At the head of the former group, "the grandfathers" of all its many tribes, stood the Delawares. In their own tongue they were known as the Lenni-Lenape, or "Original People." The Iroquois, who eventually absorbed the other group, called themselves Aquanoschioni, or "United People."[1] They were the celebrated Five, afterward Six, Nations of colonial history.[2]

Delaware traditions unfold an interesting narrative.[3] Several centuries before the eye of the white man first beheld the primeval glories of the American continent the Lenni-Lenape lived in a country of the Far West. At a time which they do not pretend to determine, and for reasons of which they are ignorant, many of their fathers emigrated toward the east, and came as far as the Mississippi. Upon its banks were encamped the Aquanoschioni, moving eastward, like the Lenape, in

---

[1] The Delawares are often represented as but one division of the Lenni-Lenape, the other being the Monseys, or Minsi. Zeisberger, however, particularly asserts the identity of the names Delawares and Lenni-Lenape, and shows that they designated one nation, consisting of three tribes, whereof the third was the Monseys.

[2] Great confusion prevails among the names of the various Indian tribes, on account of the numerous synonyms which came into use. This holds good of the Iroquois also. Iroquois is their French name; Six Nations their English; Aquanoschioni one of their original names; and Hodenosaunee, or "People of the Long House," another. It has been maintained that Aquanoschioni is a corruption of Hodenosaunee, and that they did not themselves make use of it. But the latter assertion is disproved by facts. In all the many negotiations which Zeisberger carried on with their Grand Council they invariably employed the name Aquanoschioni when speaking of themselves, as his journals abundantly show. Lafitau and Charlevoix, two Jesuit missionaries, translate it "House-Makers."

[3] Heckewelder's Hist. of the Indian Nations, chapter i. Schoolcraft, Hist. of the Indian Tribes of the U. S., Part vi. 176-178.

search of new homes. The two nations, meeting thus unexpectedly, interchanged the courtesies of Indian life. Before them rolled the mighty river of which their old men had told them when sitting in the lodges of their distant hunting-grounds, and beyond its deep waters lay an unknown country, amid whose hills and within whose valleys they hoped to find rich lands that would rejoice their hearts. But to reach these they had to traverse the territory of the Alligewi, or Allegans, a fierce and warlike people, with whom the Lenape entered into negotiations, obtaining permission to advance. Scarce a moiety of them, however, had crossed the river when the Alligewi, alarmed at the number of the strangers, treacherously attacked them. In a juncture so perilous, the Aquanoschioni, who had been watching the course of events, hastened to offer their assistance. An offensive alliance having been concluded between the two nations, they unitedly fell upon the Alligewi. Fierce battles ensued; much blood was shed; many heroic deeds were performed, until at last the Alligewi, exhausted and dismayed by a succession of defeats, fled with their women and children from the broad valley of the Ohio. The victors divided the hunting-grounds which they had gained. Around the Great Lakes, and on the banks of their tributary rivers, settled the Aquanoschioni; farther to the south the Lenape built their villages. Thus domiciliated, the two nations for a long period of time lived in amity and peace.

In the course of years some adventurous hunters of the Delawares conceived the idea of exploring the country eastward. Pressing through forests where none of their nation had ever been, they reached the Alleghany Mountains, and, crossing these, came to the West Branch of the Susquehanna. Upon the bosom of this beautiful river they launched a bark-canoe, and followed its winding current between lofty hills and through rich lowlands, until their astonished eyes beheld the broad expanse of Chesapeake Bay gleaming like a sea of silver in the noonday sun. Leaving their canoe, they plunged into the tangled thickets of the Eastern Shore, and, speeding across the level plains of Delaware, stood on the bank of a second river rolling in silent majesty to the ocean. The farther they advanced the bolder they grew. Perhaps a third stream, deep and wide, like those which they had discovered, might yet be found; nor were they disappointed. Ere long they scaled the Highlands of the Hudson, and looked down from the rocky Palisades upon the sleeping waters of Tappan Sea. They had traversed a wide territory where the smoke of not a solitary wigwam was seen; where no war-whoop met their ears; where only the carols of birds and the crashing of the bushes under the feet of the startled deer and the heavy step of the bear trudging to his den, broke the solemn silence which nature kept.

With wondering hearts the intrepid explorers hastened back to the council-fire of their nation and reported their discoveries. A part of the Lenape immediately emigrated to these new hunting-grounds, and spread their towns along the Hudson, Susquehanna, Potomac, and Delaware. Around the latter river they clustered thickly. It was the Lenapewihittuck, "the River of the Lenape."

But not all the Lenape left the western country; nor had all of them crossed the Mississippi at the time of the original emigration. Hence, in this period of its history, the nation consisted of three bodies. The one still resided beyond, the other on this side of the Mississippi; and the largest division occupied the territory stretching from the four great eastern rivers to the Atlantic Ocean. All these changes took place long before Europeans had settled on the continent.

The Atlantic Lenape were divided into three tribes. Most distinguished among them were the Unamis or Turtle tribe, who, with the Unalachtgos or Turkey tribe, lived nearest to the sea-board, from the coast to the mountains of Eastern New York, and from the upper waters of the Hudson to the region beyond the Potomac. The third tribe was the Wolf, called Minsi or Monseys. They dwelt from the Hudson to the north heads of the Delaware and Susquehanna, and southward to the Lehigh Hills of Pennsylvania, and the Musconetcong of New Jersey. From these three tribes descended, in the course of time, many others known by various names, living in different parts of the continent, and forming the great Algonquin stock of Indians. Thus far the Delaware traditions.

Whether there is any historic basis for them other than the undisputed fact that the Algonquin tribes, as we have said, all recognized the Lenni-Lenape as their "grandfathers," cannot at this day be determined. The wide diffusion of this family, however, is established beyond a doubt. It was scattered from the rocky wastes of Labrador to the pine forests of North Carolina, extending through more than twenty degrees of latitude along the Atlantic coast, and thence eastward to the Mississippi, over that vast territory which now embraces fifteen teeming commonwealths of the United States and three provinces of British America. The Abenakis, Pequods, Pokanokets or Wampanoags, Narragansetts, and Mohicans of New England; the Lenni-Lenape of Pennsylvania and New Jersey; the Susquehannocks and Nanticokes of Maryland; the Powhattan Confederacy of Virginia; the Shawanese, Kaskaskias, and Illinois west of the Ohio; the Chippewas, Ottawas, Potawatomies, and Miamis of the Great Lakes and the wild Northwest; together with others whose names need not be enumerated, all belonged to this stock. It was relatively so populous that it constituted, as has been computed, about one-half of the natives east of the Mississippi and south of the St. Lawrence.[1]

The Aquanoschioni, too, had a traditionary history, subsequent to the conquest of the Alligewi, preserved, in part, by their aged men, but, in part, imputed to them by the Lenape.

Alive to their own interests, so runs the story of the latter, as they always were, they no sooner perceived that the Lenape had discovered new hunting-grounds beyond the Alleghanies than they also moved east-

---

[1] Bancroft, iii. 243.

ward. Following the great basin of the lakes, they got to the shores of Ontario and the rushing waters of the St. Lawrence. There they established themselves, and again became the neighbors of the Lenape. But the harmony which had subsisted between the two in their western homes was marred in this new country. The Aquanoschioni, moved with envy, entangled the Lenape in wars with their own allies; the Lenape, indignant at such duplicity, turned their arms against the Aquanoschioni, determined to extirpate the whole perfidious race. A succession of wars raged for more than a century.

The fathers of the Aquanoschioni, without acknowledging such an origin of the conflict, continue the tale.

A crisis had come in their history. They were unsupported by allies, and divided among themselves; whereas numerous "grandchildren" flocked to the aid of the Lenape. How could they hope for victory in so unequal a struggle?

Quickened by the danger which threatened the very existence of his people, Thannawage, a wise and aged chief of the Mohawks, proposed the union of its five nations as one confederacy. This suggestion met with universal favor, and, about eighty years before the coming of white men, the league was organized at a council, in which the Mohawks were represented by Toganawita, the Oneidas by Otatschechta, the Onondagas by Tatotarho, the Cayugas by Togahayou, and the Senecas by Ganiatario and Satagaruges.[1]

---

[1] The above tradition is preserved in a German MS. work upon the Indians, by Christopher Pyrlaeus, a Moravian missionary. It is the

We turn from traditions to history. To the Huron-Iroquois family of Indians belonged, originally, the Hurons, or, as they were also called, Wyandots; the Tionnontates, or Tobacco Nation; the Attiwandarons, or Neutral Nation; the Eries and Andastes; together with the Five Nations of the Mohawks, Oneidas, Onondagas, Cayugas, and Senecas. These tribes all spoke dialects of the generic tongue of the Iroquois, and possessed that section of Canada which is inclosed by Lakes Huron, Erie, and Ontario, as also New York and a part of Pennsylvania. The Hurons were conquered by the Five Nations in 1649; the other tribes succumbed to the same domination, so that in the course of time the Iroquois proper were the sole but puissant representatives of their stock, with the exception of some insignificant remnants.

The supremacy which they thus gained was owing, as their traditions correctly set forth, to the league that bound them together. It existed at the discovery of the continent. To determine anything further touching the time when it was formed, or the circumstances under which it grew into being, is impossible. But its advantages are evident. The Algonquins knew nothing of a regular government. They had no system of polity, there was no unity of action among them. The affairs

---

property of the Bethlehem Archives, but deposited in the library of the American Philosophical Society, at Philadelphia. He has recorded the tradition as he found it, without meaning to imply that it is anything more than a tradition. He says, moreover, that the names of the chiefs who proposed and organized the league were perpetuated by calling, from time to time, a person in each nation after them.

even of a single tribe were managed in the loosest manner. Over the Iroquois, on the contrary, was set a Grand Council of fifty sachems, in which each tribe enjoyed equal rights. Several inferior councils, moreover, brought the idea of a government, practically, to all classes, to every age, and even to both sexes, giving them a personal interest, and, to some degree, a share in the same. Hence councils regulated tribal life in all particulars; while matters of national importance, in war and peace, were adjusted by the Grand Council. Thus they became both a political and a military power among the aborigines. The influence of their league was felt, everywhere, and their conquests extended in every direction. Sometimes they overawed the Algonquins by embassies; again, they sent war-parties into their territory for hundreds of miles, and filled the whole wilderness with the terror of the Iroquois name.

Such are the traditions and the history of the Indians up to the time when the first settlements of the white man were begun on the North American continent.

But the aborigines had been known to Europeans for more than a century before this. As early as 1497—only five years after Christopher Columbus had landed in the New World—John Cabot and his son Sebastian, sailing under a commission from Henry VII. of England, discovered the North American continent, in the latitude of the Arctic regions. In 1498, Sebastian Cabot visited the main-land again; and, turning to the south, where the cliffs of Labrador lift their hoary heads, rounded Newfoundland and Nova Scotia, and, coasting along

New England, saw the country where American liberty should be born. Passing Long Island, he looked upon the shore of New Jersey, where summer tourists now mingle in the gay scenes of fashionable watering-places, and the Absecom fisherman fills his boat with luscious oysters; and, running up, first a part of Delaware Bay, and then of Chesapeake Bay, came, at last, into the latitude of Albemarle Sound. It was a bold voyage; an era long to be remembered by the natives. Not many years after, the Spaniards visited the savannas of Florida and the inlets of South Carolina. In 1524, an Italian adventurer, John de Verrazzani, in the service of France, sailed north, and, anchoring in New York Bay, beheld the chiefs of the Mohicans, decked with their eagles' plumes, standing on the shore to bid him welcome; and stopped for two weeks in the harbor of Newport, where the red men were so friendly that he described them as "the goodliest people" he had met on his whole voyage; and, finally, approached the latitude of fifty degrees. Ten years later (1534), Cartier sailed up the St. Lawrence River, and reached the homes of the Iroquois. But all these voyages were mere explorations, and resulted in no colonies.

Nor did the brilliant discoveries of Ferdinand de Soto, in 1538 and the subsequent years, eventuate in any permanent settlements. With a proud array of mail-clad warriors, with flying banners, sounding trumpets, and prancing steeds, he began his march through Florida; and, in spite of fearful hardships and constant hostilities with the Cherokees, the Mobilian Confederacies, and the Natchez, traversed Georgia, parts of South Carolina, Alabama, and Mississippi, until he stood on a lofty bluff and beheld the Father of American rivers bearing his unequaled tribute of waters to the ocean; nor stopped there, but, crossing to the western bank, pressed through Missouri and Arkansas, and, at last, worn out in body and in mind, died amid the wilderness, and found his grave in the great stream which he had discovered. His followers, after incredible toils, reached the Gulf in brigantines, and finally escaped to the Panuco River of Mexico, without having gained a foothold in any part of the regions which they had traversed.

Twenty-two years later, Melendez, another Spaniard, whose atrocious massacre of the Huguenot colony on the St. John's River has made his name notorious, founded the town of St. Augustine, the oldest settlement in North America; but after the inroad of Dominic de Gourges, who avenged the blood of his brethren, it languished, and did not become a center of power.

The expeditions which Sir Walter Raleigh sent to the coast of North Carolina seemed to promise more abiding results. The colony on the Island of Roanoke lived to see the first convert among the Indians, in the person of Manteo, who was baptized by command of Raleigh, and received the title of "Lord of Roanoke." But when its governor, John White, returned, in 1590, from England, with supplies, the island was a desert, the settlers had disappeared, and were never heard of more. Thus the continent, with the exception of St. Augustine, again lay abandoned to its aboriginal inhabitants.

The year 1607 marks a new era. Then the foot of the European race was firmly planted upon this western buttress of the world, and never again removed. Under the auspices of the "London Company," Jamestown was founded in Virginia, amid the Powhattan Confederacy. In spite of hardships and dangers, the colony increased, and triumphantly outlived the bloody massacre of 1622. This settlement was followed, in 1608, by the permanent abode of French immigrants, under Samuel Champlain, in Canada, among the Iroquois. Five years later (1613), the Dutch established themselves at the mouth of the Hudson River, in the territory of the Mohicans; and, seven years after that (1620), the Mayflower cast anchor in the harbor of Cape Cod, and the Pilgrims landed at Plymouth to lay the foundation for the present greatness of New England.

Thus there began, on our continent, that struggle between civilization and barbarism which is now nearly at an end, leading to the extermination of the aborigines as its inevitable issue. Either they must grasp the hand of the Old World, and suffer themselves to be led in its ways, or they must be crushed under its heel.

The Delawares preserved among themselves a tradition that the coming of the white man had been foretold by aged Indians of the Algonquin stock. These prophets are said to have affirmed that the Great Spirit would send to their shores a race of men different from their own, and superior to it in power.

The Indian of that period lived in his original simplicity. He was a hunter and a warrior. In time of peace he pursued the game of his primeval forests, or speared the fish with which the rivers teemed. But when the honor of his tribe was to be upheld he sang the war-song, and went with his fellow-braves to the battle, fighting cautiously from a covert, or, boldly and fiercely, man with man. His arms were of the crudest kind. He wielded the war-club; hurled, with unerring aim, his tomahawk of stone; and sent his arrows, barbed with sharp flint-heads, deep into the breast of his foe. Nor had he other weapons when he stalked the deer or tracked the bear,—when he shot the wild-turkey or chased the raccoon. His household implements were equally simple. To hoe the corn-plant, beans, and pumpkins, which were the only staples, his women used hoes made of the shoulder-bones of the deer or the shell of a turtle, with long handles of wood; to cook his food, they took pots of clay mixed with pounded shells. He cut fuel in the forest with a heavy axe of stone, unwieldy, and slow to perform its work; or kindled a fire either with tinder made of a desiccated fungus or by rubbing together two pieces of dry wood, and brought down a tree by burning off its trunk. The skins of animals served him for clothing; his women wore petticoats of wild flax; and the blanket, that indispensable article of forest-comfort, was curiously manufactured of the feathers of the turkey. For wampum—which he used in such manifold ways, which formed his currency and jewelry, his letters of friendship, his manifestoes of war and seals of peace — he strung together bits of wood of various colors. By way of exception only it was made of sea-shells, and this latter kind he deemed precious as gold.

The moral character of the Indian, prior to his contact with the white man, has been variously estimated. It presented, without doubt, different traits in different tribes. That it was more elevated than in later times seems very probable. Zeisberger often met, especially among the Algonquins, aged men who mourned over the degeneracy they had lived to see; and he believed former generations to have been, at least relatively, far better than those natives among whom he spent his life. On the other hand, the Jesuit missionaries found licentiousness prevailing, both among the Hurons and Iroquois, to a fearful extent, although some of these chroniclers likewise speak of this as a decline from the manners of an earlier age. In general, it may be said that the primitive Indians were distinguished by hospitality, kindness to the poor and the distressed, and courtesy in their social intercourse; that some of their tribes deemed chastity in women a virtue, kept from stealing, and discountenanced lying, but among others the female sex was shamelessly dissolute, and honesty and truth were the rare exceptions; while pride, vindictiveness, cruelty, in forms which might be called devilish, were the vices common to the race. Cannibalism was of frequent occurrence, in times of war, among the Iroquois, Hurons, and some other tribes. It is evident, therefore, that the Indians even in this remote period, does not deserve, from any point of view, that exalted character which is popularly ascribed to him.

After the Dutch had settled in New York, and the French in Canada, the Iroquois became the friends of the former, and the enemies of the latter. Against these they often warred. At the same time, their protracted struggle with the Lenape was not yet over. To this period of their history relates that singular Delaware tradition with which the missionaries met.

The Iroquois, so the story begins, finding the contest in which they were engaged too great for them, as they had to cope, on the one hand, with European arms, and, on the other, with native prowess, excogitated a masterstroke of intrigue. They sent an embassy to the Lenni-Lenape, with a message in substance as follows: That it was not well for the Indians to be fighting among themselves, at a time when the whites, in ever-larger numbers, were pressing into their country; that the original possessors of the soil must be preserved from total extirpation; that the only way to effect this was a voluntary assuming, on the part of some magnanimous nation, of the position of "the woman," or umpire; that a weak people in such a position would have no influence, but a power like the Lenni-Lenape, celebrated for its bravery and above all suspicion of pusillanimity, might properly take the step; that, therefore, the Aquanoschioni besought them to lay aside their arms, devote themselves to pacific employments, and act as mediators among the tribes, thus putting a stop forever to the fratricidal wars of the Indians.

To this proposition the Lenape cheerfully and trustingly consented; for they believed it to be dictated by exalted patriotism, and to constitute the language of genuine sincerity. They were, moreover, themselves very anxious to preserve the Indian race. At a great feast, prepared for the representatives of the two nations, and amid many ceremonies, they were accordingly made women, and a broad belt of peace was intrusted to their keeping.

The Dutch, so the tradition continues, were present on this occasion, and had instigated the plot. That it was a plot to break the strength of the Lenape soon became evident. They woke up from their magnanimous dream, to find themselves in the power of the Iroquois. From that time they were the "cousins" of the Iroquois, and these their "uncles."

This tradition is as ingenious and unique as it is fabulous and absurd. It was devised by the Delawares to conceal the fact that they had been conquered. And yet history recognizes, and will ever know them, as the vassals of the Iroquois, who exercised authority over them, stationed an agent in their country, and would not permit their lands to be alienated without the consent of the Confederate Council. The story of the Delawares contradicts itself. Suspicious as Indians are, to the present day, this nation could not have been so completely duped; and brave as it was, it would never have submitted to such a degradation. The whole character of the aborigines renders the thing impossible. In the figurative language of the natives, the Delawares un-

DAVID ZEISBERGER. 47

questionably were "women," but they had been reduced to this state by force of arms.[1]

The number of the Indians, in the first era of the white man, more than two hundred years ago, cannot be determined with any degree of accuracy. They were more numerous than in Zeisberger's times, yet not to be compared with the populous nations found by the Spaniards in Mexico and Peru. The harmonious testimony of the French and English proves that, about 1660, the Iroquois, redoubtable conquerors though they were, had but two thousand two hundred warriors.[2] This gives a basis of computation which must lead to surprising results. It has been estimated that all the tribes together, east of the Mississippi and south of the St. Lawrence, numbered but one hundred and eighty thousand souls.[3] Wide tracts of that territory were, consequently, uninhabited. The explorer could travel for hundreds of miles without meeting a single human being. Between the scattered tribes lay great solitudes.

---

[1] Heckewelder (*History of the Indian Nations, Introduction and chap. i.*) argues in favor of this story. Zeisberger (*MS. History of the Indians*) and Loskiel (*History of the Indian Mission, 125 and 126*) both mention it, but merely as a tradition. It is a matter of surprise that the author of the "History of the Conspiracy of Pontiac," page 27, asserts that Bishop Loskiel records the story "with the utmost good faith." Loskiel introduces it into his work as an interesting tradition, and says not one word in its favor. As well might the brothers Grimm be accused of believing the national fables of Germany, because they collected and published them.

[2] Bancroft's Hist. U. S., iii. 244; Parkman's Jesuits of North America, Introduction, p. 66.

[3] Bancroft's Hist. U. S., iii. 253. The following is his estimate: Algonquin tribes, 80,000; Eastern Sioux, less than 3000; Iroquois, about 17,000; Catawbas, 3000; Cherokees, 12,000; Mobilian Confederacy, 50,000; Uchees, 1000; Natchez, 4000.

CHAPTER III.

NEW YORK AND PENNSYLVANIA ABOUT THE YEAR 1745.—THEIR SETTLEMENTS AND INDIAN TRIBES.

New York City.—The Counties of the Province.—Its trade, government, and religious spirit.—The Indians of New York.—Clans of Mohicans.—The Iroquois and their territory.—Relations to the English. —Population.—Pennsylvania.—Its liberal institutions and religious freedom.—Philadelphia.—The Counties of the Province and its government.—The Indians of Pennsylvania.—Delawares, Shawanese, and Nanticokes.—The West.—Its Indian tribes and French posts.—A struggle for supremacy between England and France approaching.

HAVING given an account of the Indians in general, and of the Delawares and Iroquois in particular, among whom Zeisberger labored, we will now present a picture of the country which he traversed with the feet of a messenger of peace, as it appeared at the time when he began his mission.

New York was not then the Empire State. In the eighty-one years of British sovereignty, since the inglorious end of New Netherlands, its population and resources had indeed increased, yet not in proportion to the developments expanding some of its sister colonies. But ten counties were under cultivation, scarcely a third part of its area and one-sixth of the present number.[1]

---

[1] The principal sources for the sketch of New York are: The Documentary Hist. of N. Y., in 4 vols., published by the Legislature; and History of the late Province of N. Y., from its Discovery to the Appoint-

DAVID ZEISBERGER. 49

First among them, embracing the island of Manhattan, was the County of New York, with the capital of the Province, and the seat of the Colonial government at its southern extremity. This city—the New Amsterdam of the Dutch—had existed eighty-nine years, and although, with its eleven thousand seven hundred and seventeen inhabitants,[1] it formed a place of no mean pretensions, yet it also exhibited an almost ludicrous contrast with the metropolitan magnificence which now makes it the rival of Paris and London, and one of the emporiums of the world.

Its streets were irregular, and paved with what Smith calls round pebbles; its houses, mostly of brick, covered with tiles; a City Hall, an Exchange, and Almshouse, formed its public edifices; and, ten years subsequent to 1745, it had but eleven places of worship.[2] Of the three public buildings, the most remarkable was City Hall. It was a strong, brick structure, in the shape of

---

ment of Gov. Colden, in 1762, by Hon. William Smith, late Chief Justice of Lower Canada.

[1] A census, including the county, was taken June 4, 1746. *Documentary Hist. N. Y.*, i. 695.

[2] Smith wrote the first volume of his history in 1756, and gives the following churches as existing at that time: Two Episcopal chapels, Trinity and St. George's, the former founded in 1696, the latter in 1752; two Reformed Dutch churches; two German Lutheran; one Moravian; one Presbyterian; one French Protestant; a Quaker Meeting-house; and a Jewish synagogue. The Moravian Church was organized by Count Zinzendorf, in 1743. The first church edifice was built on Fulton Street, in 1752. Smith's brief account of this church is interesting. He says (p. 261), "The Moravians, a new sect among us, a church consisting principally of female proselytes from other societies."

an oblong, two stories high, had an open walk, two jails and the apartments of the jailer on the first floor, and the rooms where the Council and Supreme Court met on the second; the cellar was a dungeon, and the garret a common prison.

New York, in accordance with a charter granted in 1730, was divided into seven wards, and governed by a Mayor, whom the Governor appointed each year, a Recorder, seven Aldermen, and as many Councilmen. Four Aldermen and four Councilmen, together with either the Mayor or Recorder, made up the Common Council.

The city could not deny its Dutch origin. The language of Holland still prevailed, to a considerable extent, and corrupted the English which was spoken; while life, both at home and in society, was marked by many Dutch customs.

In the northeastern part of the county lay the village of Harlem, surrounded by vegetable gardens, which were cultivated for the markets of the city. Like that whole region, it was inhabited, principally, by Dutch farmers.

The two islands, which the Creator has constituted arms to guard New York — to hold back the waters of its noble bay, and permit great ships, coming from all the ends of the earth, to anchor only after having passed within their reach — were well populated, and formed regular counties of the Province. But Staten Island, or Richmond County, was not the resort it now is. No summer-villas beautified it, rivaling those of Italy; no busy ferries brought jaded merchants to its refreshing shore. It presented a wild appearance, and Richmondtown, the only village, was a very poor place. Long Island, on the contrary, with its three counties, King's, Queen's, and Suffolk, and its numerous villages, formed one of the most flourishing parts of the Colony. Its soil was fertile, supporting a population of twenty-one thousand two hundred and twenty-five persons. Many of the farmers were graziers, and carried their products to Boston and Rhode Island. In the eastern section lived a remnant of Indians, in that state of semi-civilization which tends to debase rather than elevate the character of the aborigines.

On the east side of the Hudson River lay the Counties of Westchester and Dutchess. The former was rich in rough but productive land, and, among its towns, had an incorporated borough, Westchester, which enjoyed the right of representation in the Assembly. The villages of Dutchess County were few and small. In Zeisberger's history, Poughkeepsie and Rhinebeck occur. This county, however, was the abode of mixed clans of the once powerful Mohican and Wampanoag nations. The valley of Shekomeko, around the foot of the Stissing Mountain, afforded them a lovely retreat; and here the Moravian Church had established a flourishing Mission.

Skirting the west bank of the Hudson were Orange and Ulster Counties, inhabited by English, Scotch, Irish, and Dutch settlers. Tappan or Orangetown, and Goshen, already famed for its butter, were the prin-

cipal places in the one; and Esopus or Kingston,
Hurley, Rochester, and New Paltz in the other. Esopus
had a court-house, formed a town of some distinction,
and was a favorite resort of Moravian missionaries.
On Catskill Creek, now Greene County, stood a small
frontier settlement called Freehold.

The border county was Albany, whose undefined limits
were lost in the wilderness. On the site of Fort Orange,
a primitive Dutch post, had arisen an incorporated city,
now the capital of the State. It was built in the Dutch
style, governed by a Mayor and Common Council, and
growing in importance. At Albany not only treaties of
great moment were concluded with the Six Nations, but
the Colonies learned some of the rudiments of that political
philosophy which produced American independence.
Scarcely less noted was Schenectady, on the Mohawk
River, in a rich flat surrounded by hills. A very old
town, dating almost from the times of the first colonists,
and near the Indian country, it had, by common consent,
been made the general rendezvous for Iroquois, and for
traders coming to barter, or preparing to pursue their
traffic at more distant posts. To the west of it, on both
sides of the Mohawk, lay the settlements of the Palatines,
who had immigrated to New York by invitation of
Queen Anne. About 1723, many of them had removed
to Pennsylvania, but the tract had remained a German
neighborhood, and its villages, looking out from the
midst of wheat-fields and pea-patches, spread life and
industry as far as the Schoharie Creek. Beyond this,
isolated farms, reaching to the Mohawk territory, con-

stituted the western bounds of civilization. To the north, land had been reclaimed as far as Schaghticoke and Saratoga, where a fort had been erected, around which clustered a few rude homesteads. But in 1745, an attack of French Indians from Crown Point obliged the settlers to seek a safer refuge. From Saratoga to Canada reigned the solitude and grandeur of a primeval wilderness.

Exclusive of Albany County, the population of New York amounted to sixty-one thousand five hundred and eighty-nine souls, of whom fifty-one thousand eight hundred and seventy-two were whites, and the rest negroes. Four years later (1749), it had, including Albany County, increased to seventy-three thousand four hundred and forty-eight.[1] While, therefore, this Province, in most respects, was not the first among the American Colonies, it foreshadowed, in one particular, its future greatness as a commercial power. Productions of various kinds, and in large quantities, were exported to different parts of the world.

The government embraced a Governor, appointed by King's commission; a Council, numbering twelve members, designated by the King's mandamus and sign manual, and forming advisers of the Governor, exercising also legislative power and judicial authority upon writs of error and appeals; and a General Assembly of twenty-seven representatives, elected for seven years by the people.

---

[1] Doc. Hist. N. Y., i. 695. In 1746 no census could be taken in Albany County on account of the war.

New York did not afford to Christians of various persuasions the same quiet retreat which they found in Pennsylvania. Several Governors betrayed a desire to render the Episcopal Church an Establishment; the Roman Catholics were held in great abhorrence; and the Moravians suffered persecution. That the expulsion of their ministers, whose faithful labors among the Indians God crowned with abundant success, was owing to the jealousy of bigoted religionists, cannot be doubted. The Presbyterians and the Reformed Dutch were the most numerous Christian denominations; the Episcopalians comprised but a small minority. Their clergy were missionaries of the "English Society for Propagating the Gospel," and ordained by the Bishop of London, who had a commissary in the Province.

The aboriginal lords of the soil still maintained their position. However unimportant the scattered clans of Mohicans and Wampanoags, the Confederacy of the Six Nations was a power on the continent. From the limits of Orange, Ulster, and Albany Counties to the waters of the Lakes, and from Canada to Pennsylvania, stretched out their broad hunting-grounds, covering two-thirds of the present State.

Next to the settlements lived the Mohawks, who formed the strongest and brightest link in the chain of friendship that bound together the League and the Colonies.[1] They were partially civilized, enjoying the instruc-

---

[1] Zeisberger's MS. Hist. of the Indians; Morgan's League of the Iroquois, with a map of their country in 1720.

tions of Barclay, an Episcopal missionary.[1] Among them lived Sir William Johnson, the Indian agent, who knew better than any other man how to sway the proud Iroquois. His seat, at Kolaneka, the present Johnstown, in Fulton County, was a place of great celebrity, where he was accustomed to entertain their sachems and warriors.[2]

One of the chief towns of the Mohawks was Canajoharie. Between it and the plantations of the Palatines lay William's Fort, which was both an English post and a village of natives.[3]

Neighbors of the Mohawks were the Oneidas, whose territory extended from the St. Lawrence River to Pennsylvania, and, by a westward deflection of the boundary line, included the lake bearing their name. Then came the Tuscaroras, the youngest branch of the Confederacy, originally from North Carolina, whence they had been driven for attempting to extirpate the colonists of that Province. Adopted by the Iroquois in 1712, they were made the sixth tribe of the League, which was thenceforth known as the Six Nations. Tuscarora towns, on the main road to Onondaga, were Anajot, Ganatisgoa, Ganochserage, Tiochrungwe, and Sganatees.

---

[1] Smith's Hist. of N. Y., ii. 77.

[2] William Johnson immigrated to America in 1734, and undertook the management of an estate in the Mohawk valley for Sir Peter Warren, embarking also in the fur trade with the Indians, whose language he learned. Having been commissioned a General in the Colonial army, he received, in 1755, the appointment of Superintendent-General of Indian Affairs. In the same year he defeated the French and French Indians under Count de Deiskau, and for this victory was knighted.

[3] Zeisberger's Journal of a Visit to the Mohawk Country in 1745. MS. B. A.

In the middle of the Iroquois country lay the possessions of the Onondagas. This nation was the head of the Confederacy, and the custodian of the common council-fire. A few miles southeast of the Salt Lake, on the Zinochsaa,[1] stood Onondaga, the capital of the League, divided into an upper and lower town, the latter called Tagochsanagechti. It was a place of note and a seat of power. In its long and arched council-house assembled the sachems, from every part of the Confederacy, in order to deliberate upon the affairs of the same; and when the occasion was important hundreds of their followers often accompanied them, filling the village or bivouacking in the surrounding forest. Here, with the most punctilious adherence to parliamentary propriety, as established by the Indian, and with a decorum greater far than can be found in some of the legislative bodies of the white man, plans were adopted and principles settled which had an important bearing upon the history of America. Here were duly considered the overtures of friendship, which the Iroquois received from the two greatest kingdoms of Europe, whose statesmen waited, not without anxiety, for the decision of this council of American savages.

Nor were political emissaries the only visitors at Onondaga. Messengers of the Gospel of peace came there; bishops of the Moravian Church concluded alliances; and Zeisberger had a house of his own, and was regarded as a native citizen.

---

[1] The present Onondaga Creek, flowing into Onondaga or the Salt Lake.

The nearest British post, and a second rendezvous for traders, was Oswego.

West of the Onondagas lived the Cayugas, whose principal towns were Cayuga, Ganutarage, Sannio, and Ondachoe, which all enlivened the shores of the lake to which the tribe has given its name.

The remainder of New York, to the crested flood of Niagara, leaping into its deep abyss, and to the broad waters of Lake Erie, radiant in the light of the setting sun, afforded the wild Senecas a home. The most numerous and powerful people of the Confederacy, they offered a determined opposition to the encroachments of the white race. Zonesschio, Ganataqueh, and Hachniage were some of their villages.

The country of the Iroquois was well adapted to their habits. Wooded hills and beautiful lakes diversified it; salt springs poured out their abundance; a system of creeks and rivers stretched from one end of it almost to the other. Around these water-courses lay the favorite haunts of the hunter. There he trapped the beaver, or, launching his canoe of birch-bark, threw out his fish-baskets and caught thousands of eels in a single night, or, paddling up the small streams when the forests began to glow in their autumnal hues, speared the delicious salmon. The villages, too, were generally near to some stream, and environed by orchards. In many parts of the land swamps of white cedars spread their gloom, deep and silent homes of the bear. Deer were not as common as in Pennsylvania, but other game abounded.

Numerous trails intersected this country; they led to

its principal towns, and had been trodden by the Indians for generations. One of them in particular deserves to be mentioned: commencing at Albany, it followed the Mohawk River and passed through the Oneida, Tuscarora, and Onondaga cantons to the metropolis, continuing thence through the lands of the Cayugas and Senecas, it divided into two branches near its end, reached Niagara on the north and the head of Lake Erie on the south, not far from Buffalo, thus traversing the entire length of the present Empire State. This was the great highway of the Six Nations, and designated the course for the future multitudes which would sweep westward along trails of iron on the wings of steam. Other trails going south centered at Tioga, in Pennsylvania.[1]

Writers are much divided in opinion with regard to the number of the Iroquois. The middle of the seventeenth century was, in the judgment of Morgan, the era of their greatest prosperity, for he supposes them to have then had at least twenty-five thousand souls.[2] In 1745, they counted, according to some authorities, about one-half less; according to others, scarcely four thousand persons, women and children included. This latter estimate, however, is entirely too low. Many of them lived in Canada, Pennsylvania, and the West. Such emigrant Iroquois were called Mingoes.

---

[1] The Iroquois country described by *Zeisberger in his MS. Hist. of the Indians;* the trails by Morgan in his *League of the Iroquois,* 412.

[2] Morgan's Iroquois League.

Pennsylvania fills an important place in our picture.[1] When Zeisberger entered the missionary field the work of building up this Province to a broad and massive Keystone State was progressing. William Penn slept with his fathers; but the wise policy which he had initiated, and the liberal principles which he had established, had borne fruits. The first charter given by him was based upon two fundamental truths of political economy: that the happiness of society is the real object of civil power, and that freedom exists only where the laws rule and the people are parties to them.[2] Hence his Province enjoyed a greater share both of civil and religious liberty than any of its neighbors; its population rapidly increased, and its progress in other respects was extraordinary. Only sixty-three years had elapsed since the landing of Penn at New Castle, and already Pennsylvania numbered about one hundred and ten thousand inhabitants,[3] carried on a considerable trade, possessed large tracts of well-cultivated land, and had for its capital a city ranking second among all the cities of the Colonies.[4]

From many countries of Europe immigrants had

---

[1] Authorities: Gordon's History of Pennsylvania; Watson's Annals of Philadelphia; Rupp's Histories of Lancaster, Berks, and Lebanon Counties; Pennsylvania Historical Collections; and various MSS. in B. A.

[2] Gordon, 173

[3] The population, in 1745, cannot be exactly ascertained; the number I give is based upon figures for 1731 and 1751, in *Proud's History of Pennsylvania.*

[4] At that time Boston was the largest city in the Colonies. In 1742 its population was 16,582.

sought and found a home within its hospitable confines. Here lived together Quakers and Episcopalians, Presbyterians and Moravians, Schwenkfelders and Lutherans, Tunkers and Reformed, Baptists and Seventh-day Baptists, Roman Catholics[1] and Mennonites, Separatists and the Inspired, Hermits and the New Born, and there was none to make them afraid. It is true their spiritual state was often lamentable. Spangenberg draws a dark picture of the Germans especially. " Thousands," he says, " concerned themselves so little about religion that it had become a proverb to say of a person wholly indifferent to God's will and word: He is of the Pennsylvania religion."[2] Others were given up to the most extravagant fanaticism, while the young generally remained without an education, uncared for and forlorn.

Although Spangenberg is mistaken when he assigns one hundred thousand Germans to Pennsylvania,[3] yet they outnumbered all other nationalities, and, being mostly landholders, their votes at elections were eagerly solicited. The Quakers constituted not one-third of the population.[4] German industry, therefore, was changing the wilderness into fruitful farms, and developing the resources of the country. At the same time, the

---

[1] The Roman Catholics were held in such abhorrence in England that even Penn reluctantly received them.—*Gordon's History of Pennsylvania*, 570, etc.

[2] Spangenberg's Leben Zinzendorf, Part v., 1380.

[3] Spangenberg's Leben Zinzendorf, Part v., 1379.

[4] Gordon's Hist. of Penn. Proud, in his Hist. of Penn., states that in one year (1749), 12,000 German immigrants arrived.

tenaciousness with which this people clung to their mother-tongue, over against the manifest destiny of the English to become the language of the American Colonies, was the cause of the gross ignorance that still gives to many of our German farmers so unenviable a notoriety.

To Pennsylvania belonged three counties on the Delaware River—New Castle, Kent, and Sussex—which now make up the State of Delaware. In the early period of Colonial history they were known as "The Territories." Of these we will not speak, but turn to an account of the Province itself. Under cultivation was that part which is bounded by the Blue Mountains on the west, the Delaware on the east, and Maryland on the south. This section was divided into four counties—Philadelphia, Bucks, Chester, and Lancaster—of which the first three had been laid out by Penn himself as early as 1682, and the last dated to 1729. They all embraced larger areas than at presnt.

Philadelphia County, extending in a northwesternly direction to the mountains, and including a part of Berks and the whole of Montgomery, was the seat of Penn's original settlements, and of the capital of the Province.

The City of Philadelphia, founded in 1682 on the Delaware, numbered, in the first year of its existence, eighty-two houses; in 1745, it had fifteen hundred houses, and a population of thirteen thousand souls. It stretched along the river, and High or Market Street, its principal thoroughfare, reached barely to what is now Sixth. The market-houses, which for so long a period made this thoroughfare celebrated, but which to-day belong to the things that were, had been erected from Front to Third Streets.

One of the most interesting public edifices of the city, although its glory had departed in 1745, was the "Old Court House," at Second and High Streets—a quaint structure set on arches, beneath which markets were held, and having a gallery along the front gable on a level with the upper story, and steps on both sides leading down to the street. A cupola with a bell surmounted the building. Until the year 1735, it formed the "Greate Towne House," where the Assembly met, and from the gallery of which the Governors addressed the the people.[1] It was superseded by the present State House.[2] Notable, too, was the Stone Prison, at the southwest corner of Third and High Streets, consisting of two houses, joined by a lofty wall, that on High Street being the Debtor's Jail, and that on Third, the Work House. The "Carpenter Mansion," a handsome edifice on Chestnut Street above Sixth, had been set apart as the residence of the Governor. It was surrounded by grounds and orchards from Sixth to Seventh Streets, and in front of it stood a range of fine cherry-trees.

---

[1] This gallery once served Whitefield as a pulpit, where he preached with so stentorian a voice that he was heard far out on the Delaware River.

[2] Commenced in 1729, finished in 1734; afterward it underwent various changes until it assumed its present appearance.

The churches of the city numbered eleven, and were distributed among the Baptists, Presbyterians, Quakers, Moravians, Episcopalians, Lutherans, Reformed, and Roman Catholics. Particularly interesting were the Swedes' Church and the Academy. The former was the oldest place of worship in Philadelphia, having been founded by the Swedish colonists in 1677, five years before the arrival of Penn; the latter, at the instance of Whitefield, had been built by subscription, " for the use of itinerant preachers forever."

Public squares were unknown. Washington Square, which now offers its refreshing shade to the weary citizen, was a potter's-field. Instead of such artificial grounds, however, a natural park of noble trees covered the entire area between Market and South Streets, Broad Street and the Schuylkill River. It was called the " Center Wood," also " Governor's Wood."

A charter, granted in 1701, constituted the people of Philadelphia a body corporate, under the name and style of " The Mayor and Commonalty of the City of Philadelphia, in the Province of Pennsylvania." The government was composed of a Mayor, Recorder, Aldermen, and Common Council, all elected by the corporation.

Among the neighboring towns, Frankford and Germantown were best known. The latter, founded in 1683 by Francis Pastorius and a body of immigrants from Germany, was an incorporated borough; contained meeting-houses for the Friends, Dunkers, and Mennonites; and churches for the Lutherans and Reformed.

In 1746, the Moravians began a boarding-school, at the house of John Bechtel. The handsome summer-residences which now beautify the place were not seen. It was, as its name denotes, a settlement of German farmers. Germans, too, occupied parts of the present Montgomery County; both Schwenkfelders, whose plantations clustered around Skippack, and Lutherans from the Palatinate, who had a church at Trappe. Other parts were settled by Quakers, and Gwynedd Township by Welsh.

Bucks County, running in the same direction and as far as that of Philadelphia, was bounded by the same mountains. It subsequently shared its area with Northampton and Lehigh. Quakers and Irish inhabited the lower half, in which Bristol, an incorporated borough on the Delaware, was the principal town, and Pennsbury Manor, five miles from Bristol, once the handsome country-seat of William Penn, lay neglected and fallen into premature decay. The upper section bore the name of the "Forks of the Delaware."[1]

In 1737, the Indian title to its lands had been extinguished by the far-famed "walking purchase;"[2] but it

---

[1] Now Northampton County, which was established in 1752.

[2] At a treaty held by the Proprietaries in 1737, in relation to a tract of land purchased by W. Penn in 1686, but never laid off and ceded, it was agreed that the natives should alienate so much as a man could walk over in one and a half days, beginning near Wrightstown, Bucks County, and going north toward the Blue Mountains. The Proprietaries having advertised for the most expert walkers, several offered their services. Of these three were selected, who undertook the walk on the 19th and 20th of September. By noon of the 20th one of them reached the Tobihanna Creek, beyond the mountains, much to the indignation of the Indians.

DAVID ZEISBERGER.

was, as yet, sparsely settled. The first inhabitants came from North Ireland, and established themselves below Bath, in the "Irish Settlements." They were followed by Germans, among whom Zeisberger's people, the Moravians, soon attracted the attention of the entire Province. Building Bethlehem and Nazareth, having a log church at Maguntsche, laying out Christiansbruun and Gnadenthal,[1] they created centers of a wide-spread influence, both in a material and spiritual point of view; for they were no less successful as farmers and mechanics than they were zealous as missionaries and faithful as preachers of righteousness.

Easton, the flourishing county-town of Northampton, did not exist in 1745; it was begun five years later.[2] There were, in fact, no villages other than the Moravian, and these were quite small. The settlers were found at wide intervals as far as the Blue Mountains, and a few in Smithfield Township, beyond the ridge; but the larger part of that territory was a dense wilderness, the Towamensing of the Indians, where they delighted to hunt.[3] In an earlier period another of their chosen resorts had been the Minnisinks, broad flats east of the Delaware Water-Gap. There the Monseys had kindled their great council-fire; now white men's cabins usurped its place.

The County of Chester included the present Delaware

---

[1] The Indians called Bethlehem *Menagachsünk;* Nazareth, *Welagamika;* Christiansbruun and Gnadenthal, *Nolemattink.* MS. B. A.

[2] The Indian name for Easton was *Lechauwitonk.*

[3] The Moravians called this wilderness "Anthony's Wilderness," after the Rev. Anthony Seyfert, the first Moravian minister ordained in America.

County, and was first settled by Quakers. Later came Scotch-Irish Presbyterians and Welsh, the latter selecting the Great Valley for their farms. Old Chester, or Upland, was the seat of justice.

Lancaster County, the fruitful mother of the present York, Cumberland, Berks, Northumberland, Dauphin, and Lebanon, supported a numerous population, mostly of Germans. Its county seat was Lancaster Town, which had a Quaker meeting-house, a Lutheran and a Reformed church. Soon after 1745 an Episcopal chapel was erected. Ten years later there were two thousand inhabitants. A public high-way to Philadelphia had been laid out as early as 1733.

This county was divided into eight districts, whose plantations stretched along Conestoga Creek toward the Susquehanna, through Strasburg Township, where the Mennonites congregated, and along Mill Creek, in the Weber Thal. Besides these homesteads, the villages of Reamstown, Säue Schwamm, now New Holland, and Adamstown had been begun. At Ephrata were found, in all their original simplicity, under the guidance of Conrad Beissel, their "father," the Seventh-Day Baptists, living in a convent for the "brethren," and in a nunnery for the "sisters," eating their simple meals from diminutive wooden platters of their own manufacture, and sleeping at night on hard benches, with sharp-cornered blocks for their pillows. The Moravian town of Litiz was not yet in existence; on its present site George Klein garnered plentiful harvests, and Nyberg, a Lutheran minister of Lancaster, preached the

Gospel in a small log church, called St. James.[1] To the north, near the Furnace Hills, were iron-works, established in 1728, by the Grubb family.

Where Columbia sees the busy trade of the Pennsylvania Railroad, nestled a little settlement; another was visible on the opposite bank, at Wrightsville; and farther west, in York, Adams, and Cumberland Counties, were isolated farms. The Town of York, laid out in 1741, was an insignificant hamlet; but Harris's Ferry, the nucleus of the present City of Harrisburg, by the courage and indomitable perseverance of John Harris, its founder, had been made so celebrated an outpost of civilization that its fame spread not only through the Colonies, but to every country of Europe, whence immigrants had come to Pennsylvania.

That smiling valley, which lends its name to the Lebanon Valley Railroad, was well settled; but neither with Lebanon nor with any of the other thriving towns, at which the cars now stop, did the trader and the occasional traveler meet. Yet there were some points of interest. Near the site of Lebanon, the Moravians, in 1745, organized a church, and soon after erected Hebron, a large chapel of unhewn stone; in Tulpehocken Township, the new home of the Palatines from New York, another church, under the auspices of the same

---

[1] George Klein having donated his farm to the Moravian Church, Litiz was laid out in 1756, and made a Moravian settlement, like Bethlehem and Nazareth. The exclusive system, as in all former Moravian towns of this country, has long since been relinquished. St. James's Church stood on the present turnpike to Lancaster, just above the first houses of Litiz.

religionists, was built in the same year; and about half a mile east of the present Wommelsdorf lay the seat of Conrad Weisser, that distinguished Indian Agent and Government Interpreter, who exercised so great an influence over the natives, and so zealously promoted the Moravian Mission.[1] At Reading, now a prosperous city, the terminus of five railways, on one of which the coal-treasures disemboweled from the hills of Pennsylvania hourly pass by, in trains of prodigious length, to the emporium at Philadelphia, there stood probably but a single house.[2] To the south of it, was Oley Township, settled by French Huguenots, among whose descendants the Moravians had established a boarding-school and a small congregation.

In some respects the government of Pennsylvania differed from that of New York. William Penn having entered into negotiations with the Crown to sell his title and claim, but dying before they could be concluded, the proprietorship gave rise to protracted legal action. Finally, however, his three sons by his second wife, Thomas, John, and Richard, became his successors. In 1745, Thomas and John Penn lived at Philadelphia, where was their Land Office, from which warrants were

---

[1] C. Weisser, born at Herrenberg, Wurtemberg, Nov. 2, 1696, immigrated with his father to America in 1710, settled in the Mohawk valley, and lived with Quagnant, an Indian chief, from whom he learned the Mohawk and other native languages. Removing, in 1729, to Tulpehocken, he was appointed Indian Agent, Government Interpreter, and Justice of the Peace by Governor Thomas. In the Indian and French War he commanded the second battalion of the Penn. Regiment. He died July 13, 1760, and lies buried on his farm.

[2] Reading was laid out in 1748; Berks County organized in 1752.

issued for newly-purchased tracts. The Proprietaries, with the consent of the Crown, appointed the Governor or Lieutenant-Governor, as he was styled. In the period under review, George Thomas, a planter from Antigua, filled this office. The Council, whose Secretary was Richard Peters, an Episcopal clergyman, formed a body of advisers to the Governor; and the Assembly was elected annually by the people. This yearly election constituted a prerogative which Pennsylvania enjoyed over other Colonies. The Sheriffs were designated for three years by the Governor, within three days after return made to him from two persons chosen by the freemen of each county; and Clerks of the Peace were nominated in the same way, from three persons returned by the Justices. The Assembly numbered thirty persons, and was wholly under the influence of the Quakers. In 1741 there were only three members not of this persuasion.

Over all that wide country which lies beyond the Blue Mountains to the several limits of the State, and which now is its bone and sinew, roamed clans of aborigines. Some of these were without permanent homes, broken remnants of former nations, weak, poor, and degenerate; others were mixed bodies of vagrants from various tribes, having little villages in common, and even inhabiting the same wigwams;[1] while still others, like the Conestoga Indians, resided in the

---

[1] On the Susquehanna, Zeisberger found Mohicans, Shawanese, and Delawares thus living together.

counties, supporting themselves by the sale of baskets, brooms, and wooden dishes.[1]

Two tribes of the Wyoming Valley—the Shawanese and Nanticokes—were more numerous and powerful.

The former had been expelled from Florida, and adopted as nephews by the Delawares. In their new seats they increased so rapidly that a portion of them emigrated to the Ohio River, and erected their lodges below the mouth of the Scioto.[2] Those who remained in Wyoming built a village on the west bank of the Susquehanna, opposite to the confluence of the Lackawanna.[3] They were a savage and perfidious race.

The Nanticokes, having been driven from the Eastern Shore of Maryland, had likewise been adopted by the Delawares. They took up their abode below the Lackawanna, on the east bank of the Susquehanna, not far from Pittston, in sight of the Shawanese town.[4] At a later time, single parties of them moved to the north, as far as Chemung; and, in 1753, the whole tribe left Wyoming, and settled in the Iroquois country.[5] The Shawanese had, before this, joined their brothers in Ohio.

The most influential and important among the aborigines of Pennsylvania were the Delawares. Their

---

[1] Such Indians were often called "River Indians."
[2] Bancroft's Hist. U. S. iv. 77.
[3] Draft of Wyoming Valley by the Missionaries. B. A.
[4] *Ibid.* A part of the tribe came to Pennsylvania before 1745, and lived near Harris's Ferry; the main body, however, removed in that year.
[5] Zeisberger's Journal of Journey to Onondaga in 1753. MS. B. A.

favorite hunting-grounds lay along the North and West Branches of the Susquehanna. It was a rich and beautiful country. The land yielded maize in great abundance; the river swarmed with rock-fish and shad; the beaver abounded along the smaller streams; and the forests were stocked with deer, elk, foxes, and raccoons. Nor were retreats for the bear wanting,— great swamps of beech, white-pine, and spruce trees interlocked so closely, and surrounded with so thick a growth of underwood, that the rays of the sun never penetrated their deep recesses.[1]

Shamokin, the present Sunbury, was the chief town of the Indians.[2] Its importance in Pennsylvania equaled that of Onondaga in New York. It was the residence of Allemoebi, who, although a decrepit, blind, old man,[3] ranked as the "King of the Delawares." It was the post of Shikellimy, the Executive Deputy of the Grand Council of the Six Nations, and the real ruler of the Delaware dependencies. The Iroquois were still masters; the Delawares women.

About a day's journey from Shamokin lay Oston-

---

[1] Zeisberger's MS. Hist. of the Indians.

[2] David Brainerd, in his Diary, Sept. 13, 1745, gives the following description of the town: "It lies partly on the east side of the river, partly on the west, and partly on a large island in it, and contains upward of fifty houses and nearly three hundred persons, though I never saw much more than half that number in it. They are of three different tribes of Indians, speaking three languages wholly unintelligible to each other. About one-half of its inhabitants are Delawares, the others called Senekas and Tutelas."—*Brainerd's Life*, p. 167. Am. Tract Soc. Ed.

[3] Spangenberg's Journal of his Journey to Onondaga in 1745. MS. B. A.

wacken on the West Branch, where, among a mixed clan, dwelt Madame Montour, the French widow of Carondowana or Robert Hunter—an Iroquois chief who fell in a battle with the Catawbas—and her son, Andrew Montour, a warm and faithful friend of the Colonies.

Other towns on the Susquehanna were Wamphallobank, in the present Luzerne County; Neskapeke, now Nescope, at the mouth of a creek of the same name, where lived a Delaware family, named Natumus, distinguished for its relative wealth, and owning a number of negro slaves;[1] and Machiwihilusing, in Bradford County. The Alleghany, too, was enlivened by Delaware villages; while, in Ohio, they were multiplying so rapidly that they could there boast of five hundred warriors (1750).[2] They owned, moreover, a large tract of land on the Wabash, presented to them by the Kickapoos, but it was uninhabited.[3]

The Pennsylvania homes of the Delawares, in their own figurative mode of speech, were but "night-lodges." The philanthropic wish of the original Proprietary had not been realized. There was no room for the aborigines. The steady advance of the white man compelled them, at almost every treaty with the Colonial authorities, to alienate more of their land, and retire to deeper recesses of the western wilderness.

This wilderness, rich in broad lakes and noble rivers,

---

[1] Map of Wyoming Valley, by the Missionaries. B. A.
[2] Bancroft's Hist. U. S., iv. 77.
[3] Zeisberger's MS. Hist. of the Indians.

in magnificent forests and blooming prairies, one of the most luxuriant territories on the North American Continent, and big with the great future which it should bring forth, constituted the hunting-grounds of many tribes. Around the western head of Lake Erie, in Canada and Ohio, lived a remnant of the Hurons, or Wyandots; about Saginaw Bay, the Ojibwas had their wigwams; the waters of Lake Michigan reflected the council-fires of the Ottawas and Potawatomies, on the east, and of the Menomonies, Winnebagoes and Kickapoos, on the west; the Chippewas—a powerful nation mustering many braves—were scattered in Canada, along Lake Huron, and south of Lake Superior; the towns of the Sacs, Foxes, and Ottigamies lay between Lake Michigan and the Mississippi; and farther down that river were domiciliated the Illinois.

These Indians, together with numerous other clans, were claimed as allies by France, which had established military posts among them, on the Wabash, the Ohio, the Illinois, the Wisconsin, and the Mississippi. In a report made to the home government, in 1736, the French Colonial authorities asserted that no less than one hundred and three nations, comprising sixteen thousand four hundred and three warriors, and eighty-two thousand souls, were under their control.[1] However exaggerated this report may have been, or at least, however nominal such a sway, France, since the peace of Utrecht (1713), had again become a formidable rival

---

[1] Schoolcraft's Ind. Tribes, Part vi. 198.

of England, in the New World, and was active in spreading her influence through the valley of the Mississippi in particular. Hence the new war which had broken out between these two countries (1744), although it raged chiefly in Europe and on the sea, may be called the prelude to a final struggle for the supremacy of the North American Continent.

CHAPTER IV.

GOVERNMENT, MANNERS, CUSTOMS, CHARACTER, AND RELIGION OF THE DELAWARES AND IROQUOIS IN THE TIMES OF ZEISBERGER.

Idea of government.—The Iroquois polity.—Sachems.—Grand Council.—Chiefs.—Clans.—The later Iroquois different from their fathers.—The Delaware government.—National and tribal chiefs.—Counselors and captains.—Aboriginal life changed through the influence of the white men.—Hunting, its laws and charms.—Other employments.—Household utensils.—Towns and houses.—The Indian at home.—Dress of the men and the women.—Children.—Social intercourse.—Games.—Environs of a village —Magazines, rum-shops, vapor-baths, and burial-grounds.—Dances.—Moral character, and the false estimate of the same.—Zeisberger's views.—Cause of the false estimate.—Religious belief of the primitive Indians.—Outlines of their superstition in the last century.—Indian oratory.

THE idea of government, as found among the aborigines, presented interesting and peculiar features. The Indian was absolutely free, acknowledged no master, and yielded obedience to law only in so far as he chose. His chiefs did not rule, in the ordinary sense; they had no power which they could enforce; they could claim no tribute, however common it was to bring them gifts. Their authority was based upon personal influence, and upon the skill with which they guided their counselors. And yet there existed systems of government that, in spite of their many imperfections, were far in advance both of the lawlessness of some savages and the tyranny which enslaves others.

What a contrast, for example, was there not between the Indian nations of our own country and those African tribes which submitted to the cruelties of a despot, selling thousands into servitude, or putting to death wives and subjects for the most trivial offense! The grand principle of self-government appears among the former, although in a crude cast; and it may well be said, that the race which came to establish upon our Continent the great republic we have lived to see, found a faint type of it amid the children of its primeval forests.

This holds good of the Iroquois system in particular, which was the best matured and most successful. Their nations were independent in some respects, but confederated in a central government, to which certain privileges and powers had been delegated. Its distinguishing feature, however, was altogether peculiar, and constituted the League, as such, an oligarchy rather than a republic.

There existed sixty permanent sachemships, each with a title of its own, and each hereditary. The laws of descent were carefully regulated; and before a sachem could discharge the duties of his office he must be invested with his title by a council of his peers, or to use their own term for the ceremony, "raised up."

They were all of the same rank, and exercised jurisdiction, not separately or territorially, but in common, throughout the Confederacy. At its organization the Mohawks received nine such sachemships, the Oneidas the same number, the Onondagas fourteen, the Cayugas ten, and the Senecas eight. This difference in numbers, however, caused no disparity of power. The sachems, in their associated capacity, formed the Grand Council, where each representative enjoyed equal rights and the same privileges. Some, indeed, were considered more dignified than others; but this depended upon their titles. That one of the Onondago sachems who was known as Tododäho ranked first. The Council was the ruling body, and exercised legislative, judicial, and executive authority. Besides this confederate position, such sachems stood at the head of their own nations also.[1]

Next in power were the chiefs, whose office was elective, but terminated with the individual. They generally received this distinction as a reward of merit, and their number was not limited. At first, they were merely the counselors and assistants of the sachems; in the course of time, however, their influence grew to be coequal. The duties of both sachems and chiefs were altogether of a civil character. A sachem, going to war, ranked as a common brave. Indeed, there existed no regular war-chiefs. Any warrior could form and lead a band. In case of a general war, two supreme military chieftains, whose office was hereditary, directed the campaign.

Another characteristic of the Iroquois polity was the subdivision of their nations into clans or families, of which there were eight, known by the names of Turtle,

---

[1] Morgan's League of the Iroquois, pp. 62, 63. I follow this author and Zeisberger in my account of the Iroquois government.

Bear, Wolf, Beaver, Deer, Snipe, Heron, and Hawk. Each of these had for its emblem the figure of the animal or bird after which it was designated. Such emblems were called *totems*, and were tattooed on the persons of the clansmen, or painted over the doors of their huts. The clans were constituted irrespective of nationality, and embraced such as formed one family, in whatever tribe they might be found. Hence two persons of the same clan never married. The child belonged to that of its mother.

As an illustration, we may adduce the example of Zeisberger himself. He was adopted into the nation of the Onondagas and the clan of the Turtle. Consequently all those Iroquois who were comprised in this clan, whether Onondagas, Cayugas, Senecas, Oneidas, Tuscaroras, or Mohawks, acknowledged him as their kinsman.

The Turtle family, or the Anowara, was the most noble of the whole League; next came the Ochquari, or clan of the Bear, and the Oquacho, or that of the Wolf. These three were so prominent that Zeisberger hardly recognizes the others.[1]

Of the Iroquois generally, it may be said that they had grown to be, in his time, a conglomeration of nationalities, wholly different from the original Aquanoschioni. This was owing to the adoption of prisoners taken in the wars which each successive generation had

---

[1] Clark, in his *Onondaga*, i. 32, includes the Beaver among the superior clans, and adduces the Eagle and the Eel, in place of the Snipe and the Hawk.

been carrying on with nearly all the tribes of the continent. If they had not thus replenished their ranks they would have died out long before he came among them.

The Delaware government bore some analogy to that of the Six Nations, but was less of a system, and lacked a proper development.

Each of the three tribes, into which this people was divided, had a national chief at its head. The chief of the Turtle tribe stood highest, and bore the title of "King of the Delawares." It was his duty to preserve the council-bag, the belts of peace, as well as all documentary records of Colonial treaties; and, jointly with the other two chiefs, to administer the foreign affairs of the nation. A general council was sometimes called, in which all the three headmen and their advisers took part.

In addition to these rulers, however, there were many subordinate chiefs, who, together with their counselors, formed the tribal councils. They were civil officers, nominally chosen by the people, although the captains controlled the election. In case of their decease, their sons were ineligible; but grandsons, or other male relatives, might succeed them. They had the right, also, to select their own counselors, who were men of experience that not unfrequently filled, at the same time, the office of captain.

This latter position was neither hereditary nor elective, but created by the individual himself. His first claim to it generally rested upon a dream. In the visions of the night he saw himself a captain, and announced this as his destiny, substantiating it by war-parties which he led out six or seven times in succession. If he came back victorious, with scalps or prisoners, and no loss on his own side, his claim was allowed. If, on the contrary, such expeditions proved a failure, he was disgraced, and had to relinquish all hope of securing the dignity to which he aspired. Captains were intrusted with the entire management of a war. They could not, however, conclude peace. This was the province of the chiefs in council assembled.[1]

Turning now to aboriginal life, we find the Indian, in many respects, different from his fathers in a former era. The influence of a superior race, mingling freely with the Iroquois and Delawares, in particular, had become apparent. The nations farther west remained, comparatively, in their primitive state.

When the Indian was not engaged in war, the chase formed his principal occupation. It had its regular seasons. The deer-hunt began in September or October, and lasted until January. Throughout the rest of the winter, as also in spring, the fox, the raccoon, beaver, and bear were sought for. In February, the women joined their husbands in the forests, where little encampments had been provided for them, and boiled maple-sugar. Meanwhile the men continued to hunt, and supplied them with food. Next followed the

---

[1] This account of the Delaware government is based upon *Zeisberger's MS. History of the Indians*, which document is my chief authority for all that follows in this chapter.

summer deer-hunt, in June and July, when the fur of these animals assumes a reddish hue, which increases the value of their pelts. And it was, mainly, for the sake of these that they were chased during six months of the year. The meat was often wasted, lying untouched where the creature had been flayed, or hung from the branch of a tree, as a gift to the hungry. An expert hunter would shoot, in a single autumn, from fifty to one hundred and fifty head. That they rapidly decreased, even in Zeisberger's time, was a necessary consequence of such wholesale slaughter, which had never been known prior to the peltry-trade with the white men.

The agility and endurance with which the Indians pursued deer are marvelous. It was no uncommon thing for a hunter to chase one or more of them a distance of eight or ten miles, from early morning to evening, without getting a shot, until they were run down and could go no farther.

The Delawares and Iroquois used the rifle, both in war and on the chase; for small game, however, the bow and arrow were still in vogue. Western nations employed ordinary shot-guns.

There existed well-defined laws of the chase. Whenever several hunters went out in company, the oldest, especially if he was a counselor, took the command, and it was deemed disgraceful to desert such a party, and hunt independently of the rest. In case a deer was wounded by one, and afterward killed or found dead by another, the skin belonged to the first; the meat, or half the meat, to the second. If several discharged their rifles simultaneously at the same deer, so that it was impossible to determine whose bullet brought it down, the oldest received the skin, whether he had or had not fired, but the meat was divided among all. Aged men accompanying a party must be plentifully supplied by the young both with pelts and meat.

Charms, carried in the pouch, in order to make a hunt successful, were in universal use. They were for the most part prepared, by superannuated hunters, of roots, herbs, or seeds, and sold at high prices. In some cases they were administered as emetics. Zeisberger mentions an instance of a Delaware who persistently employed such a charm for three weeks, every alternate day, submitting to all its painful consequences, and yet did not shoot a single deer in that whole time.

A protracted hunt was inaugurated by a feast, given to the old men of the village, and bearing the character of a sacrifice, inasmuch as the guests invoked the aid of the good spirits on the hunter's behalf.

In addition to hunting, the men built huts and lent a hand in laying out plantations. All other work fell to the share of the women, who tilled the ground, gathered the harvest, collected fuel, and cooked. Their staples were maize, pumpkins, potatoes, and beans, as also several other vegetables introduced from the settlements, such as turnips and cabbage.

The household utensils and garments of these tribes had undergone a great change. Instead of the earthen pots of primitive times, iron or copper vessels were universal; the turkey-feather blanket had given place to the woolen; other articles of dress were mostly made of stuffs procured from the traders; and the wampum consisted almost exclusively of beads.

Indian towns were small, irregular clusters of huts on a creek or river. There was a marked difference between the houses of the Iroquois and those of the Delawares.

The former were constructed of bark, with arched roofs, and often of great length, so as to accommodate from two to four families, to each of which was assigned one of the fires that were kindled on the ground in a line down the middle of the house. Running along the entire crown of the roof was an aperture, through which the smoke escaped and the light came in. Under the roof poles were fastened, laden with haunches of venison, ears of corn, and other stores.[1]

Among the Delawares each family had a house of its own, which was of much smaller dimensions, with a peaked roof, and a frame of posts or boards covered

---

[1] Such houses were modeled after those remarkable structures which the Jesuits found among the Hurons and Iroquois in the seventeenth century, and some of which were said to have been between two hundred and three hundred feet in length, or even longer, accommodating the population of an entire village. They were made of posts and poles, or of saplings, planted in rows, covered with bark, and had two tiers of platforms stretching through the interior on both sides, with a line of fires in the open space between them.

with bark. A hole in the top gave exit to the smoke, and small openings in the sides, with sliding shutters, afforded light. Not a few, however, were well-constructed log-cabins, such as formed the homesteads of the borderers, who were occasionally hired to build them.

The center of attraction in the dwellings of both these nations was the fire, surrounded by a kind of bunk, that served as a seat and table in the daytime and as a bed at night. It was covered with deer and bear skins, or with mats of rushes, plaited and skillfully painted by the women. Such mats were also fastened to the sides of the house, in order to beautify it and keep out the cold in winter.

Let us look in upon an Indian family. The husband is lying in his bunk, the personification of indolence, sleeping or smoking, his beardless face, his broad chest, sinewy arms, and supple legs tattooed with curious figures; his head is bald, excepting a circle of hair on its crown, and two twists hanging down on either side, tricked out with strings of beads, or brass and silver ornaments. Similar trinkets dangle from his ears and nose. A small blanket, known as a match-coat, covers his shoulders, and the breech-cloth his middle. His feet are cased in buckskin moccasins, decorated with beads and embroidery.

His wife is engaged in cooking, to which she attends twice a day; her long black hair, profusely anointed with bear's grease, hangs down to the hips, and is wrapped in cloth, gay with ribbons and silver buckles.

Another piece of cloth, laid double, and reaching below her knees, is bound round her waist, like a petticoat, over which falls a white shirt daubed with red paint, or a shirt of colored cotton. Her moccasins are embroidered even more richly than her husband's. She is boiling venison, or some other meat, along with maize, taking pains to let the former be so well done that it falls to pieces — for half-cooked food, whether flesh or fish, is deemed an abomination — and occasionally looking after her corn-bread, which is baking in the ashes.

If her supply of meat is exhausted, she serves up corn, which she can prepare in twelve different ways, or mush, milk, and butter; or she gives her husband a hint that fresh meat would be acceptable, whereupon he rouses himself and goes out to hunt. Returning with game, he throws it down outside of the hut at the door, and re-enters in silence. This game belongs to the woman, who brings it in and prepares a plentiful meal, after having sent choice parts of it to her neighbors.

In one corner of the house stands a mortar, cut out of the trunk of a tree. A girl, with nothing on her person but a short skirt, is using it to pound corn; while several boys are idling around, some nude, others wearing a flap of buckskin over the groin, attached to a leathern strap that passes across their shoulders. In another corner, upon a peg, hangs a primitive cradle, consisting of a board covered with moss and surmounted by arched strips of wood, beneath which an infant is imprisoned, wrapped in furs or cloth.¹ Several lean, wolfish dogs are stretched around the fire.

The boys of such a family are left to educate themselves, receiving instruction in regard to the chase only. They do what they please; and punishment even for the worst offenses is rarely inflicted. Their parents fear that they might avenge themselves when they are grown. When they do venture to correct them, the chastisement is nothing more than a dash of cold water in the face. Girls are trained to the various duties of their slavish life, as also to make pouches and girdles.

Such girdles or bands were used for carrying burdens. They were woven of wild flax, three fingers in breadth, and ornamented with symbols and figures. Those for the women were fastened round their heads, with another band suspended behind. To this was attached the load, the strain of which, consequently, was thrown upon their foreheads, although the load itself rested on their backs. They could easily carry a hundredweight. The men secured their burdens with the band around the breast, and were accustomed, in this way, to bring the unflayed carcass of a deer, weighing perhaps one hundred and fifty pounds, from the forest to their towns.

But see! the blanket or sheet of bark which covers the door is lifted, and visitors enter.² They grasp the

---

¹ Owing to the many accidents which this mode of cradling children produced, it was given up more and more in Zeisberger's time.

² This was of very frequent occurrence; for, in spite of their ordinary

hands of their friends, addressing each one by the title which sex, or age, or station confers. After having seated themselves, they perhaps renew this ceremonial a second time, in all its details. Meanwhile the housewife hastens to prepare a kettle of food, which she places before them, giving them bowls made of wood, or of the excrescences of trees, and large spoons of the same material. When they have satisfied their hunger, they hand the bowls and spoons to the family, which proceeds to finish the meal.

Such a repast would not have been appetizing to a white man, other than a missionary or trader, whose stomachs are hardened. The cooking utensils, the bowls and spoons, are seldom washed, except by the tongues of dogs; and, not unfrequently, there is but one spoon for the whole company. The hut itself is filthy in the extreme, infested with fleas, and half-filled with smoke.

Of all this the natives are not conscious, but enjoy the visit. A pouch of otter or beaver skin, richly ornamented with beads, and containing a mixture of tobacco and sumach, is brought out; the pipes are filled and lighted; and the circle begins a chat upon the latest news of the village or the tribe, upon political affairs, hunting, and other similar topics. Intelligence known to be false, or the most improbable adventures, are rehearsed, exciting peals of laughter, but listened to without any other interruption. And, while jokes are

---

reserve, and the haughty impassiveness which they often assumed, the Indians were exceedingly fond of society. The houses of the chiefs, in particular, were visited, where the latest news might be heard.

passed, they are never offensive. Throughout the visit a courtesy prevails which is astonishing.

When the conversation begins to flag, the host produces a pack of cards, and dice made of the pits of wild plums. Both are received with silent satisfaction. Some betake themselves to a game of cards, taught them by the traders from whom they were purchased; while others put the dice in a bowl, which they lift up and then strike against the ground, each, in turn, staking some article of value upon the fall of the dice. This latter is a national and favorite game that excites the deepest interest, and is often protracted for an entire day.[1]

Weary of such in-door amusements, the visitors leave, and, followed by their host, join the other men of the village, who have assembled for more athletic sports. The town is soon full of life. One party plays ninepins, another ball; here two young men begin to wrestle,—there several try their strength in lifting boulders, or in throwing stones; while the boys bring out their bows and arrows to shoot at a mark.

Meantime the women gather in groups and look on, or, more frequently, talk of their plantations and house-

---

[1] Two towns sometimes played together. Zeisberger speaks of a game of this kind which he witnessed among the Iroquois, and which lasted eight days. The inhabitants met daily, and each one dumped the bowl once. Then they separated until the next day. The evenings were devoted, in the respective villages, to sacrifices and dancing. At the former an Indian walked around a fire, chanting incantations and strewing tobacco into the flames. The stakes were blankets, cloth, shirts, linen, and other valuable wares, which were carried off, on the eighth day, by the winning party.

hold work, or gossip and spread the plumpest lies.[1] They are not as cautious as the men, and fall to quarreling, bandying sharp words, or calling one another by the names of certain parts of the human body as the most opprobrious epithets which they can employ.

While all this is going on, we will inspect the environs of the village. Pigs, horses with bells around their necks, and a few cows, are roaming through the woods.[2] This round hole in the earth, lined and covered with dry grass, constitutes a magazine where some family has stored its harvest, the knowledge of which will be carefully kept from the other inhabitants; that isolated hut among the trees is a rum-shop, in which old women retail liquor at enormous prices; and the singular structure near it may be called a vapor bath-house, whither the Indians repair three or four times a week, when fatigued or unwell, in order to perspire.[3] Posts appear in the distance.

---

[1] The men, says Zeisberger, entertained the most sovereign contempt for the veracity of the women. Any news brought by a woman was deemed false until it had been corroborated through other sources.

[2] Horses, which were never used for agricultural purposes, belonged to the men, cows to the women. Cows were not common; but the better classes of natives began to keep them in Zeisberger's time, milk and butter being deemed great luxuries.

[3] Such bath-houses consisted of wooden ovens covered with earth, and having, at one end, a small orifice, through which the natives crept in, and squatted between stones that had been previously heated red hot in a fire built at the opening. After a time they came out and cooled themselves; then re-entered, and perspired anew. This was repeated three or four times. The bath-houses of the women were apart from those of the men.

They mark a burial-place. At the foot of each is a grave. If the post be plain and unadorned, it is the memorial of a chief; if painted red, with warlike devices, it tells of the deeds and death of a captain; if a small turtle-shell is suspended from it, it designates the tomb of a doctor.

Returning to the village, let us again visit the same house upon which we looked in before.

It is evening. The husband paints his face and entire head with vermilion, puts on a shirt over his breech-cloth, and cloth leggins stretching above the knee, ornamented along the seams with ribbons and white beads; exchanges his match-coat for a stroud, and fastens a plume to the crown of his head. His wife tinges her cheeks, eyebrows, and other parts of her face with various colors, but chiefly with red; clasps silver bracelets on her arms; winds strings of wampum or of beads around her neck; twists silver buckles in her hair, and pins them to the bosom of her shirt, or binds a girdle, glittering with such trinkets, around her forehead; decorates her petticoat with ribbons, and throws a stroud, similarly garnished, about her shoulders. They are now both in full dress, and ready for the dance, which is to take place that night in their lodge, as it does every night in some hut, except when the young men are absent hunting.

It is protracted to a late hour. The men, following a leader, and singing discordantly, dance in a circle around the fire, contorting their bodies in the most unnatural ways, assuming ridiculous attitudes, now leaping high and stamping violently upon the ground, again squatting with their necks stretched out and faces close together over the flames. The women come next, in another circle, but with a gentle motion, swaying to and fro, and demean themselves as though they were patterns of modesty, neither laughing nor talking, but grave and silent, exchanging never a word with the men. An Indian beats the time on a sort of drum; and, when one dance is ended, continues singing until another opens.

This is a picture of the home-life of the natives as seen by Zeisberger. It would, however, be incomplete if we failed to give it that finishing touch which will mar what may, possibly, have seemed attractive. The rum-shop of an Indian village was its bane and curse. Drunkenness prevailed to a fearful extent, and manifested itself in outrageous forms. It was a common occurrence to see almost the entire population in a state of wild intoxication, brawling, fighting, and giving full sway to the worst propensities of their untamed nature. At such times the Indians were little better than fiends, and it is not an extravagance to say that their towns became outlets of hell.

Nor did their general character present many redeeming traits. It is true, the pen of romance has made heroes of their warriors, and crowned their race with exalted virtues. But this is more than an error. It is absurd. The aborigines of the last century could not rightfully claim such a position in a single particular.

Morally considered, they belonged to the most ordinary and the vilest of savages. Upon this point Zeisberger's testimony is as clear as it must be deemed conclusive.

He loved the Indians. He spent his life in doing them good. It is impossible to suppose that he would have depicted their character in darker colors than truth warranted. And yet, instead of clothing it with those illustrious features which other writers have portrayed, he represents it as low and detestable. Lying, cheating, and theft were universal. The marriage relation was of the lowest kind. Husbands forsook their wives whenever they pleased. To grow weary of a woman was a sufficient cause of desertion. Fornication and adultery prevailed. The ordinary state of a majority of both sexes was unchastity. Other vices, of the most abominable kind, were common. Moreover, while the Indians continued to practice hospitality, as in the primitive times of their history, and were often steadfast friends, their vindictiveness knew no bounds, and they would spend years in seeking opportunities to avenge an injury. And although they showed themselves to be brave warriors, when put to the test, their ordinary mode of fighting was cowardly in the extreme.[1]

The false estimate which has been made of the aborigines of the last century, arose from their aptitude to dissemble and their eagerness for praise. Zeisberger

---

[1] The utter contempt with which Zeisberger, in his MS. History, speaks of the cowardice of the Indians, doubtlessly arose from the constant massacres of women and children, along the Western frontier, during the revolutionary war, in the midst of which he wrote that work.

has laid this bare by a single pithy sentence. "They love to be deemed honest and good," he writes, "even when detected in the worst of villainies." In almost every respect, therefore, they were double-faced and double-hearted; one character they assumed for show, the other was theirs in reality. This misled the casual observer. Zeisberger, however, not only saw them in all their moral deformity as savages, but was made the confidant of his numerous converts, and listened to confessions, even from the lips of sorcerers, such as other white men rarely heard.

Among such a race the triumphs of the Cross were the more wonderful. The novelist may regret to see "the noble red men" reduced to their savage and proper level; but the Christian rejoices that, in the case of this nation too, the Gospel proved to be the power of God.

The popular notion that the Indians originally believed in one Great and Almighty Spirit is incorrect. Such a belief grew into existence only after they had been brought in contact with the white race. This is shown by the earliest records, as well as by the *Relations* of the Jesuit Fathers. Not a single aboriginal language contained a word to express the idea of God. The missionaries of the last century were deceived by the fact that they everywhere met with this doctrine. Even Zeisberger was misled.[1] They did not make suf-

---

[1] Loskiel, on the contrary, instructed, without doubt, in this particular, by Bishop Spangenberg, seems to have had an intimation of the true state of the case. He says: "As the Europeans have lived so long, both

ficient allowance for the readiness with which the natives appropriated religious ideas learned from the Europeans, and moulded them to suit their own darkened understanding. And yet the scheme of the so-called preachers afforded a notable illustration, for it was substantially a parody of the Gospel.[1]

The religion of the primitive Indians was, in part, fetichism, and, in part, a vague belief in higher deities, rising, in some instances, to a Being exalted above all the rest, yet always in connection with space and time, or with bodily shape. It embraced, however, the germs of the system which the Moravian missionaries found prevalent.

Of this latter superstition we here present short outlines, that will be filled up in the course of our narrative.

The Great Spirit, or God, created the heavens and the earth, together with all beings and things that are in them. This Spirit is good, gracious, and omnipotent. Hence men must bring him sacrifices, not directly but through the agency of lesser spirits and subordinate gods, called *manitous*. These are to be found everywhere in all material things, whether animate or inanimate, in birds, beasts, and fishes, in the sun and the moon, in lakes and water-falls, in the rocky cliff and the dismal cavern, in the very stones of the earth. Each

---

in their neighborhood and among them, it may reasonably be supposed that the present religious notions of the Indians differ in many respects from those of their forefathers."—*Loskiel's History of the Indian Mission*, Part i. p. 33.

[1] For an account of these preachers, consult chapter xiv.

Indian, with rare and most unhappy exceptions, has a tutelary manitou, revealed to him in a dream, and carries about his person the animal or a part of the animal forming it, or some other emblem of its existence. In other respects, too, dreams constitute a principal part of his religion. He has implicit faith in what they tell him or in what he imagines them to prognosticate.

The devil is a wicked spirit, working evil, but chiefly among white men. Some say that he does not molest Indians at all. Subordinate spirits of evil, however, abound, and tempt them to sin. Their idea of hell is expressed by its Delaware name, *machtand owinenk*, which means "to be with the devil."

They believe in the immortality of the soul, which the Delawares call *wtellenapewoagan:* that is, "the substance of man;" and, also, *wtschitschank*, signifying "spirit." The souls of good men go to a place of happiness after death; the souls of the wicked wander about in great misery. God, add some, permits the former, if they prefer it, to migrate back to earth and to be born a second time in the person of a child.

In addition to five great sacrificial feasts, which will be described in another connection, they have numerous secondary and private sacrifices. A solitary hunter, for example, cuts up an animal in the depths of the forest, and lets the birds of prey feast on its flesh, while he stands behind a tree and watches them. The friends of the dead bring meat and drink offerings to their manes. The growing corn is propitiated with oblations of bear's meat, and the bear with ears of corn. The fish receive small cakes, and, to appease the screeching night-owl, tobacco is cast into the camp-fire. Indeed, there is scarcely an occasion on which they do not sacrifice, or a thing that they do not thus honor.

Their only idol was called, in Delaware, *Wsinkhoalican*. It was the figure of a miniature human head carved of wood and carried about their persons, or cut, life-size, out of a post, and set up in the middle of the house where they sacrificed.

The Delawares and Iroquois, particularly the latter, were native orators, and their frequent councils gave them every opportunity to practice this art. Their speeches, which they delivered in a loud tone of voice, with much gravity of manner and many gesticulations, were often instinct with beautiful imagery. They could be so clear upon any point as to make it transparent, or, if they chose, so ambiguous that it became almost unintelligible. Hence their messages required the closest attention, and every word must be carefully weighed. In regard to the things of common life, their languages were exceedingly rich. Thus the Delawares had ten different names for a bear, according to its age or sex. As touching religious ideas, on the contrary, there prevailed a dearth of words. "Nevertheless," says Zeisberger, "the more the Gospel spreads the more copious their language becomes. New words grow into use in exact proportion to the growth of the converts in the knowledge of the Word of God and of the Lord Jesus Christ."

CHAPTER V.

MISSIONARY OPERATIONS AMONG THE INDIANS PREVIOUS TO ZEISBERGER'S TIMES.—1549-1745.

Christian Henry Rauch begins a Mission among the Mohicans of New York.—The Jesuit Missions and the work of the Puritans in the seventeenth century.—Labors among the Indians in the first half of the eighteenth century.—Difficulties and success of Rauch's enterprise.—Baptism of the first converts.—Count Zinzendorf visits the Indian country.—Organizes a church at Shekomeko.—Zinzendorf in the valley of Wyoming.—Progress of the Mission in New York.—It extends to Connecticut and Massachusetts.—Church-edifice built at Shekomeko.—Persecution of the missionaries.—They are banished from New York by Act of the Legislature.

ZEISBERGER was not the first messenger of the Gospel from the Moravian Church to the Indians of New York and Pennsylvania. Three years before he devoted himself to the work of a missionary, when there was as yet no settlement of the United Brethren in any of the Northern Colonies, and a band of fugitives, from the seat of war in Georgia, constituted the whole body of that people in the country, a lone preacher landed at New York (July 16, 1740), sent from Europe to tell the aborigines the story of redeeming love. His name was Christian Henry Rauch.[1]

---

[1] Born July 5, 1718, at Bernburg, in the Principality of Anhalt After serving the Church in various capacities in America, he went to Jamaica, as a missionary among the negroes, where he died November 11, 1763.

Meeting with two Mohicans, Shabash and Wasamapah,[1] from Shekomeko, he offered to become the teacher of their tribe. In the fleeting seasons of soberness which dawned on their muddled minds, they accepted the offer; but rejected it again, as often as they were intoxicated; and, at last, slunk away to their village without him, although they had promised to take him along. Rauch followed them, asking his way from farm to farm.

Near by the Indian hamlet lay the homestead of John Rau. There he found a temporary domicile, upon condition of keeping school for the children of the family. His design to preach to the Indians was

---

[1] This Indian is called *Tschoop* by Loskiel. The same name is inscribed on his tombstone at Bethlehem,—placed over his grave about twenty-five years ago. It occurs also in the official record of his death in the Church Register, as follows: *Johannes, sonst Tschoop genannt,* that is, "John, otherwise called Tschoop." His real Indian name was *Wasamapah;* his English name, prior to his baptism, *Job;* and the name he received in baptism *John.* I incline to the opinion that he never bore the name *Tschoop* among the natives, but that it originated among the early Moravians, in consequence of their German mode of pronouncing *Job,* and that Loskiel mistook it for an original name. It is not found in any early documents other than the Church Register. Zeisberger never uses it, but calls the man either *Job* or *John,* and the official register of Indian baptisms knows nothing of it, but gives *Wasamapah.* I am strengthened in my opinion, first, by the fact that those early Moravians who came to this country from Germany often misspelt English names, so as to render them almost unintelligible; second, by the circumstance that in *Pyrlaeus's Narrative of the Work of the Brethren among the Indians of North America,* a MS. in the B. A., corrected by Count Zinzendorf, the latter, in the margin, gives this Indian the name of *Copp,* evidently another corruption of *Job;* and finally, by the opinion entertained among students of Indian history, living at Bethlehem fifty years ago, that *Tschoop* is a misnomer for *Job.*

denounced as wild and preposterous, but this did not keep him back.

Behold him, then, full of zeal and courage, going on his first visit to Shekomeko! It is the sixteenth of August. Job and Shabash welcome him; the whole tribe gathers around him, while he explains the object of his coming.

> He told us of a Mighty One, the Lord of earth and sky,
> Who left His glory in the heavens, for men to bleed and die;
> Who loved poor Indian sinners still, and longed to gain their love,
> And be their Saviour here, and in his Father's house above.
>
> And when his tale was ended—" My friends," he gently said,
> "I am weary with my journey, and would fain lay down my head;"
> So beside our spears and arrows he laid him down to rest,
> And slept as sweetly as the babe upon its mother's breast.
>
> Then we looked upon each other, and I whispered, "This is new;
> Yes, we have heard glad tidings, and that sleeper knows them true;
> He knows he has a Friend above, or would he slumber here,
> With men of war around him, and the war-whoop in his ear?"
>
> So we told him on the morrow that he need not journey on,
> But stay and tell us further of that loving, dying One;
> And thus we heard of Jesus first, and felt the wondrous power
> Which makes His people willing, in His own accepted hour.[1]

---

[1] These lines represent Job as the speaker, and are based upon an interesting account given by him after his conversion, at a missionary conference held at Bethlehem, in 1745, of the manner in which Rauch won the confidence of the Shekomeko tribe. The incident is set forth in detail by Bishop Spangenberg in his "Account of the manner in which the Protestant Church of the Unitas Fratrum preach the Gospel and carry on their Missions among the Heathen." English translation. London, 1788, pp. 62 and 63.

Thus arose a new factor in the evangelization of the aborigines of North America. Attempted by the Roman Catholic Church as early as 1549, three years after Luther's death, when Protestantism was struggling into independence; having for its forerunner Louis Cancello, a Dominican friar, who suffered death at the hands of the savages of Florida, soon after landing on their shores; its successful beginning was left to the dauntless disciples of Ignatius Loyola. The first of these reached Canada on the twelfth of June, 1611, and were the pioneers of a work which was illustrious by reason of the faith and zeal that sustained it, and unsurpassed in the sufferings it involved and the courage it evoked.

In 1634, Brebeuf, Daniel, and Lallemand inaugurated a mission among the Hurons, which prospered greatly. Christian villages clustered around the lake of this people; and upon the banks of the Matchedash, joining Lake Toronto to Huron, stood St. Mary's, the central station. Thither came, two or three times a year, the various missionaries, recounting what God had wrought in the wilderness, and preparing for new conflicts and triumphs. From 1634 to 1647, not less than forty-two Fathers traversed the wide hunting-grounds of the natives, besides eighteen evangelists not yet initiated.

Meanwhile a public hospital had been endowed at Quebec, for the benefit of Indians and of white men, a colony of converts established near the town, and a seminary founded to train Jesuits that should explore still more distant regions of the North and West.

In such explorations Charles Raymbault and Isaac Jogues had already taken the lead. They visited the Chippewas, and brought the Gospel to the tribes of Michigan. Some time after this, while on his road to the Huron Mission, Jogues was captured by a roving band of Mohawks, and made to endure the cruelties of the gantlet, all the way from the St. Lawrence to their own country. There his life was unexpectedly spared, and he wandered through the forests, writing the name of Jesus and carving the cross on the bark of trees. He was, therefore, the first to proclaim, although by these silent emblems only, the Son of God within the hunting-grounds of the Five Nations.

Nor had the East been forgotten. Among the Abenakis of Maine lived Gabriel Dreuillettes, who baptized converts, and said mass for them in a chapel erected a few miles above the mouth of the Kennebec.

Four years after his captivity, from which he had been ransomed by the Dutch, Father Jogues was sent to convert his captors. True to his vow, he obeyed the call, but expressed a presentiment that it would cost him his life. This presentiment was fulfilled. No sooner had he reached the Mohawk valley than he was condemned as a sorcerer and put to death. This brought about a new war between the Iroquois and Hurons, resulting most disastrously for the latter. Their country was invaded, its Christian villages were destroyed, the converts massacred, and some of the missionaries subjected to the most barbarous tortures. Brebeuf, cut, scorched, seared with hot iron, scalded with boiling water, and scalped while yet alive, agonized for three hours; Lallemand, cased in burning pine-bark full of rosin, lingered for seventeen hours amid excruciating pains. The Hurons, totally defeated, sued for peace; and the unfortunate remnant of the tribe was embodied with the nations of its conquerors.

Such experiences, however, could not repress the ardor of the Jesuits. The fiercer the Five Nations showed themselves to be, the more clearly it became their duty to convert them. Father Le Moyne, while on a political embassy to Onondaga (1653), preached the Gospel wherever he found hearers, opened the meetings of the Grand Council with the prayers of his church, and prepared the minds of the Iroquois for the coming of the missionaries. These appeared, two years later, in the persons of Chaumonot and Claude Dablon, who established a station in the metropolis itself, built a chapel, instituted all the ceremonies of the Romish ritual, and baptized hundreds of converts. And although, in the course of time, this mission had to be abandoned, it was eventually renewed, and stretched its branches to every canton of the League.

With the same indefatigable zeal these propagandists penetrated to the Far West. In 1670, the two extremities of Lake Superior heard the matin-bells of Ste. Marie du Sault, and the vesper hymns of the Mission du St. Esprit, while the heads of Lakes Huron and Michigan were the seats of other stations. Three years later, Marquette descended the Mississippi to the junction of the Arkansas, and he was followed by La Salle (1682), who founded colonies and missions.

Thus the Church of Rome, through that order which had been organized to crush out Protestantism from the Old World, became the herald of the Gospel in the New. In the seventeenth century, however, the glory of this work began to wane; and after the conquest of Canada, when the sway of the Continent passed into the hands of Great Britain, the most of the Fathers abandoned the field (1763).[1]

But the tribes had not been left to the spiritual embraces of Rome alone. However stern the religion of the Puritans, it could not permit heathens to perish at the very doors of its sanctuaries. As early as 1647, the clergy of New England solicited Parliament to aid in evangelizing the Indians; and, in 1649, that body passed an ordinance authorizing the organization of a "Society for the Advancement of Civilization and Christianity" among them. This society established schools, and caused the Gospel to be preached. Foremost among the men who engaged in such enterprises was John Eliot, the illustrious apostle of the New England Indians. Beginning at Nonantum, now a part of Newton, he devoted forty-four years of his life to the work, in various parts of Massachusetts and within the limits of the Plymouth patent, proclaiming Christ, teaching the Indians to read and write, translating the

---

[1] Clark's Onondaga, i. chap. vi.; Bancroft's Hist. of the U. S., i. ii. and i i.; Map of the Jesuit Missions, in 1670 and 1671; Parkman's Jesuits in North America in the Seventeenth Century.

entire Bible into their language, and bringing many of them to the personal enjoyment of faith and peace. Seconded by Mayhew, he established villages of "praying Indians" on Cape Cod, Martha's Vineyard, and Nantucket, and seven of them around Boston. And when, at last, after the toils of fourscore years and six, he slept with his fathers, other Protestant evangelists trod in his footsteps. In 1700, there were thirteen missionaries in the English Colonies supported by government, besides several who labored on their own account. At the instance of the Earl of Bellomont, Governor of New York, Queen Anne was led to interest herself in these missions. Under her auspices, clergymen of the Anglican Church were sent to "instruct the Five Nations and to prevent their being practiced upon by the French priests and Jesuits." Thoroughgood Moor came from England, on this service, in 1704; William Andrews followed, in 1712; and later, for many years, Henry Barclay and John Ogilvie, of Albany, labored among the Mohawks.[1]

It was well, however, that God had brought a new element into the work; for, at the time when the Moravians took it up, it met with little sympathy and was pining away. Neither among the Mohawks nor the Oneidas, nor the tribes of New England, were the pious efforts of God's servants successful. An evil and corrupt generation met them. "There is no hope of making them better," reported Andrews of the Mohawks after

---

[1] Clark's Onondaga, i. chapter vii.; Bancroft's U. S., ii. 94–97.

six years of toil and disappointments; "heathen they are, and heathen they still must be." David Brainerd was not yet in the rich field which was ripening for him in New Jersey; nor had Azariah Horton come to glean among the Montauks of Long Island. And as for the Jesuit Mission, its heroic days were past. The priests seldom induced their still numerous converts to lead even outwardly better lives. Baptized savages strutted among the unbaptized, decorating their persons with rosaries, as though they were strings of wampum, but were carnal and dissolute as before. Genuine conversions, manifested by a sober, righteous, and godly life, were rarely known. Hence the Indians had come to be regarded as brutish savages, whose salvation was hopeless. Earnest Christians in New York asserted this opinion in Rauch's hearing, and it was entertained even by a man like Conrad Weisser.

For a time, indeed, it appeared as if Rauch's enterprise would but serve to establish such arguments. As long as his instructions were a novelty he was welcome at Shekomeko; after that the tribe grew tired of him. But he persevered, preaching Christ from hut to hut, and quenching the suspicions that self-interested white men had excited in the minds of the natives as to the purity of his motives. A whole year passed in this way. At last a sunbeam burst through the spiritual darkness which enshrouded the village. Job, Shabash, and several others, who had for some time been struggling against their better convictions, experienced the grace of God and were converted.

Such was the humble beginning of that Moravian Mission in the service of which Zeisberger spent his life.

Meanwhile several young men, John Christopher Pyrlaeus, Gottlob Büttner, and William Zander, had come to Bethlehem from Germany, eager to aid Rauch in his work. Büttner, whose short but illustrious career makes his name a bright star in the galaxy of Indian missionaries,[1] was sent, at New Year (1742), to invite Rauch to the third Pennsylvania Synod.[2] After a protracted stay at Shekomeko, on which occasion he preached his first sermon to the Indians, he accompanied Rauch and three converts to Oley, where this Synod was to meet, in the house of John de Turck. Several days having been devoted to its ordinary business, there assembled, in the afternoon of the twenty-third of February, in Mr. de Turck's barn, the whole body of its members, consisting of Moravians, Lutherans, Reformed, Tunkers, Mennonites, Schwenkfelders, Separatists, and Hermits, in whose

---

[1] Born in Silesia, December 29, 1716; came to America, October 26, 1741; married to a daughter of John Bechtel, of Germantown, Pa.; and died at Shekomeko, February 23, 1745.

[2] The Pennsylvania Synod, as it is commonly called, embraced representatives of all the German religious denominations in that Province, and was organized at Germantown through the influence of Count Zinzendorf, January 12, 1742. Its members adopted the title of "The Congregation of God in the Spirit," and it had for its aim the union of the German churches upon the basis of experimental religion. It continued its labors for six years, although sustained, after a time, almost exclusively by the Moravians. In 1748, it was changed into a Synod of the United Brethren's Church. This interesting movement was a beautiful but premature ideal, which, in the end, served rather to augment the existing differences among religionists than to establish the unity of the spirit in the bonds of peace.

presence Rauch baptized the Indians, calling Shabash Abraham, Seim Isaac, and Kiop Jacob.[1] Under circumstances so remarkable, the first converts of the Moravian Mission among the aborigines of our country were embodied with the Church of Christ. Job, the fourth convert, was subsequently baptized at Shekomeko (April 16). He received the apostolic name of John. In autumn (October 1, 1742), Büttner became the resident missionary.

In the mean time Count Zinzendorf had himself gone to preach to the natives, accompanied by an escort of fifteen persons, among whom were his young daughter, Benigna, three of her female companions, Zander, and an Indian interpreter. Setting out from Bethlehem (July 24), they first visited Moses Tatemy,[2] on the site of the present Stockertown, as also other Indians near Nazareth. Thence they proceeded to the wilderness beyond the Blue Mountains, as far north as the Long Valley, stopping, on their way back, at Meniolagomekah.[3]

---

[1] In the morning of that day Rauch, Büttner, Pyrlaeus, and Andrew Eschenbach, the Home Missionary at Oley, had been ordained to the ministry by Bishops Zinzendorf and Nitschmann. At the baptism, Rauch first preached on Rev. v. 9; then was sung *O Welt, sieh' hier dein Leben!* during which hymn the Indians came forward. Rauch, with much emotion, addressed to them an earnest charge. The hymn *Nun ist's gethan* followed, during which they knelt around a large vessel filled with water. Thereupon Rauch baptized them, and with the imposition of hands imparted the blessing of the Lord.—*Sœlle's Hist. Account of the Origin of the Work at Oley, MS. L. A.*

[2] Tatemy, or Moses, was a Delaware chief, owning 300 acres of land, presented to him by the Proprietaries, on the present site of Stockertown, near Nazareth.

[3] This Indian village, which lay in Eldred Township, Monroe County, eight miles west of the Wind Gap, in the so-called Smith's Valley, on

Here they took a trail which is hard to trace, but which brought them through Allemaengel to the Schuylkill River, where they proclaimed Christ to a party of natives bivouacking on its banks. That same day Conrad Weisser welcomed them to his homestead in Tulpehocken.

At this place they found a delegation of Iroquois sachems, on their return from a treaty at Philadelphia, whom Zinzendorf, by Weisser's aid, won over to his project of beginning a mission among them. "Brother," they said, in reply to his overtures, "you have journeyed a long way, from beyond the sea, in order to preach to the white people and the Indians. You did not know that we were here; we had no knowledge of your coming. The Great Spirit has brought us together. Come to our people. You shall be welcome. Take this fathom of wampum. It is a token that our words are true."

This was the beginning of the friendship which existed for many years between the Moravians and the League of the Iroquois, and which gave the former a standing among all other tribes. Zinzendorf took the fathom, composed of one hundred and eighty-six pieces of wampum, to England, where he committed it to the keeping of Spangenberg, at a convocation of clergy held at Lamb's Inn, or Broad Oaks, in Essex (March 10, 1743), with instructions to use it wisely for the spread of the kingdom of God among the aborigines

---

the north bank of the Aquanshicola, afterward became a Mission station.—*Memorials of the Moravian Church*, i. 35.

of North America. Spangenberg brought it back to this country, and it was often employed in subsequent negotiations with the Iroquois.[1]

Three days after his return from Tulpehocken, the Count set out on his second journey to the Indian country, again accompanied by his daughter (August 10, 1742). By way of the Delaware Water-Gap, the Minnisinks, and Esopus, they traveled to Shekomeko, where they lodged in a bark hut, which had been constructed for them, and which they pronounced to be better than a palace. They spent eight days in the village, during which time six new converts were baptized, and the first Moravian Mission Church among the Indians was organized. It consisted of the following ten persons, who were all either Mohicans or Wampanoags: Abraham and his wife Sarah, Isaac and his wife Rebecca, Jacob, John, Thomas (Pechtawapect) and his wife Esther, Jonah (Anamapamit), and Timothy (Kaupaas).[2] John was appointed Interpreter; Abraham,

---

[1] The following sachems took part in the negotiations with Zinzendorf: Ganassateco and Caxhayion, of the Onondaga Nation; Sasislaquo and Shikellimy, of the Oneida; Cadgaradasey and Sahuchsova, of the Cayuga; and Wehvehcagy, a Shawanese chief, as the representative of the Tuscarora. Shikellimy and the two Onondagas presented the fathom.—*Buedingische Sammlung*, vol. ii. art. xxx. p. 940.

Ganassateco, called Canassetego in the Penn. Col. Records, was one of the principal men at Onondaga, and a warm friend of Zeisberger. He died in 1750. Shikellimy is called an Oneida in the *Buedingische Sammlung*, but according to the unanimous testimony of all the sources other than those of Moravian origin, he was a Cayuga. His Mohawk name was Swatana.

[2] Register of Indian Baptisms, 1742 to 1764. This invaluable record was presented to me by the late Miss Heckewelder, of Bethlehem, a

110　　　*LIFE AND TIMES OF*

Elder; Jacob, Exhorter; and Isaac, Sexton. Zinzendorf says of them, "They are incomparable Indians, true men of God among their tribe, and form a conference which we often attended with astonishment."[1]

Toward the end of September, at the head of a numerous party, he undertook his longest and most perilous tour. Among his companions were Martin and Joanna Mack,[2] Peter Boehler, Conrad Weisser, Anna Nitschmann, the Deaconess,[3] and two Indian interpreters, Joshua and David, who had recently been baptized at Bethlehem.

On their way to Shamokin, they came to a ridge of forest-crowned mountains, across which led a blind trail, full of loose, sharp stones, and close to high rocks, the rugged sides of which rendered horseback riding exceedingly dangerous. These mountains being without a name, Conrad Weisser called them "The Thürn-

---

daughter of the well-known missionary, to whom it originally belonged. After I had had it in use for a long time, I found the official Register, 1742 to 1772, in the B. A. The Register subsequent to this date must have been destroyed in the Revolutionary War.

[1] Of Zinzendorf's second journey, and of a part of the third, we have a MS. journal, written by himself, in a bark hut, at Ostonwacken. He complains of the want of a secretary, and says that he writes from memory, having taken no notes. This MS. is in the B. A.

[2] Martin Mack, born April 13, 1715, at Lysingen, in Wurtemberg, was a distinguished missionary among the Indians, and subsequently a missionary bishop among the negroes of the West Indies. He died June 9, 1784, while Superintendent of the Mission in St. Croix. His wife was a daughter of John Rau, of Shekomeko.

[3] The daughter of David Nitschmann, known as the "Founder of Bethlehem," born November 24, 1715, in Moravia, and died at Herrnhut, May 21, 1760, a woman of extraordinary talents, piety, and zeal.

stein," in honor of Zinzendorf.[1] They were the parallel chains of the Blue Ridge now known as Second, Third, and Peter's Mountains. Thence the party found their way to the Susquehanna, and, passing up the eastern bank, reached the Line and Mahanoy Mountains of Northumberland County.

Zinzendorf describes that country as the wildest he had ever seen. But its shaggy hills and precipitous cliffs seemed to inspire the Deaconess with a courage above her sex. She was on her way to heathens, who knew nothing of her God and Saviour; and, burning with impatience to proclaim His love, she dashed forward at the head of the company, and would not relinquish that place even when they crossed the Mahanoy, which was so steep that they were forced to ride linked together, like Swiss mountaineers.

At Shamokin, Shikellimy received them with all the hospitality of an Iroquois sachem. Zinzendorf had conceived a strong affection for this Indian, and looked upon him as a chosen instrument for the evangelization of the aborigines. He spent three days in his lodge, enlisting his co-operation in this great work.

Riding on to Ostonwacken, through glades tinted with the first hues of autumn, his heart was lifted up in praise to Him by whom these glorious forests of America had been created, and in whom their roving tribes should be blessed. The village received him with military salutes; Madame Montour[2] and her son An-

---

[1] Lord of Thürnstein was one of Zinzendorf's titles.
[2] Madame Montour burst into a flood of tears when she saw Zinzen-

drew[1] with a hospitable welcome. Here he preached the Gospel in French to large gatherings.[2]

In the second week of October, the party separated, Conrad Weisser and others going back to the settlements, while Zinzendorf, Mack, Joanna Mack, and Anna Nitschmann, together with Andrew Montour, proceeded to Wyoming. It was a perilous undertaking. They were in a part of the North Susquehanna wilderness, which, as far as is known, had never before been visited by a white man; and, after four days of incessant hardships, reached the plains of Skehantowanno, and encamped near the village of the Shawanese.

With this people Zinzendorf spent three weeks, preaching the glorious Gospel of the blessed God. But its cheering promises found no response in their hearts. In spite of all his efforts to gain their confidence they regarded him with suspicion, and persisted in believing

---

dorf, and heard that he had come to preach the Gospel, the truths of which she had almost entirely forgotten. She believed Bethlehem, the Saviour's birthplace, to be in France, and his crucifiers to have been Englishmen. This silly perversion originated with the Jesuits, and prevailed among the French Indians.

[1] Zinzendorf's description of Andrew Montour's appearance may prove interesting, since he was so important a character in the Colonial history of our country. "His face," he writes, "is like that of a European, but marked with a broad Indian ring of bear's grease and paint drawn completely around it. He wears a coat of fine cloth of cinnamon color, a black necktie with silver spangles, a red satin vest, pantaloons, over which hangs his shirt, shoes, and stockings, a hat, and brass ornaments, something like the handle of a basket, suspended from his ears."

[2] Here Zinzendorf's journal stops. My authority for what follows, of his visit to Wyoming, is a MS. letter (B. A.) from Martin Mack to Bishop Peter Boehler, detailing, at the request of the latter, the incidents of the journey. It was written after the Count's death.

that he wanted their land, and had come to rob them of the silver mines which were reputed to exist in that region. And although he embraced every opportunity to do them good; negotiated with the principal chief of the Shawanese; called together the Mohicans of the valley and offered these the Gospel;—his labors were unsuccessful, and the animosity of the natives but increased. To add to his distress, the provisions of the party began to fail. For ten days they lived on boiled beans. At last, Mack's wife found a Mohican squaw more friendly than the rest, who furnished corn-bread until the arrival of supplies from Bethlehem.

One afternoon, while the Count sat in his tent, which had been removed from its original site to the top of a hill, arranging his letters, Mack, who was outside in conversation with some others of the party, saw two spreading adders basking in the sunshine, but a few feet from the door. Startled by his approach, they reared their heads, dilated with rage, and passed swiftly beneath the canvas, just as Zinzendorf was stooping over his manuscripts, which he had spread upon the ground. In the next instant his ears were filled with sharp hisses, and, before he could spring to his feet, the serpents had glided over his body and disappeared among the papers. His friends rushed in, and discovered the hole of the adders within the folds of the tent. It was a wonderful escape from death. The words of the prophet, when describing, in a figure, the peace of the millennial kingdom of Christ, may be said to have been literally fulfilled in the midst of one of the heathen strongholds of the kingdom of Satan,—not a child, but a man, played on the hole of the asp, and put his hand on the cockatrice' den.¹

Not long after this, God interposed, a second time, to save his life. David Nitschmann, Anthony Seyfert, and one Kohn, having arrived from Bethlehem with a package of letters, containing reports of the work of the Church in different parts of the world, he expressed a wish to be alone, while he examined these papers. Accordingly he had his tent transferred to a solitary place, higher up the river. This excited the suspicions of the Shawanese more than ever. "Why does this white man stay on our lands? Why does he pitch his tent first here, and then there? Why do we submit to his presence?" These questions, discussed at the council-fire of the tribe, resulted in a deliberate plan to murder him. The time was fixed, and the savage designated who was to strike the blow, when, unexpectedly to all, Conrad Weisser reached the valley, alarmed by Zinzendorf's protracted absence, and filled with a presentiment of the danger which threatened him. The presence of the government agent, and the bold authority with which he treated the Shawanese, put an end to their sinister design.²

---

¹ Isaiah, xi. 8.
² These facts, given upon the authority of Mack, one of Zinzendorf's companions at Wyoming, explode the notorious rattlesnake story, first published by Chapman in his *History of Wyoming* (pp. 21, 23); repeated by Miner in his *History of Wyoming* (pp. 38, 39), and in all subsequent histories of this kind down to Stewart Pearce's latest *Annals of Luzerne County*, as also in many other works. That story is an

Count Zinzendorf, the first white man in the valley of Wyoming, sitting alone in his tent within sight of the lodges of the savages whom he had come to teach the name of Jesus, but who disdainfully refused to listen to his instructions, presents a picture which the Christian may well pause to contemplate. Descended from one of the noblest houses of Germany, counting princes and kings among his ancestors, an ornament to any royal court, trained as a statesman, and endowed with talents that might have made him a leading mind in the politics of Europe, he had turned away from these flattering prospects, had exchanged the dress of the courtier for the garb of the pilgrim, the sword of the peer for the staff of the stranger; and, cheerfully taking up as his appointed burden the displeasure of some of his own family, the scoffs of the world, the false accusations of enemies, had devoted himself and all that he possessed to the service of Christ; preaching in his own country, in America, and on the islands of the tropics, among nobles and peasants, to settlers, Indians, and negroes, the "Word of reconciliation," and glorying everywhere only in the Cross. As in all former periods of his labors, so in the dark experiences which Wyoming brought him, he remained true to the cause which he had espoused, and firm in his dependence upon God. The nights which the Shawanese spent in dancing and revelry he passed in

---

unmitigated fable, which probably grew out of the combined tradition of the incident of the adders and the plot to murder Zinzendorf. To his experience with the adders the Count himself refers in one of his poems: *Anhang*, xii. No. 1902.

wrestling with the Lord on their behalf, and on behalf of all the Indian nations; and while the fitful blasts of the autumn wind bore to his ears the shouts of inebriated savages, he lifted up the voice of impassioned intercession until his lonely tent echoed with the fervent effectual prayer of a righteous man. And these supplications availed much, according to the promise. Not at that time, but in after-years, when some of the most desperate characters among the Indians were led into the church of God; and Zeisberger established flourishing missions among the "grandfathers" of the Shawanese, and gained single converts from the midst even of this wild people. Narrow minds may deem the philanthropy of Zinzendorf misapplied, and may call his visits to the Indians quixotic; but the student of the Bible, who sees history in its light, does not entertain a doubt that this man, as he sojourned among the aborigines of America, was the priest of the Church of the Brethren, and secured a blessing which, in due time, ripened into fruits.

A proof of this was the prosperity of the Mission at Shekomeko. The converts fulfilled the highest hopes of their teachers. John especially was a living monument of grace, and an enthusiastic preacher of righteousness. According to their unanimous testimony, his eloquence was irresistible. Bishop Spangenberg used to say of him that he had the countenance of a Luther.

On the thirteenth of March, 1743, the converts received the sacrament of the Lord's Supper for the first time, and in July a chapel was dedicated. This little sanctury, nestling in the shade of the Stissing Mountain, whose leafy top is mirrored in the clear waters of Lake Halcyon, became the center of a work that spread rapidly among the tribes of New England and of Eastern New York. At the end of the year there were sixty-three baptized converts at Shekomeko, while new stations had been begun at Pachgatgoch and Wechquadnach, in Connecticut, and preaching-places at Whetak and Potatik in the same Province, as also at Westenhuc, in Massachusetts. Four additional missionaries entered the field. These were Christopher Pyrlaeus, Martin Mack, Joachim Senseman, and Frederick Post.[1]

The settlers were astonished when they saw all this. Some rejoiced in the work; others, however, opposed it with great bitterness. Among the latter, a part were actuated by the pernicious idea that their traffic with the natives would suffer if they were converted,—a part gave way to sectarian bigotry. In the spring of 1744, a formidable persecution broke out. The missionaries

---

[1] Pachgatgoch lay two miles southwest of Kent, in Connecticut, and Wechquadnach on the confines of New York and Connecticut, partly in a tract known as "the Oblong," and partly in Sharon Township, Litchfield County, Connecticut, a few miles from the town of Sharon. Whetak was near Salisbury, and Potatik about three miles northeast of Newton, Connecticut. Westenhuc was, probably, the present Housatonic, in Massachusetts. The inhabitants of these villages were Narragansetts, Mohicans, and Wampanoags. In 1859, the Moravian Historical Society erected a marble monument at Pachgatgoch, to the memory of David Bruce and Joseph Powell, two of the former missionaries.

The Mission at Shekomeko was located on what is now (1859) Mr. Edward Hunting's farm, in the Township of Pine Plains, Dutchess County, New York.—*The Moravians in New York and Connecticut.*

were accused of being Papists, in league with France, which had just joined Spain in its war against England. A Justice of the Peace was sent to Shekomeko to investigate these charges, and subsequently the missionaries were cited before the Governor and Council of New York. Their innocence, however, was invariably established. The only thing which could be shown to their prejudice was their scruples with regard to oaths and bearing arms, points which, at that time, they held in common with the Friends. Nevertheless their enemies did not rest until the Assembly of New York had passed two acts which crushed the Mission. The first required all suspicious persons to take the oath of allegiance, or emigrate; the second commanded " the several Moravian and vagrant teachers among the Indians to desist from further teaching or preaching, and to depart the Province."[1]

On the fifteenth of December, the Sheriff of Dutchess County came to Shekomeko, with three Justices of the Peace, and closed the doors of the Mission Chapel. The missionaries were recalled early in the following year. They left behind them seventy-one converts.

---

[1] *Documentary Hist. of N. Y.*, iii. 1019 and 1020. The same work contains various other papers, especially " Reasons for passing the law against the Moravians residing among the Indians," which show the inveterate prejudice that existed against the Church.

CHAPTER VI.

ZEISBERGER A STUDENT AT BETHLEHEM, A PRISONER AT NEW YORK, AND AN ENVOY TO ONONDAGA.—1744–1745.

Bishop Spangenberg.—His plans for the development of the Indian Mission.—Zeisberger a prominent member of a class of candidates for missionary service. — Sent to the Mohawk country to learn the language. — Arrested by the authorities of New York and imprisoned. — The first Delaware converts. — Zeisberger on the Mahony Creek, in Pennsylvania.—He accompanies Spangenberg to Onondaga.—Perilous journey.—Adopted into the Onondaga nation and called Ganousseracheri.—Negotiations at Onondaga and journey back to Bethlehem.

THE Moravians were not discouraged, but continued their missionary efforts with zeal, stimulated by Bishop Spangenberg, who had returned to America in the autumn of 1744.

This accomplished scholar and simple-hearted preacher was peculiarly fitted for his office. A professor of the University of Halle, an evangelist in different parts of Europe, one of the pioneers of the German colony in Georgia, an itinerant among the numerous sects of Pennsylvania,—he had passed through a school of experience which taught him to become all things to all men, to fear no reproach, shrink from no difficulties, and tremble at no dangers. Strong in faith, bold in God, burning with love to Christ,—the purpose of his whole life was Christ's glory.

One of his first measures was the organization of a Mission Board, at Bethlehem.[1] Its meetings were attended by such missionaries as happened to be in the settlement; and, influenced by these, it began to accommodate itself to the usages of the Indians, adopted their forms of address when negotiating with them, delivered written speeches, and employed belts or strings of wampum.

The next step which Spangenberg took was no less important. He instituted a class of candidates for missionary service, appointing Christopher Pyrlaeus as their instructor in the Indian languages.[2] Pyrlaeus had studied the Mohawk tongue, partly among the Mohawks themselves and partly with Conrad Weisser.

Prominent among these young men was David Zeisberger. In the corner-stone of that venerable edifice at Bethlehem, which was originally a "Brethren's House," and which still attracts the attention of the stranger by its quaint architecture, massive buttresses, and walls of unhewn stone, was deposited a scroll of

---

[1] It was called the "Mission Conference," and was subsequently absorbed by the Provincial Conference which governed the Moravian Church in America, and which bore different names at different times. As these ecclesiastical arrangements of the Moravians, in the last century, were exceedingly complicated, I employ the title "Mission Board" throughout this work, for the sake of convenience.

[2] *Spangenberg's Observations on the Evangelization of the Heathen in North America. MS. B. A.* The following were members of this class: David Zeisberger, Joseph Bull, known as John Joseph Schebosh, Michael Schnall, Joseph Möller, Abraham Bueninger, and John Hagen.

John Christopher Pyrlaeus was born at Pausa, in Swabia, in 1713, studied at the University of Leipsic, and died at Herrnhut, May 28, 1785. He married a daughter of Stephen Benezet, of Philadelphia.

parchment containing the names of the first inmates, and among these names his was recorded as follows: *David Zeisberger, destinirter Heidenbote* (1744).[1]

In the beginning of the year 1745, he set out for the Mohawk valley, accompanied by Frederick Post,[2] in order to perfect himself in the knowledge of the Mohawk tongue. On the way, they stopped at Shekomeko. It was Zeisberger's first visit to the Indian country; and his desire to preach to the natives was intensified when he beheld Job, once debased almost to brutishness, walking with God, a patriarch among his people, and heard the glad testimony of many other converts. The

---

[1] That is: *David Zeisberger, destined to be a Messenger to the Heathen.* The edifice referred to is the southwest corner-building of the present "Sisters' House." In that house the young men of the settlement lived together under the supervision of an elder, devoting themselves either to their studies or working at trades. They had a common dining-room, and daily worship in a chapel of their own. Similar establishments for young men, young women, and widows formerly existed in every Moravian settlement. There was nothing monastic in the principles by which they were governed. They were simply homes, where the inmates remained at their option, and were bound by no vow. These institutions have all been given up in America; in Germany, however, they are still to be found.

Whenever Zeisberger was at Bethlehem he lived in that building from 1744 to 1748; after that he occupied a room in the new "Brethren's House," which was the middle building of the present Moravian Seminary for Young Ladies.

[2] Frederick Post, born at Conitz, in Polish Prussia, was a distinguished missionary among the Indians, with whom he was connected by marriage. His first wife was Rachel, a Wampanoag, baptized February 13, 1743, by Büttner; and died in 1747, at Bethlehem, where she lies buried. In 1749, he married Agnes, a Delaware, baptized by Cammerhoff, March 5, 1749. She died in 1751, at Bethlehem. His third wife was a white woman. Post eventually left the service of the Moravian Church. He died at Germantown, Pa.

missionaries had been forbidden to continue their work, but they remained at the station ministering to one of their own number, Gottlob Büttner, who was wasting under the blight of an incurable disease. After his death (February 23, 1745), they left Shekomeko in a body.[1]

Meantime Zeisberger and Post, together with Rachel, who had here joined them, proceeded to Freehold, and thence to William's Fort. It was a time of great excitement, both in New England and New York. The one was preparing an expedition against Louisburg; the other rang with a false report of the disaffection of the Iroquois. The suspicions of the garrison were awakened at seeing two young men, unprovided with passports, and coming from a Church accused of sympathy with the French, on their way to the Indian country. A rigid examination was instituted by some of the soldiers, although without authority; but, as nothing appeared to prove them spies, they were allowed to go on. At Canajoharie, Hendrick, the illustrious King of the Mohawks,[2] bowing low to the salutation from Pyrlaeus which they brought him, received them into his lodge, and consented to instruct Zeisberger in the language.

---

[1] Büttner was buried at Shekomeko. A marble monument, erected in 1859 by the Moravian Historical Society, marks his grave, in a field on the farm of Mr. Edward Hunting.

[2] Soiengarahta, or King Hendrick, the principal sachem of the Mohawks, was a brave warrior, and a warm friend of England, which country he visited, and where he had an audience of King George. He was killed in the battle of Lake George, September 8, 1755.

Intelligence of their visit had, meantime, been transmitted to Albany, from William's Fort. Ten days after their arrival, as they were about going into the forest to chop wood, two strangers met them at the door, but precipitately retreated when they saw their hatchets. Upon their return, however, they were invited to a neighboring house, and there found the same men, who, displaying a warrant from the Mayor of Albany, received them with the announcement, "We are constables, and you are our prisoners!" This arrest filled the town with indignation. "Your people," said Hendrick, "have just settled their disputes with us, and now you begin a new quarrel! You deserve to be killed!" Such a threat induced the redoubtable officers of the law, who had scarce recovered from the shock produced by two domestic hatchets, to hurry their prisoners into a sleigh and speed to Albany.

There Mayor Schuyler sent them to the Court House, to be examined by the magistrates. In the course of the inquest "many filthy and scornful questions" were proposed to them, the Justices "laughing among themselves," until Zeisberger with grave dignity remarked: "We hope the Honorable Magistrates will behave more discreetly, and beg they will forbear asking us such-like questions." This silenced their ribaldry. They "seemed as if they were ashamed;" and the missionaries, having avowed themselves to be loyal subjects of King George, but, on conscientious grounds, declined to swear an oath of allegiance, were permitted to retire to private lodgings. Early the next morning, however, came a corporal and four soldiers with loaded muskets, and marched them through the streets—"as though we were the vilest malefactors," says Zeisberger—to the castle, where Captain Rutherforth committed them to the safe-keeping of a guard, with orders to convey them to New York. To their inquiries respecting the offense of which they were accused, he could give them no information, except that they had refused the oath of allegiance. The Mayor's parting words, although they, too, contained no answer to their question, were more explicit. "If you, or any of your Brethren," said he, "come here again without a pass from the Governor, I will have you whipped out of town!" Nor would he permit Rachel to accompany them, until Zeisberger pleaded in her behalf, and then he consented only on condition of her traveling as fast as the guard. The whole party being afoot, this was impossible, and, by noon of the first day, she was obliged to leave her husband, and take her way alone to Shekomeko.

At New York they were confined in the jail of City Hall. A note, which they dispatched to Thomas Noble, a merchant of the city, brought him to their assistance; while Peter Boehler and Anthony Seyfert, who were waiting for a ship to carry them to England, hastened to confer with them, but only by letter, from prudential motives.[1] They likewise sent

---

[1] The original letter is extant (MS. B. A.) which Boehler and Seyfert conjointly wrote to the two prisoners, in English, and which they were permitted to read, after it had been carefully inspected by the Sheriff.

Henry Van Vleck to Bethlehem, to notify the Board of what had occurred.[1]

The news soon spread through the city, and excited much comment. "There appears, however," writes Boehler to Spangenberg, "to be more indignation against the government than suspicion of our Church; although some persons, I am told, have declared that they would be glad to act as hangmen in the event of the execution of our two brethren as spies."[2]

On the following day (February 23d) the prisoners were cited before Governor Clinton and his Council. "We remembered," says Zeisberger, "the words of our Saviour: 'Ye shall be brought before governors and kings for my sake; but when they deliver you up, take no thought how or what ye shall speak: for it shall be given you in that same hour what ye shall speak.'[3] And we trusted in the Saviour that He would make good His words."

Zeisberger was examined first, and alone. After several preliminary questions, with regard to his birth-

---

It conveyed the warmest sympathy of the writers, without expressing any opinion upon the course of the government. Zeisberger writes in his Journal, that when Post and he had perused this communication, they "rejoiced and were exceedingly happy."

[1] Henry Van Vleck (born at New York, September 17, 1722) was a clerk in Thomas Noble's store, and subsequently became a prominent member of the Church and her Mission Agent in New York. His house was the resort of the missionaries. In 1773 he moved to Bethlehem, where he died, January 25, 1785. Thomas Noble was one of the original members of the Moravian Church in New York.

[2] Boehler's original letter to Spangenberg. MS. B. A.

[3] Matthew, x. 18 and 19.

place and arrival in America, the examination continued as follows:

"How long have you been in this government?"

"Since last New Year's Day, when we passed through here."

"How far up did you go into the country?"

"As far as Canajoharie."

"Who sent you thither?"

"Our Church."

"What church is that?"

"The Protestant Church of the United Brethren."

"Do you all do what she commands you?"

"With our whole heart!"

"But if she should command you to hang yourselves, or to go among the Indians and stir them up against the white people, would you obey in this?"

"No, I can assure your Excellency and the whole Council that our Church never had any such designs."

"What did she command you to do among the Indians?"

"To learn their language."

"Can you learn the language so soon?"

"I have already learned somewhat of it in Pennsylvania, and I went up to improve myself."

"What use will you make of this language? What is your design when you have perfected yourself in it? You must certainly have a reason for learning it."

"We hope to get liberty to preach among the Indians the Gospel of our crucified Saviour, and to declare to them what we have personally experienced of His grace in our hearts."

"Did you preach while you were among them now?"

"No, I had no design to preach, but only to learn their language."

"Were you not at William's Fôrt? Why did you not stay there?"

"We were there, but finding no Indians, as they had all gone hunting, we went farther."

"But their wives and children were at home; you could have learned of them."

"That was not proper for me, being a single man."

"You will give an account to your Church, when you come home, of the condition of the country and land?"

"I will. Why should I not? But we do not concern ourselves about that land; we have land enough of our own—we do not need that."

"You observed how many cannon are in the fort, how many soldiers and Indians in the castle, and how many at Canajoharie?"

"I was not so much as within the fort, and I did not think it worth while to count the soldiers or the Indians."

"Whom do you acknowledge for your king?"

"King George of England."

"But when you go up among the French Indians, who is your king there?"

"I never yet had any mind to go thither."

"Will you and your companion swear to be faithful subjects of King George, acknowledge him as your sovereign, and abjure the Pope and his adherents?"

"We own ourselves to be King George's faithful subjects; we acknowledge him as our sovereign; we can truly certify that we have no connection at all with the Pope and his adherents, and no one who knows anything of us can lay this to our charge. With regard to the oath, however, I beg leave to say that we are not inhabitants of this government, but travelers, and hope to enjoy the same privilege, which is granted in other English Colonies, of traveling unmolested without taking the oath."

"You design to teach the Indians, and we must have the assurance that you will not teach them disaffection to the King."

"But we have come at this time with no design to teach."

"Our laws require that all travelers in this government shall swear allegiance to the King, and have a license from the Governor."

"I never before this heard of such a law in any country or kingdom of the world!"

"Will you or will you not take the oath?"

"I will not."

Having put some other unimportant questions, the Council dismissed Zeisberger and examined Post. Then Zeisberger was recalled, and the secretary read to him the new act against the Moravians.

"Do you understand this?" he continued.

"Most of it, but not all," replied Zeisberger.

"Will you take the oath now?"

"I hope the Honorable Council will not force me to do it."

"We will not constrain you; you may let it alone if it is against your conscience; but you will have to go to prison again."

"I am content."

Zeisberger's request to be informed of the crime laid to his charge was met with the sententious remark, that it would be too late to take measures against a crime after it had been committed. "We must prevent the mischief," said a far-sighted counselor, "before it is brought about." The offer which the Council, finally, made to set him and Post at liberty, if they would give security to appear at the next term of the Supreme Court, they held under advisement. Meantime they were remanded to jail. There they were visited, the next morning, by Boehler and Seyfert, who told them to await instructions from Bethlehem.

The Mission Board had appealed to influential friends of the Church in Pennsylvania. But seven weeks passed by before the expected response came, during which period the young men remained in confinement. Zeisberger devoted the time to the study of the Mohawk, assisted by Post. Both were content to wait. "We count it a great honor," writes the former, "to suffer for the Saviour's sake, although the world cannot understand this." While in prison they saw many visitors. Not only Moravians came frequently, and, among these, Nathaniel Seidel,[1] as a special messenger of the Board; but strangers from the city and various parts of the Province called upon them nearly every day. Their extraordinary cheerfulness deeply impressed such persons; and many who had been loud in their denunciations of "Moravian priests," and "vagrant, strolling preachers," became convinced that they were victims of groundless mistrust and religious bigotry.

At last, on the eighth of April, they were enabled to send a petition to Governor Clinton, covering certificates in their favor from Conrad Weisser and Governor Thomas, of Pennsylvania, and praying to be set at liberty. These documents were considered in Council, on the same day. An order followed, relieving them from confinement, "on paying their fees," and permitting them to return to Bethlehem. On the tenth the Sheriff declared them free. Inscribing several verses, from their German Hymn Book, on the walls of their room, as an expression of their faith in God, they betook themselves to the house of Thomas Noble, and reached Bethlehem on the sixteenth.[2]

---

[1] Nathaniel Seidel was born October 2, 1718, at Lauban, in Saxony, and came to America in 1742, where he filled various offices, among others that of "Elder of the Pilgrims," or Superintendent of the Itinerating Missionaries of the Church. In this capacity he spent many years in traveling, going as far as the West Indies and South America. In 1758, he was consecrated bishop, and, in 1761, succeeded Bishop Spangenberg as President of the Mission Board.

[2] Copy of Petition; Copy of the Order of Release; Letter from Conrad Weisser to Spangenberg; and Zeisberger's Journal. MSS. B. A.

DAVID ZEISBERGER.

This experience belonged to the preparations which fitted Zeisberger for the career of a missionary. It taught him one of the most essential conditions of success. Descended from a Church of martyrs, the faith of his fathers was called into exercise; and he was thenceforth ready to suffer reproach, or even to lose his life, in the cause which he had espoused.

A few days after his return, the first converts from the Delaware nation, a chief of the Turtle Tribe and his wife, were baptized at Bethlehem. They came from Wamphallobank, and, belonging to a family of distinction, their baptism caused such a sensation among their kindred that thirty-six warriors marched to the settlement, in order to carry them off by force. But the testimony of the converts, and the friendly welcome of the inhabitants, disarmed them of their design.

The Board had not forgotten the Mission at Shekomeko. A project was set on foot to transfer it to the valley of Wyoming. This necessitated negotiations with the Iroquois Confederacy, to whose dependencies Wyoming belonged, and Bishop Spangenberg determined to visit Onondaga in person. Zeisberger and Schebosh[1] were appointed his associates.

---

[1] John Joseph Schebosh, as he was universally called, although his real name was Joseph Bull,—Schebosh (Running Water) being the name given him by the Indians, and John the name bestowed upon him when he was baptized as an adult,—was born of Quaker parents, May 27, 1721, at Skippack, Pa., and joined the Moravian Church in 1742, receiving baptism at the hands of Andrew Eschenbach, September 15, 1742. He married Christiana, a Sopus Indian, baptized by Martin Mack (July 24, 1746), and devoted his life to the service of the Indian Mission. He died in Ohio.—See *chapter xl.*

They[1] set out on horseback (May 24th), and proceeded, by way of the Heidelberg settlements, to Tulpehocken, where they were joined by Conrad Weisser, who had been commissioned by the government of Pennsylvania to treat with the Six Nations. The place of rendezvous was Shamokin. There they spent a week, preaching the Gospel to the Indians and to Madame Montour, who had recently taken up her abode in the village.

On[2] the seventh of June, the whole party, to which had now been added Shikellimy, one of his sons, and Andrew Montour, took the trail for Onondaga. Crossing the Susquehanna, they followed its West Branch, and passed the first night in the "Warrior's Camp."

It was the custom of the Moravian missionaries, in those days, when passing through the wilderness, to give to their camping-grounds names, the initials of which were carved on trees, and remained as landmarks for other evangelists. In the course of time, the valleys of the Susquehanna, and the forests of New York, were full of these mementoes of pious zeal; and as the localities were described in the journals of the itinerants, and the appellations used by subsequent visitors, a geographical nomenclature grew into existence which was peculiarly Moravian.[3]

---

[1] Spangenberg's Journal of the Tour to Onondaga. MS. B.A. The original notes, taken on the way, are extant.

[2] Weisser's Report to the Colonial Government.—*Col. Records of Pa.*, iv. 778–784.

[3] At the present day, the difficulties of a study of the old topography

The arrival of two Iroquois warriors, who noiselessly glided to the fire, suggested the name for this particular camp. They belonged to a band that had been defeated by the Catawbas, escaping with nothing but their lives. One of them, at the request of Weisser, hurried on to Onondaga, the next morning, in order to announce the coming of the party.

This proceeded more slowly. Soon after leaving Ostonwacken, they plunged into a fearful wilderness. It was that part of Lycoming County which lies between the Alleghany and Laurel Hill Mountains. Even at the present day it is a wild country; of its appearance, more than a century ago, we can scarcely form a conception. The forests were a broad waste, in many parts impenetrable to the sun; thick underwood entangled the travelers on every side; the ground, for miles, was a morass, into which the horses sank up to their knees; and, not unfrequently, gigantic trees, uprooted by the storm, were found obstructing the trail.

Amid such obstacles, they pressed through the valley of the Pine Creek—called by the Indians the Tiadaghton—and bivouacked, in the evening of the tenth, near a large salt-lick, the resort of elk. While sitting around the fire, the lurid glare of which made the night in the surrounding forest to appear more profound, Shikellimy and his son, with the formalities usual on such occasions, adopted the three envoys into the

---

of the country, from the records of the early missionaries, are enhanced in a tenfold degree by this custom. After the Pontiac Conspiracy it fell into desuetude.

Iroquois Confederacy; Spangenberg, whom they named Tgirhitontie,[1] into the tribe of the Oneidas, and the clan of the Bear, and Zeisberger, who was called Ganousseracheri,[2] into the tribe of the Onondagas, and the clan of the Turtle. Schebosh received the name of Hajingonis.[3]

Taking, now, a northeasterly course, they passed the source of the Second Fork of Pine Creek, in Tioga County, emerged from the swamps, and struck the North Branch, below Tioga Point. At its junction with the Chemung, in the small triangle formed by the two rivers and the northern extremity of Bradford County, they found a fruitful tract upon which a tribe of Mohicans had built a village. While preparing to pitch their camp, a deputation of head men came out and said: "Brothers! We rejoiced when we saw you approaching; our houses are swept; our beds are prepared; we have hung the kettle over the fire; lodge with us."

After having enjoyed this generous hospitality, they proceeded into that part of the wilderness which is now the State of New York, journeyed three days longer, in a course north by east, through Tompkins, Cayuga, and Onondaga Counties, over wastes almost as wild as those of the Alleghanies, until, in the afternoon of June the seventeenth, they reached the capital of the League. As this little body of wayworn pilgrims,

---

[1] A row of trees.   [2] On the pumpkin.
[3] One who twists tobacco. Most of the missionaries were thus adopted, and always used their Indian names when among the Iroquois.

with their Indian guides, moved into the town, Louisburg, in another part of the continent, the strongest fortress of North America, opened its gates to an undrilled army of New England husbandmen and mechanics, and the Colonies achieved a victory over France that filled the whole country with joy.

The Council met, on the twentieth, to receive the embassy. Conrad Weisser communicated two points.[1] First, in the name of the Governors of Pennsylvania and Virginia, he invited deputies from the Six Nations to a congress with deputies from the Catawbas, their hereditary enemies, to be held at Williamsburg, in order to settle the ancient feud between the League and this tribe, through the intervention of the English. Second, by authority of the Governor of Pennsylvania, he demanded satisfaction for the murders perpetrated, within the dependencies of the Iroquois, by Peter Chartier[2] and his revolted Shawanese. Bishop Spangenberg proposed to renew the friendship established with the Six Nations by Count Zinzendorf, and asked permission to begin a settlement for Christian Indians at Wyoming.

The answers of the sachems were given on the following day. To Conrad Weisser they said, that they would agree to an armistice with the Catawbas until the spring of the next year, when they were willing to treat with them at Philadelphia, but not at Williams-

---

[1] Penn. Col. Records, iv. 778, etc.

[2] A half-breed trader in the interests of France, who had incited the Shawanese to take up the hatchet against the Colonies.

burg; that the whole League, with all its chiefs and war-captains, must be consulted, before so important a question as a permanent peace with their hereditary enemies could be settled; that they would complain to the Governor of Canada of the conduct of Peter Chartier, and secure satisfaction for the Colonies. To Bishop Spangenberg they replied, that they were glad to renew their compact with Count Zinzendorf and the Brethren; and that they gave their consent to the proposed settlement at Wyoming.

The mission of Conrad Weisser was opportune. If he had arrived but a week later, the sachems would have been in Canada, listening to the persuasions of the Governor, who used every means to gain them over to his side. Now they were pledged to neutrality, and his efforts were unavailing.

After a stay of twelve days, the visitors began their homeward journey. At the first village they separated. Conrad Weisser and Andrew Montour took a circuitous trail; Spangenberg, Zeisberger, Schebosh, Shikellimy and his son followed that which had brought them to Onondaga.

The experiences of this latter party were even more trying than when they had come that way the first time. Not only had they to contend with the same horrors of the swamps, but a succession of rain-storms occurred that made traveling almost unendurable; and, greatest calamity of all, their provisions failed! They braved these hardships for eight days, until they reached Ostonwacken, almost exhausted, yet full of hope. A bitter disappointment awaited them. There was not a morsel of food to be had in the village, and not even a fire burning in a single lodge. Riding on in garments wringing-wet, and barely alleviating the worst pangs of hunger with a few fishes which they had caught in the Susquehanna, they lay down on the bank of the river at noon, of the seventh of July, utterly overcome. They could go no farther. It was an hour to try their souls. A handful of rice constituted the remnant of their provisions. Faint and silent, the bishop and his young companions waited to see what God would do; while Shikellimy and his son, with the stoicism of their race, resigned themselves to their fate. Presently an aged Indian emerged from the forest, sat down among them, opened his pouch, and gave them a smoked turkey. When they proceeded, he joined their party, camped with them at night, and produced several pieces of delicious venison. They could not but recognize in this meeting a direct interposition of their Heavenly Father. The next day they reached Shamokin, where a trader supplied all their wants.[1]

On their way to this town they came upon a rattlesnake nest, amid the hills of the Susquehanna. At first but a few of the reptiles were visible, basking in the sun.

---

[1] Loskiel, in his History, and Heckewelder, in his Biographical Sketch, both relate a wonderful draught of fishes made by Zeisberger, at Spangenberg's request, in water where fishes are not commonly found, and say that this saved the lives of the party. This incident has been often quoted by other writers. It may have occurred, but there is no authority for it, either in Spangenberg's Journal or in his original notes; hence I omit it.

No sooner, however, did they kill these than the whole neighborhood seemed to be alive with them, and a rattling began which was frightful. Snakes crawled out of holes, from crevices in the rocks, and between loose stones, or darted from thickets, and lifted up their heads above patches of fern, until there was a multitude in motion that completely surrounded the travelers, who hastened from the spot. It was a place where the reptiles had gathered in autumn and lain torpid, coiled together in heaps, during the winter.

Zeisberger says that he once met with some Indians who had found such a nest, and set fire to the dry leaves and trees around it. The result, as narrated by them, was marvelous. First a terrific concert ensued of roaring flames and hissing, rattling serpents; and then these came rolling down the mountain-side, scorched to death, in such quantities that they would have filled several wagons, while the air was laden with an intolerable stench.[1]

From Shamokin, Spangenberg and his associates hastened to Bethlehem. When they approached the ridge which formed the boundary between the wilderness and the settlements, a terrific storm of rain and hail burst upon them; but, just as they reached the top of a peak of the Second Mountain, the sun broke through the clouds in all his glory, and a rainbow spanned the firmament. Greeting this gorgeous arc as a token of God's mercy to His servants when traveling in the

---

[1] Zeisberger's MS. Hist. of the Indians.

wilderness, they encamped by the dark waters of the Swatara. On the following evening, they enjoyed the hospitality of Christopher Weisser's homestead, in Tulpehocken, and, two days later, arrived at Bethlehem.

This tour was another school of preparation for Zeisberger. It made him acquainted with the usages of the Indians at their councils, and taught him to rely ever upon God, amid all the hardships incident to his missionary life.

CHAPTER VII.

HIS LABORS AT SHAMOKIN AND IN THE VALLEY OF WYOMING.—
1745-1750.

The converts of Shekomeko refuse to emigrate to Wyoming.—
Friedenshütten near Bethlehem. — Gnadenhütten on the Mahony.
—Shamokin and its smith-shop.—The principles of the work among
the Indians.—Bishop Cammerhoff.—Zeisberger at Shamokin.—His
Iroquois Dictionary.—Exploration of the two branches of the Susquehanna.—Indian treaties at Lancaster and Albany.—Peace of
Aix-la-Chapelle.—John de Watteville.—His tour to Shamokin and
Wyoming, with Zeisberger as his interpreter.—Conversion and death
of Shikellimy.—Ordination of Zeisberger.—Running the gantlet.—
Indian treaty at Philadelphia.—Council of bishops with the sachems
of the Iroquois.—Renewal of the Missions in New York and New
England.—Act of Parliament in favor of the Moravians.—General
prosperity of the work.

AFTER his return from Onondaga, Zeisberger devoted himself anew to the study of the Indian languages. The following year (1746), however, brought him work of a different character.

Contrary to the expectations of the Board, the Indians of Shekomeko refused to emigrate to Wyoming. No persuasions availed. They were as loath to leave their pleasant homes at the foot of the Stissing, as they were afraid of the savages of the Susquehanna. But it soon became evident that they could not remain in their village, on account of the increasing animosity of the settlers. Accordingly, a temporary asylum was offered them at Bethlehem. Ten families embraced

DAVID ZEISBERGER. 141

this offer, and built a little hamlet, called Friedenshütten, on the slope and around the base of a hill near the Lehigh.[1] A tract of land which the Church had recently purchased on the Mahony Creek, in the present Carbon County, was selected as a permanent seat for the converts. Thither Mack, Zeisberger, and several other young men, together with a few Indians, now proceeded in order to lay out a town. It received the name of Gnadenhütten. A Mission was organized at this place, in July, and put in charge of Mack and Rauch.[2]

But the Board discussed still another project. Shamokin was deemed to be an important place for a missionary enterprise, in view of its metropolitan character, and its situation on the principal trail to the South, whither Indians of various nationalities were constantly going. To gain this spot was to plant the banner of the Cross upon one of the most formidable

---

[1] Friedenshütten, or "Tents of Peace," lay on, and at the base of, the hill now partly embraced in the grounds of the Moravian Seminary for Young Ladies and partly within the inclosure of the Bethlehem Skating Park, including the ridge on which the Gas Works have been erected.

[2] Gnadenhütten, or "Tents of Grace," was built on a part of a tract of land lying on both sides of the Lehigh River, and comprising altogether about thirteen hundred and eighty acres, purchased at seven different times,—the first tract in 1745, and the last in 1754. In 1747, a grist- and saw-mill was erected on the Mahony. The original town lay on the declivity of the hill which rises from the creek with a gentle slope, and the top of which is still crowned with the old grave-yard, in the outskirts of Lehighton. It consisted of three streets, built in the form of parallel arcs, and bisected by a fourth, in the middle of which stood the church.—*Plan of the Town.* MS. B. A.

strongholds of paganism in the land. The prospect of success was, indeed, not encouraging. Mack had spent a part of the autumn there, and found the savages averse to the Gospel. Nevertheless a plan, suggested by Conrad Weisser, for securing a foothold, seemed so feasible that it was adopted in faith and hope.

Ever since the introduction of fire-arms among the natives the smitheries of the white people had been in high repute, and visited both by hunters and warriors. On account of their distance from the Indian country, however, Shikellimy applied to the Colonial government to have one put up at Shamokin. The Board, by the advice of Weisser and with the consent of the Governor,[1] undertook to fulfill this request, provided that they be allowed, at the same time, to begin a Mission. To this Shikellimy agreed. In April, 1747, John Hagen and Joseph Powell[2] erected a shop and a Mission-house. The former remained as resident missionary, and was joined, in June, by Anthony Schmidt, who opened a smithery in the shop. Hagen's usefulness, however, came to a speedy end. He died in early autumn. Mack succeeded him.

The enlargement of the field of labor demanded increased faith and new zeal. In February (1747), a general meeting of the Board and of all its missionaries was

---

[1] Two letters from Charles Brockden, of Philadelphia, to Spangenberg, June 27 and November 9, 1746. B. A.

[2] Joseph Powell was an itinerant missionary, born in Shropshire, England, in 1710, and died September 23, 1774, at Wechquadnach, Conn., where, in 1859, the Moravian Historical Society erected a monument to his memory.

called, at which the character and claims of the work were discussed. It was enthusiastically resolved to carry on the evangelization of the Indians in an "apostolical manner," with resistless energy, to the glory of God; and to deem fit for this service such men and women only as were willing to lose their lives for Christ's sake.[1] Zeisberger joyfully renewed his vows on the occasion of this conference.

Among its members was Bishop Cammerhoff, Spangenberg's newly-arrived assistant.[2] Cammerhoff was a remarkable man. An alumnus of the University of Jena, a bishop at the age of twenty-five years, a divine of rare scholarship, conversant, in particular, with the church-fathers and the various systems of philosophy; amiable, devoted to the God-Man, bold in Christ, and ready to endure all things for His cause; but deeply tinctured, too, with the fanaticism of the "time of sifting;"[3] he exercised great influence among the Brethren,

---

[1] Discourse delivered by Spangenberg, February 6, 1747. MS. B. A.

[2] John Christoph Frederic Cammerhoff was born near Magdeburg, Prussia, July 28, 1721, and arrived in America in 1747.

[3] This is the term by which a brief period of Moravian history, extending from 1745 to 1750, is generally known, during which time several churches of Germany fell into fanaticism. It consisted chiefly in a religious phraseology that was antiscriptural, puerile, and extravagant. The Saviour's wounds, and especially the wound in his side, were spiritualized, and made the subject of a flood of hymns which often degenerated into irreverence. Through the exertions of Zinzendorf, Spangenberg, and others, the evil was wholly suppressed. It is owing to this temporary fanaticism that such gross slanders were spread concerning the Moravian Church, in the last century, by men like Rimius, and works like "the Moravians Detected," and are occasionally revived even at the present day.

both for good and evil. He inspired ministers and people with enthusiasm for the work of the Lord; he led many souls to a knowledge of the truth; he gained numerous converts among the Indians, and infused life into all the operations of the Church. But he also introduced the puerile sentimentality which was disgracing some of the churches in Germany, and, in spite of Spangenberg's opposition, would have made it to triumph among American Moravians likewise, had he not been removed by the hand of death after a service of but four years.

Zeisberger had now acquired great fluency in the Mohawk language, and, in April, 1748, was appointed Mack's assistant at Shamokin. There he began to prepare an Iroquois dictionary, with Shikellimy for his teacher. He found that some ideas could not be expressed by any terms in use among the natives, and was compelled to introduce words from the German or the English in Indian idioms.

In the course of the summer he accompanied Mack on an exploration of the two branches of the Susquehanna. This tour showed him the Indian in the depths of misery. Ostonwacken lay deserted and in ruins. Other villages and isolated wigwams, along the West Branch, were likewise uninhabited. After traveling for days, they at last found a Delaware, living on an island covered with rank grass. "Where are all our brothers who used to hunt along this river?" asked Zeisberger. Lifting the blanket which covered the door of his hut, he pointed, in the way of an answer, to several sufferers hideous with the small-pox. This scourge was depopulating them. Those that had escaped it were begging food in the settlements. The missionaries made similar experiences everywhere. They spent two days at Great Island, surrounded by natives ill of the disease. Others were starving. A kettle of boiled grass constituted a luxury. Gaunt figures, huddled around fires, ate voraciously of such food.

Along the North Branch, too, which they followed as far as Wyoming, a dire famine was prevailing. The most of the Indians were gone in search of provisions; such as were at home scarcely sustained life on boiled tree-bark, unripe grapes, and roots.

The missionaries went their way sorrowful and yet rejoicing. They mourned over the distress of the natives. Their hearts bled to see misery of body and soul in so frightful a combination. But, for themselves, they had peace in God; and, as they journeyed, they sang hymns to His praise until the forests of the Susquehanna were vocal with sacred melodies; or, attracted by the sanctuary-like beauty of some grove, they fell upon their knees and prayed most earnestly for the conversion of the Indians. On the first of August they reached Bethlehem and reported to the Board. This entire journey had been accomplished afoot.

Meantime two important treaties with the aborigines had taken place. The one was held at Lancaster, where commissioners of Pennsylvania formed an alliance with the Twightwees of the Far West, in accordance with their own wish;[1] the other at Albany, where Governor Clinton, of New York, and Shirley, of Massachusetts, met a large deputation of Iroquois, in order to strengthen the chain of friendship which united the League and the Colonies.[2] Some time before this the news of the peace of Aix-la-Chapelle had reached America. Preliminaries had been signed on the nineteenth of April; and now, toward the end of August, the king's proclamation was received, ordering a cessation of hostilities.[3] Thus there seemed to open, for the development of the Colonies and the spread of the Gospel among the Indians, a promising future. But ere long it became evident that a mere hollow truce, and not a lasting peace, had been concluded.

Zeisberger spent two months at Bethlehem, at which place John de Watteville arrived from Europe, on an official visit to the Moravian Churches and Missions.

Baron John de Watteville, a bishop of the Church, the principal assistant of Count Zinzendorf, and his son-in-law, was one of those lovely characters that reflect the image of Christ. Mild, gentle, persuasive, yet full of courage and zeal, he was a John among the Brethren, living in a daily fellowship with Jesus, and knowing no happiness more exalted than to show forth His praise. A character such as this attracted Zinzendorf. There subsisted between them a bond stronger and holier than

---

[1] Col. Records of Pa., v. 307.
[2] Bancroft's U. S., iv. chap. ii.
[3] Col. Records of Pa., v. 331.

even that of the family. They were one in heart, as they were one in Christ.[1]

Hence the evangelization of the Indians, concerning whom he had heard so much from his father-in-law, excited Watteville's warmest sympathies, and one of the first duties which he undertook, was a tour through their country. Bishop Cammerhoff and Martin Mack accompanied him, and Zeisberger was appointed interpreter to the party.

They[2] first visited Gnadenhütten (October 1), taking the trail through the Lehigh Water-Gap, where no shrieking steam-whistle, but only the music of nature, filled their ears. Beyond Gnadenhütten they struck to the north, and entered a wilderness of hills, clothed in their bright autumnal garb, and pregnant, even then, with untold stores of anthracite coal,—hills that should give birth to no small part of the commercial greatness and industrial power of that Commonwealth which now boasts of the mines of Mauch Chunk. At night they bivouacked under a white oak, and called their camp

---

[1] Watteville was born Oct. 18, 1718, at Walschleben, in Thuringia, and was the son of a Lutheran clergyman, named John M. Langguth. He was educated at the University of Jena, and subsequently joined the Moravian Church. Having been adopted by Baron Frederick de Watteville, he was created a Baron of the Germanic Empire by Francis I., in 1745. In the following year he married the Countess Benigna, Zinzendorf's oldest daughter, and was consecrated a bishop in 1747. At a later period, he became a member of the General Executive Conference of the Church, in which office he remained until his death, Oct. 7, 1788. In 1783, he paid a second visit to America, where he spent three years.

[2] Watteville's Journal, in his own handwriting. MS. B. A.

"John's Rest," in honor of Watteville, whose initial letter was carved on the tree. Three days later they reached Wyoming.

A visit to places that have gained a name in the fireside recollections of a family, in the traditions of a church, or the history of a people, is an occasion of deep interest and rare enjoyment. The localities are familiar and yet new, well known and yet strange; the present is linked to the past; and the past reappears in the present. With feelings such as these, Watteville, guided by Mack, explored the lovely valley which here opened to his view. They found the plain of Skehantowanno, where Zinzendorf's tent had first been pitched, the little hill where God had delivered him from the fangs of the adders, and the spot where the Shawanese had watched him with murderous designs. The very tree was still standing on which he had graven the initial of his Indian name, and they could even trace its faint outlines.

Among the inhabitants, however, many changes had taken place. The majority of the Shawanese lived by the waters of the Ohio, and but few natives of any other tribe remained, with the exception of Nanticokes. Watteville faithfully proclaimed the Gospel, Zeisberger interpreting. At nightfall of the seventh of October, he gathered his companions around him and celebrated the Lord's Supper. It was the first time that this holy sacrament was administered in that valley where many Christian churches, in this way of divine appointment, now show the Lord's death. The hymns of the little company swelled solemnly through the night, while the Indians stood listening, in silent awe, at the doors of their wigwams. And when they heard the voice of the stranger lifted up in earnest intercession, as had been his father's voice in that same region six years before, they felt that the white man was praying that they might learn to know his God.

From Wyoming the travelers followed the North Branch, visited Wamphallobank and Neskapeke, and, passing through Skogari, at present in Columbia County —the only town on the whole continent inhabited by Tutelees, a degenerate remnant of thieves and drunkards, who crowded in rude wonder around the horses of the Brethren, ejaculating in broken English, "See! Moravian preachers!"—reached Shamokin just as the sun was sinking beyond the Susquehanna in all the splendor of an October sky. Hastening from the Mission-house came Powell, and from his shop Schmidt, to bid them welcome; nor was it long before Shikellimy took them by the hand and proffered the hospitalities of the village.

Watteville's visit made a deep impression upon this sachem. Zinzendorf had sent him a costly gift[1] and an affectionate message, entreating him to remember the Gospel which he heard from his lips, and turn to Christ. Watteville urged the subject with all the

---

[1] It consisted of a silver knife, fork, and spoon, together with an ivory drinking-cup heavily mounted with silver, all inclosed in a morocco-case, to which was attached a long loop of silk.

glowing warmth of his own love, Zeisberger interpreting his words into the Mohawk language. The heart of the old chief was touched; and several weeks after the departure of the party, he arrived at Bethlehem, in order to hear more of Christ. He was daily instructed in the plan of salvation, until he experienced the power of divine grace and could make a profession of personal faith. He had been baptized by a Jesuit Father, in Canada, many years before this. Laying aside a manitou, the last relic of his idolatry, he took his way rejoicing to his forest-home. At Tulpehocken, however, he fell ill, and had barely strength to reach Shamokin. There he stretched himself on his mat, and never rose again. Zeisberger, who had returned to his post, while Watteville and Cammerhoff had gone to Bethlehem, faithfully ministered to his body and his soul. He died on the sixth of December, conscious to the last, but unable to speak, a bright smile illumining his countenance.[1]

He left three sons, James Logan or Sogechtowa, John or Thachnechtoris, and John Petty. Runners were sent out to summon them to Shamokin. James Logan arrived the next day, and, on the ninth, the sachem was buried, in the presence of the whole population. Zeisberger wrote the news to Conrad Weisser, who reported it to Governor Hamilton.[2] The Colonial government transmitted a message of con-

---

[1] Journal of Shamokin Mission. MS. B. A.
[2] Penn. Archives, ii. 23.

dolence, and the usual presents for the sons of the deceased, requesting Thachnechtoris to act as Iroquois deputy until a permanent appointment could be made by the Grand Council. To Bethlehem the intelligence was brought by Zeisberger in person, and created a profound sensation, especially among the members of the Synod, which was sitting at the time, under the presidency of Bishop de Watteville.

It had been Zeisberger's intention to go back immediately to Shamokin. But Watteville detained him, took him along on a tour to the churches of Pennsylvania and New York, and, after their return, ordained him to the ministry (February 16, 1749).[1] Then he sent him to his post, with a written message, from the bishops and the Synod, to Shikellimy's sons, sympathizing with them in their loss, telling them of their father's faith in the Lord Jesus Christ, and urging them to follow in his footsteps.[2]

Zeisberger resumed his work with new zeal, assisted by Jonathan, a Christian Indian from Shekomeko, son of the first convert. But his experiences were of a trying character. He could not stem the tide of wickedness that was sweeping through Shamokin. Not only the inhabitants themselves continued unimpressed by the truths of the Gospel, but the numerous visitors helped to maintain the supremacy of heathenism. Hunters coming to the smith-shop, and Iroquois

---

[1] Certificate of Ordination. MS. B. A.
[2] Copy of the Message. B. A.

war-parties going against the Catawbas, engaged in drunken revelries and bloody brawls, while, not unfrequently, large bodies of savages arrived in order to celebrate their sacrificial abominations, which led to debauchery in its worst forms. At other times, scenes of cruelty occurred which the missionaries were unable to prevent.

One day, for example, the death-whoop rang through the forest. A band of thirty Iroquois was returning from the country of the Catawbas, with three prisoners, one of whom was a little girl. She was spared, but the two men were obliged to run the gantlet. In this brutal sport all the Indians of Shamokin took part. Two lines were formed, between which the captives were made to run, amid furious blows dealt with fists, sticks, and war-clubs, until they reached a hut that had previously been pointed out to them as their place of refuge. Thither the warriors came and bound up their wounds; after which they were led forth again and compelled to dance for the amusement of the assembled people. To force their prisoners thus to run the gantlet, at every town to which they brought them, was the inhuman custom of the Six Nations.

In midsummer, the Board sent for Zeisberger to meet Bishop John Nitschmann,[1] who was officiating as Spang-

---

[1] John Nitschmann, Sen., was born in 1703, at Schönau, in Moravia, and emigrated to Herrnhut in 1725. He became the private tutor of Count Christian Zinzendorf, whom he accompanied to the University of Jena. In 1741 he was consecrated a bishop, and came to America in 1749, with a colony of 120 immigrants. He was President of the Board

enberg's successor,[1] and Bishop de Watteville, who had returned from a visit to the Mission in the West Indies. They had important news to communicate.

An Indian treaty had been held in Philadelphia, at which the Iroquois had sold a tract of land to Pennsylvania, extending from the Blue Mountains more than thirty miles up the Susquehanna, and thence in a straight line eastward to the junction of the Leckawacksein Creek with the Delaware River, thus alienating their dependencies to within a short distance of Shamokin, where James Logan now had his seat, as deputy of the Grand Council, in place of his father.[2] On the occasion of this treaty, Watteville, Cammerhoff, Spangenberg, Pyrlaeus, and Seidel had instituted, at the Parsonage, on Race Street, a council with the sachems of the Six Nations, at whose head stood Ganassateco, and had received permission to send an embassy to Onondaga, in the following spring, in order to arrange preliminaries for a missionary enterprise in their country.[3] This embassy was intrusted to Cammerhoff and Zeisberger; the former to be the accredited envoy, the latter interpreter.

---

until 1751, when he returned to Europe, and served the Church in England, Germany, and Holland. He died at Zeist, May 6, 1772.

[1] On the occasion of a Synod held at Bethlehem, October, 1748, under the presidency of Watteville, the "Congregation of God in the Spirit" was given up, and, at the same time, Spangenberg, owing to the jealousy of some of his fellow-laborers, was relieved of his office. He retired, deeply hurt, to Philadelphia.

[2] Indian Deed. Penn. Archives, ii. 33.

[3] At this council, Watteville was adopted into the Turtle clan of the Onondaga Nation, and received the name of Tgarihontie, or "A Messenger."

While the work at Shamokin was unsuccessful, other Missions flourished. In the early part of 1749, those in New York and New England were renewed, through the exertions of Watteville. The opponents of the cause were to be effectually silenced. In the course of the summer there was sent to America an Act of Parliament "for encouraging the people known by the name of the *Unitas Fratrum*, or United Brethren, to settle in his Majesty's Colonies." This Act allowed them "to make a solemn affirmation in lieu of an oath," exempted them from military service, and acknowledged them as "an ancient Protestant Episcopal Church."[1] Thus were those "Moravian priests," and "vagrant, strolling preachers," against whom the petty legislators of New York had taken counsel, and whom they had driven like vagabonds from their Province, recognized by the highest legislative body in the British dominions, and put on a parity with the clergy of the Anglican Church.

At Gnadenhütten, too, the cause prospered so much that a larger chapel was erected in 1749. Meniolagemekah, moreover, was now a missionary station, and had a little band of confessors under George Rex, the captain of the village, who had been baptized at Bethlehem, and received the name of Augustus; while

---

[1] 22 George II., c. xxx.; *Acta Fratrum Unitatis in Anglia*, 1749. This Act was framed, at the instance of Zinzendorf, mainly on account of the persecutions which the Church had suffered in New York. It was introduced into the House of Commons March 25, 1749, passed by the House of Lords May 12, and signed by the King, June 6.

along the Susquehanna lived single families of Christian Indians. Therefore Watteville, who sailed for Europe, with Spangenberg, on the fifteenth of October, could bear the gratifying news to his father-in-law, that the Indian Mission had increased to several hundred converts.[1]

---

[1] Loskiel (Part ii. p. 118) gives the number at five hundred, which is, unquestionably, an error. There could not have been more than about three hundred persons in fellowship with the Mission, inasmuch as there were but two hundred and thirty baptisms up to that year, as is seen from the official register.

CHAPTER VIII.

ZEISBERGER AND CAMMERHOFF ON AN EMBASSY TO ONONDAGA.—
1750.

Zeisberger and Cammerhoff at Wyoming.—Set out in a canoe, guided by a Cayuga chief.—Visit the scattered converts.—Reach the Cayuga country and take horses.—Lake Cayuga.—The historic monuments of the Cayugas.—Cayuga Town.—Arrive at Onondaga and reception by the Grand Council.—Visit the Senecas.—Great perils.—The escape from the Zonesschio.—Danger of drowning.—Return to Onondaga. Their message to the Council.—Journey home.—The rattlesnake.

The hopes awakened by the past success of the Indian Mission made the new enterprise in which Zeisberger was to engage a pleasure and a privilege, in spite of its hardships. To bear the Gospel to the powerful League of the Six Nations and bring these proud savages into the Church of Christ was the ultimate purpose of this second embassy to Onondaga. Mohicans, Wampanoags, and Delawares had been converted to the living God, and were learning the ways of civilization,— why not Iroquois also, one of whose greatest sachems had died a Christian in Zeisberger's arms?

Such were the thoughts with which he took his way to Wyoming, whither Bishop Cammerhoff had preceded him. They met in the town of the Nanticokes, and spent a week waiting in vain for their Indian guide. At last they resolved to begin the journey alone, confident that He who had led the Israelites through the wilderness would help them to find their path. A part of the way could not be missed, for Zeisberger had planned a new route. He proposed to ascend the Susquehanna in a canoe, as far as the present boundary of New York, thus avoiding the great swamp in which Bishop Spangenberg's party had suffered so many privations.

On the twenty-eighth of May, the little vessel which was to carry them lay ready, fashioned with all the ingenuity of a native builder. Their packs were put on board, the indispensable rifle and powder-horn not forgotten, the hatchet, flint, and steel securely stowed away. Surrounded by the friends who had accompanied Cammerhoff to Wyoming, they were sending messages of love to their brethren, when their long-expected guide arrived—Hahotschaunquas, a chief of the Cayugas. He had been detained by high water in the Susquehanna. An hour later, at two o'clock in the afternoon, they embarked,—Hahotschaunquas and Gajehene, his wife, in their canoe; Cammerhoff, Zeisberger, and the chief's two children — Tagita, a lad of fourteen, and Gahaea, a little girl of four years—in that belonging to the missionaries. Waving a last farewell to their friends on the bank, Zeisberger seized the paddle, and, using it with the expertness of an Indian, the canoe glided swiftly on its way to the country of the Iroquois.

The journey which the two envoys thus began was one of the most romantic ever undertaken by Moravian missionaries. Great sufferings and wonderful escapes distinguished it; faith and courage, such as the heroic age of the Church of the Brethren had never before seen, will ever render it memorable. No two men among her clergy could have been found better fitted to stand fast and endure. The intense love to Christ which filled Cammerhoff's heart gloried in tribulations; and Zeisberger's soul longed so ardently for manifestations of God's power among the Aquanoschioni that famine, nakedness, or perils were as nothing in securing such an end. Associated as the two had been on former tours through the wilderness, having many recollections in common, this mission bound them together like David and Jonathan. One in their Saviour, His divine name was continually on their lips; and the "Man of sorrows and acquainted with grief" formed the source of their daily joy and strength and peace.

In the evening of their first day's journey they fastened their canoes to the shore, and built a walnut-bark hut, in the center of which they kindled a fire. On the one side, wrapped in their blankets, lay the missionaries; on the other, the Indian family. Thus they slept in peace. Similar shelters were erected every night, and each camping-ground received a name.

Having reached a village near the line of the present Wyoming County, where Nathaniel, a convert, baptized by Cammerhoff, had his home, and near which lived other Christian Indians, the first fruits of the Mission in that valley, they stopped a day in order to visit these "brown sheep," as the bishop was accustomed to call his Indian converts, and strengthen them in their holy faith. It was a time of great encouragement. Not only did they find the baptized Indians faithful to their vows, but the savages unwittingly bore testimony to the reality of their conversion. "What have you done to our brothers," said the indignant warriors, crowding around the bishop, "that they are so entirely different from us, and from what they used to be? What is this baptism which has made them turn from our feasts and dances, and shun all our ways?" Cammerhoff's response was a fervent discourse upon the atonement of Christ.

The winding course of the river, after leaving this village, led them through a romantic country and a primeval wilderness. Wooded hills stretched from the Susquehanna to the spurs of the Alleghanies, the young foliage of early summer clothing them in a mantle of soft green, variegated by the flowers of the tulip-tree and the blossoms of gorgeous forest-shrubs. Sweeping around bluffs, the stream in many places burst into wild rapids, through which they found it almost impossible to paddle their canoes. From the coves, between the hills, ducks rose at their approach, or the startled deer bounded back into the thicket; above their heads, clouds of wild pigeons passed on their swift way; while stretched upon the rocks, basking in the sun, or coiled with head erect, appeared occasionally, and on one day in extraordinary numbers, the mottled rattlesnake, the terror of the American wilderness.

Through such scenes they journeyed for nearly ten days; Zeisberger and Hahotschaunquas shooting game for their food, and Cammerhoff speaking with the Indian family about the salvation of their souls, or listening, at night, to the tales of the chief as he related, by the fire, the heroic deeds of his ancestors. Now and then a straggling village of Delawares appeared on the bluffs, or a canoe, with its solitary hunter, crossed their track. At Tioga they turned from the Susquehanna into the Chemung, the current of which was so strong that it almost exhausted Zeisberger's strength, and reached Ganatocherat, the first village of the Cayugas, probably near the boundary of New York. Haetwe, an acquaintance of Zeisberger, met them at the bank, and invited them to stop at the hut of the chief. The latter was absent, but Haetwe took his place as host. When they entered the lodge, he turned to Zeisberger, and said with all the dignity of a well-bred gentleman, "I salute you, my brother Ganousseracheri!"

They rested at Ganatocherat for two days, and then continued their journey on horseback, still guided by the Cayuga chief. Struggling through a swamp, where the fruitful farms of Tompkins County now rejoice the tourist's eye, they reached, after four days of hard riding, the southernmost point of Lake Cayuga, or Ganiataragechiat, as it was called by the natives. Here they met a party of Indians encamped in a cave, who generously replenished their scanty stores with a supply of turtle-eggs and dried eels.

Advancing now along the eastern shore of the lake, they forded numerous creeks, and came to a spot which their guide approached with proud steps and glowing eyes. It was the rude, but to him glorious, monument of the warlike deeds of his nation. The trees all around were full of figures and curious symbols carved on the bark, — telling of battles fought and won, of scalps brought home, and of prisoners taken. He led them to one tree in particular, and pointed out the history of his own exploits.

Man, in every age, and in all states of civilization, is swayed by the same desire to leave to posterity the tokens of his renown. Gigantic blocks and pillars of stone, arrayed in mysterious hieroglyphics, formed the national chronicles of the ancient Egyptians; statues, upon which Art exhausted her highest powers, immortalized the heroes of Greece and Rome; beautiful bass-reliefs, cast out of cannon which Napoleon Bonaparte captured from the Austrians and Russians, and covering the Column Vendôme, at Paris, celebrate the victories of this mighty conqueror; a colossal obelisk of hewn granite, towering above Bunker Hill, marks that momentous struggle for American Independence which there took place. So, in the remote wilderness, by the waters of Cayuga Lake, the trees of a primeval forest published the fame of its children. But while Egypt, Greece, and Rome still live in their memorials, broken though many of them be, and while the monuments of our times are viewed by admiring thousands, the oak and the ash, which recorded Cayuga greatness, have long since bowed under the white man's axe, and the history which their bark unfolded, like the race that it concerned, is well-nigh extinct.

After nightfall, the party arrived at Cayuga Town, the capital of the nation. This was Hahotschaunquas's home, and they were hospitably entertained by his grandmother, an aged matron of more than ninety years. The village, nestling among the trees on the shore of the lake, and distinguished by its roomy and substantial houses, excited their admiration; they spent a pleasant day among its people, and joyfully anticipated the time when the true God would here have a sanctuary. Their course from this place was to the northeast, and brought them into a thick wilderness, embracing Lakes Owasco and Skaneateles, and stretching to within a short distance of Onondaga, which they reached on the nineteenth of June.

As they were entering this forest-metropolis, their guide asked them where they proposed to lodge. "At the house of Ganassateco," said Zeisberger. "Ganassateco!" echoed the chief in great surprise. "Ganassateco is a very mighty sachem!" His lodge proved to be of unusually large dimensions, and in front of it stood a flag-staff from which the English colors floated.

Ganassateco's wife welcomed them,—her husband being absent at the Council. As soon as he was informed of their arrival, however, they were invited to the Council House, where they found twenty-four heads of the League assembled, who received them with every mark of distinction. Their guide sat humbly at the door, gazing upon this reception in mute astonishment. Now that he saw the respect with which the Princes of the Aquanoschioni treated his fellow-travelers, he began to realize their dignity.

The envoys having taken the places assigned to them, a brief but profound silence ensued, until Bishop Cammerhoff rose, and spoke as follows,— Zeisberger interpreting his words into the Mohawk language : " Brothers! Gallichwio[1] and Ganousseracheri have come to visit you. They promised to visit you when they saw you at Philadelphia, and gave you a fathom of wampum. They have been sent by their brothers to bring you a message, and have reached your Council-fire, here at Onondaga, in health. They rejoice to see you all together. But first they will rest a few days from the fatigues of their long journey, and then they will meet you, and tell you their thoughts, and why they have come." This speech was greeted with applause ; whereupon the bishop presented a pipe of tobacco, which passed from mouth to mouth, and Zeisberger gave a short account of their journey. Then the Council continued its deliberations in the presence of the envoys. A plentiful meal closed the sitting.

The following day Cammerhoff and Zeisberger devoted partly to religious exercises. Retiring into the forest, they prostrated themselves before God, and

---

[1] Gallichwio, meaning " a good message," was Cammerhoff's Indian name. He had been adopted by the Six Nations on the 15th of April, 1748.

offered up fervent intercessions on behalf of the Six Nations, that this people might soon be led to embrace the Gospel of the Lord Jesus Christ. Afterward, sitting in the shade of a great tree, they celebrated the Lord's Supper, according to the solemn ritual of their Church. The "Communion Hymns" swelled in sweet harmony through Nature's lofty sanctuary, and He, whose promise to two or three gathered in His name stands fast, bestowed upon His servants the fullness of peace.

The twenty-first of June had been appointed for their negotiations with the Council, but it could not meet because a majority of its members were intoxicated; and, as days passed without any sign of returning soberness, Ganassateco, at last, advised the envoys to go back to Shamokin, and there await the answer of the sachems, which he pledged himself to send by a special runner. But they were too well acquainted with the unreliableness of the Indians to adopt such a suggestion, and knew that if they left the country the object of their mission would never be gained. Hence they persuaded Ganassateco to present their message and strings of wampum as soon as the Council could be called together, while they paid a visit to the Senecas.

They set out, first, for Cayuga Town, each carrying a pack, and Zeisberger his rifle. There they were joined by Hahotschaunquas, whom they had again engaged as their guide. Onechsagerat, a venerable old chief, gave them a farewell breakfast of corn-bread and tea, the tea service consisting of a large spoon and a wooden bowl placed on two corn-mortars instead of a table. Gannekachtacheri, a celebrated warrior, whose name had been conferred upon Secretary Peters, ferried them across the lake. They traveled afoot. Taking a trail west by north, they entered a fearful wilderness, in which they sweltered amid intense heat, unable to find a drop of water, except a turbid pool, until they had walked thirty-five miles, when they came to a stream whose murmuring current was music to their ears. An hour before sunset they reached a village lying on the outlet of Lake Seneca, which bore the name of Nugniage among the natives, probably not far from the present flourishing town of Waterloo, in Seneca County. A French trader lent them his canoe to cross the outlet to the head of the lake, where they stopped for the night, the rain descending in torrents upon their defenseless heads.

At early dawn they continued their journey in a course west-southwest, which brought them to the first hunting-grounds of the Senecas,—a beautiful valley, blooming like a garden. It was the eastern section of Ontario County. Their guide told them that a large town had enlivened this region more than half a century ago, but had been destroyed by the French in a war with the Six Nations. Contiguous to this valley, and in dismal contrast with it, lay a swamp, nearly six miles in extent. To pass this involved so many difficulties that men less determined would have relinquished the journey in despair. The gloomy wood; the tangled thickets; the deep sloughs, through which they had to creep on trunks of prostrate trees, frequently slipping into the mire up to their knees; the stifling atmosphere; the swarms of mosquitoes;—all this rendered their way arduous beyond description. A terrific thunder-storm, which burst upon them, was a relief, for it scattered the insects and purified the air. Toward evening they built a hut, and spent a dreary night, with nothing to eat except a small quantity of pounded corn. The next morning, however, they emerged from the swamp, and reached the beautiful waters of Lake Canandaigua.

Near its outlet they crossed an Indian bridge, made of small trees and poles thrown loosely upon stakes, which were bound together with thongs of bark and driven into the bottom of the lake, and came up with a Seneca hunter, from Ganataqueh, carrying a juicy haunch of venison, whereof he invited them to partake at his lodge. Nearly famished as they were, they eagerly accepted the offer. The huts of the village were all ornamented with the totems of the various clans to which the inmates belonged, painted in rude outlines above the doors. Tanochtahe—such was the name of their host—having fired a salute of four shots, to announce the arrival of distinguished guests, the headmen of the village came to welcome them.

That night Bishop Cammerhoff lay ill of a violent fever. Zeisberger was sitting by him and ministering to his wants, when a messenger summoned him to a hut in a distant part of the village. There he was unexpectedly introduced into the presence of the whole male population, engaged in an uproarious drinking-bout, shouting, laughing, and dancing in wild confusion. As soon as he entered, profound silence ensued; while the chief, who presided at the debauch, informed him that, as a mark of special respect, the people of Ganataqueh had sent for him to take part in their feast. Zeisberger's situation at that moment was critical in the highest degree. He was at the mercy of the Indians, whom rum had made mad. To offend them might prove instant death. What surety had he that a tomahawk, hurled from the midst of the drunken crowd, might not be the response if he refused the invitation? But Zeisberger was the servant of the Holy Lord. To Him he remained true. Speaking in the tongue of the Cayugas, he declined to join in the revelry, delivered a powerful speech on the evils of intoxication, and besought them to turn from the fire-water which was destroying their race. The Indians pressed around him with threatening looks, and insisted on his at least drinking their health. Zeisberger still refused, but seeing that they were determined, and that there was no other way of escape, at last took the proffered cup and barely lifted it to his lips. Then they let him go. Thus he showed himself bold and prudent, each in season. To have resisted any longer would have been courting martyrdom for an insufficient cause.

Rejoining the bishop, he prepared for rest; but there was no rest for either of them. Parties of inebriated savages burst into the lodge, shouting and singing, now heaping disgusting tokens of affection upon them, and now menacing them with fierce anger. Their situation became intolerable, especially as their guide was intoxicated like the rest. They must escape without delay, although Cammerhoff was so weak that he could barely walk. Issuing from the hut as the morning began to break, they hoped to get away unmolested, but the Indians followed them with wild whoops, jostled and worried them in many ways, pointed their rifles at them, and every few minutes sent a ball whistling just above the head, first of the one and then of the other. This cruel sport continued for a mile or two, when the savages suddenly rushed back to their town.

The next night the missionaries spent at Hachniage, where the people were sober, and a venerable chief entertained them. Having been rejoined by their guide, they continued their journey, passed Lakes Honeoye, Hemlock, and Conesus, and, on the second of July, at last reached Zonesschio,[1] the capital of the Senecas.

This village was composed of about forty large huts, and lay in a beautiful region, where, however, with the exception of occasional traders, a white man was seldom seen. The missionaries would have rejoiced to spend some days here preaching the Gospel; but the time of their visit was most inopportune, and God saw fit severely to try their faith.

They had heard shouting from afar, in every part of

---

[1] Situated in Livingston County, probably near Geneseo.

Zonesschio; and, when they entered the town, it presented an appearance that would have appalled any heart. Almost the entire adult population was intoxicated. Two hundred men and women, in all the frenzy of drunkenness, conducted them to the lodge of Garontianechqui, who had, at Philadelphia, invited Cammerhoff to be his guest. The sachem's wife received them kindly, but trembled for their lives. Her husband, inebriated like the rest, yet not to a degree that prevented him from recognizing the bishop, bade them welcome in the maudlin accents of a sot. But it was a welcome to a Pandemonium. The savages came rushing into the house and crowding around them, some as wild as maniacs, others silent, but with dark looks that boded no good to the missionaries. These retreated to a small hut near by, whither the sachem's wife sent her brother-in-law, the only sober man in the village, to protect them. His presence was of little avail. The Indians discovered their hiding-place, and tormented them as before, until they climbed up to the second bunk or platform, which, according to the Iroquois mode of constructing houses, was at a considerable elevation from the ground. It was just large enough to permit them to lie side by side; immediately above them was the roof. As soon as they had ascended, the ladder leading to this loft was removed. Here they spent the night, almost suffocated by the heat, and Cammerhoff burning with fever. The solitary Indian kept watch below. In the town the revelry continued; cask after cask of rum was drained; all the abominations of heathenism, in its worst form, made that summer night hideous; devilish laughter, yells, such as can proceed only from drunken savages, filled the air, and were borne to the ears of the missionaries. But not all the fury of Satan's reign, in this his darkest stronghold, could shake their faith in the converting and sanctifying power of the Gospel. That the savages around them might soon be transformed into children of God, and found sitting in their right mind at the feet of Jesus, was the purport of their intercessions.

The next morning Cammerhoff was so weak that all thoughts of an immediate return to Onondaga had to be abandoned. Lying in the bunk, they counted the long and weary hours that seemed to be days; or ventured occasionally to descend to the hut below, where their faithful guard still held his post. They panted for fresh water. Cammerhoff's feverish thirst, at last, became so agonizing, that Zeisberger could endure the sight no longer, but risked every danger in order to relieve his sufferings. The nearest spring lay half a mile from the village. He stole out of the hut, and reached it in safety. But, on his way back, some of the savages espied him, fell upon him, hustled him from side to side, and jerked the kettle from his hands. A fight among themselves for its contents saved him from worse treatment. Having induced them to give up the kettle, he returned to the spring, and filled it a second time. His tormentors were on the watch for him, but turning abruptly into the wood, he ran at the top of his speed, and gained the hut by a long circuit.

Toward evening, as there seemed to be less noise in the town, Zeisberger walked out once more panting for fresh air. He saw no one, and was congratulating himself upon his good fortune, when a sudden turn in the path brought him into full view of a troop of women. Some of these were nude, others nearly so, and all intoxicated. With one accord they rushed toward him, each trying lasciviously to lay hold of his person. In this disgusting dilemma, there was but one resort. Doubling his fists, and dealing out blows to the right and the left, he drove the squaws aside, and then ran for the hut. The whole party followed, their long hair streaming in the wind, their lips swelling with unearthly shrieks, their hands clutching the empty air. They seemed to be a body of incarnate fiends! Before he could reach the bunk, they were in the hut, seized the ladder on which he was ascending, and tore it from under his feet, so that he barely succeeded in grasping one of the crosspoles of the roof, and swinging himself into his retreat by the side of Cammerhoff. Their guard ejected the women, and soon night came on.

As they lay sleepless and discouraged, the bishop said to Zeisberger, "We cannot stay here; let us escape at once; although I am still very weak, I will risk the journey." Finding that the Indian below, who had been faithfully protecting them for nearly thirty-six hours, continued to sleep in spite of their repeated calls, their simple-hearted faith suggested the thought that this was a Divine intimation to leave without his knowledge.

The opening in the arch of the roof, common to all Iroquois dwellings, offered a way of flight. Through this narrow aperture Cammerhoff crept first, with great difficulty, and dropped to the ground. Zeisberger then threw out one of their packs; the other was so large that he could not force it through the hole, but had to cast down its contents singly, although every moment was precious. At last he too climbed out. It was between four and five o'clock, and the day just began to break. But perils still surrounded them. If they were detected by the intoxicated savages in the act of thus secretly leaving Zonesschio it would be equivalent to discovering a war-party stealing from an attack; and they would inevitably be made prisoners, perhaps murdered. There were, moreover, nearly one hundred fierce and hungry dogs in the village. Committing their lives into the hands of Him for whose glory they had ventured into that den of iniquity, they proceeded straight through the town. A thick fog enshrouded its straggling lodges, between which they hurried on. Zonesschio lay in a profound slumber. Not an Indian appeared; not a dog barked; not a sound was heard, except the occasional voice of a bird, hidden in the mist, and chirping its morning song. Only one hut more to pass, and they would be safe! As they approached, they saw, to their consternation, a squaw standing at the door. Their fate now hung upon a thread. If she gave the alarm, escape would be impossible. A second glance, however, reassured them; the woman was sober, returned their greeting, and let them go.

But even now their trials were not at an end. Without provisions, and unable to find any game, for it seemed to have disappeared from those hunting-grounds, they suffered greatly from hunger. In attempting to wade across the outlet of Lake Seneca, they missed the ford and were carried into deep water, struggling for their lives. After superhuman exertions, Zeisberger gained the shore; Cammerhoff, whose strength the fever had weakened, sank, and remained so long immersed that his companion gave him up as lost. At last he rose, and almost by a miracle, himself could not tell how, he too reached the land. Barely sustaining life on a pheasant which Zeisberger shot, they proceeded to Onondaga. In its vicinity they met Hahotschaunquas, who had ignobly fled from Zonesschio and left them to their fate.

The news which awaited them at the capital was not encouraging. Ganassateco had gone to Oswego without laying their message before the Council. A week passed before he returned, and then he could scarcely be persuaded to fulfill his promise. Yielding, at last, to the urgency of Zeisberger's arguments, the sachems were convened.

The message embraced three points: greetings from the Church of the Brethren; a request that two or three of her members be allowed to live at Onondaga, and in other towns of the Confederacy, in order to learn the languages of the Iroquois; and a petition from the Nanticokes of Wyoming to have a smith-shop erected among them, under the auspices of the Mission Board, like that at Shamokin.

In response the Council accepted the greetings of the Church, permitted any two of her members to live among the Six Nations and learn their languages, but rejected the petition of the Nanticokes, who were told to frequent the smithy at Shamokin.

The chief end which they had in view having thus been gained, Cammerhoff and Zeisberger took their way from Onondaga to Ganatocherat, where they found Hahotschaunquas with their horses. Having disposed of these, and bidden farewell to their guide, who, in spite of his faithlessness in the Seneca country, had served them well, they entered their canoe, and floating down the Chemung, passed into the Susquehanna. Animated by the prospect of a speedy return to the settlements, Zeisberger propelled the canoe with rapid strokes, while Cammerhoff's gushing heart found utterance in hymns of praise.

A sign from Zeisberger interrupted him. "See," he whispered as he guided the canoe to the bank, "there is a flock of wild turkeys just perched for a shot!" Seizing his rifle, he crept noiselessly through a patch of high grass, when, on a sudden, a familiar but terrible sound made him stop short. In the next instant a gigantic rattlesnake, with distended jaws, darted toward him and bit his leg. The thick buckskin leggins which he wore, heavily ornamented with fringes, saved his life.

Five days later, they reached Wyoming, and on the

sixth of August, Shamokin. Cammerhoff was very ill, and spent a week in the Mission House. Then they took horses and rode rapidly toward the settlements.

On the seventeenth, an hour after midnight, they entered Bethlehem. According to a computation made at the time—which, however, in the very nature of the case could not be exact—they had traveled more than sixteen hundred miles on horseback, afoot, and in their canoes.

CHAPTER IX.

HIS VISIT TO EUROPE AND FIRST LABORS AFTER HIS RETURN.
1750-1752.

Hostilities renewed between England and France.—The loyalty of the Moravians attacked.—Interview between Governor Hamilton and Bishop Cammerhoff.—Progress of the Mission.—Zeisberger visits Europe.—Perilous voyage.—Stay at Herrnhut.—Appointed perpetual missionary to the Indians.—Return to America.—Death of Cammerhoff.—Prosperity of the Mission.—Explorations of Gist, and treaty at Albany.—Zeisberger at Gnadenhütten, Shamokin, and Wyoming. —Bishop Spangenberg's return.—Bishop Hehl.—Zeisberger at Shamokin.—Appointed to Onondaga.—Great deputation of the Shawanese and Nanticokes to Gnadenhütten and Bethlehem.

ABOUT the time of Zeisberger's return from Onondaga an event occurred which led to serious consequences, affecting the peace of the whole country. In so far as the American Colonies were concerned, the conflicting interests of England and France had not been adjusted at Aix-la-Chapelle. Each continued to struggle for supremacy in the New World. At the head of three hundred men, De Bienville passed through the valleys of the St. Lawrence and the Ohio, and laid title to both, in the name of France, burying, under an oak on the southern bank of the Ohio, a plate of lead with an inscription setting forth this claim.[1]

The English, on their part, organized the "Ohio

---

[1] Bancroft's U. S., iv. 42, 43.

Company," and founded the town of Halifax, in Nova Scotia. Thither the French immediately began to press. At Chiegnecto, now Fort Lawrence, on the isthmus between Nova Scotia and the main-land, La Carné established himself. This post lay within the jurisdiction of Great Britain; and an expedition was sent against it from Halifax, which, however, accomplished nothing, not venturing an attack. But in August, 1750, a second attempt was made, and Chiegnecto fell into the hands of the British. Thus was blood again shed between England and France; and, sooner or later, another war became inevitable.

Under such circumstances, amid a general feeling of uneasiness which pervaded the Colonies—and which the capture of a French brigantine, off Cape Sable, by the British ship of war "Albany," served to intensify[1]—the enemies of the Moravians had abundant opportunities to malign them. That the Church stood in league with the French, formed an accusation which was not given up until five years later, when it was fearfully disproved by the bleeding corpses of her missionaries. While at Onondaga, Bishop Cammerhoff had received a letter from Aaron Stevens, Colonial Interpreter at Albany, demanding to know the purpose of his negotiations with the Iroquois. And now the newspapers made his visit the occasion of bitter attacks upon his own loyalty and that of the Church. He was proclaimed to be an emissary of France, who had

---

[1] Bancroft's U. S., iv. 73.

endeavored to entice the Six Nations from their compact with the English. Governor Hamilton, whose suspicions had thus been aroused, cited him to Philadelphia, and had an interview with him (February 8, 1751) at the house of Secretary Peters. The bishop gave a circumstantial account of his negotiations, and explained the prospect which the Church had in view to bring about the conversion and civilization of the Iroquois. Hamilton was satisfied, but not the public. Indeed, as the Governor informed him, the privileges granted by Parliament to the Moravians, and the acknowledging of their Church as an ancient Episcopal body, had excited the utmost envy among some other religious denominations. Hence their persistent accusations.[1]

Nevertheless the Indian Mission continued to flourish. During Zeisberger's absence a spirit of inquiry had been awakened in the villages of the Delawares, and of other tribes, along the Susquehanna; many visitors had come to Gnadenhütten in order to hear the word of God; in some instances, heathen Indians had voluntarily assembled to talk of Christ. The Board had sent out as many missionaries as possible, who were traversing the wilderness and breaking to its famishing children the bread of life. But their number was too small to supply all who hungered and thirsted after righteousness.

Zeisberger would have esteemed it a privilege to

---

[1] Copy of a letter, dated Feb. 9, 1751, Philadelphia, from Cammerhoff to Bishop John de Watteville.

assist in this work had not the Board commissioned him and Nathaniel Seidel to visit Europe, in order to report to Count Zinzendorf and his coadjutors the character which the Mission was assuming, as well as to explain its difficulties and necessities. They sailed in the "Irene," Captain Garrison, on the second of September.[1]

The early years of Zeisberger's missionary life were a succession of journeys, and the journeys a succession of dangers and escapes. What the apostle of the Gentiles said of himself, when writing to the Corinthian Church, this apostle of the Indians could reiterate: "In journeyings often, in perils of waters, in perils of robbers, in perils by mine own countrymen, in perils by the heathen, in perils in the city, in perils in the wilderness, in perils in the sea, in perils among false brethren; in weariness and painfulness, in watchings often, in hunger and thirst, in fastings often, in cold and nakedness."[2] He had just returned from a tour in the wilderness of America, marked by hardships and sufferings of the most extraordinary kind; and now, upon the bosom of the Atlantic, new risks surrounded him, and again brought him within a step of death. At first the voyage was prosperous, but at five o'clock on the morning of the twentieth, a tremendous hurricane struck the vessel, and raged for a day and a night with the

---

[1] The "Irene" was a *snow*, built at New York for the use of missionaries and immigrants, and owned by the Church. She cleared the port for the first time on Sept. 8, 1748, and was used until 1758, when she fell a prey to a French privateer, and while on her way to Cape Breton, in charge of a prize crew, was wrecked and totally lost.

[2] II. Cor. xi. 26 and 27.

utmost fury. "She cannot live an hour," said Captain Garrison; "our only hope is to cut away the masts." While preparing to do this, both the masts snapped asunder like dried-up reeds, and the hull rolled helplessly in the trough of the sea. On the second day after this disaster a ship hove in sight and steered for the wreck, which had hoisted signals of distress. It proved to be a Danish merchantman from St. Christopher, commanded by Captain A. Remmack, who supplied the "Irene" with yards, a top-gallant mast, and whatever else of rigging he could spare. Jury-masts were put up, and she proceeded on her voyage; but the weather continued so unpropitious that week after week passed and she made no land. At last, toward the middle of November, when provisions had begun to fail, and that most terrible of all experiences—famine at sea—threatened, the shores of England loomed into view, and, on the fourteenth of the month, the vessel dropped anchor in the harbor of Portsmouth, after a voyage of seventy-eight days.

By way of London, Zeisberger and Seidel proceeded to Holland, and thence to Herrnhut, where they arrived on the nineteenth of December. "We reached Herrnhut safely and in a happy frame of mind," writes Zeisberger. "Our coming was immediately announced to Count Zinzendorf; but we waited from day to day, until a week had passed, without being invited to visit him. We could not imagine to what this was owing. At last Bishop de Watteville informed us that the intelligence of the feud which had broken out at Bethlehem between the European and American members of the Church, and the consequent withdrawal of a number of active men, among whom was that most zealous agent of the Lord, Henry Antes, had so depressed his mind that he refused to receive any one except his son-in-law, and that not even the name America must be mentioned in his presence."[1] Finally, however, Zinzendorf desired an interview. Watteville introduced them with these words,—" Here are two messengers from the Indian country, who can tell you many things concerning the Mission there; otherwise they have nothing to say about America." The Count smiled pleasantly at this remark, and greeted them with his usual affability.

Zeisberger remained in Germany half a year, spending the most of the time at Herrnhut. He had frequent conversations with Zinzendorf, and gave him a full report of the work among the Indians. The Count was deeply interested, and conceived so high a regard for Zeisberger that he appointed him perpetual missionary to this people, and laid upon him a special blessing with the imposition of hands.[2]

On the fifth of June, 1751, Zeisberger and Seidel left Herrnhut for America. The "Irene," having been thoroughly repaired, again conveyed them across the Atlantic; and they reached New York on the twenty-fourth of September. Four days later, Zeisberger was

---

[1] Heckewelder's Biographical Sketch. MS. Lib. Mora. Hist. Soc.
[2] Heckewelder's MS. Biographical Sketch. The intention of this appointment evidently was that Zeisberger should never be employed by the Church in any work other than the Indian Mission.

once more in the midst of his associates at Bethlehem, eager to resume the work which, by an extraordinary commission of the Church, had now been given to him as the sole purpose of his life.

The first news which he heard was of a distressing character. Cammerhoff slept in death. The hardships of the journey to Onondaga had exhausted his feeble frame, and he had breathed his last on the twenty-eighth of April, universally lamented in the Church and among the Indians. His influence over the latter had been extraordinary. In the four years of his ministry he had baptized eighty-nine of them; and, more than a quarter of a century subsequent to his death, Zeisberger found warriors, in the Western country, who called him "a great man," and mentioned his name with reverence.

The Mission, however, was in a prosperous state. At Gnadenhütten the organization of the Church had been perfected, by introducing a well-devised system of discipline; and, in order to provide for the temporal wants of the visitors who were flocking to the town, an additional tract of land, on the east side of the Lehigh, had been purchased and divided among the converts by lot. Nor was their spiritual condition less encouraging. Many had been converted. Even the savages who came to the settlement had often been impressed, and had spoken to their people at home of the "great words" which had been preached to them. A Shawanese had traveled three hundred miles from the Ohio, in order to hear the Gospel. At Meniolagomekah, likewise, the work flourished, in spite of the interference of certain settlers, who claimed the land, and to escape whose persecutions George Rex and his tribe were preparing to emigrate.

In the history of the Colonies, two events of importance had transpired during Zeisberger's absence. While he was sailing across the Atlantic, that bold adventurer, Christopher Gist, at the instance of the "Ohio Company," had left the shores of the Potomac, and explored the lands in the valley of the Ohio, west of the great mountains. He had visited the Muskingum and the Scioto; crossed the Little and the Great Miami; and penetrated to within fifteen miles of the Falls of Louisville. Thus the Colonies, for the first time, obtained correct knowledge of the vast resources of that country where a republic should develop its strength in some of its most marvelous forms, and where, prior to the coming of the white man, Zeisberger should build up a community of Christian Indians that would excite the astonishment of settler and savage alike. The other event had been a great treaty, held at Albany, with the Iroquois (July, 1751), on which occasion the hereditary feud between them and the Catawbas had been settled, and the representatives of the two people had smoked together the sacred pipe of peace. At the same time, South Carolina, which had been standing aloof from confederation, joined New York, Connecticut, and Massachusetts in council, so that another step had been taken toward a future union of all the Colonies.[1]

---

[1] Bancroft's U. S., iv. 88 and 89.

Zeisberger first visited Gnadenhütten, where he introduced to the Indians John Jacob Schmick, who had come with him from Europe, in response to the call of the Board. He was an alumnus of the University of Königsberg, and took charge of the Mission School. In subsequent times he became a successful missionary in the West.[1]

The next journey which Zeisberger undertook was to Shamokin, and through the region of the Susquehanna as far as Wyoming. Gottlieb Bezold accompanied him.[2] They preached the Gospel wherever an opportunity offered, and visited the scattered lodges of the converts. In the beginning of November they returned to Bethlehem.

Thither came Bishop Spangenberg (December 10th), in order to resume his place at the head of the Church. The differences of opinion, which had estranged from him some of his brethren, were settled, and he again enjoyed, as he so richly deserved, their implicit confidence. He succeeded in healing the hurt which Bethlehem had received, by reason of those jealousies that had filled Zinzendorf's heart with sorrow, and he infused new life into the work among the Indians, particularly on the occasion of a Synod convened soon after

---

[1] Schmick was born at Königsberg, in Prussia, October 9, 1714. He was a Lutheran Pastor in Livonia, where he became acquainted with the Moravians. In 1748, he joined them.

[2] Born November 1, 1720, at Bischofswerda, Saxony; died April 1, 1762, while on a visit to Litiz. He was the Elder-General of all the unmarried men or "Single Brethren," as they were called, belonging to the American Moravian Church.

his arrival. With him was associated Bishop Matthew Hehl, an alumnus of the University of Tübingen, an eloquent preacher and a worthy successor of Cammerhoff. He took up his residence eventually at Litiz as superintendent of the churches in that part of Pennsylvania, remaining, however, a corresponding member of the Board.[1]

In the first month of the new year (1752) Zeisberger went to his old post at Shamokin. He was the bearer of a message and belt of wampum from Spangenberg to Thachnechtoris. This message, which forms a specimen of the bishop's style of addressing the Indians, ran thus:

"I have been over the Great Water, but I did not forget you. I have kept you in kindly remembrance. Now I have returned, and bring you greeting from your brother Tgarihontie and his dear father Johanan, which this belt of wampum testifies. Our dear brother, the blacksmith, we would like to see at Bethlehem. Let him come. Here is our dear brother Ganousseracheri; he will remain with you a time. Hold him dear."[2]

Zeisberger faithfully preached the Gospel at Shamokin, but his heart was with the Six Nations. In a letter to the Board,[3] written about this time, he referred to the progress of religion at Gnadenhütten in these words: "I rejoice to hear of the revival at Gnadenhütten; but I will rejoice still more when a church like that will have been established among the Aquanoschioni. I will not

---

[1] He was born in 1704 in Wurtemberg, and died at Litiz in 1787.
[2] Bethlehem Diary. MS. B. A.
[3] Copy of letter, Feb. 28, 1752, in Diary of Bethlehem. MS. B. A.

be satisfied until this is accomplished; I am on their side. Who knows what the Lord may do?" These longings for the Iroquois country were soon satisfied. He was appointed to take up his abode at Onondaga, agreeably to the compact made with the Council.

He first joined a party consisting of Spangenberg, Seidel, Schmick, and Kaske, that went to Shamokin and the valley of Wyoming, in order to preach the Gospel. In the course of this tour fifty bushels of wheat were distributed. This induced a body of one hundred and seven Nanticokes and Shawanese to visit Gnadenhütten (July, 1751) and thank the Board for their kindness. Spangenberg, Zeisberger, several other clergymen of Bethlehem, all the resident missionaries of the station, together with the converts, met them in council, and established a covenant of friendship, whose chain should never be broken as long as the great God should permit the world to stand. A few days later the most of these visitors proceeded to Bethlehem, where they were hospitably entertained, and a second council was held. Returning to Wyoming, they spread throughout the Indian country the fame of Bethlehem and its teachers.

CHAPTER X.

ZEISBERGER A RESIDENT AT ONONDAGA.—1752.

Object of Zeisberger's residence at Onondaga.—Journey thither with Rundt and Mack.—Interference of Oneida sachems.—Meeting of the Grand Council.—Speeches and replies.—Zeisberger and Rundt remain at Onondaga.—Mack returns to Bethlehem.—Indian life at the capital.—Lamentations for the dead.—Funerals and inheritances.—Widows and mourning.—Councils.—War-parties.—Cannibalism.—A day of barter with an agent of Sir William Johnson.—Drunkenness.—Zeisberger's Iroquois Dictionary.—Rundt adopted.—Zeisberger visits Oswego.—Goes to the Cayuga country.—Zeisberger attacked and cruelly beaten by a trader.—Returns to Onondaga.—Twenty kegs of Rum.—Leaves for Bethlehem.

THE purpose of the journey which Zeisberger at this time undertook to Onondaga was not, in the first instance, to officiate as a missionary, but to perfect himself in the Iroquois dialects and gain a more thorough acquaintance with their usages. Such were the instructions of the Board. He had been adopted by the Six Nations; now he was to be nationalized among them, so that he might eventually preach the Gospel to them as a brother in name and fact.

However much forethought this plan displayed, it was radically unwise. It tended to mislead the Iroquois as to the real object of the Church, and was calculated to place her missionaries in a false position. Of this Zeisberger soon became convinced.

The party leaving for the Iroquois country consisted,

besides himself, of Martin Mack and Godfrey Rundt. Mack was commissioned to take part in the negotiations with the Council, and then return to Bethlehem and report their result. Rundt, a novice in Indian life, but willing to learn its hardships, acted as Zeisberger's assistant. In his own country, he had served in the army of Holstein as a hautboyist; now he was a poet, and beguiled their weary way, and their adventurous abode among the Six Nations, by descriptions, in quaint verse, of their various experiences.[1]

In[2] the evening of the twenty-first of July, they left Bethlehem for New York, where they embarked in a sloop for Albany, and thence proceeded on foot, with one pack-horse.

Their way led them through that district of country, back of the Hudson, which the brawny arm of industry was developing, and they were astonished at the many changes that they saw. At William's Fort was an Indian Mission, in charge of Ogilvie, an Anglican minister; at Canajoharie they found a similar enterprise, inaugurated by the same church. Along the Mohawk, Dutch settlements and German plantations were multiplying; the last of these, the homestead of one Kash, lay in the Oneida

---

[1] *Eine Collection verschiedener Gedanken bei diversen Umständen und Vorgängen unserer Onondager Reise, und unsers dortigen Aufenhalts. Auctore G. Rundt.* MS. B. A. Charles Godfrey Rundt was born at Königsberg, May 30, 1713; entered the army of Holstein as a musician; joined the Church at Herrnhut in 1747; emigrated to America in 1751, and became an itinerant missionary among the Indians and white settlers; died at Bethlehem, August 17, 1764.

[2] Mack's Journal of the Journey. MS. B. A.

country, a day's journey beyond the Rapids, now Little Falls, in Herkimer County. A new source of traffic, too, had been opened in that region. The ginseng root, that much-coveted panacea of the Chinese, began to be in great demand, on account of the increasing exportations of it to their country. It was collected by the Indians and sold to traders at a high price. Zeisberger's party met a body of more than one hundred Iroquois digging up these roots.

In the vicinity of Kash's cabin were encamped four prominent Oneida sachems, with a large number of their followers. These unexpectedly forbade the missionaries to continue their journey to Onondaga. "We have been warned by a white man to beware of you and of your Brethren," they said. "He has told us many evil things of you. He has advised us to send you out of our country. To-morrow morning you must turn back and go to live in your own towns." Zeisberger's expostulations were received with a fierce threat to murder them all if they ventured to proceed.

In this dilemma, his knowledge of Iroquois usages did him good service. He proposed a council, to be held, in the manner of the Six Nations, on the next day. Such a request seemed eminently reasonable to the sachems, and they granted it at once. At this council he succeeded in overcoming their opposition by a brief speech, in the sententious style of the Indian orator, and by explaining the import of the strings of wampum which he was carrying to the Grand Council. Indeed, the Oneidas were so fully pacified that they dispatched runners to the Cayuga and Seneca nations to summon their headmen to Onondaga, in order to receive the missionaries, who reached the capital in the afternoon of the twentieth of August, and found a hospitable welcome in the lodge of Ganatschiagaje.

On the following morning they had a preliminary interview with the local council of the town. Three days after that they met a part of the Grand Council, at the hour of noon. There were present Thagechtate, Tolchactone, Hanazaeni, and Thojanoca, sachems of the Senecas; Gietterowannee, a sachem of the Cayugas; Otschinochiata, Ganatschiagaje, Garachguntie, and Hatachsocu, sachems of Upper Onondaga; Zagona and Ganechronca, sachems of Lower Onondaga; Sheguallisere, a sachem of the Tuscaroras; and more than twenty other Indians. Gietterowanne was the speaker on the one side; Zeisberger on the other. These two consulted together privately; Zeisberger unfolding the import of the strings, and Gietterowanne committing to memory what he said.

Thus prepared, he rose, and exhorted the Council to give ear to what he had to recite. By way of introduction, he chanted the Indian names of Zeisberger and Mack, and of all other Moravian missionaries and bishops known to the Six Nations, mentioning particularly Johanan as a man of note and influence. Taking up the first string of wampum, he continued:

"They are sent by our brothers Johanan (Zinzendorf), Tgarihontie (Watteville), Tgirhitontie (Spangenberg), Anuntschi (Seidel), and by the rest of the

Brethren, on this side and on the other side of the Great Water, in order to bring words to the Aquanoschioni, and they hope that their chiefs will receive these favorably, although they do not fully know how to express them."

The string was hung upon one of the poles under the roof of the house, and accepted with a loud *Juheh!*

Grasping the second string, he proceeded: "Our brothers inform the Aquanoschioni that Gallichwio (Cammerhoff) is dead. They loved him well, and know that he loved the Indians well. They were sorry to part with him, but they are assured that his spirit has gone to their God, whom he faithfully served, and therefore they do not mourn. They would have brought these news sooner, but several of their chiefs were on a visit beyond the Great Water, and they could not send an embassy until their return."

This string was disposed of and accepted in the same manner as the first.

Holding up the third, he began again: "Our brothers inform us that Tgirhitontie (Spangenberg), Anuntschi (Seidel), and Ganousseracheri (Zeisberger), who is present here, have come back from their visit beyond the Great Water, and bring to the Aquanoschioni fraternal greetings from Tgarihontie (Watteville) and Johanan, his father."

Finally the speaker took the fourth, and said: "Our brother Ganousseracheri, and a white brother, have come to live among the Aquanoschioni, according to the compact made, two years ago, with Gallichwio, that they may learn our language."

These two strings having also been received and suspended from the pole, Zeisberger delivered presents of linen, thread, and tobacco. The speaker announced each gift as it was put on a blanket, at the feet of the sachems. These directed two of the Indians who were in attendance to make three shares, one of which was given to the Cayuga chief, another to the Senecas, and the third to the Onondagas. The third share was again divided between the chiefs from Upper and Lower Onondaga. In the same manner the four strings of wampum were distributed. And now the Council once more broke out into a very loud *Juheh!*

On leaving, the sachems shook hands with the missionaries, assuring them that they would take their messages into immediate consideration, and return an answer before the sun set. Expeditiousness such as this was so contrary to their usual habits that Zeisberger doubted its reality. But in the afternoon, at four o'clock, the Council actually convened and opened with the customary formalities. The following replies were given, each corroborated by a string of wampum, to the four points presented by the embassy:

" Brothers, we have heard that Tgirhitontie and Anuntschi, our brothers, that their Brethren, and even those beyond the Great Water, among whom is a man of influence who directs the affairs of your people, also Tgarihontie, have sent messengers to the Aquanoschioni to tell them words. We have well understood their words. We were glad to hear them. We thank you that you have commissioned Ganachragejat (Mack), Ganousseracheri, and this white brother (Rundt), to come among us. We rejoice also to hear that you and your Brethren are well, and sit around your council-fire in peace.

"Brother Tgirhitontie, you and your Brethren, those also beyond the Great Water, have informed us that our Brother Gallichwio is dead. Therefore, Brother Tgirhitontie, the Aquanoschioni say to you, give diligence to seek out among your Brethren another Gallichwio; for of this we are assured that he loved the Aquanoschioni well, and was toward them an upright, honest man, in whose heart no guile was found.

"Brother Tgirhitontie, you have informed us that you and some of your Brethren have been beyond the Great Water, and have now returned bearing fraternal greeting from Tgarihontie, our brother, and Johanan, his father. We are glad that you have come back. We thank you for the greetings. Salute your brothers in turn, on the part of the united Six Nations.

"Brother Tgirhitontie, you have also assured us that the league between you and the Aquanoschioni still stands, and that you will uphold it. We too will uphold it."

Here the speaker clasped his hands together, lifted them up, and showed how firm the covenant was, saying that these were the sentiments of all the chiefs of the Aquanoschioni,—a declaration corroborated by the Council with an emphatic *Juheh!*

Having taken the fourth string, the speaker first remarked that, two years ago, Gallichwio had proposed to the Council that two of his brothers should live among the Iroquois and learn their language, so that they might tell one another their thoughts. Then he continued:

"And inasmuch as you, Brother Tgirhitontie, and your Brethren have again brought this proposition to our notice, we tell you that it is wise and good. We are well pleased that you have sent Brother Ganousseracheri and this white brother, whose name we cannot name, in order to learn our language. We believe that this is a good work. It shall be as you desire. All the chiefs of the Aquanoschioni are so minded. These two brothers shall live some years among us, and learn our tongue, that we may tell one another the thoughts of our hearts. They may begin here at Onondaga; they may then go to the Cayugas, and next to the Senecas."

After each answer, the speaker delivered the string of wampum to Zeisberger. When the latter had received the fourth string, he repeated the acclamation, in which his associates, and then the whole Council, joined, sachems and missionaries reiterating it three times with loud voices,—*Juheh! Juheh! Juheh!*

Two large kettles of boiled maize were now brought in, and the assembly partook of a hearty meal.

Taking into consideration the inordinate pride of the chiefs of the Six Nations, and the suspicion with which the aborigines regarded every attempt of white men to gain a foothold in their country, the results of this Council were remarkable, and proved the high esteem in which the Church of the Brethren was held at Onondaga, and the personal influence which Zeisberger had acquired among the same tribes whose favor the Colonial government purchased with much difficulty and by constant presents of great value.

Toward evening of the twenty-fifth of August, Mack left for Bethlehem. Zeisberger and Rundt accompanied him as far as the country of the Tuscaroras. They devoted the last night which they spent together to religious exercises, and partook of the Lord's Supper by the light of a camp-fire in the depths of the forest. Early the next day they reached Anajot. About a quarter of a mile beyond it lay a wooded hill. To the top of this they proceeded, and, standing together beneath a spreading tree, sang with deep emotion several parting hymns, the morning wind murmuring its soft accompaniment among the leaves. Then they separated. Zeisberger and Rundt returned to Onondaga; Mack, alone with his God, followed the trail through the wilderness.

[1] As the two friends, who were to remain among the Indians, pursued their way back to Onondaga, their hearts were sad; but their trust in God did not waver, and they mutually pledged themselves to stand fast by each other whatever might happen.

Domesticated as they now were among the Iroquois,

---

[1] Zeisberger's Journal. MS. Bethlehem Archives.

in the lodge of Ganatschiagaje, which had been formally assigned to them by the Council as a permanent dwelling, they had many opportunities of observing their manners and customs. Indian life, with all its strange ways, its simplicity and formalities, lay open before them.

Early one morning they were awakened by female voices, in a lodge near by, uttering the most clamorous lamentations. An Indian had died in the course of the night; and these women were the friends of the family, who gathered in his hut, at sunrise and sunset, to bewail his loss, until he was buried.

The interment took place near the town. Aged squaws dug the grave, the head of which was toward the east, and lined it with loose boards. The body, robed in new garments, of which the shirt was daubed with vermilion, the head and face being painted of the same color, was conveyed from the house of mourning in a blanket, and interred amid the dismal howls of the women. With the remains were buried the tomahawk of the dead man, a kettle, and his pouch, containing a knife, flint and steel, a pipe and tobacco. A blanket and a board were put over him; the grave was filled up, and a post erected to mark its site.

This, however, was neither the primitive mode of burial, nor that which came into vogue in Zeisberger's time. Graves were, originally, cased with bark and not filled up, but covered on the top with branches and bark, over which was raised a large mound of earth. The introduction of tools among the Iroquois and Delawares enabled them to substitute boards in place of bark, and gradually led them to make coffins similar to those of the whites. By-and-by, too, the custom was relinquished of burying weapons and other articles with the corpse.

For some weeks after a funeral, the widow, mother, and grandmother of the deceased wept at his grave every morning and evening, occasionally leaving him food, which was devoured by the dogs. After a time their visits became less frequent, and, at last, ceased altogether. But the widow remained in mourning for a year, laying aside her ornaments, wearing old clothes, and rarely washing. She was obliged to support herself, and had to forego eating meat, unless some one took pity on her and gave her an occasional supply in secret. This was owing to the absurd superstition entertained by the Indians, that their rifles would miss aim if a widow partook of the game which they had shot. At the expiration of the year, she received a new outfit of clothing, from her children and the friends of her late husband, and was at liberty to marry again. In case she wedded sooner, nothing was given her excepting evil words.

The movable property of one deceased was heaped up by the side of his grave, on the day of interment. Those who had assisted at the burial were, first of all, liberally rewarded; what remained was given to his friends of both sexes. After the funeral at Onondaga, several women made use of the lodge of the missionaries in order to divide by lot the articles which had fallen to their share. The natives know nothing of inheritances. Mementoes of the dead would revive the sorrow of the living. Widows, however, retained such effects as had been presented to them by their husbands. Hence the frequent practice of keeping distinct the property of man and wife.

Every opportunity was afforded Zeisberger to gain an insight into the operations of the system of councils which distinguished the Iroquois. The Council of Onondaga usually met in his house, and the sachems took pleasure in teaching him the import of the many belts and strings of wampum that were received, as also the mode of sending and answering messages. What he here learned was of real use to him in after-years. He became as familiar with all such details, and as ready to interpret obscure messages, as any native.

Nor did he fail to see the manner in which the Iroquois prepared for war. The night previous to the departure of a war-party was spent in feasting and dancing. Pork formed the principal dish; sometimes, however, a dog was eaten, the flesh of which was supposed to generate courage. The chiefs and the wives of the men were guests. After gorging themselves—and the women, too, swallowed dog's meat with great relish—the dance began, in which the captain led off. He either moved alone, around another warrior, with the head of the hog in his hands; or, more commonly, was followed by the whole company. Dancing and war-songs were kept up until daybreak. Then the braves, hoarse and exhausted though they were, formed in line and marched through the town. At the last hut, first the captain and next each of his men discharged their pieces; and, as they took their way into the forest, the war-song was again raised. Their first camp was, generally, but a short distance from the village. In the evening, their friends and wives joined them, and a second night was passed in dancing.

Upon the return of war-parties, the Iroquois of a former age were often guilty of the most horrible cannibalism, feasting on the bodies of the prisoners whom they had tortured to death, and distributing pieces of their roasted hearts among the boys of a village to give them courage. The Hurons and other nations of that stock did the same; and single instances occurred in Algonquin tribes. This revolting practice, of which the Jesuit Fathers have recorded such painful details, had not been entirely relinquished even in Zeisberger's times, although it seldom occurred.

Among the many traders who visited Onondaga, while he lived there, was an agent of Sir William Johnson. His coming assumed all the importance of an embassy. It was announced by a runner and a string of wampum. Having brought his boat, laden with goods, into the lake, he pitched a tent near the shore, and met the headmen in council. Zeisberger and Rundt were present by special invitation. After the usual preliminary silence, one of the sachems, in the name of his peers and people, delivered half a bushel of ginseng roots, as a gift. The trader responded by reading a speech from Johnson, which an interpreter, whom he had brought along, found great difficulty in rendering into the Onondaga dialect; and by a presentation of two barrels of rum. Meanwhile the Indians without sat in groups on the ground, patiently waiting for this Council to close. No sooner did it break up than they pushed their way into the tent from all sides, each one eager to effect a good and speedy exchange for his roots. The noise and confusion increased every moment, and at last grew so uproarious that the missionaries were glad to escape.

These are some of the views which Zeisberger had of life among the Iroquois. At the same time their moral degradation, especially in respect to drunkenness, became painfully apparent. This vice prevailed at Onondaga, at Zonesschio, and throughout the Six Nations. Indeed, the missionaries could not have remained in the country if they had not been careful to avoid the Indians whenever they were intoxicated, by retiring into the forest, where they put up a bark-hut and lived in seclusion until the revels were over.

Zeisberger devoted himself with great diligence to the study of the Onondaga dialect and the completion of his Iroquois Dictionary, assisted by Hatachsocu, one of the sachems. He became very intimate with Otschinachiatha too, the principal sachem of the town. Rundt appears not to have engaged in such studies. In the opinion of Otschinachiatha he was too old to learn the language of the Aquanoschioni. He gained their good will, however, for he was adopted into the nation of the

Onondagas and the family of the Turtle, receiving the name of Thaneraquechta.

In the beginning of November, after Zeisberger's return from Oswego, whither he had gone to make some necessary purchases, the two missionaries set out for the country of the Cayugas, with the intention of passing the winter among this people. At Ganatarage, the first of their villages which they reached, they were told that a party of traders had arrived in the country with rum; and when they came to Tgaaju they found one of them established there.

The natives gave them a cordial reception, saying that they knew of the compact subsisting between the Grand Council and the Brethren at Bethlehem; but the trader, a surly, ill-faced Dutchman, whose name remains in well-merited oblivion, had no words of welcome for them. As they were about lying down to sleep, he entered the lodge where they were guests, and seated himself by the fire in moody silence. "What are you doing in the Iroquois country?" he said, at last. "We are here," replied Zeisberger, "to learn their language by permission of the Grand Council and the Colonial government." "Produce your passports!" he continued. With this insolent demand Zeisberger refused to comply, although they had three passports,[1] telling him that he had no authority to call them to an account. A

---

[1] These passports are in the Bethlehem Archives: the first is from Squire Timothy Horsefield, of Bethlehem; the second from Daniel Schuyler, Alderman of New Brunswick, N. J.; the third from Edward Holland, Esq., Mayor of New York City.

volley of taunts and oaths was the trader's answer, in the midst of which he suddenly sprang to his feet, seized an Indian war-club, and struck Zeisberger headlong to the ground; then snatching a brand from the fire, he beat it about his head, and kicked and stamped upon him with his heavy boots. The attack was so unexpected that Zeisberger lay helpless in a moment. What Rundt, the poet, did to save his friend is not recorded; but a squaw ran for the chiefs, who rescued him, intoxicated though they were. The Dutchman, however, remained defiant, drew a knife, and would have stabbed Zeisberger had not the Indians seized and dragged him away. It is evident that he either believed the missionaries to be traffickers in disguise come to interfere with his business, or recognized their true character, and feared their influence among the natives.

Zeisberger had been severely wounded. He spent the night in great pain. The revelries of the Indians, whom strong drink was making wilder every hour, rendered his situation still more distressing. Toward morning, as soon as he had regained sufficient strength to attempt the journey, he left the town with Rundt, in spite of the assurances of their entertainer that they should be protected. The trader had come to spend the winter among the Cayugas. Under such circumstances, the missionaries could not remain there.

When Otschinachiatha was informed of what had taken place, his indignation knew no bounds that the sacred laws of Iroquois hospitality had been thus abused, and an adopted brother of the Aquanoschioni treated so outrageously. The investigation which he instituted among the Cayugas had the desired effect. Thereafter no trader ever interfered with Zeisberger.

But he could not remain at Onondaga. One of the female dealers in rum brought twenty kegs of it to her shop, soon after his return. The men of the town were nearly all absent, hunting or on the war-path. Excesses and debaucheries of the worst kind were imminent; inebriated squaws were, in some respects, more to be feared than drunken warriors; and the season would prevent the missionaries from retiring into the forest. Accordingly they were constrained to go back to Bethlehem.

In the dusk of the evening before their departure, they went to the top of a hill near the town, and, kneeling down, prayed most earnestly for the people of Onondaga, for the Six Nations, and for themselves; beseeching God to pardon whatever faults they might have committed while among the Iroquois, and to lead them safely to their distant home. Early in the morning of the twenty-fifth of November they set out, and, by the same route which they had followed in summer, reached Bethlehem after a journey of three weeks.

CHAPTER XI.

ZEISBERGER A RESIDENT OF ONONDAGA.—1753-1755.

Zeisberger in New York and New England.—Second visit of Nanticokes and Shawanese to Bethlehem.—Proposed removal of the converts from Gnadenhütten to Wyoming.—Spangenberg goes to Europe.—French aggressions.—Zeisberger and Frey go to Onondaga.—Perilous journey.—Rumors of a new war with France.—Famine.—In attempting to fetch provisions from Tioga, the two missionaries nearly perish.—Death of their hostess at Onondaga.—Sickness among the Indians.—Simples.—Indian doctors.—Treaty at Onondaga with Sir William Johnson.—Zeisberger and Frey return to Bethlehem.—Zeisberger's views upon the Iroquois Mission.—Division at Gnadenhütten and exodus of a part of the converts.—Abraham and Tadeuskund.—Site of Gnadenhütten changed.—George Washington and the French.—Zeisberger returns to Onondaga, builds a house, and begins to labor as a missionary.—Made the Keeper of the Archives of the Grand Council.—Indian cosmogony.

ZEISBERGER devoted the winter partly to his studies and partly to itinerancies in New York and New England, where the Indian Mission was progressing, and opportunities were beginning to multiply for preaching the Gospel to the settlers, whose sentiments with regard to the Church had undergone a great change.

In March, a second deputation of Nanticokes and Shawanese came to Bethlehem, agreeably to their promise, and met the Board. Two of the points which they brought forward were unexpected. The Grand

Council at Onondaga had determined to remove the Nanticokes from Wyoming to the country of the Tuscaroras, and to invite the Christian Indians of Gnadenhütten to emigrate to Wyoming. It was evident that both these measures would interfere with the work of the Gospel. The first was beyond the control of the Board; the other, however, concerned it very nearly. Some of its members suspected a plot to break up the Mission. Nevertheless, the invitation would have to be submitted to the converts.

Soon after this visit, Bishop Spangenberg left for Europe (April 20th), encouraged by the actual growth, and the bright prospect of the Mission. And yet, at that very time, complications were arising which would mar its prosperity. The Governor of Canada sent a body of armed men to the valley of the Ohio in order to substantiate the claim of the French crown, and take formal possession of that rich country. As soon as this became known at Onondaga, fleet runners hurried along the great trail of the nations to the seat of William Johnson, and warned him of the coming crisis.[1] At first, the Colonies displayed a singular want of energy and even of interest, although war was approaching with rapid strides and bloody footsteps.

The news of these events had not yet reached Bethlehem. Eager to resume his place at Onondaga, Zeisberger, four days after Johnson had received the belt

---

[1] Bancroft's U. S., 107, etc.

of warning, accompanied by Henry Frey,[1] set out for his Indian home (April 23d). At Shamokin, he heard of what was transpiring in the West; but determined to proceed, relying upon Divine protection. Frey was of the same mind.[2]

They came to Wyoming in a canoe, and found the Nanticokes preparing to emigrate.

This tribe had a singular custom in connection with the burial of their dead. Three or four months after an interment, the corpse was exhumed, its arms and legs lopped off, and the flesh cut from the bones, which were dried, wrapped in clean cloths, and then recommitted to the earth. The trunk was burned. Whenever the tribe removed to new hunting-grounds these bones were taken with them.

The missionaries, declining the invitation of the Nanticokes to join them, pushed on alone through the same country which Zeisberger had visited with Cammerhoff. It was almost depopulated. The natives were moving westward. Among the few that remained, however, they met with a hospitable welcome, as soon as it became known that they were from Bethlehem. The visits of the Nanticokes and the Shawanese had rendered that settlement famous. One

---

[1] Born May 12, 1724, at Falkner Schwamm, Pa. In 1742 Count Zinzendorf visited his parents, and, on taking leave, said: "This your son Henry you must give to me, for he is destined to devote his life to the service of the Saviour." In 1744 Frey came to Bethlehem and joined the Moravian Church, which he served in various capacities. He died at Litiz, September 25, 1784.

[2] Letter to the Board, in Bethlehem Diary, 1753. MS. B. A.

day, indeed, an exception to such kindness occurred. The missionaries were pursued by a canoe, filled with Delawares and one Oneida, and compelled to run to land. "Now give us your fire-water!" cried the Indians. "We have none," said Zeisberger. But they would not believe him, and were preparing to use force, when, fixing his eyes upon the Oneida, with whose family he was well acquainted, he remarked: "Brother, you seem not to recognize me. I am Ganousseracheri. Have you never heard of Ganousseracheri, the brother of the sachems of the Aquanoschioni, who is well known at Onondaga, and in all the Indian country?" This had the desired effect. The savages let them go, with many apologies.

Instead of entering the Chemung, at Tioga, they proceeded up the Susquehanna to Owego, a forsaken village in Tioga County, New York, intending to ascend the river as far as Zeniinge, a town of the Tuscaroras, and thence to travel to Onondaga on foot. But, after having paddled a whole day, they were obliged to turn back, finding it impossible to proceed without a guide. Sinking their canoe in a creek near Owego, they now struck out for that trail on which Bishop Spangenberg's party had traveled in 1745. It had grown so indistinct that they could not discover it, and groped for three days in the swamps, without provisions and in great distress. At last they succeeded, by the aid of a pocket-compass, in retracing their steps to Owego, where they took to their canoe once more, and ascended the Susquehanna until they came up with the Nanticokes in a little fleet of twenty-five canoes, who supplied all their wants and brought them to Zeniinge. Guided by a Tuscarora, they then advanced, on branches of the Susquehanna and affluent creeks, to within fifty miles of Onondaga. The rest of the distance they traveled afoot, and reached the town on the eighth of June. As they crossed the cornfields, the women, who were hoeing, called out, "Welcome, Ganousseracheri! welcome, brothers!"

It was a time of great excitement at Onondaga. The sachems looked grave; the warriors were eager for the conflict. Otschinachiatha showed Zeisberger a belt which the Governor of Canada had sent, with a message to the effect that he was approaching; that the Aquanoschioni should open a way for him through their country to the Ohio; that he had a hatchet in his hand, and whoever attempted to stop him would be cut down. In consequence of this message, the Council had dispatched a body of seven hundred braves to watch the French, and protect the Indians of the Ohio.

Notwithstanding these threatening troubles, Zeisberger resumed his studies and usual intercourse with the natives. Frey, too, was soon domesticated. He was adopted into the Oneida nation, and called Ochschugore. In the course of the summer a dire famine broke out, compelling the two missionaries to go to Tioga for food. Of the many journeys which Zeisberger undertook, this was perhaps the most disastrous. He and his companion both fell ill on the way, and lay in the forest without shelter, without medicine or provisions or aid of any kind, and almost perished. At last, by superhuman exertions, they dragged themselves to the door of Kash's cabin, in the Oneida country. Kash took them in; but, with all the force and plainness of speech of which the German language is capable, berated Zeisberger for wasting his life in so miserable a manner among thankless savages. He saw no glory in the very sufferings of his guest. His mind was "of the earth earthy;" it could not grasp the ideal which made Zeisberger strong when he was weak, and joyful when he was tried. In every age that philanthropy which is begotten of love to God and Jesus Christ, His Son, has been reviled as the offspring of fanatical enthusiasm.

Having recovered their health, the missionaries returned to Onondaga in a canoe laden with supplies.

Not long after this their hostess, the wife of Ganatschiagaje, died, in spite of all the efforts of her Indian doctors to save her life.

However hardy the constitution of the natives naturally was, they were subject to much sickness, on account of their manner of life, which exposed them to all the extremes of the weather, and often forced them to fast for days or subsist on insufficient food. Rheumatism, fevers, boils, and dysentery were very common among them. Small-pox and other similar diseases came from their white neighbors.

They had a thorough knowledge of simples, among which white walnut-bark and the root of the sarsaparilla were in general use, and could cure the bites of snakes with great readiness. For the poison of each species they employed a different antidote. They were expert too in healing fractures; and bled their patients with a flint or a bit of glass, in place of a lancet. The sick were laid on a bed of grass or hay near the fire, and fed with a thin soup of maize. A kettleful of a decoction of roots or herbs constituted an ordinary dose. But such simples were rarely administered without the intervention of a friend or neighbor. Superstition prevented a patient prescribing for himself. Indeed, in almost every case the doctors were called in, whom the Indians feared to offend, because they were looked upon as conjurors.

In reality, however, they were not only gross deceivers, but also the most avaricious usurers. Their fees were enormous. Goods or peltries, to the value of twenty or thirty pounds sterling, must be paid them as soon as they entered a lodge. Until this had been done, they refused to begin their incantations; and yet incantations formed the chief object of a visit. They seldom administered medicine. The patient was laid at their feet. Bending over him, they breathed into his face, or ejected a decoction of herbs from their mouths upon the affected part of his body. By-and-by they worked themselves into a fury, made the most frightful grimaces at him, screamed and howled over him with maniacal contortions, or threatened and commanded him with the authority of a master. If all this did not avail, they had him carried to a sweating-oven and placed in front of the door, while they crept in and perspired for him, frequently looking out at him, however, with faces distorted more hideously than at first. As a last expedient, he was told that he was bewitched, and must sacrifice to the angry manitou who had caused the affliction.

In case one doctor was not successful in effecting a cure, others were sent for, and a patient often squandered his entire property in satisfying their demands. Meanwhile the simples which he took really restored him to health. A poor man could count only upon a part of the incantations; and one wholly without means must forego them altogether, unless his friends contributed the required fee. Old hunters, who had retired from the fatigues of the chase, often became doctors and grew rich.

In the beginning of September Sir William Johnson reached Onondaga. The sachems had gathered, with numerous followers, from all parts of the Confederacy to meet him. He was escorted into the town by the entire population, young and old, and proceeded to hold a treaty. The chain of friendship between England and the League was brightened, and the proposal accepted to defer the great Indian Congress at Albany to the following year, on account of Governor Clinton's illness and the expected arrival of a new governor.[1]

The missionaries were present at this treaty, and made the acquaintance of Johnson. Although he manifested considerable interest in the progress of the Gospel among the Iroquois, his own conduct was grossly inconsistent. In his speeches he inveighed with much eloquence against the vice of drunkenness;[2] but at the

---

[1] Report of Treaty, Doc. Hist. of N. Y., ii. 632-641.   [2] Ibid.

close of the negotiations distributed such quantities of rum that the Indians became intoxicated, and Zeisberger and Frey had to flee into the forest for their lives.

Zeisberger had now improved so rapidly in the Iroquois languages that he was perfect master of the Mohawk, and spoke several other dialects with fluency. By the advice of Otschinachiatha, however, who deemed speedy hostilities inevitable, he broke off his studies, and returned to Bethlehem (November 12th). Frey accompanied him.

About the same time, George Washington, a young man of but twenty-one years, set out from Virginia as the special envoy of Governor Dinwiddie "to the commander of the French forces on the Ohio River, to know his reasons for invading the British dominions while a solid peace subsisted." It was a journey as full of hardships and perils as any that Zeisberger had undertaken; and led to results which hastened the impending war, and were of lasting importance in the history of freedom, opening the way for a great republican empire to be founded in the Western World.

Zeisberger's first duty at Bethlehem was to give an exposition of his views concerning the work among the Iroquois to Bishop Peter Boehler, who had just arrived from Europe as Spangenberg's temporary successor. These views he subsequently wrote out, in the form of Memoranda, addressed to Count Zinzendorf, Bishop de Watteville, and Bishop Spangenberg, and sent the document to Europe, with a letter to the latter divine.[1] From both these papers it is evident that he realized the incongruity of the principles regulating the Mission among the Six Nations; and repudiated the caution which had been observed, urging that the ultimate object which the Church had in view—the conversion of the whole League to the living God—should be impressed upon the Council. To this end, he proposed that among the students of the Iroquois languages, who should thereafter be sent to Onondaga, one should always be accredited as a minister of the Gospel.

He explained, likewise, in its true light, the invitation which the Gnadenhütten Indians had received to remove to Wyoming. The Grand Council had not given this invitation. It had been concocted by the Oneidas and the Nanticokes, but involved no evil design. According to Indian law, which sets personal liberty above every enactment of a council or order of a chieftain, the converts could do as they pleased. An offer had been made them; nothing more. The mere agitation of the subject, however, led to deplorable consequences. Some of the converts were in favor of a removal, others opposed it. Among the former, Abraham, the first convert of the Mission, and Gideon Tadeuskund, made themselves conspicuous. The one had recently been elected captain by the Mohicans

---

[1] Copy of the document. MS. B. A. Original letter to Spangenberg, dated November 25, 1753.

of New York; the other, chief, by the Susquehanna Delawares. These honors made them proud, especially Tadeuskund, who had never been distinguished for his consistency, and who now began to despise his position as a Christian. They succeeded in gaining a party of seventy converts, who left Gnadenhütten (April 24th, 1754), and proceeded to Wyoming. Afterward fifteen of them took up their abode at Neskapeke. The Board and the missionaries were overwhelmed with sorrow at this exodus; although the deserted houses at Gnadenhütten were soon filled by the converts from Meniolagomekah, who had been forced to abandon their village, on account of growing persecutions.

Not long after this, Gnadenhütten was removed to the eastern bank of the Lehigh, where the land was better suited to the wants of the natives, the soil being sandy and easy to till, whereas that on the Mahony was stiff and clayey. At this latter place, which now received the name of its creek (properly Mahonhanne), signifying a "Deer Lick," several farmers and mechanics established themselves. They were all in the employ of the Church, and in connection with the Mission, teaching the converts the arts of husbandry, and their young people various trades. The new town occupied the site of the present Weissport. Its chapel was erected in 1754.

Bishop Spangenberg, having meantime returned to America, took an early opportunity to confer with Zeisberger upon the Iroquois Mission. The Memoranda of Zeisberger had been accepted, and he received instructions to inform the Grand Council, on the occasion of his next visit to Onondaga, that the Brethren would soon begin to preach to them the Gospel of the Lord Jesus Christ.

This visit he undertook in June (1754), although the events transpiring in the country were portentous. Washington had returned, in January, from his expedition to the Ohio, and reported that the French commander had boldly avowed his purpose of seizing the valley through which that "beautiful river" runs, and, in fact, of making the entire West tributary to France. This roused England and her Colonies; and yet there existed so many conflicting interests that the measures adopted were neither prompt nor decisive. England expected the Colonies to defend themselves, or, at least, to contribute jointly toward their defense; the Colonies acted independently of each other, and produced no power adequate to the crisis. The most important step was taken by the Ohio Company, which built a fort at the confluence of the Alleghany and the Monongahela, on the site of Pittsburg. But, in April, a strong body of the French emerged from the forest, and obliged the little garrison of thirty-three men to surrender. The post was immediately strengthened by its new occupants, and received the name of Fort Duquesne. Meanwhile Washington had raised a small force and marched to the Youghiogeny, where he attacked and defeated the French, under cover of the night, at the Great Meadows. The war had, therefore, virtually begun.

Three[1] weeks after this, Zeisberger set out for Onondaga, with Charles Friedrich for a companion.[2] They reached Albany on the day of the opening of the great Congress (June 19th, 1754), composed of Commissioners from every Colony north of the Potomac, who, under the presidency of Lieutenant-Governor Delancy, of New York, deliberated upon the state of the country, and adopted Franklin's famous plan of union.[3] At the same time a new treaty was made with the Iroquois, of whom the Pennsylvania Commissioners bought a large tract of land, to the indignation of the Delawares and other tribes. In the war that followed, this sale, more than anything else, tended to embitter the French Indians against the Colonies.

Having heard from Ganatschiagaje, whom they met at Albany, that the trail to Onondaga was open, the missionaries pursued their way, and reached the capital in safety. Those sachems who were not at the Congress assembled to receive them; and Zeisberger, in words of great earnestness, brought to their recollection the ultimate object of his frequent visits to their town, which was to preach the Gospel and convert them to the living God.

With this purpose in view, his first care was to erect a substantial log-cabin as a Mission House. The natives

---

[1] Zeisberger's Journal. MS. B. A.

[2] Charles Friedrich was born at Husom, in Holstein, October 4th, 1715; labored as missionary among the Indians and negroes; and died in Surinam, January 24th, 1761.

[3] Penn. Col. Records, vi. 57–129.

rendered him every assistance in their power. He was not less welcome among them because he had officially introduced the subject of the Christian religion. He had won their respect and love. They confessed that his works were in harmony with his words. They believed that he sought their real good. They trusted him, in all respects, as one of their nation, correcting their children when these, sometimes, called after him "Assaroni" (white man), and saying, "No, Ganousseracheri is an Aquanoschioni, and not an Assaroni!" The most distinguished token of confidence, however, was given him by the Grand Council, which deposited its entire archives, comprising many belts and strings of wampum, written treaties, letters from Colonial governors, and other similar documents, in the Mission House, and constituted him the keeper of these important records.[1]

Zeisberger, on his part, faithfully strove to proclaim the Saviour of the world, not, as yet, through public ministrations, but by visits from lodge to lodge.

This gave him not only a thorough insight into the superstitions of the Indians, but made him acquainted also with their cosmogony, the absurdities of which were, however, so great and contradictory that he recorded but few of its details.

According to the saying of some old Iroquois, the natives originally lived in the interior of the earth. A

---

[1] Statements made at a missionary festival, at Bethlehem, as recorded in the Bethlehem Diary, under date of August 2, 1755.

badger burrowed his way to the surface, and was so pleased with the land he there found that he hastened back to report his discovery. Thereupon they came forth from their subterranean abode and took possession of this new country.

Others asserted that there existed in the heavens a world of men and animals. From that a pregnant woman was hurled down to the earth by her enraged husband, who had detected her faithlessness. She gave birth to twins, through whom the earth was peopled.

The legend of the Nanticokes was equally trivial. Several Indians, men and women, they said, had suddenly found themselves sitting on the sea-shore. Whence they had come, whether they had crossed the waters, or been created in America, they could not tell. From these the whole race was descended.

Those vague notions of the deluge with which Zeisberger met seem to have been a mixture of Algonquin traditions touching their great manitou, Manaboyho, and of Iroquois sayings with regard to the origin of the earth.

The earth, he was told, having been submerged, several human beings, among them two or three women, saved themselves on the back of a turtle, who had reached so great an age that his shell bore moss. These requested a loon, who happened to cross their path, to look for land. He complied, diving to the depths of the waters; but found none. At last he flew far away, and returned with a small quantity of earth in his bill. Guided by him, the turtle swam to the place, where a little spot of dry land was seen, on which the survivors settled and repeopled the world. Hence the illustrious position of the Turtle clan among the Indians.

After an abode of ten months at Onondaga, Zeisberger and Friedrich paid a visit to Bethlehem (June, 1755). The former intended to go back soon and begin to preach the Gospel in public. This intention, however, could not be carried out. His work among the Six Nations was done. A time of tribulation and blood was at hand; and when the wilderness again opened to the messengers of peace, they took their way to the Delawares and not to the Iroquois.

CHAPTER XII.

THE MONTHS PRIOR TO THE INDIAN WAR, AND THE MASSACRE AT GNADENHÜTTEN.—1755.

Renewed agitations at Gnadenhütten.—Zeisberger itinerates in the valley of Wyoming.—Preaches to a tribe of Monseys.—Braddock's defeat.—Distress of the Colonies.—Fearlessness of the Moravians.—Their loyalty questioned.—Zeisberger visits New England.—Indian war begins.—First massacre in Pennsylvania.—Zeisberger again visits Wyoming.—At Easton among the Jerseymen.—The twenty-fourth of November.—Zeisberger is sent to Gnadenhütten, and barely escapes the massacre.—The massacre.—Zeisberger brings the news to Bethlehem.—The leader of the war-party.—The Indians of Gnadenhütten retire to Bethlehem and claim the protection of the government.—Fort Allen built.

THERE had again been agitations at Gnadenhütten, during Zeisberger's absence. Tadeuskund, and Paxnous, chief of the Shawanese of the Susquehanna, had made a second attempt to entice the inhabitants to Wyoming. Although there were, at first, not a few in favor of yielding, the representations of the Board finally prevailed, and a unanimous refusal was given. To this the converts adhered, in spite of other subsequent efforts to break up their Mission.

Paxnous's visit was overruled by God to promote the glory of the Gospel. A deep impression of its truth was made upon his heart; while his wife was converted, and received baptism at the hands of Bishop Spangenberg.

DAVID ZEISBERGER. 221

The first missionary to visit the seceders from Gnadenhütten was that faithful man of God, Adam Grube,[1] who hastened to their lodges, scarcely two months after their departure, warning, admonishing, and reproving them with words of power and of love. This led to stated itinerancies in the valley of Wyoming. In this work Zeisberger now engaged, having allowed himself but ten days of rest after his return from Onondaga. Christian Seidel was his companion.[2]

They found Frederick Post at Wyoming, where he had established himself in order to minister to the converts and entertain visiting missionaries; and when they saw the dire famine which was prevailing, their first care was to relieve his wants and those of the Indians, by going back to Shamokin for supplies. Then they began to preach the Gospel to a tribe of Monseys, on the Lackawannock, not far from the present Scranton. Zeisberger was but imperfectly acquainted with their dialect, yet the women said that he spoke "words of gold," and the whole clan invited him to repeat his visit.

At Gnadenhütten, on his way back to Bethlehem, he heard of that disastrous event which had sent a thrill of dismay through every British Colony of America. Although war between England and France had not been declared, it existed. The very day (July 9th) on which Zeisberger and Seidel had pushed their canoe from the

---

[1] Born 1715, near Erfurt, Germany; died 1808, in the ninety-third year of his age, at Bethlehem.

[2] An elder of the young men of the Church. He died in North Carolina.

river-bank at Shamokin, eager to bring food to the famishing Indians of Wyoming, General Braddock, whom the British government had sent to defend the frontiers, had suffered an utter defeat, ten miles from Fort Duquesne, himself receiving a mortal wound, and, before he died, ordering a retreat to Cumberland. It was not only the victory which France had gained that caused such general consternation, but the opportunity thus given to the French Indians to ravage Pennsylvania with their murderous hatchets and their burning brands.

The Moravians, however, did not retire from the field. Strong confidence in God and great calmness of mind were vouchsafed to Bishop Spangenberg, the Board, and all the missionaries throughout this whole period. "The country," wrote Spangenberg to Count Zinzendorf, "is full of fear and tribulation. In our churches there is light. We live in peace, and feel the presence of the Saviour."[1] The missionaries not only remained at their several stations, but measures were taken to extend the work. The eighth of September, which witnessed the defeat of Count Dieskau, near the waters of Lake George, and gained a baronetcy for William Johnson, was distinguished at Bethlehem by an enthusiastic missionary conference, composed of four bishops, sixteen missionaries, and eighteen female assistants, who covenanted anew to be faithful to the Lord, and to press forward into the Indian country, as long as it was possible, in spite of wars and rumors of wars. With regard to

---

[1] Risler's Spangenberg's Leben, p. 313.

Zeisberger, this conference determined that he should continue to be a traveling evangelist, but that it should be his special work to establish a Mission among the Six Nations.[1]

Strange as it may seem, the confidence thus manifested, amid the prevailing trepidation, tended to bring the Church into still more general disfavor. The manly courage of her missionaries was imputed to a secret understanding with the French and the French Indians,— their faith perverted into an evidence of treason. A letter from an officer in Quebec appeared in the newspapers. It was said to have been intercepted by the government. The writer, addressing a friend, asserted that the French were certain of soon conquering the English, for not only the Indians had mostly espoused their cause, but the Moravians were also their good friends, and would give them every assistance in their power. This letter was a gross forgery; but it inflamed the public mind to such a degree that for a time no Moravian clergyman was safe from insult, and the whole Church was threatened with extermination. Of this state of feeling Zeisberger had abundant evidence while on a tour to the stations in New England in the month of October. The work, however, prospered notwithstanding all opposition.

Meanwhile those Indians who were hostile to the English had begun to prepare for war. The nations were divided. William Johnson had induced the

---

[1] Minutes of the Conference. MS. B. A.

Mohawks, Tuscaroras, and Oneidas to take sides with the British, and the Onondagas, Cayugas, and Senecas to remain neutral; although it required all his influence and the most strenuous efforts to bring this about. Not a few of the Canadian Iroquois, however, went over to the French. Of the Susquehanna Delawares and Shawanese, a part, influenced by Logan, John Thachnechtoris, Scarrooyady, Paxnous, The Belt, Zigarea, and Andrew Montour, remained true to the Colonies; and several of these chiefs offered to collect their people at Shamokin, and make this a post against the French.[1] But another part seized the hatchet with fierce eagerness. The Delawares and Shawanese of the Ohio, and many other Western nations, did the same. Among the leaders of these blood-thirsty enemies were Shingas, a great warrior of the Western Delawares; Buckshanoath, a Shawanese, of Wyoming; and Tadeuskund, once that "Brother Gideon" who had vowed, in holy baptism, to renounce the devil and serve the living God. He had been elevated to the dignity of "King of the Delawares;" and this had extinguished the last glimmering spark of faith. He became an apostate; made common cause with the savages; and was acknowledged as one of their boldest captains. At Neskapeke, the rendezvous of the warriors, he and Shingas planned more than one bloody massacre.

The first token of the existence of an Indian war was the burning of homesteads on the Potomac. But Penn-

---

[1] Colonial Records of Penna., Part vi. 640, etc.

sylvania soon felt its horrors. On the sixteenth of October, a band of French Indians attacked the farms on Penn's Creek—in that part of Cumberland County which is now Snyder—and murdered or captured most of the inhabitants.[1] This catastrophe was not known at Gnadenhütten when Zeisberger and Seidel arrived, on their way to the Monseys of the Lackawannock, although the settlers were fleeing to the towns, from every part of the frontier, in wild confusion. At Wyoming, too, nothing had as yet been heard of the massacre, and the missionaries began their work. But the Monseys were preparing to celebrate one of their sacrificial feasts, and had no ear for the Gospel. Its words no longer seemed golden to the women of the village. "You grieve us," said Zeisberger, as disappointed he turned back, with his companion, to Wyoming; "you listen rather to the drum at your idolatrous feast than to what we tell you of your God!"

Paxnous, who had been at Shamokin, awaited them with a letter from the missionaries of that station, detailing the massacre at Penn's Creek, and warning them of their danger.[2] They remained, however, for two days longer, preaching Christ with overflowing

---

[1] Colonial Records of Pa., vi. 645, etc.
[2] There were two missionaries at Shamokin—Roessler and Kiefer, besides Peter Wesa, the smith. The massacre occurred only six miles from the town, and the murderers came thither. Roessler and Wesa escaped to Bethlehem. Kiefer was concealed for two weeks in the lodge of a friendly Indian, and then escorted to Bethlehem by Thachnechtoris.

hearts, especially to Paxnous, whom they entreated to lay hold on eternal life. They feared that perhaps for years that lovely valley would be closed to the Gospel. On the last day of October they bent their steps homeward. At Gnadenhütten they found the converts and their teachers trusting in God; but at the Water-Gap they met two hundred excited militia-men, who overwhelmed them with eager inquiries, which were repeated at every plantation. In the night of the second of November they reached Bethlehem,[1] and immediately visited Squire Horsfield, giving him an account of all they knew respecting the movements of the hostile Indians. He took a deposition of their narrative, and sent it by express to Governor Morris.[2]

But this was not the only information which the Governor received. Conrad Weisser, John Harris, the survivors of the massacre, Logan, Andrew Montour, as well as all the friendly chiefs, urged him to adopt speedy and energetic measures for the defense of the Colony. Instead of doing this, he engaged in acrimo-

---

[1] At the end of the MS. Journal describing this tour is the following indorsement by Bishop Hehl: "Legit cum suspiriis pro prosperitate sementis inter frigora et turbines, *Matthaeus.*"

[2] *Pa. Archives*, ii. 459, etc. Timothy Horsfield was born at Liverpool, April 25, 1708, and immigrated to America in his seventeenth year. In 1748, he joined the Moravian Church in New York, and moved to Bethlehem in the following year. There he was appointed Justice of the Peace, which office he filled for about twelve years. In the Pontiac Conspiracy he was commissioned Colonel of the county, but resigned this position on account of the jealousy which his advancement had awakened outside of Bethlehem. Thereupon he was deprived of his justiceship also. He died March 9, 1773.

nious disputes with the Assembly concerning the legality of taxing, along with other real estate, the estates of the Proprietaries, in order to raise funds for the crisis. Still other points of disagreement occurred, which were tenaciously upheld by both parties, in spite of the constant entreaties of the inhabitants of the frontier counties,— in spite of the arrival in Philadelphia of a body of four hundred Germans, imploring the authorities to defer their unseasonable debates and protect the people,—in spite of the jeers of the Indian allies, and, at last, of their threats to desert the English cause and espouse that of the French if the government delayed any longer. It was not until a letter from the Proprietaries had been received—written immediately after the news of Braddock's defeat had reached England—and announcing a donation from them of £5000 toward the defense of the Province, that this shameful wrangling ceased. By that time, however, the tomahawks of the savages were reeking with blood.

After his return from Wyoming, Zeisberger spent some weeks at Bethlehem, Christiansbrunn, and Gnadenhütten, amid growing alarm throughout the Colony. He was occasionally employed by the Board as a messenger to Moravian settlements, and also as an escort to friendly Indians.[1] In the latter capacity he accompanied Thachnechtoris — who was going back to his kindred, after having acted so noble a part toward Kiefer—as far as Gnadenhütten, and brought the news

---

[1] Bethlehem Diary, Nov. 1755. MS. B. A.

from that station that savages, painted and armed for war, sometimes appeared in the neighborhood, and that they had attempted to alarm the inhabitants and induce them to forsake the town, but without success, the converts affirming their determination to live and die with their teachers. In the same capacity, Zeisberger, on the twenty-second of November, attended several natives who had arrived from Wyoming to Easton, where he testified before Squire Parsons to their peaceable disposition, and secured for them a pass to Philadelphia. On this occasion he had an opportunity to vindicate the character of the Brethren. Easton was full of armed Jerseymen. They were discussing the events of the war, accusing the Moravians of a secret understanding with the French Indians, and threatening to attack Bethlehem and lay it even with the ground.[1] Zeisberger hastened to explain to them the character of the work which the Church was carrying on in the Indian country, giving them at the same time an account of the flight of the missionaries from Shamokin, and setting forth everything known at Bethlehem with regard to the war-parties. His statements were well received, even by the most violent of the men, who confessed that they had been misinformed. Two days later the calumnies under which the Moravians were suffering were disproved in a manner that overwhelmed their traducers throughout the Colonies with shame.

The twenty-fourth of November was an exciting day

---

[1] Bethlehem Diary, Nov. 1755. MS. B. A.

at Bethlehem. Several bodies of militia arrived, on their road to the frontier, and made the little settlement as noisy with the drum and fife as though it were a military post. As some of these troops intended to pass through Gnadenhütten, Zeisberger set out on horseback to notify the missionaries of their coming. At the Lehigh Water-Gap he fell in with a company of Irish militia, who detained him for several hours as a suspicious character, when they heard that he came from Bethlehem. This delay saved his life.

At that time the Mission at Gnadenhütten was in charge of Mack, Grube, Schmick, and Schebosh, who all lived with the converts in the new town on the east side of the Lehigh. Of the settlement on the Mahony, besides the mill, the following buildings remained: the Chapel, or Congregation House, as it was called in the phraseology of the Moravians, the House of the Pilgrims, Brethren's House, store, barn, stable, kitchen, and milk-house. In the House of the Pilgrims lived Joachim and Anna Catharine Senseman, Gottlieb and Joanna Anders, Martin and Susanna Nitschmann, and George and Maria Partsch. In the Brethren's House resided John Gattermeyer, George Fabricius, George Schweigert, Martin Presser, John F. Lesly, Peter Worbass, and Joseph Sturgis. This little colony was under the pastoral care of Anders. Senseman was the overseer of the property; Fabricius, an alumnus of a European university, was engaged in studying the Delaware language, and at the same time taught the Indian school; Gattermeyer assisted both Anders and Senseman; Lesly instructed the natives in farming; Presser in carpenter-work; and Nitschmann, Partsch, Schweigert, Worbass, and Sturgis cultivated the land.

The shades of evening were falling when Zeisberger reached Gnadenhütten. Having delivered his letters, he prepared to go to the Mahony settlement. Mack earnestly begged him to wait until morning. "The tracks of French Indians," he added, "have been discovered, this very day, in the neighborhood, and if you venture across the river, now that it is nearly dark, you may expose yourself to imminent danger." "I have promised," was Zeisberger's answer, "to carry these letters to the Brethren on the Mahony this evening; I cannot stay. Be unconcerned about me. Goodnight!" So saying, he rode off.

How good and pleasant the social fellowship of Moravian settlers in those early days! They toiled in common, and in common they ate the bread of their industry. Whether as missionaries or farmers, as ministers or mechanics, their work was performed in the interests of the Gospel and to the glory of God. To them religion was not an austere principle, not the fulfilling of a code of duties; but a life of holy happiness. Her beauty smiled upon them in the midst of their labors; her sweet breath animated them in the hours of recreation; her presence made them, whenever they met, not only brethren of one fraternity, but friends, among whom existed affinity of thought and feeling and enjoyments.

An instance of all this was the circle of "Brethren"

and "Sisters" around the supper-table, in the House of the Pilgrims, toward which Zeisberger had taken his way. The whole family was present, except Mrs. Senseman and Worbass, both of whom were unwell, and had remained, the former in another apartment, the latter in the Brethren's House. The simple meal was just over. And while, without, the chill autumnal wind sighed among the fallen leaves, and, within, the crackling logs of a great chimney-fire sent up a cheerful blaze, and gave to the room that rough but welcome comfort which characterizes forest-life of evenings, the little company sat talking about the incidents of the day's work, the faith which the converts were manifesting amid the temptations of the times, and the blessedness of a communion with the Saviour. The prolonged barking of the farm-dogs interrupted this conversation. "It occurs to me," said Senseman, "that the Congregation House is still open; I will go and lock it; there may be stragglers from the militia in the neighborhood." He rose, and left the table. The rest remained together, unsuspicious of any danger.

Meanwhile Zeisberger was fording the Lehigh. Suddenly a thrilling shout of distress burst from the bank. He heard it not, amid the splashing of the water under his horse's hoofs, and the rushing of the river in its rocky bed. But the cry reached the Mission House at Gnadenhütten, where stood Mack, in great anxiety, looking into the dark night. Running to the Lehigh, he found Senseman and Partsch, who had fled across with the fearful intelligence that savages were attacking the House of the Pilgrims on the Mahony. By this time Zeisberger had almost reached the western bank. His friends called to him to turn back; but not until his horse had gained the land did their warning voices excite his attention. Then he made haste to reford the stream. Almost in the same moment young Sturgis came struggling through it; while a big volume of flames rose, with lurid glare, in the direction of the Mahony.

From Partsch and Sturgis, Zeisberger obtained the particulars of the attack. Soon after Senseman had left the house footsteps were heard approaching the door, which one of the company at the table opened to see who was coming. Great God! before them stood a band of painted savages, who, raising a terrific war-whoop, instantly discharged their rifles into the room. Martin Nitschmann fell dead on the spot; a bullet grazed the cheek of Sturgis; the rest retreated toward the stairs leading to the loft; while Partsch, being near a window, crept out unobserved and escaped. The Indians continued firing, and five more persons were killed before they could reach the attic. Nitschmann's wife had nearly gained it, when she fell backward among the savages, crying in piteous tones, "Oh, Brethren, Brethren, help me!" The entrance to the loft was a trap-door, which Schweigert succeeded in so effectually barricading that, for a quarter of an hour, the enemy were foiled. They fired, incessantly, through the floor, roof, and window, but hit no one. All at once the shooting ceased; deep silence prevailed; and hope began to awaken in the hearts of the survivors. But they soon recognized the terrible fate which awaited them. The cruel torch had been applied: the house was in flames. When Anders saw this, he went to the window, which was in the gable end, and shouted vehemently for help. No friendly voice replied; only the triumphant yells of the murderous band. But the Lord, of whom they had been conversing so joyfully a few minutes before, was with them, and made them strong. Mrs. Senseman sat down upon a bed, and exclaimed, "Dear Saviour, just as I expected!" These were her last words. Mrs. Anders, wrapping her apron around her infant daughter—who screamed in so heart-rending a manner that her cries were heard above the roar of the fire and whoops of the Indians—expressed anxiety only on her babe's account, and wished that it could be saved. Just then, Sturgis noticed that the savages had gone to the other side of the house. Quick as thought he leaped from the window and escaped.[1] Meanwhile Partsch had met Senseman coming from the Congregation House, and fled with him across the Lehigh.

Having listened to these harrowing details, Zeisberger rode at full speed to Bethlehem, where he

---

[1] Sturgis, a lad of seventeen years, who escaped in so wonderful a manner, afterward settled at Litiz, where he died in 1817, in the eightieth year of his age. He became the father of ten children, and at the time of his death had thirty-four grandchildren and three great-grandchildren. In the year 1864 there were living at Litiz more than thirty of his lineal descendants, all bearing his name.

arrived at three o'clock in the morning of the twenty-fifth, and roused Bishop Spangenberg from sleep with the startling news. Two hours later, at five o'clock, were heard the solemn tones of the church bell, calling the congregation to the early matins which were daily held. The bishop opened the service in the usual way, delivering a short discourse upon the words, "And Joseph saw his brethren, and he knew them, but made himself strange unto them."[1] In the course of his remarks, he applied the passage to the Lord's dealings with men, and, as an illustration, announced the massacre. A thrill of horror agitated the assembly; but the bishop immediately fell on his knees,—the pastors and people followed his example,—and, with earnest prayer, they all humbled themselves under the mighty hand of God.

The first of the survivors that reached Bethlehem was Worbass, who came later in the morning, alone and on foot. He had escaped from the Brethren's House. In the afternoon appeared Senseman and thirty of the Christian Indians; and, in the afternoon of the following day, Sturgis, Partsch, and Mrs. Partsch, who was supposed to be among the victims. From her further particulars were obtained.

Encouraged by Sturgis's success, she, too, sprang from the window. But having arrived at the Mahony only a few days before, she knew not where to find Gnadenhütten, and hid herself amid some bushes. From

---

[1] Gen. xlii. 7.

this shelter she saw the Indians falling upon Fabricius, who had also leaped to the ground. In a moment he lay weltering in his blood,—shot, tomahawked, and scalped. Next she beheld them running to the several buildings, plundering and setting them on fire. At the milk-house they divided the spoils, prepared a feast of the provisions which they had found, and finally applied the torch to this structure likewise. Then they left the spot which their merciless hands had made desolate. Creeping from her place of concealment, Mrs. Partsch took her way to the river, and spent the night wandering up and down the bank, with cries to God for aid. When the day broke, her prayers were heard. She descried a man and a boy crossing the stream, followed by a party of militia. They came nearer. It was her own husband and young Sturgis!

On the Mahony, amid charred logs and smoking embers, they found what the fire had spared of the remains of the victims; and, not far off, the mutilated body of Fabricius, guarded by his faithful dog.[1] Upon a stump of a tree lay a blanket and hat, with a knife stuck through them, a symbol of the savages signifying, "Thus much we have done, and are able to do more!"[2]

---

[1] These remains were subsequently interred by Anthony Schmidt, of Bethlehem, in one common grave, on the consecrated ground of the Indian congregation. Through the exertions of Bishop Ettwein, on December 2, 1788, a slab with an inscription was placed upon the grave. In 1848, a small marble monument was erected by private contributions, through the industry of the late Mr. Joseph Leibert, of Bethlehem, whose wife was the granddaughter of Martin Nitschmann. The ground is still used as a burial-place.

[2] Penn. Col. Records, vi. 522.

Thus perished ten persons: Anna Catharine Senseman, Gottlieb and Joanna Anders and their babe, John Gattermeyer, George Fabricius, George Schweigert, Martin Presser, John Lesly, and Martin Nitschmann.

A worse fate overwhelmed Susanna Nitschmann. For months she was deemed to be among the dead. But, in the following summer, the Mission Board ascertained, through a convert of Gnadenhütten who had fled to the Susquehanna at the time of the massacre, that she had been carried off as a captive.

At Wyoming believing women ministered to her wants, and unsuccessfully tried to shield her from a life more terrible than death. Her captors claimed her, dragged her to Tioga, and forced her to share the wigwam of a brutish Indian. The horror of her situation broke her strength. She relapsed into melancholy; spent her days and nights in weeping; until, after a captivity of half a year, God released her from her misery, and took her to His eternal rest.[1]

The news of the massacre was sent by Horsfield to Squire Parsons, at Easton, who dispatched an express to Secretary Peters, at Philadelphia.[2] A few days later,

---

[1] My authorities for this narrative of the massacre are the Bethlehem MSS. Diaries for November, 1755, and July, 1756; Spangenberg's Circular to the Churches; short MSS. Memoirs of the Victims; and Heckewelder's Biographical Sketch of Zeisberger.

[2] *Penn. Col. Records*, vi. 736 and 737. This letter to Parsons shows that Horsfield wrote it under great excitement, and before accurate information of the occurrence had been obtained.

Horsfield wrote a full account to Governor Morris himself.[1] The intelligence created a profound sensation throughout the country. The most violent enemies of the Moravians now acknowledged that they had done them a gross wrong.

To the churches under his charge Bishop Spangenberg sent a circular instinct with faith and resignation to God's mysterious will. The material loss which the Mission had sustained by the destruction of the buildings, he estimated at more than fifteen hundred pounds sterling.[2]

With regard to Zeisberger, all his friends confessed that his escape was providential. Nor did he fail to acknowledge this. Speaking of that memorable evening, he said, "Had I arrived at Gnadenhütten either a little earlier or a little later, I would inevitably have fallen into the hands of the savages. But such was not the will of my Saviour. He would have me serve Him longer."[3]

On his way to Bethlehem, in the night of the massacre, Zeisberger met, six miles from Gnadenhütten, the same militia who had detained him in the afternoon. These hastened to the scene of the disaster, as did likewise Colonel Anderson and his company, whom he found at the Gap, and a messenger, ordered to apply for

---

[1] Penn. Archives, ii. 520-523.
[2] By the subsequent burning of Gnadenhütten this loss was increased to over £2000.
[3] Heckewelder's Biographical Sketch of Zeisberger.

immediate reinforcements, accompanied him to the Irish settlement.¹

Meanwhile the Christian Indians gathered around their teachers, and, kindling with the fire of their warrior-days, offered to cross the river and attack the savages. But, as the missionaries would not consent to such a measure, they dispersed and fled into the forest.

The party that made the assault was composed of Monseys, and numbered about twelve braves.² It was led by Jacheabus, the chief of Assinnissink, a Monsey town in Steuben County, New York. In the Pontiac War this town was destroyed by the Mohawks and Jacheabus taken prisoner. He ended his life as a captive.³

In the course of a few days numerous volunteers hastened to Gnadenhütten, Squire Horsfield having sent out letters to call the whole neighborhood to arms. Protected by these troops, the missionaries brought the most of the converts from their hiding-places and led them to Bethlehem. The rest found their way to Wyoming. From Bethlehem the Indians sent an address to Governor Morris, professing their allegiance to the British crown, and putting themselves under its protection. "As you have made it your own choice," the Governor wrote in response, "to become members of our civil society and subjects of the same government,

---

[1] Penn. Col. Records, vi. 736.
[2] Penn. Archives, ii. 522.
[3] Zeisberger's Journal of his Exploratory Tour to the Alleghany River in 1767. MS. B. A.

and determined to share the same fate with us, I shall make it my care to extend the same protection to you as to the other subjects of his Majesty; and, as a testimony of the regard paid by the government to the distressed state of that part of the Province where you have suffered so much, I have determined to build a fort at Gnadenhütten, from which you will receive equal security with the white people under my care."[1] But before such a fort could be erected, the savages, on New Year's Day of 1756, surprised the guard of forty militiamen who were stationed there, routed them, and laid the entire village in ashes, together with the mill on the Mahony.[2] On the seventh of January, Benjamin Franklin arrived at Bethlehem, in order to superintend the defenses of Northampton County. His measures were energetic. He put up a log fort on the site of Gnadenhütten, mounting two swivels, and properly garrisoned.[3] It was called Fort Allen, and formed one of a series of posts established along the Blue Mountains, from the Delaware River to Maryland, commanding the principal passes of the chain. Bethlehem, meanwhile, had become a refuge for numerous settlers, who flocked thither from every part of the country. It was surrounded with stockades, and now formed both a frontier post and a protection for the settlements southward to Philadelphia.

Meantime those Christian Indians from Gnadenhütten

---

[1] Penn. Col. Records, vi. 747–750.
[2] Bethlehem Diary, Jan. 1756. Penn. Col. Records, vi. 772.
[3] Penn. Col. Records, vii. 15–17.

who were of the Mohican tribe were quartered at Bethlehem, in a large stone-house, near which was subsequently erected a log structure, containing a chapel. Both these buildings stood on the west side of the Monocasy Creek, near the mills and tan-yard of the settlement. The Delaware converts established themselves at Gnadenthal, in the vicinity of Nazareth. They worked industriously in the fields and farm-yards of the neighborhood, or by making wooden bowls and ladles, shovels, brooms, and sieves, for which they found a ready sale. Many of these articles were sent in wagons to New Brunswick and New York.

CHAPTER XIII.

THE FRENCH AND INDIAN WAR.—1756-1761.

War in the East and West.—Missionary work interrupted.—Zeisberger frequents the Indian treaties.—Treaty at Philadelphia, 1756.—Declaration of war against the Delawares and Shawanese.—Zeisberger escorts peace-envoys to Fort Allen.—Journey to North Carolina.—The treaties at Easton, in July and November, 1756.—The machinations of Tadeuskund.—The treaty at Lancaster, May, 1757.—Nain founded.—The treaty at Easton, July, 1757.—The reverses of England.—A new and victorious campaign in 1758.—Frederick Post, the messenger of peace.—Zeisberger at the great congress at Easton, October, 1758.—Visits Schoharie and Pachgatgoch.—Second journey to North Carolina.—Capitulation of Quebec and conquest of Canada.—Zeisberger Superintendent of the Brethren's House at Litiz.—Second great congress at Easton.—Zeisberger government-interpreter.—His literary labors during the war.

THE world was convulsed with the throes of mighty conflicts. In Europe raged the Seven Years' War; in the East, Clive was conquering a vast empire that had, for centuries, been enriching a proud but feeble race; on the bosom of the broad Atlantic the ships of England and France met in deadly strife; while, in North America, the final struggle between these ancient rivals for the supremacy of the continent was at its height, and made terrible by the wild excesses and murderous cruelties of an Indian war.

In such a crisis, it was impossible to preach the Gospel to the aborigines who roamed beyond the blood-stained frontiers of the Colonies. For six years no servants of the Most High God made known the grace of His only-begotten Son, at Onondaga or Shamokin, on the Susquehanna or in the shadow of the Blue Mountains. To care for the spiritual welfare of the refugees from Gnadenhütten, and of the converts at the stations in New England, was all that the Mission Board could undertake.

Zeisberger gave himself to the discharge of such missionary duties as the times permitted, and of such other labors as they called for. During the first four years of this period, Christiansbrunn appears to have been his place of residence. But he was sent to various settlements as a messenger of the Board. The duty, however, in which he most frequently engaged, called him to the several treaties instituted by the government of Pennsylvania. On these occasions his presence was always welcome to the natives, and they believed it would help to secure them justice.[1] He did not act as interpreter, or take part in the negotiations; but mingled with the Indians in order to embrace the only opportunities which were afforded to present the Gospel.

The first treaty which he attended was held at Philadelphia, in February, with John Thachnechtoris, The Belt, Jagrea, Captain New Castle,[2] the Conestoga Indians and others. New Castle and another Iroquois—whom Governor Morris, after an interview at Carlisle

---

[1] Heckewelder's MS. Biography.
[2] Captain New Castle, or Cashiowayah, was an Iroquois in the interests of the English, and employed as a messenger.

with several friendly chiefs, had dispatched to the Susquehanna in order to gain information of the movements of the savages—reported the result of their journey; and Thachnechtoris, who had been invited by these messengers to consult with his white brethren, assured the government of the amicable disposition of the Shikellimy family.[1]

In April, Governor Morris, with the approval of his Council, except James Logan, who entered his protest on the minutes, formally declared war against the Delawares and Shawanese, and offered large bounties for scalps or prisoners. The Quakers were shocked at the barbarity of this measure, and, by petition and otherwise, urged conciliatory measures. The way for these, unexpectedly to the Governor, was opened by Sir William Johnson, who was dissatisfied with the measures adopted by Pennsylvania, and expressed his surprise that one Province should declare war without consulting the rest. While negotiating with the Six Nations on other subjects, this far-sighted officer induced them to promise that they would exercise the authority which they claimed over the Delawares and Shawanese, and command them to lay down the hatchet. As soon as Governor Morris was informed of this, he called together his Council, invited Bishop Spangenberg to be present, and sent for Captain New Castle, Jagrea, and William Lacquis. A peace message was prepared, and intrusted to New Castle and his two associates; and Spangen-

---

[1] Penn. Col. Records, vii. 46, etc.

berg was solicited to send along with them a Christian Indian as a fourth envoy. They were to tell the hostile tribes that Onas—the Indian name for the Governor of Pennsylvania—was not averse to peace, provided that they delivered to him all their white prisoners, and instantly ceased from further attacks upon the settlements.[1]

At Bethlehem, Augustus Rex joined the envoys, and Zeisberger escorted the party as far as Fort Allen;[2] while the whole Church prayed that their mission might be crowned with success. In order to accomplish this end, the Governor suspended, in part, the declaration of war; and published a cessation of hostilities for twenty days, as far as the Susquehanna.[3] The Western tribes, however, were not included in this truce.

A few days subsequent to Zeisberger's return from Fort Allen, he was sent on a longer and more perilous journey. The Moravians had begun a settlement in western North Carolina, on a large tract of land purchased from the Earl of Granville.[4] Thither Zeisberger took his way, the bearer of letters to the infant colony from Bishop Spangenberg and other elders. After an absence of two months, he came back to Bethlehem in safety, on the thirteenth of July.

---

[1] Penn. Col. Records, vii. 107, etc. [2] Ibid., vii. 118. [3] Ibid., vii. 134.
[4] This tract embraced 98,985 acres, and was called "Wachovia," after a valley in Austria, formerly in possession of the Zinzendorf family. It lay in the present Forsyth County. Bethabara, the first town, was founded in 1753.

His arrival was opportune. New Castle and his fellow-envoys had fulfilled their mission; had reported to the Governor a favorable answer from the Susquehanna Indians; and had visited them a second time to invite them to a treaty. And now Tadeuskund and some of his warriors reached Bethlehem, on their way to the treaty which was to take place at Easton. Zeisberger failed not to be there; and, during the six days of the negotiations, moved about among the Indians with the words of eternal life upon his lips.

For these words Tadeuskund had no ear. He conceived himself to be a great man; strutted with assumed authority; pompously proclaimed that he appeared in the name of ten nations—meaning the Iroquois and four tribes on the Susquehanna—and that the Delawares were no longer women, but had been made men again.[1] The Colonial authorities bore with his arrogance. Preliminaries of peace were arranged, and another treaty was appointed to be held in November.

True to this appointment, Tadeuskund presented himself at the designated time, with a small escort, and was received by Governor Denny, who had super-

---

[1] This assertion of Tadeuskund probably refers to what Zeisberger relates in his MS. History of the Indians: that in the Indian and French War the Six Nations told the Delawares their petticoat should be shortened, so as to reach only to their knees; and that they should again receive a hatchet to defend themselves. This, no doubt, was a message from the Senecas, who at first took part in the war against the Colonies, and not from the whole Iroquois League.

seded Morris. Zeisberger was again present, accompanied by the whole male part of the Indian Congregation at Bethlehem. After nine days of speeches and deliberations, the business was finished satisfactorily to all parties, and, in conclusion, the Governor solemnly said, "Peace is now settled between us, by the assistance of the Most High."[1] Further negotiations were to take place in spring, at a third treaty; and Lancaster was designated as the place of meeting.

But these pacifications included the Susquehanna Indians only. The warriors of the West still continued their ravages along the frontiers, and the war was not at an end. That the border-men had learned to retaliate with the tactics of the savages, was triumphantly shown by a sudden assault, planned and carried out by Armstrong, upon Kittanning, on the Alleghany. There was wailing in the wigwams of the Western Delawares when the news of this exploit reached them.

On his road to the treaties at Easton, Tadeuskund was accustomed to stop at Bethlehem, where his influence upon the converts was of the worst kind. But it was not until negotiations at Lancaster began that all the evil intentions of his heart became manifest. Among the minutes which George Croghan, the deputy of Sir William Johnson, laid before the Governor, was a message received from Tadeuskund to this effect: "Brothers, there is one thing that gives

---

[1] Penn. Col. Records, vii. 313–338.

us a great deal of concern, which is, our flesh and blood that live among you at Bethlehem, and in the Jerseys, being kept as if they were prisoners. We formerly applied to the minister at Bethlehem,[1] to let our people come back at times and hunt, which is the chief industry we follow to maintain our families; but that minister has not listened to what we have said to him, and it is very hard that our people have not the liberty of coming back to the woods, where game is plenty, and to see their friends. They have complained to us that they cannot hunt where they are, and, if they go into the woods and cut down a tree, they are abused for it, notwithstanding that very land we look upon to be our own; and we hope, brothers, that you will consider this matter, and let our people come into the woods, and visit their friends, and pass and repass, as brothers ought to do."[2] Thus did this reprobate, who well knew the real sentiments of the converts, and that they were at Bethlehem of their own free will, attempt to make the government his tool in destroying that holy work which his carnal heart now hated. But the government paid no attention to this message. The Mission Board, however, when informed of it, recognized the necessity of providing a new settlement for the Christian Indians.

At the treaty (May, 1757) which brought to light this plot of the King of the Delawares, he failed to appear, although it had been appointed at his suggestion. Nev-

---

[1] Probably Bishop Spangenberg is meant.
[2] Penn. Col. Records, vii. 516.

ertheless, it proved an occasion of some importance to the British cause. A number of Nanticokes and Delawares, together with deputies from the Six Nations, were present.[1] The latter advised the Governor to hold another conference with Tadeuskund, invite the chiefs of the Shawanese to attend, and settle anew a definite peace. At the same time they prepared the way for the reconciliation of the Senecas, whom French intrigues had made the fiercest enemies of the Colonies.

In the course of the winter Zeisberger was employed as the bearer of dispatches from Bishop Spangenberg to the Governor. These dispatches contained whatever intelligence reached Bethlehem of the movements of the savages. At the treaty at Lancaster he met with several of his personal friends among the Iroquois sachems, who begged him to return to their capital. This was impossible while the war continued.

Going back to Bethlehem, he found a new enterprise in progress. By permission of the Colonial government a site for a Christian Indian town had been selected on land belonging to the Church. It lay about two miles from Bethlehem, in Hanover Township, Lehigh County, on what is now known as the Geisinger farm. The first house was put up on the tenth of June; but, owing to the unsettled state of the country, it was not until October of the following year that the chapel could be dedicated (October 18, 1758). This village received the name of Nain.

---

[1] Penn. Col. Records, vii. 519–549.

The conference, which had been suggested by the deputies of the Six Nations, was held in July, at Easton, and continued seventeen days.[1] Tadeuskund, with one hundred and fifty-nine Delawares, Paxnous, and other representatives of the Shawanese, Abraham, the Mohican, and many Senecas were present. The King of the Delawares had not grown more humble. He insisted upon having a private secretary, like the Governor, and made many other peremptory demands, all of which were granted for the sake of peace, and the articles previously agreed upon ratified. On this occasion Zeisberger did not stay at Easton, but rode over from Bethlehem almost every day. He found, however, only a few Indians with whom he was acquainted.

The two years which England, through her Colonial government in Pennsylvania, had devoted to negotiations with her savage foe, were most disastrous in her struggle with France. The Earl of Loudoun, who had been sent to America as viceroy, was wholly unfit for the position. Overbearing to the Colonies, and pusillanimous in the face of the enemy, he tried to crush out the republican spirit which was rising among the people, but suffered the Marquis de Montcalm to gain, unhindered, a series of brilliant victories. Oswego was taken; Fort William Henry, at the southern extremity of Lake George, with a garrison of two thousand men, surrendered; the whole basin of the Ohio fell into the hands of the French; the valley of the St. Lawrence and of

---

[1] Penn. Col. Records, vii. 649-714.

the Mississippi submitted to the same power. These reverses were deeply felt. England was almost in a state of anarchy. America blushed at the incompetency of her British leaders, who despised the brave provincials, but who themselves possessed neither the character nor the courage which the times demanded.

In this crisis William Pitt re-entered the cabinet and took the reins of government (July, 1757). Loudoun was immediately recalled; the conquest of Canada and of the Western territory planned; provincial soldiers were summoned to arms; and Amherst, Forbes, Howe, and Wolfe sent to carry out these measures, under the direction of Abercrombie, as commander-in-chief. The war now assumed a new aspect. Abercrombie was indeed defeated at Ticonderoga by Montcalm; but Louisburg, Frontenac (now Kingston), and Fort Duquesne passed into the possession of the English as the fruits of the campaign of 1758. In another quarter, too, France sustained a heavy loss. Her allies in the West, the fierce warriors who had so persistently refused to bury the hatchet, were at last persuaded to send deputies to a congress at Easton. It was the fearlessness of Frederick Post, who traveled through their country as the agent of the government, exposing himself to perils of every kind, that accomplished this great work.[1]

The congress began on the eighth of October, and

---

[1] Post undertook this mission in the summer of 1758. The journal of his tour was published in England in 1759. It is also found in the Penn. Archives, vol. iii. 520 to 544. A copy in MS. is in the B. A.

continued eighteen days. Nearly five hundred Indians assembled; among them Tadeuskund and many sachems of the Six Nations. They were met by Governor Denny, of Pennsylvania; Governor Bernard, of New Jersey; George Croghan, and a number of commissioners and magistrates. The result was a general pacification, embracing all the hostile tribes except the Twightwees. And when Post visited the West a second time, publishing the proceedings of the congress, the Twightwees too buried the hatchet. This brought the Indian war to an end.

On the occasion of this treaty, Zeisberger met with numerous friends among the aborigines, and had a wide field in which he silently sowed the seed of the Word. At Croghan's request he afterward escorted an old Mohawk chief as far as Schoharie, and thence proceeded to Pachgatgoch, where he assisted the missionaries in preaching the Gospel. He returned to Bethlehem in December.

About this time Nain exhibited indications of prosperity such as marked Gnadenhütten before the war. Not a few of the fugitive converts emerged from the wilderness and sought its peaceful cabins. The village was enlarged, and presented a pleasing appearance. It was built in the form of a square, of which three sides were lined with dwellings, and the south side left open, so as to permit the inhabitants to fetch water from a little stream that flowed by. In the center of the square was a well. The houses were of squared timber, and had shingle-roofs; back of them lay the gardens. Besides the chapel and school-house, there was a public building for indigent widows, whom the congregation supported.[1]

This town was an eye-sore to Tadeuskund, who did what he could to mar its prosperity, and succeeded in enticing Augustus Rex from its benign influences. Frequent efforts were made to reclaim Tadeuskund, but all in vain. His wife, however, remained true to her baptismal vows.

In August of 1759, Zeisberger undertook a second journey to North Carolina, bearing letters to Bishop Spangenberg, who had gone to cheer his isolated brethren at Bethabara. This settlement had become a green spot in the midst of a dreary wilderness.

Meantime, on the heights of Abraham, in the rear of Montcalm's fortifications at Quebec, was fought that battle which decided the future of the Western World (September 13th). Wolfe and Montcalm both fell; but victory crowned the army of Britain and gave her the sway of the continent. Four days later, Quebec capitulated, and the conquest of Canada became a question merely of time.

But the state of the Colonies and Indian country did not, as yet, admit of the renewal of missionary work. Hence Zeisberger, after his return from the South in November, spent the winter at Christiansbrunn, and in spring was appointed Superintendent of the Brethren's House at Litiz (April, 1760). In this office he spent fifteen quiet months, and had no intercourse with the

---

[1] Heckewelder's Report of the Indian Mission. MS. B. A.

Indians. At last, however, an opportunity offered to visit them again.

On the eighth of September (1760), Montreal and all Canada had been ceded to England. The French War was virtually at an end; and in August, 1761, a second General Congress was held with the Indian tribes at Easton, in order to arrange the delivery of their prisoners, and renew the peace previously concluded. Zeisberger was present at this Congress, laboring both as missionary, and, at the earnest request of Governor Hamilton, as Government Interpreter.[1] After nine days of incessant duties, he returned to Litiz, where he remained until the dedication of the new "Brethren's House" (December 5, 1761),[2] when he resigned his office and proceeded to Bethlehem, awaiting the first opportunity to resume his work among the aborigines.

In the six years of war, he wrote an Iroquois Grammar and finished his Iroquois-German Dictionary, the materials for which he had collected at Shamokin and Onondaga.

---

[1] Col. Records, viii. 630–654.

[2] This house is now the Litiz Academy for Boys, which, for half a century, was under the superintendence of John Beck, Esq., but is at present in charge of Messrs. Rickert and Hepp.

CHAPTER XIV.

ZEISBERGER'S FIRST LABORS AFTER THE FRENCH AND INDIAN WARS.—1762, 1763.

New epoch in American history.—Progress of civilization.—Traders and hunters.—The missionaries.—The Mission stations in 1762.—Bishop Spangenberg leaves America.—The wilderness in 1762, its Indian tribes and British forts.—Zeisberger at Wyoming.—Death of the first convert.—Post endeavors to draw Zeisberger away from the Church.—The dissatisfaction of the Indians with the triumph of England.—Pontiac forms a conspiracy.—Zeisberger at Wechquetank.—Indian preachers.—Their doctrines and bible.—Papunhank of Machiwihilusing.—Remarkable awakening in his town.—Zeisberger hastens thither.—Death of Tadeuskund.—The Connecticut settlers.—Zeisberger at Machiwihilusing.—Appointed resident missionary.—Papunhank baptized.—Zeisberger recalled on account of the war.

IN the year in which preliminaries of peace between England and France were signed (November 3, 1762), Zeisberger began again to preach to the Indians.

It was the dawn of a new epoch for America and the world. England had been victorious both in the East and the West. The riches of India were poured out at her feet; America was hers, from the Gulf of Mexico to the ice-fields of the Arctic lands. "To England were ceded," says Bancroft, "besides islands in the West Indies, the Floridas, Louisiana to the Mississippi, but without the island of New Orleans; all Canada; Acadia; Cape Breton, and its dependent islands." A continent, abounding in natural resources of almost every kind, and with a soil adapted to the productions of nearly every clime, opened to the Anglo-Saxon race, the English tongue, and the Protestant religion. Thus God prepared the way for a national development unparalleled in history. The British Colonies in America were to become the United States of America. A great republic was to assume its place among the kingdoms of the earth.

Sixteen years had elapsed since Zeisberger first traversed the American forests in search of their roving tribes. During this period white settlers had been advancing westward with slow but sure steps. The wilderness was dotted with flourishing settlements. There were isolated homesteads almost to the foot of the Alleghanies. The war had, indeed, put a stop to such progress; but no sooner did peace once more smile upon the land than the sturdy strokes of the backwoodsman's axe were again heard in the forest, as he came to clear his plantations and build his cabins.

In advance of him were the traders and hunters. They formed a class of their own; bold, courageous, and with a sagacity almost equal to that of the Indians, but unscrupulous and dishonest, of degraded morals, intent upon their own advantage, and indifferent to the rights of the natives.

Pioneers like them, yet of a character and with purposes altogether different—disinterested, inured to hardships, undismayed by dangers, yearning to convert and civilize the savages, in all they said and did "constrained by the love of Christ"—were the missionaries, who welcomed the return of peace with that joy which he alone can appreciate who knows what it is to "save a soul from death."

The only stations that remained to the Church, at the close of the war, were Nain; Wechquetank, a new place, begun in April, 1760, on the north side of the Blue Mountains, in the present Monroe County, by those converts who had been quartered at Gnadenthal;[1] and Pachgatgoch, where, however, the cause languished, owing to the rapid decrease of the natives. Besides these stations, Frederick Post, independently of the Board, was trying to establish a Mission in Ohio, near the site of the present Town of Bolivar, on the Tuscarawas River, and with him was associated young John Heckewelder.[2]

About this time Bishop Spangenberg, the President of the Mission Board, resigned his office and sailed to Europe (July 1, 1762), in order to take his seat in that Directory of bishops and elders which governed the Unitas Fratrum after the death of Count Zinzendorf (May 9, 1760). He was succeeded by Bishop Nathaniel Seidel, whose assistants were Bishop Boehler and Frederick de Marshall.[3]

---

[1] Wechquetank lay in Polk Township, Monroe County, Pennsylvania, between the Wechquetank and Heads Creeks. For this information I am indebted to Abraham Huebener, M.D., of Bethlehem.

[2] Born at Bedford, England, March 12, 1742. A distinguished missionary, whose labors are identified with our history, as the sequel will show.

[3] Born Feb. 5, 1721, in the garrison-town of Stolpen, Saxony, of which his father, Baron G. R. de Marshall, was commandant. He received a

The wilderness, to which the Church again turned her attention, offered to the Indian tribes the same forest-homes and broad hunting-grounds, as before the war. Some changes, indeed, had taken place. At Shamokin and Wyoming was found only a remnant of natives; the Delawares and Mohicans, on the North Branch of the Susquehanna, had dwindled away to insignificant clans; and the Shawanese had all retired to the Muskingum and the Scioto. But beyond the mountains, on the Alleghany, and farther west, on the Beaver Creeks and the Muskingum River, the Delawares were still domiciliated; and in New York the Iroquois held undisputed possession of their ancient seats; and the great Northwest continued to shelter the Ottawas and Ojibwas, the Potawatomies and many other Algonquin tribes; while along the Mississippi, in the present State which bears their name, were scattered, as of old, the villages of the dissolute Illinois.

The war had brought into existence numerous forts and military posts. Besides those in New York, among which Forts Stanwix on the Mohawk, and Brewerton at the western end of Lake Oneida, deserve to be particularly mentioned, there were, in Maryland, Fort Cumberland, and in Pennsylvania, nearest to the settlements, Fort Allen at Gnadenhütten, Augusta at Shamo-

---

strict military education. At Bethlehem, his office was that of "General Warden." Subsequently he stood at the head of the Southern District of the American Church, and died at Salem, N. C., in 1802, aged eighty-one years.

kin, and Bedford on the site of the present town of the same name. This was the starting-point of a road to the West. Another, laid out by General Braddock, passed from Cumberland across the mountains. On the former, about forty-five miles from Bedford, stood Fort Ligonier; and about fifty-five miles farther on, rose the brick-faced ramparts of Fort Pitt, a strong post constructed, in 1759, by General Stanwix, on the ruins of Fort Duquesne. Here the Western road stopped. North of Fort Pitt, at the junction of French Creek with the Alleghany River, appeared Fort Venango; still farther north, on French Creek, Le Bœuf, and on the site of the present City of Erie, Presque Isle. All these works belonged to the English, who had either built or captured them.

More remote forts were Sandusky, on Lake Erie; Detroit; Miami, on the Maumee River, near the present Fort Wayne in Indiana; Ouatanon, just below Lafayette, in the same State; Vincennes, on the Wabash River; Michilimackinac, on the Straits of Mackinaw; La Baye, on the site of Green Bay, in Wisconsin; St. Josephs, at the mouth of the river of the same name, on Lake Michigan; and Chartres, on the Mississippi above Kaskaskia, in Illinois.

These posts—of which possession had been taken, immediately after the capitulation of Canada, by Major Rogers with two hundred rangers—were important not only in a military point of view, but likewise as the nuclei of future settlements. At some of them such settlements already existed. Detroit was the home of numerous traders and Canadians; and Chartres formed the capital of a colony of two thousand souls, immigrants from Canada and disbanded French soldiers, besides nine hundred negro slaves. These settlers had founded Kaskaskia, St. Genevieve, and Cahokia, and built their huts around Forts Chartres and Vincennes.

Zeisberger paid his first visit to the Indian country in the capacity of an envoy, on the part of Sir William Johnson and Governor Hamilton, to Tadeuskund.[1] On the sixteenth of March, he left Christiansbrunn on horseback, and by nightfall reached the north foot of the Blue Mountains, where he found a large encampment of Delawares and Nanticokes. His heart was strangely stirred as he sat again by a camp-fire in the wilderness, with members of that race around him, to convert which was the exalted mission of his life. Six years, spent away from the Indians, had made him only the more eager to do them good.

The next morning he proceeded on his journey, taking with him one of the Delawares as a guide, for the whole country was covered with a deep snow. After three days of hard and perilous riding in forests obstructed by great drifts, through snow-banks from which it was almost impossible to extricate the horses, and in "weather," says Zeisberger, "the severest I ever knew,"[2] he arrived at the lodge of Tadeuskund. Having delivered his letters, he turned his attention to the con-

---

[1] Documentary Hist. of N. Y., iv. 310, and letter from Zeisberger to Spangenberg. MS. B. A.
[2] Doc. Hist. N. Y., iv. 310.

verts of Wyoming. The most of them had not heard the Gospel preached since the breaking out of the war. More than one backslider was reclaimed, among them George Rex, who, on the occasion of a subsequent visit to Nain, was readmitted to the Church. On the twenty-fourth, Zeisberger came back to Bethlehem, and thence went to Philadelphia with the answer of Tadeuskund.[1]

Toward the end of autumn, he visited Wyoming again, accompanied by Gottlob Senseman. The dysentery was raging in the valley, and many Indians were prostrated. Among these was Abraham, the first convert. He had sent an urgent request to Bethlehem: "Brethren, let a teacher come to see me ere I die!" But the missionaries arrived too late; the aged Mohican had finished his course. Yet not as a reprobate; he had repented and been forgiven; and, with his dying breath, had exhorted the Indians to remain faithful to Jesus. In the same spirit George Rex passed away, admonishing his countrymen to avoid his evil example, and professing a sure hope of eternal life. Zeisberger spent several days in comforting the sick; and a new interest was awakened among all the scattered converts of the valley. On the day of his departure, he called them together to a farewell service, and preached a touching discourse upon the words, "For the Son of Man is come to seek and to save that which is lost."[2] He reached Bethlehem on the thirtieth of November,

---

[1] Bethlehem Diary. MS. B. A.   [2] Luke, xix. 10.

bringing a petition to the Board for a resident teacher at Wyoming.

At Bethlehem, John Heckewelder, who had returned from the Muskingum, awaited him. He was the bearer of a message from Frederick Post; and delivered it in the presence of Bishop Seidel. "Cast in your lot with me," said Post to Zeisberger; "we will go out as independent evangelists, establish God's kingdom among the Indians, and extend it as far as the Mississippi." Without a moment's hesitation, Zeisberger replied: "Post is free to undertake what he pleases; I am not. I belong wholly to the Church of the Brethren."[1] This was a turning-point in Zeisberger's life. Had he embraced this offer, severed his connection with the Moravians, and joined his friend in an independent Mission, he would scarcely have earned the honorable title and the enduring fame which are accorded to his memory. For, while Post was a good and zealous man, he was unstable and erratic; wandered from the wilds of Ohio to the lagoons of Central America, accomplishing nothing; and finally withdrew altogether from missionary work.

The occupation of the military posts of the West was, in the highest degree, irritating to the Indians. Their "fathers"—the French—knew how to conciliate them; adapted themselves to their customs and prejudices, and succeeded in almost removing the impression from their minds that they were being conquered. The

---

[1] Heckewelder's Biographical Sketch.

English had not the faculty of winning their confidence. Moreover, while the struggle for supremacy between France and England continued, the natives felt their own importance, and perceived that they held the balance of power. But as soon as Canada had been ceded, and the sway of England established, there was a great change in their position. Sir William Johnson, indeed, still brightened the chain of friendship which bound the Iroquois League to his country; but, in the West, the nations fell into insignificance. At the same forts where the French had treated them with uniform kindness and urbanity, the harsh manners of the British, who despised them, formed a most galling contrast; while the systematic dishonesty of the traders, and the steady advance of the settlers, who often usurped land which had never been alienated, inflamed their proud spirits still more. There were some among them whose animosity struck deeper root, and grew to be a persistent hatred of the English. Such natives had mind enough to understand the true posture of affairs, and felt that the crisis of their race had come; that either a bold, united, and desperate effort must be made to extirpate their conquerors, or the doom of the aboriginal lords of the American continent was sealed.

No one realized this more keenly than Pontiac, the great chief of the Ottawas.[1] The Iroquois, and especially the Senecas, in spite of Sir William John-

---

[1] Bancroft's U. S., v. iii.; Zeisberger's MS. History of the Indians; Pontiac's Conspiracy, by Parkman.

son's unceasing efforts, had, for two years, been looking with extreme distrust upon the progress of the British flag, and had incited the Delawares and Shawanese to take up the hatchet; and the Delawares and Shawanese had again stirred up the tribes of the West, with the note of alarm, "The English mean to make slaves of us, by occupying so many posts in our country!" But it is not likely that a well-concerted, general rising of the natives would have occurred had it not been for Pontiac. He was the head of a confederacy which embraced his own tribe and the Ojibwas and Potawatomies, but exercised, also, undisputed and supreme influence throughout the Northwest, being "the king and lord of all that country," as Rogers called him. Endowed with natural qualifications of a high order, born to rule, brave, far-sighted, a wild statesman, and a savage hero, he organized and upheld that conspiracy which has made his name famous, which had for its aim the expulsion of the English from the American continent, which inflicted severe injury upon the Colonies, and which might have been successful had France, as he hoped, lent her aid.

As the year 1762 drew to a close, Pontiac sent out his ambassadors. They passed through the entire West to the many tribes that hunted there; they proceeded far down the Mississippi, almost to its mouth; they everywhere displayed the broad war-belt of the chief, and rehearsed his words of fiery eloquence, calling upon all red men to save the race to which they belonged from slavery and ruin. A chief of the Abanakis, who gave out that he was possessed of a prophetic spirit, and that the Great Manitou commanded the extirpation of the English, effectually seconded Pontiac's scheme, until nearly the whole Algonquin stock of Indians, the Wyandots, several tribes of the lower Mississippi, and the Senecas, were banded in a conspiracy.

With the subtleness for which the aborigines are noted, this wide-spread plot was kept a secret. In February of the new year, when the peace of Paris had been ratified (February 10, 1763), which gave a continent to England, not one of her Colonial officers suspected that, in all the villages of the West, the savages were silently preparing to wrench that continent from her grasp. On the twenty-seventh of April, Pontiac convened a council on the bank of the Ecorces, a small stream not far from Detroit. Representatives of many tribes were present; and their deep ejaculations of assent to the chief's impetuous speech showed that they were terribly in earnest. First Detroit, next the other posts and forts—the garrisons of which severally numbered a mere handful of men—were to be captured, and then desolation, with bloody strides, was to take its way to the settlements.

On the day of this council, Zeisberger was descending the Blue Mountains from Wechquetank, where he had been visiting. Wechquetank and Nain both flourished; and he little suspected that a storm was rising which would burst with such fury as almost to destroy, a second time, the work of the Gospel among the natives.

To the encouraging signs, which excited the hopes

of the Board, eminently belonged a remarkable awakening at Machiwihilusing, the seat of an Indian preacher, named Papunhank.

Preachers arose among the Indians after the introduction of the Gospel through the agency of the Moravians; and seem to have belonged especially to the Delawares. Perhaps their appearance may be fixed about the year 1750. Different from the pow-wows and sorcerers, whom the natives had always had, they constituted a distinct class, assuming the character both of prophets and teachers. As prophets, they claimed to receive revelations from the Great Spirit, to be translated into heaven, and to see him face to face. As teachers, they made known the existence of a Son of Manitou, of a devil, and a hell. Their journeys to the upper regions, they said, were always perilous; but by them they learned to know the road. This they depicted upon tanned deer-hides, as the Indian's path to heaven; also another and more circuitous way, intended for the white people; likewise God's abode, and hell, together with a pair of scales, symbolizing the dishonesty of the white man. With these hides, which were meant to take the place of the Bible, they appeared before their people, expounded the meaning of the figures, and set forth the conditions of salvation. Whoever would be saved, must purge out his sins with emetics of twelve varieties, or beat them out with twelve rods, each of a different species of wood, beginning at the feet and proceeding upward, castigating himself until all his iniquities suddenly issued from his neck; he must besides practice morality, avoiding especially the lusts of the flesh, murder, and theft.

It is evident that this singular manifestation was an attempt to counteract the influence of the missionaries, and to incite the Indians against the white race. The ideas of a Bible, of Satan, of hell, and particularly of the Son of God, were all borrowed from the Gospel. Far-sighted natives felt that they needed more than their barren creed of a Great Spirit, of manitous, and elysian hunting-grounds, at a time when the power of the Divine Word was captivating so many hearts. Hence this effort to show that the work of the white teachers was one of supererogation; that the Indians had the same and even better knowledge; and that their road to eternal happiness was the shorter.

Some of these preachers used every means to prevent the influence which the doctrine of a crucified Saviour has ever had upon the heathen. They derided it in various ways. The Son of God, they said, whom they saw in heaven, had no wounds, yet they found a place in his side, referring to the piercing of Christ's side, and whenever they came to him he gave them a piece of bread to eat as white as snow, alluding to the wafer used in the sacrament of the Lord's Supper. One of them, on a certain occasion, having prepared a beverage of the juice of whortleberries, held up a cupful and exclaimed, "See, this is the blood of the Son of God!"

The morality which they taught they failed to practice. To their example was owing the spread of polygamy, which they defended in their own case by asserting that a union with friends of the Great Spirit, such as they were, would further the salvation of the women concerned; that for them to marry several wives was therefore a work of mercy.[1]

These preachers flourished for about thirty years. At first their success was great. But when they began to predict future events, which never came to pass, and when Zeisberger had either silenced or brought into the Christian Church some of the most noted, they passed away.

Eminent among them was Papunhank, of Machiwihilusing. But God was using him for His own holy purposes. He overruled the man's discourses upon morality to the real awakening of his tribe, so that they began to seek the way of life, and sent to Bethlehem for a teacher.

To this call Zeisberger and Anthony, a Delaware convert,[2] eagerly responded. Leaving Wechquetank on the sixteenth of May, they traveled afoot in a course northwest, with the intention of striking the trail from the Minnisinks to Wyoming. This they succeeded in doing after two days of fearful hardships, amid drenching rain, in the pathless forests and swamps of the Broad Mountain, where, guided by a pocket-compass, they crept for

---

[1] This account of the Indian preachers is based upon Zeisberger's MS. History of the Indians.

[2] Baptized by Cammerhoff, Feb. 8, 1750, at Bethlehem. He came from Tunkhannock, and was for many years a faithful native assistant, one of the most brilliant illustrations of the power of the Gospel among the Indians. Nature had made him an orator, and grace sanctified his eloquence.

miles on hands and feet beneath and between laurel-bushes, the tangled mazes of which rendered walking impossible. At Wyoming they preached to the few natives who were still in the valley.

Among these Tadeuskund no longer had a place. One night in early spring, while lying intoxicated in his lodge, it was set on fire and he perished in the flames. This was, no doubt, the cruel work of Iroquois warriors, whom he had offended by his proud bearing at the Colonial treaties. Ignoble end of the King of the Delawares! Miserable fate of the apostate Gideon! His countrymen and the missionaries both mourned for him, but from different motives. The former had lost their great chief; the latter could not forget that he had remained recreant to his baptismal vows, and crucified the Son of God afresh.

Zeisberger paid a short visit to the Connecticut settlers who lived in Wyoming, the first white men, other than Moravian missionaries, that there established themselves, and found several houses erected at the mouth of Mill Creek, others a short distance below the present site of Wilkesbarre.[1] It was a settlement which not only incensed the Indians and formed one of the causes of the Pontiac Conspiracy, but which gave rise to that disgraceful episode in Colonial history known as the Pennamite and Yankee War. Both Connecticut and Pennsylvania claimed Wyoming, so that, in course of time, settlers from these two Provinces were arrayed

---

[1] Pearce's Annals of Luzerne County.

one against the other with arms in their hands. This strife continued for thirty years. Zeisberger found only six colonists, but more were on their way, and, in the course of the year, their number increased to one hundred and seventeen souls.[1]

In the evening of the twenty-third of May, Zeisberger and his companion reached Machiwihilusing. Papunhank received them into his lodge. They were very tired, but found no time to rest. The Indians flocked together from every part of the village to hear the Gospel. On the next morning the work was resumed, and continued for three days with great power. A deep impression was made upon the hearts of the natives. Tears rolled down their cheeks, and their whole frames were convulsed with emotion as they listened to that Word which is "sharper than any two-edged sword, piercing even to the dividing asunder of soul and spirit, and of the joints and marrow, and is a discerner of the thoughts and intents of the heart."[2] Papunhank seemed to be moved even more than his former disciples. On one occasion, after an earnest discourse, Zeisberger turned to him and exclaimed, "Brother, what have you to say to this people?" "Nothing," he replied, with a subdued voice, "except that they shall listen to their new teachers." On another occasion he attempted to speak, but his feelings overcame him, and the words died away on his lips.

Toward evening of the twenty-sixth, having preached

---

[1] Pearce's Annals of Luzerne County.
[2] Hebrews, iv. 12.

by turns almost without interruption from early morning, Zeisberger and Anthony went back to Bethlehem with a message from the council of the town to the Board, asking that a resident teacher might be sent them and a Mission established.

The Board responded by appointing Zeisberger to undertake this work, who retraced his steps to Machiwihilusing in the second week of June. Nathaniel, a native assistant, accompanied him.[1]

At Wyoming, he heard of Pontiac's Conspiracy. The whole valley rang with the news, and the scattered Christian and friendly Indians were preparing to leave. The war had broken out in all its vengeful fury. While nature was robing the forests of the West in the green mantle of May, the savages had silently stolen through them, seized most of the forts unawares, and massacred the garrisons. Thus fell Sandusky, St. Joseph, Miami, Ouatanon, Venango, and Michilimackinac. Detroit, the most important post of all, the honor of taking which Pontiac had reserved for himself, remained, indeed, in the hands of the English, his plot having been betrayed to Major Gladwyn; but the fort was now regularly and closely besieged by seven hundred savages. In the course of June, Presque Isle capitulated, and Le Bœuf was deserted.

What wonder that the converts at Wyoming were alarmed! Zeisberger, however, considered the reports exaggerated; and proceeded on his way. Nor did he

---

[1] A Delaware from Tunkhannock, the brother of Anthony, baptized by Cammerhoff, May 17, 1749.

turn back when he met a canoe filled with Indians and settlers, who were fleeing to Shamokin, and who corroborated all that he had heard.

At Machiwihilusing he resumed his work with fervency and joy. He was in his element; preaching and instructing; teaching the Indians to sing Delaware hymns; calling them to repentance; and unfolding to their astonished minds free grace in Jesus Christ,—a doctrine so entirely different from the absurd and painful conditions of salvation which Papunhank had made known.

While so engaged, John Woolman, a Quaker evangelist, arrived. A council was called to receive him, and he spoke to the people at first by the mouth of an interpreter, but afterward feeling "his mind covered with the spirit of prayer," he expressed a wish that the interpreting should be omitted. Divine love was shed over the meeting; and when he left, he prayed that the "great work" which Zeisberger had undertaken might be crowned with success.[1]

Papunhank grew in grace and asked for baptism. Another convert did the same. Their repentance was thorough and agonizing. Papunhank's distress of mind, at last, became so great that he could neither sleep nor eat.

On the twenty-sixth of June, the whole town gathered to a solemn assembly. Zeisberger opened the service with a Delaware hymn. Then he preached upon the

---

[1] John Woolman, an article in the "Eclectic Review," republished in No. 29, vol. xvii. of "Friend's Review."

subject of baptism, and examined Papunhank concerning his faith, who added this voluntary confession: "The Saviour has made me feel my misery and utterly depraved state. I used to preach to you; I imagined myself a good man; I did not know that I was the greatest sinner among you all. Brothers, forgive and forget everything I have said and done." So speaking, he fell on his knees, and Zeisberger baptized him in the name of the Triune God. He was called John. This was the first prophet whom Zeisberger brought into the Church of Christ, and "he rejoiced more over this convert," says Heckewelder, "than he would have rejoiced had he inherited a kingdom." In the afternoon the other convert was baptized, and received the name of Peter. "Now my heart is light," he joyfully exclaimed; "before it was heavy, so heavy that I could scarcely endure it."

Strange sight! While the hatchets of Pontiac and his fierce warriors were reeking with the blood of the race that had invaded their hunting-grounds, and were ready to spread devastation and death throughout the Colonies, these Monseys were learning to know the true God and Jesus Christ His Son, shedding tears of repentance, blessing the white man who taught them the Gospel, and, instead of the war-song, singing hymns of praise to the Prince of Peace!

The next three days Zeisberger and Nathaniel spent at Tawandaemenk, ten miles from Tioga, where an awakening had taken place, and the word of God was received with the same avidity as at Machiwihilusing.

But this work could not continue. On the thirtieth of June, a runner arrived with a letter for Zeisberger from Bishop Seidel, detailing the massacres at the Western forts, and recalling him to Bethlehem. He reluctantly obeyed the summons. The prospect of establishing a Mission was bright. But it would have been foolhardiness to remain. Pontiac's spies were beginning to visit the town.

At Wyoming, Zeisberger lodged with the Connecticut settlers. They had, unhappily, determined to stay in the valley and brave the danger. On the tenth of July he reached Bethlehem.

CHAPTER XV.

THE PONTIAC WAR AND THE PAXTON INSURRECTION.—1763, 1764.

Indians devastate the frontiers.—Battle at Bloody Run.—Fort Pitt beleaguered.—Battle of Bushy Run.—Zeisberger at Christiansbrunn.—The animosity of the settlers and the danger of the Christian Indians.—The Governor promises protection.—Their badges.—Murder of some of the converts.—The murderers killed by the savages.—The Christian Indians threatened with extermination.—One of them arrested, on the charge of murder, and taken to Philadelphia.—Marshall negotiates with the government.—The converts disarmed and brought to Philadelphia.—Refused admittance to the barracks.—The mob.—Quartered on Province Island.—Massacre of the Conestoga Indians.—Excitement in Philadelphia.—The Presbyterians and the Quakers.—The Christian Indians sent to New York.—Ordered back by the Governor of that Province.—Return to Philadelphia and are quartered in the barracks.—The Paxton Insurrection.—Great sufferings of the converts by reason of sickness.—Their release at the close of the war.

About the time of Zeisberger's return, the war drew nearer to the settlements. While an army of savages, with unparalleled obstinacy, still continued the siege of Detroit, other bodies of them menaced the posts remaining in Pennsylvania, and numerous scalping-parties attacked the frontier inhabitants. Farms were laid waste, homesteads burned, defenseless women and children butchered. Hundreds of fugitives flocked to Carlisle, or sought refuge in the woods on both sides of the Susquehanna. All the horrors of the first Indian War were re-enacted.

Toward the end of July, Captain Dalzell, from For-

Niagara, succeeded in throwing reinforcements into Detroit; but, two nights later, attempting a sortie against the Indians, contrary to the convictions of Major Gladwyn, who had given a most reluctant consent, he suffered a total defeat at Parent's Creek, which after that took the expressive name of "Bloody Run." About the same time, a furious assault was made upon Fort Pitt, and kept up for five successive days. Whether the sorely-pressed garrison could have held out much longer is doubtful, had not Colonel Bouquet, with five hundred men, advanced to its relief from Carlisle. The savages left Fort Pitt, in order to intercept him, and attacked his army (August 5th) near Bushy Run, beyond Fort Ligonier. A hard-fought battle of two days ensued. Bouquet suffered severely, but at last defeated the Indians by a bold stratagem. This victory saved Fort Pitt, and gave new hopes to the bleeding Province of Pennsylvania.

Meanwhile Zeisberger had taken up his abode at Christiansbrunn, whence he was frequently sent to Wechquetank, as the messenger of the Mission Board. Both at this station and at Nain the Indians were in no little danger. Exasperated by the many and cruel massacres that occurred, the inhabitants of the frontier counties breathed vengeance against the "Moravian Indians," as the converts were called, whom they accused of being in league with the savages. Especial bitterness was manifested by the Scotch-Irish settlers, in whom the zeal of their forefathers had degenerated into fierce fanaticism upon the subject of the aborigines of

America. They professed to believe that the Indians were the Canaanites of the Western World; that God's command to Joshua, to utterly destroy these nations,[1] held good with regard to the savages also; that, therefore, the whole Indian race ought to be exterminated; and that the war then raging was a judgment from the Most High, because this had not been accomplished.

On the twenty-second of July, the converts sent an address to the Governor claiming his protection, which he promised them.[2] At the same time, as they would be liable to great danger from the scouting-parties it would be necessary for him to send out, he suggested to Squire Horsfield, that "some visible, apparent badge of distinction should be agreed on, by which they might be known to be friends."[3]

In accordance with this suggestion, Horsfield drew up eight articles, describing their appearance, regulating their conduct when meeting white men, and calling both upon soldiers and civilians, "not to upbraid these Indians with the acts of other Indians, not spitefully to treat them, not to threaten to shoot them." These articles, having been approved at Nain and Wechquetank, were communicated to the Governor, and made known among the settlers.

The description of the Christian Indians was as follows: "They are always clothed; they are never painted, and wear no feathers, but hats or caps; they

---

[1] Deut. vii. 2.   [2] Copy of the address. MS. B. A.
[3] Letter from Governor Hamilton to Horsfield. B. A.
[4] Diary of Wechquetank. MS. B. A.

let their hair grow naturally; they carry their guns on their shoulders, with the shaft upwards." The rule to be observed by them, when meeting a white man, was this: "They will call to him, salute him, and coming near will carry their guns either reversed or on the shoulder." "Lastly, they intend, when they go out hunting, to get a pass of Mr. Timothy Horsfield, if he be at home; or else of their ministers, Mr. John Jacob Schmick, at Nain, or Mr. Bernard Adam Grube, at Wechquetank."[1] That the Christian Indians meekly submitted to such restrictions, so galling to the pride of their race, is one of the many evidences of the great change wrought in them through the power of the Gospel.

For several weeks after the issuing of the articles, they remained undisturbed. But, in the night of the twentieth of August, an event occurred which was the beginning of their troubles. Zacharias, his wife and little child, and Zipora, all Christian Indians on their way to Long Island, a village on the Susquehanna,[2] were tranquilly sleeping in a barn, near the Buchcabuchka Creek, relying for protection upon Captain Jacob Wetterhold and his company, who happened to be quartered at the same place; when, suddenly, these very protectors, who had been drinking hard, fell upon and murdered

---

[1] Copy of articles. MS. B. A.
[2] Zacharias and his family had belonged to the Mission at Wechquetank, but had withdrawn from it and removed to Long Island. They were returning from a visit to Wechquetank, and had persuaded Zipora, a member of the Mission, to accompany them.

them all, not sparing even the mother and her child, although she kneeled at their feet, in an agony, and besought them to have mercy. That this base act would excite the vengeance of Zacharias's four brothers, who lived at Wechquetank, was the prevailing opinion. Hence the militia hastened to anticipate the expected retaliation, and three several parties appeared at Wechquetank, in order to destroy the village. It was with the utmost difficulty, only by appealing to the pledge of protection received from the government, and, at last, by threatening to report Captain Wetterhold to the Governor, his Commander-in-chief, that the missionaries averted an assault.[1]

But, although Wetterhold and his troops had nothing to fear from the Wechquetank Indians, other avengers were on their track. Early in the morning of the eighth of October, while the militia were encamped on John Stinton's farm, in the Irish settlement, the savages surprised them, killed Stinton and several of the soldiers, and mortally wounded Wetterhold, who died the next day. A storm of indignation swept over Northampton County. Many of its inhabitants, indeed, thought only of their own safety, and, excited by the most extravagant rumors, flocked to Bethlehem and to the Crown, a tavern on the south bank of the Lehigh, for protection.[2] But a body of militia hastened to Wechquetank to mas-

---

[1] Diary of Wechquetank. MS. B. A.
[2] Bethlehem Diary, Oct. 1762. This tavern stood east of the old Philadelphia road, not far from the depot of the North Pennsylvania Railroad.

sacre the whole congregation, and were prevented from carrying out their purpose only by the most earnest persuasions of Grube, who, at midnight of the day of the murder, had received an express from the Board, informing him of the catastrophe, and advising immediate measures for the safety of his people.

That the Wechquetank Indians were suspected of having committed the assault on the Irish settlement, or at least of having instigated it, was natural; that, however, they were innocent does not admit of a doubt, and is fully established by evidence both circumstantial and positive.[1]

---

[1] The author of the *History of the Conspiracy of Pontiac*, p. 422, says that the charges against the Moravian Indians of having taken part in the murders in Northampton County " were never fully confuted," and adds, that " it is highly probable that some of them were disposed to sympathize with their heathen countrymen." I am sorry that he has marred his interesting and valuable work by such an imputation upon the memory of the " Moravian Indians ;" and as this is a matter of importance, because it serves to illustrate the complete change produced in their hearts by the Gospel, I here give the proofs which establish their innocence.

1. All the records of the missionaries positively assert it, which these records would not do if they had been guilty; for, in a later period, when the Mission had been transferred to Ohio, such converts as took part in the wars are mentioned in the Diaries of the Missionaries, and were excluded from church-fellowship. 2. The peculiar discipline observed in all Moravian Indian congregations rendered it almost impossible for a convert to join a war-party without being detected; and this discipline in the Pontiac War was particularly strict, the missionaries at Nain and Wechquetank keeping an exact journal of where each convert spent every day and night. (Letter from Bishop Boehler to Governer Hamilton, B. A.) 3. The Wechquetank Indians, in July and August, 1763, twice actually prevented, of their own accord, attacks upon the settlements by persuading the warriors who stopped in their town to return to the West. 4. When the Indians were removed from Wech-

Grube and his converts now fled to Nazareth, leaving their village and stores of corn to the mercy of their enemies, who destroyed both. At Nazareth they were quartered in the Widows' House.[1] Thither Zeisberger proceeded and took charge of the converts; Grube, accompanied by Squire Horsfield, Schmick, and Marshall, having gone to Philadelphia in order to report to the Governor and deliver a letter from Bishop Boehler, urgently entreating his immediate aid.[2] Meantime Zeisberger and the Christian Indians encircled Nazareth with stockades, in the event of an assault on the part of the savages.[3]

The Nain Indians too were in trouble. An attack upon their town was averted by one of their nearest neighbors, who met the party that was advancing against it, and, upon his personal knowledge, testified to their peaceable disposition.[4] After that none of them ventured to leave the Mission-land, except in company of a white man. The intelligence, received about this time, of the massacre of the Connecticut settlers at

---

quetank, their *nearest* white neighbors, who certainly knew them well, petitioned the Governor to send them back, stating that these Indians were the best safeguard they could have against assaults of the savages. (Copy of this petition as delivered to Governor Hamilton by Mr. Frederick, the minister of these settlers. MS. B. A.) 5. The Indian who was afterward accused of having aided in the attack upon the Irish settlement, and who was arrested and tried at Easton, was declared "not guilty" by a jury of white men, who could not resist the mass of evidence brought in his favor in spite of the universal desire to see him condemned and executed. This alone is conclusive.

[1] Bethlehem Diary, Oct. 1763. This Widows' House is one of the log buildings at Ephrata, near Nazareth.
[2] Copy of the letter. B. A.   [3] Grube's Diary. MS. B. A.
[4] Bethlehem Diary, Oct. 1763. B. A.

Wyoming served but to increase the apprehensions of the converts and the excitement of the country. Three anxious weeks passed by. The Indians were in constant expectation of an assault; suspicion and distrust filled the minds of the settlers; the militia were hardly restrained from acts of violence.

[1]On the twenty-eighth of October, John Jennings, Esq., High Sheriff of Northampton County, appeared at Bethlehem with a warrant from Judge Coleman, of Philadelphia, authorizing him to arrest Renatus, a member of the Nain Mission, accused by John Stinton's widow, under oath, of having formed one of the scalping-party that had murdered her husband. Renatus was a Mohican, baptized on the twenty-eighth of September, 1749, at Gnadenhütten, by Bishop Cammerhoff.[2] His father, Jacob, the venerable patriarch of the Indian Mission, was the only survivor of the first three converts.

Jennings having made George Klein[3] deputy sheriff for the occasion, the latter arrested Renatus on the following day, and then appointed Schmick, a deputy under him, to take the prisoner to Philadelphia. His father accompanied him. The party traveled in a wagon with one Lisher as the driver, and was followed a few hours later by Marshall and Klein, the former empow-

---

[1] Journal of Frederick de Marshall, from October 28, 1763, to Jan. 18, 1764. MS. B. A. This is an invaluable MS. for a proper apprehension of this interesting period of the Indian Mission.

[2] Record of Baptisms.

[3] The original owner of the land on which Litiz is built, and which he gave to the Church.

ered to represent the Mission Board at the seat of government. Not only Renatus required the services of this Board, but the Christian Indians as a body. The accusation brought against the young Mohican inflamed the minds of the people to the highest pitch,—a crisis in the Indian Mission was come; energetic measures for its safety were immediately necessary, or else its destruction would be inevitable. To negotiate such measures with the government was the purpose of Marshall's visit.

Schmick and the two Indians arrived at Philadelphia toward evening of the thirtieth, just as the inhabitants were recovering from the consternation which a severe earthquake and a loud roaring noise had occasioned. In the midst of this affrighting phenomenon, John Penn, the new Governor of Pennsylvania, stepped ashore, at High Street wharf, from the vessel that had borne him across the Atlantic.[1] Marshall and Klein reached the city later in the evening.

Eventful scenes were about to transpire in Philadelphia. A drama was maturing, which had some comic features, but more that threatened to change it into a bloody tragedy. It will be proper, therefore, to introduce those residents who were its principal characters.

First among them must be mentioned the new Governor, a son of Richard and grandson of William Penn. Desirous to redeem the promises of his prede-

---

[1] Watson's Annals of Phila., ii. 413.

cessor, he manifested a becoming interest in the Christian Indians, but, at the same time, showed his inexperience in administering the affairs of government. Associated with him was ex-Governor Hamilton, who retained his seat in the Council,—a liberally-minded man, a friend of the aborigines, acknowledging the character and importance of the work the Moravians were doing among them. Exercising great influence in the Assembly, of which he was a member, we find Doctor Benjamin Franklin, the Postmaster-General of the British Colonies in America. He had visited Bethlehem, and was well acquainted with the Moravians and their missionary labors. Another prominent member in the Assembly was Joseph Galloway, a wealthy and eminent lawyer. He had no faith in the professions of the Christian Indians, and looked upon them with disfavor, until Papunhank and his tribe voluntarily surrendered themselves. Then his views changed.[1] Particularly active in upholding their cause were two leading members of the Society of Friends,—William Logan, who belonged to the Governor's Council, and Israel Pemberton, a benevolent philanthropist, who strove to carry out the ideas of William Penn, and to gain the affection of the aborigines, instead of subjugating them by force of arms. The whole Society approved of such a course, and lent its aid. Other

---

[1] In the Revolution, Galloway espoused the cause of the British. His estates were forfeited, in 1777, for treason, and sold only about twenty years ago. Durham Furnace was a part of them.

important characters were Joseph Fox, a Commissioner on the part of the Assembly, in charge of loans; Thomas Apty, appointed by the government to lead the Indians to New York; John Dickinson, a distinguished lawyer;[1] and especially Lewis Weiss, the Attorney of the Moravian Church.[2]

The day after his arrival, the last of October, Renatus was committed to the Stone Prison, at the southwest corner of Third and High Streets. The legal services of Dickinson were engaged; and Pemberton and Logan both promised to use their influence to secure him a fair trial. Not less obliging was Ex-Governor Hamilton, who assured Marshall, with much emotion, that it was his earnest wish to assist the converts and deliver them from further persecutions, requesting him to suggest whatever measures would, in his judgment, conduce to their safety. Marshall, aided by Lewis Weiss, drew up a plan, of which the principal points were the following: That the Christian Indians, until further orders, should remain on the Bethlehem and Nazareth lands, and not go beyond these, on pain of forfeiting the protection of government; that being thus deprived of the liberty of the chase, on which they chiefly depended for a subsistence, they should receive from government each a public allowance of 3$d.$ per diem;

When a member of Congress, he refused to sign the Declaration of Independence. Afterward he was President of the State. Dickinson College is named after him.

[2] He had a brother, Jacob, who subsequently lived at Gnadenhütten, now Weissport, where he died. The present town is named after him.

that two creditable persons of Northampton County should be appointed their Muster-Masters.¹

This plan William Logan laid before the Governor and Council; but, at the instigation of other parties, it was rejected, and, in place of it, a resolution adopted to disarm and remove the converts to Philadelphia, which project the Assembly sanctioned, with little dissent.

Hamilton had not been in Council when the removal of the Indians was decided upon; nor had his advice been asked. At this he took offense; and, for a time, showed no further interest in their cause.

Governor Penn's express to the Mission Board, with the decree of the Council and the Assembly, reached Bethlehem in the evening of the fifth of November, and Nazareth on the sixth. Although distressed at the thought of being shut up in the city, the converts obeyed the mandate; and when Sheriff Jennings came first to Nain, and then to Nazareth, to disarm them, they yielded up their rifles with astonishing readiness. This was again an evidence of the reality of their conversion. They had been warriors; they prized their weapons, the insignia of their freedom, as highly as did their wild fellow-Indians; they might have dispersed, and betaken themselves to the Western hunting-grounds, where the tribes would have received them with open arms; but they valued the Gospel more than their rifles, and loved the Saviour, whom they had found precious to their souls, more than liberty or life.²

---

¹ Draft of Plan. MS. B. A.
² The author of the *History of Pontiac's Conspiracy* fails, in his

On the eighth of November, the Indians from Nazareth arrived at Bethlehem; and, after a farewell discourse delivered in the church by Bishop Boehler, upon the words, "Make thy way straight before my face,"[1] proceeded to the south bank of the Lehigh. There they were joined by the Nain Indians, under Zeisberger and Roth. The inhabitants of the town came to see their departure, bringing gifts of blankets and clothing. During their absence, Nain was intrusted to a farmer, who lived there with his family. Their cattle were sold.

Headed[2] by the Sheriff, the procession moved about the middle of the afternoon. Eight wagons, each under the charge of a white man, bore the aged, the sick, the women and children, together with Mrs. Grube and Mrs. Roth; the men followed on foot, Zeisberger, Grube, and Roth among them, passing from rank to rank with words of encouragement and peace. The total number of Indians was one hundred and twenty-five. After a journey of but five miles, they spent the night on Stoffel Wagner's farm. The next morning, they pursued their way amid a pelting rain, and passed the second night at two adjacent taverns. Having hired an additional wagon, the journey was resumed. From nearly every hamlet came curses; almost every traveler

---

narrative of these events, to make this point. He says, page 424, that the Indians "reluctantly" yielded up their arms. This is a mere supposition. The diary of Grube states particularly that it was done with astonishing "patience and resignation."

[1] Psalm, v. 8.
[2] Grube's Journal. MS. B.A.

greeted them with imprecations. When they approached Germantown, the rabble of that whole neighborhood was roused, and angry threats were made to kill them. The Sheriff restrained the people with no little difficulty. Indeed, had not a heavy rain set in, and cooled their murderous desires, he would scarcely have succeeded in preventing an assault.

Meanwhile the Governor had designated the Philadelphia Barracks as the quarters of the refugees; and, at the instance of Marshall, appointed Joseph Fox, Esq., Commissary to provide for their wants.

The "British Barracks," as they were called, were erected soon after Braddock's defeat, and extended from Tammany to Green and from Third to Second Streets, in the form of a hollow square. On Second Street was situated the parade-ground; the three other sides of the square were lined with two-story brick houses, having inside porticoes along the entire length; the quarters of the officers were on Third Street, in a three-story building. At the time of our narrative several companies of Highlanders were quartered in these barracks.

On the morning of the eleventh, Marshall, Schmick, George Neisser,[1] and Commissary Fox, proceeded thither in order to receive the Indians. They arrived about half-past nine o'clock, and the first three wagons, filled with women and children, passed in at the gate. But suddenly the soldiers divined the meaning of this strange visit. Seizing their muskets, they rushed tumultuously

---

[1] The Pastor of the Moravian Church in Philadelphia.

together, stopped the rest of the wagons, and threatened to fire among the cowering women in the yard if they did not instantly leave. Persuasions and threats were of no avail; and Fox hurried off to report to the Governor.

Meanwhile a large crowd had assembled, which soon swelled into an excited mob. Second Street rang with shouts and yells fierce as the war-whoops of the savages; maledictions and revilements poured like a torrent upon the Indians; blood-thirsty menaces passed from mouth to mouth: "Shoot them! hang them! scalp the accursed red-skins!" The presence of the missionaries, and of clergymen like Marshall and Neisser, was no restraint upon the rabble, but inflamed them still more. Zeisberger and Grube, Schmick and Roth, Marshall and Neisser, were each and all denounced and execrated most violently. From ten o'clock until three in the afternoon the converts and their teachers "were made a gazing-stock, both by reproaches and afflictions," to this Philadelphia mob, and endured every abuse which wild frenzy or ribald vulgarity could clothe in words. But they were not left altogether without sympathizers. Many Quakers came braving the scorn of the rabble, took the Indians by the hand, and called them friends. Nor did the faith of the converts themselves fail. While the crowd maligned and threatened them, they talked together of Him whose name they bore. "Jesus was despised and rejected of men," they said; "what else can we expect? Jesus was buffeted and spit upon, yet He opened not His mouth; why should we not patiently bear these indignities?"

At last Commissary Fox returned, with some members of the Council, and proposed to convey the Indians to Province Island, the government being afraid to quell the mutiny by force. Surrounded by the mob, they proceeded down Second Street "like sheep among howling wolves," said the missionaries, to the outskirts of the city. There the mob dispersed, while they were brought to the ferry, and thence taken in flats to the Island.

Province Island constituted the summer-quarantine of the port of Philadelphia,[1] and the Indians, in charge of Grube and Zeisberger, occupied two large hospital-buildings. The first weeks of their sojourn were busy weeks for Zeisberger, who officiated as minister, acted as superintendent, and labored indefatigably as purveyor, Grube having been taken ill. The measures of the government for the support of the colony were, at first, wholly insufficient. For a day they had to subsist on a few fishes caught in the Delaware, and for four days there was no fuel other than some half-rotten stumps. Hastening, therefore, to the city, he made such representations as induced the Council to provide supplies. The religious services, usually held at the Mission, were all instituted.

Not long after the arrival of the converts on the Island, John Papunhank and his family, from Machiwihilusing, joined them, and subsequently, by invitation of the Governor, Job Chilloway and others from the

---

[1] Marshall's Journal.

same village, so that the number of the Indians increased to one hundred and forty persons.

In December, Zeisberger returned to Bethlehem, and Schmick took his place. He left the Indians with the best hopes. They had a comfortable, although novel, winter home, and a safe retreat from their adversaries.

But these hopes were destined to be disappointed. Not far from Lancaster, on a tract known as the Manor of Conestoga, lived a small clan of twenty Indians, friendly to the English, as had been their fathers in the times of William Penn, semi-civilized,—a poor, squalid, inoffensive band. Not so thought the Scotch-Irish settlers of Paxton and other neighboring villages. Armed savages, it was said, were harbored in their cabins. On the fourteenth of December, Matthew Smith put himself at the head of fifty men, fell upon the hamlet, burned it to the ground, and killed six of the Indians. The remaining fourteen happened to be absent. They were hastily collected by the Sheriff of the county and lodged in the Lancaster jail. But, on the twenty-seventh, the same party galloped into town, burst open the prison-doors, and massacred every Indian, sparing neither woman nor child.

The news of these disgraceful proceedings caused intense excitement in Philadelphia, which increased still more when a rumor spread that the rioters were marching to the city in order to exterminate the Indians on Province Island. Even the Governor and his Council were alarmed, and, in the night of the twenty-ninth, ordered three flats and three boats to the Island, so that the converts could escape, "till more effectual measures should be fallen on for their protection."[1] On the thirty-first, intelligence having been sent them that the insurgents were near Philadelphia, they fled to League Island. But it proved to be a false report, and they returned to their quarters, closing the year with midnight hymns of praise to God, the strains of which were borne far down the silent Delaware.

The efforts of the government to arrest the murderers of the Conestoga Indians were unsuccessful, in spite of two proclamations, and a reward offered of two hundred pounds sterling. This apathy had its cause. Not only animosity against the Indians, without discrimination, was on the increase in the border counties, but also a general dissatisfaction with the government. The people complained that their interests were neglected; that there existed more sympathy at Philadelphia for the savages than for themselves and their families; that they were made a barrier behind which the interior settlements enjoyed peace, "ate, drank, and were merry," while they "braved the summer's heat, and the winter's cold, and the savage tomahawk."[2] Such indifference was ascribed to the influence of the Quakers and of their non-resistant principles. The Quakers, it was said, swayed the Assembly, and otherwise had an undue preponderance in the administration of the government. Against them, therefore, the anger of the inhabitants

---

[1] Col. Records of Penn., ix. 100.
[2] Lazarus Stewart's "Declaration."

of the frontier counties was inflamed almost as hotly as against the Indians. The Scotch-Irish settlers, especially, berated the whole Society of Friends in unmeasured terms. Excitement and fanaticism led them too far, making them unjust to the Quakers and cruel to the Indians; but many of their complaints were reasonable and founded in fact. The border had been neglected by the government. This was the opinion even of the principal magistrates of those counties.

Rumors and alarms ushered in the year 1764. On the twenty-ninth of December, Bishop Hehl, of Litiz, had sent an express to Bethlehem with a letter detailing the slaughter of the Conestoga Indians, and announcing that the rioters were about to move to Philadelphia.[1] This express reached Bethlehem on the thirty-first. The Mission Board, having delivered the converts into the keeping of the government, could only urge it to redeem its promises. To this end, Zeisberger and Horsfield were sent to Philadelphia as additional envoys.

Meantime the Quakers had devised a new project. Nantucket Island, belonging to Massachusetts, was peopled mostly by persons of their persuasion, among whom the Indians would find a shelter. Israel Pemberton accordingly proposed to Marshall that they

---

[1] Original MS. letter B. A. This letter states that on the evening of the day of the massacre a party of the rioters, on their return, passed through Litiz, along the present turnpike street, cursing the Moravians in chorus; and having crossed the stream which runs from the Litiz Spring, halted and fired repeated volleys in order to alarm the inhabitants.

should be conveyed thither.¹ Marshall dispatched Zeisberger to Province Island with this offer, which was, however, declined.

At the instance of Galloway, Cornelius Sturgis and Nicholas Garrison, Jr., were sent to Lancaster County as scouts; while Governor Penn wrote to General Gage, the new commander-in-chief, requesting him to put at his disposal three companies of regulars quartered at Carlisle;² and the Assembly considered and rejected a wild scheme which had been concocted, to convey the Indians to England.³

Garrison having reported that the insurgents might soon be expected, and that the popular voice in the frontier counties was in their favor, which was corroborated by other scouts, the Governor transmitted an urgent message to the Assembly, and Lewis Weiss a petition, both asking for immediate action. In response, the Assembly voted (January 4th) one thousand pounds sterling, to be used in protecting the Christian Indians in any way the Governor might deem proper.⁴ The Governor, by the advice of his Council, determined to send them to Sir William Johnson, under escort of Captain Robinson's Highlanders, and to apply this grant to the expenses of their removal. However good such a project, and however much in accordance with the wishes of the converts, its execution was strangely hurried and mismanaged; proving the trepidation of

---

[1] Marshall's Journal.   [2] Penn. Col. Records, ix. 104, 105.
[3] Votes of the Assembly, v. 293.   [4] Penn. Col. Records, ix. 108, 109.

the government. Without consulting the Governor of New York, or waiting to ascertain whether Johnson was willing to receive them, an order for their instant departure was issued.

This order Zeisberger brought to Province Island toward evening of the same day. He found the Indians assembled at worship, but they joyfully prepared for their journey. It was arranged that they should leave the Island in the night, at a preconcerted signal to be displayed from Jacob Weiss' farm, which seems to have been on the opposite bank of the river. At two o'clock in the morning of the fifth the signal was given, and they came over in flats. Lewis and Jacob Weiss received them, and led them through the city to the Moravian church on Race Street, which they reached, unobserved, at half-past five o'clock. There a breakfast had been prepared, to which they sat down girded for the journey. "It seemed like the passover-supper in Egypt," says Marshall. Commissary Fox looked on with emotion, and distributed blankets among them.

Meanwhile five large wagons drew up before the church. This excited the attention of the neighbors, who flocked together in large numbers. At half-past six o'clock the church-door opened, and, to the amazement of the people, there came forth the entire body of "Moravian Indians," followed by Zeisberger, Schmick, Grube, and Mrs. Grube, by Joseph Fox, Thomas Apty, and William Logan. A few miles beyond Philadelphia, they were joined by Captain Robinson and seventy Highlanders.

They spent the first night at Bristol, and the second in the barracks at Trenton. Here Fox and Logan took leave of them, the latter delivering a message to the Six Nations, explanatory of the massacre of the Conestoga Indians, and sending them "twenty-one black stroud matchcoats" for the relatives of the deceased, that they might "cover their graves," and "twenty-one handkerchiefs to wipe the tears from their own eyes."[1]

Apty now assumed command, and led the Indians to Princeton, where they bivouacked on Justice Lennert's plantation. On the ninth of January they reached Amboy, whence they were to sail, in two sloops, to New York. But, on the eve of embarking, an express arrived with a letter from Governor Colden to Apty forbidding them to enter his Province, and another from General Gage to Captain Robinson ordering him to prevent their advance. The reasons which Colden subsequently assigned for this course were the following:[2] That his Council unanimously disapproved of receiving the Indians, whom the government of New York was "rather disposed to attack and punish, than to support and protect;" that the Indians on the east side of the Susquehanna were the most obnoxious to the people of New York of any, having done most mischief, and consisting of a number of rogues and thieves, runaways from other nations, and for that reason not to be trusted; that the government of

---

[1] Copy of the speech and message. MS. B. A.
[2] Letter from Colden to Gov. Penn. Penn. Col. Records, ix. 120–122.

Pennsylvania ought first to have consulted the government of New York before sending on so large a body of natives. All this was the necessary result of the precipitancy with which Governor Penn had acted.

While Apty sent an express to Philadelphia, and another to Governor Franklin, of New Jersey, for instructions, the Indians spent eight days in the barracks of Amboy, holding their religious services as usual, which were attended by many visitors, upon whom their singing made a deep impression. Indeed, this whole unprecedented pilgrimage of nearly three weeks, undertaken by the Indian Mission and its teachers, through one of the most thickly populated parts of the country, seems to have been permitted by God, in order to establish the glory of His Gospel. The bearing of the converts was so extraordinary, so humble, and yet manly, so clearly the result of the Christian faith which they professed, that the reviler forgot his revilements, and the scoffer looked on amazed. Even their escorts of soldiers, among whom were such as had been at Detroit during the siege and hated Indians with all the bitterness of their past experience, began to show them respect.

Governor Penn remanded the converts to Philadelphia. In a message to the Assembly, he said:[1] "I am heartily disposed to do everything in my power to afford these poor creatures that protection and security

---

[1] Penn. Col. Records, ix. 122.

which, under their circumstances, they have an undoubted right to expect and claim from us, and shall be glad of your opinion and advice in what manner this can most effectually be done." To these sentiments the Assembly replied by advising the Governor to carry out his intentions, if necessary, by "an armed force," adding: "It will be with the utmost regret we shall see your Honor reduced to the necessity of pursuing these measures; but, with an abhorrence altogether inexpressible, we should behold 'these poor creatures,' who, desirous of living in friendship with us, as proofs of this disposition, quitting a settlement that made them suspected, and surrendering their arms, have delivered themselves, their wives and children, into our power, on the faith of this Province, barbarously butchered by a set of ruffians whose audacious cruelty is checked by no sentiment of humanity and by no regard to the laws of their country."[1]

Robinson and his command having gone on to New York, General Gage sent a guard of one hundred Royal Americans under Captain Schlosser as their escort. On the eighteenth of January they left Amboy, and reached Philadelphia in the afternoon of the twenty-fourth, amid a heavy snow-storm, entering the barracks without opposition.

Three days later Zeisberger returned to Bethlehem. While recording the faith of these converts, we must not forget the tribute of praise that is due to their

---

[1] Penn. Col. Records, ix. 122-125.

teachers. It was no ordinary heroism that induced Zeisberger and his brethren, and especially frail women like Mrs. Grube and Mrs. Schmick, to stand by them amid all these experiences, braving a tempest of ridicule and reproach and the storms of one of the severest winters.

The return of the Indians was the signal for renewed disturbances in the frontier counties. The people met at taverns and other gathering-places to hear the news and recount their grievances. Self-constituted orators harangued them and advised everything that fanaticism against the aborigines, hatred of the Quakers, and dissatisfaction with the government could suggest. Toward the end of January, a body of insurgents, variously estimated at from five hundred to fifteen hundred men, with Matthew Smith as a prominent leader, advanced toward Philadelphia, avowing their purpose to be the extermination of the "Moravian Indians" and the overthrow of that Quaker party which was said to control the government.

In the beginning of February intelligence of this movement reached the city. Popular sentiment was divided. Many respectable persons sympathized with the rioters, although they did not approve of their deeds of blood, and censured the course of the government; others, among whom were the Quakers and nearly all the men of wealth and influence, held that the government must, at all hazards, redeem its pledge to the Indians and support the authority of the laws. Between the Presbyterians and the Society of Friends there prevailed such bitterness of feeling that anonymous advertisements appeared, offering a reward of three hundred pounds for the scalps of certain prominent Quakers.

The drama opened, on the second of February, with a message from the Governor to the Assembly, asking that the English Riot Act be extended to the Province. This was done by a decided vote.[1] In the forenoon of the fourth the Governor and Council devised means of defense. The Indians were removed to the second story of the barracks; eight cannon were planted, a stockade was erected in the middle of the yard, and Captain Schlosser received written instructions "to defend the Indians to the utmost of his power, by opposing, with the detachment of the king's troops under his command, any attempt to destroy them, the Riot Act being first read by a proper civil officer."[2] In the afternoon a general town-meeting was called at the State House. Governor Penn, Ex-Governor Hamilton, the Council, Benjamin Franklin, and many members of the Assembly were present. The Riot Act having been communicated, Benjamin Chew, a councilman, addressed the meeting. He explained the posture of affairs, appealing to the citizens to uphold the laws and sustain the government; he showed that this was not the time to determine whether it had or had not done right in receiving the Indians, but that these must now be protected, since the sacred faith of Pennsylvania had been plighted

---

[1] Penn. Col. Records, ix. 129, 131, 132.
[2] Penn. Col. Records, ix. 132.

to them; he read a letter from Sir William Johnson, saying that, in the event of the massacre of these Indians, peace with the Western nations would be impossible; and finally, there being no militia-law, he called for volunteers. About five hundred persons enrolled their names, and were formed into companies, six of which were of infantry, one of artillery, and two of horse. After the meeting the Governor dispatched some of them to hold the ferries across the Schuylkill River, and then proceeded to the barracks, where he passed the night. At midnight he visited the Indians, and assured them of his protection.

The next day was Sunday, and the city remained comparatively quiet, except at the barracks, where preparations for defense were continued, many idlers looking on and trying to get a sight of the Indians. These met for the worship of God, as usual, and then received visits from several council- and assemblymen, who told them that they would be shielded whatever might happen. Israel Pemberton stayed with them through the night, and a guard of volunteers joined the regulars. At eleven o'clock the Governor received intelligence that the insurgents were approaching in two bodies on the Reading and the Lancaster roads. The Council was immediately convened; it sat until one o'clock of Monday morning, and then ordered a general alarm. In accordance with preconcerted arrangements, one of the field-pieces at the barracks was discharged, the drums beat, the bells were rung, candles were placed in the windows of the houses, and the volunteers hurried to the State House to receive their arms. Soon a confused mass of people filled the streets, especially in the neighborhood of the barracks, many of them very much excited, and many thoroughly frightened. The rabble shouted exultingly; the friends of the insurgents quietly enjoyed the prevailing alarm; the Germans gathered around the Moravian church on Race Street, and vented their spleen by cursing, in their deep vernacular, Moravians in general, and Moravian Indians in particular; a number of young Quakers astonished the multitude by seizing muskets and joining the volunteers, so that by daybreak six hundred men were under arms; while the soldiers at the barracks, full of zeal and courage, almost fired into a company of mounted butchers, who were coming up Second Street to aid in the defense of the city. Franklin and Hamilton were at the State House directing the troops, Governor Penn having been taken ill, so that he was obliged to retire to a neighboring house on Market Street.[1] Meanwhile the Indians, the cause of all this commotion, were asleep.

By this time the vanguard of the insurgents, composed of two hundred men and led by Matthew Smith, had crossed the Schuylkill at Swedes' Ford, which had remained unguarded, and had proceeded to Germantown. The measures taken for their reception, however, prevented their advancing to the city, so that the night of Monday passed without any fresh dis-

---

[1] Neisser's Letter to Marshall. MS. B. A. Another account says that he fled to Franklin's residence from fear of the mob.

turbances. But early on Tuesday morning another general alarm was sounded. Again the volunteers rushed to arms, and were clamorous for an assault. Instead of acceding to this wish, the Governor, in spite of the protestations of many citizens, sent Benjamin Franklin and several other commissioners to negotiate with the insurgents and persuade them to disperse. They gave these commissioners a respectful hearing, stated their grievances, appointed Smith and James Gibson to set them forth in writing, and, finally, asserted that among the Christian Indians were several notorious murderers, whom they pledged themselves to identify. Franklin promised them redress for their grievances, and gave them permission to send some of their party, unarmed, to the city, in order to point out the alleged murderers. Upon this they agreed to return to their homes.

But on the following morning a third alarm was raised. Four hundred men, it was said, were approaching the city. This thoroughly roused the people, and nearly one thousand of them marched forth to meet— forty frontiersmen peacefully riding to Philadelphia, as agreed upon with Franklin. Turning back, in no very placid mood, the volunteers were dismissed at the State House with the thanks of the government. The city, which for days had been a military camp, resumed its wonted appearance; shops were reopened, and business was transacted as usual.[1]

---

[1] Besides the Penn. Col. Records already cited, the following are my authorities for the narrative I have given: Marshall's Journal, MS.

The next day, Huse, one of the commissioners who had been sent to Germantown, brought to the barracks that insurgent who was pledged to identify the murderers. The Indians were mustered, but he confessed that he did not recognize a single one.[1]

Such was the serio-comic drama of the Paxton Insurrection. There followed an afterpiece less perilous but not less interesting. Smith and Gibson drew up two papers, called a *Declaration* and *Remonstrance*, addressed to the Governor and the Assembly, rehearsing the grievances of the frontier inhabitants, attacking the Quakers, and containing flagrant falsehoods concerning the Christian Indians.[2] Of these papers the Moravians took no notice; but the Quakers issued an address, in which they defended themselves against the aspersions of the borderers.[3] Thereupon the press began to teem with pamphlets, farces, dialogues, and poems. The scurrility of some of these publications is unprecedented.

At this late day it is not hard to form an impartial opinion of the Paxton Insurrection. While the bloodthirstiness of the insurgents deserves to be condemned,

---

B. A.; Grube's Diary, MS. B. A.; The Pennsylvania Gazette of February 9, 1764, preserved in the B. A.; The New York Gazette of March 5, 1764, containing a letter from an eye-witness describing the insurrection; and especially a MS. letter in the B. A. from the Rev. George Neisser to Marshall, dated Feb. 6, 1764, giving a full account of all that transpired in the city up to that date.

[1] The report which spread after this visit, that the Quakers had secreted the guilty Indians, is so evidently a fabrication, owing its origin to the chagrin of the Paxton party, that it needs no refutation.

[2] The N. Y. Gazette of March 5, 1764.

[3] The Penn. Gazette of March 1, 1764.

their sentiments and those of their fellow-frontiersmen, with regard to the Indians, are explained by the atrocities of the savages and their own indescribable sufferings. The great error into which they fell was inability, or unwillingness, to make a distinction between Pontiac's cruel warriors, and God's converted children, who, for the sake of Jesus Christ, had given up all that an Indian prizes.[1] A century has elapsed since the Pontiac Conspiracy, and, while we write, an Indian war is raging in Minnesota,[2] where the enormities of the savages are so great that many voices, and among them those of worthy citizens, are heard, as of old, demanding the extirpation of the aborigines as a race. This was the feeling which actuated the frontiersmen of Pennsylvania in 1763.

After the disturbances caused by the Paxton party were over, the Christian Indians became the object of general curiosity, so that the barracks were often crowded with visitors. On the twenty-fifth of February they celebrated the Holy Communion, for the first time since their departure from Nain and Wechquetank. Their hymns of praise swelled triumphantly through the building.

In March, Zeisberger again joined them, as they expected to go to New York, whither both their friends and foes were anxious that they should be

---

[1] A wholly one-sided article upon the Paxton Insurrection in the *Presbyterian Quarterly Review* of April, 1860, fails to make the same distinction.

[2] The above was written in 1863.

sent.[1] To this end the Governor had dispatched Thomas Apty to Sir William Johnson, who expressed his willingness to receive them. But Colden and his Council again interfered, declining to allow them to pass through New York. General Gage was also opposed to their removal.[2] They now begged Governor Penn to have them conveyed to the Pennsylvania frontier, where they would care for themselves. But to this he could not consent, as long as the war lasted. His refusal was a sore trial. Many began to lose heart; some were almost in despair. They sighed for their forests, for the liberty of the chase, for that way of living which was essential to their happiness. It was worse than death to be immured in the British barracks. To add to their afflictions, the dysentery and the small-pox broke out. Zeisberger spent two months in Philadelphia, helping Grube and Schmick to cheer them. But it was a hard task, as the journals of the missionaries show. Men of less devotedness and faith would have given up the cause as hopeless. Not less than fifty-six of the converts died in the course of the summer and autumn.

Among these was old Jacob and his daughter-in-law, the wife of Renatus. The latter was still in prison; but, soon after this, his trial took place at Easton, and he was fully acquitted.

Toward the end of September (1763) the savages

---

[1] MS. letter from Lewis Weiss to Marshall, March 2, 1764. B. A.
[2] Penn. Archives, iv. 165, 167, 168. Col. Records, ix. 170, 171.

raised the siege of Detroit, and Gladwyn concluded a truce with several of their tribes. A month later, the French commandant at Fort Chartres, which post had not yet been delivered to the English, sent a letter, by request of General Amherst, to the Indians around Detroit, assuring them that their expectations of aid from France were vain. This served to cool their ardor; and, in the following spring, when they heard of the formidable expeditions which were being organized for their subjugation, they lost heart entirely. One of these expeditions, under Colonel Bradstreet, proceeded to Detroit, where the Indians hastened to sue for peace, which was concluded in September, and embraced Pontiac, although he was not present. The other, under Colonel Bouquet, penetrated the Delaware country as far as the Muskingum, and forced this nation, as well as the Shawanese, to lay down the hatchet and give up their prisoners. The Pontiac War was at an end.

On the sixth of December, Governor Penn issued a proclamation announcing this auspicious event. The way to their own country was now open to the Christian Indians. On the twentieth of March, 1765, they left the British barracks, after having passed one year and four months in Philadelphia, and after having borne nearly one-half of their number to potter's-field.

CHAPTER XVI.

ZEISBERGER AT FRIEDENSHÜTTEN.—1765-1766.

The Christian Indians return to Nain and remove to Machiwihilusing on the Susquehanna.—Zeisberger appointed resident missionary.—Instructions of the Board.—Distressing journey across the Broad Mountain and through the Great Swamp.—A forest on fire.—A new town is built at Machiwihilusing.—Happiness of the converts.—Illness of Zeisberger.—Grant of flour and blankets.—A revival begins.—The Gospel made known among many tribes through the agency of the Mission.—Zeisberger's account of the revival.—Nitschmann "the Syndic" at Bethlehem.—The Iroquois deputy at Cayuga Town forbids the Christian Indians to remain on the Susquehanna.—Newallike, the Delaware —A deputation, led by Zeisberger, visits Cayuga Town.—Grant of land to the Christian Indians.—They enlarge their town and introduce municipal regulations.—The Christian Indians send a belt of wampum to the General Board of the Moravian Church in Europe.—Their town named Friedenshütten.—Its size and population.—Zeisberger recalled from Friedenshütten.—His last visit to Onondaga.—The Iroquois Mission abandoned by the Moravians.

ON the twenty-second of March the Indians returned to Nain, and its empty houses and deserted square once more and for the last time saw the life of a settlement of Christian natives. But it was not the life of former days. Eighty-three persons constituted the entire body of converts, and, with the exception of a handful at Pachgatgoch, the whole remnant of the once flourishing Mission. Nor could the survivors remain at Nain. The settlers were still too much excited by the events of the war to permit an Indian town in the midst of their farms. There would be, moreover, no opportunity of making it the center of new enterprises among heathen tribes.

Influenced by such considerations, and following a suggestion of the converts themselves, the Mission Board resolved to place them at Machiwihilusing, where lay hunting-grounds in their original wildness, and several tracts already cleared. Zeisberger was appointed resident missionary, and Schmick his assistant on the journey. They received written instructions in substance as follows: [1]It shall be the duty of the missionaries to study the Indian languages; to train native assistants; to teach the Indians to read and write; to translate into Delaware all the most important parts of the Bible, and as many hymns as possible; to instill principles of peace into the hearts of their converts, so that in the event of another war they may conduct themselves as children of peace, and in the event of persecutions, may forgive their enemies, and leave their cause to the Judge of all the earth, who will do right; to educate the congregation in the idea that whatever nationalities it represents and tribal distinctions it embraces, the Christian Indians are all one in the Lord Jesus Christ.

The houses of Nain having been sold at public auction[2] and a farewell-service held, that seat of native cul-

---

[1] Original Instructions. MS. B. A.

[2] They were bought by inhabitants of Bethlehem, and six of them, among these the chapel, removed to that town (Bethlehem Diary, 1765, MS. B. A.), where one of them remains. The land at Nain was put in charge of a tenant.

ture was deserted (April 3), and, like so many other similar places, thereafter never again known as a Christian village. Ere long the plowshare upturned its site.

Escorted by Thomas Apty, the Commissary of the government, Sheriff Kichline, Justice Moore, and Lieutenant Hundsecker, and led by Zeisberger, the Indians proceeded to the Rose Tavern,[1] where Marshall welcomed them, and whither many of their brethren "after the common faith," from Nazareth and Christiansbrunn, came to wish them God-speed. The evening saw them encamped at the foot of the Blue Mountains, and the next day they built a little hamlet of bark-huts on the desolate site of Wechquetank and amid its cheerless ruins. There they spent the Holy Passion-week, and engaged in all its services.

On the eleventh of April their journey was resumed. In order to open a new and direct trail from the Susquehanna to the settlements, they crossed the steep ridges of Monroe County, climbed the Broad Mountain, and traversed the Great Swamp, cutting a road through forests and tangled underwood, bridging creeks, and laying tree-trunks over deep sloughs. But the hardships of this undertaking were almost too severe even for the natives. Unable to advance more than five miles a day, two long and distressing weeks were spent in such work, and, suffering painfully from hunger, much time

---

[1] A house of entertainment built by and belonging to the Moravians, about one mile to the northeast of Nazareth. The Colonial Governors of Pennsylvania often stopped there when they were out grouse shooting. The old building was torn down only a few years ago.

was lost in hunting. On one occasion their want of food was so great, and the cry of famished women and children so heart-rending, that, while some of the most expert hunters went out just before dark to shoot game, Zeisberger and Schmick betook themselves to prayer. Their intercessions were answered. The hunters came back with six deer.

At another time they were delivered from a different but not less fearful peril. The congregation, encamped in a thick wood, lay sleeping. Suddenly the sentinels were startled by a loud, crackling noise. They knew what it portended, and gave the alarm. The wood was wrapped in a blazing sheet of fire. Gathering the women and children to the center of the camp, and bringing in the horses, the Indians encircled it, and kindled a counter-fire. It soon spread among the pine-trees; a second volume of flames, with fiery strides, leaped roaring to meet the first. The sight was grand but terrific. Night was transformed into day. For three hours this conflagration raged, sweeping down the tallest trees, devouring the forest with insatiable fury, and covering the firmament with a pall of smoke. The following day they reached the Susquehanna, ten miles above Wyoming, and, borrowing canoes of the natives, arrived at Machiwihilusing a fortnight later (May 9). Their journey from Nain had occupied five weeks.

A three days' hunt was first undertaken, and crowned with great success. Meanwhile Zeisberger, Schmick, and Papunhank, selecting the site of the old village, laid out a town, and staked off plantations. A message was sent to Togahaju, the Iroquois sachem at Cayuga Town, who ruled this part of the Delaware dependencies of the League, asking his permission to begin a settlement.

Delivered from the restraints of that city which had been to them a prison-house; at home again in the forests of their fathers' hunting-grounds, in the canoes that glided over the familiar waters of the Susquehanna, in the cornfields where many of their women had been accustomed to labor, the converts were filled with gratitude and joy. The stoical indifference into which even a Christian Indian relapses had disappeared; they were all rejuvenated. Here were men laboring with the energy of civilization, there women and children eager to do their part. The new town which came into existence rang with the melody of praise even while it was being built. In every place the feelings of the people burst into song. And when they went out to the chase, or fished in the river; when they roamed through the woods gathering roots and herbs; the game that they found, the fishes that they caught, and everything that grew upon the ground, seemed given to them by a special act of Providence.[1] "Behold," said Zeisberger, as he saw this general happiness, and heard some of his own Delaware hymns echoing through the forest, "this is making good use of their liberty! Beginning their work in this way, God will richly bless

---

[1] Heckewelder's MS. Biographical Sketch.

them. Under such circumstances it is joy to be among the Indians."[1]

Soon after this, Zeisberger was prostrated with sickness, induced by the unusual fatigues of the journey from Nain, and was obliged to intrust the Mission to young Heckewelder, whom the Board had sent to his relief. In summer, however, his health improved so much that he led the Indians to Nazareth and Christiansbrunn, where a liberal grant of flour from the Colonial government, and a lot of blankets from the Moravians of Germany, were distributed.

But God had in store for them a better benefaction. In October, the first baptism took place, and proved to be the beginning of a great revival. Not a few were converted. Upon wild Indians, in particular, descended the power of the Holy Ghost. They came from far and near, and represented different nations. Mohawks and Cayugas, Senecas and Onondagas, Mohicans and Wampanoags, Delawares and Tutelas, Tuscaroras and Nanticokes—these all heard the Word of Salvation. Many went their way believing, and scattered among their own tribes the seed of truth.

This feature of the Mission is apt to be overlooked. Statistical tables are counted the law of success. But, however correct this may in general be, success was conditioned, in the case of the aborigines of our country, not alone by the number actually added to the Church through baptism. The impression made upon indi-

---

[1] Heckewelder's MS. Biographical Sketch.

viduals who never built themselves lodges in Christian villages; the impulse which visiting warriors received to aims higher and holier than those of barbarism; above all, the ray of light from the Cross streaming into their souls as they sat in some forest-sanctuary, or stood in the shade of a tree beneath which a traveling missionary had stopped to proclaim Christ—a light, perhaps, never quenched, but, intensified through the spirit of God, showing grace, forgiveness, and heaven—this, too, must be taken into account. Many a death-bed, at which no evangelist ever prayed, may thus have been cheered by the presence of the Christian's hope; many a wigwam, never visited by a messenger of peace, may thus have become a home of peace.

The correctness of these positions will be established by the further narrative of Zeisberger's labors. His own testimony to the efficacy of the influences exerted in this respect by the present revival is important. "For several months," he writes to the Board, "a great revival has been prevailing among the wild Indians who visit here. All those who attend our services are deeply impressed, and cannot hear too much of the Saviour. It often happens, while I preach, that the power of the Gospel takes such hold of them that they tremble with emotion and shake with fear, until consciousness is nearly gone and they seem to be on the point of fainting. This shows with what violence the principalities in them oppose the Word of the Cross. As soon as such a paroxysm is over, they generally begin to weep silent tears. We have many candidates for baptism.

Anthony, who enjoys the particular esteem of the Indians, sets forth the Saviour with such feeling that not unfrequently his auditors all burst into tears, and he is constrained to weep with them."[1]

No one rejoiced more sincerely over news like this than David Nitschmann, " the Syndic," who had reached America on an official visit.[2] Zeisberger, who happened to be at Bethlehem when he arrived, found in him a countryman and a friend,—one of those five young Moravians who came to Herrnhut, exiles for conscience' sake, just as Count Zinzendorf, surrounded by the little band of fugitives who had preceded them, was on the point of laying the corner-stone for the first house of worship in that infant settlement, and in time to hear the memorable prayer of his coadjutor, Baron de Watteville, which foretold the resuscitation of the Church and her future missionary labors.

The embassy sent to Togahaju in the summer of 1765 had not been successful. He refused to permit the converts to build a town at Machiwihilusing, because it "was stained with blood," but invited them to settle at the head of Lake Cayuga. The deputies

---

[1] Copy of letter, dated Jan. 20, 1766, in Bethlehem Diary of Jan. 1766. MS. B. A.

[2] A member of the Executive Board in Europe. He arrived at Bethlehem Nov. 28, 1765. His title "Syndic" referred to the office he filled in the time of Count Zinzendorf, when he negotiated, as the representative of the Church, with various European governments. Besides itinerating in Germany, he visited Denmark, England, Russia, Switzerland, North America, the Cape of Good Hope, and the Island of Ceylon. After his return from America he became the Archivist of the Unitas Fratrum, and died at Zeist, in Holland, in 1779.

promised to lay his decision before their people, and to send an answer "when the corn would be ripe." Unfortunately, however, they failed to do this. And now the sachem dispatched a runner to the Susquehanna with the following message: "Cousins! What kind of corn have you at Machiwihilusing? You promised an answer to my proposition when your corn would be ripe. My corn has been ripe long ago. It is nearly consumed. I think of soon planting again. Why do you not fulfill your promise?"

This caused great consternation at the Mission. The authority of Togahaju was so great, and the fear which the Iroquois League inspired so general, that the Christian Indians deemed it necessary to conciliate the sachem by every proper means within their reach. Hence they applied to Newallike, an influential chief of the Delawares, at Wechpakak, on the Tunkhannock, to plead their cause, but he ungraciously refused. Thereupon Zeisberger offered to negotiate with Togahaju, and persuaded them to elect four of their number as his assistants. This embassy proceeded to Cayuga Town, where the sachem and his council received them. For the converts it was an august assembly, which they entered with awe. Encouraged by the words and presence of Zeisberger, however, they soon regained their self-possession, and delivered a succession of speeches, which he interpreted, setting forth the necessities and wishes of the Mission, as well as the advantages which Machiwihilusing offered, with such sagacity and eloquence that they gained their point. Zeisberger, too, addressed the council, and spoke as an adopted Iroquois, who had a claim on the liberality of the League. The result was a formal grant of land at Machiwihilusing, extending along the river " as far as a man can walk in two days."

Upon the return of the embassy, the town was enlarged, and a code of municipal laws adopted. Traders were forbidden to stay more than two or three days at a time; and such heathen Indians as came merely to enjoy the outward advantages of the settlement, and not to hear the Gospel, were no longer allowed to build lodges. A Synod, held at Bethlehem in May, gave to it the appropriate name of *Friedenshütten*, or Tents of Peace. Of this Synod Nitschmann was the president, and received, soon after its adjournment, a deputation of converts, with Anthony at their head. They delivered a belt of wampum and a written speech to be presented to the Executive Board in Europe in the name of the Christian Indians.

Friedenshütten continued to prosper, until it grew to be a settlement that excited the admiration of every visitor, and that we even, of to-day, must look upon as a wonderful instance of the civilizing power of the Mission. It embraced twenty-nine log-houses, with windows and chimneys, like the homesteads of the settlers, and thirteen huts, forming one street, in the center of which stood the chapel, thirty-two by twenty-four feet, roofed with shingles, and having a school-house as its wing. Immediately opposite, on the left side of the street, was the Mission House. Each lot had a front of thirty-two feet, and between every two lots was an alley ten feet wide. Back of the houses were the gardens and orchards, stocked with vegetables and fruit-trees. The entire town was surrounded by a post and rail fence, and kept scrupulously clean. In summer, a party of women passed through the street and alleys, sweeping them with wooden brooms, and removing the rubbish. Stretching down to the river lay two hundred and fifty acres of plantations and meadows, with two miles of fences; and moored to the bank was found a canoe for each household of the community. The converts had large herds of cattle and hogs, and poultry of every kind in abundance. They devoted more time to tilling the ground than to hunting, and raised plentiful crops. Their trade was considerable in corn, maple-sugar, butter, and pork, which they sold to the Indians; as also in canoes, made of white pine, and bought by the settlers living along the Susquehanna, some of them as far as one hundred miles below Friedenshütten.[1]

---

[1] *List of Houses and Plan of the Town.* B. A. *Heckewelder's Report of the Indian Mission to the Society for Propagating the Gospel.* Friedenshütten lay in Bradford County, Pennsylvania, about two miles from the present mouth of the Wyalusing Creek, on the east side of the Susquehanna, and on land now owned by the Hon. Levi P. Stalford, whose father and grandfather were on the premises before him, and whose great-grandfather, Gen. Henry Pawling, who was with Washington at Valley Forge, purchased the tract from the Indians. The site is two miles below Wyalusing, and one and a half miles above Browntown Post-office. Sugar Run is just opposite, on the west side of the river. For this interesting and valuable information I am indebted to the Rev. David Craft, pastor of the Presbyterian Church at Wyalusing, who identified the site, drew a plan of it, and had a large photographic view of the neighborhood taken. The mouth of Wyalusing Creek is now nearly a mile above where it was in Zeisberger's time.

The population had increased, from the remnant that left the Philadelphia barracks, to one hundred and fifty souls.

In September, Zeisberger was recalled, and Schmick took his place as resident missionary. A report had spread that the Iroquois Council had pronounced the grant made by Togahaju null and void. However improbable this seemed, the issues at stake justified every precaution, and Zeisberger was sent to Onondaga to ascertain the truth. Gottlob Senseman accompanied him.[1]

They reached the capital after a journey of four weeks, by way of Zeniinge, and met the Council in the Long House, over which floated the British flag. Zeisberger addressed the sachems in an elaborate speech, in which he rehearsed the history of the Mission, set forth the purpose of the Church to convert the Indians, and demanded to know whether Togahaju had acted on his own responsibility, in granting the Christian Indians land, or with the consent of his peers. Thereupon he proceeded to Cayuga Town, and conferred with Togahaju himself. He was determined to do all in his power to establish the title of the Mission, and bore himself, throughout these negotiations, with unusual dignity.

The sachem assured him that the report which had been brought to Friedenshütten was untrue; and, on

---

[1] The son of Joachim and Catharine Senseman, one of the victims of the massacre on the Mahony. His father had gone to Jamaica, as a missionary among the slaves.

his return to Onondaga, the Council gave the following answer to his speech: "The grant of land made, last spring, by Sanunawaentowa (the great pipe of peace)—which was the title of the sachemship with which Togahaju had been invested—is approved by the Council. The Aquanoschioni have a fire at Friedenshütten; let their Christian cousins, and the teachers of their Christian cousins, guard it well. Newallike, the Delaware, has no authority in the town; let him not venture to usurp authority. Their Christian cousins are to consult directly with the Council, or with Sanunawaentowa, its accredited deputy."

The sachems treated Zeisberger with great distinction, and begged him to take up his residence at Onondaga, as of old, where his Mission House was still standing. His answer was: "I am glad that you still acknowledge me as an Aquanoschioni. But I cannot consent to live among you until you want me as a preacher of the Gospel of the great God." At parting, they exacted a promise from him that, if possible, he would visit them again. Such a visit, however, was never undertaken. This was the last time that his voice was heard at Onondaga. The work of converting the Six Nations was left to missionaries of other churches, and especially to Samuel Kirkland, the distinguished teacher of the Oneidas.[1] Why the Moravians relinquished all their

---

[1] Samuel Kirkland was born at Norwich, Conn., December 1, 1741, educated at Princeton, and spent part of the year 1765 among the Senecas. Commissioned by the "Connecticut Board of Correspondents of the Society in Scotland," he began a Mission among the Oneidas, in July, 1766, which was very successful, and in which he was engaged for more than

great projects with regard to the Iroquois, and devoted themselves exclusively to the Delawares and tribes of the West, we do not profess to determine. None of the authorities we have examined explain this change in the policy of the Church.

---

forty years. He established the "Hamilton Oneida Academy," incorporated in 1793, for the mutual benefit of the frontier inhabitants and Indians. His assistant was Samson Occom, a native clergyman, from one of the Long Island tribes. Other missionaries, laboring among the Iroquois, were Ashby, Crosby, Peter and Henry Avery. In 1816, an Episcopal Mission was inaugurated by Bishop Hobart among the Oneidas and Onondagas. Eleazar Williams, an Oneida, was the first missionary. It was relinquished in 1833, owing to the removal of a majority of the Oneidas. In 1829, the Methodists began a work among the same tribe, and, in 1841, among the Onondagas. The latter is still in progress, on the Onondaga Reservation.

CHAPTER XVII.

ZEISBERGER'S EXPLORATORY TOUR TO THE INDIANS OF THE ALLEGHANY RIVER.—1767

England's weak policy in the West.—The first congress a harbinger of independence.—Zeisberger at Christiansbrunn and Bethlehem.—Visits from his Indian relatives.—Death and burial of his brother Hachsitagechte.—Message of the Board to the Onondaga Council.—Zeisberger prepares to visit the Indians on the Alleghany, at Goschgoschünk.—Anthony and Papunhank accompany him.—The journey.—Incident at Tiozinossongochto.—A feast and dance in honor of Ganousseracheri.—Arrival at Goschgoschünk.—Its situation.—Zeisberger's first sermon there.—His further labors.—The wickedness of the place.—Wangomen, the false preacher.—Discomfited by Zeisberger.—The Council asks for a resident missionary.—Return to Bethlehem.

IN the two years of Zeisberger's activity at Friedenshütten, it became evident that England's triumph on the Western Continent might prove to be but the precursor of a far greater triumph on the part of her Colonies. The children whom she had sent to the New World were no longer in their swaddling-clothes; they had grown to be a nation. England forgot this. She knew not how to rule America. Her Stamp Act was an act of folly. Her policy in the Far West displayed weakness and fear. Fort Chartres, the last remnant of French power in the valley of the Mississippi, had peacefully passed into her possession; but she "had conquered the West," says Bancroft, "and dared not make use of it; she set it apart to be kept as a desert."

Trembling lest Colonies so remote might become independent, she sent (1763) "a solemn protest," which shut all the country beyond the Alleghanies against the emigrant; while the two thousand persons of European descent already in the valley of the Mississippi were put under "the rule of the British army, with a local judge to decide all disputes."[1]

But, in the very nature of the case, such timidity and unreasonableness could not prevail. The nuclei of States already existed in the West, and no proclamation could prevent the hardy sons of America from peopling its broad prairies. Nor could schemes of unjust taxation quench their spirit of liberty. When the first congress of deputies had assembled at New York (October 7, 1765), clear-sighted eyes throughout the land saw a harbinger of independence.

After his return from Onondaga, Zeisberger took up his abode at Christiansbrunn, where he spent the winter and spring. In early summer (1767) the arrival of a deputation of chiefs and sachems called him to Bethlehem. Sent by Sir William Johnson, they were on their way to the remnant of Nanticokes in Maryland, in order to induce them to join the main body of the tribe at Zeniinge. Among these visitors were two of Zeisberger's Indian relatives, his nephew, and Hachsitagechte, his elder brother, a distinguished sachem, the Keeper of the Archives of the Iroquois Grand Council. The ties that united Zeisberger with the Onondaga family, into

---

[1] Bancroft's U. S., v. 340.

which he had been adopted, were of the closest kind. He had frequent occasions to perceive that he was honored and loved as though he had been their kinsman by birth. While attending the Synod in the previous year, Tiozihostote, one of his younger brothers, who had expected to meet him at Cayuga Town, had come all the way to Bethlehem to see him.

In September this party of Iroquois returned from Maryland, bringing with them the Nanticokes. Zeisberger again proceeded to Bethlehem. Hachsitagechte had been taken ill, and had to be left in the town. His nephew and two sachems remained behind as his escort. He grew rapidly worse, but received the Gospel, which his white brother preached to him, and died as a Christian. He was interred in the burial-ground at Nain. Immediately after the funeral his three Iroquois companions seated themselves around his grave and smoked the pipe of peace. Then they left for their own country, bearing to the Council of Onondaga the following message:

"Brothers, Onondagas! We inform you that your brother and our brother, Hachsitagechte, came to us sick from Philadelphia, and while among us left this world. We are glad that he reached our town, so that we could nurse him as our brother. We told him the great words of that God who became man, and as man shed His blood for all, that all might be saved. He received these great words into his heart, and in the hope of them he died. We buried him."

A string of wampum.

"Herewith we wipe the tears from your eyes. Grieve not. Hachsitagechte has gone to God."

A string of wampum.[1]

Immediately after these events, Zeisberger prepared to undertake a new and distinguished missionary tour. Its purpose is set forth in the opening sentence of his journal. "Intelligence having reached us," he says, "although in a very unreliable form, that there were Indians living on the Alleghany River who desired to hear the Gospel, and the Brethren having, as yet, no knowledge of that country, the Mission Board resolved upon an exploratory journey, in order to ascertain whether anything could there be accomplished for the Saviour."[2]

Anthony and Papunhank consented to accompany him; and, on the last day of September, they set out from Friedenshütten on foot, with one pack-horse. Their place of destination was Goschgoschünk.

Crossing the Susquehanna to its western bank, they came to Schechschiquanunk,[3] a Monsey town, the seat of Echgohund; and in the evening stopped at Wilawane, another Monsey village, near the junction of the Chemung. Along this river they pursued their way through prairies of tall grass, until, not far from where it is formed by the confluence of the Tioga and the Conhoc-

---

[1] Bethlehem Diary, June, July, and September, 1767. MS. B. A.
[2] Journal of Tour to the Alleghany. MS. B. A.
[3] This was old Shesequin, opposite and a little below the present town, in Bradford County, Pa.

ton, they reached the site of Assinnissink, once the home of Jacheabus, the leader in the massacre on the Mahony. They now followed the Tioga to the mouth of the Cowanesque Creek, up which they proceeded a day's journey, and then entered a dense swamp. Amid a drenching rain, they forced their way through the underwood, and over the miry ground, to the headwaters of the Alleghany, in Potter County. Around them was an almost impenetrable spruce-forest; and, as they plunged into its thickets, they lost the river, and were so completely environed by a vast wilderness that even the Indians stood amazed. Toward evening, they struck the Alleghany again, and bivouacked on its bank, perhaps not far from Coudersport.

It may, with great probability, be asserted that Zeisberger was the first white man to thread these dark forests of Northwestern Pennsylvania and build nightlodges in Potter County. Indeed, after his visit, nearly half a century elapsed before settlers were permanently located in that region, and even now it is one of the waste places of the State.

At one of the first Seneca villages which they reached, their appearance caused such suspicion that a messenger, mounted on a fleet horse, hurried to Tiozinossongochto, the next town, a distance of thirty miles, in order to inform its chief of their coming. And when they arrived there the first person whom they saw was this chief, a man of noble presence, standing at the door of his lodge on the watch for them. He barely acknowledged their greetings; but yet did not forget the rites of hospitality. They rested by his fire and were refreshed.

"Whither is the pale face going?" was the first question with which he broke the painful silence, and sat down beside his guest.

"To Goschgoschünk, to visit the Indians," answered Zeisberger.

"Is that all?"

"Yes, that is all."

"Why does the pale face come so unknown a road? This is no road for white people, and no white man has ever come this trail before."

"Seneca," replied Zeisberger, "the business that calls me among the Indians is entirely different from that of other white people, and hence the roads I travel are different too. I do not come to trade or barter; I do not undertake journeys for the sake of gain; I am here in order to bring the Indians good and great words."

"What words are these? I want to hear them."

"The words of life!" responded Zeisberger, with kindling eye. "I teach the Indians to believe in God, and by believing to be saved. Are not these good words?"

"No!" fiercely exclaimed the chief; "no, they are not good words for the Indians!"

"My friend, answer me, are the Indians not human beings? are they not to be saved? But how can they be saved unless they hear of their Saviour?"

"The Indians are as much human beings as you pale faces, but God created them for other ends than you. He gave them hunting-grounds; the game of the forest is theirs. Of the Bible they know nothing. God did not give them that; nor can they understand it. He gave the Bible to the whites; and yet what does it help even these? See how many of them live in wickedness! Explain this to me. In what respect are the whites, with their Bible, better than the Indians without it?"

This conversation was kept up for more than two hours, the chief assailing the Christian religion, and Zeisberger preaching its divine Author. "Behold," said he in conclusion, "these are the words which I come to tell the Indians. You say they are created in order to roam through the forest and run after bears and deer. Oh, no, my friend! They are made for higher purposes. Believe me, it is God's will that they, too, should be saved."

"By what name is the pale face known?" asked the chief after a time.

"I am Ganousseracheri," answered Zeisberger.

In an instant his whole demeanor changed; a smile broke over his stern face; he grasped Zeisberger's hand, called him his brother, said he had often heard of him, and begged him to excuse the coldness with which he had treated him. "I thought my brother was sent to spy out the land of the Senecas. Had I known his name he would have been most welcome."

Entire cordiality now prevailed between the two; but the chief warned Zeisberger of the perils he would encounter. "The Indians at Goschgoschünk," he said, "bear a very bad character; they use the worst kind of sorcery, and will not hesitate to murder you." Zeisberger, however, assured him that he was not afraid. "No harm can befall me if my God, in whom I believe, does not permit it. Are the Indians at Goschgoschünk very wicked? That is just the reason why I ought to go and preach to them!" At parting, he once more besought him to think of his soul and of his Saviour. All this time the chief's wife had listened to the discourse of the pale-faced stranger with that thirsty intenseness which drinks in every word. Was this first blast of the Gospel-trumpet in Tiozionossongochto, where white man had never been before, altogether in vain? The day of the Lord will tell.

At the next Seneca town were two Onondagas of Zeisberger's acquaintance, who hastened to proclaim his standing among the Iroquois. An invitation to spend the day in the village, and be its honored guest, immediately followed. Although most unwilling to accept it, the persistent kindness of the natives prevailed.

With ceremonious politeness, they led him to the largest hut, and begged him to look upon it as his own, while busy squaws hastened to serve up a feast. The woods, the river, and the cornfield yielded their choicest delicacies, and, surrounded by the warriors, painted and dressed as for a festival, he was royally entertained. Toward evening the Indians began a war-dance. At the tap of a drum—a deerskin stretched over an empty cask—they left the hut, all stripped to the breechcloth; but suddenly they returned, flourishing clubs and tomahawks, leaping into the air, filling the house with strange outcries, and going through the mazes of their dance with increasing fury, until it burst into a bewildering whirl of mad confusion. At another signal, they stopped, took seats around the fire, and, with the enthusiasm of old Scotland's bards, began to sing their own heroic deeds, the drum beating a discordant accompaniment. These savage ballads continued so long that Zeisberger's patience was quite exhausted, and he prepared to retire to rest. " Does Ganousseracheri wish to sleep?" said one of the Indians as soon as he perceived this. "Yes," he replied, "I do wish to sleep, for I am very tired." The singing ceased at once, another meal was served up, and, courteously saluting their guests, the company departed. Alone with his two Christian brethren, Zeisberger led in the worship of God by the dim light of the expiring fire.

At Goschgoschünk, which they reached on the sixteenth of October, they were entertained by one of Papunhank's friends.

Goschgoschünk had a history of but two years. Founded (1765) by Monseys from Machiwihilusing and Tioga, it comprised three straggling villages. The middle one, at which Zeisberger arrived, lay on the eastern bank of the Alleghany, near the mouth of the Tionesta Creek, in Venango County. Two miles up the river was the upper village, and four miles down, the lower. It was a region which had been the theater of important Colonial events; but since the Pontiac War, when the fort was destroyed, barbarism had again reigned supreme, and Zeisberger appears to have been the first to reintroduce civilization.

As soon as he had rested from the fatigues of the journey, he dispatched his two companions to appoint a religious service for the evening. The news that the great teacher from Machiwihilusing was come excited general interest, and the natives flocked to the Council House, where the meeting was to be held, from the middle and upper villages. Those from the lower village sent word that it was too late for them to be present that night; that they would, however, not fail to attend the next day.

Several of the Indians having witnessed the religious services of the Moravians, they arranged the Council House as much as possible like a church. Retaining the indispensable fire, which burned in the center of the building, they seated themselves in rows, the men on the one side and the women on the other.

As Zeisberger rose, every eye was fixed upon him, with curiosity or a fierce gleam. Some of the most desperate characters were before him, ruffians and murderers, whose names were a terror among the Indians. There were, moreover, several warriors present who had been engaged in the massacre on the Mahony.[1] It was no ordinary assembly even for him to address.

"My friends," he began, "we have come to bring you great words and glad tidings,—words from our God and your God, tidings of our Redeemer and your Redeemer. We have come to tell you that you will be happy if you will believe in Jesus Christ, who shed His

---

[1] Bethlehem Diary, Nov. 1767. MS. B. A.

blood and gave His life for you. These great words and glad tidings we have presented to your friends at Friedenshütten. They have received them; they are happy; they thank the Saviour that He has brought them from darkness into light. Now we bear to you the peace of God. The time is here; the visitation of God your Creator, who, as man, died for you. You are not any longer to live in darkness without Him; you are to learn to know Him, whom to know is life and peace. Say not in your hearts, these doctrines are not for us; we were not made to receive them. I tell you Jesus Christ died for me, for you, for all men. You, too, are called, and called to life eternal."

In this strain he continued, warming with his subject, until the house rang with his stirring words. No one knew better how to speak to Indians. He had studied native oratory at their councils, and he now employed it with power in the interests of the Gospel. On this occasion his hearers were spell-bound. Their countenances showed the impression which he had produced, and revealed that irrepressible conflict between truth and error into which he had forced their minds. "Never yet," he writes, "did I see so clearly depicted in the faces of Indians both the darkness of hell and the world-subduing power of the Gospel."[1]

---

[1] Of this first religious service at Goschgoschünk, Mr. Schuessele, an eminent artist of Philadelphia, has painted a large and beautiful picture, which was on exhibition some years ago in the Academy of Fine Arts, Philadelphia, and engravings of which, in the exquisite style of Mr. Sartain, have since been published. Mr. Schuessele represents the incident as taking place in the midst of a forest, and not in the Council House.

The next day all the three villages were represented, and numbers crowded the Council House, among them Allemewi, a blind but distinguished old chief, and Wangomen, the preacher of the town. Zeisberger and his assistants by turns proclaimed the Gospel, with only brief interruptions, from morning until evening, when the inhabitants of the upper and lower villages left. Those of the middle village remained, and Anthony instructed them until ten o'clock at night.

But although the Word of God made itself felt, and although some natives were impressed, it soon became evident that the majority had been attracted by the novelty of the religious services, and that the wickedness of these Monseys had not been exaggerated. The blasphemies of Wangomen, the sorceries of the powwows, the wild excesses of the young people, the powers of darkness in the worst of their heathenish manifestations, made up a sum of iniquity so appalling that Zeisberger writes in his journal, "I have never found such heathenism in other parts of the Indian country. Here Satan has his stronghold! Here he sits upon his throne! Here he is worshiped by the savages and carries on his work in the hearts of the children of darkness!

This is my fault. In 1858, when my sources of information were limited, I wrote a few articles for the *Moravian* on Zeisberger's life, and in one of these I described the incident in the manner in which Mr. Schuessele has represented it. That article was shown him, and led to his picture. Subsequent researches convinced me that I had been in error, and that the occurrence took place in the Council House, and not in the forest. I do not, however, regret my mistake, for had I not been guilty of it, Mr. Schuessele's painting would hardly have appeared.

Here God's holy name is blasphemed at their sacrificial abominations, at which they venture to take it into their unclean mouths, and to say that what they do is to His honor!" Addressing the readers of the journal, he adds: "Beloved brethren, here are needed the patience and the faith of the saints, if the Saviour is to see of the travail of His soul, if the prisoners of hope are to turn to the stronghold."

The false preacher, in particular, opposed the Gospel; but the champion of the Truth was too mighty for him. Wangomen began a disputation; Zeisberger silenced him. Wangomen announced that he would preach, and summoned the inhabitants of all the three villages to hear his refutation of the white teacher; when they had assembled, Zeisberger entered the Long House and preached in place of Wangomen, and, as soon as he was done, Anthony and John published Christianity until it was too late for the prophet to say a word. Most signal, however, was his discomfiture on the day previous to the departure of the party. Zeisberger had called a council and proposed a permanent Mission. This proposal met with favor; one voice only was dumb. Wangomen sat in moody silence. The Council called on him by name to give his opinion. He was silent still. Again the Council entreated him to speak. At last he stood up. Avoiding the question at issue, he began to declaim with all the assumed authority of his class, and to set forth, by a diagram drawn on the ground, two ways of salvation—the one for the Indians, the other for the whites. Zeisberger, deeming the matter settled, had meanwhile gone out of the house. On his return, he found Wangomen in the midst of a fiery speech, and Anthony, who was quick to reply, strangely embarrassed. Abruptly interrupting Wangomen, he exclaimed: "Did I not tell you some days ago that there is only one way of salvation, and the Saviour that way? All men, whether white or black or brown, must come to Him if they would be saved,— must feel that they are sinners, and seek forgiveness of Him. Now, what kind of a god is your god? By what attributes do you recognize him?" Wangomen was silent. "If you cannot tell me," continued Zeisberger, in a loud, stern voice, "I will tell you. The devil is your god; you preach the devil to the Indians. You are a servant of the devil, who is the father of lies; and being a servant of the devil, the father of lies, you preach lies and deceive the Indians?" The prophet was startled, and, in a much humbler tone, complained that he could not understand Zeisberger's doctrines. "I will show you the reason," said the latter. "Satan is the Prince of Darkness; where he lives all is dark. Now he lives in you; therefore your mind is dark, and you cannot understand the truth which comes from God." Then changing his invective into earnest admonition, he exhorted him to forsake his false doctrines and blasphemous practices, and give himself to Christ. "There is yet time," he said, in conclusion; "the Saviour yet grants you grace. If you will turn to Him, you may yet obtain salvation. But beware! delay not! hasten to save your poor soul!" Wangomen was utterly confounded, and throughout the Council reigned profound silence.

Zeisberger was in a den of paganism, completely in the power of this false prophet, who might have murdered him with impunity; but the honor of his Lord was at stake and made him strong. "I could not," he says, "speak otherwise, however severe my words. Ever since my arrival I had tried, by affection, to gain this man for Christ, hoping to establish the Gospel through his instrumentality. But when I saw that he willfully opposed the Saviour, and the Saviour's atoning blood, and tried to rob Him of that honor which belongs to Him, I could bear it no longer."

After a time, the Council once more asked Wangomen for his opinion with regard to the coming of a resident missionary. "Let us decide the matter now," was said on all sides. "It is decided," remarked Zeisberger with dignity. "I know your wishes; that is enough for me; I want nothing more." "I, too, am willing," said Wangomen at last.

On the twenty-third of October, after an earnest farewell-discourse, Zeisberger left the village and returned to Friedenshütten. Thence he hastened to Bethlehem, to report to the Board. His journal was read at a public meeting, and caused a great sensation.

CHAPTER XVIII.

ZEISBERGER A MISSIONARY AT GOSCHGOSCHÜNK.—1768, 1769.

Massacre of Indians in Cumberland County, Pennsylvania.—Measures to prevent an Indian War.—Treaty at Fort Pitt.—Zeisberger, Senseman, and a colony of Christian Indians begin a Mission at Goschgoschünk.—A Mission House is erected.—Conflict between the Gospel and heathenism.—Something about Indian sorcery.—The Mission opposed from without and from within.—The courage and endurance of Zeisberger and Senseman.—Two plots against the life of the former.—The influence of the Mission.—A Christian and heathen party formed.—The influence of the Iroquois League on the wane among the Delawares.—Zeisberger and several deputies go to Zonesschio.—Indian Congress at Fort Stanwix. — New boundary line settled.—The three tribal chiefs of the Delawares, and their friendly messages to the Christian party at Goschgoschünk.

AFTER his return from Goschgoshünk, Zeisberger spent the winter at Christiansbrunn. It was a time of anxiety for the frontier settlements of Pennsylvania. Ten inoffensive natives, among them three squaws and three children, encamped in Penn Township, Cumberland County, were brutally murdered (January 10, 1768) by a German, one Frederick Stump. To avenge so gross a wrong, would not the Indians seize the hatchet, and reinaugurate all the horrors of a border war?

Governor Penn took prompt measures to prevent such a calamity. He offered a reward of two hundred pounds sterling for the apprehension of the murderer, and sent conciliatory messages to Newallike, the Christian Indians, and the clans of the North Branch. Sir William Johnson came to his assistance. His runners traversed the wilderness with belts of peace, and at his own hall he mollified the anger of the Six Nations. By these efforts the storm was averted. And even when Stump, who had been arrested and lodged in the jail of Carlisle, was rescued by force, the Indians remained quiet.[1] A great treaty, to be held at Fort Pitt, absorbed their minds. George Croghan, representing the Crown, together with John Allen and Joseph Shippen, Commissioners of Pennsylvania, met (April, 1768) eleven hundred representatives of various tribes— Iroquois, Delawares, Shawanese, Mohicans, and others —and, in a figure of their own mode of speech, buried the bones of the murdered natives, while at the same place the Indians buried the bones of murdered white men, "with ours," they said, "and so deep that none of our young people may ever know that any misfortunes have happened between us." On this occasion, too, they were convinced of the sincerity of the government in its attempts to remove the squatters of Red Stone Creek, the Monongahela, and Youghiogeny, who had so long been an offense to the Councils of the Delawares and the sachems of the Six Nations. An official manifesto proclaimed " death without the benefit of

---

[1] Diary of Friedenshütten. MS. B. A. Penn. Col. Records, ix. 414, 420, 428, 436, 448, and 497.

clergy" as the penalty of a continuance of their usurpations.[1]

Toward the end of April, runners reached Friedenshütten to inquire whether the teachers, who had been promised the Monseys of Goschgoschünk, were coming. A few days later, Zeisberger and Gottlob Senseman arrived, on their way to that town.

Three families of Christian Indians—Anthony and Joanna, Abraham and Salome, Peter and Abigail—consented to accompany them and form the nucleus of a church on the Alleghany. On the ninth of May, escorted by John Ettwein,[2] and several converts, as far as Schechschiquanunk, this little colony left Friedenshütten in canoes, taking with them a small drove of cows and horses. At Wilawane, twenty chiefs, with speeches and a belt, attempted to hinder the enterprise; but Zeisberger rejected the belt and silenced their interference. "Do not imagine," said he, " so vain a thing as that you will prevent us from preaching the Gospel at Goschgoschünk." On the ninth of June they arrived at the upper town, where Wangomen received them into his lodge, which Zeisberger at once converted into a house of God, holding daily worship.

---

[1] Penn. Col. Records, ix. 481 and 482; Report of Treaty in Penn. Col. Records, ix. 514–543.

[2] Born, 1712, in the Schwarzwald, in Germany. In 1754, he emigrated to America, and served the Church both in Pennsylvania and North Carolina. In 1764, he became a member of the Mission Board. In 1784, he was consecrated a bishop, and stood at the head of the Church in Pennsylvania until his death in 1802. He was a stern, but zealous, faithful man.

He found Goschgoschünk changed. The inhabitants were scattered; the middle town was wholly deserted; the upper had no proper chiefs; and only in the lower existed somewhat of a government. The tribal relations, too, were of the loosest kind. Several other nationalities mingled with the Monseys, and even a few former converts of Gnadenhütten, fast relapsing into heathenism, had found their way thither. Of this whole motley clan the virtual head was Wangomen.

Zeisberger selected a site for a Mission House, close by a spring, about half a mile from the town, far enough to be undisturbed by the revelries of the savages, and yet not too far for such as might wish to attend his meetings. Here a log building, twenty-six by sixteen feet, was put up, and occupied (June 30) by the whole colony. Around it new converts were to erect lodges, and gradually form a separate village.

Established thus at this outpost of civilization, Zeisberger and Senseman looked hopefully into the future. They were ready to spend and be spent in the service of their Lord, and, in fellowship with their Indian brethren, mutually covenanted, in the sacrament of the Supper, to be faithful unto death.

They had need of grace and of the courage to which grace gives birth. When first they arrived, the people showed them due kindness. Had not these Monseys extended to Zeisberger a formal invitation to live and teach among them? and now that he had accepted it, should they not receive him and his friends? Had they not sent to Friedenshütten to hasten his coming? Had they not dispatched a canoe to meet him? It would have been contrary to their character to refuse a welcome. Hence they helped the converts to build their house, to plant their corn, to make themselves a home amid the rude comforts of the wilderness. And, while worship was held in Wangomen's hut, attracted by its novelty, many came to see and hear. But when they began to realize what a Christian Mission involved, their sentiments changed; bitter enmity to the Word of God broke out, and determined opposition to God's ministers. This was owing, chiefly, to the influence of the sorcerers, of whom Wangomen was the most notorious.

Sorcerers abounded among the aborigines of our country. The majority of them were cunning jugglers, or self-deluded victims of superstition. According to Zeisberger's testimony, however, some existed by whom Satan himself worked "with all power, and signs, and lying wonders."[1] He says that he disbelieved the stories he heard of what they could do until several of them were converted. These unfolded to him things, from their own past experience, which forced him to acknowledge the reality of Indian sorcery, and to adopt the opinion, which was universal among the early Church Fathers, that the gods of heathenism were not visionary beings represented by idols, but satanic powers and principalities, to worship whom was to worship demons and be under demoniacal influences. He refers to three kinds of native magic: namely, the art to pro-

---

[1] II. Thessalonians, ii. 9.

duce sudden death without the use of poison; the *mattapassigan*, a deadly charm by which epidemics could be brought upon entire villages, and persons at a distance sent to their graves; and the witchcraft of the *kimochwe*, who passed through the air by night, visiting towns, casting the inhabitants into an unnatural sleep, and then stealing what they wanted.[1]

We neither adopt these views of Zeisberger, nor pronounce them absurd. In the present aspect of demonology, opinions of this kind remain an open question.

The sorcerers of Goschgoschünk were not slow to perceive that if any should embrace Christianity whom they had initiated, their arts would be exposed. Hence, at a secret meeting held soon after Zeisberger's arrival, they bound themselves to incite the clan against him by every means in their power, while outwardly observing the semblance of friendship. Of this he knew nothing until he had removed from the town. Thus was inaugurated a desperate struggle between the lies of paganism and the truth of God. The antagonistical power of the former came from without and within.

From without, it began to show itself in the first days of the Mission. The Senecas claimed the land on which Goschgoschünk was situated, and by their permission the Monseys had built the town. To make it the seat of a Christian Church was a project which, according to aboriginal law, must be submitted for approval to the proprietaries of the domain. This Zeisberger well knew,

---

[1] Zeisberger's MS. Hist. of the Indians.

and had determined upon an embassy to Hagastaak, the sachem of Zonesschio. But while he was still the guest of Wangomen, there came a Seneca chief, with an escort, from the Onenge, who, upon hearing of the presence of the white teachers, burst into so vehement a flood of denunciation that Zeisberger had to be concealed from its fury. A week later, a mysterious message was brought: "Cousins! you that dwell at Goschgoschünk, you have cause to be afraid. Danger threatens you!" Accompanying it were alarming symbols—a string of wampum, a stick painted red, with several prongs, and a leaden bullet. This message caused much sensation, its origin being unknown, and its words enigmatical. Zeisberger, indeed, soon discovered that it had been carried by two Onondagas and a Cayuga of his acquaintance, who professed to have received it from a Seneca sachem; but it continued a source of much embarrassment. A fortnight later, it was followed by another, ostensibly from Hagastaak, and enforced by a bunch of wampum, or as many strings as a man can hold in one hand. "Cousins," this ran, "you that live at Goschgoschünk, on the Alleghany downward, and you Shawanese! I have risen from my seat and looked around to see what is transpiring in our country. I see a man in a black coat. Against him I warn you. Avoid the man in a black coat. Believe not what he tells you. He will deceive your hearts!" A message like this was, in the last degree, pernicious. The powerful sachem of Zonesschio, with all the authority of his office, as a deputy of the Grand Council, incites the Delawares of the whole Alleghany valley, and even the Shawanese, who live two hundred miles off, against Zeisberger and his work, although he knows him to be his peer in the Confederacy. However keenly Zeisberger felt the indignity, his faith wavered not, and he met it, in his journal, with an appeal to the Lord, in whose name and by whose will he had established himself on the Alleghany, leaving the issue in His hands. Not long after this, menaces came from the capital of the Delawares, obscure in their import, but yet evidently directed against the Mission. And finally, a report spread, which gained general credence, that certain New England Indians, lately returned from a visit to Old England, were the bearers of a letter from the British King, warning the natives of every name in his American Colonies to beware of the Moravians, who would lead them not to heaven, but to hell. These were some of the manifestations of the antichristian spirit that warred against the Gospel from without.

From within, this spirit was still more vehement, and rendered the situation of the missionaries far more perilous. The first instance of it was the prediction of a sorcerer, that worms would destroy the corn crop, because there were white teachers in the country. After a time, they began to perceive that their enemies, particularly among the women led on by Wangomen's sister, were doing their utmost to prevent the Indians from attending religious service. This opposition became gradually bolder; here and there squaws might be heard publicly denouncing the Christian colony, and asserting that, since its coming, the game had disappeared from the forests, the trees had ceased to produce chestnuts, and the bushes whortleberries. The young men now lent their aid. They disturbed the meetings in the Mission House, and filled the town with threats. "The two white men ought to be killed," said some of them. "Yes, and all the baptized Indians with them, and their bodies thrown into the Alleghany," added others. Incited by such sayings, the sons of the chief of the lower town formed a plot to murder Zeisberger, which was, however, detected before it could be carried out.

Toward the end of July, the principal powwow bestirred himself. "The manitous," he said, "are angry with us because we harbor white teachers. We must sacrifice to appease their wrath." Accordingly, one night a hog was slaughtered and a sacrificial feast instituted. The savages sat in a hut, in total darkness, and silently gorged themselves with meat, while the voice of the powwow was lifted up, appealing to the manitous to accept the offering of swine's flesh which he brought. After a time, he announced that they were propitiated. Thereupon the Indians emerged from the darkness—fit emblem of their wicked rites—and retired to their several wigwams.

But it was especially after the message from Zonesschio had been received that the hostility of the savages increased. Wangomen had, thus far, been passive, and treated the missionaries with courtesy; but now, supported, as he believed himself to be, by so powerful a sachem as Hagastaak, he threw off his mantle and stood revealed in the nakedness of his malice. Going from hut to hut, he forbade his people to attend Christian service in the Mission House. Not a few, who had been regular worshipers, became alarmed, and obeyed this interdict; while two young warriors broke up the next meeting which Zeisberger attempted to hold, and tried to draw him into a dispute and the utterance of harsh words, so that they might have a pretext to murder him. His calmness, however, and the firm attitude of the converts, prevented this second plot against his life. Such were some of the means employed in the town itself to hinder the spread of the Gospel.

Amid this antagonism from without and within, Zeisberger and Senseman stood fast, preaching with such power, and laboring with such energy, that they established for themselves a not inconsiderable influence, gained some souls for the Gospel, and induced others to seek the Truth.

Of their confidence, Zeisberger's journal gives frequent proofs. While his enemies were most violent, he sat in the Mission House by night, and wrote: "Will it be possible for these adversaries to prevent the spread of God's Word? They will certainly not succeed, for He that is with us is stronger than they." When informed of the plot to murder him, he recorded his presentiment of such a catastrophe, and his willingness to suffer, if God had foreordained him to a violent death, but expressed a hope that it might not occur in a religious service. And when his Indian companions began to be discouraged, and to speak of returning to Friedenshütten, he inspired them with new zeal, so that all, except Peter and Abigail, remained at their post.

The influence of the Mission was illustrated by the success with which it kept from the savages the luring cup of "fire-water." Traders were forbidden to sell it at Goschgoschünk, and a petition, drawn up by Zeisberger and signed by all the headmen of the clan, was sent to Justice Elliott, at Fort Pitt, asking him to prevent its introduction.[1] Nor was it less an evidence of Christian power in so notorious a nest of murderers, that, after the second attempt had been made to take Zeisberger's life, those Monseys who attended his preaching held a council, and appointed two of their number to administer a public reproof to the young men engaged in the plot. That God's Word was not proclaimed in vain its most vindictive opponents had to acknowledge. Goschgoschünk separated into a Christian and a heathen party. At first the former timidly succumbed to every persecution. By-and-by, however, it gained courage and stood forth openly on the side of the Gospel, while several of its adherents built themselves huts around the Mission House. The accession of Allemewi and of Gendaskund, a distinguished headman, was the crowning triumph of this party.

We have thus seen the character of the struggle between light and darkness which rendered memorable

---

[1] Copy of Petition. MS. B. A.

the establishment of the first Protestant Mission beyond the Alleghanies. This struggle was, indeed, not yet at an end, but the missionaries could no longer be driven back to the Susquehanna. Should they be obliged to retire from Goschgoschünk, which they anticipated, they would carry the Gospel westward.

Zeisberger now took into serious consideration the unfriendly attitude of the Senecas. It appeared to him important to conciliate Hagastaak by a formal embassy, but the Monseys were not of his mind. In sympathy with their fellow-tribes, their feelings toward the Six Nations had received a great shock in the Pontiac Conspiracy. The Iroquois, and especially the Senecas, had incited the Delawares to take part in that war, and had then helped the English to humble them. This duplicity received its due reward. The influence of the League was broken. The Delawares practically, if not by a national act, shook off the yoke of their vassalage and scouted the idea of being "women." Hence the Christian party at Goschgoschünk wanted to defy Hagastaak, and deemed an informal notice sufficient, which Allemewi had given him, of the establishment of the Mission. At last, however, they yielded to the persuasions of Zeisberger, and a deputation, consisting of himself, Senseman, Abraham, and two Monseys, left Goschgoschünk in October for the capital of the Senecas.

They found that Hagastaak was attending the Congress at Fort Stanwix, where three thousand Indians were gathered to settle a general boundary with the

Middle Colonies. A line was established which "began at the north, where Canada Creek joins Wood Creek, and leaving New York, passed from the nearest fork of the West Branch of the Susquehanna to Kittanning on the Alleghany, whence it followed that river and the Ohio down to the Tennessee."[1] The wide area which Pennsylvania thus secured embraced Friedenshütten and all the land of the Susquehanna Mission.

In the absence of Hagastaak, the embassy from Goschgoschünk had an interview with his councilors; and, while Abraham asked for leave to transfer the Mission to the Seneca territory on the Onenge, Zeisberger delivered an earnest protest against the warning which had emanated, at least ostensibly, from the Council of Zonesschio. He appealed to the character of his work, to his long residence among the Aquanoschioni, to his adoption into one of their nations, and asked whether these things ought not to keep the Senecas from inciting the Delawares and Shawanese, or Indians of any other name, against his doctrines and his life. The Council assured him that the warning of which he complained had never been issued by them, but had been devised by irresponsible parties; and promised to lay the petition for a grant of land on the Onenge before Hagastaak.

Meanwhile Allemewi had opened negotiations with the three tribal chiefs of the Delawares, namely, Neta-

---

[1] Bancroft's U. S., vi. 227, 228; Penn. Col. Records, ix. 554, 555; Penn. Archives, iv. 308, 309; Taylor's Ohio, 181.

watwes,[1] of the Turtle Tribe, King Beaver, or Amochk, of the Turkey Tribe, and Packanke, of the Wolf Tribe. He found that the threatening message which had been brought in their name to Goschgoschünk was likewise spurious, and that they favored the Mission. Packanke added, that the land on the Onenge was his, and did not belong to the Senecas, and that he would be glad to see it occupied by Christian Indians.

Such friendly responses were not without their influence at Goschgoschünk. The Christian party separated more completely from the heathen, and took a more decided stand in favor of the Gospel. Seven huts, inhabited by six families, now clustered around the Mission House.

---

[1] Netawatwes, who was often called King Newcomer, from Newcomerstown, or Gekelemukpechünk, his capital, was the head of the Delaware Nation. Colonel Bouquet had deposed him for refusing to attend a conference at the close of the Pontiac War, but this deposition was merely nominal, and did not invalidate his authority among the natives.

CHAPTER XIX.

ZEISBERGER AT LAWUNAKHANNEK.—1769, 1770.

Wholesale slaughter of deer.—Opposition to the Christian party breaks out afresh.—Sacrificial feasts.—The Mission temporarily removed to Lawunakhannek.—The new settlement in the heart of the present Oil Region.—Zeisberger's account of the wells.—His hopes of the ultimate triumph of the Gospel.—Glikkikan's first visit to the Mission.—He comes as the champion of heathenism and leaves convicted of sin.—Anthony's sententious arguments.—A dire famine. —Zeisberger and Senseman go to Fort Pitt to procure food.—A frontier Indian war prevented by this visit.—The ruins of Fort Venango.—Glikkikan brings an invitation from Packanke to transfer the Mission to his land.—The first baptisms at Lawunakhannek. —Allemewi baptized.—Packanke's offer accepted.—The farewell council instituted by Wangomen.—Departure from Lawunakhannek.

IN the beginning of 1769, the hunters of the clan returned from their autumnal chase, bringing the pelts of more than two thousand deer. The fur trade had greatly increased after the Pontiac War; hence such wholesale slaughter, by which the deer in the valley of the Alleghany were almost extirpated.

Some of these hunters had been violent opponents of the Gospel; but now they began to be present at the services of the Mission. This excited the heathen party anew. The same falsehoods were revived that had been used with such success when the Mission was first established. Nightly dances were, moreover, planned and sacrificial feasts inaugurated, to which the converts received urgent invitations. They continued true to their Christian vows, however, without exception.

Such feasts deserve a more particular description. They were five in number. The first three consisted of offerings of bear's meat or venison, which was procured by a hunting-party appointed for this purpose. While such a party was on the chase, women garnished the house in which the sacrifice was to be held. On their return, the hunters fired a volley in the outskirts of the town, as a signal, and then moved to the lodge in procession, carrying their game. There the guests seated themselves on litters of grass, and were supplied with meat and corn-bread. Portions of the fat, together with the bones, were cast into the fire; all the rest was eaten. A feast was repeated for three or four successive days, beginning in the afternoon, and continuing through the night until morning.

At the first sacrifice, after each meal, there was a slow and measured dance, led by an Indian rattling a small tortoise-shell filled with pebbles, and singing of dreams, or chanting the names of the various manitous which the assembled company worshiped. The second differed from this merely in the disgusting appearance of the men, who, before beginning to dance, stripped themselves to their breech-cloths and smeared their persons with white clay. At the third, ten or more tanned deer-skins were distributed among old men and women, who wrapped them around their shoulders, left the house, and, turning to the east, invoked the Great Spirit on behalf of the family which gave the feast.

The fourth was called *Machtugu*. It required an oven, constructed of twelve pieces of twelve different sorts of wood, not more and not less, and covered closely with blankets. Into this were put twelve stones of medium size, heated to their greatest intensity, and then the entertainer crept in, with eleven guests, strewing tobacco upon the stones, and praying to his manitou. Meanwhile a friend, hired with twelve fathoms of wampum, stood in front of a post covered with the head and hide of a buck, and, turning his face toward the east, called upon the same manitou. This continued until the occupants of the oven were unconscious, when they were dragged out. A feast of bear's meat began as soon as they had revived. *Machtugu*, repeated twelve times, rendered a man certain of salvation.

At the last feast the Indians gorged themselves with the flesh of the bear, which they devoured as long as they could, in the natural way. When this was no longer possible, they forced it down their throats until the stomach rejected the monstrous load. Thereupon they fell to again, passed through the same ordeal, and finally drank the liquid fat. The sicker they got, and the more frequently they vomited, the better pleased was the manitou.

There were never less than four Indians engaged to wait on the guests. Their pay was wampum, and they had, moreover, the privilege of selling refreshments to the spectators, who gathered from far and near. On the last day, rum-dealers generally made their appearance, so that drunken brawls and murders usually formed the close of these gross rites. What some of them imported, the natives were themselves unable to explain. They could not even give intelligibly the meaning of all the names by which their feasts were known. Nothing shows the low tendency of their religion more clearly than these sacrifices.[1]

About the time that they were employed at Goschgoschünk to lure the Christian party from their faith, Wangomen returned to the village, after a protracted absence, and lent all his influence to the heathen faction, whose persecutions grew to be intolerable. Another savage willfully broke the regulation with regard to strong drink, and introduced such quantities of it that drunkenness became common. The converts were discouraged, and Zeisberger recognized the necessity of removing the Mission to some other place, where it would be undisturbed, until he could determine in what part of the Western wilderness to establish it permanently. To this end he selected Lawunakhannek, three miles above Goschgoschünk, on the eastern bank of the river, whither all the Christian Indians, except two families, betook themselves in April, in spite of the opposition of the heathen party, that was glad to see the teachers go, but unwilling to have their town depopulated by the exodus of any of its native inhabitants.

---

[1] Zeisberger's MS. History of the Indians.

The new village, which consisted of substantial log-houses and a chapel, stood in the heart of the present Oil Region. Its rich springs were known in that early day. Both Indians and traders prized the petroleum for its medicinal qualities, but its excellency as a burning fluid was not appreciated.[1]

As soon as the Christian Indians had left Goschgoschünk, it relapsed into still grosser darkness. But Zeisberger's faith in the power of the Gospel remained unshaken. "We have now lived," he writes, "for ten months between the two towns of Goschgoschünk. That the Saviour has kept and preserved us amid these godless and malicious savages is wonderful. They have heard, but they resist, the Gospel, not only because they are blind, and under the influence of the Prince of Evil, but also because they are desperately wicked. I doubt not, however, that more than one among them will yet be convicted of sin, and seek forgiveness with Jesus."[2]

---

[1] Zeisberger says, "I have seen three kinds of oil springs,—such as have an outlet, such as have none, and such as rise from the bottom of creeks. From the first water and oil flow out together, the oil impregnating the grass and soil; in the second it gathers on the surface of the water to the depth of the thickness of a finger; from the third it rises to the surface and flows with the current of the creek. The Indians prefer wells without an outlet. From such they first dip the oil that has accumulated; then stir the well, and, when the water has settled, fill their kettles with fresh oil, which they purify by boiling. It is used medicinally, as an ointment, for toothache, headache, swellings, rheumatism, and sprains. Sometimes it is taken internally. It is of a brown color, and can also be used in lamps. It burns well."—*Zeisberger's MS. History of the Indians.*

[2] Zeisberger's Journal. MS. B. A.

In the beginning of June, he met Glikkikan for the first time, who subsequently became the most distinguished convert of the Western Mission. A captain, the speaker in the Council of Kaskaskunk, and Packanke's principal adviser, his fame as a warrior was eclipsed only by his reputation for eloquence. He had fought in many a battle, both in the internecine wars of the Indians and the protracted struggle of the French against the English; and he had made many a council-house ring with bursts of native oratory. Even the white man was no match for him. At Venango, he had silenced the Jesuits, who would have converted his nation; at Tuscarawas, Frederick Post had succumbed to his power. And now he came to confound the missionaries on the Alleghany. Soon after their arrival, he had sent them a tantalizing message with regard to the manufacture of gunpowder, and ever since that time this visit, which was to result in their disgraceful retreat to the settlements, had been anxiously expected by Wangomen, who was his brother, and the other leaders of paganism. These escorted him to the Mission House at Lawunakhannek in a body. He had prepared himself for the interview, considered the points of his harangue, and, in fact, committed its very words to memory; but, when in sight of the town, he could not recall a single sentence, as he afterward acknowledged, and wisely resolved first to hear what the Christians would say. Zeisberger being absent, Anthony received him. "Anthony," writes the former, "was as eager to bring souls to Christ as a hunter's hound is eager to chase the deer." Placing food before his guests, he immediately introduced the subject of religion.

"My friends," he said, "hear me; I will tell you a great thing. God made the heavens, the earth, and all things that in them are. Nothing exists which God has not made." Pausing a little, he continued, "God has created us. But who of us knows his Creator? Not one! I tell you the truth, not one! For we have fallen away from God; we are polluted creatures; our minds are darkened by sin." Here he sat down, and was silent a long time. Suddenly rising again, he exclaimed, "That God, who made all things and created us, came into the world in the form and fashion of a man. Why did He thus come into the world? Think of this!" He resumed after awhile: "I will show you. God became a man, and took upon himself flesh and blood, in order that, as man, He might reconcile the world unto himself. By His bitter death on the Cross He procured for us life and eternal salvation, redeeming us from sin, from death, and from the power of the devil." In such apothegms he unfolded the whole Gospel. When he had finished, Zeisberger, who had meanwhile entered the house, briefly corroborated his words, and exhorted Glikkikan to lay them to heart.

Glikkikan was an honest man, and open to conviction. He upheld the superstitions of his fathers because he had not yet been convinced of the reality of Christian faith. On this occasion, however, the truth began to dawn upon his mind. In place of his elaborate speech, he merely replied: "I have nothing to say. I believe your words." And when he returned to Goschgoschünk, instead of announcing the discomfiture of the teachers, he urged the people to go to hear the Gospel, and reproved them for their wickedness. He had been hired, like Balaam, to curse God's own, but, like Balaam, he was constrained to bless them.

About this time, a dire famine broke out along the Alleghany, and compelled Zeisberger and Senseman to visit Fort Pitt, where Mellegan, a trader and correspondent of William Henry, of Lancaster, supplied their wants, according to instructions from the Mission Board.

Their arrival was opportune. Depredations, committed by irresponsible bands of Senecas, on their way to the south country, had been understood by the commandant, and the settlers as far as Ligonier, to signify war. Great consternation prevailed. Many farms were deserted; from others the women and children had been sent away; while at the fort active preparations were going on to punish the savages. Coming from the heart of the Indian territory, Zeisberger knew this to be a false alarm, and reassured the commandant. A rising among the Western Indians, he said, was not thought of. He would ask them, on his return, to send peace-messages to the fort, to substantiate this assertion. With regard to the mode of treating the aborigines in general, he gave the commandant such counsel as his long residence among them suggested, and urged particularly the appointment of an Indian agent for the

West. Thus Zeisberger saved the border from a conflict which might have grown into a protracted war. In response to his appeal, the tribes of the Alleghany hastened to bring white belts and friendly messages. Confidence was restored.

The trail back to the Mission led him over the site of Fort Venango, one of the posts destroyed in the Pontiac War. "The fort," he writes, "was entirely consumed. A short distance from it stood a saw-mill. This the Indians spared, probably with the intention of using it, but not understanding its machinery, it has been neglected and fallen to pieces. On the bank above Onenge we found a cannon of curious workmanship, brought that far by the savages from the fort. Had we discovered it on our way down we would have taken it along to Fort Pitt."[1]

A second visit from Glikkikan cheered his heart. He came to tell him that he had determined to embrace Christianity, and to invite him, in the name of Packanke, to settle near Kaskaskunk, on a tract of land which should be reserved for the exclusive use of the Mission. Wangomen had been intrusted with a similar invitation, months before this, from all the three tribal chiefs, but had never delivered it. Zeisberger saw the advantages of the offer. Deeming himself, however, unauthorized to accept it, he sent two runners to the Board at Bethlehem, asking for instructions. The Board gave him unlimited power to act as he might deem best.

---

[1] Zeisberger Journal. MS. B. A.

Pleasing experiences were now in store for him. In the early hours of a December evening the first Protestant baptism in the valley of the Alleghany took place at Lawunakhannek, and was administered to Luke and Paulina. It was followed, at Christmas, by that of Allemewi, who was named Solomon. In the beginning of the new year several other converts were added to the Church.

The power of the heathen party was broken, through the unexpected defection of Glikkikan, and the persecutions, from which the Mission had so long suffered, came to an end. As the converts had accepted the offer of Packanke, and were about to withdraw from Lawunakhannek, Wangomen invited them, and their teachers, to a farewell-council, at which he proposed that they should part as friends, and apologized for the two attempts which had been made, by his young people, to take Zeisberger's life. In reply, Zeisberger forgave all the injuries which he had endured while among the tribe, and once more earnestly appealed to them to turn to the living God.

On the seventeenth of April, 1770, the Christian Indians left Lawunakhannek in fifteen canoes. As they approached Goschgoschünk, its inhabitants came down to the bank to see them pass, from which, unexpectedly to all, a solitary canoe put off and joined them. It contained Gendaskund and his family. Celebrating this open triumph in the act of their departure, the converts swept out of sight of Goschgoschünk and its iniquitous savages.

CHAPTER XX.

ON THE BEAVER RIVER, AND FIRST VISIT TO OHIO.—1770, 1771.

The Christian Indians at Fort Pitt.—Sail down the Ohio and ascend the Beaver River.—A woman's town.—Languntoutenünk, or Friedensstadt, founded.—An embassy to Packanke.—Kaskaskunk his capital.—Glikkikan becomes a Christian.—Reproaches of Packanke.—Glikkikan's calm reply.—Zeisberger is naturalized among the Monseys.—The Christian Indians and tribute.—A new Mission town built on the west bank of the Beaver.—Jungmann and his wife become Zeisberger's assistants.—Senseman returns to the settlements.—An awakening.—Zeisberger visits Gekelemukpechünk, the capital of the Delawares.—Description of the town.—First Protestant sermon in the State of Ohio.—The doctrine of emetics.—A crusade against Zeisberger proclaimed by an Indian preacher.—Dedication of a new Church at Languntoutenünk.

GLIDING down the Alleghany, the little flotilla reached Fort Pitt on the twentieth of April. When this post still bore the name of Duquesne, and French priests were as active as French soldiers, it had often been visited by baptized Indians. But now, for the first time, appeared a company of Protestant converts. It was a novel sight. Traders and the garrison thronged the camp, and beheld, with astonishment, the problem solved, that savages can be changed into consistent Christians.

Leaving this testimony behind them, they proceeded down the Ohio to the confluence of the Beaver. This region, which now teems with the traffic of the Ohio and Pennsylvania Railroad, and of the Beaver and Erie

Canal, and is enlivened by a cluster of four towns, was then a deep solitude. Not a wigwam even of a native could be seen, only the ruins of Sakunk, an Indian village abandoned long ago. They steered up the Beaver, and beyond its rapids came to the first town since leaving the fort. It was inhabited—strange to say—by a community of women, all single, and all pledged never to marry! One mile above this place was a broad plain, on the east side of the river. Here an encampment of bark-huts was put up. It must have been in Lawrence County, between the Shenango River and Slippery Rock Creek.[1]

The first business undertaken was an embassy to Packanke, whose capital, New Kaskaskunk, stood near, or perhaps on the site of New Castle, at the junction of the Neshannock Creek with the Shenango.[2] Old Kaskaskunk, the former capital, was at the confluence of the Shenango and Mahoning, which form the Beaver. Packanke, a venerable, gray-haired chief, but active as in the days of his youth, received the deputation at his own house. In response to the speeches of Abraham and Zeisberger, who thanked him for the home which he had granted the Christian Indians, and made known the principles of their faith, he said that they were welcome in his country, and should be undisturbed in the worship of their God. A great feast was in course of

---

[1] Day's Penn. Hist. Collections fixes the locality at Darlington, Beaver County. An egregious error!

[2] Day places Kaskaskunk in Butler County. This is wrong, as Zeisberger's MS. Journal proves.

preparation, and Indians were coming in from every side. Native etiquette required that the deputies should grace the occasion by their presence; but after Abraham's exposition of their views, Packanke made no attempt to detain them.

The encampment was now changed into a town, to which Zeisberger gave the name of Languntoutenünk (*Friedensstadt*, or City of Peace). It soon began to attract the Indians. The first to arrive were a number of Monseys from Goschgoschünk, who avowed themselves disgusted with its wickedness, and joined the Mission. They were followed by Glikkikan, from Kaskaskunk. Zeisberger gave him a cordial reception, but failed not to tell him all that he must relinquish, and the persecutions to which he would be subjected. Glikkikan, however, had counted the cost, and was determined to live and die with God's people. And from that day until he fell in the massacre at Gnadenhütten, he remained true to his resolution.

Not only the persecutions, which Zeisberger had predicted, followed this step, but it produced a change in the sentiments of Packanke. He was not prepared to lose his bravest warrior and best counselor. He reproached Glikkikan, and denounced the Mission. "And have you gone to the Christian teachers from our very council?" he said. "What do you want of them? Do you hope to get a white skin? Not so much as one of your feet will turn white: how then can your whole skin be changed? Were you not a brave man? Were you not an honorable counselor? Did you not sit at my side in this house, with a blanket before you and a pile of wampum-belts on it, and help me direct the affairs of our nation? And now you despise all this. You think you have found something better. Wait! In good time you will discover how miserably you have been deceived." To this burst of passion Glikkikan replied, " You are right; I have joined the Brethren. Where they go, I will go; where they lodge, I will lodge. Nothing shall separate me from them. Their people shall be my people, and their God my God."[1] Attending church at Languntoutenünk, a few days after this, he was so moved by a discourse on the heinousness of sin and the grace of the Saviour, that he walked through the village back to his hut, sobbing aloud. "A haughty war-captain weeps publicly in the presence of his former associates," writes Zeisberger. "This is marvelous! Thus the Saviour, by His Word, breaks the hard hearts and humbles the proud minds of the Indians."

Meanwhile Gendaskund had succeeded in conciliating Packanke, who resumed his friendly relations to the Mission. He could not but grant the force of the argument that if he invited preachers of the Gospel to his country, he must permit them to preach; and if they preached, he must expect the Indians to accept their religion. About the same time, moreover, Zeisberger gained a position among the Monseys which constrained the old chief to be his friend.

---

[1] Zeisberger's Journal. MS. B. A.

It grew out of a suggestion, made by Wangomen at the farewell-council with the Goschgoschünk clan, to appoint an umpire who should settle all differences between the Christian Monseys and the rest. Zeisberger rejected the plan, not understanding its object. But when this had been subsequently explained to him, he sent Gendaskund and Allemewi to consult with Wangomen. The result was a formal offer, on the part of the Monseys of Goschgoschünk, to adopt Zeisberger into their tribe, and to constitute Woachelapuehk, one of their headmen, the umpire. This offer was accepted, and the act of naturalization consummated, with due ceremony, at Kaskaskunk, in the presence of Packanke and his council (July 14). Zeisberger was invested with all the rights and privileges of a Monsey. Any complaint which he, as the head of the Mission, might have to bring against such Monseys as were not connected with the Church, was to be submitted to Woachelapuehk. It was further stipulated that the covenant thus made should be published at Gekelemukpechünk and Onondaga, to the Shawanese and Wyandots, as well as to all other friendly tribes.

On this occasion, too, the views of the Christian Indians were set forth with regard to tribute. The only tribute of which the aborigines knew consisted in wampum and peltries. The former was used for the messages which were constantly passing from tribe to tribe; the latter for the pledges interchanged at treaties. A report had spread that the converts refused to contribute their share. This Wangomen contradicted in their name and by their authority. They were willing to pay a due part, except for the purposes of war. As an evidence of their sincerity in the matter, he presented to Paskunke a string of five fathoms from Languntoutenünk.

Zeisberger's adoption among the Monseys proves the complete triumph which he had gained over the Indians of Goschgoschünk. They flocked to his village. Their preacher, who had moved all the powers of heathenism to crush the Mission, avoided an open disgrace by nationalizing the cause which a majority of his clan had espoused.

Toward the end of July, Zeisberger laid out a new and larger town, with a church, on a hill on the west side of the river, opposite the first. In October, John George Jungmann[1] and his wife arrived to aid him in his work. Senseman returned to the settlements.

Sustained by his new assistant, and especially by Mrs. Jungmann, who spoke the Delaware tongue fluently and exercised a good influence over the Indian women, Zeisberger proclaimed the Gospel with power and great success. An awakening took place. Not a few believed. Inquiry-meetings were held every evening in Abraham's new house, often lasting until midnight. The very children were impressed and talked of Jesus.

---

[1] John G. Jungmann was born, April 19, 1720, at Hockenheim, in the Palatinate. In 1731 he immigrated with his father to America, and settled near Oley, in Pennsylvania. There he became acquainted with the Moravians, whom he joined, to the great indignation of his family. In 1745 he married the widow of Gottlob Büttner, and served the Church in various capacities at Falkner's Swamp, Gnadenhütten, Pachgatgoch, Bethlehem, and Friedenshütten, until he was called to the Beaver River.

On Christmas eve, Glikkikan and Gendaskund received baptism; the former was called Isaac, and the latter Jacob. Other converts were baptized on subsequent occasions. Twenty-two persons had followed Zeisberger from the Alleghany; now his flock numbered seventy-three, of whom thirty-six had come out from Goschgoschünk. His pious anticipations were realized. Having sown in tears, he was at last reaping a harvest with joy even from that barren ground.

In March of 1771, he undertook his first visit to Gekelemukpechünk. Anthony, Glikkikan, Jeremiah, a Mingo chief, and a Delaware Indian, escorted him. The whole party was mounted. They reached the Tuscarawas River in six days, crossed it on a raft, and rode down its northern bank to a beautiful plain, rising from the lowlands in a sudden sweep, where Nugen's Bridge now spans the stream, and extending to the hills that bound the valley. Here, amid a clearing of nearly a square mile, a little distance east of the present Newcomerstown, lay Gekelemukpechünk, the capital of the Delawares and seat of their Grand Council.[1] It was a large and flourishing town of about one hundred houses, mostly built of logs. On the south side of the river were the plantations. Zeisberger was the guest of Netawatwes, whose roomy dwelling, with its shingle-roof and board-floors, its staircase and stone-chimney, formed one of those Delaware lodges that rivaled the homesteads of the settlers.

---

[1] Gekelemukpechünk occupied the out-lots of Newcomerstown, in Oxford Township, Tuscarawas County, Ohio, and extended from the field next above the school-house to Nugen's Bridge.

At noon of the fourteenth this house was filled with Indians eager to hear the teacher whose fame had preceded him. The throng was so great that many stood outside. Nearly a dozen white men, most of them traders, were present. Netawatwes having introduced him to the assembly, Zeisberger preached the first Protestant sermon within the State of Ohio. His subject was the corruptness of human nature and the efficacy of Christ's atonement. He took particular pains to expose the absurdity of the doctrine, which the Indian preachers were at that time universally urging, that sin must be purged out of the body by vomiting, and which was ruining the health of their victims. After a stay of some days, devoted to missionary labors, he returned to Friedensstadt in time for the Passion-week, which was distinguished by the baptism of new converts.

He had scarcely left the Delaware capital, when one of those preachers appeared, whose silly falsehoods he had laid bare, and proclaimed a crusade against him, denouncing him as a notorious deceiver, that enslaved the Indians, and threatening the most terrible judgments of the Great Spirit in case the people gave him any further countenance. This produced no little excitement in the town. When Glikkikan came there, sevaral weeks later, he found a strong party opposed to the Gospel, but succeeded by his earnest appeals in counteracting its influence.

On the twentieth of June, the log church at Languntoutenünk was dedicated. The Mission had increased to one hundred persons.

CHAPTER XXI.

THE SUSQUEHANNA CONVERTS SETTLE IN THE WEST.—FIRST MISSIONARY TOWN IN OHIO.—1771, 1772.

A deputation from the General Board.—Zeisberger visits Bethlehem.—Removal of the whole Mission to the West determined upon.—Zeisberger lays this plan before the Susquehanna converts.—John Heckewelder appointed his assistant.—Zeisberger's illness at Lancaster.—Return to Beaver River and second visit to Ohio.—Discovers the Big Spring in the Tuscarawas valley.—Ancient fortifications in its neighborhood.—The Christian Indians receive a large tract of land from the Delawares.—Zeisberger begins the first missionary town in Ohio.—Description of the Tuscarawas valley and of the Delaware country in general.—Homes of the Shawanese and Wyandots.—Exploration of the West by Carver and Boone.—Progress and population of Western Colonies.—Description of the site of the first missionary town.—The Mission House.—Arrival of the Susquehanna converts.—Their journey to the West.—A missionary conference at Friedensstadt.—The first church-bell in Ohio.—More land ceded to the Christian Indians.—Zeisberger's illness and its self-denying cause.—A second missionary conference.—The Statutes and Rules of the Christian Indians.—Two evangelists of the Scotch Society for propagating the Gospel come to convert the Delawares.—Progress of the Mission.—Description of Schönbrunn.—Founding of Gnadenhütten.

A DEPUTATION from the General Board in Germany, consisting of Christian Gregor,[1] John Loretz,[2] and John

---

[1] Born, 1723, in Silesia; a member of the General Board from 1764 to 1801; consecrated a bishop in 1789; died, 1801, at Berthelsdorf, in Saxony. He was one of the most distinguished hymnologists of the Church, and the editor of her German Hymn Book.

[2] Born in Switzerland, a polished man of the world, who entered the Moravian ministry after his conversion, became a member of the Gen-

Christian Alexander de Schweinitz,[1] had arrived at Bethlehem (November, 1770), in order to visit the Moravian Churches of America. Schweinitz remained in this country, became the "Administrator" of the estates of the Unitas Fratrum, a member of the Mission Board, and a warm supporter of the work among the Indians.

To meet these deputies, Zeisberger was called to Bethlehem (July, 1771), where a missionary conference was held which led to important results.

While he was preaching to the natives on the Alleghany and Beaver Rivers, the Mission at Friedenshütten, under the faithful ministry of Schmick, had prospered greatly. In 1769 a second enterprise had been begun by John Roth, at Schechschiquanunk, so that there now existed three towns of Christian Indians, two on the Susquehanna and one on the Beaver.[2] But, as has been mentioned in another connection, the land granted by the Iroquois Council to the Susquehanna converts

---

eral Board in 1769, and died in 1798. He was the author of the *Ratio Disciplinæ*.

[1] Son of John Christian de Schweinitz, and born on his father's estate of Nieder Leuba, in Saxony, October 17, 1740, where those Moravian emigrants who founded Herrnhut were entertained on their flight from their native country. His father having joined the Moravian Church, he was educated for service in the same, and appointed the first Administrator of her American estates, which important trust he discharged for twenty-seven years (1770 to 1797). In 1797 he was elected to the General Board in Germany, and died in office in 1802, after having been ordained a *Senior Civilis* the year before.

[2] The Mission at Pachgatgoch, in New England, was sustained until 1770, amid many adverse circumstances. In that year, Thorp, the last missionary, was withdrawn, and Francis Boehler, stationed at Sichem as a preacher among the white settlers, was commissioned occasionally to visit the remnant of Indians.—*Bethlehem Diary of* 1770. *MS. B. A.*

now formed a part of the tract sold by the same Council to Pennsylvania at the treaty of Fort Stanwix. Governor Penn had, indeed, forbidden the surveyors to run a line within five miles of either town; nevertheless the Mission had too often experienced the evils resulting from the proximity of settlers to be satisfied with such a guarantee. Moreover, the Yankee and Pennamite War raged in the valley of Wyoming; and the disturbances which had been inaugurated were beginning to affect Friedenshütten, whose teachers saw that it was no longer a safe retreat for the Mission. On the other hand, the Grand Council at Gekelemukpechünk had urgently invited the Christian Indians to settle among the Delawares.

In consideration of all this, Zeisberger was persuaded that the unreclaimed wilderness of the present State of Ohio constituted the future field for the missionary operations of the Church, and advised the removal of the whole body of converts to that country. The conference adopted his views, and he was commissioned to lay the project before the Indians of Friedenshütten and Schechschiquanunk. At the same time, John Heckewelder was appointed his assistant, with special instructions to perfect himself in the Delaware language.

Taking Philadelphia on his way, where he had an interview with Vice-Governor Hamilton, he came to Friedenshütten in the beginning of September and convened a council of the converts from both stations. They unanimously accepted the offers of the Delaware chiefs, and resolved to emigrate to the West in spring.

Having recovered from a severe and dangerous fever, with which he was suddenly seized at Lancaster and which brought him to the brink of the grave, Zeisberger hastened back to the Beaver River.

In early spring (1772), accompanied by several converts, one of whom was Glikkikan, he proceeded to Gekelemukpechünk to announce the coming of the Susquehanna Indians.

It is interesting to trace his route. He took the great trail from Fort Pitt to Tuscarawas, which old forsaken town formed one of the landmarks of that day. Its site was the western bank of the Tuscarawas River,[1] immediately opposite the crossing-place of the trail, on the line of Stark and Tuscarawas Counties. Turning to the south, he followed the river, and passed through that part of the valley which is now enlivened by Zoar, Canal Dover, New Philadelphia, and other towns. In the morning of the sixteenth of March, he discovered a large spring, in the midst of the richest bottom-lands, above which lay a plateau offering an excellent site for a town. The natives of a former age had recognized its advantages. "Long ago," he writes, "perhaps more than a century ago, Indians must have lived here, who fortified themselves against the attacks of their enemies. The ramparts are still plainly to be seen. We found three forts in a distance of a couple of

---

[1] In Zeisberger's time, the Tuscarawas River was called the Muskingum. At present it does not receive this name until after its junction with the Walhonding, at Coshocton. I use the names in their present acceptation.

miles. The whole town must have been fortified, but its site is now covered with a thick wood. No one knows to what nation these Indians belonged; it is plain, however, that they were a warlike race." Continuing his journey to the confluence of the Gekelemukpechünk (Still Water Creek), he here struck a direct trail, which did not wind along the river, to the Delaware capital. His negotiations with Netawatwes were eminently satisfactory. The chief suggested that the Mission should be established at the "Big Spring;" and made a grant of all the land from the mouth of the Gekelemukpechünk northward to Tuscarawas.

Three weeks later, with five families numbering twenty-eight persons, Zeisberger, leaving the Mission on the Beaver in charge of Jungmann, went to build the first Christian town in Ohio. He reached the spring at noon of the third of May, and began to clear the ground on the following morning.

He was now in that valley which was to be the scene of his greatest works and severest trials. Blooming like the rose, with its farms, its rich meadows and gorgeous orchards, it was in his day, although a wilderness, no less a land of plenty, and abounded in everything that makes the hunting-grounds of the Indian attractive. It extended a distance of nearly eighty miles, inclosed on both sides by hills, at the foot of which lay wide plains terminating abruptly in bluffs, or sloping gently to the lower bottoms through which the river flowed. These plains, that now form the fruitful fields of " the second bottoms," as they are called, were then wooded with the oak and the hickory, the ash, the chestnut, and the maple, which interlocked their branches, but stood comparatively free from the undergrowth of other forests. The river-bottoms were far wilder. Here grew walnut-trees and gigantic sycamores, whose colossal trunks even now astonish the traveler; bushy cedars, luxuriant horse-chestnuts, and honey-locusts, cased in their armor of thorns. Between these clustered laurel bushes, with their rich tribute of flowers, or were coiled the thick mazes of the vine from which more fragrant tendrils twined themselves into the nearest boughs; while here and there a lofty spruce-tree lifted its evergreen crown high above the groves. These forests were generous to their children. They gave them the elm-bark to make canoes, the rind of the birch for medicine, and every variety of game for their food. The soil was even more liberal. It produced strawberries, blackberries, raspberries, gooseberries, black currants, and cranberries; nourished the plum, the cherry, the mulberry, the papaw, and the crab-tree; and yielded wild potatoes, parsnips, and beans. Nor was the river chary of its gifts, but teemed with fish of unusual size and excellent flavor.[1]

---

[1] It may be interesting to some readers to hear what Zeisberger says of the climate of the Tuscarawas valley, in that day: "The summer is hot, especially in July and August; the winter very mild. The snow is seldom deep and soon melts. There is little frost before January. Throughout the winter rain falls in great quantities, and there are few bright days. Nevertheless the Muskingum generally freezes, once or even twice, in the course of this season. The grass of the river-bottoms remains green, and is found in full luxuriance by the end of March. East wind seldom continues longer than for half a day, and is not a sign

This valley, however, did not embrace the whole territory of the Delawares. Driven from the Delaware to the Susquehanna, from the Susquehanna to the Alleghany, and thence still farther west, they had at last settled upon that tract which formed the munificent gift of the Wyandots. Its boundary line began at the Beaver River, extended to the Cuyahoga and along Lake Erie to the Sandusky, up the Sandusky to the Hocking, down the Hocking to the Ohio, and up that river to Shingas Town, including nearly one-half of the present State of Ohio.[1] The chief seats of the Monseys were on the Beaver; in the Tuscarawas valley lived the Unamis and Unalochtgos.

The rest of Ohio was inhabited by Shawanese and Wyandots. Of the former, who were divided into four tribes—the Mequachake, to whom belonged the hereditary priesthood; the Chillicothe; the Kiskapocok, and the Piqua—some were found on the Muskingum, but more on the Scioto.[2] A part of the latter, with their Half-King, had settled at the mouth of the Sandusky; the other part near Detroit. These two tribes were nearly equal in point of population, but not as

---

of rain. This is brought by the south and west winds, and even by the northwest wind. Rain setting in with a west wind often continues for a week."

[1] Boundaries given by Glikkikan, in 1772, to John Ettwein. Ettwein's Journal. MS. B. A.

[2] Their chief towns on the Scioto were Pickaway, Kischbuki, Mocheuschay, and Chelokraty, where Henry, a white trader and gunsmith, brother of Judge Henry, of Lancaster, Pennsylvania, was domiciliated. This trader's wife, when a child, had been carried off captive by the Shawanese, and had grown up among them.

numerous as the Delawares.[1] At that time there were no settlements within the present State of Ohio, although they stretched as far as the Virginia shore of the Ohio River.[2]

More distant regions of the West were likewise becoming known. Jonathan Carver, of Connecticut, had explored the borders of Lake Superior and the country of the Sioux beyond it, bringing back glowing accounts of the copper mines of the Northwest, and of the great River Oregon, which he reported to flow into the Pacific; and Daniel Boone had traversed Kentucky. The British settlements had everywhere increased, in spite of the efforts of the Home Government to prevent their growth. Vincennes counted four hundred white persons, and Detroit six hundred. The Colonies under Spanish sway were still more flourishing. Saint Louis had become an important center of the fur trade with the Indians on the Missouri; New Orleans numbered thirty-one hundred and ninety souls, among whom were twelve hundred and twenty-five slaves; and the whole population in the Mississippi valley amounted to about thirteen thousand five hundred persons.[3]

Zeisberger's explorations around the Big Spring convinced him of the many advantages of that site. On both sides of the river were bottom-lands interspersed with small lakes, reaching, on the western

---

[1] Authorities for the above description of Ohio are: Zeisberger's MS. Hist. of the Indians; his Journal at Schönbrunn; and Ettwein's Journal, MS. B A.
[2] Doddridge's Notes, 225.   [3] Bancroft's Hist. U S., vol. vi.

bank, to the foot of a precipitous bluff, on the eastern to a declivity not quite so high. Near the base of the latter the spring gushed in a copious stream from beneath the roots of a cluster of lindens and elms, and fed a lake nearly a mile long, united by an outlet with the Tuscarawas. Both the lake and the outlet were navigable, so that the Indians could paddle their canoes from the river to the very foot of the declivity. On its top, just above the spring, where one of the old ramparts had been discovered, and not far from an ancient tumulus, was the site of the town.[1] While engaged in building it, many Delawares visited the spot. Zeisberger was so eager to instruct them that he frequently laid aside his axe, sat down on the tree he had felled, and told them of the Redeemer of the world. On the ninth of June, the Mission House was completed; and within its rude walls the converts celebrated the Lord's Supper, for the first time, on the twenty-seventh of the same month.

Not long after this, Zeisberger proceeded to Friedensstadt to welcome the Susquehanna converts.

These had (June 11th) set out in two bodies,—the one by land under John Ettwein, the other by water under Roth, numbering together two hundred and four persons.[2] They united on the West Branch, and

---

[1] The town was situated on the present (1863) farm of Rev. P. E. Jacoby, two miles southeast of New Philadelphia, in Goshen Township, Tuscarawas County. The road from New Philadelphia to Gnadenhütten passes over its site. The " Beautiful Spring " is dried up, and the lake a marsh choked with water-lilies.

[2] The Indians were mustered on the 1st of June. One hundred and

began the passage of the Alleghanies in company. Tormented by sandflies, in constant danger from rattlesnakes, suffering many other hardships, they toiled for a month across these lofty ridges, and then launched canoes on the Alleghany River, down which they passed to the Ohio, and down the Ohio to the Beaver, which brought them to Friedensstadt.

A conference of all the missionaries and native assistants, held at this station, determined to send an embassy to Gekelemukpechünk, to call the new town Welhik-Tuppeek (*Schönbrunn* or Beautiful Spring), and to revise the Delaware hymns and litanies, which work was intrusted to Zeisberger and a committee of Indians. On their way to the capital, the deputies appointed by the conference put up (August 26th) on the Mission House the first church-bell used in Ohio.

Netawatwes received them with evident satisfaction,

---

fifty-one came from Friedenshütten, and fifty-three from Schechschiquanunk. Among the latter were two sons and a nephew of King Tadeuskund. In the time of the Mission at Friedenshütten, 1765 to 1772, one hundred and eighty-six persons were added to the Church. The only equivalent which the converts received for their improvements, at the two stations, was a grant of one hundred and twenty-five pounds, Pennsylvania currency, from the Assembly of Pennsylvania, to which grant some benevolent Quakers added one hundred dollars. The lists, in Ettwein's handwriting, containing the names of the families who received the money, and the amount given to each, are still extant in the B. A. After the Indians were domiciliated in the West, they wrote a letter of thanks to their Quaker friends. It is dated Schönbrunn, May 21, 1773, and addressed to "Israel Pemberton, John Reynell, James Pench, Anthony Benezet, John Pemberton, Abel James, Henry Drinker, and the rest of the friends in Philadelphia."
—*Ettwein's Journal. MS. B. A.*

and ceded to the Mission an additional tract of land, stretching from the mouth of the original boundary-creek southward to within three miles of Gekelemukpechünk.[1] Thus a large part of the Tuscarawas valley passed into the possession of the Christian Indians.

The state of Zeisberger's health at this time caused Ettwein much anxiety. He was prostrated, and yet not by any apparent illness. Ettwein's persistent questions at last elicited the truth. In order not to burden the Mission Fund, Zeisberger had been satisfied with insufficient supplies and the coarsest fare, and was suffering from the effects of his abnegation. Against such sacrifices Ettwein protested, beseeching him not to jeopard his valuable life, and assuring him that the Board would willingly provide for all his wants.[2]

At a second missionary conference, held at Schönbrunn, the rules of the Indian Mission were revised. As these rules beautifully portray the religious and domestic character of the converts, we here reproduce them in full:

[3] *Statutes agreed upon by the Christian Indians, at Languntoutenünk and Welhik-Tuppeek, in the month of August, 1772.*

I. We will know no other God but the one only true God, who made us and all creatures, and came into this world in order to save sinners; to Him alone we will pray.

II. We will rest from work on the Lord's Day, and attend public service.

---

[1] Memoranda by Ettwein. MS. B. A.
[2] Ettwein's Journal. MS. B. A.
[3] Original copy. MS. B. A.

III. We will honor father and mother, and when they grow old and needy we will do for them what we can.

IV. No person shall get leave to dwell with us until our teachers have given their consent, and the helpers (native assistants) have examined him.

V. We will have nothing to do with thieves, murderers, whoremongers, adulterers, or drunkards.

VI. We will not take part in dances, sacrifices, heathenish festivals, or games.

VII. We will use no *tshapiet*, or witchcraft, when hunting.

VIII. We renounce and abhor all tricks, lies, and deceits of Satan.

IX. We will be obedient to our teachers and to the helpers who are appointed to preserve order in our meetings in the towns and fields.

X. We will not be idle, nor scold, nor beat one another, nor tell lies.

XI. Whoever injures the property of his neighbor shall make restitution.

XII. A man shall have but one wife—shall love her and provide for her and his children. A woman shall have but one husband, be obedient to him, care for her children, and be cleanly in all things.

XIII. We will not admit rum or any other intoxicating liquor into our towns. If strangers or traders bring intoxicating liquor, the helpers shall take it from them and not restore it until the owners are ready to leave the place.

XIV. No one shall contract debts with traders, or receive goods to sell for traders, unless the helpers give their consent.

XV. Whoever goes hunting, or on a journey, shall inform the minister or stewards.

XVI. Young persons shall not marry without the consent of their parents and the minister.

XVII. Whenever the stewards or helpers appoint a time to make fences or to perform other work for the public good, we will assist and do as we are bid.

XVIII. Whenever corn is needed to entertain strangers, or sugar for love-feasts, we will freely contribute from our stores.

XIX. We will not go to war, and will not buy anything of warriors taken in war.[1]

While the Mission was being organized, David McClure and Levi Frisbie, educated in Dr. Wheelock's Moore Charity School, at Lebanon, Connecticut, and

---

[1] This last statute was adopted at a later time, during the Revolutionary War.

sent out by the "Scotch Society for propagating the Gospel," arrived to preach to the Delawares, but relinquished this project when they found them provided with teachers. Ettwein, with that blunt honesty so characteristic of him, suggested that if the Scotch Society desired to aid in converting the Delawares, the Moravian Mission would accept any gifts it might choose to make.

Having attended to all the duties that brought him to the West, Ettwein bade his brethren farewell. Tears of gratitude bedimmed his eyes as they talked, at parting, of what God had wrought. The Mission was firmly established in its new field, and fair prospects were opening on every side. At Friedensstadt, Roth carried on the work; at Schönbrunn, which now rejoiced in a chapel dedicated September 19, labored Zeisberger, Jungmann, and Heckewelder;[1] and farther down the valley, at a spot where stood the Delaware hamlet in which King Beaver had died, admonishing his people to accept the Gospel,[2] and whence a direct trail led to the Beaver River, Joshua, a native assistant, was preparing to build for the Mohican converts a third settle-

---

[1] Schönbrunn had two streets laid out in the form of a T. On the transverse street, about the middle of it and opposite the main street, which ran from east to west, and was both long and broad, stood the church; adjoining it on the right hand, Zeisberger's house—on the left hand, Jungmann's; next to Zeisberger lived John Papunhank; next to him, Abraham; next to Jungmann, Jeremiah; and on the fifth lot, Isaac Glikkikan. At the northwest corner of the main street was the school-house. The bottom, from the foot of the bluff to the river, was converted into cornfields. The town contained more than sixty houses of squared timber, besides huts and lodges.—*Plan of Schönbrunn.* MS. B. A.

[2] A foot-note by Ettwein in one of Heckewelder's Journals. MS. B. A.

ment, afterward called Gnadenhütten.[1] Of this entire Mission Zeisberger was the superintendent. His town soon became the bright center of Christian influence in the West.

> Away in the forest, how fair to the sight
> Was the clear, placid lake as it sparkled in light,
> And kissed with low murmur the green shady shore,
> Whence a tribe had departed, whose traces it bore;
> Where the lone Indian hasten'd, and wond'ring hush'd
> His awe as he trod o'er the mouldering dust!
> How bright were the waters—how cheerful the song
> Which the wood-bird was chirping all the day long;
> And how welcome the refuge these solitudes gave
> To the pilgrims who toiled over mountain and wave!
> Here they rested—here gush'd forth salvation to bring,
> The fount of the Cross, by the "Beautiful Spring."

---

[1] Joshua arrived from Friedensstadt, with a party of Mohicans, on the 18th of September, and on the 24th laid out a town on the west side of the river, four miles above Schönbrunn, near Canal Dover. It was called the Upper Town. But, as Netawatwes insisted that this colony should go to the place agreed upon between him and Zeisberger, Joshua began to build Gnadenhütten (October 9th), the exact site of which is still preserved, it being the inclosed lot of ground at the southeastern extremity of the present Gnadenhütten, in Clay Township, Tuscarawas County. It received its name in memory of Gnadenhütten on the Lehigh, a settlement which was revived (1770) by a number of Moravians. This place is now known as Weissport, so called after Jacob Weiss, of Philadelphia, one of the settlers, the brother of Lewis Weiss, the attorney of the Moravians.

CHAPTER XXII.

ZEISBERGER'S VISITS TO THE SHAWANESE. PROGRESS OF THE MISSION IN OHIO.—1772-1774.

Zeisberger visits the Shawanese and projects a Mission among them.—The first religious service at Gnadenhütten.—Much spiritual life among the converts.—Instances of their faith and joy.—Opposition to the Gospel.—Echpalawehund a convert.—The Delawares attempt a moral reformation as a substitute for the Gospel.—The Mission at Friedensstadt relinquished.—Interview between the Delaware Council and Christian deputies.—The perplexity of Natawatwes with regard to the different creeds of Christianity.—John Jacob Schmick joins the Mission.—The first white child born in Ohio.—Death of Anthony, the national assistant.—Zeisberger's second and last visit to the Shawanese.—His meeting with White Eyes.—The opposition of the Shawanese chief to the Gospel.—His bitter philippic against the white race.—The project of a Shawanese Mission relinquished.—New church-edifices at Schönbrunn and Gnadenhütten.—The work prospers.—Baptism of Echpalawehund.—Newallike, and the first Cherokee convert.—Zeisberger offers to explore the Cherokee country.—Translates the Easter Morning Litany into Delaware.—Its first use at Schönbrunn.

No sooner had the Delaware Mission gained a foothold in Ohio than Zeisberger looked around, with faith and hope, to find other nations to which the Gospel might be brought. The Shawanese of the Muskingum, whom the Church had attempted to convert in Pennsylvania, attracted his notice. At the first of their villages he found a son of his old friend Paxnous; and, in his company, proceeded to Waketameki, their principal town, on a creek of the same name, near its confluence with the Muskingum.¹ It was known among traders as the "Vomit Town," because its inhabitants had been, for years, the miserable dupes of that doctrine which made emetics the means of salvation.

Zeisberger was well received. The native preacher, who ignorantly proclaimed this abomination, manifested a sincere desire to learn the truth, and was the first to propose that a missionary should live among his countrymen. The whole clan enthusiastically adopted this suggestion, to the great joy of Zeisberger. These Shawanese were warlike and perfidious; ever ready to instigate or begin hostilities against the Colonies. If they could be brought under the sway of the Christian religion, one of the worst elements would be removed from Western border-life.

On the road back to Schönbrunn, Zeisberger visited Gnadenhütten, where several log-houses had been finished, in one of which he held the first public service at that settlement (October 17). Like his own town, it flourished greatly. The Spirit of the Lord God came upon both places. The hearts of the converts and of many heathens were moved; and, especially at Christmas, grace was given in rich measure. Of these experiences, and of the manner in which the Indians expressed themselves upon the subject of religion, the following instances are on record:

---

¹ Waketameki was situated near Dresden, a town on the Muskingum, just below the mouth of Waketameki Creek, in Jefferson Township, Muskingum County, Ohio

Conversing with a heathen Delaware, one of the assistants said, "Why shall we not believe? The Word preached to us shows its power in our conversion." "Yes," added another, "as soon as I sought the Saviour with my whole heart I found Him, and what I asked for I received, and now I am daily growing happier, so that my heart sometimes burns with love like a flaming fire." "Ah," exclaimed a third, "heretofore I only heard, but now I believe, that my Creator became a man and shed His precious blood for me, which cleanses me from all sin." An unbaptized convert said, "When I longed for comfort and stood thinking of Jesus, it seemed to me that I could see Him on the Cross—then I found peace." "I feel," joyfully professed Michael, "as though the Saviour had taken up His abode in my heart. It is a blessed feeling! I can only weep and give myself wholly to Him." "And I," said Eve, "have never spent such a Christmas. I have obtained a deep insight into the mystery of the incarnation of God my Saviour." "As for me," remarked old Abraham, "my soul is full of joy. Oh, how good to give one's self to the Saviour!"

This religious interest spread to the Delaware capital. Echpalawehund, a noted and influential chief, who had spent Christmas at Schönbrunn and carried away impressions which he could not shake off, determined to become a Christian. This caused a great sensation. The Delawares were not willing to lose so distinguished a man, and, in the first burst of their anger, talked of expelling Zeisberger and his coadjutors from their territory. Calmer reflection, however, showed them the folly of such an attempt. The Christians constituted too powerful a party. Hence they adopted a different policy. Having called a council to devise means that would prevent the further spread of Christianity, they fell upon the idea of a reformation, not through the agency of the white teachers, but in the power of their own united will. Drunkenness, games, and whatever tended to demoralize were prohibited; traders bringing intoxicating drink, or teaching the Indians to play cards, were to be banished; ardent spirits, wherever found, were to be destroyed. Six overseers of morals were appointed to enforce the new order of things, which was actually inaugurated by staving ten kegs of rum. Thus they hoped to lead lives as correct as those of the Christians; and thus would neither chief, nor councilor, nor captain have an excuse to leave the town and build his lodge at Schönbrunn or Gnadenhütten.

But Echpalawehund assured his countrymen that such efforts would be in vain, and that faith in the Lord Jesus Christ must be the beginning of a genuine reformation. He was right. Their good intentions, like the fire of the council at which they had been adopted, flared for a little while, and then lay a heap of dead embers.

In the midst of these agitations, Shawanese from Waketameki arrived, on their way to Zeisberger, to renew their request for a teacher. Into their ears the excited Delawares poured the venom of their anger; and said so many evil things of the missionaries that the Shawanese grew distrustful and did not deliver their message. The instigator of this opposition to the Christian party was John Killbuck, a son of Netawatwes.[1]

The Mission at Friedensstadt had, meanwhile, been contending with serious difficulties. Owing to the proximity of Kaskaskunk, intoxicated Indians overran the town and disregarded its municipal regulations. Under these circumstances, Zeisberger called the converts to the Tuscarawas valley. The "City of Peace" was deserted (spring, 1773); its sanctuary laid even with the ground;[2] and its inhabitants were transferred in part to Gnadenhütten and in part to Schönbrunn.[3]

In the following June, a deputation of Christian Indians, with Glikkikan for their speaker, met the Council of Gekelemukpechünk, and once more made

---

[1] Killbuck was not an enemy of the Gospel itself; or, rather, he was willing to accept it outwardly for the sake of the advantages it would bring his nation. His opposition to the Christian party originated in his dissatisfaction with the Moravians, who, he said, were unable to protect the Indians in times of war, and, by a perverseness characteristic of his race, adduced the Paxton Insurrection as an instance, although it proved just the reverse.—*Jones's Journal*, Phila., 1865.

[2] This was done whenever the Christian Indians abandoned a town, so as to prevent their chapels from being desecrated by the heathens.

[3] In the course of the spring, the Rev. David Jones, Baptist minister at Freehold, N. J., visited the Delawares with the intention of bringing them the Gospel, and spent some time at the capital. He came likewise to Schönbrunn, where he preached. By request of the Council, he wrote a letter to Governor Penn, informing him of the reformation which the Delawares had inaugurated, especially in regard to the sale of rum.—*Jones's Journal of his Visits to some Nations of Indians.* Reprinted, Phila., 1865.

known the principles of their faith and the regulations of their communities. Glikkikan spoke not as a suppliant, but with authority and great boldness. And although the enemies of the Gospel did not believe, they were silenced for a season.

Netawatwes, about this time, was in much trouble both with regard to national affairs and the Christian religion. Anxious to promote the welfare of his people, and half convinced that their conversion to Christianity would prove the means, he was, nevertheless, weak-minded, and halted between two opinions. The differences prevailing among Christians augmented his vacillation. He could not understand that God's children were not of one name, faith, and practice. He could not believe that they were all right. He could not decide who was wrong. The Roman Catholics instituted forms and ceremonies; their rosaries and crucifixes seemed to him not different from the manitous of his own nation. The Moravians taught the necessity of personal faith and baptism, preaching Christ Jesus and Him crucified. The Quakers repudiated baptism, and gloried in the beauty of morality. The Episcopalians asserted that theirs was the true church and the apostolic ministry. Amid these conflicting views, Netawatwes, at last, devised a way of arriving at the truth. He would go to England, and consult the King as to the system of religion which the Delawares ought to adopt.

It was not a new idea. Months before this he had sent a message to Governor Penn, saying, "I am ready to go over the Great Waters to see that great King. Brother Governor and friends, I desire you to prepare a ship for me next spring."[1] And now that several Quakers visited him, he pertinaciously claimed their aid in effecting this purpose. It was, however, never carried out. The old chief remained in his rude council-house and did not see the splendor of St. James.

In August two more laborers entered the field—John Jacob Schmick and his wife—so that the corps of missionaries now embraced eight persons, namely, Zeisberger, Heckewelder, Roth, and Mrs. Roth, at Schönbrunn; Schmick, Mrs. Schmick, Jungmann, and Mrs. Jungmann, at Gnadenhütten.

A few weeks before the arrival of Schmick, there had been born, in the midst of this Mission-family, on the fourth of July, 1773, at Gnadenhütten, the first white child in the present State of Ohio. Mrs. Maria Agnes Roth was his mother, and he received in baptism, administered by Zeisberger, on the fifth of July, the name of John Lewis Roth.[2]

Simultaneously with the accession of so active a

---

[1] Penn. Col. Records, x. 62, etc.

[2] This interesting fact is established by the official diary of Gnadenhütten (MS. B. A.), which says, "July 4th, 1773. To-day God gave Brother and Sister Roth a young son. He was baptized into the death of Jesus, and named John Lewis, on the 5th inst., by Brother David Zeisberger, who, together with Brother Jungmann and his wife, came here this morning." Of the parents of this child we know the following:

His father, John Roth, was born at Sarmund, a village in the Mark Brandenburg, Prussia, February 3, 1726, and was the oldest son of teacher as Schmick, the Mission lost Anthony, its most valued native assistant. With lips eloquent even in death, he exhorted his countrymen to remain steadfast in the faith, and delivered a last testimony as bright as had been the daily testimony of his life. He passed away in the morning watches of the fifth of September, a patriarch of seventy-six years. Zeisberger mourned for him as for a brother.

In the same month, accompanied by Isaac Glikkikan and another convert named William, he paid a second visit to the Shawanese, hoping to renew the project of a work among them. At Gekelemukpechünk he found not only Hurons and Ottawas, through whom the Tus-

---

John and Anna Maria Roth. He was educated in the Catholic Church, and learned the trade of a locksmith. In 1748, he joined the Moravian Church at Neusalz, in Prussia, whence he emigrated to America, arriving at Bethlehem, where he settled, in July, 1756. In 1759, he entered the service of the Indian Mission.

His mother was Maria Agnes Pfingstag, a daughter of John Michael and Rosina Pfingstag, m. n. Ketschl, and was born at Wirsche, in the Kingdom of Würtemberg, on the 4th of April, 1735. When she was two years of age her parents emigrated with her to America (1737). She married John Roth at Bethlehem, Pa., on the 16th of August, 1770. They took up their abode at Schechschiquanunk, the Mission-station on the Susquehanna, where their oldest child, John Roth, was born, August 4th, 1771. On the 11th of June, 1772, they left that station, accompanied the Christian Indians to the West, and settled at Friedensstadt, Pa., where Roth became the resident missionary. This station having been relinquished, they proceeded to Gnadenhütten, Ohio, arriving on the 24th of April, 1773. Here their second son, John Lewis, was born. About the middle of August, of the same year, they removed to Schönbrunn. In the documents relating to the Indian Mission Roth is called Rothe; but in that church register at Bethlehem which records his marriage, the name is written Roth. That this latter was his true name becomes clear from his own signatures to letters and his official signature to records in the register of the church at York, where he died.

carawas Mission might be made known on the shores of Lake Erie, and in the great Northwest, but also that native who was destined to become its most eminent supporter at home.

Among the councilors of Netawatwes, no one enjoyed a more honorable name, and exercised a more commanding influence, than Koquethagachton, or White Eyes,[1] a Miami chief, and the first war-captain of that tribe. His achievements had given glory to the Delaware nation; and, wherever the fires of their lodges burned, his fame was rehearsed. When Zeisberger first came to the valley, he was absent on a long journey down the Ohio and the Mississippi to New Orleans, whence he returned by sea, landing at New York, and traveling from there, by way of Philadelphia, back to his kindred and his people. This tour enlarged his views. The benefits of civilization, and the contrast between the state of its children and that of the aborigines, made a profound impression upon his mind. He pondered the subject long and earnestly, until it became the all-absorbing purpose of his life to reclaim the Indian from barbarism and elevate him to an equality with the white man. That Zeisberger and Glikkikan would prove influential coadjutors in carrying out this project he was not slow to recognize, more particularly as the latter had been, for many years, his most intimate friend, to whom he could freely unfold his plans. He gave them both a cordial

---

[1] So called from the peculiar whiteness of his eyeballs.

welcome, took them to his own town, and entertained them for the night.[1] Zeisberger improved the opportunity to instruct him in the Gospel. They sat together on a little hillock, near his lodge, talking of Jesus.

It was Zeisberger's purpose to visit the Shawanese of the lower towns, but he found their chief at Waketameki. His name was Gieschenatsi, a fierce savage and bitter enemy of the white race. Among the settlers he was known as the "Hard Man." To gain him for the Gospel was worth every effort. Zeisberger approached him with its glorious truths. At first he listened patiently, but, by-and-by, his true character burst out.

"I suppose," he said, "you come to speak 'good words' to the Shawanese. Go, and see what you can do. Perhaps they will hear you. Perhaps you will succeed better than I, when I attempt to exert my authority.

"The whites tell us of their enlightened understanding, and the wisdom they have from Heaven; at the same time, they cheat us to their hearts' content. For we are as fools in their eyes, and they say among themselves, 'The Indians know nothing! The Indians understand nothing!' Because they are cunning enough to detect the weak points of our character, they think they can lead us as they will, and deceive

---

[1] White Eyes' Town was situated on the Tuscarawas, six miles below Gekelemukpechünk, near White Eyes' Plains, in Oxford Township, Coshocton County.

us as they please, even while they pretend to seek our good. See them coming into our towns with their rum! See them offering it to us with persuasive kindness! Hear them cry, 'Drink! drink!' And when we have drunk, and act like the crazed, behold these good whites, these men of a benevolent race, standing by, pointing at us with their fingers, laughing among themselves, and saying, 'Oh, what fools! what great fools the Shawanese are!' But who make them fools? Who are the cause of their madness?"

Pausing for a moment and pointing to Zeisberger, he proceeded in a furious tone:

"This man and the like of him! They are the cause of our being fools and of our madness. But they always tell us 'good words;' they always 'love' us and want 'to save our souls.' 'Behold,' they say, 'thus and so has God taught us; He has given us knowledge; we are wiser than you; we must instruct you.' Oh, certainly, they are wiser than we!—wiser in teaching men to get drunk; wiser in overreaching men; wiser in swindling men of their land; wiser in defrauding them of all they possess!"

The excited chief poured forth this tirade until after midnight, when sheer exhaustion forced him to stop. Neither Zeisberger nor Glikkikan answered him a word. The next morning, however, they sent for him, and in a series of speeches replied to his invectives, explaining the character of their missionary work, challenging him, or any other Indian, to establish a single instance of fraud on the part of a white teacher, setting forth the

Gospel as that knowledge which makes a race of Christians superior to a race of heathens, but assuring him that it constrains no one—free itself, it must be freely received. "You may not believe my words at present," remarked Zeisberger, "but the time is coming when you and I and all men will stand before God, and everything will be known and revealed. In that day it will appear that I have this day spoken the truth, and you will then acknowledge the reality of what you now denounce."

Gieschenatsi had recovered from his burst of passion and gave them a courteous hearing, but his hostility to the Christian religion continued unchanged. Indeed, it became evident that there was no prospect of founding a Mission in his tribe so long as his influence was arrayed against it. The country, moreover, was filled with rumors of an approaching Indian war. Nor could anything be accomplished at Waketameki. Those of its inhabitants who had been so eager to embrace the Gospel were gone; the rest showed themselves indifferent. Zeisberger returned to Schönbrunn, and gave up this last attempt which the Church made to convert Shawanese.

Both at Schönbrunn and Gnadenhütten new chapels were now dedicated, to which the Indians flocked in large numbers. Scarcely a day passed that did not bring such as were eager to hear the Gospel. From Christmas to the end of January (1773, 1774), more than twenty converts were baptized, among them Echpalawehund, who received the name of Peter. In the previous summer, Noah, the first Cherokee convert, had been added to the Church.[1] These baptisms encouraged Zeisberger. His Mission now embraced representatives of nine tribes. There were Unamis, Unalachtgos, and Monseys; Mohicans, Nanticokes, and Shawanese; Canais, Mingoes, and a Cherokee. And yet he was willing to let others reap, while he went to new fields in which the Word had never been sown. A letter to the Board conveys the offer to undertake an exploration of the Cherokee country, and one to Bishop Hehl says: "Upon the whole, I wish that I were free to leave here. There are so many other places where God's Word ought to be preached, and so many Indians who have not yet heard that their Maker is their Redeemer."

The Mission continued to prosper throughout the winter and spring. Scarcely two months after Echpalawehund's conversion, Newallike arrived from the Susquehanna, with his whole family, and built himself a house at Schönbrunn. "We have," said he, "no greater wish on earth than to become Christians."[2] Thus, one by one, the head men of the Delawares were gathered in. When Natawatwes heard of this alienation of another chief, he began to turn his attention still more earnestly to the claims of the Gospel.

Zeisberger now undertook an important literary work. The festival of the Lord's Resurrection was approaching, and he translated into Delaware the Easter Morning

---

[1] He was taken prisoner by the Delawares in 1753, and was now domiciliated among them, having married one of their women, who was also baptized and named Wilhelmina.

[2] He was baptized on Ascension-day, May 12, 1774, and received the name of Augustin.

Litany of the Church, that the converts might observe the occasion in accordance with the solemn usage still prevailing among Moravians throughout the world.[1]

"Very early," "when it was yet dark,"[2] the church-bell broke the silence of the night and called the Indians to the sanctuary. Standing up among the expectant worshipers, Zeisberger chanted the Easter greeting of the primitive Christians, "The Lord is risen!" and the congregation answered with a burst of song, "The Lord is risen indeed!" Then, at daybreak, they all moved out in procession, two by two, to the consecrated ground where seventeen of their number already lay enshrined, waiting for the resurrection of the just. It was the third of April; nature had flung aside her veil of morning mist, and it lay in transparent folds on the bosom of the river. The gemmed trees were gently swayed by the first breath of spring, the sky was cloudless, and over the eastern hills came the sun to awaken the valley.

Zeisberger's heart was deeply moved as he looked upon the Indians gathered around the graves of their friends, and began the Litany in their own tongue.

"Nolsittam," he said, "nekti Getanittowitink, Wetochwink, Wequisink woak Welsit Mtschitschangünk, nan gischelendangup wemi koecu untschi Jesus Christink, woak Christink achpop, mawindammenep Pemhakamiksit li hokenk."

---

[1] The Easter Morning Litany embodies the Moravian Confession of Faith. It is prayed annually early in the morning of Easter Sunday, and, wherever this is practicable, on the consecrated burial grounds of the Church.

[2] Mark, xvi. 2; Luke, xxiv. 1; John, xx. 1.

(*I believe in the One only God, Father, Son, and Holy Ghost, who created all things by Jesus Christ, and was in Christ, reconciling the world unto himself.*)

To this confession the choir sang the response: "Quawullakenimellenk Wetochemellan, Nihillataman Awossagame woak Pemhakamike, ktelli gandhattawanep julil Lelpoatschik woak netawi Nostangik, woak ktelli gemitacheaniechtauwanep Amementittak. Gohan, Wetochemellan! ntitechquo ktelgiqui wulinamenep elinquechinan."

(*We thank thee, O Father, Lord of heaven and earth, because Thou hast hid these things from the wise and prudent, and hast revealed them unto babes: even so, Father; for so it seemed good in Thy sight.*)

"Wetochemellan!" he continued, "gischachsi mehittachcaniechtol Ktellewunsowoagan!"—that is, *Father, glorify Thy name!* And with one voice the congregation answered in the words of the Lord's Prayer:

"Ki Wetochemellenk Awossagamewunk! machelendasutsch Ktellewunsowoagan. Ksakimawoagan pejewiketsch. Ktelitehewoagan leketsch talli Achquidhakamike, elgiqui leek talli Awossagame. Milineen juke Gischquik gunigischuk Achpoan. Woak miwelendamauwineen Ntschannauchsowoagannena elgiqui nilana miwelendamauwenk nik Tschetschanilawequengik. Woak katschi npawuneen li Achquetschiechtowoaganink; schukund ktennineen untschi Medhikink. Alod knihillatamen Ksakimawoagan woak Ktallewupowoagan woak Ktallowilipowoagan li hallamagamik. Amen."

(*Our Father who art in heaven, hallowed be Thy name. Thy kingdom come. Thy will be done in earth as it is in heaven. Give us this day our daily bread. And forgive us our trespasses, as we forgive those who trespass against us. And lead us not into temptation, but deliver us from evil: for thine is the kingdom, and the power, and the glory, forever. Amen.*)

Proceeding with the Litany, he confessed faith in the Father, Son, and Holy Ghost, the people adding to each confession, *This I most certainly believe;* and published the great doctrines of a Christian Church, of her sacraments, and of the resurrection from the dead, *Amen* being the solemn response. Then all united in the petition: "Niluna gettemaki Matschilipijenk patamolhummena, pendawineen echvalan Nihillalijenk Pattamawos!"

(*We poor sinners pray, hear us, gracious Lord and God!*)

"Woak glennineen," Zeisberger went on, "hallamagamik Witauchsundowoaganink li Meniechink gischtawamit, hunak woak witsche enda hallogaganitschik Kimachtennanak, woak Chesmupenank, nik metschi mentschimat juke getink, woak lelemineen tamse newitschitsch allachimuineen enda achpekok hakey."

(*And keep us in everlasting fellowship with our brethren, and with our sisters, who have entered into the joy of their Lord; also with the servants and handmaids of the Church, whom Thou hast called home in the past year, and with the whole Church triumphant; and let us rest together in Thy presence from our labors.*)

And when the *Amen* that followed this petition had

died away, there swelled from many lips the sweet-toned hymn:

"Tamse jun ugattumane,
   Ajane Wdulhewink,
Mocum nhagatamane
   Nhakeuchsowoaganink,
Wentschihhillak Erchauwesit,
   Pakantschitsch kikeuchgun,
Nenicchink hokunk epit
   Ndaan, Christ ndamuignuk-
     gun."
	When I shall gain permission
	  To leave this mortal tent,
	And get from pain dismission,
	  Jesus, thyself present;
	And let me, when expiring,
	  Recline upon Thy breast,
	Thus I shall be acquiring
	  Eternal life and rest.

Once more Zeisberger resumed the Litany, and now in exalted tones proclaimed:

"Machelemuxowoaganitetsch nanni Amuiwoaganid woak Pommauchsowoaganid! auwen welsittawot pommauchsutsch quonnatsch angel.

"Machelemo achgenimo ne talli Meniechink nik pehachtit, woak nik ika pemachpitschik hokenk."

(*Glory be to Him who is the Resurrection and the Life; He was dead, and behold, He is alive for evermore: and he that believeth in Him, though he were dead, yet shall he live.*

Glory be to Him in the Church which waiteth for Him, and in that which is around Him.)

From everlasting to everlasting, said the congregation.

Then came the benediction:

"Wulanittowoagan Nihillalquonk Jesus Christ, woak Wtahoaltowoagan Getanittowit, woak Witauchsundowoagan Welsit Mtschitschank, achpitaquengetsch wemi."

(*The grace of our Lord Jesus Christ, and the love of God, and the communion of the Holy Ghost, be with us all.*)

Loud and full of joy, ringing far over the plateau and into the depths of the forest, rose the final *Amen*.

CHAPTER XXIII.

DUNMORE'S WAR.—1774.

Rupture between Virginia and Pennsylvania.—Lord Dunmore and Connolly.—The conduct of the Western Indians since the Pontiac Conspiracy.—Irresponsible border warfare.—Unlawful sale of land by the Iroquois to Virginia.—Excitement among the Shawanese.—Massacres.—Retaliation on the part of the settlers.—Indians indiscriminately murdered near Wheeling and opposite Wellsville.—Logan's family among the number.—His revenge.—The Mission and the Delaware Council advocate peace.—White Eyes its great champion.—Glikkikan's appeal to him to become a Christian.—The converts ask the Delaware Council to naturalize all their teachers.—Roth and family return to Pennsylvania.—The subsequent life of the first white child born in Ohio.—The war begins.—Excitement among the young Delawares, and threats against the missionaries.—The nation still for peace.—Preliminary campaign against the Shawanese on the Muskingum.—Their towns destroyed.—Dunmore's and Lewis's campaign.—Battle of Point Pleasant.—Cornstalk.—Dunmore on the Scioto.—Adopts White Eyes' counsel and opens negotiations.—Peace concluded at Camp Charlotte.—Logan's speech.—White Eyes and the Delawares reap praise from Lord Dunmore.

SEASONS of spiritual refreshing, like the Easter Festival just referred to, were rudely interrupted by an Indian war, the prelude to which was a rupture between the governments of Virginia and Pennsylvania, of a most unwarrantable character on the part of the former.

Lord Dunmore, the Governor of Virginia, who favored colonization in the West because he knew how to make an official position subserve his private interests, fell upon the idea of extending his government and increasing his opportunities of self-aggrandizement by a bold act of usurpation. There came to Pittsburg (1774) a certain John Connolly, a doctor of medicine, land-jobber, and willing tool of any evil scheme, and, without notice to the government of Pennsylvania, assumed command of that post and all its dependencies, issued a proclamation announcing his commission from Lord Dunmore, and ordered a muster of the militia. In opposition to such unlawful proceedings, Governor Penn instructed Arthur St. Clair, the Clerk of Westmoreland County, to enforce the Riot Act.[1] This Dunmore pretended to take as a personal insult, and obstinately refused to settle the dispute, in spite of the most honorable offers on the part of the Council of Pennsylvania. The confusion thus prevailing along the frontier was increased by hostilities with the savages.

Whatever other writers may say to the contrary, we have the united testimony of the missionaries, whose opportunities to ascertain the truth will not be disputed, that the Indians, after the close of Pontiac's Conspiracy, remained faithful, as nations, to their treaties with the Colonies. Irresponsible parties, indeed, occasionally murdered white men. But such acts were not acts of war, and found their equivalents among the backwoodsmen themselves, the most of whom as little hesitated to shoot an Indian as to shoot a "bear or a

---

[1] Penn. Col. Records, x. 140, etc.

buffalo." Irregular and bloody proceedings of this sort are inevitable when a superior race dispossesses an inferior one of its homes.

An instance occurred in the spring of 1773. Some Shawanese who came to Gekelemukpechünk with white scalps were rebuked by the Delawares, and ordered to leave their territory.[1] Nor did they meet with anything but censure in their own towns. Soon after this, however, the Iroquois ceded to Virginia a large tract of land south of the Ohio, below the mouth of the Great Kanawha.[2] It was an illegal transaction. That country belonged to other nations and not to the League; but settlers immediately pressed forward, and built their cabins close to the Shawanese. Then first this tribe openly talked of war. Before the excitement could be allayed, another lawless massacre added to its intensity. Three traders fell victims to the cupidity of some Cherokees, with whom they were going down the Ohio, and to whom they incautiously displayed a large quantity of silver trinkets.[3] At the same time, Indians on the Great Kanawha had, it was reported, stolen a number of horses. Instead of seeking redress from the tribal authorities, the settlers began to avenge themselves by indiscriminately slaughtering Indians of any name.

A body of land-jobbers and their adherents had col-

---

[1] Zeisberger's Diary, Schönbrunn, May, 1773. MS. L. A.
[2] Ibid., July, 1773.
[3] Ibid., April, 1774. MS. L. A.

lected at Wheeling, under Captain Cresap.¹ On the twenty-seventh of April, regardless of the earnest protestations of Colonel Zane, the proprietor of the place, who predicted an Indian war as the inevitable result, they shot, in cold blood, two natives descending the river in a canoe with white traders; and, in the evening of the same day, attacked a peaceful encampment at the mouth of Captina Creek,² killing a number of Indians. A few days later, thirty-two men, under Daniel Greathouse, marched to the Baker Plantation in Virginia, opposite the present Wellsville, where was another encampment of natives, and having enticed some of them to cross the river brutally murdered them, and then killed several more who came to inquire the cause of the firing. Twelve Indians fell on this occasion, and a number were wounded.³ Among the dead was the entire family of Logan.

Hostilities so unjustifiable inflamed the Seneca Mingoes of the Ohio valley, and a majority of the Shawanese, with the desire of revenge. The Shawanese towns on the Muskingum inclined to peace,⁴ but the rest of the nations clamored for war; while Logan, his soul turned to gall against that race whose friend he and his father Shikellimy had ever been, calling around him chosen

---

[1] Doddridge's Notes on the Settlements and Indian Wars of the Western Parts of Virginia and Pennsylvania, p. 226.

[2] In Belmont County, Ohio, flowing into the Ohio River.

[3] Doddridge's Notes, p. 227.

[4] Penn. Archives, iv. 568. Deposition of Richard Butler, a trader, who vindicates the good faith of those Shawanese among whom he had been living.

followers, went out to strike blow for blow, and ceased not until for each of his thirteen murdered kinsfolk a scalp had been torn from a white man's head. "Now," he said, "I am satisfied for the loss of my relations and will sit still." Nor did he take any further part in the war.

Jungmann and Schebosh, returning from Pittsburg, were the first to bring to Schönbrunn the news of Connolly's usurpation and the approaching conflict. This intelligence was confirmed a week later, on a tranquil Sunday evening, by the arrival of a messenger from Gekelemukpechünk, who announced, with fearful warwhoops, another massacre of Indians on the Ohio. There followed, for Zeisberger and the Mission, several months of anxiety, but also of earnest labors in the interests of peace. While Lord Dunmore was collecting forces to crush the Shawanese, and his tool at Pittsburg was augmenting the complications by his brutal treatment of the Indians, the converts, in conjunction with the Delawares, encouraged by Sir William Johnson and Croghan, did what they could to avert a war. Their efforts met with varying success. A part of the Shawanese continued friendly, the rest sometimes listened to reason, and then again fiercely turned away from every attempt at a pacification, even firing upon Delaware messengers sent to conciliate them. Without doubt, however, the negotiations would eventually have been crowned with the happiest results if the impetuous young braves could have been restrained from the war-path, and the settlers could have been kept from provoking and retaliating their assaults. A council of Delawares, Shawanese, Hurons, and Cherokees, held at Gekelemukpechünk in June, seemed to promise peace; but scarcely had it separated when three Shawanese of the lower towns, who had magnanimously protected several traders and escorted them to Pittsburg, were attacked on their homeward way by a party of borderers and barely escaped with one of their number wounded.

The most active upholder of peace was White Eyes. This brought him into closer union with the Christian Indians, and he recognized, more and more, the beneficial influence which they were exerting among the Delawares. Glikkikan lost no opportunity to impress upon him the truths of the Gospel. On one occasion he made a touching appeal to him.

"Brother," said he, "you remember our ancient friendship. We pledged ourselves to be faithful one to another and love one another as long as we lived. We placed our *schewondican* (tobacco-pouch) between us, that each might take from it at will. We agreed to tell each other if either of us should discover the true way to happiness, so that both of us might walk therein. I wish to redeem that promise. I wish to testify to you that I have found this way and am following it up. It is the Word of God. This leads to salvation and life eternal. Come, go with me; share my happiness."

Tears rolled down the cheeks of White Eyes as he listened to these words, and he assured his friend that he often thought of becoming a Christian. Nor was it long before he had an opportunity of evidencing his sympathy with the Mission. The converts presented a belt to the Council at Gekelemukpechünk, and asked that all their teachers, and not Zeisberger only, should be naturalized as Delawares, and thus enjoy the protection of the tribe in the event of a war. This measure White Eyes warmly urged. It was, however, not adopted, but referred to the councilors for further consideration. Meanwhile Roth and his family—the only one of the missionaries that had children—returned to Bethlehem, by the advice of Zeisberger.[1]

Toward the end of June the war began. Eight parties of Shawanese and Mingoes lurked in the forests,

---

[1] In this way, John Lewis Roth, the first white child born on the soil of Ohio, was brought to Pennsylvania when not quite one year of age. There his parents lived successively at Mountjoy, York, Emmaus, and Hebron, at all of which places his father was pastor of the Moravian church. In 1790, his father took charge a second time of the church at York, where he died in the following year on the 22d of July. His mother died at Nazareth, February 25, 1805.

John Lewis Roth himself was educated at Nazareth Hall, and formed a member of the class of 1785, the first organized in that institution. After leaving Nazareth Hall there are no traces of him for a number of years, until he is found living on a farm near Nazareth, married, and the head of a family. In 1836, he became a resident of Bath, Pa., and joined the Lutheran church which the Rev. A. Fuchs gathered in that neighborhood. Of this church he remained a consistent and worthy member. He died on the 25th of September, 1841, in the 69th year of his age, and was buried in the Bath grave-yard, where his remains now lie. His tombstone bears the following inscription:

"*Zum Andenken an Ludwig Roth, geboren 4th Juli,* 1773. *Gestorben* 25*th September,* 1841, *Alter* 68 *Jahre,* 2 *M.,* 21 *Tage.*"

Mr. Fuchs preached his funeral sermon on the parable of the prodigal, which text Roth himself selected previous to his death. He left five children, four sons and one daughter. For these facts I am indebted to Mr. Andrew G. Kern, of Nazareth, and especially to Rev. A. Fuchs, of Bath.

while Virginia volunteers were drawing near to the Tuscarawas valley. This excited the young Delawares to the highest pitch. They snuffed the coming battles, and could hardly be restrained. Taking advantage of the absence of White Eyes, they insisted upon an offensive alliance with the Shawanese, and upon forcibly silencing the Christian Indians and their teachers. "Let the teachers be put to death!" they said. Two families of converts, one of them that of old Allemewi, yielded to these evil influences, forsook the Mission, and made common cause with the savages. Assurances sent by the volunteers, that they would not molest the Delawares, but were advancing against the Shawanese, somewhat calmed the storm; and when White Eyes arrived from Pittsburg with official messages of the same import, it came to a sudden end. Prompted by the Christian party, the Council decreed neutrality, and advised all Delawares to remain in their towns during the approaching attack upon the Shawanese.

This took place in the beginning of August.[1] Colonel Angus McDonald, at the head of four hundred men collected from the western part of Virginia, by order of Dunmore, proceeded against Waketameki, and, after a feeble resistance on the part of the Indians, destroyed this town together with four other villages. The tribe itself, however, escaped, and but three chiefs were brought back as prisoners.

---

[1] Zeisberger's Diary, Schönbrunn, MS. L. A.; Doddridge's Notes, 241-243.

The war, which had thus been inaugurated, was now carried on with vigor.[1] Two other bodies of men had been mustered: the one, composed of Southern Virginians, at Camp Union, in the Greenbrier country[2]—the other from the Northern counties, at Pittsburg, whither Dunmore had gone in person to lead it to the field. These two divisions were to unite at the mouth of the Great Kanawha.

On the eleventh of September, the Southern forces, numbering eleven hundred men, began their march through the pathless wilderness and over mountains covered with tangled thickets and massive rocks. The supplies and ammunition were transported on packhorses. After nineteen weary days of hardships, they encamped, on the first of October, at Point Pleasant, which had been designated as the place of rendezvous. On the ninth, an express arrived informing Colonel Lewis that Lord Dunmore had changed his plan of operations and ordering him to march to old Chillicothe, in the Scioto valley. The following day two of the men, while hunting, suddenly encountered a Shawanese camp, all alive with preparations for an immediate attack. One of them was shot, the other escaped and gave the alarm; but before Colonel Lewis could call out more than two detachments, eight hundred confederate Shawanese and Mingoes were upon him. At about four hundred yards from the encampment the

---

[1] Doddridge's Notes, chap. xxvi.; Bancroft's Hist. U. S., vii. 167, etc.
[2] Now Lewisburg, Greenbrier County, Virginia.

battle began. The savages were commanded by their great champion, Cornstalk, who displayed consummate generalship. After the first onset, he so manœuvred his men that the Virginians were inclosed within a triangle, of which the Ohio and Kanawha Rivers formed the two sides and the Indian army the base. All day long, from sunrise to sunset, the battle raged. Both parties fought with the utmost fury. Above the din of the conflict rose Cornstalk's voice, encouraging his men, and saying, "Be strong! be strong!" Finally the Indians fell back, crossed the Ohio in the night, and hurried to the Scioto. Their loss was never ascertained. That of the Virginians was heavy; seventy-five were killed, and one hundred and forty wounded. Yet they might well claim the victory. The foe was gone, and they moved unmolested toward his towns.

Thither Dunmore had preceded them, with White Eyes as his adviser and the representative of the Delaware Council.[1] White Eyes used every means to prevent further bloodshed. He induced the Earl to relinquish his plan of scouring the forests on his way from the Ohio to the Scioto, and advocated a treaty, urging that the mere presence of the army would bring the Shawanese to terms. Convinced of the reasonableness of this policy, Dunmore began negotiations, and sent orders to Colonel Lewis to return to Virginia. But Lewis, upheld by the sentiments of his whole command, disregarded this order, continued to advance,

---

[1] Zeisberger's Diary, Schönbrunn. MS. L. A.

and, on the twenty-fourth of October, effected a junction with the main body in Pickaway, near old Chillicothe.[1] The Earl reiterating his orders in person, he was forced to obey, although with extreme reluctance, his men burning to overrun the Scioto valley and exterminate the Shawanese.

Toward the end of October, peace was concluded at Camp Charlotte.[2] Logan refused to attend the negotiations, and sent that brief but celebrated speech which has been considered a master-piece in the annals of oratory. The Indians yielded in every particular; gave up their prisoners, restored their plunder, and pledged themselves to peace and friendship with the Colonies.[3] Lord Dunmore took occasion to extol White Eyes and his people. They had been, he said, the unflinching advocates of peace; he and they were one body; and the Shawanese must remember that only out of regard for these, their grandfathers, had he treated them so leniently.

Carrying off four Shawanese and ten Mingoes as hostages, the Earl marched back to Virginia.

---

[1] Now Pickaway Township, on the Scioto, at the southern end of Pickaway County, Ohio.
[2] On the left bank of Sippo Creek, seven miles southeast of Circleville, Pickaway County, Ohio.
[3] Zeisberger's Diary, Schönbrunn. MS. L. A.

CHAPTER XXIV.

THE GREAT PLANS OF ZEISBERGER AND WHITE EYES.—1774.

False rumors at Schönbrunn and Gekelemukpechünk concerning the results of Dunmore's War.—The Delawares send a message to the Shawanese denouncing the missionaries and the Christian religion.—Insolent behavior of young warriors and the rabble.—Zeisberger's restrospect and thoughts amid these troubles.—Determines to insist upon a formal recognition of the Mission, and hopes to build up a Christian Indian state.—White Eyes returns from Dunmore's War.—A national council called to hear his report.—His speech.—He brings back the message sent to the Shawanese, shows its illegality, rebukes his countrymen for sending it, and publicly weeps over it.—He refuses to have any further connection with Netawatwes, and resigns his councilorship.—The Christian deputies mediators between him and the chief.—White Eyes' ultimatum.—Visits Schönbrunn and unfolds his plans to Zeisberger.—Their character.—Spiritual prosperity of the Mission.

THE conclusion of peace was not known at Schönbrunn and Gekelemukpechünk. In the latter town the Indians began to grow suspicious and the evil-disposed to plot. False reports of the most alarming character came from the Scioto. Lord Dunmore, it was said, had slain or taken prisoners the whole Shawanese nation; treacherously murdered White Eyes; and was now marching against the Delawares. These rumors gained such credence that the seizure of the white teachers, to be held as protective hostages, openly found favor. And although it was not attempted, the missionaries made other unpleasant experiences. The Shawanese had taunted the

Delawares as *Schwonnaks* (Christians). This filled the young warriors of Gekelemukpechünk with indignation, and they induced Netawatwes to send the Shawanese a message, saying that they neither were nor ever would be *Schwonnaks;* that they had not invited white teachers to live among them; and that those who were in their country must have come at the bidding of foolish persons. By this message, which was so flagrantly untrue that it could have emanated from an Indian council only, the converts and the missionaries were, in a manner, outlawed. Young braves from the capital, and the most of its idle rabble, flocked to Schönbrunn, and demeaned themselves in a way no Indian had ever before ventured to do in that town, disregarding its municipal regulations, and insolently saying that it was their town; that the land on which it stood was their land; that they would act at Schönbrunn as at Gekelemukpechünk; that the Christian Indians had no special rights or privileges.

Although this state of affairs continued for several days, Zeisberger was not discouraged. Convinced that the reports from the Scioto were fictitious; that the assault upon the Mission was but the bluster of rash young men, and the weakness of timid old councilors, he hopefully waited for White Eyes' return. It was his opinion that this Indian had been chosen by God not only to deliver the Church from existing difficulties, but also to carry out lofty plans which he had long been revolving in his mind, and which these troubles but served to develop.

A retrospect of his experiences in the Tuscarawas valley showed him things in their true light. He saw now that self-interest, and not a real desire for the Gospel, had induced the Delaware chiefs to offer the Christian Indians a home. They wanted to increase the power of their nation by incorporating with it so prosperous a community. The missionaries were to be dismissed as soon as possible. But these cunning plotters had been caught in their own toils. Ignorant of the power of the Gospel, they had not taken its influences into account. The converts came and were gladly received; their teachers arrived and were hypocritically welcomed; the Word of God was preached, and—marvelous issue in the eyes of the savages!—ere the second year drew to an end, it had pierced the hearts of some of the worst abettors of this scheme of aggrandizement, and brought many others into the Church of Christ. Hence, in point of numbers and influence, the Mission had gained a standing which must be respected. It was no longer a handful of shrinking converts; it counted more than four hundred souls, and among them chiefs, captains, and councilors who had given renown to the Delaware name. This was the time, thought Zeisberger, to assert its rights. It must not be merely tolerated; the Christian Indians and their teachers must have all the privileges of citizens; be on a footing of equality with the other Delawares; hold their land, not at the will of the Council, but in their own right, so that "they would not be like a bird sitting on a bough," but have a permanent home; and throughout the nation absolute religious liberty must be proclaimed by a formal decree of the Council, allowing any Delaware, or all the Delawares, to embrace the Gospel without fear of opposition.

Zeisberger's plan challenges admiration. He aimed at nothing short of a Christian Indian state in the midst of the aboriginal domain. He would establish a center of religion and civilization, whence benign influences would stream forth and enlighten the land. He would build for the Gospel a stronghold from which it could not be driven. He would have the tribes of the South and the nations of the Northwest and the League of the Iroquois to acknowledge that a people of the living God was arisen among them—a people whose voice must be heard, whose rights must be respected, and whose principles must be honored.

While dwelling on such hopes, White Eyes returned, and invited deputies from the Christian towns to attend a national council called to hear his report of the campaign. It met in the Council House of Gekelemukpechünk (November 5) — a structure about sixty feet long by twenty-four broad, with one post in the middle and two fires — and there were present Netawatwes, together with all his advisers, many other chiefs and captains from the three tribes, a delegation of five converts, who were all former headmen of the Delawares, and a large body of spectators.

Standing in the center of the house, in the proud consciousness of having done his duty to his country, to the Colonies, and the Shawanese, White Eyes began his speech, giving a detailed narrative of Lord Dunmore's expedition to the Scioto and the treaty at Camp Charlotte, and rehearsing, in conclusion, the eulogy pronounced by the Earl upon the Delawares. This awakened general enthusiasm, the whole Council bursting into applause and complimenting their brave captain. He paid no attention to their flattering words, but continued his address.

He well knew, he said, that he had been reviled, accused of ingratiating himself with the Virginians, and endangering the prosperity and even the existence of his nation. Such reproach had been cast upon him while he was yet among the Shawanese, and repeatedly on his way home. He had been trying to deliver the Shawanese from destruction, and his own country from the presence of an army, but its chiefs and captains, his friends and companions, had impugned his motives, and incited the Shawanese to threaten him with death.

Not a word was said in reply; the whole assembly sat silent and confused. After a brief pause, he resumed: "Koquethagachton is not yet done. Returning to his lodge, he met a messenger to the Shawanese with a string of wampum and these words, 'Why do you call me a *Schwonnak*, seeing I have twenty hatchets sticking in my head?'[1] If you call me a *Schwonnak* because

---

[1] A figurative form of speech, meaning that, since the last treaty between the Colonies and the Delawares, twenty of the latter had been slain by white men.

Christian Indians and their teachers have their night-lodge on the Gekelemukpechünk, know that I do not listen to what they preach, and will never accept the Word of God—no, not in all eternity!'

"I stopped this message," continued the speaker, " and brought it back. Now I will consider its points.

" The first is unlawful. It refers to the hatchet, to war. Neither Netawatwes, nor any other chief, has the right to send a message about the hatchet, about war, without my consent. This is my prerogative. I am the principal captain and war-councilor of this nation. This point is foolish, too. Have we not been urging the Shawanese to remain at peace, and now our chief sends them a war-message!

" The second point fills me with grief. What, not in all eternity will the Delawares accept the Gospel! I spent the whole summer in efforts to restore peace, that we might sit, with our women and children, around our fires and not be disturbed by every passing wind of rumor and every rising storm of fear. To gain this end I sacrificed my health and gave my strength. I did this willingly, because I had a still higher and better purpose in view. I wanted my people, when peace should be established in the country, to turn their attention to peace in their hearts. I wanted them to embrace that religion which is preached by the white teachers. We will never be happy until we are Christians. This, I say, was the real object which I pursued all summer. I rejoiced in it, for it is good; and because I rejoiced in it, no trouble was too great for me, no hardships were too severe. But now, scarcely is peace concluded and our country delivered from danger—before ever I come back to my own fire—I hear that my people will not in all eternity accept the Word of God. This grieves me. All my trouble, anxiety, and labors have been in vain!"

A big sob shook the speaker's frame. He could say no more, but wept aloud. The Christian deputies wept with him. Strange sight! A national assembly of the Delawares awed into painful silence by the praises of the Gospel from a heathen's mouth, and he the hero of the Lenni-Lenape, a man of war and blood, shedding tears of penitence before them all, and a band of their great men, baptized and now men of God, mingling their tears with his. It was an epoch in Delaware history.

As soon as White Eyes had composed himself, he threw the confiscated belt at the feet of Netawatwes and said: "Because you sent this belt, I resign my councilorship." Wrapping his blanket around him, he immediately left the Council House, followed by Glikkikan and Echpalawehund, to whom he beckoned as he went out. In a few minutes the two latter returned, bearing a string of wampum, which they formally presented. "Koquethagachton bids us say," they added, turning to the old chief, "Look for another councilor to fill my place. I renounce all further connection with you!"

The assembly was confounded. White Eyes' services were indispensable. Without him the Delawares would be without their right arm. Hence they made every effort to conciliate him, and entreated the Christian deputies to act as mediators, Netawatwes sending him a string by their hands, with an humble apology, begging him to resume his seat in the Council. "This is satisfactory as far as it goes," said the irate councilor; "but I intend to teach Netawatwes a lesson. If he understands it, well; if he does not understand it, let him not remain chief any longer." Declining the string, he therefore returned this answer: "As regards me personally, your words are acceptable. That you usurped my authority, that you spoke evil of me and reviled me among my people and among the Shawanese, I will forgive and forget. But that you said that you and my people would not, in all eternity, receive the Word of God, I will not forget; because of these words the wound in my heart is incurable, unless you take them back."

This answer, as he told Glikkikan to explain to the chief, referred to Zeisberger's plan of a national recognition. If the Christian Indians and their teachers were made a part of the Delaware nation, and if religious liberty were granted, he would resume his seat in the Council—not otherwise.

Soon after this, White Eyes came to Schönbrunn to visit Zeisberger. He informed him of his ultimatum with Netawatwes. He believed that the chief would accept it; but if not, he would desert him and live at Schönbrunn. This would be equivalent to a deposition of Netawatwes. He added that, in his judgment, the Delaware country ought to be divided between the

Christian Indians and the rest; and that, in order to give the former more room, he intended to propose the evacuation of Gekelemukpechünk and the building of a new capital farther down the river.

With regard to his own religious views, he said that he sincerely believed the Gospel, desired to be a Christian, and hoped that God would accept him. He was debating the question in his own mind whether he ought not at once to move to Schönbrunn. Zeisberger advised him not to do this, urging the assistance which he could render the Mission by remaining at the capital. After Christianity should have been legalized in the country, he should join the Mission.

Acknowledging the force of this argument, White Eyes proceeded to unfold his other plans, which proved to be in entire harmony with those of Zeisberger. Christianity having been made the national religion, he proposed to go to England, accompanied by John Montour, and visit the King. Lord Dunmore had promised him every assistance. He would lay before the King the whole question at issue between the Delawares and white people, tell him of the westward progress of the latter, and induce him to guarantee to the former the country they then possessed, which should be the home of the Lenni-Lenape to all generations—a land respected by the whites, whereon no blood should be shed. The whites might settle beyond it, but within its confines Delawares only should dwell; not in savage wildness, but as a civilized and Christian people. And to bring about this result should be the work of the Mission.

White Eyes deserved his fame as a counselor. This was a statesman's plan. Pontiac had attempted, by deeds of cruelty and streams of blood, to secure for the aborigines their Western domain. White Eyes hoped, by tokens of peace and manly negotiations, to keep for his nation a home. Pontiac gloried in barbarism: the Indian was to remain a warrior and hunter. White Eyes deemed the plow a blessing, and every implement of civilization a good: his countrymen were to worship the true God and Jesus Christ His Son.

But however noble his thoughts—however philanthropic the corresponding plans of the missionary—their aspirations were dreams. Neither of them could anticipate the resistless westward march of that race which now possesses this Continent. In point of population and power, Ohio has grown to be the third State of the Federal Union. Gekelemukpechünk's council-fire is extinguished; a railroad traverses the site of the town. Schönbrunn has passed away. The spot where stood its chapel, to which hundreds of natives used to flock, is an object of the antiquary's explorations. And along the Tuscarawas and the Walhonding, the Muskingum, Hockhocking, and Scioto, not a solitary Indian lodge remains; from the waters of Lake Erie to the bluffs of the "Beautiful River," not a remnant of the Lenni-Lenape can be found. A great and teeming commonwealth of Americans is in the place of that home which White Eyes would have given to his people. Such was the will of God.

Amid all the perils of Dunmore's War, and the subsequent difficulties with the Delawares, the spiritual state of the converts continued encouraging. Religion grew and bore fruits. Many were baptized; others forsook the heathens and built huts in the Christian towns. Among these latter was a family of Mingoes, belonging to the Onondaga nation, and to that clan into which Zeisberger had been adopted. They became zealous members of the Church.

CHAPTER XXV.

RELIGIOUS LIBERTY IN THE DELAWARE NATION, AND GREAT PROSPERITY OF THE MISSION.—1775.

The American Revolution.—Zeisberger's views and feelings.—Great prosperity of the Mission.—Religious liberty.—The edict of the Delaware Council.—Netawatwes espouses the cause of Christianity. —General agitation among the Delawares upon the subject of the Christian religion.— The Conner family joins the Mission.— Christian deputies and the Council.—Goschachgünk, the new capital, founded.—The converts present their own belts of wampum for a national embassy to the Wyandots.—White Eyes relinquishes his projected visit to England.—Lord Dunmore's motives in furthering it.—Death of John Papunhank.—Zeisberger visits Bethlehem.—A Delaware spelling-book.—A third Christian town spoken of.—Progress of the Revolution.—The status of the Indians.— Congress resolves to secure their neutrality.—Three Indian departments organized.—The cruel and dishonorable policy of Great Britain.—Treaty at Pittsburg.—White Eyes and the Senecas.—His bold speech.—Colonel Gibson visits Schönbrunn with the "Congress Belt."—White Eyes' mysterious journey to Philadelphia.

THE American Revolution was approaching. Throughout the Colonies, and especially in New England, there prevailed that heavy stillness which precedes the storm.

Of this crisis Zeisberger heard from traders who visited Schönbrunn toward the end of January (1775). Devoted to the cause of the Indians, separated from the settlements, the wilderness his home, he had paid no attention to the political questions of the day, and his prayer to God now was that He would overrule the conflict to the spread of the Gospel in the West, and the establishment of His glorious kingdom. Nor did he allow himself to be troubled. Matters of immediate interest occupied his mind. A season of unparalleled prosperity began in the Mission. The Grand Council of the Delawares decreed religious liberty, and adopted all his other suggestions, together with those of White Eyes.

The edict of the Grand Council deserves to be recorded: 1. Liberty is given to the Christian religion, which the Council advises the entire nation to adopt. 2. The Christian Indians and their teachers are on an absolute equality with other Delawares, all of them together constituting one people. 3. The national territory is alike the property of the Christian Indians and of the native Delawares. 4. Converts only, and no other Indians, shall settle near the Christian towns; such as are not converts, but are now living near such towns, shall move away. 5. In order to give more room to the Christian Indians, Gekelemukpechünk is to be abandoned, and a new capital founded farther down the river. 6. The Christian Indians are invited to build a third town.

Netawatwes himself came to Gnadenhütten, accompanied by White Eyes, to whom he was reconciled, and by numerous other councilors, in order to promulgate this edict. He had laid aside his indecision, and boldly espoused the cause of truth. Of this his message to Packanke was an evidence. "You and I," he said, "are both old. How long we may live we know not. Let us do a good work before we die. Let us accept the Word of God, and leave it to our children, as our last will and testament." That he was sincere his whole subsequent life testified.

The Gospel now had free course and was glorified. Many still remained its foes, either openly or in secret; but the Council was pledged to its support, and the power of heathenism broken. Upon this outward prosperity the converts, by their walk and conversation, set a crown fragrant as the evergreens of their valley. Not a few heathens believed and were baptized. From every side, and even from the hunting-grounds of other tribes, visitors flocked to their towns. The chapel at Schönbrunn could hold five hundred persons, and yet it was often too small to accommodate the worshipers. Religion, as taught by the missionaries, became a subject of general inquiry among the Delawares, so that Netawatwes expected to see them all converted within five or six years; and the Christian settlements were famed in the entire West, even in remote regions of the Northwest. To this a company of traders bore witness, who came to see Schönbrunn. They had heard so much of its prosperity, in every part of the wilderness, that they had gone many miles out of their road to gratify their curiosity.

And, indeed, these villages on the Tuscarawas deserved their reputation. In them the system which Zeisberger pursued to reclaim the savages, and teach them the ways of civilization, reached its highest state of development. Such settlements were remarkable not merely as towns, built with surprising regularity and neatness, but also as communities governed, without the aid of Colonial magistrates, by a complete code of laws. In order to administer these, a council was set over each village, consisting of the missionaries and national assistants, or "helpers," as they were called. In such a council the influence of the white teachers, properly and necessarily, continued supreme; but a native element was, at the same time, brought out that reconciled personal liberty, which the Indian prizes so highly, with restrictions tending to the common good. On occasions of extraordinary importance, such as the removal of the Mission to a new locality, the decision was invariably left to a vote of the people. But, from one point of view, perhaps the most remarkable feature of these towns will appear in this, that they were centers of agriculture and not a collection of hunting-lodges. The chase was by no means abandoned, but it had become a secondary object. To raise grain, cattle, and poultry formed the principal employment of the converts. Their plantations covered hundreds of acres along the rich bottoms of the valley; herds, more numerous than the West had ever seen, roamed through the forests or were pastured in their meadows; while few farm-yards of Pennsylvania had fowls in greater variety. Men of judgment and distinction, coming from the Eastern Colonies, were often filled with astonishment when they here beheld Indians not only civilized, but changed in all their habits and growing rich.[1]

---

[1] The testimony of Colonel George Morgan, Indian Agent for the Western District, of whom more will be said in another connection,

Among those who joined the Mission about this time was a family of white persons. Richard Conner, a native of Maryland, ranging through the Indian country, met and married a captive white girl among the Shawanese. They remained with this tribe until the close of Dunmore's War, when they were delivered at Camp Charlotte, according to the stipulations of the treaty, and settled at Pittsburg. But their son had been kept back, and they now came to Schönbrunn, on their way to redeem him. Mrs. Conner stayed at the Mission while her husband proceeded to the Shawanese. Its influences captivated her. She saw Indian life, for which she had a strong predilection, developing itself in a Christian form; and recognized the Gospel as that principle which satisfies the soul. Her husband, who returned without their son, or any information concerning him, being similarly impressed, they applied for reception into the Indian Church. They said that they

---

and whose insight into the character of the natives is well known, may prove interesting. He stated, some years later, during the Revolutionary War, according to Heckewelder, in his *Report of the Indian Mission to the Society for Propagating the Gospel* (MS. B. A.), "that he was astonished at what he had seen in our towns. That the improvements of the Indians bespoke their industry; and that the cleanliness, order, and regularity which were everywhere observable, added to their devotion, gave them a claim to be ranked among the civilized part of mankind. That they deserved to be set up as an example to many of the whites. That to him it was now evident that the Indians, when living by themselves and out of connection with the white people, could easily be brought to a state of civilization and become good citizens of the United States; and that he considered our mode the surest, if not the only successful method, of training converts who had been brought from paganism, idleness, and debauchery to a state of Christianity."

would not expect any privileges other than those enjoyed by native members, but would submit to all the municipal regulations of the town. Zeisberger hesitated to grant their request, fearing that the incorporation of a white family with the Mission would awaken mistrust among the Delawares and affect its newly-acquired status. At last, however, he yielded to the urgency of the applicants. They built themselves a house at Schönbrunn, and, after a probation of an entire year, were admitted into the full communion of the Church (Easter, 1776), whereof they remained consistent and worthy members.

In accordance with Indian usage, the formal thanks of the Mission for the edict passed by the Grand Council were now delivered. At the same time, the converts sent their quota of belts for a grand national deputation to the Wyandots in acknowledgment of the land which they had ceded to the Delawares. This embassy was a long-neglected duty. The belts of the Christian Indians were half a fathom long, without devices, except a white cross at one end and a band through the middle. They had been made expressly for the occasion. From a native point of view, the converts thus assumed an important position. Their belts proclaimed their national equality with the Delawares, and yet their religious distinction from them.

Netawatwes was no longer living at Gekelemukpechünk. He had gone, with the most of his tribe, to build a new capital, which received the name of Goschachgünk, at the junction of the Tuscarawas and Walhonding. It was laid out in the form of a cross, in exact imitation of Schönbrunn.[1] There the council with the Christian deputies was held.

On their way back, they met White Eyes, at Gekelemukpechünk. He had returned from Pittsburg, and, by the advice of Lord Dunmore, given up his projected visit to England, on account of the unsettled state of Colonial affairs. The Earl regretted this necessity, for he had really fallen in with his plans. Connolly himself was to have accompanied him and urged his suit at court. But self-aggrandizement was Dunmore's motive, and not philanthropy. The Delaware country would form a convenient barrier to Pennsylvania, and keep her within her proper limits, while all around it, the noble land-jobber might give free play to his speculations.[2]

After having closed the eyes of his tried assistant, John Papunhank, once the notorious prophet of the Susquehanna country—who died (May 15, 1775) at the age of seventy years—Zeisberger spent a part of the summer at Bethlehem, in conference with the Board. Among other important resolutions which were adopted, was the issuing of a Delaware Reading- and Spelling-Book. On his return to the Mission (August 10, 1775), the Council proposed to him to build a third town, in order to bring the Gospel to that part of the nation which yet remained in heathenism, and of which John

---

[1] Goschachgünk occupied the site of the lower streets of the present Coshocton, stretching along the river bank.

[2] Letter from Arthur St. Clair to Joseph Shippen. Penn. Archives, iv. 637.

Killbuck was the implacable head. Negotiations upon this subject were, however, broken off by a treaty, held at Pittsburg, between the Western Indians and Commissioners of the American Congress.

The Revolution was advancing with rapid strides. While Zeisberger and his assistants were sitting in the Mission House of Schönbrunn, on the nineteenth of April, examining applicants for church-membership, the brave sons of Massachusetts fought the battle of Lexington. Soon after, Ethan Allan and his Green Mountain Boys surprised Ticonderoga, while Crown Point fell into the hands of Seth Warner. The struggle on Bunker Hill kindled a general enthusiasm. There existed, as yet, no formal union of the Colonies, but their Congress, which had hastened to reassemble, began to exercise all the functions of a government, and was cheerfully sustained by the people.

Next to the appointment of George Washington as commander-in-chief, and the regulation of the Continental finances, the most important subject which engaged the notice of Congress was the status of the Indians, whose neutrality must, if possible, be secured. Three Indian departments were organized (July, 1775), and treaties held with the various tribes. To the first department belonged the Six Nations and those of the North and East; to the second, the Western tribes; and to the third, all the aborigines south of Kentucky.

It was high time to adopt such measures. Not content with honorable warfare, Great Britain had inaugurated a policy of blood and cruelty against which the good of her own nation protested. In the previous year, the Governor of Quebec had been empowered to raise Indian levies and march them "into any of the plantations of America;"[1] and, recently, arms had been forwarded to Dunmore with which to equip the savages; while the King himself had sent instructions, in his own name, to the Canadian agent to persuade "his faithful allies, the Six Nations," to take up the hatchet against the rebels. Through the baneful efforts of Colonel Guy Johnson, the son-in-law and successor of Sir William Johnson, who had died suddenly in June of 1774, this policy was, in part, successful, and, after the battle of Lexington, all the Iroquois, except the Oneidas and Tuscaroras, espoused the British cause.

The treaty at Pittsburg took place in October. On the part of Congress appeared as commissioners Colonels Walker and George Clymer; on the part of the Western tribes, a large body of Delawares—including representatives of the Christian towns[2]—some Shawanese, and a few Senecas. The commissioners made known the existing war between the Colonies and the mother country, showed that the questions in dispute did not affect the interests of the natives, and exhorted them to observe a strict neutrality. To this the Delawares pledged themselves, in spite of the opposition

---

[1] Bancroft's Hist. U. S., vii. 118.
[2] The Christian deputies were Isaac Glikkikan, Nathaniel, and William.

of the Senecas, who tried in every possible way to interfere with the negotiations.

White Eyes took a prominent part in this treaty, and openly avowed that his people had embraced Christianity. His manly course and evident sympathy with the Americans gave offense to the Senecas, who haughtily reminded him that the Delawares were women.

"Women!" was his disdainful reply. "Yes, you say that you conquered me, that you cut off my legs, put a petticoat on me, and gave me a hoe and corn-pounder in my hands, saying, 'Now, woman, your business henceforward shall be to plant, hoe, and pound corn for us who are men and warriors!' Look at my legs. If, as you assert, you cut them off, they have grown again to their proper size. The petticoat I have thrown away, and have put on my own dress; the corn-hoe and pounder I have exchanged for these fire-arms; and I declare that I am a man. Yes, all the country on the other side of that river"—waving his hand in the direction of the Alleghany—"is mine!"[1]

Soon after the treaty, Colonel John Gibson, the Western agent of Virginia, and several other Americans, undertook a tour through the Indian country, bearing to its tribes the great "Congress Belt," six feet long and more than half a foot wide, as an emblem of the neutral friendship to which the Delawares had agreed. They spent some time at Schönbrunn, where a baptism, which they witnessed, so deeply impressed

---

[1] Heckewelder's Narrative of the Indian Mission, pp. 140, 141.

their hearts that they sat far into the night by Zeisberger's fire, conversing with him upon the subject of personal religion. Richard Conner accompanied them to the Shawanese territory, and returned, in the following spring, with his little son, whom he had at last succeeded in ransoming.

White Eyes did not go back to Goschachgünk from Pittsburg, but traveled alone to Philadelphia, without informing any one of his purpose. Ere long, however, a strange rumor reached Schönbrunn to the effect that he was negotiating with Congress for missionaries of a church other than the Moravian.

CHAPTER XXVI.

LICHTENAU FOUNDED ON THE MUSKINGUM.—1776.

Prosperity of Schönbrunn and Gnadenhütten.—Netawatwes desires a third town to be built near to the capital.—Its site.—A part of the heathen Delawares secede from the nation.—Lichtenau laid out and built.—The first Sunday thereat.—New converts from the families of the chiefs.—Netawatwes himself a convert.—White Eyes negotiates with Congress for missionaries and teachers other than Moravians.—The reply of Congress laid before the Delaware Council.—Zeisberger opposes the project.—Ambition its origin.—Colonel George Morgan asks for a decision.—The Delawares abide by the Moravian Church.—The first communion at Lichtenau.—Zeisberger's Delaware Spelling-Book.

THE year 1776, which formed an epoch in our national history, became illustrious in the history of the Indian Mission on account of its rapid growth. In the first five weeks eighteen baptisms occurred at Schönbrunn; others took place at Gnadenhütten; a general revival began among the children; and the project to build a third town was carried out. Netawatwes wished this settlement to be near to his capital. He argued that the evil consequences which had formerly grown out of the proximity of heathen villages were not any more to be expected, the nation having resolved to embrace the Gospel; that every opportunity must be afforded his people to hear the Word of God; and that the influence of the new enterprise ought to be felt at Goschachgünk. He confessed that he expected to lean upon Zeisberger and the converts in the administration of national affairs, and that he had already selected a site which would render this feasible. "If the Brethren," said he, "will live near me, I will be strong. They will make me strong against the disobedient."

Zeisberger acknowledged the force of these arguments, and rode out to view the spot. It was well chosen. Two and a half miles below Goschachgünk, on the eastern side of the Muskingum, a broad level of many acres stretched to the foot of the hills, with an almost imperceptible ascent. The river-bank, swelling out gently toward the stream in the form of an arc, was covered with maples and stately sycamores. Materials for building abounded, and the rich soil promised abundant crops. Numerous remains showed that the primitive aborigines of America had here had a home. Zeisberger was delighted with the place, and perceiving the great change going on in the hearts of the Delawares, and the morning of a new era dawning in their history, he gathered them around him, on his return to the capital, and delivered an animated discourse upon the words, "The glory of the Lord is risen upon thee,"[1]—setting forth that the day of salvation for the whole people was at hand.

Alarmed by the rapid progress of the Mission, and the increasing influence of the Christians, some Monseys, under Captain Pipe,[2] seceded from the Dela-

---

[1] Isaiah, lx. 1.
[2] Captain Pipe, or Kogieschquanoheel, was the principal captain of the Wolf Tribe, and became its tribal chief after the death of Packanke.

ware nation, and formed a clan of their own on the hunting-grounds of Lake Erie. As a reason for this step they did not assign the Christian religion, but White Eyes' speech at Pittsburg, and the principles he had there enunciated. They feared, they said, the wrath of the Iroquois, which he had unnecessarily provoked; and they would not stay to share the punishment to be expected from that powerful League. But, although there did prevail among the Monseys dissatisfaction with White Eyes, and although Pipe was his rival, the true cause of the secession was hatred of the Gospel. Unable to prevent its supremacy, afraid to persecute it openly, they fled from its sweet promises and words of eternal life.

This breach among the Delawares did not, however, prevent the new enterprise. On the twelfth of April, at the head of eight families, numbering thirty-five persons, and with John Heckewelder as his assistant, Zeisberger encamped on the site of the future town, and, toward evening, called his little colony together under the open canopy of heaven to worship God. The next morning the sturdy strokes of the axe began to ring through the bottom, and with a great crash tree after tree fell to the ground. Indians from Goschachgünk stood by, looking on in silence. To these the converts talked of Christ. Here was Glikkikan, hewing the branches from a prostrate trunk and at the same time magnifying his Saviour's name; there stood another, resting for a moment from his work and setting forth the communion of saints as exemplified in the towns of the Mission. Everywhere mingled in unison the energy of civilization and the eloquence of faith.

Sunday followed upon this day of toil. Netawatwes, with almost the entire population of the capital, attended religious service. On the river's bank, beneath the gemmed trees ready to burst into verdure, gathered the congregation of Christian and of pagan Indians. Zeisberger preached on the words, "Thus it is written, and thus it behoved Christ to suffer, and to rise from the dead the third day: and that repentance and remission of sins should be preached in His name among all nations, beginning at Jerusalem."[1] Afterward fires were lighted, around which the converts continued to instruct their countrymen in the way of life, until the shades of evening fell.

The new town progressed rapidly. Its Mission House served, at first, as the place of worship; the other buildings formed one street, running parallel to the river; and, midway between its northern and southern extremities, a chapel was subsequently erected. This town received the name of Lichtenau.[2]

---

[1] Luke, xxiv. 46 and 47.

[2] That is, a *"Pasture of Light"*—a green pasture illumined by the light of the Gospel. This is the explanation given in the *Bethlehem Diary of* 1776. Lichtenau was situated on what are now (1863) the farms of Messrs. Samuel Moore and Samuel Forker, in Tuscarawas Township, Coshocton County, Ohio. These two farms are separated by a long lane extending from the river to the eastern hills. The town beginning near the residence of Mr. Moore—the church probably stood in his present yard—stretched across the lane to the land of Mr. Forker.

A grandson of Netawatwes and his family of six children were the first new converts who settled there;[1] next came a son of the old chief; then arrived Welapachtschiechen, or Captain Johnny, the principal chief of the Turkey Tribe, from Assününk,[2] together with his own and ten other families; while Gelelemend, or John Killbuck, Jr., Netawatwes' destined successor, selected a lot on which to build at a future time. Owing to his position in the Council he could not leave the capital for the present. Netawatwes himself visited Lichtenau nearly every day, and became a convert, although he was not baptized.

After a silence of more than half a year, White Eyes sent word to the old chief, from Philadelphia, that

---

and, after all the converts had been concentrated at Lichtenau, was built up for a considerable distance upon his farm. On the 18th of June, 1863, my friend, Jacob Blickensderfer, Esq., of Tuscarawas County, and I discovered this site, and identified it as that of Lichtenau by numerous relics and the exact correspondence of former landmarks, as described to us by Mr. Moore, with the topography set forth in Zeisberger's manuscripts. We were greatly aided in our explorations by Mr. David Johnson, of Coshocton. The remains that date from the prehistoric times of the aborigines are a circle of five acres, quite near to the site of Lichtenau, and a mound, three quarters of a mile farther down the river.

[1] His wife, when a child of twelve years, had been baptized (Jan. 7, 1758) in the church at Bethlehem, and named Hannah, but afterward, through the influence of her mother, relapsed into heathenism.

[2] A town of the Turkey Tribe, on the Hockhocking, near the Shawanese towns. Captain Johnny's wife was a white woman from Virginia, captured (1757) in the French and Indian War. After attending the first religious service at Lichtenau, she exclaimed: "Oh, how glad I am that I am here, and, after nineteen years, can again listen to the Word of God! I have often wished to live with you, and now God has granted the desire of my heart. When I awoke this morning, I felt happier than I ever remember to have felt before."

Congress had granted the Delawares a minister and a school-teacher, and that they should build a church at Goschachgünk. It thus appeared that the rumor which had come to the ears of the converts was not without foundation. The motives which actuated White Eyes could not be divined, but the line of conduct to be pursued was plain. Moravian missionaries had brought the Gospel to the Delawares when no man cared for their souls, had led hundreds of them into the Church, and made the Christian party dominant in the nation. At such a time a new mission, begun by a minister of another persuasion, would confuse the minds of the natives and mar the existing work. It therefore became Zeisberger's duty to oppose White Eyes.

The latter having returned to Goschachgünk, a council was called to hear a report of his proceedings. He brought out an address from Congress, and asked Zeisberger to interpret it; it contained the following points: 1. White Eyes has applied to Congress for a minister and a school-teacher to labor among the Delawares. 2. If an Episcopal minister is sent, the Moravian Brethren are to be informed that he will not hinder their work. 3. White Eyes has also asked for mechanics to live among the Delawares and teach them trades. 4. Congress requests the Delawares to designate the church to which they wish the minister to belong, and to say whether they are unanimous in their application for white mechanics.

Profound silence followed the reading of this address until other and unimportant matters were introduced, which excited so little attention that the councilors, one by one, retired, including White Eyes. At last Netawatwes and two councilors, together with Zeisberger and his deputies, alone remained. "I see," said Zeisberger, "that the Council has separated without attending to the business for which it was convened. I, too, will now go home. But before I go I wish to inform you that I will have nothing to do with these plans, and will never give my consent to them; and I advise you to consider well before you sanction them." With these words he left the house and rode back to Lichtenau.

How different this Council from the one in which White Eyes had advocated the cause of the missionaries! He and Netawatwes had exchanged places. By his unauthorized negotiations with Congress—by attempting to inaugurate a new work without consulting his peers—he had transgressed against Indian law as gravely as Netawatwes when this chief had sent a war-message without his permission. White Eyes read this in the dissatisfied faces of his countrymen, and was constrained to receive Netawatwes' well-merited rebuke in silence.

On Saturday evening (May 18, 1776), the Lord's Supper was celebrated, for the first time, at Lichtenau. The next morning visitors from Goschachgünk filled the church. White Eyes was among them, friendly as of old, but ill at ease. Perceiving this, Glikkikan strolled with him into the forest, and induced him to unburden his heart. Ambition swayed it. He was no longer satisfied with the mere conversion and civilization of the Delawares, and with securing for them a permanent home; he desired to make them great and powerful, like the Americans, and to see himself at their head. In order to accomplish this, he must have ministers of a more numerous and influential church than the Moravian. The Moravians were too humble for such aspiring schemes. Upon the whole, he no longer sought personal religion, but was a friend of the Gospel only in so far as the Gospel would help him to power and glory. Glikkikan uncovered the evil of this course in language so severe and condemnatory that Zeisberger remarks in his Journal, "I would hardly have ventured to speak to him in such a way."

A few weeks later, Colonel George Morgan, the new Indian Agent for the Middle Department,[1] asked the Council to decide the matter by either sanctioning or repudiating White Eyes' application. Congress required an immediate answer. The Council sought advice of the converts, and these discouraged the project, as unjust to the Moravians and tending to confusion. White Eyes, who by this time had realized the grossness of his blunder and perceived that his popularity was waning, gladly adopted the same view. Colonel Morgan was informed that the Delawares would abide by the Moravian Church.

Zeisberger's Delaware Spelling-Book appeared at

---

[1] Colonel Morgan was a native of Princeton, N. J., and enjoyed great popularity among the Indians. He was adopted by the Delawares, who gave him the name of Tamanend, the highest honor which they could confer.

Philadelphia, and was sent to the Mission. In a letter to Bishop Hehl he expresses great dissatisfaction with its typographical arrangement; says that his instructions have been neglected; that it is more of a dictionary than of a spelling-book; and, above all, that the Delaware and the English ought to have alternated page for page.

CHAPTER XXVII.

THE MISSION DURING THE WESTERN BORDER WAR OF THE REVOLUTION.—1776, 1777.

Continued efforts of the British to stir up the Indians.—Baptism of the first convert at Lichtenau.—A new treaty with the Western tribes.—Death of Netawatwes.—Zeisberger's position in the Indian country as the advocate of peace.—A survey of the West and its military posts about 1777.—William Edwards joins the Mission.—Beginning of the Western border war.—The Delawares continue neutral.—White Eyes the champion of peace and religion.—Correspondence of the Delaware Council with Colonel Morgan respecting the missionaries.—Apostacy of the Monsey converts at Schönbrunn.—Their plot to remove the missionaries and bring back the Christian Indians to heathenism.—Schönbrunn deserted.—Schmick refuses to leave Gnadenhütten.—Heckewelder returns to Bethlehem.—All the other missionaries at Lichtenau.—Murder of Cornstalk.—The Delawares still maintain their policy.—Jungmann and Schmick retire to the settlements.—The entire Mission in charge of Zeisberger and Edwards.—Arrival of the Wyandot Half King and his warriors.—Danger of the two missionaries.—The Half King conciliated.—Edwards takes charge of Gnadenhütten.—Progress of the Indian War.—Zeisberger's influence in the Delaware Council.—Encouraging state of religion.—The Gospel preached to war-parties.—Return of the apostate Monseys.

THE tranquillity of the Mission was disturbed by the persistent efforts of the British to stir up the Indians. In July, rumors of the warlike disposition of the Iroquois, Ottawas, and Shawanese agitated the Delaware and Christian towns. The peaceful answer received from the Wyandots to a message sent by the Council relieved their anxiety for a time. But it soon became evident that a season of tribulation was at hand.

In the midst of such forebodings, the first baptism

took place at Lichtenau. The convert was that grandson of Netawatwes who had been the first heathen to build himself a house in the town. He received the name of John, and became a bold confessor. A friend advising him not to speak of his religion, lest its enemies might take his life, he replied: "If my life is in danger, I will the more cheerfully witness of the truth. Do you imagine that a baptized Indian fears your sorceries as he did when he was a heathen, and that he will hesitate to make known what the Saviour has done for him and for all men? No! While I live, I will not hold my peace, but proclaim salvation. This is the command of God."

When the autumn opened, the intentions of the British Indians could no longer be doubted. Parties of Iroquois took to the war-path, and the Wyandots, changing their policy, prepared to follow them, in spite of a second message from the Delawares, which they consented to receive only in the presence of the Governor of Detroit, who imperiously cut the belts in pieces, threw them at the feet of the deputies, insulted White Eyes, and bade them all begone within half an hour. The more cause had the Americans to make a new treaty with the Western tribes, in October, at Pittsburg. The Delawares again declared for peace, and promised to advocate it among their grandchildren.

Unusual solemnity was given to this pledge by the death of Netawatwes, who breathed his last before the treaty was ratified, beseeching his councilors, and White Eyes in particular, to uphold neutrality and the

Christian religion. It was a worthy end of the career of this aged chief, whose scheme of national aggrandizement God had overruled to the spread of the Gospel and the salvation of his own soul.

The principles which Netawatwes bequeathed to his nation he had learned from Zeisberger, who was the indomitable champion of peace in the Western border war. While the Church of God enshrines his memory as an apostle among missionaries, America must call him a benefactor, because he averted a blow that would have made her children east of the Alleghanies wail with anguish.

It has been computed that the Indians of New York, Ohio, and the Lakes could muster, at the beginning of the Revolution, not less than ten thousand warriors. But that was a time of frequent disaster to the American cause. Both the army and the people were discouraged, and had it not been for the fortitude and perseverance of Washington, the struggle would have come to a speedy and ruinous end. In such a juncture, if the British had succeeded in establishing an offensive confederation among the Indian tribes,—if ten thousand savages had advanced from the West, incited by the demon of war that changes an Indian into a fiend, and had hurled themselves upon the Colonies simultaneously with an attack from the East by the regulars of England, the result would have been fearful. But God himself did not permit such a calamity. While Samuel Kirkland secured the neutrality of the Oneidas and Tuscaroras, so that the Iroquois were divided against themselves, Zeisberger prevented the Delawares from taking up the hatchet, and thereby restrained the many tribes that acknowledged them as grandfathers.[1] Thus two ordained missionaries, the one in the East and the other in the West, prompted by the principles of a common faith and the spirit of their common Lord, tacitly joined in a compact to hinder a general rising of the savages. The greater part of the Delawares, it is true, eventually went over to the enemy; but by that time the States had gained a decisive victory through Burgoyne's surrender, and France, with all her resources, had arrayed herself on their side, quieting the Western nations by the respect which her name awakened, and rendering the issue of the Revolution no longer doubtful. It was in the most gloomy years of the conflict that Zeisberger stretched out his hand, and, in the name of humanity and the Gospel, kept back the Western hordes.[2]

---

[1] In his *MS. Hist. of the Indians*, Zeisberger says: "If the Delawares had taken part against the Americans in the present war, America would have made terrible experiences; for the neutrality of the Delawares kept all the many nations that are their grandchildren neutral too, except the Shawanese, who are no longer in close union with their grandfathers."

[2] The importance of his services, in this respect, and of the influence of the Mission among the Delawares, was acknowledged by such men as Generals Butler, Hand, Brodhead, Gibson, Irvine, and Neville. The following is the testimony of General Richard Butler, as delivered to Heckewelder: "Had the chiefs of the Delaware nation, together with the Christian Indians, pursued a different course than that which they adopted, all joined the enemy, and taken up the hatchet against the American people, it would have cost the United States much blood and treasure to have withstood them and checked their progress, besides

In order to understand the developments of the three eventful years which he spent at Lichtenau, a brief survey of the West, about the beginning of 1777, will be necessary.

Two rival centers of influence, Fort Pitt and Detroit, controlled the natives. At the former lived Colonel Morgan. Familiar with the habits of the Indians, frank, generous, and honest in his treatment of them, he enjoyed their confidence and exercised a beneficial authority. The commandant was Colonel John Neville. At Detroit, which was garrisoned by but sixty-six men,[1] Governor Hamilton had his headquarters, and associated with him were the Indian agents, who ceased not to incite the tribes to war.

The Wyandots and other British allies rendezvoused at Sandusky; the Iroquois at Niagara; and a mongrel band of some sixty or eighty, banditti and murderers of the worst sort, at Pluggy's Town, so called from the name of their leader, on the head-waters of the Scioto. In Dunmore's War, Point Pleasant, at the mouth of the Great Kanawha, had been made a fort; and, at Wheeling, Fort Fincastle had been erected. These were now American posts. In 1776, the name of the latter was changed to Fort Henry, in honor of Patrick Henry. It stood on the bank of the Ohio, about a quarter of a

---

weakening our already feeble armies on the sea-board, by draining them of troops for the Western service, and this might have proved fatal to the cause."—*Heckewelder's Report of the Mission to the Society for Propagating the Gospel.* MS. B. A.

[1] Morgan's Letter to Patrick Henry. Penn. Archives, v. 286.

mile above the outlet of Wheeling Creek. Twenty or thirty log-huts near by formed the town.

At the Delaware capital, Gelelemend had taken the place of Netawatwes. His principal advisers were: White Eyes, Memoacanund,—White Eyes' cousin,—Lehelengochwa, Paemaholend, Pegilend, Majachquicund, and Namas, or Fish, who, together with Muchusemoechtin, the messenger of the Council, warmly supported the Mission, while the remaining councilors, Tetepachkschüs—the Speaker—Machingwi Puschüs, or Big Cat, and Weliechsit, or Delaware George, were its secret enemies. The captain next in rank to White Eyes was Wenginund, living on the Walhonding, ten miles from Goschachgünk, and with him Woakaholend, another noted headman. Captain Pipe, rejoicing in war only, had made over the duties of his chieftainship to Gulpicamen, or Captain Thomson, once a convert and baptized at Gnadenhütten on the Mahony. Those Monseys who had not seceded from the nation dwelt on the Walhonding, a few miles above Goschachgünk, and were under a subordinate chief, Nachquachkschüs, or Elias, who had chosen as his councilors Unumhamen, Tenaungochwe, and Queepackange. Instigators of evil, leaders in wickedness, the oracles of the Delaware rabble, were Twegachschasu, an assistant chief, Schigalees, a councilor,—both connected with Pluggy's gang,—and Thechsallancepi, or John Snake, a Shawanese, who made common cause with the murderous Mingoes.[1]

---

[1] List of some of the headmen among the Delawares. MS. B. A.

The number of missionaries had been increased by the arrival (November 4th, 1776) of William Edwards, an Englishman, who became Zeisberger's associate at Lichtenau.[1] Heckewelder had joined Jungmann at Schönbrunn, and Schmick remained alone at Gnadenhütten.

The Western border war began in the spring of 1777. A hatchet, wrapped in a belt of red and white beads, was sent from Detroit and accepted by the Shawanese, Wyandots, and Mingoes. Rumor said that it was to be offered to the Delawares, and through them to all their grandchildren; and that, if they refused it, they were to be treated as common enemies: in any case, the Mission was to be destroyed. Cornstalk[2] himself came to Goschachgünk and reported that the Shawanese, except in his own tribe, were all for war; he could do nothing to prevent it; parties were already out; and ammunition was being forwarded from Detroit for their use.

On the ninth of March, a general council of Delawares assembled to adopt measures in so perilous an emergency. It was resolved to decline the hatchet should it be offered; to protect the missionaries; and

---

[1] William Edwards was born April 24, 1724, in the Parish of Brinkworth, Wiltshire, England. His parents belonged to the Anglican Church. He joined the Moravian Church in 1749, and emigrated to America, where he became a distinguished missionary among the Indians.

[2] On a previous visit to Gnadenhütten, with more than one hundred warriors, Cornstalk conceived so great a regard for Schmick and his wife that he adopted them both into the Shawanese nation, making Schmick his brother and Mrs. Schmick his sister.

to uphold their work. White Eyes spoke, with fervid earnestness, in favor of the Gospel. Snatching up a Bible and several of Zeisberger's Spelling-Books, he held them aloft, and said:

"My friends, all of you here present! You know what our aged chief believed, and that he told us how good a faith Christianity is. Listen to me. I, too, believe, even as these my Christian brethren, and know, even as they know, that the Word of God is true. Some of you, although you are not yet Christians, entertain the same views; others of you oppose this faith, because you think it is not good. Listen to me. Here I take my young people and children by the hand, and, with them, I kneel before that Being who gave them to us, and pray to Him that He may have mercy upon us all; that He may reveal His Word and will to us and to them, yea, to our children's children.

"My friends," turning to the Christian deputies, "you hear what I say. Let us labor together for our children, and show them our good intentions. Brethren, take pity upon me, join with me in working for their happiness."

He closed amid general emotion, the tears running down his own cheeks. On the following day, at a second session of the Council, the Christian deputies returned a warm-hearted answer to this appeal, pledging themselves to aid him in bringing all the Delawares to a knowledge of the truth.[1]

---

[1] Minutes of the Council. MS. B. A.

Anxious to provide in time against every danger that might threaten the missionaries, the councilors of Goschachgünk now sent the following message to Colonel Morgan:

"Brother Tamanend, we want your advice what we shall do with the Moravian ministers and their people, if the Mingoes should attack us. We think it would be best to bring them all together into one town, and to keep one minister only. But whatever you recommend we will adopt."

Colonel Morgan replied:

"Brothers, in case you remain in the fear that the Moravian ministers and school-teachers will be badly treated by the Mingoes and yourselves attacked, I wish that you would agree to act as the Brethren may deem best. They have been sent among you by the Almighty God to do good, and I hope the Evil Spirit will never get power to injure them.

"Brothers, I desire that you may listen to their words, and do them all the services in your power."[1]

Accordingly Gelelemend and White Eyes proposed to Zeisberger to concentrate the whole body of converts and missionaries at Lichtenau. He approved of the plan, and proceeded to Schönbrunn (March 23d), in order to carry it out.

But there confusion reigned. Ever since the preceding autumn the Monsey faction on the Walhonding

---

[1] Message and Reply recorded in the Bethlehem Diary, May, 1777. MS. L. A.

had been secretly inveigling their countrymen among the converts into a plot both against the Delaware Council and the Mission. They won over Augustin Newallike, who, apostate-like, immediately lent all his influence to seduce the rest, so that, by the end of the year, there existed a rebellious party which defied the authority of Jungmann, and was fast relapsing into heathenism. In February, Newallike openly renounced the Church and betook himself to the Walhonding.[1] The disaffected, soon after, held a secret conclave, at midnight, with one of his emissaries, at which they agreed to disown Christianity, forsake Schönbrunn, and join the Wyandots. But when their faction grew in numbers as rapidly as the influence of the missionaries waned, they became bolder, and concocted a rising of all their adherents, the seizure of the teachers, their forcible removal to Pittsburg, and the return of the converts to the faith and practice of their fathers.

It was a base conspiracy, unparalleled in the history of the Indian Mission. The machinations of the Monseys, however, did not alone give it strength; the missionaries themselves unintentionally fostered it by the differences of opinion which prevailed in their councils. Zeisberger artlessly says: "Schönbrunn was neglected. There was a want of harmony among the missionaries;

---

[1] White Eyes meeting him, said: "You joined the Brethren because nowhere else in the world could you find that happiness which your heart desired. This I have heard you say with your own lips. But hardly have you tried this happiness when you relinquish it and go back to heathenism. I call that not acting like a man."

they were jealous one of the other, and the Indians were left as sheep without a shepherd. Not slow to use this opportunity, Satan sowed tares among the wheat, and the tares grew so rapidly that the wheat was almost choked."[1]

Of all these troubles he had hitherto been kept in ignorance; but now his measures were prompt and authoritative. Supported by his colleagues, who cheerfully united to lend their aid, he announced that the Mission must forthwith be removed to Lichtenau. The faithful part of the membership agreed to go; of the apostates a number refused obedience, and declared that they no longer acknowledged him as their teacher, but others repented and withdrew from this faction. Before the settlement could be broken up, however, and after Zeisberger had returned to Lichtenau, a false report was spread by the perverts that Mingoes were on their way to murder the missionaries. Jungmann and his wife, accompanied by the Conner family, fled to Lichtenau; Heckewelder to Gnadenhütten. Thereupon the conspirators took possession of Schönbrunn, the majority of the converts retiring at their approach. As soon as Heckewelder discovered the stratagem, he hastened back to the town, but heathenism was already rampant, and the few Christians that remained seemed to be powerless. He sent for Zeisberger, who came at once, and, to some extent, restored order.

Meanwhile everything had been prepared for the

---

[1] Zeisberger's MS. Sketch of the Indian Mission. B. A.

emigration. Early in the morning of the nineteenth of April, a short religious service was held, at the close of which Zeisberger fell on his knees and offered up a fervent prayer, committing the converts to the protection of God, and interceding, with strong cries and tears, for the apostate Monseys. As soon as the benediction had been pronounced, the chapel was razed to the ground. The next day, turning their backs upon the pleasant town, and the beautiful spring, and the fair fields, the converts took their sorrowful road to Gnadenhütten, and thence to Lichtenau. Schönbrunn was left in the hands of the Monseys.

Schmick would not permit his people to join their fellow-converts, but kept them at Gnadenhütten. In a letter to Bishop Hehl,[1] he expresses his disapproval of the evacuation of Schönbrunn, denounces it as unnecessary, and Zeisberger as the cause of the evil. But Zeisberger deserves no blame. There can be no doubt that his prompt measures saved the entire Mission from ruin; and his conduct was fully vindicated by the experiences that followed.

Zeisberger, Jungmann, Mrs. Jungmann, and Edwards now lived together at Lichtenau. Heckewelder, by the advice of Zeisberger, returned to Bethlehem.

The complications of the war increased. Cornstalk, who had gone to Point Pleasant to report the movements of the Shawanese, was basely arrested, kept as

---

[1] Original Letter, May 24, 1777. L. A.

a hostage, and, soon after, murdered in cold blood, together with Ellinipsico, his son, by the soldiers of the garrison, in revenge for the loss one of their companions who, while hunting, had met his death at the hands of a British Indian. Thus fell one of the bravest and noblest of the natives of that age. That so unwarrantable an outrage did not convert the neutral tribes of the West into blood-thirsty enemies was owing more to the good fortune than to the merit of the Americans.

The Delawares firmly maintained their position. They refused the war-belt three times in the course of the summer; and although, when it was pressed upon them a fourth time, they accepted it as the easiest mode of satisfying the pertinaciousness of the Wyandots, which began to be manifested in a threatening form, they sent it back to Sandusky the moment the messengers had left their capital.

Nor were they less determined in protecting the missionaries, although it was not in their power to guarantee to them absolute security. War-parties commenced to pass that way, bringing death to the white man and destruction to his settlements. Such parties were not to be controlled. Respect for the pledges of the Delawares formed no article in their instructions. Some painted savage might, at any time, dash his tomahawk into the head of a missionary or a missionary's wife. It became the duty of these teachers to consider their danger and decide, each one for himself, what he ought to do. Jungmann, urged by

Zeisberger, left the Mission (August 6th) on Mrs. Jungmann's account, and returned to Bethlehem. A few days later, Schmick and his wife, with Schebosh, fled from Gnadenhütten to Litiz.[1] Hence the entire Mission was left in charge of Zeisberger and Edwards. In a letter to the Board, the former writes:

"My heart does not allow me even so much as to think of leaving. Where the Christian Indians stay I will stay. It is impossible for me to forsake them. If Edwards and I were to go, they would be without a guide, and would disperse. Our presence gives authority to the national assistants, and the Lord gives authority to us. He will not look upon our remaining here as foolhardiness. I make no pretensions to false heroism, but am, by nature, as timid as a dove. My trust is altogether in God. Never yet has He put me to shame, but always granted me the courage and the comfort I needed. I am about my duty; and even if I should be murdered, it will not be my loss, but my gain, for then will the fish return to his native element."[2]

The confidence of the missionaries was soon put to the test and the crisis of their fate brought on. There arrived at Goschachgünk, with two hundred warriors from Sandusky, Pomoacan, the wild and haughty Half

---

[1] At Litiz, Schmick assisted Bishop Hehl, and preached in the U. S. Hospital which had been established in the town, until early in the next year, when he died, January 23, 1778, in the 64th year of his age.

[2] Zeisberger's Letter. L. A.

King of the Wyandots. According to the barbarous usage of Indian warfare, the two white teachers were at the mercy of these savages, who might scalp them, or carry them into captivity, as they pleased. "No exceptions," writes Zeisberger, "had theretofore occurred; no white persons found in the Indian country during a time of war had ever been saved by friendly natives from the hands of passing warriors, unless they were prisoners adopted into a tribe; on the contrary, many cases were known of headmen and chiefs trying in vain to rescue their white friends."[1]

Zeisberger and Edwards were equal to their perilous situation. Calm in the strength of their faith, they said one to another, "If we perish, we perish!"[2] Prudent in their efforts to save their lives, they employed all the means of conciliation common among the aborigines. A speech was prepared, setting forth that the believing Indians of Lichtenau and Gnadenhütten had accepted the Word of God; that they prized it as a great treasure; that they held daily councils at which it was made known; that they had two white teachers who proclaimed it; and that they begged the Half King to recognize these teachers as their own flesh and blood. Sending a large quantity of their choicest provisions in advance, a deputation of converts, headed by Isaac Glikkikan, sought an interview with Pomoacan. It was the eighth of August.

---

[1] Zeisberger's MS. Sketch of the Indian Mission. B. A.
[2] Ibid.

He met them in the Council House of Goschachgünk. The missionaries remained at Lichtenau, where a canoe was launched ready to convey them to a place of safety; while at the door of the Council House stood a messenger on the watch, who was to mount his horse at the first token of unfriendliness on the part of the Wyandots, and bring Zeisberger timely notice.

Glikkikan delivered the speech and several fathoms of wampum. Both were well received, and after a brief consultation with his captains, the Half King replied: "I rejoice to hear that the believing Indians have accepted the Word of God, and have two white teachers among them to proclaim it. Let them continue to hold their daily councils, undisturbed by passing warriors. Their teachers I herewith acknowledge as my fathers; the Wyandots are their children. I will make this known among the nations, and tell it to the Governor of Detroit." The next day he visited Lichtenau with his warriors, all of whom, one by one, pledged their hands to Zeisberger and Edwards. "Thus," writes the former, "was suddenly removed a mountain of difficulties." The missionaries were now under the protection of the warriors themselves; and although, shortly after, an army of Mingoes, Ottawas, Chippewas, Shawanese, Wampanoags, Potawatomies, and French Canadians encamped near their town, their work was carried on as freely as though it were a time of profound peace.

Edwards now hastened to Gnadenhütten, and took charge of that forsaken station. Zeisberger remained at Lichtenau, where hardly a week passed without the arrival of a war-party. But no harm befell him. He was treated with the respect due to a "father," even when he ministered to the wants of prisoners and interdicted the running of the gantlet in his town.

The Half King's band, after totally defeating a body of borderers who were advancing against the Delaware capital without authority from Pittsburg and in spite of the orders of its commandant, gathered around Fort Henry, toward the end of September, and on the twenty-seventh attacked it with the utmost fury. But although its garrison was a mere handful, the assault was unsuccessful, and, the following day, they left on their homeward march.

The news of the attempt against Goschachgünk startled its councilors; and when further intelligence reached them, that General Hand, the new commandant of Pittsburg, and said to be a bitter enemy of the Indians, was on his way with four hundred men to devastate the country, the excitement grew so intense that it carried along even White Eyes, although he had letters both from Hand and Morgan assuring him of the unwavering friendship of the Americans. The Council would inevitably have declared war had not Zeisberger, the same night in which he heard of its intentions, sent several Christian Indians, at the full speed of their horses, to prevent such an issue. He expostulated with the members upon their impetuosity; proved from their letters that they were misled by false rumors; and besought them not to leave their neutral ground. His arguments prevailed. War was not declared.

But Captain Pipe and his faction were indefatigable in their attempts to bring about a rupture. By dark hints and open persuasions, by alternately exciting their fears and appealing to their honor as Indian braves, by filling the whole month of October with incessant agitations, they, at last, caused a majority in the Council and nation to incline to war. But again Zeisberger interposed. By his authority it was proclaimed at Goschachgünk, that the very day the Delawares took up the hatchet the whole body of Christian Indians would leave their country. Alarmed by this threat, and well knowing that if it were carried out the prosperity of the nation would wane, Gelelemend and White Eyes called a general council at which the neutrality of the Delawares was reaffirmed.

In the letter which reported these events to the Board, Zeisberger expresses his belief that he will be able to maintain his position at Lichtenau. It is clear, too, from the same missive, that he was, at this time, the most influential councilor among the Delawares, and, in conjunction with White Eyes and Gelelemend, virtually ruled the nation. His connection with national affairs, he says, is not agreeable to him, but it is necessary, and gives him great authority. What he most fears is the evil influence of the warriors upon the religious state of the converts. In conclusion, he writes: "Edwards and I commend ourselves, with all our people, to your prayers and earnest intercessions, which the Lord will certainly hear."

His apprehensions were, however, not fulfilled. In spite of the frequent enticements which surrounded them, the people grew in grace and in the knowledge of God, distinguishing themselves at this time, even more than in other periods, by their consistency and zeal. The national assistants were full of holy fire, and often went to Goschachgünk to preach, where they gained new converts, some of whom were not ashamed to rise publicly in the Council and confess Christ. Nor were the warriors forgotten. To band after band, as it came and went, was the Gospel proclaimed with great boldness. Painted braves with their nodding plumes often filled the chapel at Lichtenau to overflowing. By far the most encouraging experience, however, was the return of the majority of the apostate Monseys, who confessed their sins, and entreated Zeisberger to receive them again into fellowship. In all the history of the Mission there is not a more brilliant evidence of the power of the Gospel.

CHAPTER XXVIII.

THE MISSSION DURING THE WESTERN BORDER WAR OF THE REVOLUTION (CONTINUED).—1778, 1779.

New perils threaten the Mission.—Governor Hamilton's reputed letter ordering the missionaries to arm their converts.—Alexander McKee, Matthew Elliot, Simon Girty.—Their intrigues among the Delawares.—Captain Pipe and his party clamor for war.—Its declaration postponed for ten days at the instance of White Eyes.—Arrival of Heckewelder with peace-messages, and complete discomfiture of Pipe's faction.—Heckewelder's meeting with Zeisberger.—All the converts concentrated at Lichtenau.—Major Clark's dash on the posts of the Mississippi.—Governor Hamilton incites the savages to greater violence.—The Delawares maintain their position.—Treaty at Pittsburg.—Its stipulations and baneful results.—The commissioners give the Delawares the war-belt.—Indignation of Morgan and Zeisberger. —McIntosh's expedition against the Sandusky towns.—Requisition for Delaware warriors.—Zeisberger's protest against enlisting converts.—Fort Laurens.—Death of White Eyes.—Hamilton's expedition against Goschachgünk and Lichtenau frustrated.—Plots of the British Indians in these towns.—The Council and Zeisberger call McIntosh's army to their aid.—Siege of Fort Laurens.

In the early spring of 1778, Zeisberger unexpectedly found himself again in the midst of perilous complications. They came upon him from two different sides.

One day a Wyandot entered the Mission House and handed him a letter with an official seal. It purported to be from Governor Hamilton, and commanded the Moravian missionaries to arm their Indians, put themselves at their head, and march against the "rebels" beyond the Ohio, whom they were indiscriminately to attack on their farms and in their settlements, slaying without mercy and bringing the scalps to Detroit.[1] Terrible threats were added if they refused to obey this order.

Zeisberger was horror-stricken. To an ordained minister of Christ, preaching peace, having for years devoted his strength of body and mind to civilize the savages, using every effort, at this time, to stop the massacres and alleviate the misery of the border war, the idea that a Christian man and British officer should require missionaries to incite their converts to deeds of blood seemed iniquitous beyond expression. Hurrying to the fire-place, he threw the sheet into the flames. But he could not forget its contents. It plunged him into a state of mental depression which he vainly endeavored to shake off. Unburdening his heart, several weeks later, to Heckewelder, he said: "Oh, what sorrow that letter has caused me! I cannot think of it without dying a sort of death—it was too horrible a production!"

It appears not to have occurred to him that the letter was a forgery He believed that it had been written by Hamilton. And yet, although the truth was never ascertained, it is more than probable that this missive was an attempt on the part of some subordinate and perhaps irresponsible agent to alarm the missionaries and drive them from the Delaware country. Whatever the character of Hamilton, he would not have ventured officially to bid ministers of the Gospel be-

---

[1] Heckewelder's MS. Biographical Sketch.

come murderers, tear reeking scalps from the heads of their countrymen, and lead Christian Indians to those scenes of carnage in which the savages engaged. Against such a measure the civilized world would have protested.

Zeisberger was alone, harassed by many responsibilities, worn out by much labor. It is not surprising that, under such circumstances, his usual sagacity failed him and he accepted as true what was so evidently false.

The other cause of trouble was more serious. There came to Goschachgünk some disaffected persons from Pittsburg, with Alexander McKee, Matthew Elliot, and Simon Girty, an ignoble trio of go-betweens and desperadoes.

McKee was an Indian agent of the British government, a prisoner released on parole, hurrying, in flagrant violation thereof, to Detroit, in order to give all the information he had gathered while among the Americans. Elliot, a trader, but secretly holding the commission of a British captain, had been at Pittsburg as a spy. Simon Girty, an adopted Seneca, an inveterate drunkard, a blustering ruffian, seduced by British gold to forsake the Americans, whose interpreter he had been, was now espousing the royal cause with all the baseness of his character.[1]

Soon after the arrival of this party a second appeared, consisting of a serjeant and twenty privates, deserters

---

[1] *Taylor's Ohio*, 281, 282. Girty had two brothers, George, an adopted Delaware, and James, an adopted Shawanese. They were all three Pennsylvanians, and carried off prisoners by the Indians, about 1755.

from the fort, who joined the British Indians.[1] These men all vied one with another in spreading falsehoods among the Delawares. The Americans, they said, had been totally defeated in the Atlantic States; driven westward, they were now about to wage an indiscriminate war against the Indians. Such reports produced a general excitement in the nation. Captain Pipe, who had been eagerly watching for an opportunity to supplant White Eyes and overthrow the policy of the Council, hastened to the capital, called upon his countrymen to seize the hatchet and defend their homes. Who would venture to prate of treaties now? White Eyes barely succeeded in having the declaration of war postponed for ten days, that time might be given to ascertain whether the reports were true or false. But this did not hinder preparations for the conflict. Goschachgünk rang with the war-song; rifles were cleaned and tomahawks sharpened; the warriors painted their faces and selected their plumes. Meanwhile Zeisberger sat alone at Lichtenau, unable to control this storm. His words were as a whisper amid its fury.

But it was ruled by a higher hand. The Board having, for a long time, heard nothing from the Mission, Heckewelder and Schebosh were sent to Pittsburg (March 23d), to gather what intelligence they could, or to visit the Indian churches in person should the trail be open. They found the fort in great alarm at the escape of the spies and deserters and the success of their intrigues among the Delawares. In order to

---

[1] Penn. Archives, vi. 445.

prevent the rising of this nation and its numerous grandchildren, peace-messages must at once be sent to Goschachgünk. Such messages were prepared, but not a runner could be induced to take them. General Hand's offers of the most liberal rewards were all in vain; the risk was too great.

In this emergency, Heckewelder and Schebosh volunteered their services. Riding three days and two nights without stopping, except to feed their horses, in constant danger from the war-parties that lurked in the forests, they reached Gnadenhütten an hour before midnight of the fifth of April. The next day was the ninth of the stipulated term. No contradiction of the reports spread by Girty and his confederates had been received. War was accepted as a necessity even by White Eyes. Of that crisis John Heckewelder was the illustrious hero. Although scarcely able any longer to sit upon his horse, and although it was at the risk of his life, he pressed on, after but a brief rest, accompanied by John Martin, a native assistant, and got to Goschachgünk at ten o'clock in the morning. The whole population turned out to meet him. But their faces were dark and sinister. There was no welcome given. Not a single Delaware reciprocated his greetings. He extended his hand to White Eyes, but even White Eyes stepped back.

Holding aloft the written speeches of which he was the bearer, Heckewelder addressed the Indians from his horse. He told them that they had been deceived; that the Americans, instead of being defeated in the

Atlantic States, had gained a great victory and forced Burgoyne and his whole army to surrender; and that, so far from making war upon the Delawares, they were their friends and had sent him to establish a new alliance. Such news brought about a sudden change in the aspect of affairs. A council was called; the missives of General Hand were delivered and accepted in due form; the warlike preparations ceased; and, while Captain Pipe and his adherents left the town in great chagrin, the instigators of this whole plot fled to more congenial tribes.

Heckewelder now hastened to cheer Zeisberger with the glad tidings. Entering the Mission House at Lichtenau with all the pleasurable excitement of one about to surprise a friend, he was startled to see him sitting by the fire, pale, emaciated, the image of despair. "Ah, my dear John!" exclaimed Zeisberger as he rose to welcome him, "are you here? You have come into the midst of the fire! If God does not work a miracle the Mission is at an end! The Indians of Gnadenhütten are on the point of fleeing hither for safety. But there is no safety here! Satan rules! One evil follows the other! All Goschachgünk is preparing for war! What will be the issue of these things? What will become of the Mission? If the Delawares really go to war, we are lost! I care not for myself—but oh, my poor Indians!" Thus burst forth the pent-up emotions of his breast until tears choked his utterance. In all the dark days that boded ruin to his work, he had no friend to whom to open his heart, and now that his faithful coadjutor unexpectedly stood before him, he sought relief in these wails of agony. Heckewelder seated himself at his side and recounted the events of the morning. Then his drooping faith renewed its youth like the eagle's.[1]

In consequence of the disturbances caused by the war, and the refractory spirit of some of the young people, the Gnadenhütten Indians were brought to Lichtenau, so that the whole body of converts might be concentrated at one place, under the combined care of Zeisberger, Edwards, and Heckewelder. Zeisberger regained his influence in the Council, and caused a deputation to be sent to Pittsburg in response to General Hand's dispatches. In a letter to the Board, written about this time, he said that the three united churches hoped to be able to hold out until the end of the war. If, however, this should prove impossible, he would put himself at their head and lead them to the south country far beyond the reach of danger.

Stirring events now transpired in the West. Commissioned by Virginia, Major George Rogers Clark, a brave Kentuckian, set out from the Falls of Ohio, with a small force of volunteers, for the British posts on the Mississippi. At midnight of the third of July, he took Kaskaskia by surprise and sent the commandant, together with important papers, to Williamsburg.

---

[1] Heckewelder's MS. Biographical Sketch.

In the same way, Parraderuski, St. Philipps, and Cahokia fell into his hands. Vincennes, where the French element predominated, voluntarily yielded as soon as he had conveyed to its inhabitants the news of the alliance between France and the American States.

These unexpected disasters roused Governor Hamilton, who was holding a treaty with the Indians at Detroit. He gave them the hatchet anew, and urged them to more general and violent assaults upon the frontiers. The Delawares who were present in vain attempted to advocate peace. Their words were scorned and their towns soon filled again with Wyandot and Mingo war-parties. By one of these Hamilton sent the Council a menacing letter, and once more, and "for the last time," called upon it, in his own name and that of the confederate nations, to join them against the Americans. But the Council replied: "Years ago we promised Sir Willian Johnson to remain at peace with the white people, and this promise we intend to keep."

On the seventeenth of September, an Indian treaty, on the American side, took place at Pittsburg. Andrew and Thomas Lewis, special commissioners of Congress, General McIntosh, commander of the Western department, and numerous other officers, represented the States. It was stipulated, on the one hand, that the Americans should, at any time, be allowed to march troops through the Delaware country and erect a fort within it; and, on the other, that the Delawares should be admitted to a perpetual alliance and confederation with the United States.[1] But, however propitious such a result seemed to be, this very treaty formed one of the reasons of the subsequent alienation of the Delawares. The commissioners secretly gave the war-belt to the chiefs, and thus subverted the whole past policy of their young republic. It was an unpardonable blunder. Morgan, who was absent at Philadelphia, condemned the proceedings in the most unqualified manner. "There never was," he wrote, "a conference with the Indians so improperly or so villainously conducted as the late one at Pittsburg." Similar sentiments he expressed in a letter to Zeisberger, who was himself highly displeased. The war-belt was in flagrant opposition to all that he was urging in the Council of the Delawares, by the request, and upon the authority of the Indian agents. It is not likely, however, that the commissioners acted under instructions from Congress. The measure rather seems to have been urged by the West, in retaliation for its terrible sufferings.

McIntosh had come to Pittsburg in the spring, with a small force of regulars, for the defense of the frontier,

---

[1] *Taylor's Ohio*, 291, 422, etc. At this treaty White Eyes' favorite scheme of an independent Delaware nation was adopted in a modified form. One of the articles of the treaty reads as follows: "It is further agreed on between the contracting parties, should it for the future be found conducive for the mutual interests of both parties, to invite any other tribes, who have been friends to the interests of the U. S., to join in the present confederation, and to form a state, whereof the Delaware nation shall be the head, and have a representative in Congress: provided nothing in this article to be considered as conclusive until it meets with the approbation of Congress."

and had constructed a stockade fort at Beaver, named after him, with four bastions, each mounted with a six-pounder. Toward the end of September, he undertook an expedition against the Sandusky towns. His army consisted of about one thousand men. Upon the Delaware Council he had made a requisition for two captains and sixty warriors. Whether these were furnished does not appear, but White Eyes joined his command.

As soon as Zeisberger heard of this requisition, he wrote to the Board and urged a petition to Congress for a special act forbidding the officers of the United States to enlist Christian Indians.[1] Such an enlistment, however, was never attempted.

McIntosh encamped at Tuscarawas and built Fort Laurens, so called in honor of the President of Congress. This delayed him so long that advancing winter rendered the further campaign impracticable. Leaving a garrison of one hundred and fifty men, under Colonel Gibson, he prepared to move back to Pittsburg.[2]

It was at Tuscarawas—that ancient seat of the aborigines where their old men had, for generations, rehearsed their deeds of glory—that White Eyes, one of the greatest and best of the later Indians, finished his career, in the midst of an army of white men to whom he had ever remained true. He died of the small-pox, on the tenth of November, 1778. No unbaptized native,

---

[1] Letter to Bishop Seidel. B. A.
[2] Doddridge's Notes, chap. xxix.

of any tribe or name, did so much for the Mission and the Gospel. The period in which ambition alienated him was but as the time of autumnal clouds, that darken the firmament for a little while, and then leave it brighter and clearer. Where his remains are resting no man knows; the plowshare has often furrowed his grave. But his name lives; and the Christian may hope that in the resurrection of the just he, too, will be found among the great multitude redeemed out of every kindred, and tongue, and people, and nation.

White Eyes' death caused deep sorrow throughout the Indian country. Runners hastened from Goschachgünk to every part of the West bearing the sad intelligence; and many embassies were sent to condole with the Delawares. At the head of their Council now stood Gelelemend, Big Cat, and Tetepachkschüs. Captain Pipe still continued the leader of the war faction.

When Governor Hamilton received the Council's answer to his letter, he grew infuriated, and devised means to wreak his vengeance upon the councilors, and especially upon Zeisberger, whom he professed to regard as an emissary of the Americans. A formidable expedition against Goschachgünk and Lichtenau was set on foot. It consisted of Indians and a few British soldiers, and was commanded by two captains. Orders were given to bring back, without fail, the heads or scalps of White Eyes, Gelelemend, and Zeisberger.[1] The day of marching was already fixed, when, suddenly, both cap-

---

[1] Zeisberger's Letter to Bishop Hehl, Jan. 4, 1779. L. A.

tains died. This the Indians deemed so bad an omen that the undertaking had to be relinquished.

Hamilton now incited the Wyandots, Mingoes, and seceding Monseys to attack the Delawares. They refused, indeed, to lift up the hatchet against them, but began an assault with the weapons of intrigue that was even more alarming. Many, and among the converts too, wavered in their neutrality and clamored for war. At last, seeing no better way to silence such outcries, the Council and Zeisberger dispatched a runner to General McIntosh, and begged him to come to their aid with his troops. He was on the point of breaking camp at Fort Laurens, and immediately complied with the request. No sooner did the British Indians, who were filling Goschachgünk and Lichtenau with their plots, hear of his approach than they hurried off, as Zeisberger had anticipated.

In the beginning of 1779, an army of several hundred Shawanese, Wyandots, and Mingoes passed through Lichtenau on their way to Fort Laurens, which they besieged for six weeks, reducing the garrison to terrible straits. Soon after they had raised the siege, McIntosh arrived with supplies and a relief of seven hundred men. Major Vernon assumed the command of the post, and McIntosh returned to Pittsburg, where he was relieved by Colonel Daniel Brodhead.

CHAPTER XXIX.

LICHTENAU ABANDONED AND NEW SCHÖNBRUNN AND SALEM BUILT.—1779, 1780.

The border war abating.—Governor Hamilton taken prisoner.—Division of the Christian Indians into three colonies.—Founding of New Schönbrunn.—Simon Girty's attempt to capture or kill Zeisberger.—A second attempt to murder him.—The campaign against the Iroquois.—Lichtenau deserted and Salem built.—Arrival of new missionaries.—Marriage of John Heckewelder.—Adam Grube's visit.—Michael Jung.—Prosperity of the Mission.—The Delawares scatter and mostly join the British Indian

THE border war was abating. Governor Hamilton, the main instigator of it, could no longer promote its cruelties. After having recaptured Vincennes, which he found garrisoned by a captain and one private only, he fell into the power of Major Clark, who suddenly made his appearance a second time at this post and took it by assault (February 24, 1779). The "hair buyer" was carried to Williamsburg, where the Virginia Council ordered him to be confined in irons and fed on bread and water, as a punishment for his barbarities. But Washington interposed, and secured for him the treatment of a prisoner of war.

Zeisberger now determined to divide the Christian Indians into three colonies again. They had spent a year at Lichtenau, and had been a shining light to their neighbors and hundreds of warriors from the Western villages. But the permanent success of the Mission required smaller churches, as soon as the war would admit of their reorganization. Besides, there no longer existed that cordiality between him and the Delaware Council which had prevailed while White Eyes was its ruling mind. Tetepachkschüs and Big Cat, as we said in a former chapter, were secret enemies of the Gospel, and although Gelelemend ranked among its supporters, he was too weak a character to be its champion.

The division took place on the sixth of April, 1779. Edwards, with a part of the converts, reoccupied Gnadenhütten; Zeisberger, with another part, proceeded to Schönbrunn, which had been destroyed in the course of the war, and encamped amid its ruins; the rest stayed at Lichtenau in charge of Heckewelder.

Nearly opposite to the Big Spring, on the western bank of the Tuscarawas, were broad and fruitful bottoms skirted by a plateau that extended to the foot of the hills. Here Zeisberger's colony began a new town.[1] It progressed but slowly, and for eight months they lived in their encampment close by the spring.

Zeisberger passed much of his time in visiting the other stations, especially at Communion-seasons. In the early part of July, he spent such a season at Lichtenau, and was about to return to Schönbrunn, when Alexander McCormick, a trader and friend of the Mission, arrived with evil tidings. McKee, Elliot,

---

[1] It was situated on what is now (1863) the farm of Mr. John Gray, in Goshen Township, Tuscarawas County, a quarter of a mile from Lockport, and one and a quarter miles south of New Philadelphia. In constructing the Ohio Canal, a part of its site was dug away.

and Girty, he said, were still plotting Zeisberger's ruin; a party of Indians, led by Girty himself, was on his trail, with orders either to bring him alive to Detroit, or to shoot him down and take his scalp. It was a most timely warning, to which, however, he listened unmoved, and mounted his horse to go. "My life," he said to Heckewelder, who would have detained him, "is in the hands of God. How often has not Satan desired to murder me? But he dare not! I shall ride to Schönbrunn." Seeing that he was not to be kept back, Heckewelder persuaded him to take along a guard of Indians. To this he consented, but as their horses could not immediately be found, he proceeded alone, calling back: "I will slowly push on; send the Brethren after me; farewell!" A short distance from Lichtenau, the trail forked, one branch leading to a salt-lick about two miles distant. Down this branch he turned, lost in meditation, and did not perceive his mistake until he had advanced a considerable distance. Retracing his steps, he got to the fork just as his escort came up. If he had not missed the road they would not have overtaken him, and he would have been at the mercy of his enemies. For, suddenly, at the foot of a little hill, Simon Girty and his band stood before them. "That's the man!" cried Girty to the Indian captain, pointing out Zeisberger. "Now do what you have been told to do!" But in that instant there burst through the bushes two athletic young hunters of Goschachgünk. Divining at a glance the posture of affairs, they placed themselves in front of Zeisberger, drew their tomahawks, and began deliberately to load their rifles. As soon as the Wyandot captain saw this, and moreover recognized among Zeisberger's escort the great Glikkikan, he shook his head, motioned to his men, and disappeared with them in the forest. Girty followed him, gnashing his teeth in impotent rage.[1]

Not long after this, Zeisberger was again in imminent danger. An Indian noted for his inveterate enmity to the Gospel came to Schönbrunn, and sought an interview with him. The usual salutations of friendship were interchanged. But, suddenly, drawing a tomahawk, which he had secreted under his blanket, the savage exclaimed, with a fierce gleam of his eyes, " You are about to see your grandfathers!"[2]—lifted up his arm, and was in the act of striking the fatal blow, when Boaz, a convert, who suspected and had been closely watching him, sprang forward and wrenched the weapon from his hand. Zeisberger maintained "his usual presence of mind," says Mortimer, from whom we have this incident,[3] and spoke to him with such "serious friendliness" that the man repented of his sins, joined the Mission, and, in the course of time, was baptized, receiving the name of Isaac. He re-

---

[1] Heckewelder's MS. Biographical Sketch.

[2] This was a common saying among the Indians when they murdered a man, or supposed that he was otherwise on the point of death.

[3] *Mortimer's Journal, December,* 1779. MS. B. A. Mortimer, of whom more will be said in another connection, was Zeisberger's assistant during the last years of his life.

mained a worthy member of the Church until the general dispersion, and held out bravely against the seductions of heathenism even when he was separated from his teachers.

In the same summer in which Zeisberger was thus marvelously delivered out of the hands of his enemies, a terrible retribution overwhelmed the Iroquois, in whom he continued to take a deep interest. The valleys of the Mohawk and the Scoharie, where they had been raging with the brand and the tomahawk, and the nameless atrocities of the Wyoming massacre, called for vengeance, and the Americans prepared to strike a fearful blow. Washington himself planned the campaign, which was intrusted to General Sullivan. On the last day of July, 1779, the army marched from Wyoming, and, toward the end of August, defeated the allied Indians and British, eighteen miles above Tioga Point. For an entire month, the besom of destruction swept over the Iroquois country. Orchards, fields, towns, and every other vestige of culture were demolished. About the same time, Colonel Brodhead marched to the head-waters of the Alleghany, burned many villages, laid waste five hundred acres of corn, and captured a valuable booty of pelts. In spite of these reverses, however, the Six Nations were not subdued. They merely abandoned their hunting-grounds.

Toward the end of the year (December, 1779), Zeisberger's colony moved into their town, which received the name of New Schönbrunn; and in the spring of

1780, Heckewelder's division left Lichtenau (April 6th), in order to begin a settlement farther up the valley. It was an exodus which the conduct both of the Goschachgünk Indians and of the Wyandot and Mingo warriors rendered necessary. The former were growing more and more unfriendly; the latter had made Lichtenau a place of rendezvous and the starting-point for a new war-path to the Ohio.

A few miles from Gnadenhütten, on the site of a Delaware village, the inhabitants of which had been removed by the Council, in a beautiful plain on the western bank of the Tuscarawas, Heckewelder founded the town of Salem.[1]

In its chapel, dedicated on the twenty-second of May, there gathered, on the fourth anniversary of American Independence (July 4, 1780), a large congregation of Indians from the three towns, together with the whole Mission-family, recently increased by the arrival of Gottlob Senseman, Mrs. Senseman, and Miss Sarah Ohneberg. In the presence of this assembly, that veteran missionary, Adam Grube, whom the Board had sent

---

[1] It was situated in Salem Township, Tuscarawas County, one and a half miles southwest of Port Washington, on what is now (1863) Mr. Henry Stocker's farm, just opposite three bald hill-tops, and between the track of the Steubenville and Indiana Railroad and the Tuscarawas River. On the twentieth of June, 1863, Mr. Blickensderfer, to whom I have referred in a former note, and I discovered the site of Salem. The plain in which it stood was well known; but we succeeded in identifying the very spot which it once occupied, and clearly traced the line of its houses by the discoloration of the soil, at regular intervals, in a field of young corn, and by numerous relics which we dug up.

on an official visit to the valley, united John Heckewelder and Miss Ohneberg in marriage. It was, doubtless, the first wedding of a white couple in the present State of Ohio.[1]

Grube spent six weeks at the Mission, in conference with his brethren, and then went back to Bethlehem to report to the Board. In the following autumn, Michael Jung arrived as Edward's assistant.[2] Senseman was stationed at New Schönbrunn, and Zeisberger, as superintendent of the Mission, itinerated from church to church. The whole year was one of peace and prosperity, distinguished, too, by the return of the rest of the apostate Monseys. In the course of the winter, Zeisberger wrote that lengthy account of the manners and customs of the North American Indians which forms the basis of the Introduction to Loskiel's History of the Mission.[3]

---

[1] The party from Bethlehem, consisting of Grube, Senseman, Mrs. Senseman, and Miss Ohneberg, was escorted from Pittsburg to Schönbrunn by a number of Christian Indians. Upon these three American scouts fired from an ambush, in spite of the presence of white persons, with the intention of taking their scalps, for which bounties were now paid. A bullet passed through the sleeve of the Indian leading Grube's horse.

[2] Michael Jung was born, January 5, 1743, at Engoldsheim, in the old province of Elsass, or Alsace, in Germany. His parents belonged to the Reformed Church. In 1751, he immigrated with them to America. They settled at Broadbay, in Maine, where he joined the Moravian Church. In 1767, he proceeded to Bethlehem, and remained an inmate of the Brethren's House until he was called to serve the Indian Mission, in 1780. He was a faithful missionary, and labored among the Indians for thirty-three years. In 1813, he retired to Litiz, Pa., where he died December 13, 1826.

[3] Comp. chap. ii. note 2.

Meantime Captain Pipe had gained the ascendency at Goschachgünk. Gelelemend and those of his councilors who sided with the Americans fled from the town; the most of the other chiefs were scattered; the great council-fire which Netawatwes and White Eyes had made to burn with so bright a flame was dying out. Distracted, without a proper head and a national center, the majority of the Delawares yielded to the persuasions of the British Indians and joined them. Pipe built a town near the Half King's, and stood in open league with him against the United States. When this alienation became known to the converts, they renounced, by several formal embassies, all further fellowship with the Delawares.

CHAPTER XXX.

ZEISBERGER'S MARRIAGE AND LAST VISIT TO THE SETTLEMENTS.—1781.

Zeisberger visits Bethlehem.—Bishop Reichel.—Interview with President Reed at Philadelphia.—Zeisberger's views on the expediency of his remaining a single man.—Yields to the persuasions of his friends and marries.—Broadhead's expedition against the Delawares.—His proposal to the missionaries.—The Christian towns disturbed by war-parties.—Narrow escape of Edwards and Jung.—Zeisberger returns to the Mission with his wife and Jungmann.

IN the spring of 1781, Zeisberger visited Bethlehem in order to attend a Synod convened by Bishop Reichel,[1] from Germany, who had been spending two years in the United States on an official visit to the Moravian churches. He found his old friend, Bishop Seidel, with whom he had followed up many a forest-trail, weak and weary, longing to be at rest. But the other members of the Board—Ettwein, Schweinitz, and Huebener[2]—

---

[1] John Frederick Reichel was born at Oberlödel, in Altenburg, in 1731, and was the son of the Rev. Jacob Daniel Reichel, of the Lutheran Church. Having studied at Jena, he took charge of the parish of Taubenheim. In 1758, he resigned this parish, joined the Moravians, and became pastor of the church at Nisky, Prussia. In 1769, he was elected to the General Executive Board of the Unitas Fratrum, and in 1775 consecrated bishop. He died November 17, 1809.

[2] John Andrew Huebener (born June 16, 1737, at Aschersleben, in Halberstadt) joined the Moravian Church in 1759, and filled various offices in Germany. In 1780, he came to America as a member of the Mission Board and pastor of the church at Bethlehem. In 1790, he was

were in the midst of their activity, which the complications of the Revolutionary War rendered both arduous and embarrassing.

After the adjournment of the Synod, Zeisberger proceeded to Philadelphia with a letter of introduction from Colonel Broadhead to President Reed, of the Supreme Executive Council of Pennsylvania. Brodhead wrote: "I have requested him to go to Philadelphia, as I expected the Honorable Executive Council, Congress, and the Board of War would be glad of an opportunity to examine him respecting his Mission and the disposition of the Indians in general. He is a faithful man, and what he says may be relied on."[1] President Reed received him with great distinction, and thanked him, in the name of the whole country, for his services among the Indians, particularly for his Christian humanity in turning back so many war-parties that were on their way to rapine and massacre.[2]

Zeisberger now spent several weeks in conference with Bishop Reichel and the Mission Board. He was sixty years of age, thirty-seven of which had been devoted to the service of God among the Indians. Of days of comfort, or the cheering presence of a wife and the joys of a family, he had scarcely thought. Indeed, applying the contrast drawn by the Apostle

---

consecrated bishop, and took up his residence at Litiz, of which church he was, at the same time, the pastor. In 1801, he was elected a member of the General Board in Europe, and filled that office until his death, December 26, 1809.

[1] Penn. Archives, ix. 57.
[2] Philadelphia Diary, May, 1781. MS. P. A.

Paul between the married and single state[1] to the circumstances and work of his own life, he had long since made up his mind never to marry.[2] On this occasion, however, his friends urged him to abandon such a determination, reminding him of the dreariness of his old age, on a distant frontier, without a helpmate. He yielded to these persuasions, and made proposals of marriage to Miss Susan Lecron, of Litiz, who accepted him.[3]

On the first of June, he left Bethlehem, which he had helped to found forty years ago, and which he never saw again, and, in the evening of Whit-Monday (June 4th), the marriage took place in the church at Litiz, the patriarch Grube performing the ceremony.

During Zeisberger's absence, events of importance transpired in the Tuscarawas valley. Informed of the disaffection of the Delawares, Colonel Brodhead organized an expedition of about three hundred men, nearly one-half of whom were volunteers, and having rendezvoused at Wheeling, where he was joined by John Montour and several friendly Indians, advanced into their country to punish them for their breach of faith. By a rapid march he surprised Goschachgünk and Lichtenau, in the evening of the nineteenth of April, killing fifteen warriors and taking twenty prisoners. Among the latter were five Christian Indians, from Salem, on a visit

---

[1] I. Cor. vii. 32, 33.
[2] Heckewelder's MS. Biographical Sketch.
[3] Susan Lecron was born at Lancaster, Pa., February 17, 1744. In 1758, her parents, who were Lutherans, removed with her to the neighborhood of Litiz, where she joined the Moravian Church.

to their former home. These he set at liberty. But, as they were going up the Muskingum in a canoe, some of the militia, contrary to orders, stealthily followed and made a furious attack upon them from a convenient ambush. The converts took to the hills, and succeeded in reaching Salem with but one of their number wounded.

Having destroyed both Goschachgünk and Lichtenau,[1] together with the corn, poultry, and cattle of the Indians, the army proceeded up the valley to Gekelemuckpechünk, where Gelelemend and the remnant of friendly Delawares were living. At the request of Brodhead, the missionaries and native assistants visited his camp. He proposed to them to break up their settlements and accompany him to Pittsburg. It was a well-meant overture. The Delawares having joined the British Indians, the Mission would be exposed to their attacks. But, in the very nature of the case, the invitation could not be accepted. Gelelemend and his band, however, were glad to profit by a similar offer, and put themselves under the protection of the United States. The rest of the nation had set up their lodges in the Wyandot country, among the Shawanese, and farther west; so that the entire valley of the Tuscarawas now embraced no Indians other than the Christian converts in their three towns.

Brodhead's apprehensions were fulfilled. A few days after his departure, a body of eighty savages, led by

---

[1] After the exodus of the Christian Indians, Lichtenau was occupied by the Delawares, who named it Indaochaie.—*Penn. Archives*, ix. 161.

Pachgantschihillas, a noted Delaware captain, surprised Gnadenhütten, demanding the surrender of Gelelemend and his followers. When it was found that this party had retired to Pittsburg, the Delaware band endeavored to break up the Mission by persuading the converts to seek a refuge among the Wyandots. Some of the warriors made three several attempts to murder Heckewelder, whom they considered a stumbling-block in the way of their purpose. At last, alarmed by a false report of the approach of an American army, they departed, carrying with them more than a dozen of the Salem Indians, who renounced the Gospel and fell back into heathenism. As he was about leaving the town, Pachgantschihillas, with almost the vision of a prophet, warned the converts against raids on the part of the Americans. "If you pass safely through this war," he said, "and I see you all alive at the close of it, I will regret not to have joined your Mission."

After this, marauding-parties prowled through the valley, stealing horses and whatever else they could find. One of these parties lay in ambush near a field of Gnadenhütten. Into this field came Edwards and Jung, and began to plant potatoes. Instantly seven of the savages cocked their rifles, took aim, and were upon the point of shooting them down, when the captain, seized by an unaccountable impulse of mercy, persuaded his men to spare their lives. The band crept away, and the two missionaries continued working in the field, ignorant of the death which had threatened them.

On the twelfth of June, Zeisberger and his wife, together with John Jungmann and Mrs. Jungmann, who had consented to resume their labors among the Indians, set out from Litiz for the West. They traveled on horseback, and, after crossing the Alleghanies, found themselves in such constant danger from the savages, who were on the war-path in great numbers, that they took refuge in New Store, on the Monongahela, eighteen miles from Pittsburg, whither Zeisberger proceeded alone for a boat and guard of soldiers. At the fort an escort of twenty Christian Indians awaited them, under whose protection they reached New Schönbrunn in safety, on the fifteenth of July.

CHAPTER XXXI.

CAPTURE OF THE MISSIONARIES, AND OVERTHROW OF THE MISSION ON THE TUSCARAWAS.—1781.

The Mission family and its labors.—Causes of the overthrow of the work in the Tuscarawas valley.—An expedition against the Christian towns planned.—The tribes that took part in it, and their motives.—Intelligence of the approaching raid.—Arrival of the Wyandot Half King and his warriors.—Elliot the British captain.—Friendly words and base purposes.—McCormick and his secret information.—Zeisberger's trust in God.—Arrival of more warriors.—The encampment at Gnadenhütten.—Speeches of the Half King, and reply of the Christian Indians.—Differences of opinion among the latter.—Zeisberger's message to Bethlehem.—Quarrels between Elliot and the warriors.—He insists upon the seizure of the missionaries.—The Half King and his Council deciding their fate.—Hesitation of the savages to take their lives.—The missionaries refuse to flee.—The morning service of the third of September at Gnadenhütten.—Final demand of the Half King, and answer of the missionaries.—Their motives in giving this answer.—They are seized and held as captives.—The night of the third of September.—Their wives are seized and brought to Gnadenhütten.—Scalp-yells.—Flight of a young squaw with the news to Pittsburg.—Anger of the warriors.—Capture and release of Glikkikan.—The missionaries set free on promising to leave the valley with their converts.—Their last Communion at Salem.—The news at Bethlehem.

There were now six missionaries on the Tuscarawas:[1] Zeisberger and Jungmann at New Schönbrunn; Sense-

---

[1] Sources for this chapter are: Diary of Bethlehem, April to December, 1781, MS. B. A.; Diary of Litiz, April, 1781, MS. L. A.; Zeisberger's Journal of 1781, compendium, in his own handwriting, MS. B. A.; the same journal more in detail, copied, MS. B. A.; Heckewelder's Diary of Salem, 1781, MS. B. A.; Heckewelder's English Narrative of the Capture of the Missionaries and Massacre of the In-

man and William Edwards at Gnadenhütten; Heckewelder and Michael Jung at Salem. They all zealously preached the Word, dispensed the sacraments, instructed the children, comforted the aged, and ministered to the sick; while their wives went about among the women, taught them to be Christian mothers and fill the position which the Gospel assigns to their sex. Peace reigned in the churches, until that storm burst upon them which swept them from the valley. The elements which produced it had silently been gathering ever since the commencement of the war.

Placed in the heart of a country which lay between the frontier settlements of the Americans and the western posts of the British, the situation of the missionaries was, in the highest degree, embarrassing. They and their people were neutral. But, while they never attempted to interfere with legitimate warfare, the case was different in regard to the massacres perpetrated by the Indians. They were pledged by their responsibilities to God to prevent such massacres, as far as lay in their power. It was not enough to theorize in the Delaware Council upon the wickedness of burning homesteads and butchering women and children. Their sacred office, their ordination vows, the Gospel which they proclaimed, all forbade them to enjoy the security of their houses and rich abundance of their plantations, without bestirring

---

dians, 1781 and 1782, MS. B. A.; Heckewelder's Biographical Sketch of Zeisberger, MS. Lib. Morv. Hist. Soc.; Heckewelder's Corrections of Loskiel's History of the Capture of the Missionaries, MS. B. A.; Jungmann's Autobiography, MS. B. A.; Susanna Zeisberger's Autobiography, MS. B. A.; Penn. Col. Records, xii. xiii.; Penn. Archives, ix.

themselves to save other non-combatants from death. Hence they frequently persuaded war-parties, stopping in their towns, to turn back, and, by request of the Delaware Council, wrote letters to the commandant at Pittsburg reporting the movements of the savages. But these acts were not the acts of American spies. They were not performed in the interests of the Americans politically considered; they were done in the name of humanity and by the authority of the Prince of Peace. With the political aspects of the Revolution Zeisberger and his coadjutors wished to have nothing to do; they espoused neither cause, but waited until the struggle should be over, in order then to obey those powers that should be ordained of God. If to induce bloodthirsty savages to go back to their villages and not dash their tomahawks into the brains of women and sucking children militated against such neutrality—if to fulfill the solicitations of the Delaware councilors, themselves unable to write, and transcribe messages to American officers whereby border families were warned of the approach of murderous gangs, was to take sides with the "rebels" against the crown—then, in both cases, they followed the higher law, the law of God, which supersedes every other. But a position like this the British agents would not, and indeed could not, understand. Blunted by the associations of the Indian war they had evoked, they did not realize that their policy deserved to be condemned at the bar of nations, not to speak of a divine tribunal. The Moravian missionaries and their converts were to them, not upholders of principles which necessarily grew out of their sacred vocation, but abettors of the American rebellion, on a par with its frontier scouts.

To none were they more hateful than to Elliot, McKee, and Simon Girty. Ever since the first visit of these men to Goschachgünk, where they saw the influence which Zeisberger was exercising, they had persistently plotted the ruin of the Mission. Thus far their efforts had been without success. Now, however, another attempt was to be made. A treaty with the Iroquois took place at Niagara. Thither went McKee, as Agent of Indian Affairs, and proposed, by authority of the commandant of Detroit, an expedition against the Christian towns. The Six Nations were unwilling themselves to engage in it, but sent, first, to the Chippewas and Ottawas, saying, "We give you the believing Indians and their teachers to make broth of;" and when they had declined the gift, the same message was transmitted to the Half King of the Wyandots. He accepted it, but, as he protested, merely in order to save the lives of the Christian Indians. At a barbecue in a Shawanese town, on the Scioto, the raid was planned, in the presence and by the help of British officers, and under the folds of the British flag. Wyandots, Mingoes, and Delawares, together with a few Shawanese, formed the troop. To the captains only was the real object of the expedition made known. They received secret instructions to drive the Christian Indians from their seats, to seize their teachers, and either to convey them as prisoners to Detroit, or put them to death and bring their scalps. The Wyandot and Mingo captains consented for the sake of the plunder and the promised reward; of the Delaware captains the Unamis were actuated by their implacable animosity to the Gospel, the Monseys by the desire of revenge for the neutral policy which the Goschachgünk Council had maintained in opposition to Pipe, and which they correctly ascribed to the influences of the Mission, and for Broadhead's ravages on the Muskingum, unjustly laid to its charge.

The first intelligence which the missionaries received of this threatening invasion was brought during Zeisberger's absence, and induced them to hold a consultation (June 11) with the national assistants, at which it was determined not to leave the Tuscarawas valley except by force. Of this resolution Zeisberger approved when he got back; but, as no further tidings came from the Scioto, he began to hope that the expedition had been given up. In the first days of August, however, reports of its speedy arrival again circulated; and, on the ninth, they were unhappily verified by two runners who came to Salem from the Half King himself, announcing that he and his warriors were on their way to have a talk with their father, Zeisberger, and with their cousins, the Christian Indians, and requesting to be informed in which of their towns they should encamp. Zeisberger, to whom this message was referred, designated Gnadenhütten as the place of rendezvous.

In the afternoon of the tenth, at four o'clock, the first party reached Salem with a painful attempt at martial array. Most of them were mounted, and rode in the following order: the Half King and his men, from Upper Sandusky; Abraham Coon[1] and Wyandots, from Lower Sandusky; Wyandots from Detroit; Mingoes; two Shawanese captains, John and Thomas Snake; Captain Pipe and Captain Wenginund, with Monseys and Delawares; Matthew Elliot, in his capacity of British captain, attended by Alexander McCormick, as ensign, bearing a British flag, as also by Michael Herbert and five other Englishmen and Frenchmen; stragglers from various tribes bringing up the rear. The whole troop numbered one hundred and forty men. They encamped on the plain between Salem and the river, and were hospitably entertained. The Half King, the captains, and Matthew Elliot visited the Mission House, where Heckewelder received them in the presence of the native assistants. The interview was of the most friendly character. With a polite impudence, possible only among arch-deceivers like the Indians, Pomoacan addressed Heckewelder:

"Father, I thank the great God in heaven that He has preserved us both until this day, and permitted us to see one another again.

"Father, I rejoice to be with you, and beg you to fill my tobacco-pipe."

Turning next to the assistants, he complimented them with all the phrases usual on occasions of amity. Not the remotest hint was given of the evil designs which

---

[1] Abraham Coon was a white man, captured by the Indians in the first French War, adopted by the Wyandots, and now a captain among them. He was the interpreter of the expedition

had brought the party to Salem. Elliot, too, consummately acted the hypocrite. His words were soft and kind; his heart full of gall and bitterness. Of this McCormick, who had been forced, against his will, to accompany the expedition, assured Heckewelder, with whom he had arranged a secret meeting under cover of the night. "Elliot is the real leader of these men," he said, "and you missionaries and all your Indians are to be carried away from your towns. At first they intended to kill you, but now they have concluded to begin with milder means. Agree to their demands, Mr. Heckewelder; there is no other alternative. This is my earnest advice."

Several hours later a rider was hastening through the silent forests to New Schönbrunn with a letter to Zeisberger containing this calamitous intelligence. It was not unexpected. "Satan appears indeed," he wrote in reply, "to be about to trouble and persecute us again, and to make merry at our expense. What wonder!— seeing the many subjects he loses by our preaching. But his roaring must not frighten us. We have a heavenly Father. Without His will Satan dare not touch us. Let us rely on that Father who has so often delivered us!" These noble sentiments were reiterated by all the missionaries at a conference which they held, on the twelfth, at Gnadenhütten. They could not, as yet, agree upon measures to meet the emergency because Pomoacan did not make known his intentions, and Elliot still professed friendship, accepting Heckewelder's hospitality, and but occasionally dropping vague hints about the insecurity of the Mission in the Tuscarawas valley.

Meanwhile the troop had proceeded to Gnadenhütten, where it was augmented by other parties of Delawares and Wyandots, which arrived from time to time, until, by the seventeenth, it mustered three hundred warriors, besides a number of old men and squaws who came to take charge of the spoils. An encampment was put up on the green which crowned the lofty riverbank west of the town, one part being appropriated to the Wyandots, the other to the Delawares; in the center stood Elliot's tent surmounted by the British flag.

On the twentieth, the Half King, at last, called a council of the national assistants, and unfolded the purpose of the expedition, the missionaries being present.

"My cousins," so ran his speech, "ye believing Indians in Gnadenhütten, Schönbrunn, and Salem!

"I am much distressed on your account. You live in a dangerous place. Two exceedingly mighty and wrathful gods stand opposed one to another with extended jaws, and you, seated between them, will be destroyed by the one or by the other, perhaps by both, and will be crushed between their teeth.

"You must not any longer remain here. Remember your young people, remember your women and your children. Care for their lives; here they will all perish.

"Therefore I take you by the hand, lift you up, and set you where I have my lodges. There you will be safe and can dwell in peace.

"Do not regard your houses, fields, and property. Rise up and come with me.

"Take your teachers along. Hold your religious councils as you are accustomed to do. You will find an abundance of provisions in my country, and our English father beyond the lake will care for you. To tell you this I have come."

A string of wampum.

The next day, the national assistants returned the following answer:

"Uncle, and ye captains of the Delawares and Monseys, who are our friends, and one nation with us, ye Shawanese, our grandchildren, and all ye who are assembled here!

"We have heard your words, that we live in a dangerous place; that we ought to remember our young people, our women and children; that we must bring them to a place of safety, and care for their lives; that we are to rise up and go with you ere evil befall us. We have heard and understood your words.

"But we do not see the danger of which you speak; we do not believe that we cannot stay here. We are at peace with all men. We have no interest in the war. We interfere with none; and all we desire is that none shall interfere with us.

"You see yourselves that we cannot now go with you. We are heavy and must have time. But we promise to keep and consider your words; and, next winter, after we shall have reaped our fields, we will give you a reply upon which you may depend."

So well was this speech received by the Half King

and the majority of his captains that the missionaries imagined the danger to be past, and each returned to his town.

But Elliot was not satisfied. He persuaded Pipe, and Pipe persuaded Pomoacan, to insist upon an immediate removal. On the twenty-fifth, the Half King accordingly convened the national assistants of Gnadenhütten, and told them that he was not pleased—first, because no string of wampum had been given him; and secondly, because the term which they had set was too long. The Christian Indians must leave their towns now.

Zeisberger having been sent for, a second speech was delivered, setting forth that the converts could not lose their crops and all their property; that it would be wrong to expose their women and children to the danger of starvation; that time should be given them at least to gather their corn; that the Half King should have pity and think of the distress into which he was plunging them.

Several days of great anxiety for the missionaries followed. It was a grievous burden to feed three hundred warriors, whose frequent association with the young members of the Church was bearing evil fruits; and—worse than all!—differences of opinion began to prevail among those of maturer years and even among the assistants. Misled by the artful words of the captains and their men, not a few believed that the country to which they were to be taken was a land flowing with milk and honey, and favored a speedy emigration. Zeisberger and his fellow-laborers did what they could to undeceive such as these, crying to God for aid. It was not their personal safety which affected them, but the prosperity of the Mission,—the eternal welfare of the souls intrusted to their care. Wisdom to guide them aright, amid such dark experiences, was the boon for which they prayed. With regard to themselves, they had no fears, as is shown by a message which Zeisberger succeeded in conveying to Colonel Brodhead for transmission to the Board at Bethlehem. "We are beset," he wrote, "by upwards of three hundred warriors of different nations. They are determined to take us away from our settlements, and threaten to kill us and carry off our scalps if we do not yield. We are resigned to our fate."

Pomoacan and his captains were in perplexity. The request of the Christian Indians for time to gather their corn was reasonable, and ought, they said, to be granted. But as Elliot would not hear of this, they fell to quarreling, and some of the warriors conceived such disgust for his pertinacity that they insulted him and shot at the British flag. This roused his anger. "Of whom are you afraid?" he exclaimed. "If you go home without these ministers, expect no favor from your English father; if you fail to seize them, I will leave this place and report your faithlessness. Then you will have not a father, but a powerful enemy at Detroit; and, the English and the Americans both against you, what awaits your tribes but destruction?" With this threat he instantly began to prepare for his departure, and made it appear that he was in great haste to return to Detroit. The Half King took the alarm, and promised immediate compliance with his wishes.

Council after council was now called to decide the fate of the missionaries. At length, it was resolved to put them to death, provided this should meet with the approval of a noted sorcerer who accompanied the expedition. But he pronounced the decision unwise, inasmuch as the national assistants would then fill the place of the teachers, and nothing would be gained. Another council thereupon included the national assistants in the sentence of death. "What!" stormed the sorcerer when this new plan was submitted to him, "you have determined to kill my countrymen, and friends, and near relations! Lay but a finger upon a single one of them, and I know what I will do!" So great was the fear of this man that the project immediately fell through. Finally the council determined to spare the lives of the missionaries, but to carry them off to Detroit. The converts, it was believed, would follow of their own accord.

God undoubtedly here made, as He often does, an agent of Satan to praise Him; but the Indians were influenced by other motives also, and hesitated to shed the blood of the white teachers, because they had always received kindness at their hands, because their fame was in all the land, and their towns were everywhere known to be the seats of generous hospitality. Many of these savages were ill at ease. They would not have scrupled to murder the innocent; but to slay men who had so often fed them when they were hungry and given them to drink when they were thirsty, was contrary to their instincts. This explains, what would otherwise be an enigma, why three hundred armed warriors wavered for an entire week before seizing a handful of missionaries.

On the first of September, the Half King again summoned them to an interview at Gnadenhütten. Zeisberger, Senseman, Edwards, and Heckewelder appeared. Jungmann, with his wife, Mrs. Zeisberger, and Mrs. Senseman—who had but two days before given birth to a son[1]—remained at New Schönbrunn; Michael Jung with Mrs. Heckewelder at Salem.

Gnadenhütten, by this time, presented a dreary scene of rioting and ruin. Savages filled it, running about with terrific war-whoops, dancing and singing, shooting down cattle and hogs, and leaving the carcasses to rot in the streets and the stench to infect the air. The missionaries kept the house, their meeting with Pomoacan having been appointed for the following day. Late at night, a national assistant came and begged them to flee to Pittsburg, saying that the converts were all ready to aid and protect them. But they declined. In no case, they added, would they desert the Mission. Their lives were in the hands of God. The next morning, Saturday, September the third, John Martin pre-

---

[1] Christian David Senseman, born August 30, 1781, who afterward settled at Nazareth, Pa., where he was a merchant for many years, and at which place he died in 1834.

sented himself, and with tearful eyes informed them that that day would decide their fate. "A warrior," he said, "a relative of mine, who was at the Half King's council last night, assures me of this, and tells me, too, that there again exists a difference of opinion. Some have changed their minds and want to kill you in spite of the sorcerer's judgment. Dear brethren, it is certain that to-day you will either be put to death or taken prisoners."

Never did Zeisberger's Christian heroism shine more brightly than on this occasion. In all the towns of the Mission a public service was held daily, at 8 o'clock. To omit it that morning would have been but natural. Not so, however, thought this stanch confessor, who had so often stood up to his duty "in perils among the heathen," and so often found his father's God "a sun and shield." At the appointed hour, he gave directions to ring the bell of the chapel. Its clear tones filled Gnadenhütten and sounded through the encampment and were borne to the plantations of the river-bottom, until they died away in the forest beyond. The converts heard them, and flocked to the sanctuary from every house, hut, and field; the warriors heard them, and many bent their steps to the same place; the Half King heard them, and a shade of remorse fell upon his heart at the thought that that bell would never ring again; the British captain heard them, and, with an uneasy mind, sought the recesses of his tent; the ensign heard them, and hastened to take part in the worship of the men whom he loved; the distant scouts, guarding the trails, heard them, and wondered whether that morning's prayers would be the last the teachers would bring to the white man's God. When Zeisberger entered the church he found it filled to overflowing and the doors wide open, that the throng without might catch his words. His tried associates were calm and self-possessed; the national assistants manifested deep anxiety; the converts sat with sorrow in their eyes; the warriors looked grave as when gathered to a council. Deep silence pervaded the assembly.

Zeisberger gave out a hymn in the Delaware language. That roused the faith of the congregation, and there ensued such a burst of song as had never before been known within those walls. His discourse, which now followed, had for its text the passage appointed for that day in the churches of the Brethren: "Behold, thou art wroth; for we have sinned: in those is continuance, and we shall be saved."[1] The spirit of the Lord God was upon him. Taking for his theme divine love, which, while the Lord is wroth because of their sins,

---

[1] Isaiah, lxiv. 5. Both in his *MS. Biographical Sketch* and in his published *History of the Mission*, Heckewelder adduces a different text, namely, Is. liv. 8. This, however, is manifestly an inadvertency. I have before me his own official diary of Salem, written a few days after the event, and in that he gives the text I have cited. His MS. Sketch was written twenty-seven, and his history thirty-nine, years later.

The Moravian Church annually publishes a little volume, in the German, English, French, Dutch, Swedish, Danish, Esquimaux, and Negro-English languages, containing two texts—the one from the Old, the other from the New, Testament—for each day in the year, with appropriate stanzas from the Hymn Book annexed. This manual has appeared ever since 1731, and is, consequently, now in its one hundred and fortieth year. It was from it that Zeisberger took his text.

prompts Him to chasten men that they may repent and be saved, he illustrated the subject, first, by the example of ancient Israel, and then by that of the converts from heathenism in modern times. He showed that in Greenland and Labrador, in South Africa and the West Indies, in South America and the Western wilderness, where they then were, God had chosen for himself a people redeemed from pagan errors, delivered from Satan's snares, and waiting to join those who were already before His throne. It was a people that He would never forsake, however much He might try them in His righteous wrath.

"We here," he continued, "are a part of this chosen nation. And shall we who have thus been brought out of darkness to the light, who have experienced the goodness of the Lord, and in so many instances seen His protecting hand over us, who have braved so many storms and the threatenings of the children of darkness, who have never yet been disappointed in our hopes— shall we forget this? Did we not frequently hear the same menaces? Were we not told, time and again, what would be done to us if we did not leave our habitations and live among the heathen? And did we obey? or were we molested for not obeying? No! And why not? Because we put our trust in the Lord and depended upon His protection. Will we, then, not continue in the same faith and place the same trust in Him, assured that He is both willing and able to protect us at all times? Have we grown weaker in our faith instead of stronger? Will we give the heathen cause to mock and laugh at us that they may say, 'These pretend to believe what they believe not'? No, my brethren! Not only will we abide in that faith which, through grace, we have received, but we will endeavor to grow in such faith. Death itself shall not rob us of this treasure. And though, in times of old, the Lord was sometimes wroth with His people, and permitted the heathen to chastise them a little when they became indifferent and departed from His ways; yet, as soon as they repented, He turned to them again in mercy. Let it be so with us also, and particularly with those who, at this time, have been led astray, who have been overwhelmed by fear and timidly would choose rather to submit to the dictates of the heathen than to rely upon Him to whom all power has been given both in earth and heaven, and who is able to withstand Satan and his whole host.

"My brethren, our present situation, in some respects, is indeed unparalleled. We are surrounded by a body of heathen, by enemies to the glorious Gospel, by those who threaten to take our lives if we do not go with them and make them our near neighbors. Nevertheless we trust in the Lord and submit to our fate. He will not forsake us. We will quietly await whatever He permits. We will not defend our lives by force of arms, for that would be putting ourselves on a level with the heathen, and we are the children of God. Neither will we hate our enemies. They know not what they do. We are Christians, and will therefore rather pray for them, that the Lord God may open their eyes and turn their hearts, that they may repent and be saved. Perhaps we may yet see some of these who are here now, seeking Christ and joining His holy church, against which the gates of hell shall not prevail."

Deep feeling agitated the congregation during the delivery of this discourse, of which the foregoing are but mere extracts; tears were shed on every side, not of fear, but of repentance and joy in the Lord; even the savages, of whom Zeisberger spoke so fearlessly, and whose wicked designs he laid bare with so unsparing a hand, bowed their proud heads in shame. The power of God was so manifest, that Heckewelder affirms he never witnessed anything like it, and that it seemed almost as though Jesus himself were visibly present. A fervent prayer followed, in which the missionaries and converts were commended to the protecting care of their heavenly Father, and His benediction was invoked upon the warriors present, upon those in the camp, upon every person in the town, that they might all be converted.

At eleven o'clock, the Half King, with his councilors and captains, repaired to the Mission House, whither the missionaries and assistants had retired immediately after the morning service. He told them that their speech of a week ago, asking for time to harvest, was not acceptable, and that he had called them together in order to afford them one opportunity more to yield voluntarily to his demands. They must leave their towns at once, and accompany him to the Wyandot country; if they refused, it would be at their own peril. According to a previous understanding, one of the assistants, in the name of Zeisberger as the head of the Mission, replied: "We have already informed you of our determination. We repeat it now. We cannot leave our towns at once. We ask for time at least to harvest. We have nothing further to say." As soon as they had received this answer, the Half King and his captains left the house.

In declining to submit freely to the will of the savages, the missionaries were moved by a high sense of duty. It was clear to their minds that they would, in the end, have to give way; but every effort, consistent with their principles, must first be made to avert such a catastrophe. They must uphold the Mission as long as it was possible, even if it should cost them their lives. A forcible abduction they could not prevent; but not until this was attempted would they feel at liberty to leave a spot where their work prospered so abundantly, and expose the converts to the perils which would surround them in the Wyandot country.

Word had been brought to Zeisberger, by one of his converts, from a Monsey captain, that he should assert his rights as a naturalized citizen of their nation, promising him full protection if he did so. But his fellow-missionaries not being included in the offer, he did not deem it worthy of his notice. In the afternoon, about one o'clock, as he was walking with Senseman and Heckewelder back of the Mission garden, this captain himself hurried up and renewed the suggestion, telling him that he must make the claim at once, or it would be too late. While in the act of declining, a guard of three Wyandots, sent by Pomoacan, rushed upon the three missionaries, took them prisoners, and, with loud scalp-yells, dragged them to the Delaware camp. Thither the Wyandots came running, and while some stripped them to their shirts, others plundered the Mission House, wantonly destroying whatever they did not want. One savage only—an "ugly-looking" Wyandot—attempted to excite the cruelties of the gantlet by aiming several blows with his tomahawk at Senseman's head; another—a dark-faced Monsey—seized each of them by the hair, shook them violently, and said: "I salute thee, my friend!" But a third hastened to their assistance. "You vile fellow," he exclaimed, "what have these done that you treat them thus? You are a worthless Indian! leave this camp instantly!" The Delawares generally did not participate in the pillage of the Mission House. The captains withdrew in evident disgust, remembering too well the good works which these teachers had wrought in their nation. Indeed, the treatment which they experienced was far more lenient than would have been meted out to other captives. This Heckewelder ascribed to Zeisberger's public declaration in the morning that they would not allow the converts to resist by force of arms.

The prisoners were now conveyed to Elliot's tent. There stood God's ordained servants, almost naked, in the presence of this British captain who had frequently enjoyed their hospitality! For a moment he was overwhelmed with shame; then made some lame apologies, and finally ordered them to be taken to the Wyandot camp, after having induced the savages to restore to them a few old rags and torn garments, that they might to some extent at least cover their nakedness. Zeisberger and Heckewelder were put in one hut, and guarded by Coon; Senseman came into the keeping of Snip, a Mingo captain, notorious for his cruel murders, who was with difficulty dissuaded from fastening his feet in stocks. The prison-huts were mere roofs supported by low poles. Edwards had been overlooked when his brethren were seized. He now gave himself up, of his own accord, and shared their confinement.

A band of thirty warriors set out for Salem, and another of but two, accompanied by a squaw, for New Schönbrunn, in order to capture the rest of the Mission family. The prisoners saw them wildly riding off with fearful yells, and knew that their wives and children were at their mercy. Soon night came on and a cold rain began to fall. It was a night memorable amid all the eventful experiences of their lives. Wrapped in blankets, brought by the Christian Indians, they lay on the ground, each silently wrestling with God that He would protect their loved ones, and all expecting death in the morning.

The party sent to Salem broke into the Mission House, which Jung had barricaded. He was immediately attacked with tomahawks, from which Captain Coon rescued him upon his promising to surrender. The house having been sacked, he was hurried to Gnadenhütten, and, at midnight, brought to his associates. "Good-evening, my brethren," was his greeting; "our earthly career seems to be near its end; we have reached the borders of eternity, but we die in a good cause." At the urgent entreaty of the Salem women, Mrs. Heckewelder and her babe of five months had been permitted to remain with them until morning.[1]

The family at New Schönbrunn had spent an anxious day. Toward evening they heard of the events at Gnadenhütten and that warriors were approaching their own town. But when only two arrived, they took them to be visitors, and while Jungmann went to entertain them at his house, to which they had ridden, the ladies, deeming the danger past, retired for the night in Zeisberger's dwelling. Jungmann found at his door a Wyandot captain, together with his sister and one of his men. This captain had, on the previous day, paid a friendly visit to the Mission House and requested to be

---

[1] This child was Joanna Maria Heckewelder, born April 6, 1781, at Salem, and, in all probability, the second white child born in the State of Ohio. She remained at the Mission until 1785, when her parents sent her to Bethlehem with the Jungmann family, where she was educated. In 1801, she was appointed a teacher in the Ladies' Boarding-School at Litiz, Pa., but was obliged to retire, after five years, on account of her impaired hearing. Eventually she lost her hearing altogether. After the death of her parents, she took up her residence in the Sisters' House at Bethlehem, where her room became the resort of visitors from far and near, anxious to see one of the first white children born in Ohio, and to make the acquaintance of a lady who impressed every one that approached her by her high culture, her gentle ways, her deep Christian piety, and the childlike resignation with which she bore her affliction. Communication was carried on with her by writing on a slate, which she always had lying on her table. She was a life-long friend of the Indians, and never ceased to pray for them. Her many friends will always remember her as a handmaid of Jesus, with whom it was a privilege to associate. She died on the 19th of September, 1868, aged 87 years, 5 months, and 2 days.

shown through the premises. Jungmann was immediately seized and the house plundered. Going next to Zeisberger's, the two savages pretended to be friends anxious to protect the pale-faced women and save their property, inducing Mrs. Zeisberger to rise and help them pack up her own linen. But soon they grew tired of the part they were acting, threw off the mask, robbed the house, destroyed what they could not use, including the books and papers of the Mission, forced Mrs. Senseman out of bed, although it was but the fourth day after her confinement, and dragged her, together with Mrs. Zeisberger and Mrs. Jungmann, all shivering in their night garments, through the pelting rain to a canoe, where Jungmann had been previously secured. The young men of the Church would have flown to arms and rescued them, but were prevented by the assistants, in accordance with Zeisberger's instructions, of which the Wyandots were well aware, else they would have dispatched more than two of their warriors to overawe the population of an entire village. Amid the wails of the Indian women, who, writes Zeisberger, "lifted up their voices and wept aloud until the night was filled with lamentations," the canoe put off and proceeded down the river.

On Sunday morning, the fourth of September, while it was yet dark, the prisoners at Gnadenhütten caught the faint sounds of scalp-yells in the direction of New Schönbrunn. These yells grew louder, and were answered by their guards, until, as the day broke, their wives and Jungmann landed from the canoe, and were taken to the Delaware camp, where the whole body of savages, in terrific chorus, repeated the whoop twelve times in succession for the twelve members of the Mission family.[1] But all this was mere show. The cruel import of the halloo was not carried out; and the missionaries were even permitted to have an interview with their wives, who came guarded to the Wyandot camp, and fell weeping into their husbands' arms. After this outflow of feeling, they grew calm, and during all their subsequent hardships not a murmur or a complaint fell from their lips. Of Mrs. Senseman, Zeisberger's journal says: "He to whom all things are possible did not permit the slightest injury to befall her, or her babe, from the unnatural events of that night." Later in the morning, she and her female companions were set at liberty, and betook themselves to Schebosh's house. Jungmann was also released; and only Zeisberger, Senseman, Edwards, Jung, and Heckewelder remained captives.

The Wyandots spent the day in dividing the spoils; dressed themselves in the clothes which they had stolen, and strutted about the camp with childish vanity; or brought linen to the ladies and obliged them to make it up into shirts. But the Delawares took no part in all this; some of them spoke kindly to the prisoners

---

[1] Heckewelder says the scalp-yell consists of the sounds *aw* and *oh*, successively uttered, the last drawn out at great length, as long indeed as the breath will hold, and raised about an octave higher than the first. He adds, that it is a fearful yell, and the impression it makes, when heard for the first time, is not to be described.

and expressed their regret at their sufferings. An unexpected occurrence, however, exposed them to new danger.

A young woman of Salem, a repentant prostitute, possessed herself of Pipe's horse and rode off toward Pittsburg for assistance, moved by the tribulations which her teachers, to whom she owed so much, were enduring. She was followed, in hot haste, by a whole party of warriors, who caught sight of and galloped after her for many miles, but being better mounted, she succeeded in effecting her escape. Intense indignation raged against the missionaries. "You have sent for the Long Knives!" was the cry. "We will kill you!" With dark looks and threatening gestures the savages crowded around them, until their anger found a new vent. It became known that the woman was a relative of Isaac Glikkikan. Twelve men were instantly sent to Salem with orders to bring him alive or dead. So great, however, was the fear which his name still inspired that these warriors manifested no little trepidation when he stood before them and heard the object of their coming. "There was a time," said he, "when I would never have yielded myself prisoner to any man; but that was the time when I lived in heathenish darkness and knew not God. Now that I am converted to Him, I suffer willingly for Christ's sake." So saying he allowed his hands to be bound behind his back. He was dragged to Gnadenhütten with triumphant scalp-whoops. As he passed the hut where his teachers were confined, one of them called to him: "Be of good cheer, Isaac, you are our fellow-prisoner!" He looked back with a smile of manly trust unintelligible to his captors. Nor did he forget his profession amid the abuse that was now heaped upon him. His own countrymen were his worst traducers; they both hated and feared him; and having got him in their power, at last, wanted to tomahawk him on the spot. But the Half King interposed. He was arraigned, in regular form, before a council, which found him as innocent of all complicity with his relative as the missionaries had shown themselves to be.

After an imprisonment of three days and three nights, the captives in the Wyandot camp perceived that they were not to be put to death but to be forced to break up the Mission. Having done all in their power to prevent this, even to the offering of their lives, they finally yielded to an imperative necessity. On Tuesday, the sixth of September, the national assistants delivered a speech to the Half King and his captains, intimating that their teachers were willing to do what was required of them, and praying that they might be liberated. They were, accordingly, set free.

Zeisberger appointed Salem as the place of rendezvous, where the whole Mission family met on the eighth, and, the next day, in fellowship with the church of that town, celebrated the Lord's Supper in faith and hope.

The woman who had fled from Gnadenhütten went to Fort McIntosh, and the commandant of this post sent the intelligence which she brought to Pittsburg, whence Jacob Haymaker transmitted it by letter, dated September 7th, to John Heckedorn, the pastor of the

Moravian church at York, Pennsylvania. Heckedorn dispatched this letter to the Board at Bethlehem, where it arrived on the twenty-seventh.[1] Its statements were not fully credited. There were those who treated them as an idle tale. Zeisberger's message had not yet been received.

---

[1] Original letter, and Bethlehem Diary of 1781. MSS. B. A.

CHAPTER XXXII.

THE MISSIONARIES AND CHRISTIAN INDIANS CARRIED OFF TO THE SANDUSKY.—1781.

Departure from Salem.—Losses sustained by the Mission.—Reflections.—Journey to Gokhosing.—The prisoners in the hands of the Wyandots.—Their harsh treatment.—Arrival at the Sandusky, and building of Captives' Town.—Pomoacan's visit.—Other visits.—The missionaries summoned to Detroit for trial.

ON the morning of Monday, the eleventh of September, the whole body of Christian Indians, with the missionaries and their families, left Salem, closely guarded by some Delaware and Wyandot warriors. They traveled in two divisions, the one in canoes on the Tuscarawas, the other on land driving the cattle, of which there was a large herd.

It was a sad journey. They were turning their backs upon the scene of more than eight years' industry, and of a Christian communion never equaled in the history of the Indians. They were leaving behind rich plantations, with five thousand bushels of unharvested corn, large quantities of it in store, hundreds of hogs and young cattle loose in the woods, poultry of every kind, gardens stocked with an abundance of vegetables, three flourishing towns, each with a commodious house of worship, all the heavy articles of furniture and implements of husbandry,—in short, their entire property, excepting what could be carried on pack-horses or stowed in canoes.

But it was not the loss of earthly goods that caused Zeisberger the bitterest pang as he looked back, for the last time, upon the settlements which his faith and energy had called into existence. Nor was it the mere removal from the Tuscarawas valley that bowed him down. He had often, before this, led the converts to new places of the wilderness and built new sanctuaries to his God. It was, rather, the conviction that a fatal blow had been given to his work; that the prestige of the Mission was gone; that the independence of the Christian Indians had been destroyed; that under the most favorable circumstances, their influence in the West would decline, and they would themselves suffer spiritual harm. A philanthropist, in the highest sense of the word, had been rudely stopped in mid-career as he was establishing a Christian nation which bade fair to hold the balance of power among the Western savages, and to bring them, as docile children, from a barbarism that fiercely struggled for existence into the school of a generous civilization and common faith. Who can tell all the thoughts that crowded his mind while riding, a prisoner, down the river-bank which his feet had so often trod as a free messenger of peace?

Mysterious, too, is the providence that permitted the overthrow of the Mission at this time. The surrender of Cornwallis at Yorktown (October 19, 1781) took place less than four weeks after the abduction of the Christian Indians. It was the virtual close of the war which had drawn upon them the animosity of the British.

After having passed the ruins of Goschachgünk, the

troop spent six days in camp, at two different places on the Walhonding, partly in order to wait for Pomoacan and the main body of Wyandots, who had remained behind plundering the towns, and partly on account of a freshet that swamped the canoe laden with what little property the missionaries had saved from the hands of the savages. On the twenty-second, they reached the junction of the Walhonding and Vernon, and, following the latter, arrived at Gokhosing on the twenty-fifth, where, as its name denotes, they found the wilderness alive with owls.[1]

From Goschachgünk, Elliot and his escort had taken their way to the Scioto to rejoice with McKee over the success of their plot; the Monseys and the Shawanese captains had also dispersed to their villages; and now the rest of the Delawares turned off on another trail, so that the prisoners were left in charge of the Half King and his Wyandots. These grew harsh and insolent, especially in their treatment of the missionaries, whom they carried off, on the twenty-seventh, in advance of the converts, striking their horses until they were mad with fright and plunged through the swamps at a fearful rate, refusing the mothers time to nurse their babes, and pushing forward in a wild, reckless career. Mrs. Zeisberger was twice thrown from her saddle and dragged some distance, her foot catching in the stirrup. Michael Jung, who was afoot, received a cruel blow to make him walk faster. At last the Half King

---

[1] Gokhosing, "a habitation of owls." It was in Knox County, probably near Mount Vernon.

ordered a halt for the night, and the Christian Indians rejoined them.

At noon of the first of October, they reached the Sandusky River. Here Pomoacan, not deigning a word of explanation or an offer of assistance, drew off his band to Upper Sandusky and left the captives to their fate. Deserted thus in a howling wilderness, without provisions, and no game to be seen, they were compelled to trust to their own exertions for subsistence. Having selected a better camping-place two miles down the river, in a small wood on a bluff of the eastern bank, not far from a Wyandot village,[1] they proceeded to survey the country for the site of a town in which they might spend the winter. About one mile above their camp they found timber, and on that spot put up a village of very small log-houses. It stood on the north bank of the Sandusky, one mile above the junction of the Broken Sword Creek, in Antrim Township, Wyandot County.

---

[1] The Christian Indians must have reached the Sandusky, in Antrim Township, Wyandot County, ten miles below Upper Sandusky—now the capital of that county—which was the Half King's residence. Zeisberger particularly mentions that the place was ten miles from the Half King's town. The camp, two miles farther down the river, no doubt was quite near to the junction of the Broken Sword Creek and the Sandusky, and the village in its vicinity was Upper Sandusky Old Town. All this is evident from a comparison of the map of Ohio with Zeisberger's Journal. Taylor, in his otherwise excellent *History of Ohio*, has (pages 381 and 382) wholly mistaken these localities. He fixes the Half King's town at Springville, in Seneca County. But the original manuscripts of the missionaries show that the Half King's town was on the Sandusky, whereas Springville is nearly ten miles away from it. Moreover, at the rate the Indians were traveling, it is quite impossible that they could have gone, in three and a half days, from Mount Vernon, in Knox County, to Seneca County.

As this village received no name at the time, we will call it Captives' Town. Here the Zeisberger and Jungmann families occupied a cabin in common, suffering for want of clothing and blankets, and with hardly enough food to satisfy the worst cravings of hunger. The rest of the missionaries made similar experiences.

As if in derision of all this, Pomoacan came to congratulate the converts upon their safe arrival in his country, the abundance of which he put at their disposal. At the same time he proclaimed himself their chief, and announced that he would organize them into war-parties and lead them out against the Americans. Soon after this, however, when news reached him of the death of two of his sons, who fell in an attack upon the frontiers, he conceived a bitter dislike to them, especially to their teachers, and, with a perverseness characteristic of the Indian, blamed the missionaries for his loss. Other visitors were not wanting. Such Delawares as had persistently opposed the Gospel flocked to the town in triumph; while an agent of McKee hastened to bargain with them for their cattle at reduced prices.

On the fourteenth of October, Wingenund and Captain Pipe's brother brought the missionaries a summons from the commandant at Detroit to present themselves before him for trial, with their families and some of the national assistants.

Meanwhile the most conflicting reports of the fate of the Mission had been agitating Bethlehem. The Board dispatched John Wiegand to Pittsburg to ascertain the truth.

CHAPTER XXXIII.

THE TRIAL AND ACQUITTAL OF THE MISSIONARIES.—1781.

Journey of the missionaries to Detroit.—Schebosh and a party of Christian Indians captured by American militia.—The Black Swamp.—Preliminary hearing at Detroit.—The missionaries at Tybout's house.—Negotiations with Captain Pipe.—News at Bethlehem of the destruction of the Mission.—The trial of the missionaries.—Pipe's speech in their favor.—Their examination by the commandant.—They are acquitted.—The commandant's private interview with them.—His kindness and character.—Return of the missionaries to their converts.—The night-gathering on the bank of the Sandusky.—A church built and dedicated.

THE teachers were ready to go to Detroit, but not to carry along their families.[1] By permission of the captains who had brought the summons, their wives and children remained at Captives' Town, with Jungmann and Jung as their protectors; while Zeisberger, Senseman, Edwards, and Heckewelder, together with the national assistants, William, Tobias, and Isaac Eschicanahund, set out for Detroit on the twenty-fifth of October. At the same time Schebosh led a party of converts to their plantations in the Tuscarawas valley to gather corn, there being a dire famine along the Sandusky.

At Pipe's Town, where they arrived in the afternoon,[2]

---

[1] Zeisberger's Journal, 1781; Heckewelder's English Narrative. MSS. B. A.

[2] Pipe's Town was, therefore, only a few hours' ride from Captives' Town. Hence Taylor (*Hist. of Ohio*, 382) is wrong when he puts it on the Tymochtee, eight miles above its junction with the Sandusky.

the missionaries expected to put themselves under the orders of Pipe and Wingenund, who had been detailed as their escort. But the former had not waited for them, and the latter was unwilling to take them in charge. Hence they pursued their journey alone. Strange anomaly,—prisoners, to be tried as spies, are left to themselves! Without a guard, opportunities opening on every side to flee to the settlements, they are allowed to find their own way into the presence of their judge!

Three days' hard riding brought them to the Maumee River, on whose bank Pipe was encamped with many Delawares. Here they stopped to rest; and, by a strange coincidence, met with Elliot going to distribute among the warriors of his late command the rewards which had been sent by the British government to Maumee Bay, in a sloop from Detroit. Here, too, they received intelligence of the capture of Schebosh's party by a body of American militia, under Colonel David Williamson. These militia had invaded the Tuscarawas valley in order to remove the Christian Indians to Pittsburg, by force if necessary, ignorant of the fact that the inglorious achievement of breaking up the Mission had already been accomplished by the British.[1]

Following the Maumee down to the lake, Zeisberger and his companions saw many Indians gliding home with the gifts thus ignobly earned. Whatever feelings this might have awakened under other circumstances,

---

[1] Doddridge's Notes, 262.

the hardships of the trail precluded every thought of the past. They were in the midst of the horrors of the Black Swamp. Plunging through mud-holes, creeks, and half-frozen morasses, or entangled in undergrowth that was almost impassable, they had to rouse all their energies in surmounting these obstacles, especially as they were benumbed with cold, against which their thin and scanty garments offered but an insufficient protection. Even men used as they were to the trials of the wilderness acknowledged that day to have been one of unprecedented sufferings.[1] At last they reached the outlet of the Rouge into the Detroit River, with Detroit itself only five miles off. They could see the fort in the distance, but there was no means of crossing the stream. They spent the night on a bleak point, exposed to a chilling wind, without a morsel to eat, or a fire to warm them, until, early next morning, a canoe with Indians hove in sight, who set them over, in answer to their signals. Tattered and weary, hungry and friendless, they arrived at the western gate of the town, where they were kept waiting for hours on the drawbridge, and then led to the house of Major de Peyster. A sentinel ushered them into his presence.

---

[1] In a lecture on "the Moravians in Michigan," delivered before the Historical Society of that State, in March, 1858, Judge Campbell, of Detroit, says of this journey: "The journey through the Black Swamp, from Sandusky to Detroit, can be appreciated by those who have lived here long enough to experience the inconvenience of that almost impassable barrier between Michigan and the rest of the world."

"Are you the Moravian missionaries from the Muskingum?" began the commandant.

"We are."

"Are you all here? I have heard that there are six of you. Where are the rest?"

"Two of our number remained on the Sandusky with our wives and children, whom we could not leave alone."

"Why did you not bring along your wives and children, as I expressly ordered? I intend to send you all back to Philadelphia."

"We asked the chiefs whether our families must accompany us, and they said it was not necessary."

"I have heard that you correspond with the rebels to the injury of this government; many accusations have been brought against you; for these reasons I have had you removed from your settlements on the Muskingum."

"We do not doubt that many accusations have been brought against us; the treatment we have received sufficiently proves that. But we know that you have been told much that is false, and which, when examined into, will appear in a light very different from that in which you have been made to see it."

"Where are your Indians? What is their number? How many of them are men?"

"Our Indians are on the Sandusky, numbering about four hundred persons. The exact number of men we cannot give."

"Did your Indians ever go to war?"

"Never, while under our charge."

"Do you intend to return to them?"

"That is our earnest desire. We would deeply regret, and it would be wholly unjustifiable, if we were prevented from rejoining them. In that case the Mission would be ruined and the work of the Moravian Brethren among the Indians, which has now existed forty years, would come to an end."

"Do you think so? But what if your Indians injure the British government?"

"They will not injure the British or any other government, as you will understand when you know them and us better; they are civilized, and have learned of us to be industrious and to work."

After this preliminary examination, of which he took notes, the commandant dismissed the missionaries to the house of a Frenchman, one Tybout, there to await their regular trial, which was to take place upon the arrival of Captain Pipe, their principal accuser. They were not required to give their parole, nor put under arrest. Having traveled, unguarded, more than two hundred miles to present themselves before a court-martial, this was, no doubt, deemed a sufficient guarantee that they would not now attempt to escape.

Their arrival excited much attention, and many officers called to see them, including several of the American army, prisoners of war at Detroit. The French priest, an aged Jesuit, also visited them. Sympathy with their misfortune was the general feeling in the town.

Zeisberger made repeated attempts to get another audience of the commandant, and, when these failed, to present a memorial. But no communication, he was told, would be accepted until the trial. Hearing that Pipe was come and lay encamped near the fort, he turned to him for aid, sent him a string and speech, and entreated him to advocate the cause of the teachers, that they might get back to their families and Indians. "How sad it is," he writes in his Journal, "to know that our fate depends upon a savage, and he a bitter enemy of the Gospel, when we are among persons who call themselves Christians!" Pipe accepted the string and speech, but gave no promise of assistance.

On the same day on which these negotiations took place, Wiegand returned to Bethlehem from Pittsburg, with a letter from Colonel Brodhead containing the first reliable intelligence of the abduction of the missionaries. The congregation being upon the point of assembling for evening worship, the news was immediately announced, and fervent intercessions went up to God for the safety of His servants. Where they then were had not yet been ascertained. Joseph Horsfield hastened, the next morning, to New York to inform Bishop Reichel and Schweinitz of what had occurred, that the former, who was about to sail to England, might plead the cause of the missionaries in that country, and the latter endeavor, through the government of New York, to ascertain their fate and send them aid.[1]

---

[1] Bethlehem Diary, Nov. 1781. MS. L. A.

Captain Pipe's band entered Detroit in procession on the eighth of November, with their prisoners and scalps, whooping the scalp-yell. The trial took place the next day in the council-chamber of the commandant's house. Major de Peyster occupied the head of a table in the center of the room; to his right Mr. Bawbee, the Indian Agent; to his left, a secretary. Behind them were numerous officers; and behind these, interpreters and servants. The missionaries and national assistants were ranged on a bench opposite the table; on one side of them sat Pipe and the Delawares; on the other, Mingoes and Indians of various nationalities.

A few words from the commandant, setting forth the purpose of the "council," as he called it, opened the proceedings. Then Pipe rose and made a formal speech,[1] giving an account of his recent exploits, and delivering a stick to which were fastened seven human scalps. A Mingo chief followed in a second speech, and presented a stick with three scalps; he was succeeded by other warriors, each of whom brought forward the scalps which his band had taken. These trophies of barbarism having been placed in a corner, the "live flesh"—a term by which prisoners were known—was turned over to the keeping of the guard.

Pipe now rose again. "Father," said he, " you commanded me to remove the Christian Indians and their

---

[1] This speech has been preserved by Heckewelder in his *Hist. of the Indian Nations* (pp. 121-124). It is full of ironical allusions to the war between Great Britain and the Colonies, in which the Indians had been inveigled to take part.

teachers from the Muskingum. I have done as you commanded me.

"Father, when I had conducted the Christian Indians and their teachers to the Sandusky, you sent me word that I should bring the teachers and some of the Christian Indian chiefs to Detroit, that you might see and speak with them.

"Father, they are now here, and you can see and speak with them as you wished to do.

"Father, I hope you will speak kindly to them. I say to you, speak good words to them. They are my friends. I do not want them to be treated with severity."

Repeating the last sentence two or three times, he sat down.

The commandant answered by rehearsing the charges against the missionaries; the messages he had transmitted to them to leave the Muskingum and settle elsewhere; and the measures he had finally adopted to remove them by force. "Now tell me," he continued, addressing Pipe, "whether all these accusations are correct and founded in fact, and, especially, whether these men have or have not corresponded with the rebels."

"There may be some truth in the accusations," replied the captain. "I am not prepared to say that all that you have heard is false. But now nothing more of that sort will occur. The teachers are here."

"I infer, therefore," rejoined the commandant, "that these men have corresponded with the rebels; and sent letters to Fort Pitt. From your answer this seems evident. Tell me, is it so?"

Pipe grew confused. He whispered to his councilors, urging them to speak; but they hung their heads in silence. At last, springing to his feet, he exclaimed:

"Father, I have said that there may be some truth in the reports that have reached you; but now I will tell you exactly what has occurred. These teachers are innocent. On their own account they never wrote letters; they had to do it! I," striking upon his breast, "and the chiefs at Goschachgünk are responsible. We induced these teachers to write letters to Pittsburg, even at such times when they, at first, declined. But this will no more occur, as I have said, because they are now here."

A further examination elicited the fact that Pipe and the other Delaware captains had pledged their word to the Christian Indians that their teachers should remain with them, and that the nation considered itself bound by this promise.

Turning to the missionaries themselves, the commandant inquired:

"Are you all ordained ministers?"

"We are."

"Is any one the superior among you?"

"Yes, the Rev. David Zeisberger."

"Mr. Zeisberger, how long have you and your colleagues been with the Indians?"

"Forty years ago the Mission was begun; thirteen years ago I came to the West; the others followed at different times."

"Did you go out among the Indians of your own accord, or were you sent, and if sent, by whom?"

"We were sent by our Church, which is an ancient Episcopal Church."

"Where are your bishops?"

"In Europe and America."

"Whence do your American bishops come?"

"From Europe."

"Were you ordained and sent out by your bishops?"

"We were."

"Did you receive instructions from Congress when you went out among the Indians."

"We did not, but from our bishops."

"Did Congress know of your being among the Indians, and give you permission to labor among them?"

"Congress knew of it, and in no way hindered our work, but never gave us instructions."

"Have you taken the test-oath?"

"We have not, and have never been asked to do so."

"Then I will not exact from you an oath of allegiance to the British government."

After this conversation, Major de Peyster gave his verdict. To the missionaries he said that he was not opposed to the preaching of the Gospel among the Indians, on the contrary, heartily favored it; but that they must not meddle with the war; that having been falsely accused, they were at liberty to return to their converts as soon as they pleased; that he would consult the commander-in-chief, at Quebec, with regard to their future place of residence; that he would further confer with them; and that, as they had been plundered, he would supply them with clothing from the public stores.

To the national assistants he said that he was glad to see them; that they should obey their teachers, and not interfere with the war; that he would provide for their wants, and if any of their people hereafter visited him they should not go away with empty hands. Then the council broke up.

At a subsequent interview with the missionaries, he excused himself for having removed them from the Tuscarawas valley, assuring them that his duty, as a sworn officer of Great Britain, had demanded the measure; but earnestly protested that he had never given orders to maltreat and rob them, or plunder their homes, and had never intended that anything of this kind should be done. True to his promise, he furnished them with clothing, and redeemed their watches which the Wyandots had sold to Detroit traders. His example was followed by others in the town, who voluntarily restored to them such articles of their property as had been disposed of by the Indians.

The readiness with which De Peyster accepted the explanations of Captain Pipe presents his character in a favorable light when compared with that of Hamilton. Like his predecessor, he encouraged, indeed, the cruelties of the Indian War, but these belonged to that inhuman policy which the Americans had, by this time, learned almost as well as the English. It was deemed, by the one side, a legitimate means to reduce the rebels, and, by the other, a just mode of retaliation. But while

Hamilton pursued it with ungenerous vindictiveness, De Peyster looked upon it as a necessary evil. The one was a vulgar ruffian; the other a high-toned gentleman.

Supplied with a passport which permitted them to resume their missionary labors,[1] Zeisberger and his brethren hastened back to their families and people, arriving at Captives' Town on the twenty-second of November. Five days later the Christian Indians and their teachers met around a large fire, on the bank of the river, under the open canopy of heaven. The night was clear, the stars looked down with solemn brightness, the crackling logs threw a lurid glare upon the houses of the town, and conjured into existence fantastic shapes in the dark forest beyond. Standing in the center of the circle, Zeisberger gave the converts a narrative of the journey, trial, and acquittal of their teachers, exhorting them to render the glory unto God. A unanimous resolution to erect a church, as a thank-offering, was the response; and in less than a fortnight it was completed and dedicated to the worship of the Most High (December 8). It was a structure of poles laid horizontally between upright stakes, the crevices being filled with moss.

---

[1] By Arent Schuyler de Peyster, Esq., Major of the King's 8th Regiment, Commandant of Detroit and its Dependencies, etc. The bearers, David Zeisberger, John Heckewelder, William Edwards, and Gottlob Senseman, are hereby permitted to return to Sandusky, there to remain with John George Jungmann and Michael Jung, and to follow their spiritual functions among the Christian Indians unmolested, they behaving as becometh.

Given under my hand and the seal of Detroit, November 12, 1781.

CHAPTER XXXIV.

THE MISSIONARIES AT CAPTIVES' TOWN UNTIL THEIR REMANDMENT TO DETROIT.—1781, 1782.

Severity of the winter.—A famine.—Sufferings of the missionaries.—Mrs. Zeisberger's testimony.—Return of the captured converts from Pittsburg.—Visit of the Half King, and Glikkikan's stinging rebuke.—Insolent conduct of the heathen Indians.—Zeisberger's influence among them at an end.—A party of converts go to the Tuscarawas.—The missionaries remanded to Detroit.—Zeisberger's anguish of heart.—The scattered converts recalled to Captives' Town.—Rumor of a massacre on the Tuscarawas.—Departure and journey of the missionaries to Lower Sandusky.—Authentic news of the massacre.

THE missionaries, as well as their converts, had need of all the faith which the assembly on the bank of the Sandusky had evoked. The winter that followed was uncommonly rigorous, and the contrast between its hardships and the comforts of their homes in the Tuscarawas valley painful in the highest degree.

In spite of McCormick's friendship, who sent them provisions from Lower Sandusky, and the assistance rendered by the Shawanese of the Scioto, in remembrance of what the Moravians had done for them, thirty years ago, in a time of scarcity, when they were living in Wyoming, the insufficiency of their supplies grew more and more aggravated, and, at last, caused a terrible famine. A bushel of corn sold at eight dollars. The missionaries reduced their allowance to one pint a day for each member of their families; the Indians often had nothing to eat but wild potatoes and the flesh of their dead cattle, of which one hundred and forty head miserably pined away and perished. The cold, too, became extreme, and, owing to the smallness of the houses, no generous fires, such as had warmed their former dwellings, could be kindled. In a brief autobiography, written after her retirement from the Mission, Mrs. Zeisberger gives a dreary glimpse of the sufferings of that winter: "Many a time," she says, "the Indians shared their last morsel with me, for many a time I spent eight days in succession without any food of my own."

In the midst of this distress, some of those converts whom Williamson's men had carried off to Pittsburg returned to the Mission, having been set at liberty by General Irvine, Broadhead's successor in the command of the Western Department.[1] As soon as the Half King heard of their arrival, he came with a troop of warriors to learn the news. At Zeisberger's request, Isaac Glikkikan undertook the entertainment of these visitors, but found absolutely nothing to eat in the whole town, excepting carrion. With deep indignation he presented himself before Pomoacan, described his bootless

---

[1] Schebosh did not return with them, but proceeded to Bethlehem to report to the Board, which, for more than one-quarter of a year, could not ascertain whither the Christian Indians had been abducted. The first intelligence which reached the Board of the settlement on the Sandusky was conveyed to Bishop Hehl by a letter from Schebosh, written while a prisoner, and forwarded from Litiz to Bethlehem, where it arrived on the 15th of December, 1781.

search for food, contrasted it with the plenty that had prevailed in the Tuscarawas towns, and reminded him of his promise to take the Christian Indians to a better land than theirs. "Yes," said he, " you have brought us to another, but not to a better land. It is a miserable country; and you have not offered us one single grain of corn. We suffer; you rejoice. We are perishing; you triumph over us!" So unexpected and yet well deserved was this rebuke, that the Wyandots knew not what to answer, and hurried away.

But the heathen Indians were not often thus abashed. On the contrary, they showed themselves rude and insolent, glorying in the distress of the converts, and saying that now these Christians were not above other Indians, but as poor as any. And when they found them erecting a chapel, they threatened the lives of the missionaries. There should be no more praying and preaching in the Indian country. Or when they met with converts who had rendered themselves liable to discipline, they incited such to resist Zeisberger's authority. The teachers were their prisoners, and had no right to punish a red man. In short, the relationship between the Mission and the unconverted natives was completely changed; and Zeisberger, accustomed to mould the savage mind almost at will, whether as a councilor or a preacher, saw himself suddenly without influence, and even laughed at if he attempted to proclaim the unsearchable riches of Christ.

The famine increasing, about one hundred and fifty Christian Indians, by permission of the Half King, set out for the Tuscarawas to gather corn; others visited the Shawanese; and still others roamed through the forests, boiling maple sugar. By the end of February, almost the entire Mission had scattered; the teachers and a few old people remained in the town.

On the first of March, a runner called Zeisberger to the Half King's village. He found a council of Wyandots and Delawares assembled, and Simon Girty in attendance, who gave him a letter to read which he had received from Major de Peyster. It contained the following passage: "You will please to present the string I send you to the Half King, and tell him that I have listened to his wishes. I therefore hope he will give you such assistance as you may need in order to bring the teachers and their families from the Sandusky to this place. I will by no means allow you to suffer them to be plundered or in any way ill treated."

Never did blow fall more unexpectedly upon a troubled heart. In spite of the difficulties which surrounded him, Zeisberger had anticipated a gradual reorganization of the Mission, either in the Sandusky valley, or at some other place, on the plan which had proved so successful in the valley of the Tuscarawas. He had the written promise of the commandant that he should not be hindered in his work; and there existed no other cause which could make the future hopeless. But now came this order. To obey it, was to disperse the converts; to render void, in a day, the labor of forty years. Hence the anguish of Zeisberger's soul. "We cannot be satisfied," he writes in his Journal, "to leave our Indians. It seems impossible that the Lord will permit it. If we were to be slain it would be better, we would then be relieved, at last, of all our troubles; but now we seem to be reserved for many deaths. Our thoughts stand still; our counsels come to naught."

Zeisberger having given a written pledge to meet Girty, with the whole Mission family, in two weeks at Lower Sandusky, runners were dispatched to the Shawanese villages, the Tuscarawas valley, and the forests around Captives' Town to recall the converts. Those near by came at once, and when informed that the missionaries were to leave them, wept and lamented " in a way," writes Zeisberger, "that might have moved a stone." Confessions of sin and sentiments of manly faith were not wanting. Said one: "That I have lost all my property and am poor, that my cattle are dead, that I must suffer hunger—all this I bear and complain not; but that our enemies are about to deprive us of our teachers, and keep food from our souls—this I cannot bear, it deeply wounds my heart. They shall, however, see that I will have no communion with them, and will not be enticed back to heathenism. They shall not get me into their power, or force me to grieve the Saviour. Rather will I flee to the forest and miserably eke out my life alone!"

On the twelfth of March, some of the converts returned from the Shawanese country, but not one from the Tuscarawas. Zeisberger sent another urgent message, bidding them hasten to their teachers. And still they came not. He could not divine the cause. At last there arrived a Delaware warrior with the news that they had been captured by American militia, and subsequently, report said, put to death. So great, however, was Zeisberger's confidence in the integrity of the officers at Pittsburg, that he gave no credit to the rumor of a massacre. He deemed it possible that they had been carried off; but he could not be induced to believe that Indians, whom the whole West knew to be professors of Christianity, had been slain in cold blood.

Nevertheless the uncertainty of their fate was distressing, more especially as the missionaries could no longer postpone their departure. With those converts that had gathered at Captives' Town Zeisberger held a farewell service, on the fifteenth; commending them to God; exhorting them to stand fast in the faith and endure to the end. The separation itself wrung his soul. He was filled with the darkest forebodings; and when, at last, he tore himself away, "it was," says Heckewelder, "with an agony almost like the agony of death."

Guided by Francis Levallie, a Frenchman, whom Girty had deputed to take his place, the little band of teachers moved off, in the presence of the Half King, who watched them with exultant eyes. Not being able to muster enough horses, some of them had to travel afoot. The two children of the Mission,[1] wrapped in blankets, were carried by Indian women on their backs.

A weary journey of four days brought them to Lower

---

[1] Joanna Maria Heckewelder, who was nearly a year old, and Christian David Senseman, not yet seven months of age.

Sandusky,[1] where they were hospitably received by Messrs. Arundle and Robbins, traders from Detroit. Lower Sandusky was at the head of navigation, and they were here to take boats, which Major de Peyster had promised to send. While waiting to embark, Joshua and Jacob arrived from Captives' Town with their luggage (March 23), and brought at the same time the most heart-rending corroboration of the reported massacre in the Tuscarawas valley. Of the converts who had gone thither nearly two-thirds—men, women, and children—had been put to death.

---

[1] A trading-post, near which lay a small Wyandot village. The present Fremont, in Sandusky County, occupies the old site.

CHAPTER XXXV.

THE MASSACRE AT GNADENHÜTTEN.—1782.

The suspicions to which the Tuscarawas towns of the Christian Indians expose them.—They bear the ill-will both of the Americans and the British.—The animosity of the borderers against all Indians.—The first attack upon the frontier in 1782.—Moravian Indians accused of having taken part in it.—Williamson's militia.—The converts arrive in the Tuscarawas valley, and harvest their corn.—Warning of a war-party.—Williamson's command takes Gnadenhütten.—The Indians duped by a pretense of friendship.—The Salem Indians snared in the same way.—Salem burned to the ground.—Religious conversation with the militia on their way to Gnadenhütten.—The Indians seized, bound, and put under guard.—The accusations against them rebutted.—A majority of Williamson's command vote in favor of putting them to death.—The preparations of the converts for their end.—The massacre.—Escape of two lads.—Number and names of the victims.—Their heroic death.—Gnadenhütten and New Schönbrunn burned to the ground.—Escape of the New Schönbrunn Indians.—The character of the expedition against the Christian towns.—Doddridge's views.

WHILE[1] living in their towns on the Tuscarawas, the Christian Indians were an object of suspicion not to the British only; frontiermen on the American side looked upon them with equal distrust, ignorant of the benefits which the settlements were deriving from the Mission. The officers of the military posts might, indeed, have enlightened them; but their lips were sealed by pru-

---

[1] Sources for this chapter are: Zeisberger's Journal, March, 1782, MS. B. A.; Heckewelder's English Narrative of the Massacre, MS. B. A.; Heckewelder's History of the Mission; Doddridges Notes; Pennsylvania Archives, vol. ix.; Taylor's History of Ohio.

dential reasons. Thus the converts were placed in a false position. Their towns, it was commonly said, formed "half-way houses," where the warriors rendezvoused and gained strength for their murderous expeditions. That they entertained war-parties is undeniable; but this was a necessity, forced upon them by the sacred laws of hospitality and by a local situation that put them at the mercy of the savages. This situation was their misfortune. It brought them the ill-will of both parties. The British heaped maledictions upon them as American spies; the Americans burned with indignation against them as allies of the British. Taylor well says: "It was the peculiar hardship of these inoffensive religionists, that every act of benevolence or humanity, on their part, was sure to excite distrust and hostility in some quarter. But whatever appeared like a complication with the savage enemy was so notorious as to provoke exaggeration, while the evidence of an opposite or friendly disposition was diligently guarded by Morgan, McIntosh, or Broadhead as confidential communications."[1]

In addition to all this, there prevailed along the Western border an intense hatred of Indians in general, who, by common consent, were outlawed. Their barbarous cruelties had evoked this spirit. The last years of the Revolution, in the West, were years of blood. From early spring to the beginning of winter, murders were committed in every direction. The frontier was almost uninhabitable; the people lived

---

[1] Taylor's Ohio, p. 345.

in stockade forts; worked their little fields in parties under arms with scouts on the watch; had their cattle killed, their horses carried off, and their cabins burned; and saw the plantations which they had reclaimed with heavy toil lapsing again into their original wildness. Moreover, few families could be found that had not lost some members by the merciless hands of the savages. It may well be said, that in the Pontiac Conspiracy Pennsylvania never thirsted for vengeance as the West did now, amid the closing acts of the Revolutionary War.

Such was the state of feeling when, in the beginning of 1782, war-parties from Sandusky appeared much earlier than usual, before the last of the winter months was past. One of these bands attacked the farm of William Wallace, murdered his wife and five children —impaling one of the children with its face toward the settlements and its belly toward the Indian country— and carried off John Carpenter as a prisoner.

This monstrous deed roused the whole frontier, and the opinion gained ground that the Christian Indians had either themselves been engaged in it, or that the savages had spent the winter in their towns. In either case, these "half-way houses" must be destroyed. About ninety men,[1] many of them mounted, mainly from the settlements on the Monongahela, were collected in great haste, rendezvoused at the Mingo Bottom,[2] and

---

[1] Some authorities estimate the number to have been more than one hundred and fifty men.

[2] Mingo Village, or Mingo Bottom, was on the west bank of the Ohio, seventy-five miles below Pittsburg.

thence set out for the Tuscarawas, with Colonel David Williamson as their commander.

Meanwhile the converts were on their peaceful way to the same place, unsuspicious of danger, and encouraged to proceed by several of their friends who had been with Schebosh's party, and were loud in their praises of General Irvine and his officers at Pittsburg. Arrived in the valley, the Indians scattered to their towns, each family occupying its former house, and organized three little churches, of which the national assistants took charge. Soon after this, the warriors that had murdered the Wallace family passed through Gnadenhütten, and warned the inhabitants of the peril to which they were exposing themselves. Carpenter, with noble magnanimity, did the same, pointing out its imminency, however peaceable their intentions. "My captors," he added, "will undoubtedly be pursued and tracked to this place."

The converts were alarmed, but the national assistants allayed their fears. In conformity with the suggestions of a council held at Salem, it was determined to finish the harvest, relying, in the event of the appearance of American militia, on their innocence, their friendship for the States, and their common religion. The seventh of March was designated as the time of their departure.

In the morning of the sixth, they accordingly resumed their work, laboring hard to complete it that day. The plantations were alive with activity. Some gathered the corn in heaps; some bagged it; while others stored what could not be transported in such rude but safe garners as the forest afforded. Into the midst of this scene of peaceful industry burst the pitiless destroyer.

Williamson's command had reached the neighborhood of Gnadenhütten the evening before, and lay encamped, all night long, but one mile from the town, without being discovered. And now preparations began for an immediate attack. The men were formed into two divisions, of which the one received orders to cross the river and gain the fields on the western side, where the scouts had reported Indians, while the other was to advance upon the village itself by a circuit through a wood.

On reaching the Tuscarawas, the first division found no canoes; but what appeared to be one was seen moored to the opposite bank. A young man, named Sloughter, swam the river and brought back not a canoe, but a trough for maple-sap, and large enough to accommodate but two persons. In order to expedite their passage, a number of the men stripped off their clothes, put them into this trough, and, holding fast to its sides with one hand, swam across with the other. Sixteen of them had passed over in this manner, when Joseph Schebosh was seen coming from the plantations in search of his horses. One of the two scouts, who had been thrown forward, immediately fired upon him, breaking his arm; the rest of the men ran up, and, in spite of his protestations that he was Mr. Schebosh's son, the son of a white man, buried their tomahawks in his head and tore off his scalp. Fearing that the shot might have alarmed the Indians, they pressed on, without waiting for the other part of the division, and reached the fields where their victims were at work. These they greeted, as previously agreed upon, with all the tokens of amity usual among the natives, and told them that they were come to convey them to a place of safety, where they would be housed, clothed, and fed. Duped by these protestations, the converts received the militia with joy and escorted them to Gnadenhütten. There they found the second division, which had meanwhile quietly possessed itself of the town, killing but one Indian, who was crossing the river in a canoe. To this act Jacob, Schebosh's son-in-law, who stood on the bank tying up his corn-sacks, was a witness. Had he given the alarm, the most of the converts might have been saved. But he was so confounded by what he saw, having taken the militia to be friends, and recognizing among them some of his personal acquaintances at Pittsburg, that he fled to the forest and hid himself amid its bushes. The entire command was hospitably entertained at Gnadenhütten, and the rest of the day passed in an interchange of the most friendly courtesies.

John Martin, a national assistant, and his son, returning from a distant part of the forest, noticed the tracks of shod horses, and mistrustfully crept to the top of a hill, on the western bank of the river, whence the town could be seen. But when they beheld their people associating on the most familiar terms with the white men that filled the place, their suspicions vanished. Young

Martin hastened across, while his father went to Salem to tell the news. There the opinion, which he urged, that the Americans were come to deliver the Christian Indians from their troubles, found general favor, and was corroborated by the belts and strings of wampum which Israel had received, in his former capacity of chief, as tokens of the friendship of the States, and which he now spread before the gratified eyes of his countrymen.

Taking with him Adam and Henry, John Martin returned to Gnadenhütten, and informed Colonel Williamson that the Salem Indians, too, would put themselves under his protection, and follow him to the promised place of safety. He was assured that they would be cared for; and that a part of the command would, the next morning, escort them from their town, which could not be done at once, because the men were engaged in helping their Gnadenhütten friends to collect from the forest such of their goods as had been hidden at the time of the Wyandot invasion. Overjoyed to hear all this, John Martin, in the simplicity of his heart, made the colonel his confidant with regard to another project. Some of the converts, he said, deemed it best to establish a branch Mission in the place of refuge to which they were going; they would send to Bethlehem for new teachers, and have churches and schools of their own, while their brethren on the Sandusky would continue to enjoy the ministrations of their old teachers. What did their friends think of this plan? Williamson approved of it, and all his men, to whom it was mentioned, said it was well thought of, and praised the Indians for their piety.

Amid such converse night came on. Murderers and victims lay down to sleep like brothers, in the same town and the same houses, the one dreaming of scalps, the others of new and happy homes. Never were Indians more guileless; never was the most marked trait in their character more completely wiped out. Christians had faith in Christians. Though of different races, they worshiped one God and adored one Saviour.

Early in the morning of the seventh, a division, with Adam and Henry as guides, set out for Salem, and found the Indians not only ready to accompany them, but prepared to yield to all their demands. They surrendered their arms—"for safe-keeping," said the militia—without a shadow of doubt. They acquiesced in the firing of their town—"to prevent warriors from harboring there"—and pleasantly remarked that their American friends would soon build them another. They put themselves wholly into the power of their escort, and did not entertain the remotest idea of treachery. Indeed, even from a spiritual point of view, it was for them a day of joy. They had opportunities to glorify their God. The white men seemed deeply interested in religion, asked many questions with regard to it, and listened to what they told them of their personal experiences with the profoundest attention. Samuel Moore, who was a Jersey Indian, Christian, a national assistant, and Tobias, an aged servant of the Lord—who all spoke English fluently—proclaimed the unsearchable riches of Christ, with the eloquence of faith. "Truly, you are good Christians!" exclaimed the militia. Meanwhile the Indian boys sported with some half-grown lads of the command, taught them to make bows and arrows, and frolicked gleefully through the forests.

On the bank opposite Gnadenhütten the eyes of the deluded converts were suddenly opened. Coming upon a pool of fresh blood and a bloody canoe, they stopped in mute surprise; but in that moment the militia seized them, bound their hands behind their backs, and hurried them across the river, where they found the rest of the Indians also prisoners, confined in two houses, and closely guarded.

The militia now tried to criminate them, bringing forward the following accusations: First, that they were warriors and had taken part in the war against the Americans; second, that they had harbored and fed, in their towns, British Indians on the march to the American frontiers; third, that their horses must have been stolen from the Americans, inasmuch as they were branded with letters like the horses of the frontier settlers, a thing unknown among the natives; fourth, that those articles of clothing and children's caps, those tea-kettles and household equipments, those saws, axes, and chisels, and all those many other implements found among white people only, of which both Gnadenhütten and Salem were full, constituted a positive proof that they had helped to plunder farms and attack settlements.

The prisoners clearly rebutted every one of these charges. They appealed to their friendship for the white people—of which the militia could not be ignorant, since all the West knew of it—and to the efforts which they had, for years, successfully made to keep the Delawares neutral, as evidence that, since their conversion, they had never gone to war. They explained the necessity which compelled them to entertain British Indians passing through their towns, but showed that they had, at the same time, persuaded many a war-party to turn back; and, further, that when Colonel Broadhead had come into their country, on his expedition against Goschachgünk, they had furnished his army, too, with provisions. They reminded them, that Gnadenhütten and Salem were towns belonging to civilized natives, to Christian Indians, to Indians who had been taught to dress like the whites, to work their horses like the whites, and to use the same household utensils, mechanical tools, and agricultural implements.

But this vindication did not satisfy the militia, because they were predetermined not to be satisfied.[1] A

---

[1] On their return to the settlements, the militia asserted that they had found among the clothes of the converts the blood-stained garments of Mrs. Wallace, whose own husband recognized them, and that this was an unanswerable proof that these Indians had been engaged in the atrocious murder of his family. But this was, by no means, a valid evidence of their guilt, even granting that such garments were discovered, a thing which, as it rests solely upon the authority of the murderers themselves, is, to say the least, open to serious doubt. It is known that the warriors who murdered the Wallace family put up their plunder at public auction, a mode of disposing of spoils not unusual among the natives. This sale took place one mile from Gnadenhütten.

council of war was called to decide upon their fate. The officers, unwilling to assume the responsibility, agreed to submit the question to the men. They were accordingly drawn up in a line, Colonel Williamson stepping forward and saying: "Shall the Moravian Indians be taken prisoners to Pittsburg, or put to death? All those in favor of sparing their lives, advance one step and form a second rank!" On this but sixteen men—another report says eighteen—stepped out of the line, leaving an overwhelming majority for the sentence of death.

The mode of execution created not a little debate. At last it lay between two proposals: one was to set fire to the houses in which the captives were kept and burn them alive; the other, and this prevailed, to tomahawk and scalp them, so that there might be trophies of the campaign.

Although startled when informed of the fate which awaited them, the Indians soon recovered their self-possession. Solemnly protesting their innocence, they nevertheless declared themselves willing to die, and asked no favor other than time to prepare for death.

Now, although it was a law among the Christian Indians never to buy booty thus offered for sale, and although the national assistants had, on this very occasion, prohibited their companions from doing so, it is possible that some of the young people secretly attended the sale and purchased that dress. It is just as possible, however, and not at all in conflict with the warnings which they gave the converts, that it was intentionally left by the warriors in one of the houses of Gnadenhütten, without the knowledge of the inmates, in order to fasten suspicion upon the Christian Indians.

This was granted them, and the following morning fixed for the execution.

There now ensued a scene that deserves to find a place in the history of the primitive martyrs. Shut up in their two prisons, the converts began to sing and pray, to exhort and comfort one another, to mutually unburden their consciences and acknowledge their sins. Abraham, surnamed the Mohican, took the lead in humbling himself under the mighty hand of God. "Dear brethren," said he, "we are soon all to go to the Saviour. You well know that I am a bad man; that I have grieved my Lord; that I have caused our teachers much sorrow; and have not done the things that I ought to have done. But now I give myself anew to Jesus. I will hold fast to Him until I die. I believe that He will not cast me off, but pardon all my sins." As the hours wore away, and the night deepened, and the end drew near, triumphant anticipations of heaven mingled with their hymns and prayers. Converted heathens taught their Christian slayers what it means to die "as more than conquerors."

At last the morning broke. It was the eighth of March. Impatient to begin their work of blood, the militia selected two buildings, which they wantonly denominated "slaughter-houses," the one for the killing of the men, the other for the massacre of the women; and brutally called to their captives, who continued to sing and pray in exultant tones, whether they would not soon be ready. "We are ready now," was the reply; "we have committed our souls to God, who has given us the assurance that He will receive them."

Several of the men immediately seized Abraham, whose long, flowing hair had attracted their notice the day before as fit for making "a fine scalp," tied him and another convert with a rope, and dragged them to the appointed house. There they were deliberately slain, and afterward scalped. The rest suffered in the same way, two by two. When all the men and boys were dead, the women and small children were brought out, two by two as before, taken to the other house, and dispatched with the same systematic barbarity. Judith, a venerable widow, was the first among these victims. Christiana, another widow, who had been an inmate of the Bethlehem "Sisters' House" in her youth, spoke English and German fluently, and was a woman of education and refinement, fell on her knees before Colonel Williamson, as she was being led away, and, addressing him in English, besought him to spare her life. "I cannot help you!" was his cold reply. She rose and submitted to her fate, patiently like the others. Tomahawks, mallets, war-clubs, spears, and scalping-knives were used to effect the slaughter, in which, however, only some of the militia appear to have taken an active part.[1]

---

[1] There are various discrepancies in the accounts of the massacre that have come down to us. Heckewelder, in his English MS., and also in his printed history, says that the militia entered the two houses in which the Indians were confined, and murdered them with a wooden mallet, taking turns in the slaughter. Zeisberger, in his Journal, says they were led out singly to the "slaughter-houses," and implies that there

It was not a carnage perpetrated in the flush of victory, ere the heat and passions of battle have passed away. It was not as when a long-beleaguered city is taken, and half-intoxicated horsemen dash through the streets, hewing right and left with their sabers, and sparing neither age nor sex. It was a butchery in cold blood, without the least excitation of feeling, as leisurely and dispassionately done as when animals are slaughtered for the shambles.

Two lads, Thomas and Jacob, escaped the common fate. The former received a blow that merely stunned him, and revived toward nightfall. Hearing footsteps approaching, he gave no signs of life. A militiaman entered the house to view the bodies, and dispatched Abel, who had likewise been but stunned and

---

were two massacres, that of the Gnadenhütten Indians on the seventh of March, and that of the Salem Indians on the eighth, the latter being brought to Gnadenhütten after its inhabitants had been put to death. Loskiel agrees with the representation which I have given. Its correctness is proved by a careful examination of all the sources extant, including those not of Moravian origin. Zeisberger's Journal was written soon after the occurrence, when the different reports brought in had not yet been sifted. It is, moreover, impossible, as his Journal seems to indicate, that John Martin and the two Salem Indians should have come to Gnadenhütten, on the seventh of March, after all its Indians had been murdered, should have treated with the militia, and then led a part of them to Salem, without discovering what had taken place. There exist two lists of the victims, both of which, it is true, say that they were killed on the seventh and eighth of March; but this, no doubt, refers to the fact that four of them were shot the day before the massacre, two while attempting to escape. Its whole history rests upon the testimony of Samuel Nanticoke, a national assistant of New Schönbrunn; of two lads who fled from the very midst of the slaughter; and of the militia themselves, who boastfully detailed, on their return home, all the incidents of the campaign.

was in the act of rising. Thomas kept close amid the ghastly corpses until it was dark, and then made his way to the forest, although suffering excruciating pain from the loss of his scalp.[1] Jacob succeeded in slipping, unobserved, from the house in which the women suffered, into the cellar by means of a trap-door, and when their blood began to stream upon him through the floor, forced an exit out of a narrow window, concealed himself in some hazel-bushes, and at night also gained the forest. The day before the massacre, Anthony and Paul, John Martin's sons, had not been so fortunate. They got out of their prison and fled, but were shot down by the sentinels.

According to a careful computation made by the missionaries, with the aid of the national assistants, the whole number of victims was ninety. The militia brought back ninety-six scalps; hence six of the murdered ones must have been heathen Indians, probably visitors at Gnadenhütten.

It is proper that their names should be enshrined in history. Here follows the roll:

National Assistants.	*Their Wives.*
Isaac Glikkikan.	Anna Benigna, Glikkikan's wife.
Jonah.	Amelia, Jonah's wife.
Christian.	Augustina, Christian's wife.
John Martin.	
Samuel Moore.	
Tobias.	

---

[1] Thomas lived four years longer, and was commonly known as the "scalped boy." On the thirtieth of June, 1786, when the Mission was located on the Cuyahoga, he was found drowned in a creek, where he had been fishing, and into which he had fallen in a fit, having been subject to such attacks ever since the loss of his scalp.

Other Men.	Other Women.
Adam.	Cornelia, Adam's wife.
Henry.	Joanna Salome, Henry's wife.
Luke.	Lucia, Luke's wife.
Philip.	Lorel, Philip's wife.
Lewis.	Ruth, Lewis's wife.
Nicholas.	Joanna Sabina, Nicholas's wife
Israel (Captain Johnny).	Hannah, Joseph Peepi's wife.
Abraham, the Mohican.	Catharine.
Joseph Schebosh.	Judith.
Mark.	Christiana.
John.	Mary.
Abel.	Rebecca.
Paul, of Salem.	Rachel.
Henry.	Maria Susanna.
John.	Anna, a daughter of the assistant Joshua.
Michael.	
Peter.	Bathseba, the same.
Gottlob.	Julianna.
David.	Elizabeth.
	Martha.
	Anna Rosina.
	Salome.

All of these were baptized adults

Boys.	Girls.
Christian.	Christiana.
Joseph.	Leah.
Mark.	Benigna.
Jonathan.	Christina.
Christian Gottlieb.	Gertrude.
Timothy.	Anna Christina.
Anthony.	Anna Salome.
Jonah.	Maria Elizabeth, a daughter of Mark.
Gottlieb, a son of Joanna.	
Benjamin, the same.	Sarah, a daughter of Philip.
John Thomas.	Hannah, a daughter of Mary.
	Anna Elizabeth.

All of these were baptized children.

There were, besides, twelve babes and five adults not yet baptized. Of the latter but one name has been preserved, namely, Scappihillen, the husband of Helen. Thus it appears that of the victims twenty-nine were men, twenty-seven women, and thirty-four children.

Their death was the beginning of the decline of the Mission; but it was also the most illustrious exemplification of what the Church and Zeisberger, her apostle, had accomplished among the aborigines. Never did Christian Indians leave a brighter testimony. Their very murderers confessed that, by their faith and patience, by their fearlessness and resignation, they had glorified God. Successive generations have brought a tribute to their memory. There is not a writer of the history of our country who does not mourn over their fate. Even at this late day the traveler, as he passes through the blooming valley of the Tuscarawas, stops to see the spot where they suffered. The heathens themselves, while vowing vengeance on their slayers, acknowledged the piety of the dead. "We sought," they said, "to compel our Christian countrymen to return to the wild sins in which we live; but the great Manitou loved them too well; he saw our schemes; he saw their pious lives; he took them."

After the massacre had been consummated, the militia spent the day in securing their plunder; then, setting fire to the "slaughter-houses," with their mangled corpses, and to the whole village, marched off to New Schönbrunn to kill its Indians.

In the execution of this new atrocity, they were, however, happily disappointed. The messenger whom Zeisberger had commissioned to summon the converts to

Sandusky, reached New Schönbrunn on the same day on which the command came to Gnadenhütten. Too much fatigued to continue his journey, he sent two of the Schönbrunn Indians to the other stations. These found the body of Joseph Schebosh, saw at a glance that he had been murdered, and discovered the tracks of Williamson's horses. Allowing themselves barely time to bury their comrade, they sped back to the town and gave the alarm. The Indians immediately fled, and the militia had to content their bloodthirstiness with plundering and burning its houses. Some of the converts watched them from their hiding-places.

The expedition against the Christian Indians was wholly unnecessary, and the massacre at Gnadenhütten an act of inhuman barbarity. Williamson's men anticipated a safe campaign, relied upon the pacific principles of the converts, and expected no resistance, thus tacitly giving the lie to their own accusations against them. They went out, at least the major part of them, with the intention of murdering and not of fighting. All this is evident from the unjustifiable looseness, in a military point of view, with which the attack upon Gnadenhütten was conducted. At the same time, it is but right to adduce what may be said in extenuation of their crime. Hence we append the following extract from Doddridge, who writes with commendable fairness, and, having spent his youth among the men who engaged in the campaign, must be a well-informed witness:

"The longer the war continued, the more our people

complained of the situation of the Moravian villages. It was said that it was owing to their being so near us that the warriors commenced their depredations so early in the spring, and continued them until so late in the fall.

"In the latter end of the year 1781, the militia of the frontier came to a determination to break up the Moravian villages on the Muskingum. For this purpose a detachment of our men went out under the command of Colonel David Williamson, for the purpose of inducing the Indians with their teachers to move farther off, or bring them prisoners to Fort Pitt. When they arrived at the villages, they found but few Indians, the greater number of them having removed to Sandusky. These few were well treated, taken to Fort Pitt, and delivered to the commandant of that station, who, after a short detention, sent them home again.

"This procedure gave great offense to the people of the country, who thought that the Indians ought to have been killed. Colonel Williamson, who, before this little campaign, had been a very popular man, on account of his activity and bravery in war, now became the subject of severe animadversions on account of his lenity to the Moravian Indians.

"In justice to the memory of Colonel Williamson, I have to say that, although at that time very young, I was personally acquainted with him, and from my recollection of his conversation, I say with confidence that he was a brave man, but not cruel. He would meet an enemy in battle and fight like a soldier, but not murder a prisoner. Had he possessed the authority of a superior officer in a regular army, I do not believe that a single Moravian Indian would have lost his life; but he possessed no such authority. He was only a militia officer, who could advise, but not command. His only fault was that of too easy a compliance with popular opinion and popular prejudice. On this account his memory has been loaded with unmerited reproach.

"Several reports unfavorable to the Moravians had been in circulation for some time before the campaign against them. One was, that the night after they were liberated at Fort Pitt, they crossed the river and killed, or made prisoners of a family of the name of Monteur. A family on Buffalo Creek had been mostly killed in the summer or fall of 1781, and it was said by one of them who, after being taken a prisoner, made his escape, that the leader of the party who did the mischief was a Moravian. These, with other reports of a similar import, served as a pretext for their destruction, although, no doubt, they were utterly false.

"Should it be asked what sort of people composed the band of murderers of these unfortunate people, I answer, they were not miscreants or vagabonds; many of them were men of the first standing in the country; many of them were men who had recently lost relations by the hand of the savages. Several of the latter class found articles which had been plundered from their own houses, or those of the relations, in the houses of the Moravians. One man, it is said, found the clothes of his wife and children, who had been murdered by the Indians but a few days before. They were still bloody; yet there was no unequivocal evidence that these people had any direct agency in the war. Whatever of our property was found with them had been left by the warriors in exchange for the provisions which they took from them. When attacked by our people, although they might have defended themselves, they did not. They never fired a single shot. They were prisoners, and had been promised protection. Every dictate of justice and humanity required that their lives should be spared. The complaint of their villages being 'half-way houses for the warriors' was at an end, as they had been removed to Sandusky the fall before. It was, therefore, an atrocious and unqualified murder. But by whom committed? By a majority of the campaign? For the honor of my country, I hope I may safely answer this question in the negative. It was one of those convulsions of the moral state of society in which the voice of the justice and humanity of a majority is silenced by the clamor and violence of a lawless minority. Very few of our men imbrued their hands in the blood of the Moravians. Even those who had not voted for saving their lives retired from the scene of slaughter with horror and disgust. Why, then, did they not give their votes in their favor? The fear of public indignation restrained them from doing so. They thought well, but had not heroism enough to express their opinion. Those who did so, deserve honorable mention for their intrepidity. So far as it may hereafter be in my power, this honor shall be done them; while the names of the murderers shall not stain the pages of history, from my pen at least."

CHAPTER XXXVI.

ZEISBERGER AT LOWER SANDUSKY AND DETROIT.—1782.

Funeral service in memory of the dead.—The converts at Captives' Town after the massacre.—Conversation with Samuel Nanticoke. Massacre at Pittsburg, and dispersion of the Christian Indians.—Zeisberger's wail of anguish —The missionaries leave Lower Sandusky and reach Detroit.—Major de Peyster's reasons for removing them.—They determine to renew the Mission in the Chippewa country.—De Peyster's message to the Christian Indians.—The religious state of Detroit. —Zeisberger and a few converts embark in order to begin a settlement on the Huron River.

HAVING listened, with bursting heart, to all the details of the massacre which Joshua and Jacob could give him, Zeisberger called together his fellow-missionaries in Arundle's house, and read the burial-service of the Church in memory of the dead. From the orphaned flock at Captives' Town he often heard. Among others, Robins visited there, and reported that the converts sang and prayed together in the most touching manner, exhorted one another to stand fast in the faith, but often, in the midst of their assemblies, fell to sobbing like children. Deprived of their teachers, overwhelmed by the massacre in which the most of them had lost a kinsman, as in Rama of old, so in Captives' Town now, there was a voice heard, lamentation, and weeping, and great mourning.

With Samuel Nanticoke, who came to see him, Zeisberger had a conversation upon the state of the Mission and the sufferings of the Christian Indians. Zeisberger pointed out to him the chastising hand of God. The fiery trial through which the converts were passing had not occurred by chance; their own disobedience had helped to produce it. "We well know," he added, "that the most of you have been true to your profession in spite of all your afflictions, but we also know that some of you are recreant. I refer to those who advised the Wyandots, at the time of the invasion, to carry us off from the Muskingum; and who now, instead of acknowledging what we are enduring for your sakes, and what we have borne in the many years of our missionary service, are base enough to impute the blame of your present trials to us, and even to assert that we were aware of the projected massacre. We hope that such deluded souls will seek forgiveness of the Lord. With the rest of you we deeply sympathize.'

This conversation affords an interesting glimpse of the state of feeling both among the converts and in the heart of their leader. Many of the former recognized the judgments of God as well deserved. "We have drawn all this misery upon ourselves," said Abraham, a national assistant, in one of their meetings; "we have sinned against the Saviour; every one of us is guilty; I, too, am guilty. Let us return again to the Lord our God and pray for mercy." But others, staggered by their misfortunes, without a teacher's hand to guide them, lost their faith, let their love grow cold, and like the Israelites of old, murmured against their Moses and against God. Zeisberger, on the other hand, while he felt for them and confessed that theirs was no ordinary sorrow, was deeply wounded that among his own spiritual children there should be those who requited his long-tried devotion with such low suspicions and unmanly ingratitude.

His cup of woe was filled to the brim by the intelligence that Colonel Williamson's command, on their return to Pittsburg, had massacred the majority of friendly Delawares encamped near that post, under the protection of the American flag; and that the converts at Captives' Town had been forced by the Half King to disperse. Mark, at the head of one body, had gone to the Shawanese of the Scioto; Abraham, William, Cornelius, and Samuel Nanticoke had led the rest to the vicinity of Pipe's Town, whence they thought of proceeding to the Maumee. "Where shall we find a retreat," he writes in his Journal, "nay, but a little spot of earth whither we may flee with our Indians? The world is not wide enough. From the whites, who call themselves Christians, we can hope for no protection; among the heathens we no longer have any friends. We are outlawed! But the Lord reigneth. He will not forsake us. I believe that He is punishing us for our sins, but will afterward gather us with greater mercies. I believe that, in His own time, He will stop the mouth of our enemies, who mock us and say, 'Where is now their God? Let us see whether He of whom they preach, and on whom they depend, will protect them. Let us see whether their God is stronger than our god!'"

After an abode of four weeks at Lower Sandusky, the missionaries took the long-expected boats to Detroit, with an escort of fourteen rangers under command of Sergeant Rau (April 14). Levallie still accompanied them. Sailing down the river, they entered Lake Erie, and, after rounding Marblehead Point and leaving a group of islands on the right, infested in summer by such a multitude of rattlesnakes that they were uninhabitable, coasted westward, crossed Maumee Bay on the nineteenth, and at noon of the following day reached Detroit, where convenient quarters were assigned them in the barracks. Subsequently they removed to Jenky Hall, beyond the gates of the town.

Major de Peyster gave them a cordial welcome, and explained the cause of their removal. The Half King had again accused them of corresponding with the American commandant at Pittsburg; he had insisted upon their immediate deportation from his country, avowing that he could not prosper while they were near; that their presence brought him misfortune; that they were an eyesore and a stumbling-block to him; he had even threatened to murder them, if they were not called away. "Hence, Mr. Zeisberger," continued the major, "you see that I was compelled to have you conveyed hither. Your own personal safety demanded it. I did it most reluctantly, but there was no alternative. You may now either stay here or go to Bethlehem, as you may deem best. While you remain at this post, I will provide for all your wants."

There was but one sentiment among the missionaries.

They determined to revive the Mission. Nothing but absolute necessity could induce them to forsake their converts.

Such a self-sacrificing spirit awakened the warmest sympathies of the commandant. He induced the Chippewas to grant them permission to begin the work on those of their hunting-grounds which stretched along the Huron River; and he transmitted both a written and a verbal message to the Christian Indians, offering his services. This message, which was sent off on the third of May, ran, in substance, as follows: That their teachers were about to settle in the Chippewa country, and resuscitate the Mission; that Detroit was to be the rendezvous, whither he earnestly invited them to come, and where he would supply them with provisions; that he was sorry for their sufferings, but had not been the willing author of them, inasmuch as a time of war often rendered things necessary which, in themselves, were most distasteful to those who executed them; that he did not wish to bear the name of destroyer of so flourishing a work as the Indian Mission, — no, not for the whole world, and would therefore do all in his power to aid its renewal.

Weeks passed by without an answer. Conner and his family arrived, but not an Indian. It was a time of anxious suspense, which Zeisberger endeavored to render profitable by proclaiming the Gospel to the people of Detroit. He found religion at its lowest ebb. The Roman Catholics had one priest, an old man, who never preached, but read mass, which was attended by the French inhabitants and such baptized Indians of the Jesuit Mission as passed that way. The Protestants had no minister, or public service of any kind. A justice of the peace attended to their weddings and funerals, administering, occasionally, even the sacrament of baptism. Iniquity abounded in all its forms.

At last two families, Samuel Nanticoke's and Adams's, reached the town. They said that the commandant's message had been received, but subsequently contradicted through the machinations of the enemies of the Mission, who were determined to prevent its renewal. A second, more urgent message, dispatched by Zeisberger, shared the same fate. After a time, however, two more families arrived, so that there were now gathered at Detroit nineteen Christian Indians. With this little band, Zeisberger resolved to begin the new enterprise. Leaving Heckewelder and Senseman in the town, in order to take charge of such other converts as might come, he embarked, on the twentieth of July, in boats well laden with supplies, and ascended the Detroit River.

He had led the Indians along the Susquehanna, the Alleghany, and the Ohio, the Tuscarawas, and the Muskingum, — ever seeking a home for the Gospel. And now, with a mere remnant of them, his course was westward still, to a strange land, amid a new nation, "hoping all things, believing all things."

CHAPTER XXXVII.

SECOND CAMPAIGN AGAINST THE CHRISTIAN INDIANS, AND NEWS OF THE MASSACRE IN THE STATES.—1782.

Crawford's expedition. — The march to Sandusky. — Battle with the savages.—Indian reinforcements.—Flight and rout of the Americans.—Cruel fate of the prisoners.—Crawford burned at the stake.—His conversation with Wingenund. — Retaliation for the Gnadenhütten massacre.—Reports of the occurrence at Bethlehem.—Leinbach's and Schebosh's negotiations with Congress and Executive Council of Pennsylvania.—Schebosh goes to Pittsburg.—General Irvine's letter.—Sentiments at Pittsburg.—President Moore's message to the Assembly of Pennsylvania.—Publications authorized by the Mission Board.

Soon after the return of Williamson's command from the massacre, a second campaign was inaugurated, with the purpose of destroying the rest of the Christian Indians, and attacking the Wyandot settlements as well as Pipe's Town.[1]

"It was," says Doddridge, "the resolution of all those concerned in this expedition not to spare the life of any Indians that might fall into their hands, whether friend or foes. It would seem that the long continuance of the Indian War had debased a considerable portion of our population to the savage state of our nature. Having lost so many relatives by the Indians and witnessed their horrid murders, and other depredations on so extensive a scale, they became sub-

---

[1] Doddridge's Notes, chap. xxxii.

jects of that indiscriminating thirst for revenge which is such a prominent feature in the savage character, and having had a taste of blood and plunder, without risk or loss on their part, they resolved to go on, and kill every Indian they could find.

"It was intended to make what was called, at that time, 'a dash,' that is, an enterprise conducted with secrecy and dispatch. The men were well mounted on the best horses they could procure, and furnished themselves with all their outfits, except some ammunition."

On the twenty-fifth of May, nearly five hundred volunteers mustered at Mingo Town, and elected Colonel Crawford as their commander. Williamson was his unsuccessful competitor. Following "Williamson's trail," they came to the ruins of New Schönbrunn, where they encamped, and fed their horses on the unharvested corn of the plantations. A glimpse of two Indian scouts, watching their movements, threw them into such confusion that dark forebodings filled the mind of their leader. On the sixth of June, they reached Sandusky, and prepared to surprise the Christian Indians as they had done at Gnadenhütten. But Captives' Town was deserted, its huts lay in ruins, its gardens and fields were covered with rank grass. The Half King's brutal expulsion of the converts had saved them from a second massacre.

The disappointed volunteers held a council, and resolved to proceed one day longer in search of the Indians, but if they did not fall in with them by that time, then to march back to Pittsburg. They knew not that they had already advanced too far, that warriors were reconnoitering all their movements, and that they would meet not the inoffensive religionists of the Mission, but braves, painted and plumed, and burning to avenge the blood of their murdered countrymen. The very next afternoon, about three miles north of Upper Sandusky, and one mile west of the river, a large body of savages suddenly rose from the high grass of the plains and disputed their progress. A battle immediately ensued, and continued until dark. Both parties lay on their arms during the night. In the morning, the Indians did not resume the engagement, but sent for reinforcements, which arrived in such numbers as to threaten the Americans with an overwhelming discomfiture. Their only hope was an instant retreat. It began in the night, in good order. But some shots, in the direction of the enemy, caused a disastrous panic; the cry was raised that their design had been discovered, straggling parties broke away from the army and sought safety in headlong flight, until the retreat became a general rout. In the midst of this confusion, the savages fell upon the volunteers with the utmost fury, but ceased their attack on the main body, in order to pursue the stragglers, nearly all of whom were either cut down on the spot, or taken prisoners. The victory of the Indians was complete. Scarcely three hundred Americans reached the settlements.

A terrible fate awaited the captives. They were tortured to death with all the arts of savage cruelty. Among these sufferers was Colonel Crawford himself, who fell into the hands of Captain Pipe. He was taken to an Indian village for execution. A post, about fifteen feet high, was set in the ground and a large fire of hickory poles kindled around it, at a distance of six yards.

While these preparations were going on, Crawford recollected that Captain Wingenund had been several times entertained at his house, and that they had parted as friends who would stand by one another in adversity. He requested that this warrior might be sent for. Wingenund obeyed the summons, but with extreme reluctance. Approaching the colonel, he waited in silence for the communications he might choose to make.

"Do you recollect me, Wingenund?" began Crawford.

"I believe I do. Are you not Colonel Crawford?"

"I am. How do you do? I am glad to see you, captain."

"Ah!" replied Wingenund, with much embarrassment. "Yes, indeed!"

"Do you recollect the friendship that always existed between us, and that we were always glad to see each other?"

"I recollect all this. I remember that we have drunk many a bowl of punch together. I remember also other acts of kindness that you have done me."

"Then I hope the same friendship still exists between us."

"It would, of course, be the same were you in your proper place and not here."

"And why not here, captain? I hope you would not desert a friend in time of need. Now is the time for you to exert yourself in my behalf, as I should do for you were you in my place."

"Colonel Crawford, you have placed yourself in a situation which puts it out of my power and that of others of your friends to do anything for you."

"How so, Captain Wingenund?"

"By joining yourself to that execrable man, Williamson and his party; the man who but the other day murdered such a number of the Moravian Indians, knowing them to be friends—knowing that he ran no risk in murdering a people who would not fight, and whose only business was praying."

"Wingenund, I assure you that had I been with him at the time this would not have happened; not I alone, but all your friends and all good men, wherever they are, reprobate acts of this kind."

"That may be; yet these friends, these good men, did not prevent him from going out again to kill the remainder of these inoffensive yet *foolish* Moravian Indians! I say *foolish*, because they believed the whites in preference to us. We had often told them that they would be one day so treated by those people who called themselves their friends! We told them that there was no faith to be placed in what the white men said; that their fair promises were only intended to allure us, that they might the more easily kill us, as they have done many Indians before they killed these Moravians."

"I am sorry to hear you speak thus; as to Williamson's going out again, when it was known that he was determined on it, I went out with him to prevent him from committing fresh murders."

"This, colonel, the Indians would not believe were even I to tell them so."

"And why would they not believe it?"

"Because it would have been out of your power to prevent his doing what he pleased."

"Out of my power! Have any Moravian Indians been killed or hurt since we came out?"

"None; but you went first to their town, and finding it empty and deserted you turned on the path toward us. If you had been in search of warriors only, you would not have gone thither. Our spies watched you closely. They saw you while you were embodying yourselves on the other side of the Ohio; they saw you cross that river; they saw where you encamped at night; they saw you turn off from the path to the deserted Moravian town; they knew you were going out of your way; your steps were constantly watched, and you were suffered quietly to proceed until you reached the spot where you were attacked."

"What do they intend to do with me? Can you tell me?"

"I tell you with grief, colonel. As Williamson and his whole cowardly host ran off in the night at the whistling of our warriors' balls, being satisfied that now he had no Moravians to deal with, but men who could fight, and with such he did not wish to have anything to do; I say, as he escaped, and they have taken you, they will take revenge on you in his stead."

"And is there no possibility of preventing this? Can you devise no way to get me off? You shall, my friend, be well rewarded if you are instrumental in saving my life."

"Had Williamson been taken with you, I and some friends, by making use of what you have told me, might perhaps have succeeded in saving you; but, as the matter now stands, no man would dare to interfere in your behalf. The King of England himself, were he to come to this spot, with all his wealth and treasures, could not effect this purpose. The blood of the innocent Moravians, more than half of them women and children, cruelly and wantonly murdered, calls aloud for *revenge*. The relatives of the slain, who are among us, cry out and stand ready for *revenge*. The nation to which they belonged will have *revenge*. The Shawanese, our grandchildren, have asked for your fellow-prisoner; on him they will take *revenge*. All the nations connected with us cry out, *Revenge! revenge!* The Moravians whom they went to destroy having fled, instead of avenging their brethren, the offense is become national, and the nation itself is bound to take *revenge!*"

"Then it seems my fate is decided, and I must prepare to meet death in its worst form?"

"Yes, colonel!—I am sorry for it; but cannot do anything for you. Had you attended to the Indian principle, that as good and evil cannot dwell together in the same heart, so a good man ought not to go into evil company, you would not be in this lamentable situation. You see, now, when it is too late, after Williamson has deserted you, what a bad man he must be! Nothing now remains for you but to meet your fate like a brave man. Farewell, Colonel Crawford,— they are coming!"[1]

So saying, Wingenund burst into a flood of tears and turned away, seeking a place where he could not see the approaching torture. He never, afterward, spoke of the fate of his unfortunate friend without strong emotions of grief.[2]

The savages now stripped Colonel Crawford, and, having first beaten him with sticks, tied him to the post by a rope long enough to allow him to walk two or three times around it. Then they began to discharge gunpowder at his person, and to burn him with brands, coals, and hot ashes. In a little while the space between the fire and the post was covered with coals, on which he was made to walk. Simon Girty stood by and looked on, answering with a derisive laugh his appeal to shoot him that he might be relieved from his misery.[3] Thus the unfortunate officer

---

[1] This conversation is recorded by Heckewelder, in his *History of the Indian Nations*, pp. 281-284, who had it, word for word, from Wingenund himself, with whom he was well acquainted. As Heckewelder's work has become exceedingly rare, I have inserted the dialogue, which serves to illustrate the feelings of the savages with regard to the massacre at Gnadenhütten.

[2] To this Heckewelder again bears testimony, who was a frequent witness of such emotions.—*Heckewelder's Hist. of Ind. Nations*, p. 284.

[3] Another account says that Girty, at first, tried to ransom Crawford, which so incensed Pipe that he threatened to put Girty to a similar torture, whereupon he made common cause with the savages.

suffered for three hours, until death mercifully came to his aid.

The Indians distinctly avowed, as is clear from the conversation between Wingenund and Crawford, that they inflicted such tortures in retaliation for the massacre at Gnadenhütten; and, indeed, a number of their victims had actually taken part in that atrocious deed. We here recognize that law in the government of the world which men have so often been made to feel, and which is thus written in the statutes of God: "Vengeance is mine; I will repay, saith the Lord."[1]

Crawford's doom awakened universal sorrow in the States. He was the friend of Washington and greatly beloved. We will neither detract from his fame nor reproach his memory; but that he lent himself, after a confession of the principles of the Prince of Peace such as had been given under the blows of the tomahawk and the crash of the war-club at Gnadenhütten, to the command of an expedition destined to slay the remnant of God's people among the Western Indians, can be palliated only by the barbarism which the Revolution evoked on the frontiers.

Meantime the news of the massacre had reached Bethlehem and spread throughout the States. The first Moravian who heard of it was Frederick Leinbach, who had charge of the church-store at Hope, in New Jersey. One of his neighbors had been at Pittsburg, and seen the bloody scalps of the converts displayed as trophies

---

[1] Romans, xii. 19.

and their property put up at auction. Leinbach, in person, hurried to report to the Board. At Nazareth, he met Bishop Seidel, and with him proceeded to Bethlehem. The intelligence was so authentic that it could not be doubted, and, at one o'clock in the afternoon (April 5), the congregation was publicly informed of the calamity. On the same day the Board received a missive from Krogstrup, pastor of the church at Lancaster, detailing the occurrence in the words of a traveler fresh from Pittsburg, only with this difference, that the majority of the victims were said to have been warriors and not Moravian Indians. Then followed communications from nearly every quarter where the Brethren had churches, all describing the event as set forth by different authorities. Ettwein, too, who was on a journey, wrote to say that he had met with a German who boastfully claimed to have been one of Williamson's party.

The Board sent Leinbach to Philadelphia to notify Congress of what had occurred, and to petition for measures which would insure the safety of the rest of the converts. He received from Lewis Weiss the following letter to Charles Thomson, its secretary:

To CHARLES THOMSON, ESQUIRE, *Secretary of Congress, per* MR. FREDERICK LEINBACH.

SIR—I received, this afternoon, a letter from the Reverend Nathaniel, Bishop of the United Churches of the Brethren, residing at Bethlehem, dated the 5th instant. He informs me that the same day a melancholy report was brought to him, by one Mr. Leinbach, relative to a murder committed by white men upon a number of Christian Indians, at a place called Muskingum. He continues, in his letter, that the same Mr. Leinbach is to proceed, the next day, to Philadelphia, in order to give Congress information how he came to the knowledge of that event, so that Congress, unless it had already a better account of the affair than he can give, might, upon his report, take some measures with respect as well of the mischief already done as more which might be done, and thus prevent the total extirpation of a congregation of Indians converted to the faith of Jesus Christ, and the judgments of Almighty God against our dear country, which stands much in need of His divine protection. The Bishop desires me to give attention to Mr. Leinbach's report (I have done it), and to direct him where he should make his addresses. I make bold, Sir, to address him to you, and to beg the favor that you introduce him, if possible, this night, with the Delegates of the State of Virginia, from whence it is said the mischief originated, and to-morrow morning with Congress.

Your humanity, Sir, gives me confidence to use the freedom to trouble you this day—the day set apart for the service of men to their God—about a cause which is most properly His own. The tragic scenes of erecting two Butcher Houses, or Sheds, and killing, in cold blood, 95 brown or tawny sheep of Jesus Christ, one by one, is certainly taken notice of by the Shepherd, their Creator and Redeemer.

I am, with particular respect, Sir,
Your most obed. humble servant,
L. WEISS.[1]

SUNDAY, 7 April, 1782.

Congress referred the case to President Moore, of Pennsylvania, and his Chief Executive Council, requesting that body to begin an investigation. The Council sent, by Schebosh, who was going to Pittsburg as the messenger of the Mission Board, a dispatch to General Irvine as follows:

IN COUNCIL,
PHILADA., April 13th, 1782.

SIR—The Council have received information, thro' various channels, that a party of militia have killed a number of Indians, at or near Muskingham; and that a certain Mr. Bull (Joseph Schebosh) was killed at the same time. The Council being desirous of receiving full information on a subject of such importance, request you will obtain and

---

[1] Penn. Archives, ix. 523.

transmit to them the facts relative thereto, authenticated in the clearest manner.[1]

But Schebosh was not satisfied with letters. He wanted action on the part of the government. Writing from Litiz, he said that both the Council and the Board of War were, indeed, much concerned about the massacre, but protested that they could do nothing except order the commandant at Pittsburg to use all his authority to prevent such occurrences in the future. "God must help us," adds Schebosh, "we cannot reckon upon the help of man."

Returning from Pittsburg to Bethlehem, three days after the second expedition against the Christian Indians had mustered at Mingo Town, he brought the following lines from General Irvine to Bishop Seidel:

FORT PITT, May 8th, 1782.

SIR—I received your letter of the 11th April last, by Mr. Sheboshe; any attention paid him, when a prisoner, by me, was not meant to lay him, or any person for him, under the smallest obligation, it was dictated by humanity.

As he can inform you verbally of the transaction at Muskingham, it will be unnecessary for me, at this time, to trouble you with an account of it. He can also inform you of my intentions respecting future measures.

I believe the Missionaries are safe, and I can assure you it will always be pleasing to me to be able to render them service. I hope (and think it probable) they have removed farther than Sandusky, that being now a frontier, and one of the British and Indian Barrier Towns, they cannot rationally expect to be safe at it.

I am, Sir,
Your obedient, humble servant,
WM. IRVINE.[2]

THE REV. MR. NATHANIEL SEIDEL.

---

[1] Penn. Archives, ix. 525.   [2] Original Letter. MS. B. A.

Schebosh reported, further, that the commandant, a majority of his officers, and many intelligent men disapproved of the massacre, and would do all in their power to protect the remnant of Christian Indians. From this it is evident that Crawford's "dash" was either undertaken without the knowledge of General Irvine, or that he was unable to hinder it. That Schebosh was correct in his view of the sentiment prevailing at Pittsburg is shown by a letter which President Moore received from Lieutenant-Colonel Edward Cook, of Westmoreland County, dated the second of September, 1782. In this communication he says:

> I am informed that you have it reported that the massacre of the Moravian Indians obtains the approbation of every man on this side of the Mountains, which I assure your Excellency is false; that the better part of the community are of opinion the perpetrators of that wicked deed ought to be brought to condign punishment; that without something is done by Government in the matter, it will disgrace the annals of the United States, and be an everlasting plea and cover for British cruelty.[1]

Prior to the receipt of this letter, President Moore had sent a message to the Assembly of Pennsylvania (August 14th), in the course of which he said:

> We had great reason to apprehend a severe blow would be aimed at the frontiers by the Indians Our fears, in this respect, have been but too well justified by events that have since happened, and there is reason to believe that the blow has fallen with redoubled force, in consequence of the killing of the Moravian Indians at Muskingham, an act which never had our approbation or countenance in any manner whatever.

---

[1] Penn. Archives, ix. 629.

DAVID ZEISBERGER. 577

On this message a committee was appointed, which reported, Thursday, August 15, as follows:

> Your Committee are of opinion that an enquiry, on legal principles, ought to be instituted respecting the killing of the Moravian Indians at Muskingham; an act disgraceful to humanity, and productive of the most disagreeable and dangerous consequences.
>
> Resolved, therefore, that this House will give every support in their power to the Supreme Executive Council toward prosecuting an enquiry respecting the killing of the Moravian Indians at Muskingham.[1]

Some newspapers having excused the massacre, and represented the victims as warriors, and the Moravian Indians generally as fit subjects for extermination, the Mission Board published all the documents within its reach relating to the occurrence, and thus removed unfavorable impressions from the public mind. Legal proceedings, however, such as had been recommended by the Assembly of Pennsylvania, never took place. The fatal issue of Crawford's campaign, and the terrible defeat of the Kentuckians, at the Big Blue Lick, by a large body of Indians, under Simon Girty and others, closed the scenes of Indian warfare in the great drama of the Revolution; and soon after came the general peace. A subsequent grant of land, by Congress, to the Christian Indians was the only official act of indemnity.

---

[1] A MS. Record of the Message and Report. B. A.

CHAPTER XXXVIII.

ZEISBERGER AT NEW GNADENHÜTTEN, IN MICHIGAN.—1782-1786.

Encampment on the Clinton.—Character of the country.—New Gnadenhütten.—The scattered converts.—Sir John Johnson, and English views of the abduction of the missionaries.—Instructions from the home government.—Peace between Great Britain and the United States.—Renatus, the Mohican.—New mode of hunting and fishing.—The Chippewas.—Schebosh again joins the Mission.—Letters from the Board.—Death of Bishop Seidel.—A winter of unexampled severity.—Complications in Indian affairs of the West.—Jungmann, Senseman, and Michael Jung retire to Bethlehem.—Edwards's visit to Pittsburg. —Letters from Bishop de Watteville.—A grant by Congress.—Uncertainty with regard to the future of the Mission.—Treaty at Fort Finney.—The Mission removed from New Gnadenhütten.—The Conner family remains in that town.

A HALF day's sail brought Zeisberger and his party to Lake St. Clair. Having anchored off Point Clinton, they entered the Clinton—or, as it was then called, Huron River—next morning, and followed it up until evening, when they encamped.

On the south bank extended a plateau, unobstructed by trees, but surrounded on all sides with woods, and springs of limpid water gushing from its base. Fat bottoms, with fine timber, skirted the stream. The sycamore, beech, and lime, the ash, oak, poplar, and hickory abounded; sassafras-trees of unusual size were found; and wild flax grew luxuriantly. The forests were not open, as in Ohio, but tangled with dense thickets, and interspersed with morasses.

In the evening of the twenty-second of July, the little band of Indians gathered around Zeisberger and set apart this spot, by prayer to God, as the site of a Christian settlement, to be called Gnadenhütten.[1] When finished, it consisted of one street of log-houses, with a church, which was dedicated on the fifth of November. Toward the end of August, Senseman and Heckewelder joined the Mission, and, on the twenty-fifth of September, the Holy Communion was celebrated for the first time in the new village.

The scattered converts came in very slowly, owing to the machinations of the heathen, as well as to an unfortunate difference among themselves. Mark, with all the authority of a national assistant, denounced the gathering on the distant Clinton, and urged the Christian Indians to settle among the Twightwees. By the end of the year, but fifty-three persons were living at New Gnadenhütten.

Zeisberger frequently visited Detroit. On one occasion, he was introduced to Sir John Johnson, the General Superintendent of Indian Affairs, who had recently arrived from England, bringing with him letters from Ignatius La Trobe,[2] the British Secretary of the Unitas Fratrum, and Wollin, the Mission Agent in London.

---

[1] In his *History of the Indian Mission*, Loskiel changed this name into New Gnadenhütten, for the sake of convenience, and I will follow him. The town was situated on the south side of the Clinton River, between Mt. Clemens and Frederick, in Clinton Township, Macomb County, Michigan. — *Judge Campbell's Lecture before the Michigan Historical Society*, in 1858, published in the *Detroit Daily Advertiser*.

[2] A distinguished clergyman of the British Moravian Church, born, 1758, at Fulneck, in Yorkshire. He filled the office of "Secretary of

These letters inclosed a draft for one hundred pounds sterling, from the "Society for Propagating the Gospel among the Heathen,"[1] and were to the hearts of the missionaries like sunbeams after dark days. They had not heard from their own Board for more than a year.

Sir John Johnson told Zeisberger that the abduction of the Moravian teachers from the Tuscarawas, and the overthrow of their flourishing Mission, had produced a great stir in England. Well might he say this. Not a nameless church had been injured, but one acknowledged by Parliament, and invited to labor in the British Colonies. Some of the most influential men of the kingdom were her upholders. Johnson himself spoke of her "powerful friends" in England. Of all this the instructions which he had received were an evidence. The Mission was to be protected in every way, and the Moravian ministers to be treated with all respect and distinction. These instructions were a passport to still closer intimacy with the commandant, and to general favor at Detroit.

With the genial breezes of spring (1783) came joyful experiences. On his return from a visit to Detroit, Edwards brought the first news of a general peace. Pre-

---

the Unity of the Brethren in England," and also that of "Secretary of the Society for the Furtherance of the Gospel," was a *Senior Civilis* of the Church, and did much to develop her literature and sacred music. Among his works is the English translation of "Loskiel's History of the Missions among the Indians in N. A." He died May 6, 1836.

[1] A Moravian Missionary Society organized in England in 1741, and one of the oldest in existence.

liminaries had been signed at Paris in the previous year (November 30), and on the nineteenth of April a cessation of hostilities was proclaimed. About the same time that such intelligence filled New Gnadenhütten with praise, forty-three converts arrived from the Shawanese towns, in order again to cast in their lot with God's people. These were followed by Renatus, the Mohican, whose name occurs in the history of the Paxton Insurrection, now a poor wanderer, who had been erring and straying for many years. He had left the church at Friedenshütten and relapsed into heathenism; but his conscience gave him no peace until, accompanied by his whole family, he sought out the remnant of the Mission, confessed his sins, and vowed to live to God. He was readmitted to church-fellowship, and died soon after in the full hope of eternal life. Thomas, the grandson of Netawatwes, breaking away from the Delaware chiefs, who tried their utmost to detain him, also arrived and reunited with the converts.

In their new homes they had to learn new ways. There being but few hills, and the country covered with thick forests, they could not hunt singly, as in the Tuscarawas valley, but, for the most part, went to the chase in a body. The best marksmen formed a semicircle around the skirt of a wood, toward which the rest drove the game from the opposite side. When fishing, they followed the example of the Chippewas, and built weirs in the river. And, as Detroit was not far off, they began an extensive trade in canoes, baskets, and other articles of native manufacture. The only heathens they met were Chippewas, whose habits were peculiar. These Indians often spent a whole winter in the forests hunting. In spring, they gave up the chase and boiled maple sugar. This they sold at Detroit, and then passed the summer fishing in Lake Erie. Thus a party of Chippewas would be absent from its village for almost a year.

In the beginning of July, Schebosh arrived from Bethlehem. His Indian wife and daughters, who had been living among the Shawanese since the massacre, had previously come to New Gnadenhütten, so that this much-tried family was, at last, reunited.

John Weigand accompanied Schebosh, as a special messenger from the Board, with letters to the missionaries, the first which reached them in two long and weary years. These letters brought the news of the death of Bishop Seidel (May 17, 1782), who had gone down to his grave mourning for his Indian brethren, and lamenting the inevitable decline of the Mission which he foresaw. For twenty years he had devoted his energies to its extension, rejoiced over its prosperity, and gloried in its growing influence. The unexpected catastrophe at Gnadenhütten was an enigma which he could not solve. Other intelligence from Bethlehem, however, was more encouraging. Ettwein, who had succeeded Bishop Seidel, aided by Huebner and Schweinitz, was preparing to lay a petition before Congress, asking for a grant of land, on which the Christian Indians might live and worship God in peace. The whole Board was animated by the determination to do all in its power to resuscitate the Mission.

The winter set in with unprecedented severity. Such weather had not been known in the dependencies of Detroit, and the Indian country generally, for a quarter of a century. For months in succession the ground was covered with deep snow. In the Shawanese country many cattle perished, and, in other parts, even deer and buffaloes froze to death. Provisions failed everywhere, and although the converts obtained supplies from Detroit, furnished by the government, these proved insufficient as the spring advanced, so that they were obliged to repair thither in person and earn a livelihood as best they could. For some time New Gnadenhütten was inhabited by the missionaries only.

Occasional visits from the scattered members of the Mission broke the monotony of this dreary period. Some were still among the Shawanese; others had followed Mark to the Twightwees, on the Maumee. Mark himself, however, was dead. He had been stricken suddenly by the hand of God. A Delaware councilor succeeded him as the chief of the Christian Indians, who still hesitated to join their brethren.

After harvest, which was a plenteous one, the converts at New Gnadenhütten began to build a larger chapel; but relinquished this work again at the suggestion of Vice-Governor John Hay, who had succeeded Major de Peyster in the command of Detroit. There prevailed, he said, much uncertainty with regard to the future government of that part of the West, and it was doubtful whether the Mission could remain in its present place. This warning was corroborated by a threatening message from the Chippewas, who said that they had given the Christian Indians a refuge merely until the end of the war. Under these circumstances, Zeisberger resolved to establish the Mission elsewhere in spring; but when spring came (1785), new complications arose, and it was deemed best to defer the projected removal until autumn. Of these complications we must proceed to give a brief account.

By the sixth article of the definitive treaty of peace between the United States and Great Britain, signed on the third of September, 1783, the King renounced and yielded "to the United States all pretensions and claims whatever of all the country south and west of the great Northern Rivers and Lakes, as far as the Mississippi." No reservation was agreed upon in favor of the Indian tribes of that vast territory. These were left to make their own terms with the young republic. After much opposition on the part of single States, Congress took the administration of Indian affairs into its own hands, and inaugurated a series of conferences with the natives, in order to settle their future relation to the government and fix the boundaries of their hunting-grounds. The first of these treaties was held with the Six Nations (October 3d to 22d, 1784) at Fort Stanwix, Oliver Wolcott, Richard Butler, and Arthur Lee being the commissioners.

During the Revolutionary War, the Cayugas and Oneidas had been the consistent friends of the American cause—the Mohawks, on the contrary, its bitter opponents. Influenced by Johnson, this nation eventually emigrated to Canada, and their land fell to the State of New York, although the French Mohawks, near St. Regis, who were called Cagnawagas, claimed a part of it. A new line was now run for the Six Nations. It began four miles east of Niagara, bearing south to Pennsylvania, and passing along the eastern boundary of that State to the Ohio. All claims west of this line they relinquished with a bad grace, and merely from necessity.[1]

The second treaty took place at Fort McIntosh (January 21, 1784) with the Wyandots, Delawares, Chippewas, and Ottawas. George Rogers Clark, Richard Butler, and Arthur Lee were the commissioners, who established a line beginning at the mouth of the Cuyahoga, and extending to the portage between this river and the Tuscarawas, along which it passed to the crossing place above Fort Lawrence, thence west to the portage of the Miami and Maumee, down the Maumee to its mouth, and along the southern shore of Lake Erie to the Cuyahoga again. Within these narrow limits the Western tribes might live and hunt.[2] The land was not theirs; it belonged to the United States; they were merely tolerated. Hostages for the delivery of prisoners were invariably exacted.

Congress was of opinion that the treaty of peace with Great Britain absolutely invested the United States with the fee of all the Indian territory embraced within their limits, and that the American government had the

---

[1] Butler's Journal in Craig's Olden Time, ii. 404, etc.
[2] N. Y. Statutes, vii. 16.

right to assign, or retain, whatever portions of it should be judged proper.[1] Such an idea, however, originated a policy different from that of Colonial times, and not calculated to bring about a real pacification of the West. In the period of British supremacy, the natives never alienated their land without receiving a due equivalent. And it was not to be supposed that they would now, in good faith, submit to a principle so novel, and, as they thought, so unjust; more especially as the British garrisons, which still held the Western posts, sustained them in their opposition. A general feeling of distrust prevailed, and, throughout the spring, the question of war was agitated. Even after the policy of the United States had been changed, affairs continued in this posture for years, and finally produced that last struggle of the Western nations for the homes of their fathers which cost the government two armies, and drove Zeisberger, with his Indians, to Canada.

There being no immediate prospect of such an enlargement of the work as would require the services of all the missionaries, Jungmann and Senseman returned to Bethlehem (May 17), whither Michael Jung had previously gone, leaving Zeisberger, Edwards, and Heckewelder to take sole charge of the Mission.[2]

Edwards, soon after, visited Pittsburg, in order to obtain information with regard to the treaties, the lands

---

[1] American State Papers, v. 13.

[2] Jungmann retired from active service, spending the rest of his days at Bethlehem, where he died, July 17, 1808, in the eighty-ninth year of his age.

that had been ceded, and other points of importance concerning which the missionaries remained in ignorance. He brought back news of the treaty at Fort McIntosh, and of the passage in Congress of "an ordinance for ascertaining the mode of disposing of lands in the Western Territory," by which a corps of surveyors, one from each State, under Thomas Hutchins, Geographer of the United States, was instructed to survey the lands that had been ceded and to divide them into townships. At the same time he delivered letters from Bishop John de Watteville, who had arrived at Bethlehem, in the summer of the previous year (June 2, 1784), on an official visit to the churches, informing Zeisberger that the ordinance of May reserved for the Christian Indians their three towns on the Tuscarawas, and so much land as the Geographer might see fit to give.[1]

---

[1] In October, 1783, Ettwein, Huebner, and Schweinitz drew up a memorial, setting forth the claims of the Christian Indians, which Ettwein himself took to Princeton, where Congress was then in session. He found this body on the point of adjourning to Annapolis, and delivered the paper to Charles Thomson, its secretary. It was presented and referred to a committee, which reported favorably (March, 1784). Inasmuch, however, as no action was taken on this report, the Mission Board sent a second petition, in May, as also letters to the President and Secretary. But nothing was done at that time. In the following year, when Congress was in session at New York, Ettwein again appeared in person, and now, at last, the report was accepted and the reservation made (May 20, 1785). The news of this favorable issue was brought to Ettwein by the Hon. William Henry, of Lancaster, a member of Congress and a Moravian.—*Drafts of Petitions and Letters*, MSS. B. A.; *Ettwein's Historical Statement*, MS. G. A.

Previous to the receipt of Watteville's letter containing such cheering information, Zeisberger had received through him (March, 1785) an epistle from the General Board of the Unitas Fratrum, in Germany,

The future now appeared plain. Leaving New Gnadenhütten in autumn, they might pass the winter on the Cuyahoga, proceed to their old seats in spring, and re-establish the Mission in the valley where it had so greatly prospered. This Zeisberger announced to the scattered converts and invited them to join their brethren. But the autumn brought from the Western tribes rumors of war, denunciations of the proposed exodus, and the most violent menaces, in case it were carried out. To come forth from their secure retreat, in the face of all this, would have been foolhardiness. There was no alternative but to spend another winter at New Gnadenhütten.

In January, 1786, the Shawanese concluded a treaty with the United States, at Fort Finney,[1] submitting to the new government, and accepting the same terms which had been offered to the Ottawas, Wyandots, and Delawares.

Major Ancrum, the successor of Vice Governor Hay, believed this to be a definitive treaty, and deemed all the points in dispute between the United States and the Indian nations finally settled. His views were honest, but he wholly mistook the situation. By his advice, the long-projected removal of the Mission was, accord-

---

condoling with the missionaries in their distress and protracted afflictions, and encouraging them to stand fast and endure. The original of this missive, which deserves to be called an apostolical epistle, I found at Gnadenhütten, among some old papers.

[1] A post established for the occasion on the left bank of the Miami at its junction with the Ohio. George Rogers Clark, Richard Butler, and Samuel Parsons were the commissioners at this treaty.

ingly, undertaken. In conjunction with John Askin, a merchant of Detroit, and warm friend of the Mission, he bought the improvements at Gnadenhütten for four hundred dollars, protesting, after a personal inspection, that they excelled everything of the kind he had seen within the circuit of his command, and that the Christian Indians had done more in three years than the French settlers in twenty. This purchase was an act of real kindness to the Mission. At noon of the twentieth of April the congregation embarked in canoes for Detroit.

Richard Conner and his family remained behind. Advanced in years, he could no longer follow his Indian brethren on their many wanderings, but wished to spend the remainder of his days in the homestead which he had acquired at New Gnadenhütten. His family was confirmed in its rights to the "Conner Farms," became well known in the Northwest, and some of his descendants are still living at Detroit and in Indiana. Ancrum and Askin were less fortunate. When Detroit and its dependencies were occupied by the United States, the Commissioners pronounced their title to the land illegal, and refused to ratify it. New Gnadenhütten fell back into the hands of the Chippewas, who occupied it conjointly with Conner.[1]

---

[1] Judge Campbell's Lecture; Zeisberger's Journal.

CHAPTER XXXIX.

ZEISBERGER ON THE CUYAHOGA, OHIO.—1786, 1787.

Askin's offer to convey the Indians in sloops across Lake Erie.—Their character at Detroit.—Fearful gales.—The vessels at anchor for four weeks. — Breaking up of the expedition. — Journey by land, and encampment on the present site of Cleveland —The converts settle on the Cuyahoga.—Flour depot at the lake.—Visits from traders. —Zeisberger's unsuccessful attempt to reclaim the scattered converts.—The speech sent them by the missionaries.—Conversation between two brothers, a Christian and an apostate.—Zeisberger's illness.—Council of the Western tribes, and their proposals to Congress.—Change of the Indian policy.—Zeisberger's correspondence with General Butler touching a removal to the Tuscarawas.—Such a removal postponed, but the Mission on the Cuyahoga given up.

THE Indians encamped in the government ship-yard, where they were welcomed by John Askin, who offered to convey them to the Cuyahoga in vessels across Lake Erie. This offer Zeisberger eagerly accepted. Two sloops, the *Beaver*, Captain Godrey, and the *Mackinaw*, Captain Anderson, belonging to the Northwest Company at Michilimakinac, of which Askin was a partner, having been fitted out, the congregation embarked at noon of the twenty-eighth of April.

Detroit was loath to see them go. In all their intercourse with its inhabitants they had sustained the reputation of the Mission, dealing honestly, and paying their debts, which, at the time of their departure, amounted to hundreds of pounds sterling, with scrupulous exactness. The town could not but acknowledge the great difference between these natives and all the others, whether heathens or Romanists, who had, for generations, been coming to its trading depots and gathering in its council-house.

In the evening of the twenty-ninth, the sloops anchored in six fathoms of water, between Van Renssalaer and Bass Islands. That night a succession of easterly gales began, unprecedented in the experience of the oldest sailor on the lake. For four weeks, varied only by one unsuccessful attempt to make headway against the storm, the Indians were forced to inhabit these islands, living on fish, ducks, wild pigeons, and raccoons. The missionaries remained aboard the vessels, whose anchorage had to be repeatedly shifted, until a deep harbor, which received the name of Hope's Cove, was found on Bass Island, where the sloops were moored close by the shore and fastened with cables to trees. The island itself abounded in beautiful red cedars and ginseng, but was infested with a multitude of rattlesnakes.

Toward the end of May, Askin sent a pilot-boat to look after the expedition, and to order back the *Beaver*. The Indians, accordingly, disembarked at Rocky Point,[1] and formed two divisions—the one with Zeisberger proceeding by land; the other, in charge of Heckewelder, coasting along the southern shore in canoes; while Ed-

---

[1] The promontory at Scott's Point, or Ottawa City, in Ottawa County, Ohio.

wards, with the household goods, sailed for the Cuyahoga in the *Mackinaw*.

Zeisberger's party were all afoot, and all had packs to carry. There was no trail. With Samuel Nanticoke for a guide, they plunged through the wilderness, as far as Sandusky. There they hired canoes of Ottawa Indians, and crossed the waters of the bay. Having celebrated Whitsuntide on the eastern bank of the Pettquotting Creek,[1] they resumed their march, meeting numerous hunting- and fishing-parties, and being joined, occasionally, at night, by Heckewelder's division. They were unable to procure a horse for Mrs. Zeisberger, until within two days' travel of the Cuyahoga, which river they reached on the eighth of June, and pitched their camp where the city of Cleveland now stands in all the beauty of its shady avenues. Both the *Mackinaw* and Heckewelder's party had arrived before them.

As their stores were nearly exhausted, and game was scarce, Schebosh proceeded to Pittsburg to buy provisions, while Zeisberger explored the river. He found the banks covered with a dense forest, offering no place for a settlement; but toward the end of the second day, a clearing came into view, a lofty plateau, the site of a former Ottawa village. Here the Indians began to erect huts and plant corn, with the intention of proceeding to the Tuscarawas after harvest. By the end of June, they were housed as comfortably as could be

---

[1] The Huron River.

expected. A chapel was subsequently built, and dedicated on the tenth of November.[1] Meantime Schebosh had returned, with an order from Duncan and Wilson, good friends of the Mission, directed to their agents on the lake, to sell Zeisberger provisions to any amount. These agents had charge of a depot of flour, forwarded from Pittsburg by long trains of pack-horses. The chase, too, grew more successful, yielding elks in particular. Moreover, a large quantity of goods, dispatched three years before by the Church at Bethlehem, at last arrived, — so that all danger of famine was removed. A connection with Pittsburg was kept up by frequent visits from traders. Among these were Isaac Williams and Duncan, who united in assuring Zeisberger that the hinderances which had prevented the immediate return of the Mission to the Tuscarawas were providential, amid the existing troubles in the Indian country. Any attempt to resuscitate the work in its old field would have led to misery and bloodshed.

The scattered converts caused Zeisberger many anxious thoughts. He longed to reclaim them, and prayed for their speedy coming; but they continued recreant. One day, Samuel Nanticoke, while boiling salt at the springs of the Pettquotting, met a party of them, among whom was Anthony, once a faithful Christian, now decked in the trappings of a warrior, which, as he said

---

[1] The Indians gave no name to their new village, but Loskiel calls it *Pilgerruh*, or Pilgrims' Rest. It was situated on the eastern bank of the river, in Independence Township, Cuyahoga County, probably not far from the northern line of that township.

himself, were an evidence of the apostasy of his heart. Having lost all his children, and nearly all his other kin, at Gnadenhütten, he had cast away both his faith in God and trust in man, and accused the missionaries of being the instigators of the massacre. Samuel succeeded, with much difficulty, in convincing him of his error. At last he said: "I will come to greet our teachers. You may tell them my suspicions with regard to them." Zeisberger's inmost soul was moved with pity when he heard of this conversation, and, summoning the national assistants, he suggested the propriety of sending a deputation to the scattered converts, and inviting them to a conference. Samuel and Thomas undertook this mission, and set out, in September, bearing the following speech from the missionaries:

To all our scattered Brethren, this our salutation:
We have not forgotten you. We think of you constantly, and wish that you could again be in fellowship with us, believing that you, on your part, have not forgotten the Word of God which we have taught you. Hence we desire to know your mind as to how you may again be brought to hear this Word and experience its divine influences. To this end, we invite some of your understanding men to visit us, that we may consult with them. Do not cast away your confidence, or give up your hope; do not imagine that this effort to reclaim you will be in vain, that you have strayed too far away, and sinned too grievously, to be gathered again as a congregation of the Lord. Do not say, "The Saviour and the Brethren have cast us off!" Take courage. Turn to the Saviour, who is merciful and gracious, full of compassion and truth, and who will forgive your sins. As for us, we do not seek an opportunity to reprove you. We ask you to hold a conference with us, that we may, together, determine how to relieve you from your present unhappy mode of life, and to bring you back to the Lord Jesus Christ, whose blood was shed for the worst of sinners.

In a month's time the deputies returned. They had

been kindly welcomed by those who lived in the Shawanese towns, but their mission was unsuccessful. Some, indeed, expressed a wish to rejoin the Church; others avowed that nothing could induce them ever again to cast in their lot with Christians. The massacre, perpetrated by Christians, had completely extinguished their faith. The remnant on the Miami did not even notice the urgent message sent by Samuel, whom a severe illness prevented from visiting them in person. They were fast relapsing into heathenism, to the joy of the savages.

Perhaps the wide contrast between the spirit which animated the apostates and that which filled the faithful ones, cannot better be shown than by a conversation that Samuel had with his own brother. "By the waters of the Tuscarawas," said the latter, "the whites gained the end for which they strove so long. There lie all our many murdered friends. I avoid the whites and flee from them. No man shall induce me to trust them again. Never, while I live, will I reunite with you Christians. If your town were near, I might, perhaps, visit you; but that would be all. Our forefathers went to the devil, as you say, and where they are I am content hereafter to be." To which Samuel replied: "I have heard your views. Hear mine. Nothing shall bring me from the Saviour and His Church—nothing while I live; neither tribulation, nor distress, nor persecution, nor famine, nor nakedness, nor peril, nor sword. None of these things move me. To be in communion with Jesus Christ and save my soul is all I want. And, while I abide in Him, my salvation is certain. It cannot be taken from me."

While these fruitless negotiations were progressing, Zeisberger fell ill, in consequence of the hard work which he had done, with his own hands, in order not to be a burden to the Mission Board. When this became known to its members, they united in a fraternal remonstrance, begging him to draw on them whenever he needed assistance. "It is our earnest desire," they wrote, "to make the declining years of your life easy in every way within our power, so that you may continue to nurse and minister to the remnant of God's people among the Indians; and that He may be pleased to use you longer in this field is our unceasing prayer."[1] At such a time, it was particularly unfortunate that Heckewelder was obliged to leave the Mission, owing to the ill health of his wife. They returned to Bethlehem (October 9), so that Zeisberger and his ever-faithful friend, Edwards, were left alone.

In November, at the instance of Brant, a confederation of Western tribes held a grand council in the Huron village, opposite Detroit (November 28 to December 18, 1786). The Six Nations, Wyandots, Delawares, Shawanese, Ottawas, Chippewas, Potawatomies, Twightwees, Cherokees, and the Wabash Confederates were represented, and conjointly issued a missive to Congress, which expressed their desire for peace, but insisted that "all treaties carried on with the United States should be with the general voice of the whole

---

[1] Ettwein's letter to Zeisberger. MS. B. A.

Confederacy," attributing to the separate conferences the many mischievous consequences that had lately become apparent, and proposing a new treaty in the following year. These overtures were well received by Congress, and led to a change of its Indian policy. The aborigines were recognized as the rightful owners of the soil, and an appropriation was voted to purchase their claims to such lands as they had already ceded to the States.

The favorable report which he received of this Council, induced Zeisberger to consider the propriety of returning to the Tuscarawas. This report was brought by a vile fellow, named Mamasu, who had taken part in the raid on the Mission and had made several attempts to murder the missionaries, but who now came, humbled and repentant, asking to be accepted as a candidate for baptism. Addressing a letter to General Richard Butler, Superintendent of Indian Affairs for the Northern District, Zeisberger asked his advice touching a return to the Tuscarawas valley. Butler dissuaded him; but a communication from the Mission Board, received simultaneously with the General's answer, urged him to take this step, and a written "speech" from Lieutenant-Colonel Harmar, inclosing the resolution adopted by Congress in favor of the Christian Indians, and announcing a grant of five hundred bushels of corn, one hundred blankets, twenty axes, and twenty hoes, appeared to open the way and render it safe.[1] This speech ran as follows:

---

[1] The resolution of Congress was the following:
"By the United States in Congress assembled, August 24, 1786:

FT. HARMAR, AT THE MOUTH OF THE MUSKINGUM.
December 6, 1786.

BROTHERS!

The Honorable Congress have been pleased to pass the enclosed resolve in your favor. I have directed that the corn and other articles shall be sent down to this post, where they will be ready to be delivered to you. In obedience to the orders of Congress, I have to inform you that that honorable body are well pleased to hear of your arrival, and have granted you permission to return to your former settlements on the Muskingum, where you may be assured of the friendship and protection of the United States.

I should wish to know the names of the principal men who have the direction of your affairs, and shall be happy in rendering you every assistance in my power. I am, Brothers, your friend,

JOS. HARMAR,
Lt.-Col. Com'd. of the troops in the service of the U. S.

TO THE MORAVIAN INDIANS AT OR NEAR CUYAHOGA.

Zeisberger determined to disregard the advice of Butler and carry out the wishes of his Board. But a second message from the General, sent by Duncan and Wilson, assured him that this would be madness, in the face of the settled opposition which the Indian tribes of every name manifested to the project. This warning was, soon after, corroborated by the most

---

Resolved, that the Secretary at War give orders to Lt.-Col. Harmar that he signify to the Moravian Indians, lately come from the River Huron to Cuyahoga, that it affords pleasure to Congress to hear of their arrival, and that they have permission to return to their former settlement on the Muskingum, where they may be assured of the friendship and protection of the United States; and that Lt.-Col. Harmar supply the said Indians, after their arrival at Muskingum, with a quantity of Indian corn, not exceeding five hundred bushels, out of the public stores on the Ohio, and deliver the same to them at Fort McIntosh as soon after next Christmas as the same may be procured; and that he furnish the said Indians with twenty Indian axes, twenty corn-hoes, and one hundred blankets; and that the Board of Treasury and Secretary at War take order to carry the above into effect."—*Certified Copy of the Resolution, signed by Chas. Thomson, Secretary of Congress.* MS. B. A.

violent menaces from the savages themselves. Hence Zeisberger was reluctantly constrained again to postpone the return of the Mission to its old seats. He proposed, however, that it should be transferred from the Cuyahoga to some more favorable site, near the Pettquotting. To this the Indians agreed, and began immediate preparations for their journey. In the midst of these, came a letter from Heckewelder, announcing his arrival in Pittsburg, with Michael Jung and John Weigand, who were to be assistants in the work of the Mission.

Sending a few Indians to escort them to Pilgerruh, and leaving Schebosh with several families to receive them, Zeisberger, on the nineteenth of April, set out with the rest to seek a new home. In the language of the natives, Pilgerruh had been but a "a night lodge."[1]

---

[1] A place inhabited for one year.

CHAPTER XL.

ZEISBERGER FOUNDS NEW SALEM ON THE PETTQUOTTING.— 1787-1789.

The valley of the Black River selected as the new site of the Mission. — Interference of Delaware and Wyandot chiefs. — The Christian Indians yield at first, but afterward stand their ground. — New Salem founded. — Great prosperity of the town and Mission. — A revival and numerous baptisms.—Death of John Joseph Schebosh.— The Convention of 1787 and the Continental Congress.—Ordinance for the government of the Northwest Territory.—Sales of Western land, and first white settlements in Ohio.—The reservation in the Tuscarawas valley. — Organization of the Society of the United Brethren for Propagating the Gospel among the Heathen. — John Heckewelder appointed its agent.—Unsuccessful attempt to survey the reservation.—Treaty of Fort Harmar.—George Washington inaugurated President of the United States.—Visit of the head chief of the Chippewas to New Salem.—His offer to receive the Christian Indians into a peace confederation accepted.—Second futile effort to survey the Tuscarawas tract.

SEVERAL of the converts had been sent in advance to prospect for a settlement. Directed to the fruitful valley of the Black River, by a party of Ottawas, they found a delightful spot, about five miles from the lake, in Lorain County, which, on the arrival of the rest, was accepted by all as the new site of the Mission. But, in a few days, Titawachkam, a Monsey captain, made his appearance, and, in the name of Pipe, the Half King, and Welendawecken, of Gigeyunk,[1] who stood at the head of the Delaware war faction, forbade them to settle there. They must come to the Sandusky, he continued, where the Half King would give them land between the Lower Wyandot and the Monsey towns, but at such a distance from both that they could live and worship God in peace. To Zeisberger he brought a special message: "Listen, my friend," it ran; "you are my grandfather. I am not ignorant of the fact that our chiefs received you into our nation. Therefore no harm shall befall you. You need not fear to come to Sandusky."

Amid the plots and counterplots of Indian diplomacy, it is hard to understand to what this ill-timed interference was owing. Pipe no longer opposed, but was rather inclined to favor the Mission. He had, more than once, expressed his regret at the part he had taken in removing it from the Tuscarawas. Indeed, the frequent reproaches of the Unamis and Unalachtgos had made the Monseys, as a tribe, ashamed of that measure. Even Pomoacan had become tolerant. Perhaps the instigator was Luke, a renegade Christian. He had left Pilgerruh, and was making common cause with Titawachkam, who aspired to a chieftaincy, and hoped to swell the number of his clan by incorporating with it the Moravian Indians.

But, whatever the origin of the mandate, both Zeisberger and the national assistants deemed it best to yield. They foresaw far greater annoyances in case

---

[1] Fort Wayne, Indiana.

they resisted, and constant attempts to seduce their Indians. And although even a tacit concession that these three chiefs, or any chiefs, had authority over them, was very distasteful, and although this claim of authority was ridiculous in a land which the Indians had just alienated to the United States, and where the Delawares lived merely on sufferance, yet the converts took comfort from the thought that it might be God's will, by bringing the Mission into closer connection with the heathens, to make it a power again among the Western tribes.

Accordingly when Jung and Weigand[1] had joined them, the Christian Indians broke up their encampment, and continued their journey in several divisions. Zeisberger and his party were the first to reach the Huron River, at whose mouth lived a French trader, Monsieur Huno, who gave them a cordial welcome. There they learned from one of the scattered converts, whom they chanced to meet, that they had been deceived,—that the place set apart for the Mission was so near to the Monsey town as to subject them to unceasing disturbances. The rest of the missionaries and Indians having come up, this intelligence called forth a unanimous determination to proceed no farther, but to settle on the Huron and brave the anger of the chiefs. These, however, attempted no new interference.

A few miles from the mouth of the river, and on its eastern bank, where they found some old plantations,

---

[1] Weigand returned to Bethlehem after the lapse of a few weeks, as his services were not required.

the converts began to build a town, which is known as New Salem.¹ By the sixth of June, a chapel was erected, and on the ninth the Lord's Supper was administered for the first time. In the preparatory agapæ, a farewell letter from the venerable Bishop de Watteville was communicated, who sent his blessing to the Indian church, on the eve of his return to Europe.²

New Salem, like Gnadenhütten of old among the Lehigh Hills, and Friedenshütten on the Susquehanna, and the villages of the Tuscarawas valley, grew to be a thriving town, and a center of Christianity, whose light beamed over the Indian country.

God laid a blessing upon its industrial pursuits. The products of the wilderness and the crops of the fields combined to fill the measure of its plenty. From the beach of Lake Erie the Indians gathered turtle-eggs by the thousand; from the forests, large quantities of wild grapes and nuts; and from the plantations, rich harvests of corn. Their cattle, too, increased until they had herds almost as large as those which filled the meadows of the Tuscarawas.

The spiritual state of the Mission was still more encouraging. Not only did the members walk with God and adorn their profession, but the Gospel once more began to be a power among the heathens. At

---

[1] New Salem was probably in the vicinity of Milan, in Milan Township, Erie County, Ohio. It did not receive its name from Zeisberger, but from Loskiel, who was at that time completing his *History of the Mission*.

[2] He left Bethlehem June 4th, and arrived at Herrnhut September 13th.

New Gnadenhütten and Pilgerruh scarcely any baptisms had taken place. Now, however, Indians from different parts, Delawares, Chippewas, Ottawas, and, occasionally, Wyandots, flocked together to hear the Word of God. Of these a large number joined the Church. A revival began, genuine and deep, as in former times. Nothing like it had been known since the abduction from the Tuscarawas; and nothing like it occurred again in all the subsequent history of the Mission. There were other seasons of prosperity, but they could not be compared with this. The palmiest days of the Mission came back again. The Western wilderness rang anew with the fame of its apostle, and the village of the Christians was once more the rock to which the heathen came thirsting for the waters of life.

Amid such experiences Zeisberger grew young again. His afflictions were forgotten. Sustained by Edwards and Jung, and zealously aided by the national assistants, he labored with joy and thankfulness. The work continually increased. In the summer of 1788, hardly a day passed which did not witness heathen Indians visiting the Mission to hear of Christ; and sometimes the town was crowded with them. Among the most distinguished baptisms, in this period, were those of Mamasu, who received the name of Jeremiah; of Gegeshamind, a notorious sorcerer, who was called Boaz; and of Gelelemend, whose career, as the chief of the Delaware nation, fills an important page of American history. He was named William Henry, at his own request, after Judge Henry, the Congressman.

In the midst of these triumphs of the Gospel, the Mission sustained a heavy loss, by the death of John Joseph Schebosh, or, more properly, John Bull, aged sixty-eight years (September 4, 1788). Identified with its history from its very inception, laboring for its welfare with untiring zeal, his name will be illustrious while men rehearse the works of faith which are done in God. "He was always ready," writes Zeisberger, "to serve his fellow-men, whether whites or Indians. He bore his cross with patience. He seldom knew of easy days or the comforts of life, but he never complained, not even when suffering the severest hardships and enduring dire famine. He loved his neighbors and his neighbors loved him. Of this his last illness was an evidence. The Indians vied one with another in ministering to his wants, and watched at his bedside, singing hymns. He will be missed among us. But his labors of love will remain in blessed memory. He is at rest, in peace and happiness. We rejoice over his lot, but weep that he is gone." [1]

A convention was called at Philadelphia, in the spring of 1787, to revise the articles of confederation which proved insufficient as a basis for the union of the States. Meantime the Continental Congress continued its work, and adopted measures of importance, which gave a mighty impetus to the development of the country. On the eleventh of July, the

---

[1] Schebosh's Indian wife, Christiana, died the year before, after a union with him of forty-one years. At the time of his death, there remained, among the Christian Indians, one daughter with two children.

celebrated "ordinance for the Government of the Territory of the United States Northwest of the Ohio" was reported, and, on the thirteenth, passed by the unanimous vote of the eight States represented.[1] This ordinance brought the blessings of civil and religious liberty to the West, and opened the way for that galaxy of new States which now shine with such luster. In the same month (July 23), a contract was entered into with an association of New Englanders, styling themselves the "Ohio Company," for the sale of a tract of five millions of acres, extending along the Ohio from the Muskingum to the Scioto; and, subsequently, a similar contract was made with John Cleves Symmes, of New Jersey, for the sale of a tract of two millions of acres between the Great and Little Miamis.[2] And as the Mission could not, for the present, return to the Tuscarawas, Congress enacted (July 27), "that the property of ten thousand acres, adjoining to the former settlements of the Christian Indians, should be vested in the Moravian Brethren of Pennsylvania, or a society of said Brethren for civilizing the Indians and promoting Christianity, in trust and for the uses expressed in the ordinance of May 20, 1785, including Killbuck (Gelelemend) and his descendants, and the nephew and descendants of the late Captain White Eyes, Delaware chiefs, who have distinguished themselves as friends of the cause of America." Before adjourning, Congress appointed its President, Arthur St. Clair, to be Governor of the new territory.

---

[1] Hildreth's History of the United States, iii. 527, etc. [2] Ibid., iii. 529.

It was not long before settlements grew up within its broad area. A colony came from Massachusetts (April 7th, 1788) to the mouth of the Muskingum, led by General Rufus Putnam, and founded the town of Marietta, the first white settlement in Ohio. It lay near Fort Harmar.[1] Governor St. Clair arriving in July, a code for the Territory was published, and the district around the fort erected into the County of Washington. Soon after this three more settlements were formed on Symmes's grant, namely, Columbia, Fort Washington, now Cincinnati, and at Great Bend, near the mouth of the Miami.[2]

Not less active was the Mission Board of the Moravian Church. The Board of Treasury, which had been empowered to treat with its representatives, touching the grant in the Tuscarawas valley, resolved "that each of the three towns should have allotted four thousand acres of land, and that each tract might be surveyed in an oblong square, twice as long as broad; and that a free deed, without any expense, should be given to the Society."[3] In September, 1787, a warrant was granted to survey the tracts; and, on the twenty-first of the same month, "The Society of the United Brethren for

---

[1] Erected on the right bank of the Muskingum River, at its junction with the Ohio, by United States troops, under Major Doughty, in the autumn of 1785.

[2] Hildreth's History of the United States, iii. 541; Burnet's Notes on the Early Settlement of the Northwest Territory, pp. 46 and 56.

[3] *Ettwein's Historical Statement.* MS. G. A. Ten thousand acres, exclusive of the town plats, had been granted by Congress. The three town plats were $666\frac{2}{3}$ acres each, making an entire grant of 12,000 acres.

Propagating the Gospel among the Heathen," was organized at Bethlehem. This association, which was incorporated by an act of the Legislature of Pennsylvania (February 28, 1788),[1] held the land granted by Congress, in trust for the Christian Indians.

Having appointed John Heckewelder its agent, he set out for the Northwest Territory (September 10, 1788), accompanied by Matthias Blickensderfer, in order to have the tract surveyed. At Pittsburg, he met Hutchins, with whom he proceeded down the Ohio to Fort Harmar. Here he waited until the beginning of winter, in daily expectation of a treaty which was to be held with the Indians for the pacification of their country, and upon the issue of which depended the survey. At last he was forced to return to Bethlehem without accomplishing his object.[2]

It was not the fault of the United States that this treaty did not take place. The Indians held back. They were dissatisfied and turbulent; many of them eager for war. Not until the winter was far advanced could they be induced to begin negotiations.

The treaty was opened on the ninth of January, 1789, at Fort Harmar. The boundaries previously settled were re-established, but under the new principle of paying for the land. To the Six Nations were given, pay-

---

[1] The first officers were: Bishop Ettwein, President; Bishop Ettwein, John Huebner, John Christian Alexander de Schweinitz, Directors; Bernard A. Grube, Frederick Peter, Jacob Van Vleck, Assistant Directors; John Christian Alexander de Schweinitz, Treasurer; Jacob Van Vleck, Secretary.—*Bethlehem Diary*, Sept. 1787. MS. B. A.

[2] Journal of Heckewelder's Journey. MS. L. A.

able in goods, three thousand dollars for the cessions they had made; to the Western tribes, of which the Wyandots, Delawares, Ottawas, Chippewas, Potawatomies, and Sacs were represented, six thousand dollars.

The Six Nations were disposed to accept these terms in good faith. By particular treaties, not with the United States authorities, they had ceded large tracts in Western New York, retaining, however, extensive reservations, and some among them were rapidly progressing in civilization, especially the Oneidas, on whose reservation the Stockbridge Indians and other remnants of Northeastern clans had been established.[1] But the Western tribes were as insincere as they were malcontented. Comparatively few of them had been in attendance, and these had been sent but to blind the eyes of the government. General Harmar, however, as well as the Commissioners, believed that the treaty had given peace to the Northwest Territory, and rejoiced in this consummation,—for the power of the aborigines was not to be despised. According to the estimate of the War Department, there were five thousand warriors between the Ohio and the Lakes, and a population of twenty thousand persons. But the true number was considerably larger.[2]

The Christian Indians had sent deputies to the fort, who, however, grew so discouraged by the long-protracted delay, that they did not await the opening of the treaty. But their interests were not forgotten.

---

[1] Hildreth's U. S., i. 138, etc.   [2] Ibid., i. 139.

General St. Clair formally notified the tribes of the grant which Congress had made, and added that he would invite Zeisberger to re-establish the Mission on the Tuscarawas at once. No objections were made, and yet, soon after, Welendawacken sent a message to New Salem, protesting against the attempt. This new interference incensed the converts, and they transmitted a spirited reply.

The new Constitution of the United States, framed by the Convention of 1787, having been ratified, the Continental Congress gave way to the first Congress of the United States; and, on the last day of April, 1789, George Washington was inaugurated President. One of his earliest acts was to lay before the Senate the treaty of Fort Harmar. It was not only approved, but a bill passed substantially reaffirming the ordinance of the Continental Congress for the government of the Northwest Territory.

About this time Zeisberger gained a correct insight into the real state of the Indian country, through Ekuschuwe, the head chief of the Chippewa nation, who came to New Salem, attended by a body-guard of ten warriors, in order to bring "good words" to the Mission. The treaty, he said, was a mere delusion; a majority of the tribes were for war. In opposition to these the Chippewas, Ottawas, Potawatomies, and Wyandots had formed a confederation, in order to uphold peace with the United States by all the means in their power. Pipe and the Half King had broken with Welendawacken and joined the confederates. The

Half King, however, had died at Detroit, in the summer of 1788, before any decisive measures could be taken. Not long after this, the other chiefs had met in council, at the same place, and, while deeming an immediate return of the Christian Indians to their old seats impossible, had determined to recognize and protect them, in their present town, as a part of their confederacy, in case they were willing to assume such a position.

The preservation of peace being one of the fundamental laws of their code, the converts gladly assented to the proposal. Ekuschuwe was royally entertained, and departed amid the firing of salutes.

A few weeks later, Heckewelder and Abraham Steiner arrived, in order to consult Zeisberger with regard to the propriety of a survey in the Tuscarawas valley. After what he had heard from the Chippewa chief, he could not but dissuade them. As long as an Indian war impended, the attempt would be perilous in the extreme. Hence Heckewelder was obliged to return to Bethlehem a second time, without gaining his object.

CHAPTER XLI.

ZEISBERGER AT NEW SALEM AMID THE FIRST INDICATIONS OF WAR.—1789–1791.

Indian schools, and Zeisberger's literary labors.—New Salem thrives in the midst of a famine.—Emigration of Delawares and scattered converts to the Mississippi.—The Mission in the height of its prosperity.—Senseman rejoins the Mission.—First signs of war.—Scott's raid.—Harmar's expedition and defeat.—A general war begins.—The plots of the Indian Council against the Mission.—Zeisberger applies to the confederate chiefs, and then to the Canadian government, for a refuge during the war.—Reasons which induced him to seek an asylum in Canada —Manners and customs of the Chippewas.—Mode of adopting prisoners.—Exodus from New Salem.—Andrew Montour's sister.—Zeisberger's opinion of Loskiel's History of the Indian Mission.

THE further stay of the Mission at New Salem afforded Zeisberger an opportunity to devote himself particulrly to schools. He established three of them, in all of which he gave daily instructions. They numbered about one hundred pupils, including not a few adults, who were anxious to learn to read and write. At the same time, he engaged in literary labors, translating into Delaware a selection of hymns and a Harmony of the History of the Saviour's Passion.[1]

In the course of the summer and autumn, a dreadful famine prevailed at Detroit and along the Lakes. Men actually starved to death. But New Salem continued to prosper. God laid upon its plantations a twofold

---

[1] Zeisberger's Letters to Ettwein and Huebener, 1789. MS. B. A.

blessing. They yielded richer harvests than ever before. Of this the Indians were not slow to take advantage. They flocked in from all sides. A single family sometimes entertained as many as thirteen guests, for weeks together. There was, however, no complaint on the part of the converts. They showed their faith by their works.

Induced by this famine, a part of the Delaware nation emigrated to the Mississippi, and settled near the Spanish colonies. The most of the scattered members of the Mission accompanied these emigrants, and were never again heard of. A number had died before this exodus, and of these some repented in their last hours, and left behind a sweet savor of the Gospel.

In the year 1790, New Salem reached the height of its prosperity; but, at the same time, the complications in the West grew so portentous as to render the settlement untenable.

The year opened with the genial weather of spring. Wild flowers in full bloom were found in the forests. They formed a type of the spiritual beauty of the Mission. The Gospel was proclaimed with power, and received with joy. Many heathens were converted and baptized. Others died full of hope.[1] The congregation numbered two hundred and twelve persons, a larger membership than at any time, since the massacre, and

---

[1] Among these was a white woman, once a member of John Harris's family, at the Susquehanna Ferry, who had been taken prisoner in the French and Indian War, and had wandered about among the tribes until she became an Indian in all things except color.

the town, with its improvements, increased so much that Zeisberger thought of beginning a second settlement, and asked for more laborers. Gottlob Senseman and his wife hastened to answer this call, and rejoined the Mission on the ninth of November. The prospect of bringing it back to its former strength and influence was continually brightening, when the clouds of war that had been hanging over the distant horizon, instead of melting away, unexpectedly began to rise in such dark masses as to obscure these hopes.

Instigated by British agents and officers, and encouraged particularly by Sir John Johnson,[1] the hostile tribes infested the banks of the Ohio, which they claimed as the only rightful boundary of their country, and commenced to waylay emigrants from the States. A lofty rock above the mouth of the Scioto, on the Virginia shore, was their favorite lookout, whence they could see boats at a great distance. In other places they committed murders and carried off horses. Instances of this kind became so common, that both Governor St. Clair and General Harmar could no longer deny that war existed.

The first attempt at retaliation was abortive. Two hundred and thirty Kentuckians, and one hundred regulars from Fort Washington, under General Scott, marched as far as the Scioto (April, 1790) without meeting any savages, or finding any traces of them except deserted villages. In autumn, a more formidable expe-

---

[1] Hildreth's Hist. U. S., Second Series, i. 247, etc.; Burnet's Notes, 94, 102, etc.

dition was undertaken against Gigeyunk and the other towns of the Maumee, by a body of eleven hundred men, regulars and militia, called out by the President. General Harmar commanded in person. At first he, too, saw only deserted villages, which his troops destroyed, together with about twenty thousand bushels of corn and large fruit-orchards. By-and-by, however, he got upon the trail of the Indians, and sent two detachments in pursuit. This was a most imprudent measure. The Indians turned upon the detachments and totally defeated them. Harmar retreated with such haste as to leave his dead in their hands. The scalped and mutilated remains became food for birds and beasts of prey.[1]

A cry for vengeance passed through the Indian country when the burning of the Maumee villages was known; and a yell of triumph followed as soon as the news spread of the victory which the warriors had gained. The peace-confederation, under Ekuschwe and Pipe, lost all influence. A council, held on the ruins of Gigeyunk, determined to begin a general war, and to force the Christian Indians to take part in it. So intense was the excitement, that a project to seize them and their teachers at once was prevented by the more prudent of the chiefs, only after they had pointed out an internecine war as the inevitable result. The confederates would, they said, make common cause with the converts. A plot was, accordingly, concocted

---

[1] *Zeisberger's Letter to Bishop Hehl.* At his own request, Harmar was tried by a court-martial and acquitted, but resigned his commission.

to invite the Mission to come to Gigeyunk, under the semblance of friendship, but, in reality, for the purpose of destroying its liberty and coercing its members into the ranks of war-parties, upon pain of death.

These machinations were not known at New Salem. Nevertheless, in any case, it became necessary to secure a retreat during the approaching storm. In the early part of the next year (1791), an embassy was sent to the confederate chiefs, and to Pipe in particular, asking their aid on behalf of the Mission, in accordance with the offers which they had made. Pipe expressed his willingness to do all he could, and promised to consult the other confederates. Meantime two runners arrived at New Salem, from the war-council at Gigeyunk. "Friends and inhabitants of Pettquotting!"—ran their message—"we hereby inform you that you cannot remain in your town. Make ready to go. In two months you will hear more. Obey us, or what you suffered at Muskingum will come upon you again." This was the first coil which the wily savages wound around the Mission. But the Christian Indians refused the string that accompanied the message, and replied: "Friends! We are preparing to go. We do not sit in darkness. We know what to do. We have appealed to three chiefs. They will care for us. We do not need your advice, but thank you for it."

Unfortunately, however, the confederates delayed their answer so long that Zeisberger was constrained to apply to the English government for protection. In March, Edwards went to Detroit to negotiate with

Major Smith, the commandant, and McKee, the Indian agent, for the lease of a tract of land in Canada, where the Mission might be carried on temporarily, as long as war existed. Smith and McKee, on their part, suggested a grant, in place of a lease, and wrote to the government at Quebec upon the subject, advising Edwards to spend another planting-season at New Salem.

This Zeisberger deemed impossible. A general war had virtually begun. The United States were engaged in great preparations to humble the savages. Meanwhile irresponsible bodies of militia made incursions into their country, shooting all they found, whether friends or foes. On the Beaver River several Indians had been slain who were connected with the Mission. The converts were not to be pacified. Their rich plantations and flourishing town were as nothing to them in comparison with a safe retreat. All the harrowing recollections of the massacre came up again, and Zeisberger well knew, from former experiences, that at every alarm his Indians would take to the woods and disperse. He believed them to be, moreover, in real danger. On the other hand, he was not ignorant of the risks which the Mission would run in the event of an exodus from the soil of the United States. Congress might resent as an insult his appeal to those British authorities who were tampering with the savages, and revoke the grant in the Tuscarawas valley. But all these considerations were outweighed by the personal safety of the converts. Zeisberger, too, could not forget the massacre. Another war would produce all the accessories of another massacre. And although Bishop Ettwein pointed out Presque Isle, or the French Creek, as a suitable locality; and told him of the renewal of the ancient friendship of the Church with the Six Nations, at the house of Governor Mifflin, where he had been in council with Cornplanter, Half Town, and Big Tree, noted sachems of the Senecas, of their desire for the Gospel, and of his own hopes with regard to the Iroquois in case the Mission were, for the time being, transferred to Pennsylvania;[1] yet Zeisberger

---

[1] *Ettwein's Letter to Zeisberger*, Feb. 1791. MS. B. A. At the time of writing this letter, Bishop Ettwein entertained high hopes of extending the Mission in Pennsylvania. On the eleventh of January, 1791, the Society for Propagating the Gospel had petitioned the Assembly of Pennsylvania for a tract of land near Lake Erie, or on French Creek, partly in order to gain an increased income for defraying the expenses of its work among the Indians, and partly with the view of beginning a settlement of natives, which, "by the blessing of God, would become a means of bringing many savages to the Christian religion, to industry, and to social life with the citizens of the United States." This petition was shown to Governor Mifflin, who favored the project, and was presented by Mr. Mahollen. Having been read a second time, on the twelfth of January, a committee of five was appointed to report on it. This committee strongly urged the propriety of granting the prayer of the petitioners, upon the following grounds: 1. Moravian Indian settlements near Lake Erie would tend to civilize the natives. 2. Would prove a protection to the infant settlements of white people in that country. 3. Would open a connection with distant tribes and divert a considerable quantity of the fur trade into the State of Pennsylvania. Accordingly another committee was appointed, which brought in an act that was adopted, and approved by the Governor, April, 9, 1791, granting the Society five thousand acres in two tracts, one of twenty-five hundred acres on Conneaut Creek, the other of twenty-five hundred acres on the heads of French Creek. Warrants for the survey were issued May 28, 1791. Owing to the war, it could not, however, be undertaken until May and June, 1794, when Jacob Eyerly and Mr.

remained true to his convictions that the only place of real security in the approaching conflict was the neutral ground of a British colony. Hence he sent Edwards back to Detroit to secure an asylum, without delay, somewhere on English territory, even if it were only a "night-lodge."

With regard to himself, this prospect of another migration elicited the following sentiments in a letter to a member of the Board: "My time is short. I begin to anticipate my rest with God. But as long as I am here, I will be diligent to do my part in establishing the glory of the Saviour among the heathen. I would very much wish to finish, before I die, the literary labors in which I am engaged. Our frequent journeys hinder them greatly."[1]

During his stay at New Salem, Zeisberger had many opportunities to observe the manners and customs of the Chippewas. Whenever they came to the town, they engaged in what was called their begging-dance. Beginning at one end of the village, they danced from house to house till they had reached the

---

Rees accomplished it, amid considerable danger. The tract on the Conneaut, which stretched to the lake, was called "Hospitality;" that on French Creek, "Good Luck." They were both in Erie County, Pa., and comprised, in addition to the Assembly's grant, five hundred and eighty-two acres purchased by the Society, and four hundred and three acres presented to the same by Jacob Eyerly and George Huber, in all fifty-nine hundred and eighty-five acres. The hoped-for Indian town was, however, never built, and the Society, in course of time, sold the land, some of it but twenty years ago.—*Drafts, Letters, and other MSS. in the Society's Archives.*

[1] Original Letter. MS. L. A.

other end, and at the same time begged from door to door. Besides the string or belt of wampum, their messages were always accompanied with a piece of tobacco, which the recipients were expected to smoke while in consultation. To cure a sick person they slaughtered a dog, feasted on its flesh, and chanted incantations.

A chief, who died near New Salem, was buried in great state. His face having been painted red, and his body robed in the best of garments, he was placed in a coffin such as the Christian Indians used. A wreath of silver buckles encircled his head, on one side of which were apples and on the other onions. Around his neck and arms were wrapped belts of wampum with silver trinkets. Close by his one hand lay his tobacco-pouch, pipe, knife, and flint; near the other, his hunting-pouch, powder-horn, lead for bullets, and a loaf of wheat bread; at his feet were a pot, bowl, spoon, hatchet, and a pair of shoes.

The canoes of the Chippewas consisted of a frame of cedar wood, around which was a covering of birch-bark sewed together in bands, the seams being cemented with gum. They were so light that two men could carry the largest of them, and yet so strong that they plowed even the waves of Lake Erie with ease.

The custom of adoption into a family by force prevailed among various tribes. In case of the death of a son or daughter, the parents, with a black belt, hired a captain to procure a substitute. Collecting his band, this captain went out as for war, and took a prisoner. If he was a white man, his head was shaved and painted; in every case, the belt was wrapped around his neck, and he was carried off to the bereaved family, which received him with all affection.

On the last day of March, thirty large canoes having been completed, the Indians sent their goods and chattels to Sandusky, which was to be the place of rendezvous. Soon after, the greater part of them followed, leaving Zeisberger and a few of his companions in the town. On the tenth of April, he officiated, for the last time, in the chapel, preaching on the words: "Verily, verily, I say unto you, If a man keep my saying, he shall never see death."[1] Immediately after this service, the structure was taken down, and the bell removed. On the fourteenth, he, too, departed. One of the latest converts, who accompanied him, was a sister of Andrew Montour. She was a living polyglot of the tongues of the West, speaking the English, French, Mohawk, Wyandot, Ottawa, Chippewa, Shawanese, and Delaware languages.

From every part of the neighborhood Indians had flocked to New Salem to see the exodus of the congregation. Into their hands the town fell. Some fifty applicants for church-membership declined accompanying the Mission.

While at New Salem, Zeisberger received a copy of *Loskiel's History of the Indian Mission*, of which he is the hero. In a letter to the Board, he says of this

---

[1] John, viii. 51.

work: "I have read the History of the Mission with much pleasure, but the orthography of the Indian words is a disgrace to the book. I wish the English translation could be postponed. There are persons still living whose names occur as enemies of our Mission, who have now wholly changed their views and sentiments, and are our friends. They ought not to be exposed. Perhaps the best plan would be to omit their names altogether." This is an interesting instance of Zeisberger's forgiving spirit. He refers to such persons as Elliot and McKee, who were the real cause of all the misfortunes that had come upon the Mission, however friendly they now showed themselves under orders from the British government. Zeisberger's suggestion was carried out. In La Trobe's translation, published in 1794, the names of all former enemies of the Mission are omitted.

CHAPTER XLII.

ZEISBERGER AT THE MOUTH OF THE DETROIT RIVER.—1791, 1792.

Journey from Sandusky to the Detroit.—The Watch-Tower.—Scott's raid on the Wabash.—Message to the Christian Indians, requiring them to take part in the war.—Excitement among the young men.—Zeisberger's policy. — Fruitless attempts at negotiations. — Indian "talk" at Quebec.—Joseph Brant.—Wilkinson's raid.—March of St. Clair's army.—His plan of operations.—Surprised by the Indians at the head-waters of the Wabash.—The news at the Watch-Tower.—Death of Job Chilloway and Abraham.—Report of the Secretary of State of the United States upon the exodus of the Mission.—Explanatory memorial of the Society for Propagating the Gospel.—A more permanent settlement undertaken in Canada.—Departure from the Watch-Tower.

THE *Saginaw*, a sloop chartered from the Northwest Company for fifty pounds sterling, came to the rendezvous at Sandusky and took on board Senseman, Jung, the aged and infirm, together with the goods of the Mission. The rest proceeded in two bodies, one by land with the cattle, the other, led by Zeisberger and Edwards, in canoes, encamping, each night, on the shore of the lake. One of their halting-places was at the mouth of the Maumee, on which lay Gigeyunk, the seat of savage power, where so many threats had been breathed against the Mission. Gathering the converts around a fire, Zeisberger sang with them a number of Delaware hymns, expressive of their faith and confidence in God, as though he would send up the river that defiance with which Christians meet the plots of heathens.

On the third of May, his party reached the mouth of the Detroit, and was, soon after, joined by the other division. The *Saginaw* had been awaiting them. On the eastern or Canada side, lay a tract of land belonging to McKee and Elliot, which had been put at the disposal of the Mission. This land was cleared, ready for cultivation, and had several houses. In one of these Zeisberger took up his abode; in another, close by, Jung, both on McKee's plantation; a quarter of a mile nearer to the river, Senseman and Edwards found a home in houses owned by Elliot. Between these several buildings the Indians put up bark-huts. This little settlement, which they called the *Warte*, or the "Watch-Tower," stood in full view of the lake.[1] Opposite to it, on the American side of the river, was a Wyandot village. A few Canadian farmers lived in the vicinity, among them a steward of Elliot, with a number of negroes. Otherwise the converts were isolated.

But even this refuge did not completely secure them against the machinations of the hostile tribes.

It is true, the war-parties which gathered on the Maumee, the Wabash, and the heads of the Miami, came from the north, and passed on the opposite bank of the river, yet messages were sent to disturb them, particularly after the campaign of early summer.

While an army of three thousand men was being

---

[1] The village must have been at or near what is now the garrison-town of Amherstburg.

raised for Governor St. Clair, who had been commissioned as major-general, Washington called out Kentucky volunteers for immediate relief. They crossed the Ohio in May, numbering five hundred men, under General Scott, and proceeded to the villages on the Wabash. The Indians made but little resistance, fleeing in great confusion; their towns were taken and burned (June 1st). The next day, Colonel Wilkinson marched against Kethtipecanwak, an important Kickapoo village eighteen miles distant, which he captured and destroyed, together with all its stores and property. The inhabitants, however, escaped. Many of these were French settlers, and, as their papers showed, in correspondence with Detroit.[1]

This expedition brought out a message to the Christian Indians. It professed to come from the General War Council, although it was, in reality, sent by the Delawares alone, and called upon the young men to join the warriors and fight for their country, threatening death to the whole congregation if they refused. The young men were thrown into the wildest excitement, which the reproaches of a French captain served to intensify, who taunted them with the assertion that all the Indians of the West, except the Christians, were making an effort to save the land of their fathers. A band of ten was formed, determined to join the Indian army. Zeisberger did not attempt to keep them back, seeing that this would be impos-

---

[1] Hildreth's U. S., New Series, i. 281; Burnet's Notes, 117, etc.

sible, but persuaded them to accept two of the national assistants as their leaders. These received instructions to prevent them from actually taking part in the war, and to protest, in the Council, against further interference of this sort with the Mission. It proved to be a successful policy. After some weeks the assistants brought back the young men, who were satisfied with a mere sight of the army, and a promise from the Council that the Christian Indians should not again be molested. This promise was, indeed, constantly broken, but thé influence of the War Council over the young of the Mission came to an end. Public opinion among the converts, which had for a moment wavered, recovered its normal state, and sternly interdicted all further connection with warriors.

Amid the warlike preparations which were going on, negotiations were not left untried. Cornplanter, a Seneca sachem, agreed to be the mediator with the hostile tribes; but the unwillingness of the British commandant at Fort Erie to render him the necessary assistance put an end to his friendly effort. Nor did the "talk" which they had at Quebec with their English Father, lead to any better results. They laid their grievances before him, and professed their readiness to conclude peace, if the United States would give up their boundaries and accept the Cuyahoga and Muskingum as the line. But neither the Indians nor the Canadian authorities were sincere. The former hoped for aid from the latter, and these would have furnished it had they dared; for it galled them to see the abundant fruits which the United States were reaping from their independence.

In this treaty Joseph Brant[1] took an active part. He had passed with Elliot through the Christian settlement, on his way to Quebec, and made the acquaintance of Zeisberger; and now he delivered a speech in favor of the Christian Indians, to the astonishment of their teachers, who could not divine his object.

The negotiations which had been attempted were followed by new campaigns. In August, a body of Kentuckians, under Colonel Wilkinson, destroyed several towns on the Wabash, and large quantities of corn in the stalk; and, on the seventeenth of September (1791), St. Clair's army, although lacking nearly one thousand men of its complement, began its march from Fort Washington. St. Clair proposed to open communication between the Ohio and the Maumee by a line of posts, to build a strong fort on the latter river, and to garrison it with a force sufficient to overawe the Indians.

In pursuance of this plan, Fort Hamilton[2] was constructed on the Miami, at a distance of twenty-four miles from Fort Washington; and forty-five miles farther north, Fort Jefferson. Reduced in numbers by garrisons for these posts and by desertions, and wait-

---

[1] A celebrated Mohawk sachem, Thayendanega, born about 1742, died 1807, civilized and educated, attached to the interests of the Johnson family and of Great Britain,—a brave warrior and a man of great ability. He published the Gospel of Mark in Mohawk. In England, wherever he traveled, he was received with distinction.

[2] Now Hamilton, the county-seat of Butler County, Ohio.

ing anxiously for supplies, the army spent two weeks in marching the next twenty-nine miles. On the third of November, fourteen hundred men encamped at the head-waters of the Wabash, in Mercer County, Ohio, which stream St. Clair mistook for the St. Mary's. Early the next morning, about sunrise, as the troops were dismissed from parade, and while he was lying sick in his tent, a sudden and furious attack was made by the Indians. The militia fled in dismay; the first line of regulars was thrown into confusion; General Butler fell mortally wounded; many other officers were killed in their attempts to rally the men; and, at last, the remnant of the army retreated precipitately to Fort Jefferson, leaving in the hands of the savages all the baggage and artillery, a large quantity of arms, besides six hundred killed and numerous prisoners. The entire loss, in killed, wounded, and prisoners, amounted to more than nine hundred men, including fifty-nine officers. It was a total and most disastrous defeat, which filled the frontiers with alarm.

On the fifteenth of the month, a dispatch-boat, on its way to Fort Erie, anchored off the missionary settlement, and sent ashore the intelligence. Zeisberger was distressed. He feared a long and bloody war, and immediate interference, of the most serious character, with the Mission. But the Indians did not follow up their victory, so that the converts remained undisturbed, and peacefully worshiped in their new church, which had been dedicated on the nineteenth of June. Two of the most distinguished among them, and both national assistants, here finished their earthly course. The one was William, or Job Chilloway, who died on the twenty-second of September. In his youth a special favorite of Sir William Johnson, and one of his interpreters, he had joined the Mission in 1770, and served it for twenty years with ability and faithfulness, especially in negotiations with heathen chiefs. The other was Abraham, who passed away on the third of November. Of him it may be said that he was a prince and a great man among his people. Besotted, fierce, and cruel as a heathen, he was consistent, bold, and faithful as a Christian. He had led a holy life ever since his baptism at Friedenshütten, in 1765, preaching the Gospel with eloquence and power, helping Zeisberger to establish the stations on the Alleghany and in Ohio, and filling the office of Steward to the Mission until his death. "We have had," says Zeisberger, "but one Abraham, and will painfully miss him. But praise be to God that He permitted this witness of the truth to be among us for so many years!"

In his report of November eighth, 1791, Thomas Jefferson, Secretary of State, noticed the transfer of the Mission to British soil in the following terms: "The Indians, however, for whom the reservation was made, have chosen to emigrate beyond the limits of the United States, so that the lands reserved for them still remain to the United States." This induced the Society for Propagating the Gospel to memorialize Congress upon the subject, explaining the necessity which compelled the Indians to seek an asylum in Canada.[1] Meanwhile Zeisberger took measures to secure a more permanent seat in that Province (1792), justified, as he thought, by the continuance of the war. An application to McKee for a grant of land was forwarded to Sir John Johnson, and well received. Owing to the organization of separate governments for Upper and Lower Canada, which was taking place at the time, an immediate answer could not be given. Hence, as it was important to leave the Detroit in time for planting, McKee, upon his own responsibility, permitted the Christian Indians to remove to the Retrenche River.[2] On the twelfth of April, they left in two parties,—one by land, the other in canoes up the Detroit and across Lake St. Clair. They were to meet at the mouth of the Retrenche.

---

[1] Draft of Memorial. MS. B. A.   [2] Now the Thames.

CHAPTER XLIII.

ZEISBERGER FOUNDS FAIRFIELD, IN CANADA.—1792–1795.

Arrival of the Christian Indians on the Retrenche.—Site for a town.—Influence of the war.—Attempts of the United States to bring about a pacification.—Murder of Major Trueman—General Putnam and John Heckewelder at Port Vincennes. — Grand Council on the Maumee.—Joseph Brant's views on the war.—The Peace Commission and its Quaker assistants.—The gift and letter of the Quakers to the Christian Indians.—The Commission at the mouth of the Detroit. —Violent debates in the Indian council.—Pipe's speech against the Shawanese.—Failure of the negotiations.—Wayne's Legion at Greenville.—A township donated to the converts.—Description of Fairfield. —Wayne's victory at the Rapids of the Maumee.—The position of the British.—Anarchy among the Western Indians.—The Delawares released from their position as women by the Six Nations.—Conclusion of peace.—The Western posts relinquished to the Americans.

AFTER severe experiences off the mouth of the Retrenche, Zeisberger's party landed on the sixteenth of April, and came, the next day, to Sally Hand, a colony composed of English, German, and French settlers. Here they waited for the arrival of the rest, while Senseman and Edwards explored the river. Toward the end of the month, the whole congregation followed, and, in the beginning of May, pitched upon a site admirably suited to their wants. It lay on the west side of the river, about eighty-five miles from its mouth, and consisted of a sandy bluff more than seventy feet high. On the east bank were three large bottoms of the richest soil, and not hard to clear; while numerous springs gushed into the river. A town was laid out, which received the name of Fairfield, and grew rapidly. Farther up the Retrenche were several Monsey and Chippewa villages.

With these neighbors the Mission soon came in contact; and, at the very outset of its work, made a discouraging experience. A Monsey captain enticed ten young men to join his war-party. It is true the majority of them came back again, praying to be forgiven; and the captain himself, having been taken dangerously ill, was, at his earnest request, brought to Fairfield, where he expressed the most agonizing concern for his soul, and received baptism just before his death, at the hands of Zeisberger. But yet it became evident that the war had evoked a carnal spirit among the young, and that great circumspection and watchfulness would be required on the part of the missionaries to lead their people safely through these evil times.

Active military operations were, however, not going on. Congress had voted another army, to be commanded by General Wayne. While it was being slowly raised, various attempts were made to bring about a pacific settlement. The first ended most disastrously. Major Trueman was sent by the President to negotiate with the savages. From Fort Washington, where Colonel Hardin joined him, he took his way, in June, to the Indian country, but never returned. The savages murdered him and his whole party. The next essay proved more successful. General Rufus Putnam and John Heckewelder, the latter appointed Assistant Commissioner by the War Department, ventured as far as Port Vincennes, on the Wabash, where they held a treaty (September 24 to 27, 1792), and concluded peace with some Wiachtenos, Potawatomies, Kickapoos, Kaskaskias, and Piankeshaws. Sixteen chiefs accompanied them to Philadelphia to visit President Washington.[1]

A grand council of nearly all the Northwestern tribes soon after convened at the confluence of the Maumee and the Au Glaize, at which Simon Girty was the only white man permitted to be present. By request of the government, however, forty chiefs of the Six Nations attended, and earnestly counseled peace. The result was that the Indians agreed to hold a treaty, next summer, with Commissioners of the United States.[2]

The converts heard of these negotiations while busily engaged in building their town and clearing the plantations. Joseph Brant with forty warriors, and many other parties of Indians, passed that way to attend the council. Brant told Zeisberger that he did not believe the negotiations would result in peace; and spoke rather favorably of the claims of the United States, although he was, in fact, one of their most formidable opponents. On the occasion of a later visit, he confessed, with singular far-sightedness, that the war then raging would be the turning-point in the history of the American aborigines, and would end in their irremediable ruin.

---

[1] Rondthaler's Life of Heckewelder, 116, etc.
[2] Hildreth's U. S., New Series, i. 380, etc.

In the spring of the following year (1793), three Commissioners, General Lincoln, Colonel Pickering, the Postmaster-General, and Beverly Rudolph, late Governor of Virginia, with whom John Heckewelder was again associated as Assistant Commissioner, set out to hold the proposed treaty. At the suggestion of the Six Nations, and in conformity with the wishes of the Western tribes themselves, several Quakers accompanied them, namely, John Parrish, William Savery, and John Elliot, of Philadelphia; Jacob Lindley, of Chester County; William Hartshorne and Joseph Moore, of New Jersey. Arrived at Niagara, they were hospitably entertained by Colonel Simcoe, the new Lieutenant-Governor of Upper Canada, at his seat, Navy Hall.

From Niagara, Heckewelder paid a visit to Fairfield, arriving quite unexpectedly on the thirteenth of June. Zeisberger had ten days' delightful intercourse with his old friend; while the Indians reaped a special benefit. Finding them in want of provisions, as their last year's crops had failed, he represented their necessities to the Quakers, who sent them an order for supplies to the amount of one hundred dollars, accompanied with a letter of good wishes.[1]

---

[1] The following was the letter (*Original letter*, G. A.):

DETROIT, 26th of the 6th mo., 1793.

TO OUR BRETHREN THE MORAVIAN INDIANS, *settled on the River La Trench.*

ESTEEMED FRIENDS—We, the subscribers, are your well-wishing Friends of the people called Quakers. We have left our homes and

Senseman, who had gone to Niagara to negotiate with the Governor for a grant of land, and had there

---

near connections in Pennsylvania and New Jersey, in and near Philadelphia, with no other motives but from a sense of Religious duty to endeavour to promote peace in our Country, and the welfare of our Indian Brethren in general, and we particularly sympathize with you, as many and deep have been your trials. We are thankful there is yet a little Flock of your people preserved, who love peace, and are endeavouring to pursue it in the Lord's fear. We wish and pray that in all your afflictions you may look up to Him for his blessing and support, and not sink under discouragement, for indeed many are the trials and afflictions of his Children and People in this world. We hope you will be industrious in your business, and follow peace with all men, pressing daily after a life of purity and holiness, that so your Latter end may be glorious, is the sincere desire of your Brethren the Quakers. We are also Men of peace and do not fight, nor go to war on any occasion; we wish you to live in Love one with another, and hope you may be now settled, and may be driven about no more, and that you and us may endeavour to persuade and convince other warlike Indians by our example and by our peaceable and godly conversation that this is the right way.

We have with satisfaction and gladness seen five or six of your People, who informed us of your present difficulty, and tho' we are strangers here far from home, yet as a small testimony of our sincere Love and esteem for you, and a desire for your preservation and prosperity, have allowed our mutual friend Matthew Dolsen here, to furnish you with provision to the amount of One Hundred Dollars, which is Forty Pounds New York Currency, on our account, which we hope will be useful to you, and a token of our regard for your People. With Love and sincere regard to old and young, male and Female, we subscribe ourselves your affectionate Friends, wishing you health and salvation.

JOHN PARRISH,
JOSEPH MOORE,
JACOB LINDLEY,
WILLIAM SAVERY,
WILLM. HARTSHORNE,
JOHN ELLIOTT.

P. S.—ESTEEMED FRIEND, DAVID ZEISBERGER—We have taken the Liberty to direct the above lines to thee, desiring thou may communicate them to the friendly society of Indians under thy care generally.

With love and regard to thee and thy wife, tho' strangers to most of us, we are thy Friends.

witnessed the satisfactory interview between the Commissioners and a body of chiefs, headed by Captain Brant, the representatives of the nations assembled at the Rapids of the Maumee, brought back to Fairfield flattering hopes of a permanent peace. In a little while, however, these hopes were disappointed.

Embarking at Fort Erie (July 2d), the commission reached the mouth of the Detroit River in safety. There they were met, toward the end of the month, by Pachgantschihillas and about thirty other chiefs, who came to inquire whether they would consent to the Ohio as the boundary line of the Indian territory. The Commissioners replied that this was impossible, but offered large presents if the nations would confirm those limits which had been agreed upon at the treaties of Forts McIntosh and Harmar. This answer was reported to the council on the Maumee. A violent debate ensued. Some were in favor of peace on these terms, others advocated a renewal of the war. To the latter party belonged the Shawanese, who were under the evil influence of Simon Girty and other British emissaries; among the former Captain Pipe was prominent. He earnestly contended for peace, and delivered a scathing rebuke to the Shawanese.

"See the Shawanese," he said, turning to Captain Henry, the chief of the Mohawks. "You brought him to me when he was a little boy; you gave him to me, saying, 'Have mercy on this child; receive him that he may live; you are old, and he may help you, fetch you a drink of water occasionally, and shoot you a squirrel!' Moved with pity, I consented; received the Shawanese; adopted him as my grandson, because, without a single friend in the world, he went about forsaken and forlorn. I kept him with me; I instructed him in that which is good; I educated him; he was always about me. But no sooner had he reached manhood than he became disobedient. I admonished him; I punished him; but he grew more wicked continually. And now he listens neither to me nor to any one else, but does evil only. Therefore I am of the opinion that the Great Spirit did not create the Shawanese, but that the devil created him."[1]

After protracted discussions of this character, a written speech was at last prepared (August 13th), denying the validity of the treaties at Forts McIntosh and Harmar, refusing the proffered gifts, claiming the Ohio as the boundary, and declaring the negotiations at an end. This speech, which bore the marks of British influence, and which had been worded not in the manner usual among the nations, but with an insolence characteristic of Simon Girty, was delivered on the sixteenth by two young Wyandots. The Commissioners were greatly disappointed, but sent a dignified reply, rehearsing the pacific efforts made by the United States, and assuring the tribes they would now have to bear the consequences of their own folly.

---

[1] This sarcastic speech was reported to Zeisberger by Captain Henry himself. It referred to the circumstance that when the Shawanese were but a remnant in Florida, the Mohicans brought them to Pennsylvania and induced the Delawares to adopt them as grandchildren.

A party of Mohawks, Chippewas, and Mohicans, returning from the treaty, brought the first news to Fairfield of the abrupt close of the negotiations and the renewal of the war. The most of them were dissatisfied with this result, the entire blame of which they laid upon the Shawanese, Wyandots, and Twightwees.

As soon as General Wayne had been informed of what had taken place, he hastened with such troops as he had to Fort Washington, and thence marched into the Indian country (October 7). Arriving at Stillwater Creek, a fork of the southwest branch of the Miami, on the thirteenth, he constructed a fortified camp, on a high plain, six miles in advance of Fort Jefferson, and called it Greenville.[1] There he spent the winter, with about twenty-six hundred men.

Amid these renewed hostilities the refuge in Canada was more welcome than ever to the Christian Indians. It promised to become a permanent home. In January, (1794), McNeff, the government surveyor, came to Fairfield, and, under instructions from Governor Simcoe, who had visited the settlement and expressed his best wishes for the spread of the Gospel, laid off an entire township, twelve miles long and six broad, which was donated to the Mission, the deed being assigned in trust to the "Brethren's Society," in London, "for Propagating the Gospel among the Heathen."[2]

---

[1] On the site of the town of the same name, the capital of Darke County, Ohio.

[2] Simcoe's Original Letter. G. A.; Draft of Address of Missionaries. G. A.

The improvements upon this tract advanced rapidly. Upwards of forty houses were built, forming one street, which began at the road to Detroit, and ran southwest to northeast. On the north side, near the upper end, stood the church, beside it Zeisberger's house, and immediately opposite a dwelling occupied by Edwards and Jung in common. Next to theirs was Senseman's comfortable home, and close by the school-house. North of the lower end of the town lay the burial-ground.[1] The church, dedicated on the nineteenth of October, was a log structure, boarded, with windows framed and glazed, and a small steeple with a bell. It was one of the most commodious chapels belonging to the Mission in the West. The plantations embraced several hundred acres; and the entire tract was surrounded by white settlers. Some of these would have purchased lots if Zeisberger had consented; but he held that the land given by government constituted a reservation exclusively for the use of the Indians.

The opening spring brought many messages from the hostile Indians, invoking the aid of their Christian brothers against the Americans. Of these messages the converts took no notice.

There was good cause for the anxiety which the tribes manifested. They had to deal with a man of sound judgment, great resolution, and indomitable perseverance, who, moreover, took every precaution to

---

[1] Plan of Fairfield. B. A.

avoid surprises. As soon as the season permitted, the Legion—the name by which Wayne's army was known—advanced from Greenville to St. Clair's battle-field, and built Fort Recovery. This was attacked by the savages, aided by many British (June 13); but the assailants suffered a terrible repulse. Reinforced by eleven hundred volunteers under Scott, from Kentucky, the Legion again advanced, in the first week of August, to the confluence of the Au Glaize and the Maumee. Here was the "grand emporium" of the Indians, who were taken by surprise, and fled in the utmost confusion, leaving Wayne in possession of their wide fields of corn, their well-stocked gardens, and clusters of villages extending on both rivers for several miles.[1] In order to hold so important a position, he erected Fort Defiance, a strong stockade post, and between it and Fort Recovery, built Fort Adams, on the St. Mary's River. About forty miles farther down the Maumee are rapids, at the foot of which the British had constructed an improved fort. Thither the savages retired. Moved by the humane desire to avoid further bloodshed, Wayne proposed a treaty. But being met with evasive answers he attacked and completely defeated the Indians, in full sight of the British garrison. This battle decided the fate of the Western nations. The bow of their strength was broken.

Of all these events Zeisberger was kept informed by

---

[1] Burnet's Notes, 169.

the numerous expresses which passed through Fairfield, on their way to British posts. The day before the battle, a Chippewa runner appeared, calling all the Indians along the Retrenche to the Maumee. This message was sent in the name of the British Colonial government, whether by its authority or not remains uncertain. At the same time, Senseman and Jung, who were on the road to Detroit, returned with the intelligence that it was impossible to reach the post, the whole country being roused, and the British militia called out.

The prudence with which Wayne acted under these circumstances forms an unfading leaf of his laurels. There existed provocation enough to justify him in attacking the British fort, which would have led to a new war with England. He saved his country from so great an evil, and yet maintained the honor of its flag and made its cause triumphant.

The defeat of the Indians brought on dissensions among them, and quarrels with the British. Anarchy reigned supreme. The Delawares were in a miserable state. Captain Pipe, the most illustrious of their headmen, and the last chief identified with the great days of the Mission, had died shortly before the battle.

It was in this disastrous period of their history that the Six Nations conceived the idea of formally releasing them from their position as women. Joseph Brant was the master-spirit on the occasion,—inaugurating ceremonies, delivering speeches, and causing a war-club to be presented to them with the words, "Go forth, now, in the fashion of a man!" But the Delawares received these mummeries very ungraciously. "What shall we do," they said, "with this murderous club, except to use it against you, our uncles, who have so often and so richly deserved such treatment at our hands?"

Zeisberger, who had all the particulars from Brant himself, explains the proceeding as an attempt, on the part of the Six Nations, to entangle their old enemies irreconcilably with the United States, and thus to debar them from the benefits of the peace which was at hand. Whether this be correct or not, it is evident that mischief of some kind was intended. For, in the following year, when Brant was on his way to the treaty with Wayne, he no sooner heard that the Delawares suspected him of a plot against their nation than he precipitately returned home.[1]

Misrule and disorder continually increasing among them, they sent an urgent message to William Henry Gelelemend to resume his office of chief. In reply he reminded them of the testament of his grandfather, Netawatwes, appealed to them to accept the Gospel, and declined the chieftaincy. Famine added its horrors to their national distress, and extended to many other of the Western tribes, so that their sufferings, according to the testimony of a British agent, were unprecedented. Many Indians died. The Nanticokes, although not from this cause alone, dwindled to four or five families.

---

[1] Zeisberger's Journal, Fairfield. MS. B. A.

All these experiences inclined the nations to peace. On the third of August, 1795, a treaty was concluded at Greenville, between General Wayne and the Wyandots, Delawares, Shawanese, Ottawas, Chippewas, Potawatomies, Miamis, Weas, Kickapoos, Piankeshaws, Kaskaskias, and Eel River Indians. The whole eastern and southern portion of the State of Ohio fell into the hands of the United States, which gave, as an equivalent, twenty thousand dollars in presents, and an annual allowance of nine thousand five hundred dollars. Thus the Indians ceded a much larger domain than the American government had asked for before the war began. They were the more willing to accept these terms, because the Western posts which Great Britain still held were now, at last, to be given up to the United States, according to an arrangement effected between the two countries.

CHAPTER XLIV.

FURTHER STAY OF ZEISBERGER AT FAIRFIELD.–1795-1798.

State of the Mission.—Work among the white settlers.—Zeisberger's labors.—A great penitential council.—The grant on the Tuscarawas renewed by Congress.—Its survey.—The site of the massacre after fifteen years.—An emigration from Fairfield agreed upon.—Benjamin Mortimer joins the Mission.—His sermon to the Indians prior to the departure of Zeisberger.—Senseman's remarks on Zeisberger's lifework.—Prosperity of the town.—Zeisberger leaves for the Tuscarawas with a part of the converts.

THE war prevented an increase of the Mission. The Gospel was preached to the many heathens that came to Fairfield; but the great struggle going on for their Western homes filled their minds to the exclusion of higher interests. Some were occasionally impressed; yet there was no general movement, as at New Salem, or in the towns on the Tuscarawas. The ears of the tribes remained heavy. Among the white settlers, however, whose numbers continually augmented, especially in the spring of 1796, when the Chippewas sold their land and emigrated, the missionaries had frequent opportunities of doing good. Senseman and Jung preached to them statedly, and baptized their children. Jung had an appointment at the house of Francis Cornell, a settler from Connecticut, where many attended. Senseman gained such repute by his energy and eloquence, that he was almost unanimously selected as a candidate for the Canadian Assembly. He declined this position as irreconcilable with his missionary duties.

The spiritual state of the Mission itself was encouraging. To this Zeisberger devoted himself. The mode which he adopted to bring the subject of religion directly to the hearts of the converts, was peculiar. He opened a correspondence with them in the Delaware language. Selecting an appropriate topic, he expounded it in missives to the heads of families and others. These replied in writing, each one bringing him a letter, which he read aloud and commented upon in the presence of the bearer. He also developed the native agency, so that, both among men and women, national assistants labored in accordance with a regular system. The young people manifested great interest in the school, which Senseman taught. He had pupils who wrote a better hand than many of the mercantile clerks in Detroit.

Toward the end of the year 1797, Zeisberger perceived that a contaminating influence was beginning to proceed from some of the neighboring settlements. The converts grew careless and fell into open sin, especially drunkenness, of which even national assistants were guilty. Determined to resist such evils at the very outset, he convened the entire membership, on the tenth of December, in a special council. He addressed them with all the fire of his youthful years, and the authoritative dignity of his matured age, beseeching them to repent and turn to God. The effect was wonderful. The Spirit that convicts of sin was poured out upon that meeting. A general and deep emotion ensued. One by one the Indians rose and publicly acknowledged their transgressions. It was not a mere momentary excitement. The weeping and mourning and rending of hearts continued for days. Little companies gathered for prayer and confession. Every face was full of shame; every mouth overflowed with self-reproach; the whole town presented the appearance of a penitential fast. A celebration of the Lord's Supper sealed this return to their covenant.

Meantime the "Society for Propagating the Gospel among the Heathen" took measures to secure the land granted by Congress. This grant had been renewed by an act dated June 1st, 1796; and President Adams had issued the necessary deed.[1] In the following spring (1797), John Heckewelder and William Henry, with whom were associated as assistants, John Rothrock and Christian Clewell, of Schoeneck,[2] as also Kamp, of Graceham,[3] undertook the survey. From Charlestown, a new and flourishing settlement at the confluence of the Buffalo Creek and the Ohio,[4] they proceeded, on the seventh of May, accompanied by John Carr, their guide, John Messemer, a Tunker preacher of Detroit, on his way home, and two Indians, Captain Bull and Joseph White Eyes, a son of the celebrated captain, to

---

[1] Ettwein's Hist. Statement. MS. G. A.
[2] A village half a mile north of Nazareth, Pa.
[3] A village in Frederick County, Maryland.
[4] Now Wellsburg.

the site of Gnadenhütten, where they arrived on the evening of the eleventh. Heckewelder went on to Marietta to notify General Rufus Putnam and his son, who were to represent the government; while the rest prepared for the survey. The site of the town was a dense wilderness of bushes and trees, and infested with rattlesnakes. Here and there the ruins of a chimney projected from the midst of a blackberry or sumac thicket. To this wilderness they set fire. When it had been consumed, a spectacle presented itself which awoke thrilling emotions within their hearts. The ground was covered with human bones, that gave evidence of having been dragged about by wild beasts, and formed the sole relics of the murdered converts. For the first time in fifteen years men cared for the sepulture of these remains.[1]

The party having been joined by the two Putnams, and Schmick, of Nazareth, the work of surveying began, and was completed by the beginning of July. Three plats, each of four thousand acres, were laid out, and called respectively the Gnadenhütten, Schönbrunn, and Salem tracts.[2] Of these a part of the converts were invited to take speedy possession.

---

[1] In October, 1799, the bones of the murdered Indians were reinterred in one of the cellars of the old town by John Heckewelder and David Peter. There they remain to this day. The site of this grave, which had been intentionally left without a stone, that it might not be desecrated by evil-disposed white men, was lost in the course of time. In 1847, however, it was again discovered. An association has been formed to erect a monument to the memory of the victims, and inter their remains at its base. That this design may soon be carried out is the wish of many hearts.

[2] *William Henry's Journal.* MS. L. A. Schmick, Rothrock, and

But it was not until the next year (1798) that the necessary arrangements could be made. Then Heckewelder came to Fairfield (May 22d) with instructions from the Board. Pursuant to these, it was agreed that he and Edwards should proceed to the Tuscarawas valley with a few pioneers; and that Zeisberger and Benjamin Mortimer should follow with a larger colony. Mortimer had come to Fairfield with Heckewelder, as assistant to Zeisberger.[1]

This indefatigable laborer was seventy-seven years of age, and might well have left new enterprises to younger hands. But it was his life-purpose to spread the Gospel among the Indians, and he deemed this last emigration a joy and not a burden. It permitted him, moreover, to end his days in that valley where his greatest works had been performed.

On the thirty-first of May, Heckewelder and Edwards, together with Nicholas, Leonard, Renatus, Bartholomew, Christian Gottlieb, and Samuel, all of whom were native members of the Mission, left Fairfield. Zeisberger remained until the middle of August, translating into Delaware the liturgical services of the

---

Clewell had made an attempt, June 5th, to explore the site of Salem; but, after a hard day's toil, were obliged to return without accomplishing their object. The whole country was overgrown and the trail lost. The next day, accompanied by William Henry, they set out again, and reached the spot by noon. They found very few remains. The bottom was covered with a thicket of scrub oak, known as the red-jack. The spot where Salem stood was called, in that country, *Massas Town,* " where the swallow used to live."

[1] He was born in England. Subsequently he became pastor of the Moravian church in New York city, where he died November 10th, 1834.

Church. On Tuesday, the twelfth, Mortimer delivered a farewell sermon upon the words of the apostle: "Therefore we are buried with him by baptism into death: that like as Christ was raised up from the dead by the glory of the Father, even so we also should walk in newness of life."[1] His theme was, divine grace imparted to believers through baptism into the death of Jesus, whereby they enter into a communion with Him and His people, and are strengthened to lead a new life. In the course of his remarks he said:

"For a number of years you have constituted one body, as you moved from place to place. Now a part of you are to begin a settlement in your old home, that the Gospel may spread among your countrymen. Your beloved father, David Zeisberger, will likewise go to the Tuscarawas. He has preached to you the whole counsel of God; he has faithfully made known to you the way of salvation; he has baptized the most of you into the death of Jesus; he has consecrated his whole life to your service, gone with you where you went, and endured with you what you suffered. Love to the Saviour and to your souls prompted him to do all this. His sharpest reproofs were for your good. That some of you have become faithless has caused him many a sleepless night of sorrow and of prayer. He yearns over you all; and his heart's desire before God is that you may all know, love, and serve the Lord Jesus Christ. Those of you who remain here will see the face of this your faithful

---

[1] Romans, vi. 4.

teacher and venerable father no more. But, although you be bodily separated, remain united, I beseech you, with him, and with all of us who will accompany him, in the glorious communion of saints. In that communion we will intercede for each other, and by the grace of God continue true to our baptismal vows."

During the delivery of this sermon, the deepest feeling pervaded the hearts of the people. The next day Senseman called them together again, and spoke once more of Zeisberger's departure, of his fearless courage, his self-sacrificing spirit, his readiness to lose his life for the Indian's sake, and of all that had rendered illustrious the many years of his missionary service. In conclusion, he made a covenant between the converts of Fairfield and those going to the Tuscarawas, to the end that they would all be faithful unto death and meet again around the throne of God and of the Lamb. Afterward, the Lord's Supper was celebrated.

In reviewing his labors at Fairfield, Zeisberger had reason to be encouraged. He left the Mission in a prosperous state, spiritually, and the town growing in resources and importance. Three hundred acres were under cultivation; two thousand bushels of corn were annually furnished to the Northwest Trading Company; an extensive trade in cattle, canoes, baskets, and mats was carried on; and five thousand pounds of maple sugar were made and sold every winter. Moreover, the station was well calculated to become the starting-point for other Missions in the West.

On the fifteenth of August, the whole population of

Fairfield gathered by the river to bid farewell to their leader, counselor, and friend. He came among them, and grasped each one by the hand with emotions too deep for utterance. Precisely at noon, he entered a canoe, paddled by three young Indians who had begged for this honor, and put off from the bank amid the sobs of the converts. Thirty-three of them, forming the colony for the Tuscarawas valley, followed in other canoes.

CHAPTER XLV.

ZEISBERGER RETURNS TO OHIO, AND FOUNDS GOSHEN.—1798–1807.

Journey to the Tuscarawas.—Detroit in 1798.—Arrival on the Schönbrunn tract.—John Heckewelder on the reservation as agent of the Society for Propagating the Gospel.—Goshen founded.—Increase of emigration.—A prohibitory liquor-law passed for the reservation by the Legislature of the Northwest Territory.—First baptisms at Goshen.—A part of the reservation leased to white settlers.—The first inhabitants of the present town of Gnadenhütten.—Zeisberger among them at the sacramental table.—Lewis Huebner their pastor.—Death of Gottlob Senseman and William Edwards.—The new council-fire of the Delawares on the White River.—Kluge and Luckenbach begin a Mission among them.—Indian deputation to President Jefferson.—Visit of the Stockbridge Indians.—Denke among the Chippewas.—Quakers at Goshen.—Contaminating influence of the traders.—Bishop Loskiel holds a missionary conference at Goshen.—The church at Beersheba.—George Godfrey Mueller.—New Missions on the Pettquotting and in Georgia.—Drunkenness the destroying vice of the Indians of the reservation.—Carnal spirit at the other stations.—The Missions among the Chippewas and on the White River broken up.—Zeisberger's health fails.—Visit of Forestier and Cunow.—Zeisberger's marvelous deliverances from deadly serpents.

THE inhabitants of the various settlements along the Retrenche, numbering more than one hundred families, hailed the missionary canoe as it passed down the river, that they might bid farewell to Zeisberger and bring him the best fruits of their gardens and orchards. The improvements, which everywhere presented themselves, filled him with astonishment. Sixteen miles below Fairfield was a flour-mill; near by a saw-mill; and, fourteen miles farther down, Dolson's place, an inn and farm, the proprietor of which was a warm friend of the Mission. Hamlets, embowered in fruit-trees, lined the banks of the Detroit above the town. These villages were inhabited by French Canadians, who had intermarried with the Indians, and formed an idle, but good-tempered and jovial race. Detroit itself had increased to a population of about two thousand persons. It was now in the hands of the United States, and commanded by Lieutenant-Colonel Strong. Opposite to it, on the Canada side, the English were building a town, and, at the mouth of the river, Fort Malden, on the site of the "Watch-Tower."

Passing the outlet of the Rouge, a place which Zeisberger had cause to remember, where the missionaries had camped, seventeen years before, shivering and distressed, on their way to the court-martial, and where the Northwest Trading Company now had its ship-yard, the colony spent two days at Stony Point, and reached Sandusky Bay on the first of September. Thence they proceeded to the site of New Salem, which the heathen Indians had destroyed, and buried a child in the graveyard, that was still discernible. Re-entering the lake, they coasted eastward to the mouth of the Cuyahoga, up which they passed to the ruins of Pilgerruh. Beyond this point lay a wilderness with which they were not familiar, and their journey became very arduous. The river was shallow, full of rocks, and obstructed by gigantic tree-trunks. Fortunately, however, they fell in with Nicholas, one of Heckewelder's party, who had come to meet them. Guided by him, they reached the portage between the Cuyahoga and the Tuscarawas, on the waters of which they joyfully launched their canoes, and, after a sail of nine days, entered the well-remembered lake and landed by the Beautiful Spring of old Schönbrunn (October 4). This last journey which Zeisberger undertook, through the wilderness of the West, occupied fifty-one days.

The pioneer-party had encamped on the site of Gnadenhütten, where Heckewelder's house formed the nucleus of the present town.[1] Heckewelder took up his abode there as agent of the Society for Propagating the Gospel, and was not any longer connected with the Mission. Zeisberger's colony pitched their tents near the center of the Schönbrunn tract. A suitable place for a permanent settlement was found on the river-bank, opposite to an island to which General Putnam had given Zeisberger's name, seven miles northeast of Gnadenhütten, just below the fork in the present New Philadelphia Road, where one branch crosses Goshen Hill and the Hill Road goes up a gorge in the mountains. Here a little village was laid out and called Goshen. Schmick and the brothers Colver having arrived from Nazareth to assist in the work, the Mission House was completed and occupied on the thirteenth of November. A temporary church was erected in the following month.[2]

---

[1] *Church Book of Beersheba.* G. A. Heckewelder's house was finished September 9, 1798.

[2] Goshen was situated in Goshen Township, Tuscarawas County, on the farm owned, in 1863, by Jacob Keller. East of the New Philadelphia

A treaty with the Southern tribes followed that of Greenville, and brought about a pacification of all the Indians (1796), much to Washington's joy, who made this one of the special objects of his administration. The result was a rapid development of the Northwest Territory, into which a stream of immigrants began to pour from many parts of the States. That this would bring temptation to the Christian Indians, past experience had recorded. It is true, there were no settlements nearer to Goshen than Charlestown and Marietta, distant respectively about sixty-five and fifty miles. Nevertheless it was necessary to adopt precautionary measures in time. Accordingly the missionaries sent a memorial to Governor St. Clair (October 28, 1798), asking that they and their successors be legally authorized, "in such manner as to his wisdom might best seem meet, to prevent any spirituous liquors from being offered for sale or barter, or used as an enticement to trade, in any town or settlement of Indians that might be made under their direction within the limits of his jurisdiction." They enforced this request by the following considerations: "The practice of introducing spirituous liquors into Indian towns is, in its consequences,

---

Road is a frame house erected over the cellar of Zeisberger's dwelling. A part of the apple orchard remains on the west side of the road.

Zeisberger visited the site of New Schönbrunn, November 11. Single posts of the garden-fences formed the only parts of the town that were still standing. A great many Indian implements and vessels, however, lay scattered on the ground. The place where Schönbrunn stood was called, in that country, *Tuppakin*, or, by some, *Opakin*, or the *Upper Moravian Town*. The whole region was thickly overgrown with bushes and rank weeds.

highly inimical to every attempt to reform and civilize the Indian nations. Not to enlarge on the wickedness of taking advantage of the weakness of a race of our fellow-men, for purposes of deceit, and to their manifest destruction, we believe, also, that the habits of idleness and vice to which it leads, by enervating their constitutions, and diminishing their numbers, are inconsistent with the interests of that very trade which it is meant to promote. We conceive, therefore, that it must be the ardent wish of every benevolent and patriotic mind, that, if possible, an end might be put to so immoral and pernicious a practice."[1] This memorial was signed by David Zeisberger and Benjamin Mortimer, as also by John Heckewelder, in his capacity of agent of the Society. In response, the Governor sent a message to the territorial legislature, which passed a bill in harmony with the wishes of the missionaries.[2]

Zeisberger began his work in the valley, as of old, preaching regularly in the chapel, and conversing upon religion with the numerous Indians who came to visit him. His venerable age and earnest words made a deep impression upon their hearts. On the twenty-fourth of March, 1799, he baptized Pemahoaland and his wife, as the first fruits of the renewed Mission. She was the widow of his old friend White Eyes. Some time after, Hakinkpomsgu, Captain Pipe's successor, came to Goshen. William Henry Gelelemend made him the bearer of a message to the Delaware nation, informing

---

[1] Copy of the Memorial. MS. G. A.
[2] Burnet's Notes, 312 and 384.

them of the return of the Christian Indians, and inviting them to frequent Goshen and hear the Word of God.

But, however auspicious this resuscitation of the missionary enterprise in the Tuscarawas valley at first appeared, the entire reservation could not be used for the Christian Indians. Hence the Society for Propagating the Gospel leased a part of it to settlers from the States, some of whom took up land at Gnadenhütten, and others on the site of Salem.[1] In the course

---

[1] As this is a point of local interest to the present inhabitants of that portion of the Tuscarawas valley, we will give, in this note, a brief history of the first settlements. The Society had foreseen that the land could not all be used by the Christian Indians, even before their arrival, and had issued a circular inviting members and friends of the Church to settle there (Sept. 13, 1796). Certain conditions were fixed upon which lots of 100 to 150 acres would be leased. In order that there might be no misconception concerning this point, Bishop Ettwein drew up an historic statement (MS. G. A.) setting forth the principles according to which the Society acted, and which he had previously explained to a committee of Congress : 1st. All the former inhabitants and their descendants, together with Killbuck and White Eyes and their descendants, should have land rent free, as long as they remained in allegiance to the United States and observed the rules of the Mission. 2d. Land not needed by the Indians was to be let out to white settlers, the rent to be used for the benefit of the former, in providing them with ministers, schoolmasters, books, and churches. He adds: "The trustees will not, and cannot, make any other use of the produce but what is for the benefit of the Christian Indians, and hold the whole undivided for them, forever, in performance of the patent or deed for the land. No part can be given away or sold." In response to the circular of the Society, the first to arrive were Jacob Bush and two other settlers, May 6, 1799. On the twenty-ninth of the same month came Paul Greer, Peter Edmonds, Ezra Warner, and Peter Warner from Gnadenhütten on the Mahony; and, on October 18th, David and Dorcas Peter from Bethlehem. Peter had been appointed to take charge of a store opened by the Society. Soon after more families arrived from the Mahony. The first teams with goods reached the settlement in June, Henry Bollinger, of Nazareth, and Jacob Ricksecker, of Litiz, being the drivers. John Jung-

of the summer, Zeisberger paid them a visit, and, at their request, administered the Holy Supper of the Lord (July 13). The associations of Gnadenhütten awakened such deep feelings in his heart that he delivered an address full of sad reminiscences, and yet instinct with unquenchable faith. For the little band of communicants it was one of those occasions that memory enshrines.[1] Lewis Huebner subsequently became the regular pastor of this colony (July, 1800), which erected a church-edifice, dedicated by Zeisberger to the Triune God, July 10, 1803.[2]

While God thus permitted His aged servant to labor, awhile longer, among the settlers and the Indians, two of the other heroes of the Western Mission were called to receive their crowns. On the fourth of January, 1800, Gottlob Senseman died at Fairfield; and on the eighth of October, 1801, William Edwards, at Goshen, aged seventy-eight years. Both had been faithful coadjutors of Zeisberger. They had toiled and suffered, reaped and triumphed, together. The summons came to Senseman in the midst of his activity; Edwards, broken down by the infirmities of old age, was longing to be at rest. For several years he had been unable to

---

mann, a son of the missionary, was sent out to superintend the clearing of the land, and bore the title of Steward. He returned to the States in November.—*Church Book of Beersheba,* G. A., *and various MSS. in the Archives of the Society for Propagating the Gospel.*

[1] Church Book of Beersheba. G. A.

[2] Huebner was born, August 8, 1761, at Nazareth, where he was educated. Prior to his emigration to the West, he was pastor of various Moravian churches in Pennsylvania, at Bethel, York, and other places.

DAVID ZEISBERGER.

attend to his duties, but declined retiring to the States. He wished to die among the Indians.

About this time, the Delawares were trying to kindle a national council-fire on the White River. Tedpachxit was their chief, and they had six towns, of which the largest were Woapikamikunk, Monsey-Anderson, and Sarah Town. From these villages there came, at last, an answer to the speech of Gelelemend, sent a year previously. The tribe congratulated the converts upon their return to the Tuscarawas, and expressed a desire for white teachers and a Christian colony. This wish having been reported to the Board, John Peter Kluge[1] and Abraham Luckenbach[2] were appointed to begin a Mission. They spent the autumn and winter of 1800 at Goshen, studying the Delaware language under the instructions of Zeisberger, and proceeded, in spring, to the White River, with fifteen converts, where they established themselves twenty miles below Woapikamikunk.

---

[1] Born October 3, 1769, at Gumbinnen, in Prussia. In 1789, he joined the Moravian Church at Kleinwelke, Saxony, and in 1794 went to Surinam, as a missionary to the Arawack Indians. In 1800, he came to the United States and served the Indian Mission. After leaving the West he was pastor of various Moravian churches, and died at Bethlehem January 30, 1849, in the eighty-first year of his age.

[2] Born May 5, 1777, in Lehigh Co., Pa.; entered Nazareth Hall, a boarding-school for boys, at Nazareth, Pa., as a teacher, in 1797; became a missionary among the Indians in 1800, and labored as such, with great faithfulness, at various stations for forty-three years, when he retired to Bethlehem, where he died March 8, 1854. He edited the second edition of Zeisberger's Delaware Hymn Book, and published "Select Scripture Narratives from the Old Testament translated into Delaware."

Many hopeful signs followed the birth of this new enterprise. In November, 1802, twelve Delaware chiefs, among them Tedpachxit himself, and the representatives of ten other nations, arrived at Goshen, on their way to Washington, to visit President Jefferson, and consolidate the amity subsisting between the United States and the Indians.[1] A few months later, the East responded to this act of friendship on the part of the West, and there appeared a deputation of Stockbridge Indians, headed by Hendrich Aupaumut and John Metoxen, who had been educated at Bethlehem, going from tribe to tribe, throughout the territory, and exhorting their brothers of every name to receive the Gospel and adopt the ways of civilization and peace.[2] In the same year, Christian Denke, who had succeeded Senseman at Fairfield, and with whom another new-comer, Oppelt by name, was associated, set up a cabin among the Chippewas, on the Jongquahamik, in the midst of eight villages, and preached Christ; while a young man from Fulneck, in England, John Ben Haven, reached Goshen, eager to assist in the work of the Lord. Nor was interest in the natives of the West confined to the Moravians. The year after Zeisberger's arrival at

---

[1] The interpreter of this party was John Conner, a son of Richard, born at Schönbrunn, and baptized by Zeisberger.

[2] These Indians lived at New Stockbridge, in Massachusetts. Their clan was composed of Mohicans and others, with whom had amalgamated the descendants of Brainerd's New Jersey Indians, who had sold their land to that State. They were Christians; engaged in farming; and had a missionary among them, named Sargent, a Congregationalist, who had devoted his whole life to this remnant. John Konkaput, a former pupil of Nazareth Hall, lived among them.

Goshen, an aged Quaker preacher, with six members of his Society, came to consult him upon the best mode of evangelizing the Indians, in view of extensive Missions which his people wished to inaugurate among the Chippewas and Delawares.

All these efforts to spread the Gospel filled Zeisberger's heart with joy. The prospects for a general conversion of the Indians seemed to him to have been never more favorable. He took new courage and labored with fresh zeal; baptizing converts, among them Joseph White Eyes, a son of the captain; finishing the manuscript of his Delaware Hymn Book (1802); and instructing the various young missionaries who entered the field.[1] The only drawback from such cheering experiences was the introduction of ardent spirits by traders, in spite of the prohibitory law and the prompt measures which Zeisberger adopted, who, on one occasion, seized the casks and had them emptied into the river. These grasping and unprincipled men succeeded in eluding his utmost vigilance, and the Indians became contaminated.

Meantime the Board, which had so long and faithfully directed the affairs of the Mission, had undergone an entire change of members. Ettwein had died at Bethlehem (January 2, 1802); Schweinitz at Herrnhut, but four years after entering the Directory of the Unitas Fratrum; and Huebner had become a mem-

---

[1] At the close of 1800, the church at Goshen counted seventy-one souls, the largest number that Mission ever had.

ber of the same body. Bishop Loskiel,[1] the historian of the Indian Mission, was now President of the Board, and John Gebhard Cunow had taken Schweinitz's place.

In the autumn of 1803, Loskiel paid an official visit to Goshen; and held a conference of missionaries (October 10 to 21), which was attended by Schnall, as the deputy from Fairfield, who had recently joined that post. The whole work was fully discussed, and a renewal of the Mission at New Salem determined upon. Zeisberger gave his matured experience, and many a word of advice and monition fell from his lips. He spoke in particular, and very pointedly, upon the degeneracy of the younger missionaries when on journeys. Formerly, he said, evangelists went out into every part of the wilderness with scanty provisions but a firm trust in God; now well-laden pack-horses were deemed essential. Hence exploratory tours, to look up new places where the Gospel could be preached, had almost come to an end. At the conclusion of the conference, Bishop Loskiel ordained Haven (October 21, 1803), the first ordination ever witnessed by the

---

[1] George Henry Loskiel, born November 7, 1740, at Angermünde, in Curland, the son of a Lutheran minister, joined the Moravian Church in 1759, and filled various offices until 1782, when he became Superintendent of the Domestic Mission in Livonia, and agent for the Unitas Fratrum in Russia. During this period he wrote his History. In 1789, he became pastor of the church at Gnadenfeld, Silesia, and subsequently of other German churches. In 1802, he was consecrated a bishop and came to America, as President of the Board, from which he retired in 1810, and lived at Bethlehem, where he received an appointment to the Directory in Europe, in 1812, but could not leave America on account of the war and his failing health. He died February 23, 1814.

Indians; and distributed Zeisberger's Hymn Book, which had been printed at Philadelphia.

Another result of his visit was the religious development of the colony of white settlers. In response to the earnest application of those living on the west side of the Tuscarawas, he gave them authority to begin an organization of their own. They built a second Moravian church, which was dedicated (December 15, 1805), in the presence of about two hundred persons, by Zeisberger, who performed the act with patriarchal unction, offering up, says Heckewelder, a prayer of extraordinary fervor. This station received the name of Beersheba,[1] and was in charge of George Godfrey Mueller, Huebner having been recalled. Mueller preached, statedly, in English at Beersheba, and in German at Gnadenhütten.[2]

In the spring of 1804, Oppelt and Haven led out a colony from Fairfield, and began the enterprise, projected on the Pettquotting, near to the site of New Salem. Meantime John Joachim Hagen joined the Mission at Goshen; and Abraham Steiner and Gottlieb Byhan commenced a work among the Cherokees of Georgia (1801), after Steiner and Frederick de Schweinitz had undertaken two exploratory tours through their country (1799 and 1800).

---

[1] It was situated on the west side of the Tuscarawas, in Clay Township, Tuscarawas County, on the farm now (1863) owned by Benedict Gross.

[2] *Church Book of Beersheba.* G. A. Mueller was born, May 22, 1762, at Hennersdorf, near Herrnhut, in Saxony. He immigrated to America in 1784, and was pastor of various Moravian churches prior to his appointment to Beersheba.

But this rapid increase of the Indian Mission, which now numbered twelve laborers and six stations, was its last spasmodic effort to subdue the aboriginal domain, and bring its natives under the sway of righteousness and truth. The very next year (1805) brought on a mournful change.

In consequence of the influx of settlers, the prohibitory law could not be carried out on the reservation. Not only passing traders, but its near neighbors, tempted the Indians in every possible way. They looked them up in the forest especially, when hunting or sugar-boiling, supplied them with liquor, and then entrapped them in bargains which were as advantageous to themselves as they were ruinous to the natives. A regular gang of thieves and desperadoes infested the vicinity of Goshen, who worked incalculable injury to the Mission.

During the Holy Passion-week, most of the converts were intoxicated. Zeisberger did what he could to stop the evil; and the Indians gave earnest promises to reform. But a demon had been let loose among them, and they fell into his power so often that drunkenness became the mortal sin and the destroying vice of the little flock. Some of them, indeed, like Gelelemend, remained faithful to the last; and the majority of them erred, not with premeditation, but through that want of stability which is everywhere characteristic of the aborigines, as soon as they meet the white man holding out the inebriating cup.

This state of affairs continued to grow worse. Indians

from beyond the reservation instituted carousals at Goshen, defying all control; and, in the course of time, the prohibitory law was repealed, at the instance of traders, as being an infringement on the rights and liberties of a free people. At the other stations, too, a carnal and rebellious spirit manifested itself. Hitherto, amid the greatest trials of the Mission, even when it was reduced to a mere handful, it had remained vigorous, because of its faith and spiritual life. But now it was shorn of its strength, and its glory was departing, because inward corruption preyed upon its vitals.

Other distressing experiences occurred. In 1806, Denke left his post, on account of the ill-will which the Mission was exciting among the Chippewas, without having gained a single convert. At the same time excesses broke out among the Delawares on the White River. Incited by that notorious prophet and fierce warrior, Tecumseh, the young men of the nation usurped the government, asserting that there were sorcerers at work whose arts must be suppressed, and murdered Joshua, a worthy and consistent member of the Christian colony, throwing his body into the flames. The same fate befell their aged chief, Tedpachxit, whose own son was a ringleader in these outrages. Kluge and Luckenbach were forced to abandon the Mission. In the following year (1807), the contaminating influences of a debauched clan of Monseys, as well as the alienation of the land to white settlers, broke up the station on the Pettquotting. The few converts that were left, removed to the west bank of the Sandusky River.

All these events overwhelmed Zeisberger with such poignant sorrow, that his health began to fail, and he often expressed a desire to depart and be with Christ. In June, 1807, Charles de Forestier, a member of the Directory in Europe, on an official visit to the Moravian churches of America, came, with John Gebhard Cunow, to cheer him; but he had little to say to them, and mostly kept his bed. His eventful career was drawing to a close.

And yet even now that particular providence was displayed which had accompanied him through the world, from his infancy to his hoary age — from the time his parents fled with him out of Moravia to the days in which he was to be set free forever from bondage in every form. In the course of his long abode in the wilderness, he had been often delivered from the murderous hands of savages; but his escapes from deadly serpents had been almost numberless. The last of such deliverances occurred during the summer. One morning, as he woke from sleep, he found that a huge rattlesnake had been coiled up, all night long, beneath the pillow on which his head had been resting. If ever the promise given by the Lord Jesus, touching one of the signs which should "follow them that believe," namely, "they shall take up serpents," was fulfilled since the apostolic age, such a fulfillment may be found in David Zeisberger's life.

CHAPTER XLVI.

THE LAST YEAR OF ZEISBERGER'S LIFE.—1808.

Zeisberger's literary labors.—Indians from Pettquotting at Goshen.—Their scandalous behavior.—Zeisberger's last public discourse a denunciation of their conduct.—His health fails.—His testimony respecting his life and his hopes in view of death.—Interview with the Christian Indians.—Farewell to the Mission family.—His sufferings and death.—A review of his work among the Indians.—Sketch of his character by Heckewelder and Mortimer.—His funeral and interment.

ZEISBERGER'S[1] general health grew better, but the infirmities of old age began to distress him. His hearing was impaired, and his eyesight fast failing. He could no longer read or write. This was a heavy trial, but he thanked God that it had been withheld until his literary labors were completed.

Of these, besides the Hymn Book, the most important was a translation into Delaware of *Lieberkühn's Harmony of the Four Gospels*, a work that cost him infinite trouble, and upon which he expended the greatest care. He also finished his Delaware Grammar, which was, however, never printed. Of his Spelling-Book, he edited a second edition.

He now often spoke of dying, and longed to be at

---

[1] Mortimer's Journal, MS. L. A.; Heckewelder's Biographical Sketch; Mueller's Diary of Beersheba, MS. G. A.; Mortimer's Narrative of Zeisberger's Last Days and Characterization, appended to Heckewelder's Sketch.

rest. Whenever Mortimer, or others, expressed a hope that he would be spared awhile, he replied: "Why shall I stay here? I can be used no longer. My work is done."

About midsummer, forty Indians from Pettquotting arrived, for the most part heathens, with the intention of staying at Goshen for some time. Several weeks later, they were joined by a second party, so that the village was full of visitors. Gelelemend welcomed them in Zeisberger's name, but besought them to abstain from strong drink. "Your aged father cannot bear to see you intoxicated," he added. "It pierces his heart. You will shorten his days if you give way to this sin." They promised to avoid everything that would grieve him. Not long after, however, a boat came up the Tuscarawas laden with rum. The Pettquotting Indians were out hunting; but they no sooner heard of it than they forgot their promises, flocked to the river, like vultures around carrion, and began a carousal so wild and fearful that the Goshen converts fled to the woods, and the neighboring settlers, seizing their rifles, hastened to guard the Mission property and protect the missionaries.

Soon after this, a part of the savages left Goshen; but the rest continued in debaucheries of every kind. This stirred up the old fire within Zeisberger's heart. Summoning all the Indians, both converts and heathens, to the chapel, he addressed them in substance as follows:

"When our friends from Pettquotting came here, we

admonished them to lead a sober, righteous, and godly life, while at Goshen. They promised to do so, but they have not kept their promise. Therefore I herewith notify them that the time has come for returning to their own lodges.

"But this is not all I have to say. There is a house here in which the following persons"—mentioning them by name—" are living, who have given themselves up to every kind of vice. They act like wild beasts, and not like men. They do not belong to our people; and yet they want to be masters in this town. Therefore I herewith command these persons instantly to leave Goshen, and never again to show themselves among us.

" Before they go, however, I will add a few words for their special benefit, and in the way of warning for you all. As a general thing, your teachers speak kindly to you, cheer and comfort you, and tell you of the love of God. But I wish you to know that the Bible contains not only sweet promises, but also fearful denunciations upon the children of darkness, and says, particularly, that neither drunkards, nor harlots, nor fornicators, nor murderers, nor evil-doers of any kind will inherit the kingdom of God, but will, unless they repent, be cast, with the devil and his angels, into hell-fire, where they will be tormented for ever and ever, without the possibility of escape, or the hope of salvation. I wish you to hear this, once more, from my lips ere you leave this place; so that, on the day of judgment, you may not bring forward as excuse for your wickedness that I and your other teachers did not tell you the consequences if you persist in your present course."

This was the last public address ever delivered by Zeisberger. After having, for more than sixty years, proclaimed the grace of the Lord Jesus Christ, he was constrained to close his ministrations with a threat of terrible woe to the ungodly. The result was the dispersion of the whole gang. Fear fell upon all. Some left that same day; others followed in a few days; in a week's time there was not a savage to be seen at Goshen.

In October a sickly season set in, and Zeisberger again fell seriously ill. The Rev. Mr. Espich, a Lutheran clergyman and physician, who had recently settled at New Philadelphia,[1] attended him. On the twenty-ninth, the sacrament of the Lord's Supper was administered to him, at his request, in the circle of the Mission family. He now failed rapidly, and, with a composedness which was characteristic of him, began to contemplate his approaching end and all its circumstances. To Mortimer he said, that he was ready to die, and that nothing troubled him except the spiritual state of the Indians.

This had cast a deep shadow upon the last years of his life and brought him into many an agony of prayer. "I may truthfully assert," writes Heckewelder, "that he wrestled every day with God, from whom alone help could come, and cried to Him that He would heal the diseases of His people."[2] It seemed to Zeisberger as though he could not leave the converts, while they were

---

[1] The county town of Tuscarawas County, founded, by about fifty persons, in the spring of 1804.—*Mortimer's Journal.*

[2] Heckewelder's Biographical Sketch.

so lukewarm, so weak in resisting temptation, so prone to commit sin.

Mortimer called them together and told them what Zeisberger had said, beseeching them first to repent before God, and secure His forgiveness, and then to go to their dying father, who had spent his life among them, confess their sins to him also, and ask his pardon for all the sorrow they had caused him. This would be acceptable to the Lord. Their father must not pass away with such a weight upon his mind. The Indians were moved, and promised compliance.

The next day, Zeisberger remarked to Mortimer: "As my weakness is continually increasing and my appetite gone, I believe that the Saviour intends to take me to Himself. Lying here, often sleepless, on my bed, I have employed the time in reviewing my whole past life, and find so many faults, and so much cause for forgiveness, that nothing remains to me but His grace. Nevertheless, I know that I am His. I trust in the efficacy of His atoning blood, which makes one clean from all sin. The Saviour is mine. The Saviour's merits are mine. Some Christians die rejoicing, with joy unspeakable and full of glory. This is not my case. I leave the world as a poor sinner. My spirit God will receive. I am certain of that. This mortal with all its sinfulness, I leave behind."

This remarkable testimony, unveiling his innermost experiences, to which he had never been in the habit of referring, given at the brink of eternity, as a legacy to all who should come after him, was delivered with great meekness of spirit and humility of manner, but also with the confident boldness of a child of God and an heir of heaven.

The converts now came to visit him, one by one, and, amid many tears, prayed him to forgive all the sorrow they had caused him, assuring him that they had reconsecrated their lives to Christ. He received them with that gentleness and authority which he knew so well how to blend in his intercourse with the Indians; told them of his unabated interest in their welfare; warned them against drunkenness as the sin which so easily beset them, and which would ruin their souls if they did not renounce it; declared to them that in heaven he would be in the midst of the great cloud of witnesses, and would see whether they followed Christ, adding, that even if but one among them remained behind, he would grieve in the midst of his glory.

After this he grew weaker and seldom sat up. But he wanted the latest intelligence of the spread of the Gospel among the heathen read to him, from some missionary reports which had been sent to the station.

On the twelfth of November, the cramp in his bowels from which he had often suffered, in the last years, returned with great vehemence. He was now confined to his bed. Mortimer and the Indians vied with each other in ministering to him. The following day, he called the whole Mission family around him, thanked his wife, with deep fervor, for the willingness with which she had shared the hardships, privations, and trials to which his missionary life had exposed them, and for twenty-six years of true love in all other respects; bade an affectionate farewell to Mortimer and Mrs. Mortimer; and laid his patriarchal blessing upon their children. Toward midnight he seemed to be dying; and Mortimer commended his spirit into the hands of the Lord Jesus Christ.

But this was not the hour of his release. He lived for several days longer, in great pain. It was the last cross which he had to bear, and he took it up with resignation, praying much in a voice scarcely audible. Once he was heard to say: "Lord Jesus, I beseech Thee, come and take my spirit to Thyself." Again, being in great agony: "Thou hast never forsaken me in any of the severe trials of my life; Thou wilt not forsake me now!" Soon after, as though an answer had come from the world above, he exclaimed: "The Saviour is near! Perhaps He will soon call and take me home!" Nothing soothed him so much as Delaware hymns, from his Hymn Book, especially those appointed for the dying, which the Indians sang, grouped around his bed.

On the seventeenth, Heckewelder came from Gnadenhütten, and Mueller from Beersheba, to see him once more. He expressed his satisfaction by signs, but could not speak. Soon after they had taken leave of him, the hour of dissolution drew near. The chapel bell was tolled. At that signal, all the adult Indians of Goshen silently entered, and surrounded the couch, which had been moved to the center of the room, and close by which his wife and Mortimer were sitting. At the open door were several Indian boys, and among them Samuel Fry, the son of a white settler. Zeisberger lay calm, without pain, and perfectly conscious. The converts sang hymns, treating of Jesus the Prince of Life, of death swallowed up in victory, and of Jerusalem the Church above. He occasionally responded by signs expressive of his joy and peace. Amid such strains, at half-past three o'clock in the afternoon, he breathed his last, without a struggle, and went to God. All present immediately fell upon their knees. The Indians sobbed aloud, and Mortimer, with much emotion, thanked the Lord that He had delivered His servant from death, and that He had blessed his testimony while living, to the conversion of so many souls among the aborigines of America, beseeching Him to strengthen the converts that remained, so that they might follow their father's footsteps and meet him in heaven. Zeisberger's age was eighty-seven years and seven months.

Looking back upon his missionary career of sixty-two years, we are led to reflections of a peculiar character.

From one point of view, a cloud hung over his death-bed, after all his labors, perils, courage, and faithfulness. For himself, he was certain of his reward; but for his life-work, the future was dark. True, he did not cease to hope. "In the last years of his pilgrimage," says Heckewelder, "whenever the conversation turned upon the former blessed seasons of grace and glory, which he had seen among the Indians, his spirit revived, and he expressed a hope that, in His own time,

God would renew the days of His people as of old."[1] But as long as such a change was withheld, he knew that the Mission would continue to decline. It had flourished like a glorious sycamore by the rivers of Western valleys; but now he saw that a worm was gnawing at its roots and its beauty withering away.

Many of his aspirations had not been fulfilled. There was no Mission, bearing the ancient name of his Church, among the Six Nations, and although others had gathered into Christ's fold some of their number, the Iroquois, as a people, were not converted. There was no Christian state of Delawares in Ohio, flourishing in the arts and ways of civilization, a center of power, whence messengers were going to the West and the South to lead other nations to the knowledge of the truth. A broken remnant of the Lenni-Lenape, steeped in all the worst abominations of heathenism, eked out their existence far away from their former council-fires. There was no station among the Chippewas. The servant of God, who had brought them the Gospel, had turned back disappointed from their lodges. There was no prosperous church anywhere as a monument of Zeisberger's prayers and work. Fairfield was not what it had been; on the Sandusky stood but a cottage in a vineyard; around his own little chapel, at Goshen, clustered the huts of barely a score of natives.

He looked to other lands, and he beheld the Zion of his fathers victorious in her conflict with paganism, in

---

[1] Heckewelder's Biographical Sketch.

nearly all the ends of the earth. In the West Indies, in Surinam, on the ice-bound coasts of Greenland and Labrador, amid the groves of South Africa, thousands had been reclaimed. The missionary fame of the Unitas Fratrum rang through the Christian world. Not only single souls, but whole nations were converted. Yet in the Indian country, where faithfulness and endurance had been manifested, and hardships and dangers experienced, unparalleled elsewhere, that evangelization which leads tribes to the God of Jacob had proved a failure.

This result was, however, not peculiar to his Church. On the contrary, it seems to be the end of every missionary work in the midst of races that are dying out. At no time has there been a Mission among the North American Indians which grew statedly, from year to year, spreading abroad its influences, and keeping pace with other enterprises among the vigorous nations of the heathen world. Eliot's communities prospered for a time, and then passed away, like the leaves of the woods where his converts hunted. Not a vestige of the tribe remains. But one man is still living, it is said, who can read the Indian Bible which he translated with so much labor. On the lands where his Indians worshiped, are communities of the Anglo-Saxon race that have never seen a native. A few descendants of Brainerd's Indians may yet exist, but soon they, too, will all be gone. Kirkland's work is almost forgotten in the regions where it prospered. In the West and South everywhere, Indian Missions have always been feeble, and languish now.

The discouragements amid which Zeisberger died grew, therefore, originally, out of the character and mournful destiny of the race to which he brought the Gospel. At the same time it does not admit of a doubt that he might have counted his converts by thousands, if he had forsaken the principles of his Church and acted contrary to his own convictions. The aim of the Moravians, in their work among the heathen, was the real conversion of souls. Hence they not only withheld baptism until evident signs of a change of heart appeared, but used precautions unknown to other Christian denominations, and long since set aside in the Moravian Church, because they proved to be a barrier of doubtful propriety.

But, from another point of view, Zeisberger's hoary head was crowned with glory. Taking into account the character of his work, and comparing it with that of other missionaries among the aborigines of our country, he stands foremost of all the men that entered the same field in the eighteenth century. Indeed, in some respects, he far outranks Eliot himself, whose labors belong to a preceding age. This apostle of the Indians remained in New England, and preached to its tribes; but the apostle of the Western Indians traversed Massachusetts and Connecticut, New York, Pennsylvania, and Ohio, entered Michigan and Canada, preaching to many nations in many tongues. He brought the Gospel to the Mohicans and Wampanoags, to the Nanticokes and Shawanese, to the Chippewas, Ottawas, and Wyandots, to the Unamis, Unalachtgos, and Monseys of the Delaware race, to the Onondagas, Cayugas, and Senecas of the Six Nations. Speaking the Delaware language fluently, as well as the Mohawk and Onondaga dialects of the Iroquois; familiar with the Cayuga and other tongues; an adopted sachem of the Six Nations; naturalized among the Monseys by a formal act of the tribe; swaying for a number of years the Grand Council of the Delawares; at one time the Keeper of the Archives of the Iroquois Confederacy; versed in the customs of the aborigines; adapting himself to their mode of thought, and, by long habit, a native in many of his own ways;—no Protestant missionary, and but few men of any other calling, ever exercised more real influence and was more sincerely honored, among the Indians; and no one, except the Catholic evangelists, with whom the form of baptism was the end of their work, exceeded him in the frequency and hardships of his journeys through the wilderness, the numbers whom he received into the Church of Christ, and brought to a consistent practice of Christianity, and the conversion of characters most depraved, ferocious, and desperate.

Then, too, the frequent removal of the Mission from place to place, while it hindered the work in some respects, served to spread the Gospel in others. Zeisberger, at the head of the Christian Indians, with the open Bible in his hands, was a messenger of the truth to nations from nearly every section of the West, that, in their turn, often became its herald among their own countrymen. It was thus made known in regions where no missionary ever appeared.[1]

But, perhaps, the most illustrious feature and successful part of his work were the Christian communities which he established. They were the wonder of all who saw them, whether white men or natives; and they seem even to us, who can only read of them, miracles of energy and faith. A hunter and a warrior, the Indian was constrained to give up his wild habits and cruel ways; to quench all the instincts of his savage nature; to change most of the customs of his race; to acknowledge woman as his equal; to perform the labor himself which for generations had been put upon her; to lay aside his plumes, paint, and traditional ornaments of every kind; to assume the dress which white men wore; to plow and plant and reap like any farmer; to rove no longer through the wilderness at pleasure, building lodges here and there, but to remain with his family in one town; and, above all, to submit to municipal enactments, which were of necessity so stringent that nothing could be more galling to the native pride of American aborigines.[2]

---

[1] "By the dispersal and the constant wanderings of the Indian Congregation," writes Mortimer in his *Journal* of October, 1798, "a general knowledge of them has been spread abroad, their faith and character are known and spoken of even beyond the Mississippi River. Many who heard the Gospel through them have witnessed among their own countryman of a Saviour, in life or death."

[2] In an article on Gnadenhütten, published in the *Atlantic Monthly* of January, 1869, the author says: "The success of the good men who effected this change seems like a poet's dream, in view of what we know of Indian life."

Nor must we look upon Zeisberger as a missionary only; he was one of the most notable pioneers of civilization our country has ever known. We find him among the settlers who developed the infant Colony of Georgia. He came to Pennsylvania, and helped to found towns in the Forks of the Delaware, in the Lehigh valley, and in what is now Northumberland County. He continued to labor in the same Province, and built Friedenshütten on the Susquehanna, Lawunakhannek on the Alleghany, and Friendensstadt on the Beaver. He passed into Ohio, laying out Schönbrunn, Gnadenhütten, New Schönbrunn, and Goshen, on the Tuscarawas; Lichtenau on the Muskingum; Pilgerruh on the Cuyahoga; and New Salem on the Huron. He pressed forward even to Michigan, and brought into existence a third Gnadenhütten. He found his way to Upper Canada, erected a Watch-Tower at the mouth of the Detroit, and made Fairfield a center of industry and trade. Thirteen villages sprang up at his bidding, where native agents prepared the way for the husbandman and the mechanic of the coming race.

Zeisberger was a man of small stature, but well proportioned. His face wore the marks of constant exposure and of a hardy life. It was furrowed with deep lines, yet always cheerful and pleasing. His dress was very plain, but scrupulously neat and clean. Except for medicinal purposes, he never used spirituous liquors. His words were few. He had adopted the reticence of the natives among whom he spent his life. In conversation, one of their social ways had become a habit with him. When questioned, especially in later years, regarding any incident of his life, or experience of the Mission, he often observed a profound silence, instead of giving a reply, and allowed the conversation to turn upon other topics. After a time, however, he addressed the querist and delivered an answer somewhat in the way of a speech at an Indian council.

A sketch of his character is best given in the words of two of his fellow-missionaries.

Heckewelder, who was associated with him for many years, when he was yet in the full tide of activity, says:

"He was endowed with a good understanding and a sound judgment; a friend and benefactor to mankind, and justly beloved by all who knew him, with perhaps the exception of those who were enemies of the Gospel which he preached."[1]

"His reticence was the result of the peculiar circumstances of his life. He undertook many solitary journeys, and, in the first half of his life, lived at places where there either was no society, or such as was not congenial. Hence he withdrew within himself, and lived in a close communion with his unseen but ever-present heavenly Friend. In all his views he was very thorough, not impulsive, not suffering himself to be carried away by extraneous influences, not giving an opinion until he had come to a positive and settled conclusion in his own mind. Experience invariably

---

[1] Heckewelder's History of the Indian Mission, 427.

proved the correctness of his judgment. To this the missionaries who served with him all bear witness. Receiving, as it were, a glimpse of the future, through the deep thoughts and silent prayers in which he engaged, he stood up, on most occasions, full of confidence, and knew no fear. Amid distressing and perilous circumstances, not only his fellow-missionaries, but the Indian converts, invariably looked to him; and his courage, his undaunted readiness to act, his comforting words cheered them all."[1]

"He would never consent to have his name put down on a salary-list, or become a 'hireling,' as he termed it; saying, that although a salary might be both agreeable and proper for some missionaries, yet in his case it would be the contrary. He had devoted himself to the service of the Lord among the heathen without any view of a reward, other than such as his Lord and Master might deign to bestow upon him."[2]

To this Mortimer, who was daily about him, in the last nine years of his life, and knew him as a patriarch, adds the following:

"Zeisberger was fully convinced that his vocation to preach the Gospel to the Indians and spread the kingdom of God was of divine origin, and therefore he sacrificed all vanities of the world, all convenience, and whatever is highly esteemed among men, and took up the mission of his life in strong faith, relying upon the blessing and aid of that Lord whom he served, and with

---

[1] Heckewelder's Biographical MS. Sketch.
[2] Heckewelder's History of the Indian Mission, 426.

joyous courage, in the midst of scorn and reproach, persecutions and menaces, hunger and perils, triumphing at last, in spite of every foe. His work was distinguished by perseverance, faithfulness, zeal, and courage. Nothing afforded him more satisfaction than the genuine conversion of those to whom he preached. This was the highest goal of his ambition. If he could gain but one soul, and bring it to a saving knowledge of Christ, it was for him a more precious gift than if he had come into possession of the whole world. To describe the joy he experienced when an erring sheep returned to the fold is impossible. In his ministry he neither forgot that he had to contend with 'the prince of the power of the air, the spirit that worketh in the children of disobedience,' nor that God was on his side. And, truly, he did overcome Satan, in an illustrious way, by the blood of the Lamb, and by the word of his testimony; and loved not his life unto the death.

"He was not only bold in God, fearless and full of courage, but also lowly of heart, meek of spirit, never thinking highly of himself. Selfishness was unknown to him. His heart poured out a stream of love to his fellow-men. In spite of his constant journeys and exposure, he never needlessly sacrificed his health. His whole bearing was extremely venerable. He was an affectionate husband; a faithful and ever-reliable friend. In a word, his character was upright, honest, loving, and noble, as free from faults as can be expected of any man this side of the grave."

The twentieth of November was the day appointed for

the burial of his mortal remains. It was a Sunday, shrouded at dawn in a thick fog, but later, clear, warm, and radiant. From Gnadenhütten came many of its inhabitants, from Beersheba Mueller, and from the vicinity of Goshen a large body of settlers. The corpse, arrayed in the ministerial surplice of the patriarch, was placed in front of the chapel, which was filled with mourning hearers. At eleven o'clock, Mortimer opened the service, delivering, in English, which John Henry interpreted into Delaware, a sermon on the words, "And they overcame him by the blood of the Lamb, and by the word of the testimony; and they loved not their lives unto the death."[1] A brief memoir of Zeisberger's life was then communicated; after which Mueller preached, in German, on the text, "The memory of the just is blessed,"[2] the whole service concluding with a fervent prayer. Then a procession was formed. First walked Mortimer and Mueller; next came the coffin, borne by three Moravians of Gnadenhütten and three Christian Indians of Goshen, and followed by Mrs. Zeisberger, supported by Mrs. Mortimer, and the Indians; the settlers bringing up the rear. On the left of the Hill Road to New Philadelphia, a few rods from the fork, still lies the Goshen burial-ground. There they buried Zeisberger, according to the solemn ritual of the Church of his fathers; and there, under the shade of a small tree, with occasionally a moss-rose blooming on the lowly mound, planted by the

---

[1] Rev. xii. 11.   [2] Prov. x. 7.

pious hand of neighboring residents, his body awaits the resurrection of the just. A marble slab, simple and unostentatious as his life, bears this epitaph:

> DAVID ZEISBERGER,
> *who was born* 11 *April,* 1721,
> *in Moravia, and departed
> this Life* 17 *Nov.* 1808,
> *aged* 87 *Years,* 7 *M. and* 6 *Days.*
> *This faithful Servant of the
> Lord laboured among the
> American Indians as a Mis-
> sionary, during the last*
> 60 *Years of his Life.*

The traveler, descending Goshen Hill, who turns into this way-side cemetery to read its tombstones, and finds Zeisberger's resting-place, stands by the grave of a hero. While the chronicles of America magnify the men who wielded the sword and were great in war, or swayed her councils and earned illustrious names under the dome of her capitol, the church of God enshrines the memory of this humble missionary of the Cross, who, for twelve years more than half a century, used the sword of the Spirit, wrestled against principalities and powers of evil where spiritual wickedness reigned in high places, and fulfilled all the biblical conditions of heroism, watching, standing fast in the faith, quitting himself like a man, being strong. And when national annals shall belong to that past from which shall proceed no more influences, when statesmen and men of war shall be forgotten amid the glory of the saints, he shall be one of those who, having turned many to righteousness, shall shine "as the stars for ever and ever."

CHAPTER XLVII.

THE LITERARY WORKS OF DAVID ZEISBERGER.

His literary activity.—Published works.—Works remaining in manuscript.—Collections in the Library of the American Philosophical Society and the Library of Harvard University.

In the course of our history we have frequently referred to the literary labors of Zeisberger. This chapter is devoted to a more complete account of them, and to a list of his various works.

He did more than any other man of his century to develop both the Delaware language and the Onondaga dialect of the Iroquois. Unfortunately, however, the most important of his works, from a philological point of view, remain in manuscript. These manuscripts have been placed, partly, in the Library of the American Philosophical Society of Philadelphia, and partly in that of Harvard University, at Cambridge, Massachusetts. Those at Philadelphia continue the property of the Moravian Church, having been merely deposited; those at Cambridge have been presented to the University.

We proceed to give, first, a list of Zeisberger's published works.

I. PUBLISHED WORKS OF DAVID ZEISBERGER.

1. *Essay of a Delaware Indian and English Spelling Book, for the use of the Schools of the Christian Indians on Muskingum River.* By David Zeisberger, Missionary among the Western Indians. Philadelphia: Printed by Henry Miller, 1776, pp. 113.

To this work are appended the Lord's Prayer, the Ten Commandments, with Scripture passages illustrating them, and a short Litany, an abbreviation of the Church Litany of the Moravians, all in Delaware and English.

A second edition appeared at Philadelphia in 1806. This omits the Appendix.

The original manuscript of the first edition of this work is preserved in the Bethlehem Archives. Upon comparing it with the printed copy, it is evident that there was cause for the dissatisfaction which Zeisberger expressed with the manner in which the book was brought out. The manuscript does not contain the Appendix described above, but, in place of it, the following articles:

1. A Short History of the Bible, evidently original, in Delaware and English, in parallel columns.

2. Reading Lessons in Delaware, being Biblical and other Narratives.

3. Conjugations of the verbs "to say" and "to tell," in Delaware and English.

4. The Delaware Numerals.

All these articles have been omitted in the printed copy.

2. *A Collection of Hymns, for the use of the Christian Indians, of the Missions of the United Brethren, in North America.* Philadelphia: Printed by Henry Sweitzer, at the corner of Race and Fourth Streets, 1803, pp. 358.

On the reverse of the English title-page stands the Indian:

Mawuni Nachgohumewoaganali enda auwegenk Welsittangik Lenapewinink, untschi Nigasundewoagano enda Nguttimachtangundink, li Lowanewunk Undachqui America.

Then comes a dedication to the Society of the United Brethren for Propagating the Gospel among the Heathen, signed David Zeisberger, and dated Goshen, River Muskingum, September 30, 1802.

The hymns are translated from the German Hymn Book of the Moravian Church, edition of 1778, and from the English Hymn Book, of the same Church, edition of 1801. The Easter Morning Litany is introduced after the Hymns treating of the Resurrection of Christ; the Litanies for the Baptism of Children and of Adults after the Hymns on Holy Baptism; the Church Litany after the "Supplicatory Hymns," as they are called; and the Burial Litanies after the Hymns relating to Death and the Resurrection of the Body. The hymns themselves are arranged nearly in the same order as in the German Hymn Book, and have the first lines, as also the numbers, of their originals, either in the German or English Hymn Book prefixed.

The original manuscript of this work is preserved in the Bethlehem Archives.

A second edition was issued in 1847, printed at Bethlehem, and edited by the Rev. Abraham Luckenbach, in an abridged form. The Litanies precede the Hymns, as in the Moravian Hymn Books at present in use; but those relating to baptism, as also all hymns treating of this sacrament, are omitted.

3. *Sermons to Children.* Translated by David Zeisberger. *Ehelittonhenk li Amemensak Gischitak Elleniechsink.* Untschi David Zeisberger. Philadelphia: Printed by A. and G. Way, 1803, pp. 90.

These sermons are translated into Delaware, and are seventeen in number. The original manuscript is in the Bethlehem Archives.

4. *Aug. Gottl. Spangenberg. Something of Boduy Care for Children.* Translated by David Zeisberger. *Aug. Gottl. Spangenberg Kechitti Koecu Hokeyiwi Latschachtowoagan Untschi Amemensak Li.* Gischitak Elleniechsink Untschi David Zeisberger. Philadelphia: 1803.

This is a Delaware translation of a treatise written by Bishop Spangenberg in German. It forms a part of the preceding volume, the Sermons and this Treatise being bound together, filling, in all, one hundred and fifteen pages. The original manuscript is in the Bethlehem Archives.

5. *The History of our Lord and Saviour Jesus Christ:* comprehending all that the Four Evangelists have recorded concerning Him; all their relations being brought together in one Narration, so that no circumstance is omitted, but that inestimable History is continued in one Series, in the very words of Scripture. By the Rev. Samuel Lieberkühn, M.A. Translated into the Delaware Indian Language by the Rev. David Zeisberger, Missionary of the United Brethren. New York: Printed by Daniel Fanshaw, No. 20 Slote-Lane, 1821, pp. 222.

Elekup Nihillalquonk woak Pemauchsohalquonk Jesus Christ Seki Ta Lauchsitup Wochgidhakamike.

There follows an "Address of the late Rev. David

Zeisberger to the Christian Indians, on his presenting them with his translation of the history of our Lord and Saviour Jesus Christ. The address was prefixed by him to the work, and entitled Preface." It is dated Goshen, on the Muskingum, May 23, 1806.

The original manuscript of this work is in the Bethlehem Archives. A very complete Table of Contents, prepared by Zeisberger, has been omitted in the printed copy.

6. *Verbal Biegungen der Chippewayer,* von **David Zeisberger.** Published in Vater's Analekten der Sprachkunde, Leipzig, 1821.

This work is a collection of Delaware conjugations, and the title ought to read "Delawaren," instead of "Chippewayer," which is a mere inadvertence.

II. MANUSCRIPT WORKS OF DAVID ZEISBERGER.

A. MANUSCRIPTS DEPOSITED IN THE LIBRARY OF THE AMERICAN PHILOSOPHICAL SOCIETY, AT PHILADELPHIA.

1. *Deutsch und Onondagaisches Wörterbuch,* von David Zeisberger, 7 Bände.

(Lexicon of the German and Onondaga Languages, in 7 vols.)

This is one of the most important of his works, which he began early in life, and upon which he bestowed the greatest care and the most persevering diligence, calling in the aid of Iroquois sachems, who rendered him valuable assistance.

2. *Onondaga and German Vocabulary,* by David Zeisberger.

A shorter work of the same character as the above.

3. *Essay toward an Onondaga Grammar, or a Short Introduction to learn the Onondaga, or Maqua tongue,* by David Zeisberger. Quarto.

4. *Onondagaische Grámmatica,* von David Zeisberger.

A complete grammar of the Onondaga language.

This work was translated into English by Peter S. Duponceau, LL.D., a Vice-President of the American Philosophical Society, which version, however, also remains in manuscript.

5. *Onondagaische Grammatica.*

The same work as the preceding (No. 4), but in an incomplete form, appearing to be the author's first attempt.

6. *A Grammar of the Language of the Lenni-Lenape, or Delaware Indians,* translated from the German MS. of the Rev. David Zeisberger, and presented to the American Philosophical Society by Peter S. Duponceau. MS. For the original of this work, see below, No. 5.

B. MANUSCRIPTS PRESERVED IN THE LIBRARY OF HARVARD UNIVERSITY, AT CAMBRIDGE.

We present the titles, in brief, as they were given to us by the Librarian of the University.

1. *A Dictionary in German and Delaware.*
2. *Delaware Glossary.*
3. *Delaware Vocabulary.*
4. *Phrases and Vocabularies in Delaware.*
5. *Delaware Grammar.*
6. *Harmony of the Gospels in Delaware.* This is evidently a duplicate MS. of the work published in 1821.
7. *Hymns for the Christian Indians in Delaware.* This is a duplicate MS. of the Delaware Hymn Book.
8. *Litany and Liturgies in Delaware.*
9. *Zeisberger's own MS. Hymn Book in Delaware.*
10. *Sermons by Zeisberger in Delaware.*
11. *Seventeen Sermons to Children.* This is a duplicate MS. of the printed work.
12. *Church Litany in Delaware.*

13. *Short Biblical Narratives in Delaware.*
14. *Vocabulary in Maqua and Delaware.*

The above fourteen manuscripts, together with some fragmentary papers, procured from the Archives of the Church at Gnadenhütten, Ohio, were delivered to Judge Lane, of that State, by him transmitted to the Hon. Edward Everett, and received at the University Library, January 21, 1850.

The Librarian adds: " The manuscripts were sorted, handsomely bound at Mr. Everett's expense, and placed in a trunk provided and lettered expressly for the purpose, and put in a conspicuous place in the Library, under lock and key, that they may be carefully preserved for posterity, and at the same time often call the attention of visitors to the labors and sacrifices and zeal of as worthy a class of missionaries as have ever gone forth conquering and to conquer the sins of the world, since the days of the Apostles."

CHAPTER XLVIII.

THE INDIAN MISSION FROM THE DEATH OF ZEISBERGER TO THE PRESENT TIME.—1809-1870.

Mrs. Zeisberger leaves the Mission and retires to Bethlehem.—Her death.—Goshen.—Death of William Henry Gelelemend.—The War of 1812.—Its ruinous consequences.—Fairfield destroyed.—Rebuilt in 1815.—Cherokee Mission in Georgia.—The reservation in the Tuscarawas valley given back to the United States.—Goshen abandoned.—Emigration of a part of the Fairfield Indians to the West.—The Cherokees expelled from Georgia.—The stations that remain.

AFTER the death of her husband, Mrs. Zeisberger lingered for ten months in the valley where he had labored. The Indians revered her as a friend whose devotedness to their interests had been tried by many self-denials and constant afflictions, and had never been found wanting. On the fourth of August, 1809, they assembled in the Goshen chapel to bid her farewell. Heckewelder, Mueller, and others from Gnadenhütten were present, and Mortimer rehearsed and commented upon the last messages of her deceased husband to the Indians, beseeching these to consecrate themselves anew to God.

A week later, Mrs. Zeisberger left the Mission and took up her abode at Bethlehem, where she spent the remainder of her life in the "Widows' House." She died on the eighth of September, 1824, aged eighty years, and was buried in what is now the old graveyard, where fifty-six representatives of the race among which she and her husband spent their days are sleeping by her side. She left no children to perpetuate the name of Zeisberger. It has died out in the Church.

In the second year after her departure from Goshen, William Henry Gelelemend finished his earthly course. He was one of the last converts of distinction that had come down from the heroic times of the Mission, and bore an irreproachable character. The vices of the generation which he had lived to see caused him deep sorrow, and he protested, even with his dying breath, against its degeneracy.[1]

The war that began in 1812, between the United States and Great Britain, gave a severe blow to the work of the Church among the aborigines. The station on the west bank of the Sandusky was broken up; and Fairfield, with all its improvements, was destroyed.

The battle of the Thames (October 5, 1813) took place near this town, which was overrun by the victorious Americans, under General Harrison. It was alleged that some of its Indians had been foremost in the massacre on the Raisin; and although the imputation remained without the least proof, the village was plundered and burned to the ground, including the Mission House and the chapel. The converts took to the woods. Of the missionaries, Schnall and Michael Jung, the latter, by this time, an aged man and infirm in health,

---

[1] He was born in 1737, near the Lehigh Water-Gap, in Northampton County, Pa.

proceeded to Bethlehem, while Denke remained to care for the Indians. He succeeded in bringing them from their hiding-places, and, toward the end of the year, they built a village of bark-huts on Lake Ontario. In the following spring this was abandoned, and a new town put up about ten miles from Burlington Heights. After the close of the war, the converts returned to Fairfield, and lived in huts on its site until they had built a permanent settlement, which received the name of New Fairfield, and was situated about a mile and a half from the former village, on the opposite bank of the Thames, but back from the river (1815).

Meantime the Mission among the Cherokees in Georgia flourished. It embraced two stations: the one called Spring Place, on the site of the town of that name in Murray County, the other at Oochgelogy, in Gordon County (1819).

Goshen, on the contrary, declined, and the reservation in the Tuscarawas valley, which had always proved a source of expense and not of revenue to the "Society for Propagating the Gospel," grew at last to be an intolerable burden. Accordingly, after having carried on protracted negotiations with Congress, at Washington, Lewis David de Schweinitz, the representative of the Society, met Lewis Cass, the Commissioner of the United States, at Gnadenhütten, and concluded a treaty with him (August 4, 1823), according to the stipulations of which the Society was divested of its trust of land. On the eighth of November, a second treaty was held with the Christian Indians, at which they ratified the former. The United States promised them, in lieu of the land, an annuity of $400; or, if they preferred removing to some other part of its domains, a new grant of twenty-four thousand acres. On the first of April, 1824, the deed of retrocession was executed.

Goshen was now abandoned, and the little remnant of converts joined the Mission in Canada.

In August, 1837, nearly two-thirds of the Indians emigrated to the Far West. Some of them spent two years near Stockbridge, a Mohican station, on Lake Winnebago, in Wisconsin; the rest settled in Nebraska Territory, now the State of Kansas, on the Kansas River, eight miles from its junction with the Missouri, calling the place Westfield. They were joined by their brethren from Wisconsin, in 1839. Westfield was abandoned in 1853, and a new station begun on the bank of the Missouri, near to what is now Leavenworth City. After the lapse of six years, it was again moved a distance of fifty miles to the southwest, on the Little Osage, where New Westfield arose. This station remains.

The Cherokee Mission in Georgia came to an end in consequence of the troubles which broke out between the settlers and the natives, and their forcible expulsion from that State. In the autumn of 1837, the majority of the converts emigrated to the territory beyond Arkansas. The rest followed in 1838. A new Mission was inaugurated on the Barren Fork of Illinois, a branch of the Arkansas River, about thirty miles west of the State line, and thirty-five miles northeast of Fort Gibson.

In 1840, this Mission was transferred to the neighborhood of Beattie's Prairie, where a station was established which received the name of Canaan. Two years later, a second station, New Spring Place, was begun, and subsequently a third, known as Mt. Zion. The entire Mission among the Cherokees came to a violent end in the Southern Rebellion, a national assistant being murdered by the seceding party, and the other missionaries obliged to flee for their lives (1862). In 1866, New Spring Place was resuscitated.

Thus it appears that the Church, at the present day, has but three missionary stations among the aborigines of our country—the one in Canada West, the second in Kansas, and the third in the Cherokee country. The time may not be far distant when even these will disappear, and nothing remain of the Moravian Mission among the North American Indians, as nothing remains of the work of the Jesuit Fathers, except its wonderful history, to teach future generations zeal for God and faithfulness unto death.

APPENDIX.

A BRIEF SKETCH OF THE MORAVIAN CHURCH.

The Church of the United Brethren, or *Unitas Fratrum*, commonly called the Moravian Church because her first members at the time of her resuscitation came from Moravia, was founded, in 1457, on the barony of Lititz, in Bohemia, by pious followers of the Bohemian reformer and martyr, John Huss. Her original ministers were priests of the Calixtine or National Church. In 1467 she obtained the episcopacy from a Bohemian colony of Waldenses, who had themselves received it from the National Establishment. In spite of frequent persecutions she flourished greatly, and about the time that Martin Luther began the reformation of the sixteenth century, had more than four hundred churches in Bohemia and Moravia, together with a membership of at least two hundred thousand souls, among whom were some of the oldest and noblest families of the land. From this point of view the Brethren properly bear the title of "Reformers before the Reformation." In the course of time they established themselves in Poland also. The three branches of their Church were organically united as one, through the agency of a General Synod; hence the name *Unitas Fratrum*.

In the first quarter of the seventeenth century, Ferdinand of Tyrol began the Anti-reformation in Bohemia and Moravia. The Church of the Brethren, and all other evangelical churches of these two countries, were destroyed. The Polish branch continued for some time longer, but was gradually amalgamated with the Reformed Church. In Moravia, however, many families secretly maintained the faith and practice of their fathers;

while Bishop John Amos Comenius, filled with an almost prophetical anticipation of the renewal of the Church, cared for the preservation of the episcopacy, with which clergymen in the Reformed Church were invested, from time to time, that the succession might not die out.

His hopes were fulfilled in 1722, when an awakening took place among the descendants of the Brethren, through the instrumentality of Christian David, and a number of them fled from Moravia to Saxony, where they found an asylum on the estate of Berthelsdorf, belonging to Count Nicholas Lewis Zinzendorf.

This pious nobleman, born May 26, 1700, at Dresden, eventually resigned a high office which he held at the Saxon court, and devoted himself and his property to the interests of the refugees. They built the town of Herrnhut, introduced the discipline of the Bohemian Brethren, and, in 1735, received the episcopacy, from Bishops Jablonsky and Sitkovius, the two survivors of the ancient line. Thus the Church was renewed, and soon spread on the Continent of Europe, to Great Britain, and to North America. Her first bishop was David Nitschmann and her second Count Zinzendorf.

During the lifetime of the latter he was her virtual head. After his death (May 9, 1760), a system of government was introduced, which still exists in a modified form.

The present *Unitas Fratrum* embraces three ecclesiastical provinces—the Continental, the British, and the American. Each province is independent in all provincial matters, and governed by a Provincial Synod, which elects an Executive Board, called the "Provincial Elders' Conference;" but all the provinces are united in matters of doctrine, ritual, and discipline, and carry on the work of Foreign Missions as one church. Hence there is a General Synod, which meets every ten years, and consists of an equal number of delegates from the Continent of Europe, Great Britain, and the United States. This Synod elects an Executive Board, known as the "Unity's Elders' Conference," to which is committed the general oversight of the Unitas Fratrum and the control of the various foreign missions. It has its seat in the castle of Count Zinzendorf, at Berthelsdorf, about one mile from Herrnhut, in Saxony.

The work of foreign missions is the principal field of labor in which the Church engages. This field embraces Greenland, Labrador, parts of the Indian country of North America, the Mosquito Coast, the islands of St. Thomas, St. John, St. Croix, Jamaica, Antigua, St. Kitts, Barbadoes and Tobago, Surinam, South Africa, Australia, and Thibet. There are eighty-seven regular stations; three hundred and seven preaching places; three hundred and thirteen laborers from Europe and America, including one hundred and fifty-two female assistants; one thousand and fifteen native assistants; eight normal schools; two hundred and thirty other schools; and seventy thousand three hundred and eleven converts.

For further information in regard to the Church, consult "The Moravian Manual," second edition, Bethlehem, 1869.

GEOGRAPHICAL GLOSSARY.

This Glossary contains the names of those Indian towns, early settlements, forts, rivers, and creeks which occur in the "Life and Times of David Zeisberger," with the exception of such as are well known and can readily be found on any map of the United States.

A.

ADAMSTOWN.—An early settlement in Lancaster County, Pennsylvania, twenty miles north of the City of Lancaster.

ALLEMAENGEL.—Lynn Township, in Lehigh County, and Albany Township, in Berks County, Pennsylvania. The name signifies *general destitution*.

ANAJOT.—An Iroquois town, in the Tuscarora country, on the main trail from Albany to Onondaga.

AQUANSHICOLA.—A creek flowing through the first valley north of the Blue Mountains, in Pennsylvania, and emptying into the Lehigh at the Gap.

ASSINNISSINK.—A Monsey town in Steuben County, New York, near the confluence of the Tioga and the Conhocton. The residence of Jacheabus, the leader of the war party that committed the massacre on the Mahony, in 1755.

ASSÜNÜNK.—A town of the Turkey Tribe of Delawares, in the Revolutionary War, on the Hockhocking, in Ohio.

B.

BEERSHEBA.—Formerly a Moravian church, in Clay Township, Tuscarawas County, Ohio, on the west side of the Tuscarawas River. It stood on the farm of Benedict Gross.

BETHLEHEM.—A borough in Bethlehem Township, Northampton County, Pennsylvania, twelve miles southwest of Easton. It was formerly a Moravian town, where none but Moravians were permitted to own real estate, and it is still their chief seat in the United States. The exclusive polity was relinquished in 1843.

GEOGRAPHICAL GLOSSARY.

BLACK RIVER.—A river flowing through Lorain County, Ohio, into Lake Erie.

BRISTOL.—A borough in Bucks County, Pennsylvania, on the Delaware River, nineteen miles above Philadelphia, and one of the earliest settlements in the State. Founded in 1697.

BROKEN SWORD CREEK.—A creek in Ohio flowing into the Sandusky River, in Wyandot County.

BUCHCABUCHKA CREEK.—The same as the Pocopoco or Big Creek, in Carbon County, Pennsylvania, emptying into the Lehigh River at Parryville.

BUFFALO.—See *Charlestown.*

BUFFALO CREEK.—A creek flowing through the "Panhandle" of Virginia, and emptying into the Ohio River, at Wellsburg.

C.

CATSKILL CREEK.—A creek in Greene County, New York, flowing into the Hudson, at Catskill.

CAPTINA CREEK.—A creek in Belmont County, Ohio, flowing into the Ohio River.

CAMP UNION.—Lewisburg, Greenbrier County, Virginia.

CAHOKIA.—A French, and later a British village and post on the east bank of the Mississippi, in St. Clair County, Illinois.

CAYAHAGA.—The Cuyahoga River of Ohio, flowing into Lake Erie, at Cleveland.

CANAJOHARIE.—An Iroquois town of the Mohawk nation, on the right bank of the Mohawk, in Montgomery County, New York, on the site of the present town of the same name.

CAYUGA.—An Iroquois town, the capital of the Cayuga nation, on the site of the present village of the same name, on the eastern shore of Lake Cayuga, in Cayuga County, New York.

CANAL DOVER.—A town in Tuscarawas County, Ohio, on the west bank of the Tuscarawas River.

CAMP CHARLOTTE.—The spot where Lord Dunmore concluded peace with the Shawanese and Mingoes, in 1774, on the left bank of Sippo Creek, seven miles southeast of Circleville, in Pickaway County, Ohio.

CAPTIVES' TOWN.—The name given, in the "Life and Times of David Zeisberger," to the village built by the Christian Indians, in 1781, on the Sandusky River, about eleven miles below Upper Sandusky, in Antrim Township, Wyandot County, Ohio.

CHRISTIANSBRUNN.—Formerly a Moravian farm and small settlement, with a chapel, two miles from Nazareth, on the road to Bath, in Northampton County, Pennsylvania.

GEOGRAPHICAL GLOSSARY. 703

CHARLESTOWN.—Now Wellsburg, at the confluence of Buffalo Creek and the Ohio River, in Brooke County, Virginia. This settlement was also called Buffalo.

CHOANSCHICANUENK.—An Indian name for Virginia.

CHELOKRATY.—A Shawanese town at the heads of the Scioto, in Ohio, in 1772.

CHAWANO.—One of the lower Shawanese towns of the Muskingum valley, Ohio, in 1772.

CHILLICOTHE.—See *Old Chillicothe*.

CLISTONWACKIN.—An Indian village on the Delaware River, fifteen miles south of the Gap.

COLUMBIA.—One of the first settlements on the Miami Tract, in Hamilton County, Ohio, five miles from Cincinnati.

COLUMBIA.—A borough in Lancaster County, Pennsylvania, on the left bank of the Susquehanna.

ÇOWANESQUE CREEK.—A creek of Pennsylvania, rising in Potter County and flowing into the Tioga River, in Steuben County, New York.

COUDERSPORT.—The capital of Potter County, Pennsylvania, on the Alleghany River.

CONHOCTON.—A river of New York, rising in Steuben County and uniting with the Tioga to form the Chemung.

COSHOCTON.—The capital of Coshocton County, Ohio, on the left bank of the Muskingum, just below the junction of the Tuscarawas and Walhonding.

CROWN, THE.—A tavern belonging to the Moravians, and opened in 1745, on the south side of the Lehigh, opposite Bethlehem, Pennsylvania. The building stood near the Depot of the Lehigh Valley and North Pennsylvania Railroads.

D.

DAMASCUS.—Name of the lower town of *Goschgoschünk*, which see.

DANSBURY.—Stroudsburg, Monroe County, Pennsylvania.

E.

EASTON.—The capital of Northampton County, Pennsylvania, at the junction of the Lehigh with the Delaware River.

EPHRATA.—The seat of the Seventh-Day Baptists, in Ephrata Township, Lancaster County, Pennsylvania, thirteen miles northeast of Lancaster City.

ESOPUS.—Now Kingston, the capital of Ulster County, New York.

F.

Fairfield.—A Christian Indian town on the right bank of the River Thames, in the Township of Oxford, Canada West.

Falckner Schwamm.—Falckner Swamp, so named after Daniel Falckner, who settled there about 1700. It included the Townships of Hanover and Frederick, in Montgomery County, Pennsylvania.

Falls of the Ohio.—Louisville, Kentucky.

Fort Adams.—On the St. Mary's River, Ohio, between Fort Defiance and Fort Recovery.

Fort Allen.—On the site of Weissport, Carbon County, Pennsylvania.

Fort Bedford.—On the site of Bedford, the capital of Bedford County, Pennsylvania.

Fort Brewerton.—At the west end of Lake Oneida, in New York.

Fort Bull.—On the site of Rome, Oneida County, New York. See *Fort Stanwix*.

Fort Chartres.—On the Mississippi, in Illinois, above Kaskaskia.

Fort Crown Point.—On the site of Crown Point, on the western shore of Lake Champlain, in Essex County, New York.

Fort Cumberland.—On the site of Cumberland, on the left bank of the Potomac, in Maryland.

Fort Defiance.—At the junction of the Auglaize and Maumee Rivers, in Defiance County, Ohio.

Fort Detroit.—On the site of the City of Detroit, in Michigan.

Fort Duquesne.—On the site of the City of Pittsburg, in Pennsylvania.

Fort Fincastle.—On the site of Wheeling, Virginia.

Fort Finney.—On the left bank of the Miami River, at its junction with the Ohio, in the southwestern extremity of the State of Ohio. A post established for the treaty held there in 1786.

Fort Frontenac.—On the site of Kingston, in Canada.

Fort Hamilton.—On the site of Hamilton, Butler County, Ohio, on the Miami, twenty-five miles from Cincinnati.

Fort Harmar.—On the right bank of the Muskingum, at its junction with the Ohio.

Fort Henry.—The same as Fort Fincastle. It received the name of Fort Henry in 1776.

Fort Jefferson.—In Jefferson Township, Preble County, Ohio, near the line between Ohio and Indiana, forty-five miles from Fort Hamilton.

Fort La Baye.—On the site of Greenbay, Wisconsin.

Fort Laurens.—On the right bank of the Tuscarawas, a little below Sandy Creek, in Lawrence Township, Tuscarawas County, Ohio.

GEOGRAPHICAL GLOSSARY. 705

FORT LE BŒUF.—On French Creek, in Erie County, Pennsylvania, about fourteen miles south of Erie.

FORT LIGONIER.—On the road from Bedford to Pittsburg, in Pennsylvania, a few miles west of the Laurel Hill Mountains.

FORT MCINTOSH.—On the site of Beaver, at the mouth of the Beaver River, in Beaver County, Pennsylvania.

FORT MIAMI.—On the Maumee River, near Fort Wayne, Indiana.

FORT MICHILLIMACKINAC.—On the south side of the Straits of Mackinaw, between Lakes Michigan and Huron.

FORT NIAGARA.—On the right bank of the Niagara River, at its entrance into Lake Ontario.

FORT OSWEGO.—On the site of Oswego, on Lake Ontario.

FORT OUATANON.—A short distance below Lafayette, in Indiana.

FORT PITT.—On the site of the City of Pittsburg, in Pennsylvania.

FORT POINT PLEASANT.—At the mouth of the Kanawha River, in Mason County, Virginia.

FORT PRESQUE ISLE.—On the site of the City of Erie, Pennsylvania.

FORT RECOVERY.—In Recovery Township, Mercer County, Ohio, on St. Clair's battle-field.

FORT SANDUSKY.—Near the site of Sandusky City, Ohio, on Sandusky Bay.

FORT STANWIX.—On the site of Rome, Oneida County, New York. This fort and Fort Bull formed one post.

FORT ST. JOSEPHS.—On Lake Michigan, at the mouth of the St. Joseph's River, in Berrien County, Michigan.

FORT VENANGO.—At junction of French Creek with the Alleghany River, in Venango County, Pennsylvania, on the site of Franklin.

FORT VINCENNES.—On the site of Vincennes, on the left bank of the Wabash, in Knox County, Indiana.

FORT WASHINGTON.—Cincinnati, Ohio.

FORT WAYNE.—On the site of Fort Wayne, at the confluence of the St. Joseph's and St. Mary's Rivers, in Allen County, Indiana.

FORT WILLIAM HENRY.—At the southern extremity of Lake George, New York.

FRANKFORD.—An early settlement in Philadelphia County, Pennsylvania, now a part of the City of Philadelphia.

FREEHOLD.—An early settlement in Greene County, New York, on Catskill Creek.

FRIEDENSSTADT.—"City of Peace" (*Languntoutenünk*). A Christian Indian town, first on the east then on the west bank of the Beaver River, between the Shenango River and Slippery Rock Creek, in Lawrence County, Pennsylvania.

FRIEDENSHÜTTEN (*The first*).—"Tents of Peace." A Christian Indian town near Bethlehem, Pennsylvania, at the foot of the ridge crowned with the Gas-Works and on the slope of the hill above the Skating-Park.

FRIEDENSHÜTTEN (*The second*) —"Tents of Peace." A Christian Indian town, on the east side of the Susquehanna River, opposite Sugar Run, two miles below Wyalusing, and one and a half miles above Browntown P. O., on the farm of the Hon. Levi P. Stalford, in Bradford County, Pennsylvania.

G.

GANATARAGE.—An Iroquois town of the Cayuga country.
GANIATARAGECHIAT.—Lake Cayuga, in New York.
GANATISGOA.—An Iroquois town of the Tuscarora country.
GANOCHSERAGE.—An Iroquois town of the Tuscarora country.
GANUTARAGE.—An Iroquois town, of the Cayuga country, on Lake Cayuga.
GANATAQUEH.—An Iroquois town of the Seneca country.
GANATOCHERAT.—An Iroquois town of the Cayuga country, on the Chemung River, near the New York line.
GERMANTOWN.—An early settlement in Philadelphia, County, Pennsylvania, now a part of the City of Philadelphia.
GEKELEMUKPECHÜNK.—The first capital of the Delaware nation in Ohio, on the north bank of the Tuscarawas River, in Oxford Township, Tuscarawas County. It occupied the outlots of Newcomerstown.
GIGEYUNK.—Fort Wayne, Indiana.
GNADENHÜTTEN (*The first*).—"Tents of Grace." A Christian Indian town on the Mahony Creek, near its junction with the Lehigh, in Carbon County, Pennsylvania. It occupied the slope of the hill crowned with the burial-ground of Lehighton.
GNADENHÜTTEN (*The second*).—A Christian Indian town on the east bank of the Lehigh River, in Carbon County, Pennsylvania, occupying the site of Weissport.
GNADENHÜTTEN (*The third*).—A Moravian settlement of white persons on the same site as *Gnadenhütten the second*. This settlement grew into the town of Weissport.
GNADENHÜTTEN (*The fourth*).—A Christian Indian town on the Tuscarawas River, in Clay Township, Tuscarawas County, Ohio, lying in the outskirts of the present Gnadenhütten.
GNADENHÜTTEN (*The fifth*).—A Moravian village on the Tuscarawas River, in Clay Township, Tuscarawas County, Ohio, founded after the return of a part of the Christian Indians from Canada to the reservation granted by the Congress of the United States.

GNADENTHAL.—Formerly a Moravian settlement near Nazareth, in Northampton County, Pennsylvania; now the County Poor House.

GOKHOSING.—"Habitation of Owls." Owl Creek, now the Vernon River, flowing through Knox County, Ohio, and emptying into the Walhonding.

GOSCHGOSCHÜNK.—A Monsey Indian town on the east bank of the Alleghany, not far from the mouth of Tionesta Creek, in Venango County, Pennsylvania, and the place where Zeisberger established a Mission after the Pontiac War.

GOSCHACHGÜNK.—The second capital of the Delaware nation in Ohio, built on the site of Coshocton, on the left bank of the Muskingum, just below the junction of the Tuscarawas and Walhonding, in Coshocton County.

GOSHEN.—An early settlement in Orange County, New York.

GOSHEN.—The last Christian Indian town founded by Zeisberger, on the west bank of the Tuscarawas River, in Goshen Township, Tuscarawas County, Ohio, seven miles northeast of Gnadenhütten. It was situated on what is now the farm of Jacob Keller.

GREENVILLE.—General Wayne's fortified camp in 1793, on the site of Greenville, the capital of Darke County, Ohio.

GREAT MEADOWS.—Ten miles east of Uniontown, Fayette County Pennsylvania, on the Youghiogheny.

GREAT ISLAND.—Lock Haven, on the right bank of the West Branch of the Susquehanna, in Clinton County, Pennsylvania.

GREAT SWAMP.—Called also the *Pine Swamp*, or *Shades of Death*, on the plateau of the Broad Mountain, in Monroe and Carbon Counties, Pennsylvania.

GREENBRIER COUNTRY.—Lewisburg, Greenbrier County, Virginia.

H.

HACHNIAGE.—An Iroquois town of the Seneca country.

HAARLEM.—An early settlement of New York, now a suburb of the City of New York.

HARRIS'S FERRY.—Harrisburg, the capital of Pennsylvania.

HEIDELBERG.—Formerly a Moravian log church, in North Heidelberg Township, Berks County, Pennsylvania.

HEBRON.—Formerly a Moravian stone church and parsonage, in the outskirts of Lebanon, Lebanon County, Pennsylvania. The building was used as a military prison for the Hessians in the Revolutionary War.

HOPE.—Formerly a Moravian town, in Sussex County, New Jersey.

HOCKHOCKING RIVER.—A river of Ohio, rising in the southeastern central part of the State and flowing into the Ohio River, twenty-five miles below Marietta.

HURON RIVER.—Now the Clinton River, flowing through Macomb County, Michigan, into Lake St. Clair.

I.

INDAOCHAIE.—The name given by the Delawares to Lichtenau (*which see*), after the exodus of the Christian Indians.

IRISH SETTLEMENT.—An early settlement of Scotch-Irish below Bath, in Northampton County, Pennsylvania.

J.

JOHNSTOWN.—The seat of Sir William Johnson, in the Mohawk country, in Fulton County, New York. Called also *Kolaneka*.

K.

KASKASKUNK.—A Monsey Indian town originally at the junction of the Shenango and Mahoning Rivers, in Lawrence County, Pennsylvania; afterward removed to the site of New Castle, the capital of Lawrence County. It was the residence of Packanke, chief of the Wolf Tribe.

KASKASKIA.—On the right or west bank of the Kaskaskia River, two miles east of the Mississippi River, in Randolph County, Illinois.

KISCHKUBI.—A Shawanese town, at the heads of the Scioto, in Ohio.

KITTANNING.—An Indian town on the Alleghany, about twenty miles above Fort Duquesne.

KOLANEKA.—See *Johnstown*.

KUEQUENEKU.—An Indian name for Philadelphia.

L.

LAWUNAKHANNEK.—A temporary Christian Indian town, three miles above Goschgoschünk (*which see*), on the east bank of the Alleghany River, in Venango County, Pennsylvania.

LANGUNTOUTENÜNK.—See *Friedensstadt*.

LAAPHAWACHTINK.—An Indian name for New York.

LACKAWAXEN CREEK.—Also called *Lechawacksein*, rises in the northern part of Pennsylvania, in Wayne County, and enters the Delaware in Pike County.

LACKAWANNOCK CREEK.—Rises in the northeastern part of Pennsylvania, and falls into the North Branch of the Susquehanna River, about ten miles above Wilkesbarre.

LECHAUWEEK.—The Lehigh River, in Pennsylvania.

LECHAUWITONK.—Easton, Pennsylvania.

GEOGRAPHICAL GLOSSARY.

LEHIGH RIVER.—A river of Pennsylvania rising in the pine swamps of Luzerne, Pike, and Monroe Counties, flowing through the coal region of Carbon County, and emptying into the Delaware at Easton.

LEHIGH HILLS.—A ridge bounding, on the south, the lower part of the Lehigh valley, in Northampton County, Pennsylvania.

LENAPEWIHITTUCK.—The River Delaware.

LEHIETAN.—The Bushkill Creek near Nazareth, Pennsylvania, emptying into the Delaware at Easton.

LICHTENAU.—A Christian Indian town, on the east bank of the Muskingum, two and a half miles below Coshocton, on the farms of Samuel Moore and Samuel Forker, in Tuscarawas Township, Coshocton County, Ohio.

LITIZ.—Formerly an exclusively Moravian town, in Warwick Township, Lancaster County, Pennsylvania, eight miles from the City of Lancaster. The exclusive system was abrogated in 1855.

LONG ISLAND.—Jersey Shore, a borough of Lycoming County, Pennsylvania, on the West Branch of the Susquehanna River.

LOGSTOWN.—A French and Indian village, fourteen miles below Pittsburg, on the right bank of the Ohio.

LOUISBURG.—Formerly a strong fortress and sea-port of the French, on the southeastern shore of Cape Breton.

LOWER SANDUSKY.—A trading post and Wyandot village, the present Fremont, capital of Sandusky County, Ohio.

M.

MAGUNTSCHE.—Emmaus, Lehigh County, Pennsylvania. It was originally a Moravian town; now it is an incorporated borough.

MACHIWIHILUSING.—An Indian town in Bradford County, Pennsylvania, on or near the site of *Friedenshütten the second*, which see.

MARIETTA.—The first town of white settlers in Ohio, on the left bank of the Muskingum River, at its confluence with the Ohio, the capital of Washington County.

MENAGACHSUENK.—An Indian name for Bethlehem, Pennsylvania.

MENIOLAGOMEKAK.—An Indian town and afterward a Mission station in Smith's valley, eight miles west of the Wind Gap, on the north bank of the Aquanshicola, in Eldred Township, Monroe County, Pennsylvania.

MICHENSCHAY.—A Shawanese town, at the heads of the Scioto, in Ohio (1772).

MINGO BOTTOM.—Called also *Mingo Village*, on the west bank of the Ohio River, seventy-five miles below Pittsburg.

MINNISINKS.—Flats above the Delaware Water-Gap, on both shores.

GEOGRAPHICAL GLOSSARY.

MONOCASY.—A creek of Northampton County, Pennsylvania, emptying into the Lehigh River, at Bethlehem.

MONSEY-ANDERSON.—A Delaware Indian town on the White River, Indiana, in 1800.

MUSCONETCONG HILLS.—Bounding the valley through which the Musconetcong River flows, in Warren and Morris Counties, New Jersey.

N.

NAIN.—A Christian Indian town in Hanover Township, Lehigh County, Pennsylvania, on the "Geisinger Farm."

NAZARETH.—Formerly an exclusive Moravian town, now a borough of Northampton County, Pennsylvania, seven miles northwest of Easton. The exclusive system was abrogated in 1850.

NESKAPEKE.—Nescopec, Luzerne County, Pennsylvania.

NEW FAIRFIELD.—A Moravian Indian Mission in the Township of Oxford, Canada West. This Mission still exists.

NEW GNADENHÜTTEN.—A Christian Indian town on the south side of the Clinton River, between Mt. Clemens and Frederick, in Clinton Township, Macomb County, Michigan.

NEW PALTZ.—An early settlement in Ulster County, New York.

NEW PHILADELPHIA.—The capital of Tuscarawas County, Ohio.

NEW SALEM.—A Christian Indian town on the Huron River, in Erie County, Ohio, near or on the site of Milan.

NEW SCHÖNBRUNN.—A Christian Indian town on the west bank of the Tuscarawas River, one and a quarter miles south of New Philadelphia, on the farm of John Gray, in Goshen Township, Tuscarawas County, Ohio.

NEW SPRING PLACE.—A Moravian Mission station among the Cherokees, in the Cherokee country. This Mission still exists.

NEW WESTFIELD.—A Moravian Mission station on the Little Osage, in Kansas.

O.

OLEY.—Formerly a Moravian church in Berks County, Pennsylvania.

OLD CHILLICOTHE.—Pickaway Township, on the Scioto, in Pickaway County, Ohio.

ONENGE.—French Creek, or Venango River, in Pennsylvania, flowing into the Alleghany at Franklin, in Venango County.

ONONDAGA.—The capital of the Iroquois Confederacy, a few miles southeast of Lake Onondaga, on Onondaga Creek, in Onondaga County, New York.

OSTONWACKEN.—An Indian town, the seat of Madame Montour, on the site of Montoursville, on the West Branch of the Susquehanna, in Lycoming County, Pennsylvania.

ONDACHOE.—An Iroquois town of the Cayuga country, on Lake Cayuga, New York.

OWEGO —An old Iroquois village in Tioga County, New York.

OWL CREEK. — The Vernon River, flowing through Knox County, Ohio, and entering the Walhonding in Coshocton County. See *Gokhosing*.

P.

PACHGATGOCH.—An Indian town and Mission station, two miles southwest of Kent, in Connecticut.

PARRADERUSKI.—A British town on the Mississippi, fifteen miles above Kaskaskia, *which see*.

PENN'S CREEK.—A creek in the central part of Pennsylvania, flowing into the Susquehanna a few miles below Sunbury.

PETTQUOTTING CREEK.—The Huron River of Ohio, flowing through Huron and Erie Counties into Lake Erie, at Huron village.

PICHUWAY.—A Shawanese town at the heads of the Scioto, in Ohio, in 1772.

PILGERRUH.—" Pilgrims' Rest." A Christian Indian town on the east bank of the Cuyahoga River, in Independence Township, Cuyahoga County, Ohio.

PIPE'S TOWN.—An Indian village in Ohio, about ten miles from Captives' Town, *which see*.

PICKAWAY.—Now Pickaway Township, on the Scioto, at the southern end of Pickaway County, Ohio.

PLUGGY'S TOWN.—The seat of a mongrel band of Indians, in 1777, on the head-waters of the Scioto, in Ohio.

POINT HURON.—Now Point Clinton, a promontory in Lake St. Clair, Michigan.

POTATIK.—An Indian village and Mission station three miles northeast of Newton, in Connecticut.

PURYSBURG.—An early German settlement in Beaufort County, South Carolina, twenty miles from Savannah, between Savannah and Port Royal Harbor.

Q.

QUEKELININK.—An Indian name for Pennsylvania.

R.

REAMSTOWN.—An early settlement in Lancaster County, Pennsylvania.

RETRENCHE.—The River Thames, in Canada, flowing into Lake St. Clair.

RED STONE CREEK.—A creek of Fayette County, Pennsylvania, falling into the Monongahela River near Brownsville.

ROCHESTER.—An early settlement in Ulster County, New York.

Rocky Point.—A promontory now known as Scott's Point, or Ottawa City, in Ottawa County, Ohio.

Rouge River.—A river of Michigan, rising in Oakland and Washtenaw Counties, and flowing into the Detroit River, five miles from the City of Detroit.

Rose, The.—A tavern belonging to the Moravians, built in 1752, one mile north of Nazareth, Pennsylvania.

S.

Säge Schwamm.—New Holland, Lancaster County, Pennsylvania.

Saratoga.—An old tract of land on the Hudson River, in New York, now a county of this name.

Sannio.—An Iroquois town of the Cayuga country, on Lake Cayuga, New York.

Sakunk.—An old abandoned Indian town (1770), at the confluence of the Beaver River with the Ohio, in Beaver County, Pennsylvania.

Salem.—Formerly an exclusive Moravian town, now a borough, in Forsyth County, North Carolina. The exclusive system was abrogated in 1856.

Salem.—A Christian Indian town on the western bank of the Tuscarawas River, one and a half miles southwest of Port Washington, on the farm of Henry Stocker, in Salem Township, Tuscarawas County, Ohio.

Sarah-Town.—A Delaware village on the White River, in Indiana, in 1800.

Schenectady.—An old settlement in New York, now the capital of Schenectady County.

Schaghticoke.—A township of Rensselaer County, New York.

Schönbrunn.—*Welhik-Tuppeek* (Beautiful Spring). A Christian Indian town two miles southeast of New Philadelphia, on the east bank of the Tuscarawas, in Goshen Township, Tuscarawas County, Ohio, on the farm of Rev. E. P. Jacobs.

Schechschiquanunk —A Monsey town and Mission station on the west bank of the Susquehanna, opposite but a little below Shesequin, in Bradford County, Pennsylvania.

Schoharie Creek.—A creek of New York, flowing into the Mohawk, in Montgomery County.

Schoeneck.—A Moravian village near Nazareth, in Northampton County, Pennsylvania.

Sganatees.—An Iroquois town of the Tuscarora country, in New York.

Shamokin.—An Indian town on the site of Sunbury, in Northumberland County, Pennsylvania.

Shekomeko.—A Christian Indian town, in Pine Plains, Dutchess County, New York, on the farm of Edward Hunting, twenty miles southeast of Rhinebeck.

SICHEM.—Formerly a Moravian Home Mission station, in the so-called "Oblong," bordering on New York and Connecticut. The Mission House was on the farm of Douglass Clark, in Dutchess County, New York, quite near to the Connecticut line.

SKIPPAC.—An early settlement in Skippack Township, Montgomery County, Pennsylvania.

SKEHANTOWANNO.—Plains in the valley of Wyoming, Pennsylvania.

SKOGARI.—A village of Tutelees in Columbia County, Pennsylvania. It was the only village of this tribe remaining in 1748.

SOPUS.—See *Esopus*.

ST. PHILIPPS.—A British town on the Mississippi, nine miles above Parraderuski.

STOCKERTOWN.—A village of Northampton County, Pennsylvania, a few miles from Nazareth.

STONY POINT.—A promontory of Monroe County, Michigan, in Lake Erie.

STINTON'S FARM.—Or *Stinton's Tavern*, where Captain Wetterhold's party was attacked by the Indians, in the Pontiac War, one mile and a quarter northwest of Howertown, in East Allen Township, Northampton County, Pennsylvania. It is now Simon Laubach's place.

T.

TAGOCHSANAGECHTI.—The name of the lower village of Onondaga, which see.

TAPPAN.—Orange Town, in Orange County, New York.

TAWANDAEMENK.—A Monsey village, ten miles from Tioga, in Bradford County, Pennsylvania.

TADEUSKUND'S TOWN.—The village of Tadeuskund, the "King of the Delawares," a little below Wilkesbarre, in the Wyoming valley, Pennsylvania.

TGAAJU.—An Iroquois village of the Cayuga country, in New York.

THÜRNSTEIN, THE.—The name given by Conrad Weisser to the Second, Third, and Peter's Mountains of Pennsylvania, in honor of Count Zinzendorf.

TIOCHRUNGWE.—An Iroquois town of the Tuscarora country, in New York.

TIADAGHTON.—Also called *Diadaghton*, the Pine Creek, rising in the northern part of Pennsylvania, and entering the West Branch of the Susquehanna, near Jersey Shore.

TIOGA.—Also called *Tioga Point*, on the North Branch of the Susquehanna, in Bradford County, Pennsylvania.

TIONESTA CREEK.—A creek of Pennsylvania, rising in the northwestern part of the State and flowing into the Alleghany River, in Venango County.

GEOGRAPHICAL GLOSSARY.

Tiozionossongochto.—An Iroquois town of the Seneca country, in Alleghany County, New York.

Tobyhanna Creek.—A Creek of Monroe County, Pennsylvania, flowing into the Lehigh River.

Towamensing.—The wilderness north of the Blue Mountains, in Monroe County, Pennsylvania.

Trapp, The.—An early settlement in Upper Providence Township, Montgomery County, Pennsylvania.

Tulpehocken.—A township of Berks County, Pennsylvania.

Tuscarawas.—An old, abandoned Indian town, on the west bank of the Tuscarawas River, opposite the crossing-place of the trail from Pittsburg, on the line of Stark and Tuscarawas Counties, Ohio.

Tuscarawas River —A river of Ohio, rising in the northeastern part of the State, flowing through the Tuscarawas valley, and uniting with the Walhonding, at Coshocton, to form the Muskingum.

U.

Upland.—Old Chester, the seat of justice of the original Chester County, Pennsylvania.

Upper Sandusky.—The Huron Half King's town, now the capital of Wyandot County, Ohio.

Upper Sandusky Old Town.—A Wyandot village, twelve miles below Upper Sandusky, on the Sandusky River.

V.

Vernon River.—See *Owl Creek*.

W.

Wamphallobank. —A Delaware Indian town in Luzerne County, Pennsylvania, on the Susquehanna.

Waketameki.—A Shawanese town, near Dresden, on the Muskingum River, just below the mouth of Waketameki Creek, in Jefferson Township, Muskingum County, Ohio.

Walhonding River.—A river of Ohio, called also the *Mohican* and *White Woman River*, uniting with the Tuscarawas, at Coshocton, to form the Muskingum.

Warte, Die.—"The Watch-Tower." A temporary Indian Mission station (1791, 1792) at the mouth of the Detroit River, on the Canada side, at or near Amherstburg.

Wechquetank.—A Christian Indian town, in Polk Township, Monroe County, Pennsylvania, between the Wechquetank and Head's Creeks.

Wechpakak.—A Delaware Indian town on the Tunkhannock, in Bradford County, Pennsylvania.

WECHQUADNACH.—An Indian village and Mission station on Indian Pond, on the boundary of Dutchess County, New York, and Connecticut.
WELHIK-TUPPEEK.—See *Schönbrunn*.
WELAGAMIKA.—An Indian name for Nazareth, *which see*.
WESTCHESTER.—An early settlement in Westchester County, New York.
WESTENHUC.—An Indian village and Mission station in Massachusetts, on the site of Housatonic.
WHETAK.—An Indian village and Mission station, near Salisbury, Connecticut.
WHITE RIVER.—A river of Indiana, falling into the Wabash, nearly opposite Mount Carmel, Illinois.
WHITE EYES' TOWN.—An Indian village in Ohio, the seat of White Eyes, near White Eyes' Plains, Oxford Township, Coshocton County.
WHEELING CREEK.—A creek rising in Pennsylvania, and falling into the Ohio River, at Wheeling, Virginia.
WILLIAM'S FORT.—An Indian village and British post in the Mohawk country, New York, between Freehold and Canajoharie.
WILAWANE.—A Monsey Indian town in Bradford County, Pennsylvania, near the junction of the Chemung and the Susquehanna.
WILLIAMSBURG.—In Colonial times the seat of government of Virginia, now the capital of James City County.
WOMMELSDORF.—A town on the Lebanon Valley Railroad, in Berks County, Pennsylvania.
WOAPIKANNIKUNK.—A Delaware Indian town on the White River, Indiana, in 1800.
WOOD CREEK.—A Creek of Oneida County, New York, emptying into the east end of Oneida Lake.
WRIGETSVILLE.—A town on the Susquehanna, in Pennsylvania, opposite Columbia.
WYALUSING CREEK.—A creek of Pennsylvania flowing into the North Branch of the Susquehanna River, in Bradford County.

Y.

YOUGHIOGHENY RIVER.—A river rising in Virginia, flowing through Maryland into Pennsylvania, and entering the Monongahela eighteen miles southeast of Pittsburg.

Z.

ZENIINGE.—An Iroquois town of the Tuscarora country, in New York.
ZINOCHSAA.—The Onondaga Creek of New York.
ZONNESSCHIO.—The capital of the Seneca country in New York, probably near or on the site of Geneseo, the capital of Livingston County, New York.

INDEX.

A.

Abenakis, an Indian tribe, 36; Jesuit Mission among them, 101.
Abraham, first Moravian Indian convert, 107; entices some converts from Gnadenhütten, 213, 214; at the treaty of Easton in 1757, 249; death, 260.
Abraham, the Mohican, a convert, 548; his confession at the massacre at Gnadenhütten, *ib.;* the first victim, 549.
Abraham, the steward of the Mission, 629; helps to begin Mission at Goschgoschünk, 338; confesses his sins after the Gnadenhütten massacre, 559; leads the Christian Indians to Pipe's Town, 560; death and character, 629.
Adam, a convert, leads American militia to Salem, 544.
Adam, a convert, one of the first to rejoin the Mission after the massacre, 563.
Adoption compulsory among Indians, 620, 621.
Algonquins, an Indian race, 31; its wide diffusion, 36.
Alligewi or *Allegans*, an Indian tribe, 33.
Allen, Fort, on the site of Gnadenhütten, 239.
Allemwi, Monsey chief at Goschgoschünk, 332; negotiates with Delaware chiefs about the Mission, 348; his baptism, 359; forsakes the Mission, 406.
Amochk. See *King Beaver.*
Andastes, an Indian tribe, 38.

Anowara, or Turtle family, among the Iroquois, 78.
Andrews, William, a missionary among the Indians, 104.
Anuntschi, Nathaniel Seidel's Indian name, 190.
Anders, Gottlieb and Joanna, killed in the massacre on the Mahony, 229, 233, 236.
Anthony, a native assistant, 267 and *note* 2; accompanies Zeisberger to Machiwihilusing, 267; to Goschgoschünk, 324; settles at Goschgoschünk, 338; preaches the Gospel to Glikkikan, 355, 356; accompanies Zeisberger to Gekelemukpechünk, 366; his death, 389.
Anthony, one of the scattered converts after the massacre, 593; his suspicions with regard to the missionaries, 594.
Anthony's Wilderness, 65, note 3.
Ancrum, Major, commandant of Detroit, 588; advises Zeisberger to leave New Gnadenhütten, *ib.;* buys the improvements of the Mission, 589.
Anderson, Captain, commands a sloop on Lake Erie, 590.
Apty, Thomas, has charge of the Christian Indians in the Paxton Insurrection, 284, 294, 295, 296, 305, 309.
Aquanoschioni, a name for the Iroquois, 32. See *Iroquois.*
Armstrong, General, attacks the Indians on the Alleghany, 246.
Arundle, a trader at Lower Sandusky, 536; entertains the missionaries, *ib.;* burial service at his

(717)

house in memory of the Indians massacred at Gnadenhütten, 558.

Askin, John, a merchant of Detroit, 589; buys the improvements of the Mission at New Gnadenhütten, *ib.*; offers to convey the converts in sloops across Lake Erie, 590, 591.

Attiwandarons, an Indian tribe, 38.

Aupaumut, Hendrick, a Stockbridge Indian, 660.

B.

Barclay, Henry, a missionary among the Indians, 104.

Barnard, Governor, at the treaty of Easton, in 1758, 251.

Bawbee, Mr., a British Indian agent, 524.

Beautiful Spring, the, in Ohio, 371; its prehistoric remains, 371, 372; site of a Mission town, 372; description of the neighborhood, 375, 376.

Belts of wampum of Christian Indians, 426.

Beersheba, second Moravian church in Ohio, 663 and *note* 1.

Bethabara, first Moravian settlement in North Carolina, 252.

Bear family, among the Iroquois, 78.

Bethlehem founded, 24; the Economy, 24, *note* 1; threatened with destruction, 228; receives the news of the Gnadenhütten massacre, 233, 234; a refuge in the French and Indian War, 239, 240; events at, during the war, 244, 245, 247, 248, 251; during the Pontiac War, 278, 285; receives the news of the captivity of the missionaries, 512; the news of the massacre of the Christian Indians, 572, 573.

Bezold, Gottlieb, a Moravian clergyman, biography, 184, *note* 2; visits Wyoming with Zeisberger, 184.

Black Swamp, 520 and *note* 1.

Blickensderfer, Matthias, Heckewelder's companion on a surveying expedition, 608.

Boaz. See *Gegeshamind.*

Boehler, Peter, Moravian bishop, biography, 22, *note* 1; in South Carolina, 22; at the Whitefield House, 23; visits Shamokin with Zinzendorf, 110; consults with Zeisberger during his imprisonment in New York, 124, 125; Spangenberg's temporary successor, 212; assistant of Bishop Seidel, 256; writes to Governor Penn on behalf of the Christian Indians, 280; farewell discourse to the Christian Indians, 286.

Bollinger, Henry, drives first teams to the Tuscarawas reservation, 657, *note* 1.

Boone, Daniel, explores Kentucky, 375.

Bouquet, Colonel, defeats the Indians in the Pontiac War, 275; conquers the Delaware country, 306.

British Barracks, in Philadelphia, 287.

Brodhead, Colonel Daniel, assumes command of Pittsburg, 471; campaign against the Iroquois in 1780, 476; introduces Zeisberger to President Reed, 481; campaign against the Delawares, 482; offers to convey the Christian Indians to Pittsburg, 483.

Brant, Joseph, Iroquois chief, biography, 627, *note* 1; originates the Western confederation, 596; his speech in favor of the Christian Indians, 627; conversation with Zeisberger about the Indian War, 633; makes the Delawares men, 641, 642.

Bradstreet, Colonel, expedition against the Indians, 306.

Brebeuf, a Jesuit missionary, 100; his martyrdom, 101.

Brainerd, David, a missionary among the Indians, 105; his description of Shamokin, 71, *note* 2.

Braddock, General, defeated by the French and Indians, 222.

Butler, General Richard, Superintendent of Indian Affairs, 597; his testimony concerning the importance of the Indian Mission during the Revolution, 444, *note*

INDEX. 719

2; commissioner at Indian treaty, 584, 585; correspondence with Zeisberger about the return of the Mission to the Tuscarawas, 597, 598; killed in battle, 628.

Bush, Jacob, one of the first settlers on the Tuscarawas reservation, 657, *note* 1.

Buckshanoath, a Shawanese warrior, 224.

Burial-places, among the Indians, 90.

Büttner, Gottlob, a Moravian missionary, 106; biography, 106, *note* 1; missionary at Shekomeko, 107; death, 122; grave, 122, *note* 1.

Byhan, Gottlieb, a Moravian missionary among the Cherokees, 663.

C.

Cancello, Louis, the forerunner of the Jesuit missionaries, 100.

Cannibalism among the Indians, 44, 199.

Canaan, a Moravian mission station among the Cherokees, 697.

Catawbas, an Indan tribe, 31.

Cayugas, an Iroquois tribe, 38, 57.

Cayuga Town, the capital of the Cayugas, 162.

Cabot, John, voyages of discovery, 39.

Cabot, Sebastian, voyages of discovery, 39.

Cartier, Jacques, voyages of discovery, 40.

Camping-places of Moravian missionaries, 132.

Cammerhoff, Frederick, a Moravian bishop, biography, 143, *note* 2; character, 143, 144; visits the Indian country with Watteville, 147–150; visits Onondaga with Zeisberger, 156–175; cited before Governor Hamilton, 178; death, 182.

Carver, Jonathan, explores the Northwest, 375.

Cass, Lewis, appointed commissioner of the United States to treat about the Tuscarawas reservation, 695.

Cagnawagas, an Indian tribe, 585.

Captives' Town, the Moravian Mission town built after the breaking up of the Tuscarawas Mission, 516 and *note* 1, 517; the assembly of converts there by night, 529; a chapel erected, 529; the town forsaken by the converts, 560.

Carpenter, John, captured by the Indians, 539; warns the Christian Indians against the American militia, 540.

Charlestown, an early settlement in the West, 646, 655.

Cherokees, an Indian tribe, 30; first Moravian convert, 394; Moravian Mission among them in Georgia, 663; mission broken up, 696; renewed in the West, 697; given up again in Southern rebellion, *ib.*; renewed since the war, *ib*.

Chickasas, an Indian tribe, 31.

Choctas, an Indian tribe, 31.

Chippewas, an Indian tribe, 36, 73; refuse to engage in a raid upon the Mission, 489; grant the Christian Indians land, 562; notify them to leave the land, 584; their begging-dance, 619, 620; manner of burying, 620; canoes, *ib.*; habits, 582; villages in Canada, 632; a Moravian Mission among them, 660; the Mission given up, 665.

Champlain, Samuel, 42.

Christian, a convert killed at Gnadenhütten, converses on religion with the militia, 544.

Christiana, a convert, appeals to Colonel Williamson for mercy, at the massacre, 549.

Children of the Indians, 85, 86.

Chilloway, Job or *William*, a native assistant, flees to Province Island, 289; baptized at Friedenshütten, 629; accompanies Zeisberger to the Shawanese, 389; accompanies the missionaries to the court-martial at Detroit, 518; leads the converts to Pipe's Town after the massacre, 560; his death, 629.

Chew, Benjamin, a Philadelphia councilman, 299.

Chillicothe, a tribe of the Shawanese, 374.
Church-bell, the first, used in Ohio, 377.
Clans, among the Iroquois, 77, 78.
Clewell, Christian, assistant at the survey of the Tuscarawas land, 646, 647, *note* 2.
Clymer, Colonel George, United States commissioner at the treaty of Pittsburg in 1775, 429.
Clark, George Rogers, takes the British posts on the Mississippi, 466; captures Governor Hamilton, 472; United States commissioner at an Indian treaty, 585.
Comenius, John Amos, a bishop of the Unitas Fratrum, 699.
Conestoga Indians, 69; massacred, 290.
Conestoga Manor, 290.
Convention at Philadelphia in 1787, 605.
Congress of commissioners at Albany in 1754, 216.
Congress, Continental, exercises the functions of a government, 428; organizes Indian departments, *ib.*; takes into its hands the administration of Indian affairs, 584; its views with regard to the Indians, 585, 586; grants land to the Christian Indians, 587 and *note* 1; its ordinance for the government of the Northwest Territory, 605, 606; sells land, 606; vests its grant to the Christian Indians in the Moravians of Pennsylvania, 606.
Congress of the United States opens, 610; reaffirms ordinance for the Northwest Territory, *ib.*
Congress Belt, the, 430.
Connecticut settlers in Wyoming, 268; visited by Zeisberger, 269; massacred in the Pontiac War, 280.
Conner, John, a white member of the Indian Mission, 425, 426; ransoms his son from the Shawanese, 431; rejoins the Mission after the massacre, 562; remains at New Gnadenhütten after the exodus of the converts, 589; his subsequent history, *ib.*
Conner, John, son of the preceding, interpreter of the Delaware chiefs who visit President Jefferson, 660, *note* 1.
Connolly, John, agent of Lord Dunmore, 400.
Cooking, among the Delawares and Iroquois, 84, 85.
Cook, Lieut.-Colonel Edward, denounces the Gnadenhütten massacre, 576.
Coon, Abraham, takes part in the expedition against the Tuscarawas towns, 491, *note* 1, 506.
Cosmogony, Indian, 217–219.
Colden, Governor, of New York, refuses to receive the Christian Indians, 295; his reasons, *ib.*; his second refusal, 305.
Colver, two brothers, help to build Goshen, 654.
Cornplanter, a Seneca, offers to mediate for the United States with the hostile tribes, 626.
Cornell, Francis, a Canadian settler at whose house the missionaries preach, 644.
Cornstalk, Shawanese chief, commands at the battle of Point Pleasant, 408; advocates peace with the Colonies in the Revolution, 447; adopts Schmick and his wife, *ib.*, *note* 2; murdered, 452, 453.
Cornelius, a convert, leads the Christian Indians to Pipe's Town after the massacre, 560.
Crawford's expedition against the Christian Indians, 564–572; Doddridge's account of it, 564, 565.
Crawford, Colonel, elected commander, 565; encamps at New Schönbrunn, *ib.*; finds Captives' Town deserted, *ib.*; defeated by the savages, 566; taken prisoner, *ib.*; his conversation with Wingenund, 567-571; tortured, 567, 571; character, 572.
Crown, The, a tavern near Bethlehem, 278 and *note* 2.
Croghan, George, deputy of Sir W. Johnson, 246; at the treaty of

INDEX.

Easton in 1758, 251; tries to prevent Dunmore's War, 403.
Cresap, Captain, murders Indians in Dunmore's War, 402.
Creeks, an Indian tribe, 31.
Cunow, John Gebhard, a member of the Mission Board, 662; visits Goshen, 666.

D.

Dablon, Claude, a Jesuit missionary, 102.
Daniel, a Jesuit missionary, 100.
Dances, among the Indians, 90, 91, 198, 199, 328.
Dahcotas, an Indian tribe, 31.
David, Christian, a Moravian elder, 14, note 2; 699.
Dalzell, Captain, reinforces Detroit, 275.
Denny, Governor, at the treaty of Easton, in 1758, 251.
Detroit, its population in 1771, 375; British center of influence in the Revolution, 445; the Moravian missionaries on trial there, 520–529; rendezvous for the Christian Indians, 562; its condition and morals, 562, 563; terrible winter at, in 1783, 583; testimony of its inhabitants to the character of the converts, 590, 591; the town in 1798, 653.
Denke, Christian, a Moravian missionary at Fairfield, 660; begins a Mission among the Chippewas, 660; abandons it, 665; gathers the scattered converts in the war of 1812, 695.
Delawares, an Indian tribe, 32; identical with the Lenni-Lenape, 32, note 1; early traditions, 32–35; divisions, 35; their three tribes, ib.; tradition of the coming of white men, 42; their women by the Iroquois, 45, 46; their nation about 1745, 70–72; their hunting-grounds on the Susquehanna, 71; their government, 79, 80; baptism of first Moravian converts, 131; refuse to be considered women, 245 and note 1, 347; invite the Christian Indians to settle among them, 370; their hunting-grounds in Ohio, 372–374; begin a moral reform, 385; neutral in Dunmore's War, 403, 406; denounce the Mission to the Shawanese, 411; their real object in inviting the converts, 412; their grand council decrees religious liberty, 422; remain neutral in the Revolution, 441, 442; importance of their neutrality to the United States, 443, 444, and notes 1 and 2; names of their headmen, in 1777, 446; decide anew for peace, 447, 448, 453, 467; change in their policy, the majority going over to the British Indians, 479; take part in the expedition against the Mission, 489; their boundaries after the Revolution, 585; a part of them emigrate to the Mississippi, 613; their miserable condition after the Indian War, 641; made men by the Iroquois, 641, 642; beg Gelelemend to be their chief, 642; settle on the White River, Indiana, 659; ask for Christian teachers, ib.; send a deputation to President Jefferson, 660; excesses and murders among them, 665.
Dickinson, John, a lawyer in Philadelphia, 284 and note 1; employed to defend a Christian Indian charged with murder, 284.
Doctors, Indian, 210, 211.
Doddridge, Joseph, his account of the massacre at Gnadenhütten, 554–557.
Dreuillettes, Gabriel, a Jesuit missionary, 101.
Dress, of the Delawares and Iroquois, 84, 85, 90.
Duncan and Wilson, merchants of Pittsburg, 593; bring Zeisberger a message from General Butler, 598.
Dutch, the, on the Hudson River, 42.
Dunmore's War. See War, Dunmore's.
Dunmore, Lord, Governor of Virginia, 399; his usurpations, 400; quarrels with the Council of

Pennsylvania, *ib.;* commands the northern forces in the war, 407; marches to the Scioto, 408; opens negotiations with the Indians, *ib.;* concludes peace, 409; promises to help White Eyes to visit England, 418; his motives in promising this, 427.

E.

Easton, a borough in Pennsylvania, 65, *note* 2; Jerseymen congregate there, 228; Indian treaties, 245, 246; the treaty of 1757, 249; the Indian congress of 1758, 250, 251; the second Indian Congress of 1761, 253.
Easter Morning, at Schönbrunn, 395–398.
Echpalawehund, a convert, 384; baptized, 393; at the grand council of the Delawares after Dunmore's War, 416.
Edmonds, Peter, one of the first settlers on the Tuscarawas reservation, 657, *note* 1.
Edwards, William, a Moravian missionary, biography, 447, *note* 1; joins the Mission, 447; Zeisberger's sole companion among the Indians, 454; at Gnadenhütten, 456; at Lichtenau, 466; returns to Gnadenhütten, 473; in danger of his life, 484; his experiences during the British expedition against the Mission, 498, 506, 509; tried at Detroit, 518; brings the news of peace to New Gnadenhütten, 580; visits Pittsburg to inquire about the Indian treaties, 586, 587; sails across Lake Erie, 591, 592; his labors at New Salem, 604; negotiates with Canadian authorities for a refuge for the converts during the Indian War, 616, 617, 619; leads the converts to the mouth of the Detroit, 623; leads a colony from Canada to the Tuscarawas reservation, 648; his death, 658, 659.
Ekuschuwe, head chief of the Chippewas, 610; visits New Salem, *ib.*
Ellinipsico, son of Cornstalk, murdered, 453.

Elliot, John, a missionary among the Indians, 103, 104, 677.
Elliot, John, a Quaker peace commissioner in 1793, 634.
Elliot, Matthew, a British captain, 462; incites the Delawares against the United States, *ib.;* his animosity against the Mission, 489; real commander of the British expedition against the Mission, 491; incites the Huron Half King to seize the missionaries, 495, 496; leaves the expedition, 515; distributes rewards among the Indians, 519.
Ephrata, the seat of the Seventh-Day Baptists, 66.
Eries, an Indian tribe, 38.
Eschicanahund, Isaac, a convert, accompanies the missionaries to Detroit, 518.
Espich, Rev. Mr., Lutheran clergyman and physician, attends Zeisberger in his last illness, 670.
Ettwein, John, a Moravian bishop and member of the Mission Board, biography, 338, *note* 2; has a marble slab placed over the grave of the victims in the massacre on the Mahony, 235, *note* 1; escorts Zeisberger's colony on its way to Goschgoschünk, 338; leads the Christian Indians to Ohio, 376; returns to Bethlehem, 380; active in the Mission Board during the Revolution, 480; meets a German who helped to kill the Christian Indians at Gnadenhütten, 573; negotiates with Congress for a grant of land for the Christian Indians, 582; desires to remove the Western Mission to Pennsylvania, 618 and *note* 1; his historic statement about the Tuscarawas reservation, 657, *note* 1; death, 661.

F.

Fabricius, George, killed in the massacre on the Mahony, 229, 235.
Fanaticism in the Moravian Church, 143, *note* 3.
Fairfield, a Moravian Mission town,

INDEX. 723

632; its site, 631, 632; its growth, 639; a general repentance among its inhabitants, 645, 646; its trade and exports, 650; the improvements around it, 652, 653; destroyed by American troops, 694.
Feasts, sacrificial. See *Sacrifices.*
Fire, a, in the forest, 310.
Floridian Indians, 31.
Forks of the Delaware, 64.
Foxes, an Indian tribe, 73.
Fox, Joseph, a commissioner of the Pennsylvania Assembly in the Paxton Insurrection, 284, 294, 295.
Forts, Colonial, after the French and Indian War, 257-259.
Forestier, Charles de, a member of the Directory of the Unitas Fratrum, visits Goshen, 666.
Friedenshütten (the first), a Moravian Mission town, 141 and *note* 1.
Friedenshütten (the second), a Moravian Mission town, laid out, 310; revival at, 311, 313; enlarged, 316; description and site of, 316, 317 and *note* 1; the land on which it was situated sold by the Iroquois to Pennsylvania, 348, 370; prosperity of the Mission there, 369; the town abandoned by the converts, 376; number of its inhabitants, 376, *note* 1.
Friedensstadt, a Moravian Mission town, 362; awakening at, 365 366; prosperity of the Mission there, 367; abandoned, 386.
Frisbie, Levi, visits the Delawares in Ohio, 379.
Franklin, Governor, of New Jersey, 296.
Franklin, Benjamin, at Bethlehem and Gnadenhütten, 239; in Philadelphia during the Paxton Insurrection, 283, 301, 302.
Friedrich, Charles, a Moravian missionary, biography, 216, *note* 2; visits Onondaga with Zeisberger, 216-219.
Frey, Henry, a Moravian missionary, biography, 206, *note* 1; visits Onondaga with Zeisberger, 206-212.
France, influence of, among the Indians, 73, 74; usurpations in America, 176, 177, 205, 208.

G.

Gage, General, commander-in-chief, 293; refuses to allow the Christian Indians to enter New York, 295; sends them an escort, 297; second refusal to permit them to enter New York, 305.
Galloway, Joseph, a member of the Pennsylvania Assembly, 283 and *note* 1, 293.
Gallichwio, Bishop Cammerhoff's Indian name, 163 and *note* 1.
Gantlet, running of, 152.
Garrison, Nicholas, Jr., a scout in Paxton Insurrection, 293.
Garrison, Nicholas, biography, 25, *note* 1; commands the "James," 25.
Gattermeyer, John, killed in the massacre on the Mahony, 229, 236.
Ganassateco, Iroquois sachem, 109, *note* 1; at Philadelphia, 153; entertains Cammerhoff and Zeisberger, 162.
Ganousseracheri, Zeisberger's Indian name, 134.
Ganachragejat, Mack's Indian name, 193.
Gegashamind, a sorcerer, baptized, 604.
Gendaskund, a convert, 359; conciliates Packanke, 363; baptized, 366.
Gekelemukpechünk, capital of the Delawares in Ohio, 366 and *note* 1; first Protestant sermon in Ohio preached there, 367; religious interest begins there, 384; a moral reformation attempted, 385; council at, with the Christian Indians, 386; grand council at, after Dunmore's War, 413 -417; its council-house, 413; abandoned by the Delawares, 426.
Gelelemend, a grandson of Neta-

watwes, biography, 694, *note* 1; at Lichtenau, 436; the head of the Delaware nation, 470; faithful to the United States, flees from the Delaware capital, 479; puts himself under the protection of the United States, 483; his baptism, 604; refuses to be head chief, 642; invites the Delawares to visit Goshen, 656, 657; entreats heathen Indians at Goshen to abstain from strong drink, 668; his death, 694.

Gigeyunk, head-quarters of hostile Indians in the West, 615; Zeisberger's defiance sent thither, 623, 624; his protest in its council against any interference with the Mission, 626.

Girty, Simon, his character, 462, *note* 1; incites the Delawares against the United States, 462, 463; tries to capture Zeisberger, 474; his animosity toward the Mission, 489; summons the missionaries to Detroit, 533, 534; is present at Colonel Crawford's torture, 571; defeats the Kentuckians, 577; at the council on the Maumee, 633; his influence exerted against the peace commission, 636, 637.

Gieschenatsi, a Shawanese chief, denounces the white race, 391, 392; bitter enemy of the Gospel, 393.

Gibson, James, a leader of the Paxton insurgents, 302, 303.

Gibson, Colonel John, Western Agent of Virginia, 430; visits Schönbrunn, 430; commands Fort Laurens, 469.

Ginseng root, traffic in, 189.

Gist, Christopher, explores the Western country, 183.

Girdles, Indian, 86.

Gideon. See *Tadeuskund*.

Gladwyn, Major. at Detroit, in the Pontiac War, 275.

Glikkikan, a distinguished convert, 355; comes to the Alleghany to refute Zeisberger, 355, 356; declares his belief in the Gospel, 357; becomes a convert, 358; joins the Mission, 362; persecuted, 362, 363; baptized, 366; accompanies Zeisberger to the Delaware capital and there preaches the Gospel, 366, 367, 371, 386; accompanies Zeisberger on his visit to the Shawanese, 389; appeals to White Eyes to become a Christian, 404; at the grand council after Dunmore's War, 416, 417; reproves White Eyes, 438, 439; his speech to the Half King in favor of the missionaries, 456; seized by the British Indians and tried by the Half King, 510, 511; reproves the Half King, 531, 532; killed in the massacre at Gnadenhütten, 551.

Gnadenthal, a Moravian settlement, 65.

Gnadenhütten, on the Mahony, a Moravian Mission town, 141 and *note* 2; its prosperity, 182; exodus of a part of its inhabitants, 214; removed to a new site, 214; destroyed by the French Indians, 239.

Gnadenhütten, in Ohio, a Moravian Mission town, 380, 381, *note* 1; first public service there, 383; its prosperity, 383; its new chapel, 393; its municipal system, 423, 424; revival there, 432; the British Indians encamped there, 490; massacre at, 537–557; its appearance fifteen years after the massacre, 647.

Gnadenhütten, the present town in Ohio, 654 and *note* 1; it increases, 657; its first inhabitants, 657, *note* 1.

Goshen, a Moravian Mission town, 654 and *note* 2; a colony goes out from there to Indiana, 659; its population, 661, *note* 1; a missionary conference there, 662; overrun by a gang of desperadoes, 664; its converts intoxicated, *ib.;* frequented by Indians from the Pettquotting, 668; abandoned, 695, 696.

Goschgoschünk, an Indian village on the Alleghany, 324, 326, 327,

329; visited by Zeisberger, 329–335; the town in 1768, 339; a Mission begun there, 339–349; the Mission removed, 353; wickedness of the town, 354; a number of its inhabitants join the Mission at Friedensstadt, 362, 365.
Goschachgünk, the second capital of the Delawares in Ohio, 426, 427 and *note* 1; destroyed by Colonel Brodhead, 483.
Gokhosing, a stopping-place of the converts on their journey to the Sandusky, 515 and *note* 1.
Godfrey, Captain, commands a sloop on Lake Erie, 590.
Gourges Dominic, 41.
Good Luck, the name of a tract of land in Pennsylvania, granted to the Moravian Missionary Society, 618, *note* 1.
Great Britain struggles with France for the supremacy in North America, 176, 177; triumphs over France, 254, 255; introduces a foolish policy after her victory, 321, 322; a cruel policy in the Revolution by inciting the Indians to war, 428, 429, 441; interferes in the war between the United States and the Western Indians, 641; relinquishes the Western posts to the United States, 643.
Grube, Bernard Adam, a Moravian missionary, biography, 221, *note* 1; visits Wyoming, 221; at Gnadenhütten on the Mahony at the time of the massacre, 229; in Philadelphia during the Pontiac War, 280; accompanies the Christian Indians on their way to New York, 294; visits the Ohio Mission, 477, 478 and *note* 1; officiates at the marriage of Heckewelder, 477; at the marriage of Zeisberger, 482.
Grant of land to Christian Indians. See *Society of the U. B. for Propagating the Gospel.*
Gregor, Christian, a Moravian bishop, biography, 368, *note* 1; visits America, 368.
Greathouse, Daniel, murders Indians in Dunmore's War, 402.
Greer, Paul, one of the first settlers on the Tuscarawas reservation, 657, *note* 1.

H.

Hagen, John, a Moravian missionary, 142; his death, *ib.*
Hagen, John Joachim, a Moravian missionary, 663.
Hajingonis, Joseph Schebosh's Iroquois name, 134.
Hahotschaunquas, Cammerhoff's and Zeisberger's guide to Onondaga, 157, 159, 161, 162, 164, 173, 174.
Hard Man, the. See *Gieschenatsi.*
Hamilton, Governor of Pennsylvania, interview with Cammerhoff, 178; espouses the cause of the Christian Indians, 283, 284, 285, 301.
Hamilton, Governor of Detroit, forged letter from him sent to Zeisberger, 460–462; incites the Indians against the United States, 467; organizes an expedition against the Mission, 470, 471; taken prisoner by the Americans, 472.
Harris family, the, a member of dies among the Christian Indians, 613, *note* 1.
Hachsitagechte, Zeisberger's Indian brother, 322; dies at Bethlehem, 323; message concerning his death, 323, 324.
Hagastaak, a Seneca sachem, 342; Zeisberger negotiates with his council, 347, 348
Harmar, Lieut.-Colonel Joseph, his speech to the Christian Indians, 597, 598 and *note* 1; disastrous campaign against the Indians, 615 and *note* 1.
Hardin, Colonel, murdered by the Indians, 632.
Hartshorne, William, a Quaker peace commissioner in 1793, 634.
Hakinkpomsgu, Captain Pipe's successor, 656.
Half King of the Wyandots, 374;

visits Lichtenau, 454, 455; protects Zeisberger, 456; defeats American militia and attacks Fort Henry, 457; commands British expedition against the Mission, 489; announces his coming, 490; interview with Heckewelder, 491; his speech to the Christian Indians, 493, 494; hesitates to lay hands on the missionaries, 494–498; his last speech, 503, 504; deserts the Christian Indians in a wilderness, 516; proclaims himself their chief, 517; reproved by Glikkikan, 531, 532; forces the converts to leave Captives' Town, 560; demands the removal of the missionaries, 561; forbids the converts to settle on the Black River, 600, 601; his death, 611.

Hand, General, commandant at Pittsburg, 457; sends peace messages to the Delawares by Heckewelder, 463–465.

Harrison, General William Henry, destroys Fairfield, 694.

Haymaker, Jacob, sends the news of the capture of the missionaries to the States, 511.

Hay, Vice-Governor John, commandant at Detroit, 583.

Haven, John Ben, a Moravian missionary, 660; ordained at Goshen, 662; begins a Mission on the Pettquotting, 663.

Heckewelder, Joanna Maria, born at Salem, 507; biography, 507, *note* 1; taken to Detroit, 535 and *note* 1.

Heckewelder, John, a Moravian missionary, biography, 256, *note* 2; his father, 20; with Post in Ohio, 256; bearer of a message from Post to Zeisberger, 261; Zeisberger's assistant at Friedenshütten, 312; in Ohio, 370; at Schönbrunn, 380, 447; returns to Bethlehem, 452; goes to Pittsburg, 463; carries peace-messages to the Delawares, 464, 465; visits Zeisberger at Lichtenau, 465; takes charge of the Lichtenau Mission, 466, 473; founds Salem, 477; married in its chapel, 477, 478; in danger of his life, 484; his experiences during the British expedition against the Mission, 491, 492, 498, 504, 506, 509; goes to Detroit to be tried, 518; at Detroit again, 563; at New Gnadenhütten, 579; on the way to the Cuyahoga, 591, 592; leaves the Mission, 596; visits the Mission, 599; Agent of the Society for Propagating the Gospel, 608; unsuccessful attempts to survey the Tuscarawas reservation, 608, 611; assistant peace commissioner of the United States, 632, 633, 634; surveys the reservation, 646–648; at Fairfield, 648; leads a colony to the reservation, *ib.;* his house at Gnadenhütten, 654 and *note* 1; his memorial to Governor St. Clair about the sale of ardent spirits on the reservation, 656; visits Zeisberger on his death-bed, 673; his sketch of Zeisberger's character, 681, 682.

Henry, Captain, chief of the Mohawks, 636, 637, *note* 1.

Henry, a convert, leads militia to Salem, 544.

Henry, Mr., a trader among the Shawanese, 374, *note* 2.

Henry, Judge William, a member of Congress, 357; Gelelemend named after him, 604; helps to survey the Tucarawas reservation, 646–648.

Hehl, Matthew, a Moravian bishop, member of the Mission Board, 185 and *note* 1; sends an express to Bethlehem about the Conestoga massacre, 292.

Hendrick, the King of the Mohawks, 122 and *note* 2.

Herrnhut, 15.

Herbert, Michael, takes part in the British expedition against the Mission, 491.

Heckedorn, John, forwards the news of the capture of the missionaries to Bethlehem, 511, 512.

Houses of the Iroquois, 83 and *note* 1.
Houses of the Delawares, 83, 84.

INDEX.

Horton, Azariah, a missionary among the Indians, 105.
Hodenosaunee, a name for the Iroquois, 32, *note* 2.
Hospitality, the name of a tract of land in Pennsylvania granted to the Society for Propagating the Gospel, 618, *note* 1.
Horsfield, Timothy, biography, 226, *note* 2; takes Zeisberger's deposition, 226; his dispatches concerning the massacre on the Mahony, 236, 237, 238; his rules for the Christian Indians in the Pontiac War, 276; negotiates with the government in the Paxton Insurrection, 292.
Huebner, Lewis, a Moravian clergyman, biography, 658, *note* 2; pastor of the white settlers on the Tuscarawas reservation, 658; leaves the reservation, 663.
Huebner, John Andrew, a Moravian bishop, biography, 480, *note* 2; a member of the Mission Board, 480, 582; a member of the Directory in Europe, 661, 662.
Huss, John, 16, 698.
Hutchins, Thomas, Geographer of the United States, 587, 608.
Hundsecker, Lt., escorts Christian Indians, 309.
Huron-Iroquois, a race of Indians, 31.
Hurons, the same as *Wyandots*, which see.
Hunting, among the Delawares and Iroquois, 80, 81; laws of hunting, 81, 82; wholesale slaughter of deer, 350.

I.

Idol, of the Delawares, 96.
Illinois, a tribe of Indians, 36, 73.
Indians, general remarks, 28; generic stocks, 30; description of, in primitive times, 43; early moral character, 44; cannibalism, 44; population in early times, 47; the tribes of Pennsylvania in 1745, 69–72; the nations of the West, 72–74; general government, 75, 76; their manner of life at home in Colonial times, 80–91; their moral character in the same period, 91–93; false notions concerning their early religion, 93, 94; later superstition, 94–96; oratory, 96; lamentations for the dead and funerals, 196, 197; inheritances, 197; sickness, 209, 210; doctors, 210, 211; cosmogony, 217–219; tribes and hunting-grounds after the French and Indian War, 257; dissatisfied with the occupation of Western forts by the English, 200, 261, 262; faithful to their treaties after the Pontiac War, 400, 401; hated by the whites in the West during the Revolution, 538, 539; no reservations for them after the Revolution, 584; boundaries of the Western tribes, 585; dissatisfied with the policy of the United States, 586; form a confederation in the West and send a message to Congress, 596, 597; their condition and number after the treaty of 1789, 609; hostile demonstrations, 614; hold a grand council on the Maumee in 1792, 633; break off negotiations with the United States, 637; totally defeated by Wayne, 640; great sufferings among them, 642, 643.
Indians, the Christian, quartered at Bethlehem and Gnadenthal, 239, 240; their industry and trade, 240; claim the protection of the Governor of Pennsylvania, 276; their personal appearance, 276, 277; false accusations against them, 279; proofs that they took no part in the Pontiac War, 279; *note* 1; disarmed and removed to Philadelphia, 285–289; quartered on Province Island, 289; flee to League Island, 291; set out for New York, 294; at Trenton and Princeton, 295; at Amboy, 296; return to Philadelphia, 297; no murderers found among them, 303, *note* 1; sickness among them, 305; leave Philadelphia, 306; their journey from Nain to

Machiwihilusing, 309, 310; their happiness, 311; negotiate with the Iroquois sachem at Cayuga Town, 315, 316; send a speech and belt of wampum to the Directory in Europe, 316; receive a message from Governor Penn, 337; their views with regard to tribute, 364, 365; invited by the Delaware chiefs to settle in Ohio, 370; journey to the Beaver River, 376, 377; receive a grant from the Assembly of Pennsylvania, 376, *note* 2; their statutes, 378, 379; instances of their joy in believing, 384; the tribes from which they are gathered, 394; try to prevent Dunmore's War, 403; ask that all the missionaries may be adopted among the Delawares, 405; secure religious liberty, 422; their growing prosperity, 423; settlements on the Tuscarawas, 423, 424; Colonel Morgan's testimony concerning them, 424, *note* 1; their belts of wampum, 426; conspiracy among some of them to overthrow the Mission, 449-452; the faith and zeal of the rest during the Revolution, 459; all concentrated at Lichtenau, 466; divided again into three congregations, 472, 473; the apostates return, 459, 478; their experiences during the British expedition against the Mission, 493-512; leave the Tuscarawas as prisoners, 513; their losses, *ib.*; journey to the Sandusky, 514-517; erect a chapel at Captives' Town, 529; their sufferings, 530, 531; regarded with suspicion both by the Americans and the British, 537, 538; at Captives' Town after the massacre, 558; their feelings in view of the massacre, 559, 560; settle at New Gnadenhütten, 578, 579; their life at New Gnadenhütten, 581, 582; receive a grant of land from Congress, 587 and *note* 1; leave New Gnadenhütten, 589; journey to the Cuyahoga, 591, 592; settle at Pilgerruh, 592, 593; leave Pilgerruh, 599; settle at New Salem, 602; accept the protection of the peace confederation, 611; disturbed by the Indian War, 615, 616; leave New Salem, 621; settle at the mouth of the Detroit, 624; settle in Canada, 631, 632; spiritual state at Fairfield, 645, 646; exodus of a part of them to the Tuscarawas, 651; exodus of a part from the Tuscarawas to Indiana, 659; of a part from Fairfield to the Pettquotting, 663; great decline of spiritual life among them, ·664, 665; the Goshen Indians at Zeisberger's death-bed, 672-674; exodus of a part from New Fairfield to the West, 696.

Indians, the Christian, massacred at Gnadenhütten, go from Captives' Town to the Tuscarawas, 532, 533; warned by warriors and Carpenter, 540; meet with the militia, 541, 542; their joy that the Americans will care for them, 543; murderers and victims sleeping together, 544; the converts seized by the militia, 545; rebut the charges against them, 545, 546; their innocence, 546 and *note* 1; condemned to death, 547; their faith and joy, 548; they are murdered, 548, 549; names of the victims, 551, 552; their bright testimony as Christians, 553; their remains found and buried, 647 and *note* 1.

Indians, the Christian, scattered after the massacre, leave Captives' Town, 560; hesitate to rejoin the Mission, 579; forty-three come to New Gnadenhütten, 583; they receive a message from Zeisberger, 588; a written speech inviting them to a conference, 593, 594; their reception of these overtures, 595; emigrate to the Mississippi and disappear, 613.

Indaochaie, the name of Lichtenau after the exodus of the converts, 483, *note* 1.

Irene, the Moravian missionary ship, 179 and *note* 1, 180, 181.

INDEX.   729

Irvine, General, commander at Pittsburg, 531; liberates the Christian Indians taken by Williamson, 531; receives a dispatch from the Executive Council of Pennsylvania, 574, 575; his letter to Bishop Seidel, 575.

Iroquois, synonyms for them, 32, *note* 2; early traditions, 36, 37; organization of their league, 37; their supremacy, 38, 39; account of them in 1745, 54–57; description of their country, 57; the trails, 57, 58; population, 58; government, 76, 77; clans or families, 77, 78; the Iroquois a conglomeration of other nationalities, 78, 79; their monuments, 161; their feud with the Catawbas settled, 183; preparations for the war-path, 198, 199; missions among them, 319, *note* 1; cede land to Pennsylvania in 1773, 401; relations to the United States in the Revolution, 441, 443, 444; their country devastated by the Americans, 476; give the Christian Indians to heathen tribes to make broth of, 489; their boundaries after the Revolution, 585; their condition after the treaty of 1789, 609; advise the Western nations to conclude peace with the United States, 633; make the Delawares men, 641, 642.

Iroquois Grand Council, 76, 77; receives Cammerhoff and Zeisberger, 162, 163; negotiates with Cammerhoff and Zeisberger, 173, 174; negotiates with Zeisberger, Mack, and Rundt, 190–194; negotiates with Zeisberger and Senseman, 318, 319.

Israel. See *Johnny, Captain.*

J.

Jacob, a convert, brings news of the massacre to Zeisberger, 536.

Jacob, a lad, escapes from the massacre, 550, 551.

Jacob, son-in-law of Schebosh, fails to give the alarm to the converts when the militia attack Gnadenhütten, 542.

Jamestown founded, 42.

Jacheabus, leader of the war-party that committed the massacre on the Mahony, 238.

Jablonsky, Daniel Ernst, a bishop of the Unitas Fratrum, 699.

Jesuit Relations, 29, *note* 1.

Jesuit Missions, 100, 103.

Jeremiah. See *Mamasu.*

Jefferson, Thomas, reports the emigration of the Christian Indians to Canada, 629; receives visits from Indian chiefs, 660.

Job, one of the first Moravian Indian converts, 98, 99; baptized, 107; eloquent preacher of the Gospel, 116.

John. See *Job.*

John, grandson of Netawatwes, the first convert at Lichtenau, 436, 442.

Johanan, Count Zinzendorf's Indian name, 190.

Johnson, Sir William, biography, 55, *note* 2; his seat, 55; visits Onondaga, 211, 212; his efforts in the French and Indian War, 224; renewed efforts to bring about peace, 243; conciliates the Indians after the war, 262; his views regarding the Christian Indians in the Paxton Insurrection, 300; is willing to receive them, 305; mollifies the anger of the Six Nations, 337; tries to prevent Dunmore's War, 403; his death, 429.

Johnson, Sir John, General Superintendent of Indian Affairs in Canada, 579; his interview with Zeisberger, 579; instructions from the British government in regard to the Mission, 580; instigates the Indians against the United States, 614.

Johnson, Colonel Guy, incites the Indians against the United States, 429.

Johnny, Captain, a convert at Lichtenau, 436 and *note* 2; produces belts of peace previous to the massacre, 543.

Jones, David, visits the Delawares, 386, *note* 3.
Joshua, a native assistant, founds Gnadenhütten, 380, 381, *note* 1; brings the news of the massacre to Zeisberger, 536; murdered by the Delawares of the White River, 665.
Judith, the first woman murdered at Gnadenhütten, 549.
Jung, Michael, a Moravian missionary, biography, 478, *note* 2; joins the Ohio Mission, 478; in danger of his life, 484; his experiences during the British expedition against the Mission, 498, 506, 507, 515; protects the wives of the missionaries at Captives' Town, 518; goes to Bethlehem, 586; returns to the Mission, 599, 602; his labors at New Salem, 604; sails to the mouth of the Detroit, 623; preaches to white settlers in Canada, 644; leaves the Mission, 695.
Jungmann, John, steward on the Tuscarawas reservation, 657, *note* 1.
Jungmann, John George, a Moravian missionary, 365; biography, 365, *note* 1; at Friedensstadt, 372; at Schönbrunn, 380; brings the news of Dunmore's War to Schönbrunn, 403, 447; goes to Bethlehem, 453, 454; returns to the Mission, 485; his experiences during the British expedition against the Mission, 498, 507, 508, 509; protects the wives of the missionaries at Captives' Town, 518; retires from the Mission, 586; his death, 586, *note* 2.

K.

Kamp, Mr., assistant surveyor on the Tuscarawas reservation, 646.
Kash, a German settler in the Iroquois country, 188; denounces missionary work among the Indians, 209.
Kaskaskias, a tribe of Indians, 36.
Kiefer, Rev. Mr., a Moravian missionary, escapes from the massacre at Penn's Creek, 225, *note* 2.
Kichline, Sheriff, escorts the Christian Indians, 309.
Killbuck, John, a Delaware opposed to the Moravian Mission, 386 and *note* 1, 428.
Killbuck, John, Jr. See *Gelelemend*.
King Newcomer. See *Netawatwes*.
King Beaver, chief of the Turkey tribe of the Delawares, 349; place of his death, 380.
King of the Delawares, popular title of the head chief, 79.
Kirkland, Samuel, a missionary among the Iroquois, 319 and *note* 1; secures the neutrality of two nations in the Revolution, 443.
Kickapoos, an Indian tribe, 73.
Kiskapocok, a Shawanese tribe, 374.
Klein, George, his farm the site of Litiz, 66, 67, *note* 1; deputy sheriff in the Pontiac War, 281.
Kluge, John Peter, a Moravian missionary, 659; biography, 659, *note* 1; on the White River, Indiana, 659; leaves the Mission, 665.
Kogieschquanoheel. See *Pipe, Captain*.
Kolaneka, seat of Sir W. Johnson, 55.
Konkaput, John, a Stockbridge Indian educated at Nazareth Hall, 660, *note* 2.
Koquethagachton. See *White Eyes*.
Krogstrup, Rev. Mr., reports the massacre at Gnadenhütten to the Mission Board, 573.

L.

Lallemand, a Jesuit missionary, 100; martyrdom, 101.
Languntoutenünk. See *Friedensstadt*.
La Salle, a Jesuit missionary, 103.
La Trobe, Ignatius, the British secretary of the Unitas Fratrum, 579 and *note* 2; sends money to the missionaries, 579, 580.
Lawunakhannek, a Moravian Mission town, 353; first baptisms there, 359; abandoned, *ib.*

INDEX.

Lecron, Susan, biography, 482, *note* 3; marries Zeisberger, 482.
Leinbach, Frederick, brings the news of the massacre to Bethlehem, 572, 573; notifies Congress of the massacre, 573.
Lee, Arthur, United States commissioner, 584.
Lenni-Lenape, a name of the Delaware Indians, 32.
Le Moyne, a Jesuit missionary, 102.
Lesly, John F., killed in the massacre on the Mahony, 229, 236.
Leibert, Joseph, places a monument over the grave of the missionaries killed on the Mahony, 235, *note* 1.
Lewis, Andrew and Thomas, United States commissioners, 467.
Lewis, Colonel, commands Southern forces in Dunmore's War, 407, 408, 409.
Lichtenau, a Moravian Mission town, 433, 435, *note* 2; founded, 434, 435; first celebration of the Lord's Supper there, 438; first baptism there, 442; all the Christian Indians concentrated there; 466; forsaken by the converts, 477; destroyed by Colonel Brodhead, 483.
Lindley, Jacob, a Quaker peace commissioner, 634.
Lincoln, General, a United States peace commissioner, 634.
Litiz, a Moravian town, 66.
Litiz, barony of, 698.
Logan, James, an Iroquois sachem, son of Shikellimy, 150; at Shamokin as deputy of the Grand Council, 153; a friend of the Colonies in the French and Indian War, 224; his family murdered, 402; his revenge, 402, 403; his celebrated speech, 409.
Logan, William, a member of the Pennsylvania Council, 243; his protest against the Indian war, *ib.*; espouses the cause of the Christian Indians in the Paxton Insurrection, 283, 284, 285, 294, 295.
Loretz, John, a member of the Directory in Europe, 368, *note* 2; visits America, 368.
Loskiel, George Henry, a Moravian bishop, 662; biography, 662, *note* 1; his history of the Indian Mission reaches Zeisberger, 621, 622; President of the Mission Board, 662; visits Goshen, *ib.*; ordains Haven, *ib.*
Lower Sandusky, the missionaries stop there, 535, 536, and *note* 1, 561.
Luckenbach, Abraham, a Moravian missionary, 659; biography, 659, *note* 2; begins a Mission on the White River, in Indiana, 659; abandons this Mission, 665.
Luke, a renegade convert, 601.

M.

Mack, Martin, a Moravian missionary, 110; biography, 110, *note* 2 visits Wyoming with Zinzendorf 110; in New England, 117; at Gnadenhütten, 141; at Shamokin, 142; explores the Susquehanna, 144, 145; visits Shamokin and Wyoming with Watteville, 147-150; accompanies Zeisberger to Onondaga, 188-195; at Gnadenhütten on the Mahony at the time of the massacre, 229.
Machtugu, a sacrificial feast, 352.
Machiwihilusing, an Indian town, awakening there, 265, 267; visited by Zeisberger, 269
Mahony settlement, the, 214.
Maguntsche, a Moravian settlement, 65.
Mamasu, a wicked Indian, 597; applies for baptism, *ib.*; baptized, 604.
Mantee, first convert among the North American Indians, 41.
Manitous, 94, 95.
Marquette, a Jesuit missionary, 102
Mark, a native assistant, 560; leaves Captives' Town, *ib.*; opposes the resuscitation of the Mission at New Gnadenhütten, 579; his sudden death, 583.
Martin, John, a native assistant warns the missionaries of their

danger during the British expedition, 498, 499; at the massacre at Gnadenhütten, 542, 543; his conversation with Colonel Williamson, 543.

Marshall, *Frederick de*, biography, 256, *note* 3; Bishop Seidel's assistant, 256; in Philadelphia during the Pontiac War and the Paxton Insurrection, 280, 281, 282, 284, 287.

Massacre of the missionaries on the Mahony, 229–236; of the Christian Indians in Ohio, 537–557; discrepancies in the account of the massacre in Ohio, 549, *note* 1.

Marietta, the first white settlement in Ohio, 607, 655.

McDonald, *Colonel Angus*, attacks the Shawanese, 406.

McClure, *David*, visits the Delawares in Ohio, 379.

McCormick, *Alexander*, a trader and friend of the Mission, 473; warns Zeisberger of his danger during the Revolution, *ib.*; ensign to the British expedition, 491; warns Heckewelder of its object, 492; sends provisions to the Christian Indians, 530.

McIntosh, *General*, commands the Western department, 467; constructs a fort at Beaver, 468, 469; makes a requisition on the Delaware council for warriors, 469; builds Ft. Laurens, 469; marches into the Delaware country at Zeisberger's request, 471; relieves Ft. Laurens, *ib.*

McKee, *Alexander*, a British Indian agent and enemy of the Mission, 462, 489; proposes an expedition against the Mission, 489; bargains for the cattle of the Christian Indians, 517; assists the Christian Indians to secure land in Canada, 617, 630.

Mequachake, a Shawanese tribe, 374.

Meniolagomekah, a Moravian Mission station, 107 and *note* 3.

Menomonies, an Indian tribe, 73.

Melendez founds St. Augustine, 41.

Metoxen, *John*, a Stockbridge Indian educated at Bethlehem, 660.

Miamis, an Indian tribe, 36.

Mingoes, emigrant Iroquois, 58; engage in Dunmore's War, 402, 405; take part in the battle of Point Pleasant, 407, 408; a family of them, Zeisberger's relatives, join the Mission, 420; side with Great Britain in the Revolution, 447; besiege Ft. Laurens, 471; take part in the British expedition against the Mission, 489.

Mingo Bottom, 539, and *note* 2.

Missionaries, *Moravian*, their heroism, 298; their instructions, 308; their influence among the natives, 312, 313; hold a conference at Friedensstadt, 377, 378; jealousy among them, 450 and *note* 1, 451; their position with regard to the Indian Border War, 487, 488, 489; resolve to remain with the converts in spite of every danger, 490, 492, 504; their capture and sufferings at the hands of the British Indians, 493–512; refuse to flee, 498; their trial and acquittal at Detroit, 518–529; remanded to Detroit, 533; their farewell to the converts, 535; determine to revive the Mission, 561, 562; receive a letter from the Directory in Europe, 587, *note* 1; memorialize the Governor of the N. W. Territory about the sale of ardent spirits, 655, 656.

Mission Board, *the*, organized at Bethlehem, 120; enthusiastic meeting of, in 1747, 142; council with Iroquois sachems, 153; meeting of, at the beginning of the French and Indian War, 222, 223; its instructions to the missionaries, 308; relinquishes the Mission among the Iroquois, 319, 320; removes the Mission to Ohio, 370; its difficulties during the Revolution, 481; publishes the documents relating to the massacre at Gnadenhütten, 577; active in resuscitating the Mission, 582; a change among its members, 661.

Mobilian Indians, 31.

INDEX. 733

Mohicans, an Indian tribe, 36.
Mohawks, an Indian nation, 38, 54.
Montauks, an Indian tribe, 105.
Montour, Madame, 72; entertains Zinzendorf, 111; her ignorance of the Gospel, 111, *note* 2.
Montour, Andrew, 72; Zinzendorf's description of his appearance, 112, *note* 1; accompanies Zinzendorf to Wyoming, 112; accompanies Spangenberg to Onondaga, 132–137; a sister of his joins the Mission, 621.
Moor, Thoroughgood, a missionary among the Indians, 104.
Moore, Joseph, a Quaker peace commissioner, 634.
Moore, President, receives a report of the massacre at Gnadenhütten, Ohio, from Congress, 574; his message to the Assembly of Pennsylvania about the massacre, 576, 577.
Moore, Samuel, a convert, talks on religion with the militia at the massacre, 544.
Moore, Justice, escorts the Christian Indians, 309.
Morgan, Colonel George, the Indian Agent for the West, 424, *note* 1, 439, *note* 1; his testimony concerning the Christian Indians, 424, *note* 1; correspondence with the Delawares about an Episcopal missionary, 439; at Pittsburg, 445; correspondence with the Delawares about the Moravian missionaries, 449; dissatisfied with the treaty of 1778, 468.
Morris, Governor, receives Zeisberger's deposition, 226; disputes with the Assembly in the Indian and French War, 227; receives an address from the Christian Indians, 238; promises them protection, 239; declares war against the Shawanese and Delawares, 243; sends peace-messages to the Indians, *ib.*
Moravian Church, in general, origin 698; an account of, 698–700; increase, 698; destruction, 698, 699; renewal, 699; present government, 699, 700; foreign missions, 700.
Moravian Church, in America, accused of sympathy with the French, 177; courage of her members in the French and Indian War, 222; maligned and persecuted, 223, 228.
Mortimer, Benjamin, a Moravian missionary, biography, 648, *note* 1; joins the Mission, 648; farewell discourse at Fairfield, 649, 650; his memorial to Governor St. Clair, 656; admonishes the Goshen Indians to repent, 671; ministers to Zeisberger in his dying hours, 672; his prayer at Zeisberger's death-bed, 674; sketch of Zeisberger's character, 682, 683; remarks about the frequent journeys of the Christian Indians, 679, *note* 1; preaches Zeisberger's funeral sermon in English, 684.
Mount Zion, a Moravian Mission station among the Cherokees, 697.
Mueller, George Godfrey, biography, 663, *note* 2; the pastor of the white settlers on the Tuscarawas reservation, 663; visits Zeisberger on his death-bed, 673; preaches his funeral sermon in German, 684.

N.

Nain, a Moravian Mission town, 248; description of it, 251, 252; threatened with destruction, 275; an attack upon it prevented, 280; the town abandoned and its houses sold, 307–309.
Nanticokes, an Indian tribe, 36; in the Wyoming valley, 70; visit Gnadenhütten and Bethlehem, 186, 204; emigrate to the Iroquois country, 206, 208; their mode of burial, 206; a remnant of the tribe joins those in the Iroquois country, 322, 323; they dwindle to a few families, 642.
Nanticoke, Samuel, a convert, his conversation with Zeisberger about the massacre, 558, 559;

leads the Christian Indians to Pipe's Town, 560; rejoins the Mission, 563; guides the converts to the Cuyahoga, 592; his conversation with one of the scattered converts, 593; goes on an embassy to them, 594; his conversation with his brother, 595.

Narragansetts, a tribe of Indians, 36.

Natchez, a tribe of Indians, 30.

Nathaniel, a native assistant, 270, note 1; accompanies Zeisberger to Machiwihilusing, 270.

Nazareth, a Moravian settlement, 65; in the Pontiac War, 280, 285.

Neisser, George, a Moravian clergyman, 287.

Netawatwes, the head chief of the Delawares, 349 and note 1; entertains Zeisberger, 366; grants the Christian Indians land, 372; troubled about the differences among Christian churches, 387, 388; his disputes with White Eyes, 413–417; reconciled to White Eyes, 422; promulgates the edict of religious liberty at Gnadenhütten, *ib.*; sends a message about the Gospel to Packanke, *ib.*; urges Zeisberger to build a third town, 432, 433; his death, 442, 443.

Neutral Nation, a tribe of Indians, 38.

Neville, Colonel John, commandant at Fort Pitt in 1777, 445.

Newallike, a Delaware chief, 315; receives a message from Governor Penn, 337; joins the Mission, 394 and note 2; becomes an apostate, 450 and note 1.

New Castle, Captain, an Iroquois friendly to the Colonies, 242 and note 2; 243.

New Fairfield, a Moravian Mission town, 695.

New Gnadenhütten, a Moravian Mission town, 578, 579 and note 1.

New Kaskaskunk, the capital of the Monseys in 1770, 361.

New Orleans, population in 1771, 375.

New Salem, a Moravian Mission town, 602, 603 and note 1; a revival there, 604; its prosperity amid a famine, 612, 613; abandoned, 621; destroyed, 653; a child buried in its grave-yard, 653.

New Schönbrunn, a Moravian Mission town, 473 and note 1; occupied by the converts, 476; destroyed, 553, 554; revisited by Zeisberger in 1798, 655, note 1.

New Spring Place, a Moravian missionary station, 697.

New Westfield, a Moravian Mission station, 696.

New York Province, description of, 48, 50–54.

New York City, description of, 49, 50.

New York Government, 53.

Nicholas, a convert, Zeisberger's guide on his last journey, 653, 654.

Nitschmann, David, a Moravian bishop, biography, 16, note 1; leads emigrants to Georgia, 16; founds Bethlehem, 23; visits Zinzendorf in Wyoming, 114.

Nitschmann, David, the Syndic, biography, 314, note 2; visits America, 314; convenes a Synod at Bethlehem, 316.

Nitschmann, Anna, biography, 110, note 3; accompanies Zinzendorf on his last journey to the Indian country, 110, 111, 112.

Nitschmann, John, a Moravian bishop, biography, 152, note 1; President of the Mission Board, 152.

Nitschmann, Martin, killed in the massacre on the Mahony, 229, 232, 236.

Nitschmann, Susanna, carried off as a captive by the Indians, 229, 232; her sufferings and death at Tioga, 236.

Noah, the first Moravian convert from the Cherokees, 394 and note 1.

Noble, Thomas, aids Zeisberger and Post during their imprisonment, 124, 125, note 1.

INDEX.   735

Northwest Territory, ordinance for its government, 606; its first white settlements, 607; great increase of settlers, 655; its legislature prohibits the sale of ardent spirits on the Tuscarawas reservation, 656; the prohibitory act repealed, 665.

O.

Ochquari, or Bear family, among the Iroquois, 78.
Ochschugore, Henry Frey's Indian name, 208.
Oglethorpe, James, founds the Colony of Georgia, 15; assists Zeisberger and Schober, 19, 20.
Ogilvie, John, a missionary among the Indians, 104, 188.
Ohio Company buys land of Congress, 606.
Ohneberg, Sarah, marries Heckewelder, 477, 478.
Oil Wells, in Zeisberger's times, 354 and *note* 1.
Ojibwas, an Indian tribe, 73.
Old Kaskaskunk, the first capital of the Monseys in Western Pennsylvania, 361.
Oneidas, an Iroquois nation, 38, 55; neutral in the Revolution, 443.
Onondagas, an Iroquois nation, 38, 56.
Onondaga, the capital of the Iroquois League, 56.
Oochgelogy, a Moravian Mission station, 695.
Opakin, a name for New Schönbrunn, 655, *note* 1.
Oppelt, a Moravian missionary, 660; begins a mission on the Pettquotting, 663.
Oquacho. or Wolf family, among the Iroquois, 78.
Ostonwacken, an Indian town, 72; visited by Zinzendorf, 111.
Otschinachiatha, an Iroquois sachem and friend of Zeisberger, 200, 202, 208, 212.
Ottawas, an Indian tribe, 36, 73; side against the United States in the Revolution, 441; refuse to take part in the British expedition against the Mission, 489.
Ottigamies, an Indian tribe, 73.

P.

Pachgatgoch, a Moravian Mission station, 117 and *note* 1, 256, 369, *note* 2.
Pachgantschihillas, a Delaware captain, at Gnadenhütten, 484; meets the peace commissioners of the United States, 636.
Packanke, head chief of the Wolf tribe of Delawares, 349; invites Zeisberger to begin a Mission, 358; welcomes the converts, 361; upbraids Glikkikan, 362, 363; receives a message about the Gospel from Netawatwes, 422.
Papunhank, John, an Indian preacher, 267; baptized, 271, 272; goes to Province Island, 289; helps to lay out Friedenshütten, 310; accompanies Zeisberger to Goschgoschünk, 324–335; his death, 427.
Parliament, Act of, in favor of the Moravians, 154.
Parrish, John, a Quaker peace commissioner, 634.
Partsch, George and Maria, escape from the massacre on the Mahony, 229, 231, 232, 234, 235.
Paxton Insurrection, 282–304.
Paxton Insurgents leave Lancaster County, 298; reach Germantown, 301; receive commissioners, 302; return home, *ib*.
Paxnous, a Shawanese chief, 220; interferes with the Mission at Gnadenhütten, *ib*.; baptism of his wife, *ib*.; a friend of the Colonies in the Indian War, 224, 225, 226; at the treaty at Easton in 1757, 249.
Peace of Aix-la-Chapelle, 146, 176.
Peace of Paris, 580, 581.
Peace Confederation, Indian, in 1789, 610, 611; offers to protect the Christian Indians, 611; loses its influence, 615.
Pemahoaland, the first convert at Goshen, 656.

Pemberton, Israel, espouses the cause of the Christian Indians in the Paxton Insurrection, 283, 292, 300.

Penn, William, his policy, 59.

Penn, John, Governor of Pennsylvania, 282; applies to General Gage for troops, 293; sends Christian Indians out of the Province, 293; his message to the Assembly, 296, 297; taken ill in the midst of the Paxton Insurrection, 301; negotiates with the insurgents, 302; his proclamation of peace, 306; his measures to prevent an Indian war in 1768, 336, 337; forbids the surveyors to run a line near Friedenshütten, 370; his relations to Lord Dunmore, 400.

Pennamite and Yankee War. See *War, Pannamite and Yankee*.

Pennsylvania, description of, in 1745, 59–69.

Pennsylvania, government of, 68, 69.

Pennsylvania Synod, the, 106 and note 2; 153, note 1.

Pequods, an Indian tribe, 36.

Petty, John, a son of Shikellimy, 150.

Pettquotting Mission, the second, 663; abandoned, 665, 666.

Peters, Richard, Secretary of the Pennsylvania Council, 69; his Indian name, 165; Cammerhoff at his house, 178; receives an express about the massacre on the Mahony, 236.

Peter, a convert, helps to begin the Mission at Goschgoschünk, 338; leaves Goschgoschhünk, 346.

Peter, David and Dorcas, early settlers on the Tuscarawas reservation, 657, note 1; David buries the bones of the murdered converts, 647, note 1.

Peyster, de, Major, commandant of Detroit, 520; examines the missionaries, 521, 522; conducts their trial, 524–528; his character, 528, 529; gives the missionaries a passport, 529 and note 1; remands them to Detroit, 533, 536; his reasons for this measure, 561; helps to revive the Mission, 562.

Philadelphia, description of, in 1745, 61–63.

Pickering, Colonel, United States peace commissioner, 634.

Pilgerruh, a Moravian Mission town, 592, 593, and note 1; abandoned, 599; its ruins, 653.

Pilgrims at Plymouth, 42.

Pipe's Town, 518 and note 2.

Pipe, Captain, of the Wolf tribe of Delawares, 433, note 2; secedes from the nation, 433, 434; advocates war against the United States, 458, 463, 470, 479; takes part in the British expedition against the Mission, 491; on his way to the trial of the missionaries, 519, 522, 523; advocates their cause, 524–526; has Colonel Crawford tortured, 567; his regret at having taken part in the British expedition, 601; joins the peace confederation, 610; aids the Christian Indians, 616; his death, 641.

Pitt, Fort, and Pittsburg, visited by Zeisberger in 1769, 357; the Indian converts there, 360; seized by John Connolly, 400; the American Western center in the Revolution, 445.

Piqua, a Shawanese tribe, 374.

Pluggy's Town, a Western Indian village, 445, 446.

Point Pleasant, battle of, 407, 408.

Pokanokets, an Indian tribe, 36.

Pomoacan. See *Half King of the Wyandots*.

Pontiac Conspiracy. See *War of Pontiac*.

Pontiac, a chief of the Ottawas, 262; his character, 263; his conspiracy, 263, 264.

Post, Frederick Christian, a Moravian missionary, biography, 121, note 2; in New England, 117; in the Mohawk country, 121; arrested and imprisoned, 123–130; in Wyoming, 221; his embassies to the Western Indians during the War, 250, 251; in

INDEX. 737

Ohio, 256; tries to induce Zeisberger to leave the Moravian Church, 261.

Potatik, a Moravian Mission station, 117 and *note* 1.

Potawatomies, an Indian tribe, 36, 73.

Powhattan Confederacy, 36.

Powell, *Joseph*, biography, 142, *note* 2; at Shamokin, 142, 149.

Preachers, *Indian*, an account of, 265–267.

Presser, *Martin*, killed in the massacre on the Mahony, 229, 236.

Putnam, *General Rufus*, founds Marietta, 607; treats with the Western Indians, 632, 633; surveys the Tuscarawas reservation, 647.

Pyrlaeus, *Christopher*, a Moravian missionary, 106; biography, 120; *note* 2; in New England, 117; teaches the Indian languages, 120.

Q.

Quakers, *the*, espouse the cause of the Christian Indians in the Paxton Insurrection, 283, 288; accused of swaying the Assembly of Pennsylvania, 291, 292; propose to send the Christian Indians to Nantucket Island, 292; rewards offered for the scalps of prominent men among them, 299; assailed through the press, 303; send a present to the Christian Indians, 376, *note* 2; a party of them accompanies the peace commission of 1793, 634; their letter and gift to the Christian Indians, 634 and *note* 1; send a deputation to Zeisberger to consult about the conversion of the Indians, 660, 661.

R.

Raleigh, *Sir Walter*, his American expeditions, 41.

Randolph, *Beverly*, a United States peace commissioner, 634.

Rattlesnake nest, 137, 138.

Rau, *John*, a settler near Shekomeko, 98.

Rau, *Sergeant*, in command of a guard sent to protect the missionaries, 561.

Rauch, *Christian Henry*, the first Moravian missionary to the Indians, 97; biography, 97, *note* 1; difficulties, and success of his work, 105; baptizes the first converts, 107 and *note* 1; at Gnadenhütten, 141.

Reichel, *John Frederick*, a Moravian bishop, biography, 480, *note* 1; visits America, 480.

Renatus, a convert, arrested for murder, 281; imprisoned in Philadelphia, 284; acquitted, 305; subsequent history and death, 581.

Reservation, *Christian Indian, on the Tuscarawas*, laid out, 647; ardent spirits prohibited on it, 656; part of it leased to white settlers, 657; the first settlers, 657, *note* 1; receive a minister of their own, 658; evil influences of the traders, 661; a second church organized for the settlers, 663; prohibitory law repealed, 665.

Revolution, *the*. See *War of the Revolution*.

Rex, *Augustus*, a convert, 154; carries peace-messages, 244; forsakes the Mission, 252; rejoins the Mission and dies, 260.

Risecker, *Jacob*, drives the first teams to the Tuscarawas reservation, 657, *note* 1.

Robinson, *Captain*, escorts the Christian Indians, 294.

Robbins, a trader, entertains the missionaries, 536; visits Captives' Town, 558.

Roessler, a Moravian missionary, escapes from the massacre at Penn's Creek, 225, *note* 2.

Rose, *The*, a tavern, 309.

Rothrock, *John*, assistant surveyor on the Tuscarawas reservation, 646, 647, *note* 1.

Roth, *John*, a Moravian missionary, biography, 388, *note* 2; leads the Christian Indians to Philadelphia, 286; on the Susquehanna, 369; leads the Christian Indians to the West, 376; at Friedensstadt, 380; at Gnadenhütten and Schönbrunn, 388; leaves the Mission, 405; subsequent history and death, 405, *note* 1.

Roth, John Lewis, the first white child born in Ohio, 388 and *note* 2; his subsequent history and death, 405, *note* 1.

Roth, Maria Agnes, the mother of the first white child born in Ohio, 388 and *note* 2; her death, 405, *note* 1.

Rundt, Godfrey, a Moravian missionary, 188; biography, 188, *note* 1; visits Onondaga with Zeisberger, 188-203.

Rutherforth, Captain, at Albany, 124.

S.

Sacs, an Indian tribe, 73.

Sachemships, among the Iroquois, 76, 77.

Salem, a Moravian Mission town, 477 and *note* 1; first wedding of a white couple in Ohio in its chapel, 477, 478; British Indians encamp there, 491; the last Lord's Supper, 511; its ruins, 647, *note* 2; white settlers occupy its site, 657.

Sally Hand, a colony in Canada, 631.

Sacrifices, among the Indians, 95, 96, 344, 351-353.

Savery, William, a Quaker peace commissioner, 634.

Scalp-yell, among the Indians, 508, 509 and *note* 1.

Schebosh, John Joseph, an assistant Moravian missionary, 131; biography, 131, *note* 1; accompanies Spangenberg to Onondaga, 131; adopted among the Iroquois, 134; at Gnadenhütten, 229; brings the news of Dunmore's War to Schönbrunn, 403; flees to Litiz, 454; goes to Pittsburg, 463; carries peace-messages to the Delawares, 464; captured with a party of converts by American militia, 518, 519; liberated by General Irvine and goes to Bethlehem, 531 and *note* 1; visits Pittsburg after the massacre, 574, 575, 576; reunited with his family at New Gnadenhütten, 582; purchases provisions for the Mission at Pittsburg, 592, 593; receives Heckewelder at Pilgerruh, 599; his death, 605; his character, *ib.;* his family, 605, *note* 1.

Schebosh, Joseph, son of the preceding, killed by American militia, 541.

Schmidt, Anthony, the smith at Shamokin, 142, 149; buries the remains of the victims in the massacre on the Mahony, 235, *note* 1.

Schmick, John Jacob, a Moravian missionary, 184; biography, 184, *note* 1; at Gnadenhütten at the time of the massacre, 229; in Philadelphia during the Pontiac War, 280, 281, 287; accompanies the Christian Indians on their way to New York, 294; on their journey to Friedenshütten, 308, 309; at Friedenshütten, 318, 369; in Ohio, 388, 447; adopted among the Shawanese, 447, *note* 2; disapproves of Zeisberger's course in the Revolution, 452; flees to Litiz, 454; his death, 454, *note* 1.

Schmick, assistant surveyor on the Tuscarawas reservation, 647 and *note* 2; helps to build Goshen, 654.

Schober, John Michael, 18; runs away from Herrendyk with Zeisberger, 19; his death, 20.

Schweigert, George, killed in the massacre on the Mahony, 229, 232, 236.

Schönbrunn, a Moravian Mission town, 372; its site, 376 and *note* 1; its name, 377; the plan of the town, 380, *note* 1; its chapel dedicated, 380; a revival there, 383, 393; its municipal system, 423, 424; a revival in 1776, 432; a conspiracy against the Mission among some of its inhabitants, 449-451; abandoned, 452.

INDEX.

Schechschiquanunk, a Moravian Mission station, 369; abandoned, 376; number of its inhabitants, 376, note 1.
Schweinitz, John Christian Alexander de, biography, 369, note 1; comes to America, 369; a member of the Mission Board, *ib.*; active in the Board during the Revolution, 480, 582; endeavors to ascertain whither the missionaries have been carried by the British Indians, 523; his death, 661.
Schweinitz, Frederick de, explores the Cherokee country, 663.
Schweinitz, Lewis David de, a Moravian clergyman, treats with Congress and the United States commissioner about the Tuscarawas reservation, 695, 696.
Schnall, a Moravian missionary, 662; leaves the Mission, 695.
Schlosser, Captain, escorts the Christian Indians, 297; commands the British barracks in the Paxton Insurrection, 299.
Schuessele's painting of Zeisberger preaching to the Indians, 331, note 1.
Schuyler, Mayor, at Albany, 123; his parting words to Zeisberger and Post, 124.
Scotch-Irish settlers, their animosity toward the Indians, 275, 276; murder the Conestoga Indians, 290; their hatred of the Quakers, 292.
Scott, General, his campaigns against the Western Indians, 614, 625.
Seidel, Christian, accompanies Zeisberger to Wyoming, 221 and note 2, 225.
Seidel, Nathaniel, a Moravian bishop, biography, 130, note 1; visits Zeisberger and Post in jail, 130; travels to Europe with Zeisberger, 178-181; president of the Mission Board, 256; recalls Zeisberger from Machiwihilusing, 273; hears of the massacre at Gnadenhütten in Ohio, 573; his death, 582.

Senseman, Joachim, a Moravian missionary in New England, 117; escapes from the massacre on the Mahony, 229, 231, 234.
Senseman, Anna Catharine, killed in the massacre on the Mahony, 229, 233.
Senseman, Gottlob, a Moravian missionary, accompanies Zeisberger to Wyoming, 260; to Onondaga, 318-320; to Goschgoschünk, 338-349; to Fort Pitt, 357, 358; goes to Bethlehem, 365; rejoins the Mission 477; at New Schönbrunn, 478; his experiences during the British expedition against the Mission, 498, 504; 505, 506, 509; trial at Detroit, 518; at Detroit again, 563; at New Gnadenhütten, 579; goes to Bethlehem, 586; returns to the Mission, 614; sails to the mouth of the Detroit, 623; at Niagara, 635, 636; preaches to the white settlers in Canada, 644; refuses to serve in the Canadian Assembly, 645; teaches the school at Fairfield, *ib.*; his discourse previous to the departure of Zeisberger, 650; his death, 658.
Senseman, Christian David, born at the time of the British expedition against the Mission, 498 and note 1; taken to Detroit, 535 and note 1.
Senecas, an Iroquois nation, 38, 57.
Settlements in the West, about 1771, 375.
Seyfert, Anthony, the first Moravian clergyman ordained in America, 16; visits Zinzendorf in Wyoming, 114; advises with Zeisberger and Post during their imprisonment, 124, 125.
Shawanese, an Indian tribe, 36; in the Wyoming valley, 70; visit Gnadenhütten and Bethlehem, 186, 204; their hunting-grounds in Ohio, 374; their towns on the Scioto, 374, note 2; visited by Zeisberger, 382, 383, 389-393; incline to war in 1773, 402; defeated in Dunmore's War, 406; take part in the battle of Point

Pleasant, 407, 408; take sides against the United States in the Revolution, 441, 447; besiege Fort Laurens, 471; take part in the British expedition against the Mission, 489; send the Christian Indians provisions, 530; submit to the United States, 588; active in the new Indian War, 636; Captain Pipe rebukes them, 636, 637.

Shabash, one of the first converts of the Moravian Mission, 98, 99.

Shamokin, the principal Indian village in Pennsylvania, 71 and *note* 2; visited by Zinzendorf 111; by Spangenberg, 132; a smithy and Mission there, 141, 142; wickedness of its inhabitants, 151, 152.

Shekomeko, the first Moravian Mission station, 98, 99; a church organized, 109; a chapel dedicated, 117; the site of the village, 117, *note* 1; the Mission broken up by the New York Assembly, 118.

Shikellimy, Iroquois sachem at Shamokin, 71; at Tulpehocken, 100, *note* 1; entertains Zinzendorf, 111; entertains Watteville, 149; receives a gift from Zinzendorf, 149 and *note* 1; his conversion and death, 150.

Shingas, a Delaware warrior, 224.

Sioux, an Indian tribe, 31.

Six Nations. See *Iroquois.*

Sitkovius, Christian, a bishop of the Unitas Fratrum, 699.

Simcoe, Colonel, Governor of Upper Canada, 634; grants land to the Christian Indians, 638.

Smith, Major, commandant at Detroit, 617.

Smith, Matthew, a leader of the Paxton Insurgents, 290, 298.

Snake, John and Thomas, two Shawanese captains, 491.

Sogechtowa, another name for James Logan, 150.

Solomon. See *Allemęwi.*

Sorcerers, among the Indians, 340, 341.

Society for the Advancement of Civilization and Christianity among the Indians, 103.

Society for the Furtherance of the Gospel among the Heathen, in England, 579, 580; holds the deed for the Mission land in Canada, 638.

Society of the United Brethren for Propagating the Gospel among the Heathen, in America, organized, 607, 608; its first officers, 608, *note* 1; the Tuscarawas reservation vested in it, 606; dimensions of the tract, 607 and *note* 3; appoints John Heckewelder its agent, 608; receives land from the Assembly of Pennsylvania, 618, *note* 1; memorializes Congress about the removal of the Mission to Canada, 629, 630; has the Tuscarawas reservation surveyed, 646-648; leases a part of it to white settlers, 657 and *note* 1.

Soto, Ferdinand de, his discoveries, 40, 41.

Spring Place, a Moravian Mission station, 695.

Spangenberg, Augustus Gottlieb, a Moravian bishop, biography, 15, *note* 2; obtains land from the trustees of Georgia, 15, 16; his character, 119; organizes a Mission Board and a school for young missionaries, 120 and *notes* 1 and 2; visits Onondaga, 131-139; adopted among the Iroquois, 134; goes to Europe, 155; returns to America, 184; visits Europe again and returns, 205, 214; at the Governor's Council in 1756, 243; enters the Directory of the Unitas Fratrum, 256.

St. Augustine, 41.

St. Clair, Arthur, clerk of Westmoreland County, Pennsylvania, 400; Governor of the Northwest Territory, 606, 607; notifies the Indians of the grant made to the Christian Indians, 610; a major-general, 625; his disastrous campaign against the Indians, 627, 628; receives a memorial from the missionaries, 655.

INDEX.   741

St. Louis, a center of the fur trade in 1771, 375.
Steiner, Abraham, a Moravian missionary, accompanies Heckewelder to the West, 611; among the Cherokees, 663.
Stockbridge, a Mission station, 696.
Stockbridge Indians, where established, 609, 660, *note* 2; a deputation of them visits Goshen, 660.
Strong, Lt.-Colonel, the American commandant at Detroit in 1798, 653.
Stinton, John, murdered by the savages, 278.
Sturgis, Joseph, escapes from the massacre on the Mahony, 229, 232, 233 and *note* 1, 235.
Sturgis, Cornelius, a scout in the Paxton Insurrection, 293.
Stevens, Aaron, a Colonial interpreter, writes to Cammerhoff about his visit to Onondaga, 177.
Stump, Frederick, murders peaceable Indians, 336; imprisoned and rescued, 337.
Susquehannocks, a tribe of Indians, 36.
Sullivan, General, commands the expedition against the Iroquois in 1780, 476.
Sweating Ovens, among the Indians, 89 and *note* 3.
Symmes, John Cleves, buys land of Congress, 606.

T.

Tadeuskund, Gideon, a convert, chief of the Delawares, 213; interferes with the Gnadenhütten Mission, 220; becomes an apostate and the King of the Delawares, 224; at Bethlehem and Easton, 245, 246; incites the Colonial government against the Mission, 246, 247; at the treaty of 1757, 249; entices Augustus Rex to leave the Mission, 252; visited by Zeisberger in Wyoming, 259; his death, 268.
Tatemy, Moses, a Delaware chief, 107 and *note* 2.

Tawandamaenk, an Indian village, visited by Zeisberger, 273.
Tecumseh, an Indian prophet, 665.
Tedpachxit, chief of the Delawares in Indiana, 659; visits President Jefferson, 660; murdered by his tribe, 665.
Tgarihontie, John de Watteville's Indian name, 153.
Tgirhitontie, Bishop Spangenberg's Indian name, 134.
Thachnechtoris, a son of Shikellimy, 150; temporarily the Iroquois deputy at Shamokin, 151; a friend of the Colonies in the Indian War, 224; escorts a missionary to Bethlehem, 225, *note* 2; escorted by Zeisberger to Gnadenhütten, 227; at a treaty in Philadelphia, 242, 243.
Thaneraquechta, Godfrey Rundt's Indian name, 201.
Thomas, a Christian lad, escapes, scalped, from the massacre, 550, 551 and *note* 1.
Thomas, a convert, grandson of Netawatwes, rejoins the Mission after the massacre, 581.
Thomson, Charles, the Secretary of Congress, receives a letter about the massacre, 573, 574.
Thürnstein, the, the name given to a mountain-range in honor of Zinzendorf, 110, 111.
Thayendanega. See *Brant, Joseph*.
Tiozinossongochto, an Iroquois village, visited by Zeisberger, 325–328.
Tionnontates, an Indian tribe, 38.
Titawachkam, a Monsey captain, 600; interferes with the Mission, 600, 601.
Tobacco Nation, an Indian tribe, 38.
Tobias, a convert, accompanies the missionaries to Detroit, 518; at the massacre, 544.
Togahaju, an Iroquois sachem, 311; refuses to allow the converts to remain at Friedenshütten, 314, 315; visited by Zeisberger and Senseman, 318.
Totems, among the Indians, 78.
Traders, among the Indians, an agent of Sir William Johnson at

Onondaga, 199; a Dutch trader beats Zeisberger, 201, 202; their general character, 255.

Treaties, Colonial, at Lancaster with the Twightwees, in 1747, 145; at Albany with the Iroquois in 1747, 146; at Philadelphia with the Iroquois in 1749, 153; at Albany with the Iroquois in 1751, 183; at Albany with the same in 1754, 216; at Philadelphia with several chiefs in 1756, 242, 243; at Easton in July and November, 1756, 245, 246; at Lancaster in May, 1757, 246–248; at Easton in July, 1757, 249; at Easton in October, 1758, 250, 251; at Easton in 1761, 253; at Fort Pitt in April, 1768, 333; at Fort Stanwix in October, 1768, 347, 348.

Treaties of the United States, with the Western tribes at Pittsburg, in 1775, 428–430; at Pittsburg in 1776, 442; at Pittsburg in September, 1778, 467, 468; with the Iroquois at Fort Stanwix in 1784, 584; with the Delawares and other tribes at Fort McIntosh in 1784, 585; with the Shawanese at Fort Finney, in 1786, 588; with the Western tribes at Fort Harmar in 1789, 608, 609; with some of the Western tribes at Port Vincennes in 1792, 633; unsuccessful treaty with the Western tribes at the mouth of the Detroit, 634–637; treaty of peace with the Western tribes at Greenville, in 1795, 643; with the Southern tribes in 1796, 665; with the Christian Indians and the Society holding their land in 1823, 695, 696.

Trueman, Major, murdered by the Indians, 632.

Tschoop, a misnomer for Job, 98, note 1. See *Job*.

Tuppakin, a name for New Schönbrunn, 655, *note*.

Turck, John de, the first Moravian Indians baptized in his barn, 106.

Turtle, a clan among the Iroquois, 78.

Tuscarawas Valley, a description of it, 372, 377; its climate, 373, *note*, 1.

Tuscaroras, an Iroquois nation, 55; neutral in the Revolution, 443.

Tutelees, remnant of, 149.

Twightwees, treaty with, 145; engage in the war against the United States, 638.

Tybout, a Frenchman, entertains the missionaries at Detroit, 522.

U.

Uchees, an Indian tribe, 30.
Unamis, a Delaware tribe, 35.
Unalachtgos, a Delaware tribe, 35.
Unitas Fratrum. See *Moravian Church*.

V.

Van Vleck, Henry, biography, 125, *note* 1; sent to Bethlehem with the news of Zeisberger's and Post's imprisonment, 125.

Venango, Fort, ruins of, visited by Zeisberger, 358.

Vernon, Major, commands Fort Laurens, 471.

Verrazzani, John, his voyages of discovery, 40.

Vincennes, its population in 1771, 375

W.

Walker, Colonel, United States peace commissioner, 429.

Walking Purchase, 64, *note* 2.

Wallace, William, his family murdered by the Indians, 539.

Wampanoags, an Indian tribe, 36.

Wangomen, an Indian preacher, 332; discomfited by Zeisberger, 333–335; his relation to the Mission at Goschgoschünk, 338, 339, 344, 345, 353, 359; naturalizes Zeisberger among the Monseys, 364; explains the views of the Christian Indians with regard to tribute, 364, 365.

Warner, Ezra and Peter, early settlers on the Tuscarawas reservation, 657, *note* 1.

INDEX. 743

Warte, Die, or the *Watch Tower,* a Moravian Mission station, 624 and *note* 1.
War between England and Spain, in 1739, 22.
War between England and France, in 1744, 53, 74, 118, 122.
War, French and Indian, in 1755, preliminary complications, 205, 208, 212, 215; Braddock's defeat, 222; the names of the tribes engaged in it, 223, 224; first massacres, 224; progress of the war, 241-253; reverses of England, 249; William Pitt's energy, 250; decisive battle at Quebec, 252; Canada ceded to England, 253.
War of Pontiac planned, 263, 264, breaks out, 270; the forts captured, *ib.;* progress of the war, 274, 275; triumph of the Colonies, 306.
War, Pennamite and Yankee, 268, 269, 370.
War, Dunmore's, 399-409.
War of the Revolution, approaching, 421; progress of, 428; Western border war, 441-471.
War of the United States with the Western Indians, 614-616, 624, 625, 627, 628, 632, 633, 638-640.
War of the United States with Great Britain, in 1812, 694.
Wasamapah. See *Job.*
Washington, George, his mission to the French on the Ohio, 212, 215; defeats the French, 215; commander-in-chief of the American armies, 428; plans a campaign against the Iroquois, 476; inaugurated President, 610; receives a visit from Indian chiefs, 633; the pacification of the Indians a special object, 655.
Watteville, Baron John de, biography, 147, *note* 1; character, 146; arrives in America, *ib.;* visits the Indian country, 147-150; adopted among the Iroquois, 153, *note* 3; returns to Europe, 155; second visit to America, 587; his letter to Zeisberger about the reservation, 587; his farewell letter to the Christian Indians, 613; returns to Europe, 603, *note* 2.
Wayne, General, commands an expedition against the Western Indians, 632; his victorious campaign, 638-640; his prudence, 641.
Wechquetank, a Moravian Mission town, 256 and *note* 1; threatened with destruction, 275, 278, 279; destroyed, 280.
Wechquadnach, a Moravian Mission station, 117 and *note* 1.
Weigand, John, a messenger of the Mission Board, 517, 582, 599, 602.
Weiss, Lewis, attorney of the Moravians, 284; his letter to the Secretary of Congress about the massacre, 573, 574.
Weisser, Conrad, biography, 68, *note* 1; his seat, 68; entertains Zinzendorf, 108; visits Shamokin with Zinzendorf, 110; protects Zinzendorf in Wyoming, 114; accompanies Spangenberg to Onondaga, 132-136; suggests to the Moravians to establish a smithy at Shamokin, 142.
Welandawecken, a Delaware chief inciting to war, 600, 601, 610.
Wesa, Peter, escapes from the massacre at Penn's Creek, 225, *note* 2.
Wesley, John, in Georgia, 16.
Westenhuc, a Moravian Mission station, 117 and *note* 1.
West, the, a survey of, in 1777, 445, 446.
Westfield, a Moravian Mission station, 696.
Wenginund, Captain, takes part in the British expedition against the Mission, 491; summons the missionaries to Detroit, 517; refuses to take them to Detroit, 519; his conversation with Colonel Crawford at the stake, 567-571.
Wetterhold, Captain Jacob, murders Christian Indians, 277; is murdered, 278.
Welhik-Tuppeek See *Schönbrunn.*
Whitefield, George, 23.
Whitefield House, the, 23.

White child, the first, born in Ohio. See *Roth, John Lewis.*

White Eyes, a Delaware captain, 390; his views regarding the Indians, 390; meets with Zeisberger, 390, 391; his town, 391, *note* 1; advocates peace in Dunmore's War, 404; Glikkikan's appeal to him, 404; urges the adoption of all the missionaries, 405; Lord Dunmore's adviser in the war, 408; his speech in the Delaware Council after the war, 413-416; his great plans, 418-420; relinquishes his project of going to England, 427; his speech at the treaty of Pittsburg in 1775, 430; negotiates with Congress for Episcopal missionaries, 431, 436, 437; at the Delaware Council after his return from Philadelphia, 437, 438; his conversation with Glikkikan, 438, 439; his appeal to the Delawares in favor of the Gospel, 448; advocates peace in the Revolution, 463; his plan concerning the Delaware nation partly adopted by the United States, 468, *note* 1; his death, 469, 470.

White Eyes, widow of, baptized, 656.

White Eyes, Joseph, baptized, 661.

William, a convert. See *Chilloway, Job.*

William Henry. See *Gelelemend.*

Wilkinson, Colonel, his expeditions against the Indians, 625, 627.

Williamson, Colonel David, captures Shebosh and his party of converts, 519; commands the expedition against Gnadenhütten, 540-542; leaves it to his men to decide the fate of the Christian Indians, 547; refuses to save Christiana, 549; his character according to Doddridge, 555, 556.

Winnebagoes, an Indian tribe, 31, 73.

Wollin, John G., sends the missionaries money from England, 579, 580.

Wolcott, Oliver, United States commissioner, 584.

Wolf, a clan among the Iroquois, 78.

Woolman, John, a Quaker preacher at Machiwihilusing, 27.

Worbass, Peter, escapes from the massacre on the Mahony, 229, 231, 234.

Wyandots, an Indian tribe, 38; conquered by the Iroquois, *ib.;* remnant of, 73; Jesuit Mission among them, 100; their hunting-grounds in Ohio, 374; take sides against the United States in the Revolution, 442, 447; besiege Fort Laurens, 471; take part in the British expedition against the Mission, 489; in the Indian War after the Revolution, 638.

Wyoming, the Indian tribes there, 70; visited by Count Zinzendorf, 112-116; by Baron de Watteville, 148, 149; the first Lord's Supper administered in its valley, 148; visited by Cammerhoff and Zeisberger, 156, 174; by Zeisberger and Bezold, 184; by Spangenberg and his party, 186; stated itinerancies there of Moravian missionaries, 221; Christian Frederick Post establishes himself there, *ib.;* Zeisberger's visit there at the outbreak of the French and Indian War, 225, 226; Zeisberger itinerates there after the war, 259-261.

Z.

Zane, Colonel, protests against murdering the Indians in Dunmore's War, 402.

Zander, William, a Moravian missionary, 106.

Zauchtenthal, Zeisberger's birthplace, 13.

Zeisberger, David, his birth, 13; ancestors, 14; parents, 13, 16, 20, 24, *note* 2; flees to Herrnhut, 15; early years in Germany and Holland, 17, 18; runs away from Herrendyk and escapes to Georgia, 19, 20; his stay in Georgia and South Carolina, 21, 22; goes to Pennsylvania, 22, 23; at the Whitefield House and Bethlehem, 23, 24; his return to

INDEX. 745

Europe prevented, 24, 25; conversion, 26; devotes himself to missionary work among the Indians, 26, 27; a member of Pyrlaeus's class of students of Indian languages, 120; inmate of the Brethren's House at Bethlehem, 120, 121, *note* 1; sent to the Mohawk country, 121; at Canajoharie with King Hendrick, 122; arrested as a spy, 123; examination at Albany, trial at New York, and imprisonment in the jail, 123–130; first journey to Onondaga with Spangenberg, 131–139; adopted among the Iroquois, 134; his Indian name, *ib.;* helps to lay out Gnadenhütten, 141; Mack's assistant at Shamokin, 144; explores the two branches of the Susquehanna with Mack, 144, 145; interpreter to Watteville's party at Shamokin and Wyoming, 147–150; brings the news of Shikellimy's death to Bethlehem, 151; his ordination, *ib.;* labors at Shamokin, 151, 152; second visit to Onondaga with Cammerhoff, 156–175; escape from a rattlesnake, 174; visit to Europe, 178–181; appointed perpetual missionary to the Indians, 181; his return to America, *ib.;* visits Wyoming with Bezold, 184; missionary at Shamokin, 185, 186; third visit to Onondaga, 187–190; negotiations with a part of the Grand Council, 190–194; among the Cayugas, 201; attacked and beaten by a trader, 201, 202; itinerates in New York and New England, 204; fourth visit to Onondaga, 205–212; his views concerning the Iroquois Mission, 212, 213; fifth visit to Onondaga, 215–219; builds a Mission house at Onondaga, 216; is made the keeper of the archives of the Grand Council, 217; his labors among the Indians of Wyoming, 221, 225, 226; barely escapes the massacre at Gnadenhütten, 229–233; brings the news of the massacre to Bethlehem, 234; present at Colonial treaties during the French and Indian War, 242–251; visits North Carolina, 244, 252; superintendent of the Brethren's House at Litiz, 252, 253; government interpreter at the Indian congress at Easton in 1761, 253; first visit to the Indian country after the war, 259, 260; itinerates in the Wyoming valley, 260, 261; refuses to leave the Moravian Church and join Frederick Post, 261; visits the Connecticut settlers in Wyoming, 268; his work at Machiwihilusing, 269–273; messenger of the Mission Board in the Pontiac War, 275; leads the Christian Indians to Philadelphia, 286; further connection with the Christian Indians during the Pontiac War and Paxton Insurrection, 289, 290, 292, 294, 304, 305; appointed missionary at Machiwihilusing, 308; leads the Christian Indians from Nain to Machiwihilusing, 308–310; his illness, 312; letter to the Board reporting a revival at Friedenshütten, 313; meets David Nitschmann, the Syndic, 314; leads a deputation of Christian Indians to Cayuga Town, 315, 316; leaves Friedenshütten, and last visit to Onondaga, 318–320; spends the winter of 1766 at Christiansbrunn, 322; meets with his Indian relatives at Bethlehem and buries one of them, 322, 323; his exploratory tour to the Indians of the Alleghany at Goschgoschünk, 324–335; his conversation with the chief of Tiozinossongochto, 325–328; his bold refutation of Wangomen, the Indian preacher, 333–335; begins a Mission at Goschgoschünk, 338–349; removes the Mission from Goschgoschünk to Lawunakhannek, 353–359; visits Fort Pitt and prevents an Indian war, 357, 358; visits the site of Fort Venango, 358; journey with the converts from the Alleghany to the Beaver River, 359–361; naturalized among the Monseys, 363, 364; first visit to Ohio, 366, 367; meets deputies from Europe at Bethlehem, 369; presents an invitation from the Delaware chiefs to the Susquehanna converts to come to Ohio, 370; dangerously ill at Lancaster, 371; second visit to Ohio, 371; begins the first Mission station in Ohio, 372; receives the Susquehanna converts at Friedensstadt, 376; his illness in Ohio, 378; missionary at Schönbrunn, 380, 381; first visit to the Shawanese of Ohio, 382, 383; second visit to the Shawanese, 389–393; interview with Gieschenatsi, 391–393; offers to leave Ohio and explore other parts of the West, 394; his position during Dunmore's War, 399–409; his views with regard to White Eyes, 411; his great plans concerning the Mission, 412, 413; his views concerning the Revolutionary War, 421, 422; visits Bethlehem in 1775,427; negotiates with Netawatwes about a third Christian town, 432, 433; founds Lichtenau, 434, 435; opposes White Eyes in his efforts to secure teachers other than Moravians, 436–438; secures the neutrality of the Delawares and their grandchildren in the Revolution, 443, 444; importance of his services acknowledged by United States generals, 444, note 2; Zeisberger at Schönbrunn amid the conspiracy of some of the converts, 449–452; the Mission in charge of Zeisberger and Edwards only, 454; Zeisberger's views with regard to their situation, *ib.*; saved from the danger of passing war-parties by the Huron Half King, 454–456; maintains his position at Lichtenau and sways the Delaware council, 456–459; further stay at Lichtenau amid the difficulties and dangers caused by the war, 460–471; his dissatisfaction with the treaty at Pittsburg in 1778, 468, 469; leaves Lichtenau and founds New Schönbrunn, 472, 473; saved from the hands of Girty's war-party, 473–475; his life saved again, 475, 476; last visit to Bethlehem, 480; interview with President Reed, at Philadelphia, 481; his marriage at Litiz, 481, 482; returns to the Mission with his wife, 484, 485; is taken prisoner and forced to break up the Mission on the Tuscarawas, 486–512; his public discourse at Gnadenhütten while the town is in the power of the British Indians, 499–503; refuses to claim his rights as a Monsey, 504; his feelings at leaving the Tuscarawas towns, 514; journey to the Sandusky region, 514–517; at Captives' Town, 517; on trial at Detroit, 518–529; returns to Captives' Town, 529; loses his influence among the heathen Indians, 532; remanded to Detroit, 533; his distress of mind, 533, 534; his agony at parting from the converts, 535; receives news of the massacre at Gnadenhütten, 536, 558; reads the burial service in their memory, 558; conversation with Samuel Nanticoke about the massacre, 558, 559; his feelings at the unjust suspicions of some of the converts, 560; his agony of mind with regard to their future, *ib.*; at Detroit after the massacre, 561, 562; goes to Michigan to resuscitate the Mission, 563; at New Gnadenhütten in Michigan, 578–589; interview with Sir John Johnson at Detroit, 579, 580; on the Cuyahoga, at Pilgerruh, in Ohio,590–599; sends a written speech to the scattered converts, 594; his illness, 596; receives a comforting letter from the Mission Board, 596; at New Salem, on the Pettquotting, 600–611; further stay at New Salem, 612–622; applies to the Canadian government for a refuge during the Indian War, 616–619; his opinion of Loskiel's History of the Mission, 622; at the mouth of the Detroit, 623–630; negotiates with Canadian government for the permanent establishment of the Mission in Canada, 630; at Fairfield in Canada, 631–651; resolves to begin a new town on the reservation in Ohio, 648; leaves Fairfield, 651; last journey to Ohio, 652–654; founds Goshen, 654; visits the site of New Schönbrunn, 655, *note;* signs a memorial to Governor St. Clair about the sale of ardent spirits, 656; labors at Goshen, *ib.;* administers the Lord's Supper to the white settlers on the reservation, 658; continues to labor at Goshen, 661; his health begins to fail, 666, 667; deliverance from serpents, *ib.;* last public address to the Indians, 668; his health continues to fail, 670; receives the Lord's Supper, *ib.;* his testimony concerning his hopes as a Christian, 671; his dying hours, 672, 673; his death, 674; his work, 674–680; his personal appearance and habits, 680, 681; his funeral, 683, 684; his epitaph, 685.

Zeisberger's, David, literary works, general remarks, 686; MS. History of the Indians, 29, *note* 2, 478; his MSS. in Harvard University, 691; Iroquois German Dictionary, 144, 200, 253, 690; Iroquois Grammar, 253, 690, 691; Delaware Easter Morning Litany, 394–398; Delaware Spelling Book, 427, 439, 440, 663, 667, 687; Delaware Hymn Book, 612, 661, 667, 688, 689; Delaware Grammar, 667, 691; Delaware Harmony of the Gospels, 612, 667, 689, 690; Delaware Sermons to Children, 689; a Delaware treatise on the Bodily Care for Children, 689.

Zeisberger Island, in the Tuscarawas, 654; named by General Putnam, *ib.*

Zeisberger, Susan (see *Lecron, Susan*), arrives at the Mission, 484, 485; captured by the British Indians, 508; thrown from her horse, 515; sufferings at Captives' Town, 531; leaves the Mission, 693; residence and death at Bethlehem, 693, 694.

Zinzendorf, Count Nicholas Lewis, biographical notices, 699; Herrnhut on his estate, 15; lays the corner-stone for the first chapel, 314; secures retreats for the Moravians, 15; arrives at Bethlehem, 23, 24; first visit to the Indian country, 107–109; treaty with Iroquois sachems, 108; visits Shekomeko, 109, 110; visits Wyoming, 110–116; the adders, 113; plot to murder him, 114; the rattlesnake story a fable, 114, *note* 2; his Indian name, 148, 190; returns to Europe, 24; his morbid sensibility with regard to American affairs, 180, 181; his death, 256.

Zonesschio, capital of the Senecas, 168.

The First American Frontier
AN ARNO PRESS/NEW YORK TIMES COLLECTION

Agnew, Daniel.
A History of the Region of Pennsylvania North of the Allegheny River. 1887.

Alden, George H.
New Government West of the Alleghenies Before 1780. 1897.

Barrett, Jay Amos.
Evolution of the Ordinance of 1787. 1891.

Billon, Frederick.
Annals of St. Louis in its Early Days Under the French and Spanish Dominations. 1886.

Billon, Frederick.
Annals of St. Louis in its Territorial Days, 1804-1821. 1888.

Littel, William.
Political Transactions in and Concerning Kentucky. 1926.

Bowles, William Augustus.
Authentic Memoirs of William Augustus Bowles. 1916.

Bradley, A. G.
The Fight with France for North America. 1900.

Brannan, John, ed.
Official Letters of the Military and Naval Officers of the War, 1812-1815. 1823.

Brown, John P.
Old Frontiers. 1938.

Brown, Samuel R.
The Western Gazetteer. 1817.

Cist, Charles.
Cincinnati Miscellany of Antiquities of the West and Pioneer History. (2 volumes in one). 1845-6.

Claiborne, Nathaniel Herbert.
Notes on the War in the South with Biographical Sketches of the Lives of Montgomery, Jackson, Sevier, and Others. 1819.

Clark, Daniel.
Proofs of the Corruption of Gen. James Wilkinson. 1809.

Clark, George Rogers.
Colonel George Rogers Clark's Sketch of His Campaign in the Illinois in 1778-9. 1869.

Collins, Lewis.
Historical Sketches of Kentucky. 1847.

Cruikshank, Ernest, ed,
Documents Relating to Invasion of Canada and the Surrender of Detroit. 1912.

Cruikshank, Ernest, ed,
The Documentary History of the Campaign on the Niagara Frontier, 1812-1814. (4 volumes). 1896-1909.

Cutler, Jervis.
A Topographical Description of the State of Ohio, Indian Territory, and Louisiana. 1812.

Cutler, Julia P.
The Life and Times of Ephraim Cutler. 1890.

Darlington, Mary C.
History of Col. Henry Bouquet and the Western Frontiers of Pennsylvania. 1920.

Darlington, Mary C.
Fort Pitt and Letters From the Frontier. 1892.

De Schweinitz, Edmund.
The Life and Times of David Zeisberger. 1870.

Dillon, John B.
History of Indiana. 1859.

Eaton, John Henry.
Life of Andrew Jackson. 1824.

English, William Hayden.
Conquest of the Country Northwest of the Ohio. (2 volumes in one). 1896.

Flint, Timothy.
Indian Wars of the West. 1833.

Forbes, John.
Writings of General John Forbes Relating to His Service in North America. 1938.

Forman, Samuel S.
Narrative of a Journey Down the Ohio and Mississippi in 1789-90. 1888.

Haywood, John.
Civil and Political History of the State of Tennessee to 1796. 1823.

Heckewelder, John.
History, Manners and Customs of the Indian Nations. 1876.

Heckewelder, John.
Narrative of the Mission of the United Brethren. 1820.

Hildreth, Samuel P.
Pioneer History. 1848.

Houck, Louis.
The Boundaries of the Louisiana Purchase: A Historical Study. 1901.

Houck, Louis.
History of Missouri. (3 volumes in one). 1908.

Houck, Louis.
The Spanish Regime in Missouri. (2 volumes in one). 1909.

Jacob, John J.
A Biographical Sketch of the Life of the Late Capt. Michael Cresap. 1826.

Jones, David.
A Journal of Two Visits Made to Some Nations of Indians on the West Side of the River Ohio, in the Years 1772 and 1773. 1774.

Kenton, Edna.
Simon Kenton. 1930.

Loudon, Archibald.
Selection of Some of the Most Interesting Narratives of Outrages. (2 volumes in one). 1808-1811.

Monette, J. W.
History, Discovery and Settlement of the Mississippi Valley. (2 volumes in one). 1846.

Morse, Jedediah.
American Gazetteer. 1797.

Pickett, Albert James.
History of Alabama. (2 volumes in one). 1851.

Pope, John.
A Tour Through the Southern and Western Territories. 1792.

Putnam, Albigence Waldo.
History of Middle Tennessee. 1859.

Ramsey, James G. M.
Annals of Tennessee. 1853.

Ranck, George W.
Boonesborough. 1901.

Robertson, James Rood, ed.
Petitions of the Early Inhabitants of Kentucky to the Gen. Assembly of Virginia. 1914.

Royce, Charles.
Indian Land Cessions. 1899.

Rupp, I. Daniel.
History of Northampton, Lehigh, Monroe, Carbon and Schuykill Counties. 1845.

Safford, William H.
The Blennerhasset Papers. 1864.

St. Clair, Arthur.
A Narrative of the Manner in which the Campaign Against the Indians, in the Year 1791 was Conducted. 1812.

Sargent, Winthrop, ed.
A History of an Expedition Against Fort DuQuesne in 1755. 1855.

Severance, Frank H.
An Old Frontier of France. (2 volumes in one). 1917.

Sipe, C. Hale.
Fort Ligonier and Its Times. 1932.

Stevens, Henry N.
Lewis Evans: His Map of the Middle British Colonies in America. 1920.

Timberlake, Henry.
The Memoirs of Lieut. Henry Timberlake. 1927.

Tome, Philip.
Pioneer Life: Or Thirty Years a Hunter. 1854.

Trent, William.
Journal of Captain William Trent From Logstown to Pickawillany. 1871.

Walton, Joseph S.
Conrad Weiser and the Indian Policy of Colonial Pennsylvania. 1900.

Withers, Alexander Scott.
Chronicles of Border Warfare. 1895.

V

E99.M9 Z44 1971
De Schweinitz

DISCARDED